JAVA™ EXAMPLES

IN A NUTSHELL

Other Java™ resources from O'Reilly

Related titles

Ant: The Definitive Guide
Head First Java™
Head First EJB™
Java™ & XML
Java™ Cookbook
Java™ Enterprise in a Nutshell
Java™ Extreme Programming Cookbook

Java™ Web Services in a Nutshell
Java™ Security
JavaServer™ Pages
Learning Java™
Programming Jakarta Struts
Tomcat: The Definitive Guide

Java Books Resource Center

java.oreilly.com is a complete catalog of O'Reilly's books on Java and related technologies, including sample chapters and code examples.

OnJava.com is a one-stop resource for enterprise Java developers, featuring news, code recipes, interviews, weblogs, and more.

Conferences

O'Reilly & Associates brings diverse innovators together to nurture the ideas that spark revolutionary industries. We specialize in documenting the latest tools and systems, translating the innovator's knowledge into useful skills for those in the trenches. Visit *conferences.oreilly.com* for our upcoming events.

Safari Bookshelf (*safari.oreilly.com*) is the premier online reference library for programmers and IT professionals. Conduct searches across more than 1,000 books. Subscribers can zero in on answers to time-critical questions in a matter of seconds. Read the books on your Bookshelf from cover to cover or simply flip to the page you need. Try it today with a free trial.

JAVA EXAMPLES

IN A NUTSHELL

Third Edition

David Flanagan

O'REILLY®

Beijing • Cambridge • Farnham • Köln • Paris • Sebastopol • Taipei • Tokyo

Java™ Examples in a Nutshell, Third Edition
by David Flanagan

Copyright © 2004, 2000, 1997 O'Reilly & Associates, Inc. All rights reserved.
Printed in the United States of America.

Published by O'Reilly & Associates, Inc., 1005 Gravenstein Highway North, Sebastopol, CA 95472.

O'Reilly & Associates books may be purchased for educational, business, or sales promotional use. Online editions are also available for most titles (*safari.oreilly.com*). For more information, contact our corporate/institutional sales department: 800-998-9938 or *corporate@oreilly.com*.

Editor:	Brett McLaughlin
Production Editor:	Genevieve d'Entremont
Cover Designer:	Edie Freedman
Interior Designer:	Melanie Wang

Printing History:

September 1997:	First Edition.
September 2000:	Second Edition.
January 2004:	Third Edition.

ISBN: 0-596-00620-9
[M]

Table of Contents

Part II. Core Java APIs

Part III. Desktop Java APIs

Preface

This book is a companion volume to my previous books *Java in a Nutshell*, *Java Foundation Classes in a Nutshell*, and *Java Enterprise in a Nutshell*. While those books are quick-references at heart, they also include accelerated introductions to various Java™ programming topics and example code, usually in the form of program fragments. I wrote *Java Examples in a Nutshell* to pick up where those books leave off, providing a suite of complete working examples, ready to compile and run, suitable for novice Java programmers and experts alike.

The first edition of this book came about when Java 1.1 was released at more than double the size of Java 1.0. While I was busy writing additional examples for the second edition of *Java in a Nutshell*, the engineers at Sun were busy turning Java into something that could no longer fit in a nutshell. With its quick-reference section expanding so much, *Java in a Nutshell* could no longer hold many examples. The examples in *Java in a Nutshell* were one of its most popular features, and it was hard to have to cut them.

This book is the result of those cuts, and I am glad that we made the decision we did. Given the freedom to devote an entire book to examples, I was able to write the examples I really wanted to write. I was able to go into more depth than I ever would have before, and I found myself really enjoying the exploration and experimentation that went into developing the examples. For the second edition of the book, I had the pleasure of exploring and experimenting with new parts of the Java API: Swing™, Java 2D™, servlets, and XML. And for the third edition, I got to play around with New I/O, Java Sound, and several new minor APIs, such as logging and preferences. I hope you will use these examples as a starting point for your own explorations, and that you feel some of the same excitement I felt while writing them.

As its name implies, this book teaches by example, which is how many people learn best. There is not a lot of hand-holding, nor will you find detailed documentation of the exact syntax and behavior of Java statements. This book is designed to work in tandem with *Java in a Nutshell*, *Java Foundation Classes in a Nutshell*, and *Java Enterprise in a Nutshell*. You'll probably find those volumes quite useful while studying the examples here. You may also be interested in the other books in the O'Reilly Java series. Those books are listed at *http://java.oreilly.com*.

This book is organized into four parts. Chapters 1 and 2 are introductions to the Java language itself, suitable for programmers who are just learning Java. Chapters 3 through 10 cover the core Java APIs. The APIs covered in these chapters are documented in *Java in a Nutshell*. Chapters 11 through 17 form the third part of the book. These chapters demonstrate Java's graphics and graphical user interface APIs, which are documented in *Java Foundation Classes in a Nutshell*. Finally, Chapters 18 through 21 contain examples of server-side or "enterprise" APIs and complement the book *Java Enterprise in a Nutshell*.

You can read the chapters in this book in more or less whatever order they strike your interest. There are some interdependencies between the chapters, however, and some chapters really ought to be read in the order they are presented. For example, it is important to read Chapter 3 before you read Chapter 5. Chapters 1 and 2 are aimed at programmers just starting out with Java. Seasoned Java programmers will probably want to skip them.

By their very nature, nontrivial programming examples are rarely about only a single topic, and there are many examples here there could be placed in more than one chapter. The final chapter of this book is a special "Index of Examples" in which you can look up a class, method, or programming topic and find examples that cover that topic. This example index is distinct from, and provided in addition to, the regular index that appears at the back of the book.

New in This Edition

Readers of the second edition will find this edition much improved. New chapters cover the New I/O API and the Java Sound API. The chapters on servlets and XML have been completely overhauled, and there are many new and improved examples throughout the book. To save typing, the package prefix for all examples has changed from the correct but awkward "com.davidflanagan.examples" to the succinct and easy "je3".

Java Examples Online

The examples in this book are available online, so you don't have to type them all in yourself! You can download them from the author's web site, at *http://www.davidflanagan.com/javaexamples3*, or from the publisher's site, *http://www.oreilly.com/catalog/jenut3*. As typos and bugs are reported, you will also find an errata list at the publisher's site. The examples are free for noncommercial use. If you want to use them commercially, however, I ask that you pay a nominal commercial licensing fee. Visit *http://www.davidflanagan.com/javaexamples3* for licensing details.

Related Books from O'Reilly

O'Reilly publishes an entire series of books on Java. These books include *Java in a Nutshell*, *Java Foundation Classes in a Nutshell*, and *Java Enterprise in a Nutshell*, which, as mentioned earlier, are quick-reference companions to this book.

A related reference work, written and published by the author, is *Jude*, an innovative software package that combines the popular quick-reference format of *Java in a Nutshell* with the definitive javadoc documentation from Sun, and with the instant search and navigation commands of an online help application. See *http://www.davidflanagan.com/Jude* for details.

You can find a complete list of Java books from O'Reilly at *http://java.oreilly.com*. Individual chapters in this book refer to specific books that may help you understand that material in more detail.

Conventions Used in This Book

The following formatting conventions are used in this book:

Italic

> Used for emphasis and to signify the first use of a term. Italic is also used for commands, email addresses, web sites, FTP sites, file and directory names, and newsgroups.

Bold

> Occasionally used to refer to particular keys on a computer keyboard or to portions of a user interface, such as the **Back** button or the **Options** menu.

`Constant Width`

> Used in all Java code and generally for anything that you would type literally when programming, including keywords, data types, constants, method names, variables, class names, and interface names. Also used for command lines and options that should be typed verbatim on the screen, as well as tags that might appear in an HTML document.

`Constant Width Italic`

> Used for the names of method parameters and generally as a placeholder to indicate an item that should be replaced with an actual value in your program. Also used for variable expressions in command-line options.

Request for Comments

Please address comments and questions concerning this book to the publisher:

> O'Reilly & Associates, Inc.
> 1005 Gravenstein Highway North
> Sebastopol, CA 95472
> (800) 998-9938 (in the United States or Canada)
> (707) 829-0515 (international or local)
> (707) 829-0104 (fax)

The examples in this book are professionally written and have been tested, but that does not mean that they are guaranteed to be bug-free or to work correctly with your version and your platform's implementation of Java. If you have problems, find bugs, or have suggestions for future editions, please email them to:

   bookquestions@oreilly.com

There's a web page for this book that lists errata, examples, and any additional information. You can access this page at:

   http://www.oreilly.com/catalog/jenut3

For more information about books, conferences, Resource Centers, and the O'Reilly Network, see the O'Reilly web site at:

   http://www.oreilly.com

Acknowledgments

Brett McLaughlin was the editor for the third edition of this book. He tried his best to keep me on schedule, and generally pulled things together at the end to get this book out the door. Thanks also to Paula Ferguson, who edited the second and first editions. And Frank Willison and Tim O'Reilly deserve credit for being willing and enthusiastic to try this all-example book format.

I've had the help of a number of O'Reilly's other Java authors with this book. Jonathan Knudsen, author of several Java books from O'Reilly, reviewed the graphics and the printing chapters. Bob Eckstein, coauthor of *Java Swing*, reviewed the Swing chapter. Jason Hunter, author of *Java Servlet Programming* and webmaster of *servlets.com*, reviewed the servlets chapter for the second edition, and then carefully reviewed it again when I rewrote it for the third edition. Brett McLaughlin, author of *Java and XML*, reviewed the XML chapter in both the second and third editions. George Reese, author of *Database Programming with JDBC and Java*, was kind enough to look over the database chapter. Jim Farley, author of *Java Distributed Computing* and coauthor of *Java Enterprise in a Nutshell*, reviewed the RMI examples. The expertise contributed by these reviewers has dramatically improved the quality of my examples. I am indebted to them all and recommend their books highly!

Other reviewers are not O'Reilly authors but, given the quality of their reviews, they probably ought to be. Alvin Wen of Westbridge Technology reviewed the New I/O chapter, pointed out omissions, and even debugged one of the examples for me. The chapter on the Java Sound API was reviewed by Florian Bomers and Matthias Pfisterer, maintainers of the excellent Java Sound Resources web site, *jsresources.org*. Their careful explanations greatly improved the chapter.

The production team at O'Reilly & Associates has again done a great job of turning the manuscript I submitted into an honest-to-goodness book. As usual, I am grateful to and awestruck by them.

Finally, my thanks and love to Christie.

—David Flanagan
http://www.davidflanagan.com
October 2003

Learning Java

Part I introduces the Java language with simple examples. Chapter 1 focuses on language constructs such as conditionals and loops. Chapter 2 introduces Java's object-oriented programming features.

Chapter 1, *Java Basics*
Chapter 2, *Objects, Classes, and Interfaces*

Java Basics

This chapter contains examples that demonstrate the basic syntax of Java; it is meant to be used in conjunction with Chapter 2 of *Java in a Nutshell*. If you have substantial programming experience with C or C++, you should find the material in this chapter straightforward. If you are coming to Java from another language, however, you may need to study the examples here more carefully.

The most important step in learning a new programming language is mastering the basic control statements of the language. With Java, this means learning the if/else branching statement and the while and for looping statements. Learning to program well is like learning to do word problems in high-school algebra class: you have to translate the problem from an abstract description into the concrete language of algebra (or, in this case, the language of Java). Once you learn to think in if, while, and for statements, other Java statements, such as break, continue, switch, and try/catch/finally, should be easy to pick up. Note that although Java is an object-oriented language, we won't discuss objects until Chapter 2.

So, with that as an introduction, and with mastery of basic syntax as our goal, let's jump right in and start writing Java programs.

Hello World

As long ago as 1978, Brian Kernighan and Dennis Ritchie wrote, in their classic book *The C Programming Language*, that "the first program to write is the same for all languages." They were referring, of course, to the "Hello World" program. The Java implementation of Hello World is shown in Example 1-1.

Example 1-1. Hello.java

```
package je3.basics;                       // A unique class name prefix
public class Hello {                      // Everything in Java is a class
    public static void main(String[ ] args) { // All programs must have main( )
```

Example 1-1. Hello.java (continued)

```
        System.out.println("Hello World!");    // Say hello!
    }                                          // This marks the end of main( )
}                                              // Marks the end of the class
```

The first line of this program is the package declaration. It specifies the name of the *package* of which this program is part. The program's name (as we'll see in the second line) is Hello. The package name is je3.basics. We can combine these two names to produce a fully qualified name, je3.basics.Hello. Using packages provides a unique namespace for every Java program. By placing this Hello program in a package, I've helped to ensure that no naming conflict will arise if someone else defines a program that is also named Hello. Each chapter of this book has its own package that begins with the prefix je3 (for JavaExamples3). In this case, since this is the basics chapter, the package name is je3.basics.*

The value of "Hello World" is that it is a template that you can expand on in your later experiments with Java. The second and third lines of Example 1-1 are a required part of the template. Every program—every piece of Java code, really—you write is a class. The second line of the example says that we're writing a class named Hello. It also says the class is public, which means it can be used by anyone.

Every standalone Java program requires a main( ) method. This is where the Java interpreter begins running a Java program. The third line of the example declares this main( ) method. It says that the method is public, that it has no return value (i.e., its return value is void), and that it is passed an array of strings as its argument. The name of the array is args. The line also says that main( ) is a static method. (In this chapter, we work exclusively with static methods. In Chapter 2, when we start working with objects, you'll learn what a static method is, and you'll see that nonstatic methods are actually the norm.)

In any case, you might as well go ahead and memorize this line:

```
    public static void main(String[ ] args)
```

Every standalone Java program you ever write contains a line that looks exactly like this one. (Actually, you can name the array of strings anything you want, but it is usually called args.)

The fifth and sixth lines of Example 1-1 simply mark the end of the main( ) method and of the Hello class. Like most modern programming languages, Java is a block-structured language. This means that such things as classes and methods have bodies that comprise a "block" of code. In Java, the beginning of a block is marked by a {, and the end is marked by a matching }. Method blocks are always defined within class blocks, and as we'll see in later examples, method blocks can contain such things as if statements and for loops that form subblocks within the

---

* In the second edition of this book, I was more rigorous about preventing naming conflicts: I created the package name by reversing my Internet domain name, a procedure that should guarantee that there will be no naming conflicts. The resulting package name for this chapter was com. davidflanagan.examples.basics. For this edition, I've settled on a less rigorous but much easier to type alternative.

method. Furthermore, these sorts of statement blocks can be nested arbitrarily deep within each other.

The first three lines and the last two lines of Example 1-1 are part of the basic framework of a Java application. It is the fourth line of the example that is of primary interest to us. This is the line that prints the words "Hello World!" The System.out.println( ) method sends a line of output to "standard output," which is usually the screen. This method is used throughout this chapter and in many other chapters in this book. It isn't until Chapter 3, however, that you'll really understand what it is doing. If you are curious before then, look up the java.lang. System and java.io.PrintStream classes in *Java in a Nutshell* (or some other Java reference manual).

One final point to note about this program is the use of comments. Example 1-1 uses C++-style comments that begin with // and continue until the end of the line. Thus, anything between the // characters and the end of a line is ignored by the Java compiler. You'll find that the examples in this book are thoroughly commented. The code and the comments are worth studying because the comments often draw your attention to points that are not mentioned in the main text of the book.

Running Hello World

The first step in running our program is to type it in.* Using a text editor, type in the Hello program as shown in Example 1-1. For now, however, omit the package declaration on the first line. Save the program in a file named *Hello.java*.

The second step is to compile the program. If you are using the Java Software Development Kit (SDK) from Sun, you compile code with the *javac* command.† *cd* to the directory that contains your *Hello.java* file, and type this command (assuming that *javac* is in your path):

```
% javac Hello.java
```

If the Java SDK has been properly installed, *javac* runs for a short while and then produces a file named *Hello.class*. This file contains the compiled version of the program. As I said earlier, everything you write in Java is a class, as the *.class* extension on this file indicates. One important rule about compiling Java programs is that the name of the file minus the *.java* extension must match the name of the class defined in the file. Thus, if you typed in Example 1-1 and saved it in a file named *HelloWorld.java*, you would not be able to compile it.

To run the program (again using the Java SDK) type:

```
% java Hello
```

This command should produce the output:

```
Hello World!
```

---

* Although this example is included in the online example archive, I'm suggesting that you type it in so that you start imprinting basic Java idioms in your brain. I'm also going to have you modify the example, in order to explain certain aspects of running the program.

† If you are using some other Java programming environment, read and follow the vendor's instructions for compiling and running programs.

The *java* command is the Java interpreter; it runs the Java Virtual Machine. You pass *java* the name of the class that you want to run. Note that you are specifying the class name, Hello, not the name of the file, *Hello.class*, that contains the compiled class.

The previous steps have shown you how to compile and run Java programs that don't have package declarations. If you omitted the package declaration when you typed in *Hello.java*, these instructions should have worked for you (if they didn't, check that you typed the program in correctly). In practice, however, all nontrivial Java programs (including the examples in this book) do have package declarations. Using packages makes compiling and running Java programs a bit more complicated. As I just noted, a Java program must be saved in a file that has a name that matches the class name. When a class is in a package, there is a further requirement that the class be saved in a directory that matches the name of the package.

Go ahead and reinsert the package declaration into *Hello.java*:

```
package je3.basics;
```

Now make yourself a new directory (or folder) in which you'll do all your work with the examples from this book. For example, on a Windows system, you might create a folder named *c:\Examples*. On a Linux system, you might use *~/Examples*. Within this directory, create a subdirectory named *je3*. Then create a subdirectory of *je3* named *basics*. Now copy your *Hello.java* program (with the package declaration) into this directory. On a Windows system, the resulting file might be:

```
c:\Examples\je3\basics\Hello.java
```

After you've created the directory structure and put your Java program in it, the next step is to tell the Java compiler and interpreter where to find it. The compiler and interpreter simply need to know the base directory you've chosen; they will look for the *Hello.class* file in subdirectories of this base directory, based on the package name. To tell Java where to look, you have to set the CLASSPATH environment variable in the manner appropriate for your operating system. If you used the suggested name for your base directory on a Windows system (*c:\Examples*), you can use a command like the following:

```
C:\> set CLASSPATH=.;c:\Examples
```

This tells Java to look first for classes in the current directory (.), followed by the *c:\Examples* directory.

On a Unix system using the *csh* shell, you can use the following command:

```
% setenv CLASSPATH .:/home/david/Examples
```

With the *sh* or *bash* shell, the command is:

```
$ CLASSPATH=.:/home/david/Examples; export CLASSPATH
```

You may want to automate this process by setting CLASSPATH in a startup file, such as *autoexec.bat* on Windows systems or *.cshrc* on Unix systems (under *csh*).

With your CLASSPATH set, you can now go ahead and compile and run the Hello program. To compile, change directories to the *examples/basics* directory that holds *Hello.java*. Compile the program as before:

```
% javac Hello.java
```

This creates the *Hello.class* file.

To run the program, you invoke the Java interpreter as before, but now you must specify the fully qualified name of the program, so that the interpreter knows exactly which program you want to run:

```
% java je3.basics.Hello
```

Because you've set the CLASSPATH, you can run the Java interpreter from any directory on your system, and it will always find the correct program. If you get tired of typing such long class names, you may want to write yourself a batch file or shell script that automates the process for you.

Note that all Java programs are compiled and run in this way, so we won't go through these individual steps again. Of course, one step you don't have to repeat is typing in all the examples. You can download the example source code from *http://www.davidflanagan.com/javaexamples3*.

FizzBuzz

FizzBuzz is a game I learned long ago in elementary-school French class, as a way to practice counting in that language. The players take turns counting, starting with one and going up. The rules are simple: when your turn arrives, you say the next number. However, if that number is a multiple of five, you should say the word "fizz" (preferably with a French accent) instead. If the number is a multiple of seven, you should say "buzz." And if it is a multiple of both, you should say "fizzbuzz." If you mess up, you're out, and the game continues without you.

Example 1-2 is a Java program named FizzBuzz that plays a version of the game. Actually, it isn't a very interesting version of the game because the computer plays by itself, and it doesn't count in French! What is interesting to us is the Java code that goes into this example. It demonstrates the use of a for loop to count from 1 to 100 and the use of if/else statements to decide whether to output the number or one of the words "fizz", "buzz", or "fizzbuzz". (In this case, the if/else statement is used as an if/elseif/elseif/else statement, as we'll discuss shortly.)

This program introduces System.out.print( ). This method is just like System.out.println( ), except that it doesn't terminate the line of output. Whatever is output next appears on the same line.

The example also shows another style for comments. Anything, on any number of lines, between the characters /* and the characters */ is a comment in Java and ignored by the compiler. When one of these comments begins with /**, as the one in this example does, then it is additionally a *doc comment*, which means its contents are used by the *javadoc* program that automatically generates API documentation from Java source code.

Example 1-2. FizzBuzz.java

```
package je3.basics;

/**
 * This program plays the game "Fizzbuzz".  It counts to 100, replacing each
 * multiple of 5 with the word "fizz", each multiple of 7 with the word "buzz",
```

Example 1-2. FizzBuzz.java (continued)

```
 * and each multiple of both with the word "fizzbuzz".  It uses the modulo
 * operator (%) to determine if a number is divisible by another.
 **/
public class FizzBuzz {                             // Everything in Java is a class
    public static void main(String[ ] args) {  // Every program must have main( )
        for(int i = 1; i <= 100; i++) {          // count from 1 to 100
            if (((i % 5) == 0) && ((i % 7) == 0)) // Is it a multiple of 5 & 7?
                System.out.print("fizzbuzz");
            else if ((i % 5) == 0)                  // Is it a multiple of 5?
                System.out.print("fizz");
            else if ((i % 7) == 0)                  // Is it a multiple of 7?
                System.out.print("buzz");
            else System.out.print(i);               // Not a multiple of 5 or 7
            System.out.print(" ");
        }
        System.out.println( );
    }
}
```

The for and if/else statements may require a bit of explanation for programmers who have not encountered them before. A for statement sets up a loop, so that some code can be executed multiple times. The for keyword is followed by three Java expressions that specify the parameters of the loop. The syntax is:

```
for(initialize ; test ; update)
    body
```

The *initialize* expression does any necessary initialization. It is run once, before the loop starts. Usually, it sets an initial value for a loop counter variable. Often, as in this example, the loop counter is used only within the loop, so the *initialize* expression also declares the variable.

The *test* expression checks whether the loop should continue. It is evaluated before each execution of the loop body. If it evaluates to true, the loop is executed. When it evaluates to false, however, the loop body is not executed, and the loop terminates.

The *update* expression is evaluated at the end of each iteration of the loop; it does anything necessary to set up the loop for the next iteration. Usually, it simply increments or decrements the loop counter variable.

Finally, the *body* is the Java code that is run each time through the loop. It can be a single Java statement or a whole block of Java code, enclosed by curly braces.

This explanation should make it clear that the for loop in Example 1-2 counts from 1 to 100.

The if/else statement is simpler than the for statement. Its syntax is:

```
if (expression)
    statement1
else
    statement2
```

When Java encounters an if statement, it evaluates the specified *expression*. If the expression evaluates to true, *statement1* is executed. Otherwise, *statement2* is evaluated. That is all if/else does; there is no looping involved, so the program continues with the next statement following if/else. The else clause and *statement2* that follows it are entirely optional. If they are omitted, and the *expression* evaluates to false, the if statement does nothing. The statements following the if and else clauses can be either single Java statements or entire blocks of Java code, contained within curly braces.

The thing to note about the if/else statement (and the for statement, for that matter) is that it can contain other statements, including other if/else statements. This is how the statement was used in Example 1-2, where we saw what looked like an if/elseif/elseif/else statement. In fact, this is simply an if/else statement within an if/else statement within an if/else statement. This structure becomes clearer if the code is rewritten to use curly braces:

```
if (((i % 5) == 0)&& ((i % 7) == 0))
    System.out.print("fizzbuzz");
else {
    if ((i % 5) == 0)
        System.out.print("fizz");
    else {
        if ((i % 7) == 0)
            System.out.print("buzz");
        else
            System.out.print(i);
    }
}
```

Note, however, that this sort of nested if/else logic is not typically written out with a full set of curly braces in this way. The else if programming construct is a commonly used idiom that you will quickly become accustomed to. You may have also noticed that I use a compact coding style that keeps everything on a single line wherever possible. Thus, you'll often see:

```
if (expression) statement
```

I do this so that the code remains compact and manageable, and therefore easier to study in the printed form in which it appears here. You may prefer to use a more highly structured, less compact style in your own code.

The Fibonacci Series

The Fibonacci numbers are a sequence of numbers in which each successive number is the sum of the two preceding numbers. The sequence begins 1, 1, 2, 3, 5, 8, 13, and goes on from there. This sequence appears in interesting places in nature. For example, the number of petals on most species of flowers is one of the Fibonacci numbers.

Example 1-3 shows a program that computes and displays the first 20 Fibonacci numbers. There are several things to note about the program. First, it again uses a for statement. It also declares and uses variables to hold the previous two numbers in the sequence, so that these numbers can be added together to produce the next number in the sequence.

Example 1-3. Fibonacci.java

```
package je3.basics;
/**
 * This program prints out the first 20 numbers in the Fibonacci sequence.
 * Each term is formed by adding together the previous two terms in the
 * sequence, starting with the terms 1 and 1.
 **/
public class Fibonacci {
    public static void main(String[ ] args) {
        int n0 = 1, n1 = 1, n2;              // Initialize variables
        System.out.print(n0 + " " +          // Print first and second terms
                         n1 + " ");          // of the series

        for(int i = 0; i < 18; i++) {        // Loop for the next 18 terms
            n2 = n1 + n0;                     // Next term is sum of previous two
            System.out.print(n2 + " ");       // Print it out
            n0 = n1;                          // First previous becomes 2nd previous
            n1 = n2;                          // And current number becomes previous
        }
        System.out.println( );                // Terminate the line
    }
}
```

Using Command-Line Arguments

As we've seen, every standalone Java program must declare a method with exactly the following signature:

```
public static void main(String[ ] args)
```

This signature says that an array of strings is passed to the main( ) method. What are these strings, and where do they come from? The args array contains any arguments passed to the Java interpreter on the command line, following the name of the class to be run. Example 1-4 shows a program, Echo, that reads these arguments and prints them back out. For example, you can invoke the program this way:

```
% java je3.basics.Echo this is a test
```

The program responds:

```
this is a test
```

In this case, the args array has a length of four. The first element in the array, args[0], is the string "this", and the last element of the array, args[3], is "test". As you can see, Java arrays begin with element 0. If you are coming from a language that uses one-based arrays, this can take quite a bit of getting used to. In particular, you must remember that if the length of an array a is n, the last element in the array is a[n-1]. You can determine the length of an array by appending .length to its name, as shown in Example 1-4.

This example also demonstrates the use of a while loop. A while loop is a simpler form of the for loop; it requires you to do your own initialization and update of the loop counter variable. Most for loops can be rewritten as a while loop, but the compact syntax of the for loop makes it the more commonly used statement. A for loop would have been perfectly acceptable, and even preferable, in this example.

Example 1-4. Echo.java

```java
package je3.basics;

/**
 * This program prints out all its command-line arguments.
 **/
public class Echo {
    public static void main(String[ ] args) {
        int i = 0;                          // Initialize the loop variable
        while(i < args.length) {            // Loop until the end of array
            System.out.print(args[i] + " "); // Print each argument out
            i++;                            // Increment the loop variable
        }
        System.out.println( );              // Terminate the line
    }
}
```

Echo in Reverse

Example 1-5 is a lot like the Echo program of Example 1-4, except that it prints out the command-line arguments in reverse order, and it prints out the characters of each argument backwards. Thus, the Reverse program can be invoked as follows, with the following output:

```
% java je3.basics.Reverse this is a test
tset a si siht
```

This program is interesting because its nested for loops count backward instead of forward. It is also interesting because it manipulates String objects by invoking methods of those objects and the syntax starts to get a little complicated. For example, consider the expression at the heart of this example:

```
args[i].charAt(j)
```

This expression first extracts the ith element of the args[ ] array. We know from the declaration of the array in the signature of the main( ) method that it is a String array; that is, it contains String objects. (Strings are not a primitive type, like integers and boolean values in Java: they are full-fledged objects.) Once you extract the ith String from the array, you invoke the charAt( ) method of that object, passing the argument j. (The . character in the expression refers to a method or a field of an object.) As you can surmise from the name (and verify, if you want, in a reference manual), this method extracts the specified character from the String object. Thus, this expression extracts the jth character from the ith command-line argument. Armed with this understanding, you should be able to make sense of the rest of Example 1-5.

Example 1-5. Reverse.java

```java
package je3.basics;

/**
 * This program echos the command-line arguments backwards.
 **/
public class Reverse {
    public static void main(String[] args) {
        // Loop backwards through the array of arguments
        for(int i = args.length-1; i >= 0; i--) {
            // Loop backwards through the characters in each argument
            for(int j=args[i].length()-1; j>=0; j--) {
                // Print out character j of argument i.
                System.out.print(args[i].charAt(j));
            }
            System.out.print(" ");  // Add a space at the end of each argument.
        }
        System.out.println();       // And terminate the line when we're done.
    }
}
```

FizzBuzz Switched

Example 1-6 is another version of the FizzBuzz game. This version uses a switch statement instead of nested if/else statements to determine what its output should be for each number. Take a look at the example first, then read the explanation of switch.

Example 1-6. FizzBuzz2.java

```java
package je3.basics;

/**
 * This class is much like the FizzBuzz class, but uses a switch statement
 * instead of repeated if/else statements
 **/
public class FizzBuzz2 {
    public static void main(String[] args) {
        for(int i = 1; i <= 100; i++) { // count from 1 to 100
            switch(i % 35) {        // What's the remainder when divided by 35?
            case 0:                             // For multiples of 35...
                System.out.print("fizzbuzz ");  // print "fizzbuzz".
                break;                          // Don't forget this statement!
            case 5: case 10: case 15:   // If the remainder is any of these
            case 20: case 25: case 30:  // then the number is a multiple of 5
                System.out.print("fizz ");      // so print "fizz".
                break;
            case 7: case 14: case 21: case 28:  // For any multiple of 7...
                System.out.print("buzz ");      // print "buzz".
                break;
            default:                            // For any other number...
                System.out.print(i + " ");      // print the number.
                break;
```

Example 1-6. FizzBuzz2.java (continued)

```
        }
    }
    System.out.println( );
  }
}
```

The `switch` statement acts like a switch operator at a busy rail yard, switching a train (or the execution of a program) to the appropriate track (or piece of code) out of many potential tracks. A `switch` statement is often an alternative to repeated `if`/`else` statements, but it only works when the value being tested is an integer (i.e., `long`, `float`, `double`, `boolean`, and reference types such as `String` objects are not allowed) and when the value is being tested against constant values. The basic syntax of the `switch` statement is:

```
switch(expression) {
  statements
}
```

The `switch` statement is followed by an *expression* in parentheses and a block of code in curly braces. After evaluating the *expression*, the `switch` statement executes certain code within the block, depending on the integral value of the expression. How does the `switch` statement know where to start executing code for which values? This information is indicated by `case:` labels and with the special `default:` label. Each `case:` label is followed by an integral value. If the *expression* evaluates to that value, the `switch` statement begins executing code immediately following that `case:` label. If there is no `case:` label that matches the value of the expression, the `switch` statement starts executing code following the `default:` label, if there is one. If there is no `default:` label, `switch` does nothing.

The `switch` statement is an unusual one because each case doesn't have its own unique block of code. Instead, `case:` and `default:` labels simply mark various entry points into a single large block of code. Typically, each label is followed by several statements and then a `break` statement, which causes the flow of control to exit out of the block of the `switch` statement. If you don't use a `break` statement at the end of the code for a label, the execution of that case "drops through" to the next case. If you want to see this in action, remove the `break` statements from Example 1-6 and see what happens when you run the program. Forgetting `break` statements within a `switch` statement is a common source of bugs.

Computing Factorials

The factorial of an integer is the product of that number and all of the positive integers smaller than it. Thus the factorial of 5, written 5!, is the product of 5*4*3*2*1, or 120. Example 1-7 shows a class, `Factorial`, that contains a method, `factorial( )`, that computes factorials. This class is not a program in its own right, but the method it defines can be used by other programs. The method itself is quite simple; we'll see several variations of it in the following sections. As an exercise, you might think about how you could rewrite this example using a `while` loop instead of a `for` loop.

Example 1-7. Factorial.java

```java
package je3.basics;
/**
 * This class doesn't define a main( ) method, so it isn't a program by itself.
 * It does define a useful method that we can use in other programs, though.
 **/
public class Factorial {
    /** Compute and return x!, the factorial of x */
    public static int factorial(int x) {
        if (x < 0) throw new IllegalArgumentException("x must be >= 0");
        int fact = 1;
        for(int i = 2; i <= x; i++)     // loop
            fact *= i;                  // shorthand for: fact = fact * i;
        return fact;
    }
}
```

Recursive Factorials

Example 1-8 shows another way to compute factorials. This example uses a programming technique called *recursion*. Recursion happens when a method calls itself, or in other words, invokes itself recursively. The recursive algorithm for computing factorials relies on the fact that n! is equal to n*(n-1)!. Computing factorials in this fashion is a classic example of recursion. It is not a particularly efficient technique in this case, but there are many important uses for recursion, and this example demonstrates that it is perfectly legal in Java. This example also switches from the int data type, which is a 32-bit integer, to the long data type, which is a 64-bit integer. Factorials become very large, very quickly, so the extra capacity of a long makes the factorial( ) method more useful.

Example 1-8. Factorial2.java

```java
package je3.basics;
/**
 * This class shows a recursive method to compute factorials.  This method
 * calls itself repeatedly based on the formula: n! = n * (n-1)!
 **/
public class Factorial2 {
    public static long factorial(long x) {
        if (x < 0) throw new IllegalArgumentException("x must be >= 0");
        if (x <= 1) return 1;                // Stop recursing here
        else return x * factorial(x-1);      // Recurse by calling ourselves
    }
}
```

Caching Factorials

Example 1-9 shows a refinement to our previous factorial examples. Factorials are ideal candidates for caching because they are slightly time consuming to compute, and more importantly, there are few factorials you actually can compute, due to the limitations of the long data type. So, in this example, once a factorial is computed, its value is stored for future use.

Besides introducing the technique of caching, this example demonstrates several new things. First, it declares static fields within the Factorial3 class:

```
static long[ ] table = new long[21];
static int last = 0;
```

A static field is kind of like a variable, but it retains its value between invocations of the factorial( ) method. This means that static fields can cache values computed in one invocation for use by the next invocation.

Second, this example shows how to create an array:

```
static long[ ] table = new long[21];
```

The first half of this line (before the = sign) declares the static field table to be an array of long values. The second half of the line actually creates an array of 21 long values using the new operator.

Finally, this example demonstrates how to throw an exception:

```
throw new IllegalArgumentException("Overflow; x is too large.");
```

An exception is a kind of Java object; it is created with the new keyword, just as the array was. When a program throws an exception object with the throw statement, it indicates that some sort of unexpected circumstance or error has arisen. When an exception is thrown, program control transfers to the nearest containing catch clause of a try/catch statement. This clause should contain code to handle the exceptional condition. If an exception is never caught, the program terminates with an error.

Example 1-9 throws an exception to notify the calling procedure that the argument it passed is too big or too small. The argument is too big if it is greater than 20, since we can't compute factorials beyond 20!. The argument is too small if it is less than 0, as factorial is only defined for nonnegative integers. Examples later in the chapter demonstrate how to catch and handle exceptions.

Example 1-9. Factorial3.java

```
package je3.basics;

/**
 * This class computes factorials and caches the results in a table for reuse.
 * 20! is as high as we can go using the long data type, so check the argument
 * passed and "throw an exception" if it is too big or too small.
 **/
public class Factorial3 {
    // Create an array to cache values 0! through 20!.
    static long[ ] table = new long[21];
    // A "static initializer": initialize the first value in the array
    static { table[0] = 1; }  // factorial of 0 is 1.
    // Remember the highest initialized value in the array
    static int last = 0;
```

Example 1-9. Factorial3.java (continued)

```java
    public static long factorial(int x) throws IllegalArgumentException {
        // Check if x is too big or too small.  Throw an exception if so.
        if (x >= table.length)   // ".length" returns length of any array
            throw new IllegalArgumentException("Overflow; x is too large.");
        if (x<0) throw new IllegalArgumentException("x must be non-negative.");

        // Compute and cache any values that are not yet cached.
        while(last < x) {
            table[last + 1] = table[last] * (last + 1);
            last++;
        }
        // Now return the cached factorial of x.
        return table[x];
    }
}
```

Computing Big Factorials

In the previous section, we learned that 20! is the largest factorial that can fit in a 64-bit integer. But what if you want to compute 50! or 100!? The java.math. BigInteger class represents arbitrarily large integer values and provides methods to perform arithmetic operations on these very large numbers. Example 1-10 uses the BigInteger class to compute factorials of any size. It also includes a simple main( ) method that defines a standalone test program for our factorial( ) method. This test program says, for example, that 50! is the following 65-digit number:

```
30414093201713378043612608166064768844377641568960512000000000000
```

Example 1-10 introduces the import statement. This statement must appear at the top of a Java file, before any class is defined (but after the package declaration). It provides a way to tell the compiler what classes you are using in a program. Once a class like java.math.BigInteger has been imported, you no longer have to type its full name; instead you can refer to it simply as BigInteger. You can also import an entire package of classes, as with the line:

```
import java.util.*
```

Note that the classes in the java.lang package are automatically imported, as are the classes of the current package, which, in this case, is je3.basics.

Example 1-10 uses the same caching technique Example 1-9 did. However, because there is no upper bound on the number of factorials that can be computed with this class, you can't use a fixed-sized array for the cache. Instead, use the java.util.ArrayList class, which is a utility class that implements an array-like data structure that can grow to be as large as you need it to be. Because an ArrayList is an object rather than an array, you use such methods as size( ), add( ), and get( ) to work with it. By the same token, a BigInteger is an object rather than a primitive value, so you can't simply use the * operator to multiply BigInteger objects. Use the multiply( ) method instead.

Example 1-10. Factorial4.java

```
package je3.basics;

// Import some other classes we'll use in this example.
// Once we import a class, we don't have to type its full name.
import java.math.BigInteger;  // Import BigInteger from java.math package
import java.util.*;  // Import all classes (including ArrayList) from java.util

/**
 * This version of the program uses arbitrary precision integers, so it does
 * not have an upper-bound on the values it can compute.  It uses an ArrayList
 * object to cache computed values instead of a fixed-size array.  An ArrayList
 * is like an array, but can grow to any size.  The factorial() method is
 * declared "synchronized" so that it can be safely used in multi-threaded
 * programs.  Look up java.math.BigInteger and java.util.ArrayList while
 * studying this class.  Prior to Java 1.2, use Vector instead of ArrayList
 **/
public class Factorial4 {
    protected static ArrayList table = new ArrayList(); // create cache
    static { // Initialize the first element of the cache with !0 = 1.
        table.add(BigInteger.valueOf(1));
    }

    /** The factorial() method, using BigIntegers cached in a ArrayList */
    public static synchronized BigInteger factorial(int x) {
        if (x<0) throw new IllegalArgumentException("x must be non-negative.");
        for(int size = table.size(); size <= x; size++) {
            BigInteger lastfact = (BigInteger)table.get(size-1);
            BigInteger nextfact = lastfact.multiply(BigInteger.valueOf(size));
            table.add(nextfact);
        }
        return (BigInteger) table.get(x);
    }

    /**
     * A simple main() method that we can use as a standalone test program
     * for our factorial() method.
     **/
    public static void main(String[ ] args) {
        for(int i = 0; i <= 50; i++)
            System.out.println(i + "! = " + factorial(i));
    }
}
```

Handling Exceptions

Example 1-11 shows a program that uses the `Integer.parseInt( )` method to convert a string specified on the command line to a number. The program then computes and prints the factorial of that number, using the `Factorial4.` `factorial( )` method defined in Example 1-10. That much is simple; it takes only two lines of code. The rest of the example is concerned with exception handling, or, in other words, taking care of all of the things that can go wrong. You use the try/catch statement in Java for exception handling. The try clause encloses a block of code from which exceptions may be thrown. It is followed by any number of catch clauses; the code in each catch clause takes care of a particular type of exception.

In Example 1-11, there are three possible user-input errors that can prevent the program from executing normally. Therefore, the two main lines of program code are wrapped in a try clause followed by three catch clauses. Each clause notifies the user about a particular error by printing an appropriate message. This example is fairly straightforward. You may want to consult Chapter 2 of *Java in a Nutshell*, as it explains exceptions in more detail.

Example 1-11. FactComputer.java

```
package je3.basics;

/**
 * This program computes and displays the factorial of a number specified
 * on the command line.  It handles possible user input errors with try/catch.
 **/
public class FactComputer {
    public static void main(String[ ] args) {
        // Try to compute a factorial.
        // If something goes wrong, handle it in the catch clause below.
        try {
            int x = Integer.parseInt(args[0]);
            System.out.println(x + "! = " + Factorial4.factorial(x));
        }
        // The user forgot to specify an argument.
        // Thrown if args[0] is undefined.
        catch (ArrayIndexOutOfBoundsException e) {
            System.out.println("You must specify an argument");
            System.out.println("Usage: java FactComputer <number>");
        }
        // The argument is not a number.  Thrown by Integer.parseInt( ).
        catch (NumberFormatException e) {
            System.out.println("The argument you specify must be an integer");
        }
        // The argument is < 0.  Thrown by Factorial4.factorial( )
        catch (IllegalArgumentException e) {
            // Display the message sent by the factorial( ) method:
            System.out.println("Bad argument: " + e.getMessage( ));
        }
    }
}
```

Interactive Input

Example 1-12 shows yet another program for computing factorials. Unlike Example 1-11, however, it doesn't just compute one factorial and quit. Instead, it prompts the user to enter a number, reads that number, prints its factorial, and then loops and asks the user to enter another number. The most interesting thing about this example is the technique it uses to read user input from the keyboard. It uses the readLine( ) method of a BufferedReader object to do this. The line that creates the BufferedReader may look confusing. For now, take it on faith that it works; you don't really need to understand how it works until we reach Chapter 3. Another feature of note in Example 1-12 is the use of the equals( ) method of the String object line to check whether the user has typed "quit".

The code for parsing the user's input and computing and printing the factorial is the same as in Example 1-11, and again, it is enclosed within a try clause. In Example 1-12, however, there is only a single catch clause to handle the possible exceptions. This one handles any exception object of type Exception. Exception is the superclass of all exception types, so this one catch clause is invoked no matter what type of exception is thrown.

Example 1-12. FactQuoter.java

```java
package je3.basics;
import java.io.*; // Import all classes in java.io package.  Saves typing.

/**
 * This program displays factorials as the user enters values interactively
 **/
public class FactQuoter {
    public static void main(String[] args) throws IOException {
        // This is how we set things up to read lines of text from the user.
        BufferedReader in=new BufferedReader(new InputStreamReader(System.in));
        // Loop forever
        for(;;) {
            // Display a prompt to the user
            System.out.print("FactQuoter> ");
            // Read a line from the user
            String line = in.readLine();
            // If we reach the end-of-file,
            // or if the user types "quit", then quit
            if ((line == null) || line.equals("quit")) break;
            // Try to parse the line, and compute and print the factorial
            try {
                int x = Integer.parseInt(line);
                System.out.println(x + "! = " + Factorial4.factorial(x));
            }
            // If anything goes wrong, display a generic error message
            catch(Exception e) { System.out.println("Invalid Input"); }
        }
    }
}
```

Using a StringBuffer

One of the things you may have noticed about the String class that is used to represent strings in Java is that it is immutable. In other words, there are no methods that allow you to change the contents of a string. Methods that operate on a string return a new string, not a modified copy of the old one. When you want to operate on a string in place, you must use a StringBuffer object instead.

Example 1-13 demonstrates the use of a StringBuffer. It interactively reads a line of user input, as Example 1-12 did, and creates a StringBuffer to contain the line. The program then encodes each character of the line using the *rot13* substitution cipher, which simply "rotates" each letter 13 places through the alphabet, wrapping around from Z back to A when necessary. Because a StringBuffer object is being used, you can replace each character in the line one-by-one. A session with this Rot13Input program might look like this:

```
% java je3.basics.Rot13Input
> Hello there.  Testing, testing!
Uryyb gurer.  Grfgvat, grfgvat!
> quit
%
```

The main( ) method of Example 1-13 calls another method, rot13( ), to perform the actual encoding of a character. This method demonstrates the use of the primitive Java char type and character literals (i.e., characters that are used literally in a program within single quotes).

Example 1-13. Rot13Input.java

```java
package je3.basics;
import java.io.*;  // We're doing input, so import I/O classes

/**
 * This program reads lines of text from the user, encodes them using the
 * trivial "Rot13" substitution cipher, and then prints out the encoded lines.
 **/
public class Rot13Input {
    public static void main(String[] args) throws IOException {
        // Get set up to read lines of text from the user
        BufferedReader in = new BufferedReader(new InputStreamReader(System.in));
        for(;;) {                                    // Loop forever
            System.out.print("> ");                  // Print a prompt
            String line = in.readLine( );            // Read a line
            if ((line == null) || line.equals("quit")) // If EOF or "quit"...
                break;                               // ...break out of loop
            StringBuffer buf = new StringBuffer(line); // Use a StringBuffer
            for(int i = 0; i < buf.length( ); i++)   // For each character...
                buf.setCharAt(i, rot13(buf.charAt(i)));// ..read, encode, store
            System.out.println(buf);                 // Print encoded line
        }
    }

    /**
     * This method performs the Rot13 substitution cipher.  It "rotates"
     * each letter 13 places through the alphabet.  Since the Latin alphabet
     * has 26 letters, this method both encodes and decodes.
     **/
    public static char rot13(char c) {
        if ((c >= 'A') && (c <= 'Z')) {  // For uppercase letters
            c += 13;                     // Rotate forward 13
            if (c > 'Z') c -= 26;        // And subtract 26 if necessary
        }
```

Example 1-13. Rot13Input.java (continued)

```
        if ((c >= 'a') && (c <= 'z')) {  // Do the same for lowercase letters
            c += 13;
            if (c > 'z') c -= 26;
        }
        return c;                        // Return the modified letter
    }
}
```

Sorting Numbers

Example 1-14 implements a simple (but inefficient) algorithm for sorting an array of numbers. This example doesn't introduce any new elements of Java syntax, but it is interesting because it reaches a real-world level of complexity. The sorting algorithm manipulates array entries using an if statement within a for loop that is itself within another for loop. You should take the time to study this short program carefully. Make sure that you understand exactly how it goes about sorting its array of numbers.

Example 1-14. SortNumbers.java

```java
package je3.basics;

/**
 * This class demonstrates how to sort numbers using a simple algorithm
 **/
public class SortNumbers {
    /**
     * This is a very simple sorting algorithm that is not very efficient
     * when sorting large numbers of things
     **/
    public static void sort(double[ ] nums) {
        // Loop through each element of the array, sorting as we go.
        // Each time through, find the smallest remaining element, and move it
        // to the first unsorted position in the array.
        for(int i = 0; i < nums.length; i++) {
            int min = i;   // holds the index of the smallest element
            // find the smallest one between i and the end of the array
            for(int j = i; j < nums.length; j++) {
                if (nums[j] < nums[min]) min = j;
            }
            // Now swap the smallest one with element i.
            // This leaves all elements between 0 and i sorted.
            double tmp;
            tmp = nums[i];
            nums[i] = nums[min];
            nums[min] = tmp;
        }
    }

    /** This is a simple test program for the algorithm above */
    public static void main(String[ ] args) {
```

Example 1-14. SortNumbers.java (continued)

```
        double[ ] nums = new double[10];      // Create an array to hold numbers
        for(int i = 0; i < nums.length; i++) // Generate random numbers
            nums[i] = Math.random( ) * 100;
        sort(nums);                           // Sort them
        for(int i = 0; i < nums.length; i++) // Print them out
            System.out.println(nums[i]);
    }
}
```

Computing Primes

Example 1-15 computes the largest prime number less than a specified value, using the Sieve of Eratosthenes algorithm. The algorithm finds primes by eliminating multiples of all lower prime numbers. Like Example 1-14, this example introduces no new Java syntax, but is a nice, nontrivial program with which to end this chapter. The program may seem deceptively simple, but there's actually a fair bit going on, so be sure you understand how it is ruling out prime numbers.

Example 1-15. Sieve.java

```
package je3.basics;

/**
 * This program computes prime numbers using the Sieve of Eratosthenes
 * algorithm: rule out multiples of all lower prime numbers, and anything
 * remaining is a prime.  It prints out the largest prime number less than
 * or equal to the supplied command-line argument.
 **/
public class Sieve {
    public static void main(String[ ] args) {
        // We will compute all primes less than the value specified on the
        // command line, or, if no argument, all primes less than 100.
        int max = 100;                        // Assign a default value
        try { max = Integer.parseInt(args[0]); } // Parse user-supplied arg
        catch (Exception e) { }                // Silently ignore exceptions.

        // Create an array that specifies whether each number is prime or not.
        boolean[ ] isprime = new boolean[max+1];

        // Assume that all numbers are primes, until proven otherwise.
        for(int i = 0; i <= max; i++) isprime[i] = true;

        // However, we know that 0 and 1 are not primes.  Make a note of it.
        isprime[0] = isprime[1] = false;

        // To compute all primes less than max, we need to rule out
        // multiples of all integers less than the square root of max.
        int n = (int) Math.ceil(Math.sqrt(max));  // See java.lang.Math class

        // Now, for each integer i from 0 to n:
        //   If i is a prime, then none of its multiples are primes,
```

Example 1-15. Sieve.java (continued)

```
//    so indicate this in the array.  If i is not a prime, then
//    its multiples have already been ruled out by one of the
//    prime factors of i, so we can skip this case.
    for(int i = 0; i <= n; i++) {
        if (isprime[i])                          // If i is a prime,
            for(int j = 2*i; j <= max; j = j + i) // loop through multiples
                isprime[j] = false;              // they are not prime.
    }

    // Now go look for the largest prime:
    int largest;
    for(largest = max; !isprime[largest]; largest--) ;  // empty loop body

    // Output the result
    System.out.println("The largest prime less than or equal to " + max +
                       " is " + largest);
    }
}
```

Exercises

Exercise 1-1. Write a program that counts from 1 to 15, printing out each number, and then counts backward by twos back to 1, again printing out each number.

Exercise 1-2. Each term of the Fibonacci series is formed by adding the previous two terms. What sort of series do you get if you add the previous three terms? Write a program to print the first 20 terms of this series.

Exercise 1-3. Write a program that takes two numbers and a string as command-line arguments and prints out the substring of the string specified by the two numbers. For example:

```
% java Substring hello 1 3
```

should print out:

```
ell
```

Handle all possible exceptions that might arise because of bad input.

Exercise 1-4. Write a program that interactively reads lines of input from the user and prints them back out, reversed. The program should exit if the user types "tiuq".

Exercise 1-5. The SortNumbers class shows how you can sort an array of doubles. Write a program that uses this class to sort an array of 100 floating-point numbers. Then, interactively prompt the user for numeric input, and display the next larger and next smaller number from the array. You should use an efficient binary search algorithm to find the desired position in the sorted array.

2

Objects, Classes, and Interfaces

This chapter contains examples that illustrate the object-oriented nature of Java and show you how to define and use classes and interfaces. It is designed to be read in conjunction with Chapter 3 of *Java in a Nutshell*, which offers a complete introduction to the object-oriented concepts and syntax you must understand to program in Java. As a refresher, the following paragraphs summarize Java's object-oriented terminology.

An *object* is a collection of data values, or *fields*, plus *methods* that operate on that data. The data type of an object is called a *class*; an object is often referred to as an *instance* of its class. The class defines the type of each field in an object, and it provides the methods that operate on data contained in an instance of the class. An object is created using the new operator, which invokes a *constructor* of the class to initialize the new object. The fields and methods of an object are accessed and invoked using the . operator.

Methods that operate on the fields of an object are known as instance methods. They are different from the static, or class, methods that we saw in Chapter 1. Class methods are declared static; they operate on the class itself, rather than on an individual instance of the class. Fields of a class may also be declared static, which makes them class fields instead of instance fields. While each object has its own copy of each instance field, there is only one copy of a class field and it is shared by all instances of the class.

The fields and methods of a class may have different visibility levels, including public, private, and protected. These different levels of visibility allow fields and methods to be used in different contexts. Every class has a *superclass*, from which it *inherits* fields and methods. When a class inherits from another class, it is called a *subclass* of that class. Classes in Java form a *class hierarchy*. The java.lang. Object class is root of this hierarchy; Object is the ultimate superclass of all other classes in Java.

An *interface* is a Java construct that defines methods, like a class, but doesn't provide any implementations for those methods. A class can *implement* an interface by defining an appropriate implementation for each method in the interface.

A Rectangle Class

Example 2-1 shows a class that represents a rectangle. Each instance of this Rect class has four fields, x1, y1, x2, and y2, that define the coordinates of the corners of the rectangle. The Rect class also defines a number of methods that operate on those coordinates.

Note the toString( ) method. This method overrides the toString( ) method of java.lang.Object, which is the implicit superclass of the Rect class. toString( ) produces a String that represents a Rect object. As you'll see, this method is quite useful for printing out Rect values.

Example 2-1. Rect.java

```
package je3.classes;
/**
 * This class represents a rectangle.  Its fields represent the coordinates
 * of the corners of the rectangle.  Its methods define operations that can
 * be performed on Rect objects.
 **/
public class Rect {
    // These are the data fields of the class
    public int x1, y1, x2, y2;

    /**
     * The is the main constructor for the class.  It simply uses its arguments
     * to initialize each of the fields of the new object.  Note that it has
     * the same name as the class, and that it has no return value declared in
     * its signature.
     **/
    public Rect(int x1, int y1, int x2, int y2) {
        this.x1 = x1;
        this.y1 = y1;
        this.x2 = x2;
        this.y2 = y2;
    }

    /**
     * This is another constructor.  It defines itself in terms of the above
     **/
    public Rect(int width, int height) { this(0, 0, width, height); }

    /** This is yet another constructor. */
    public Rect() { this(0, 0, 0, 0); }

    /** Move the rectangle by the specified amounts */
    public void move(int deltax, int deltay) {
        x1 += deltax; x2 += deltax;
```

Example 2-1. Rect.java (continued)

```
        y1 += deltay; y2 += deltay;
    }

    /** Test whether the specified point is inside the rectangle */
    public boolean isInside(int x, int y) {
        return ((x >= x1)&& (x <= x2)&& (y >= y1)&& (y <= y2));
    }

    /**
     * Return the union of this rectangle with another.  I.e. return the
     * smallest rectangle that includes them both.
     **/
    public Rect union(Rect r) {
        return new Rect((this.x1 < r.x1) ? this.x1 : r.x1,
                        (this.y1 < r.y1) ? this.y1 : r.y1,
                        (this.x2 > r.x2) ? this.x2 : r.x2,
                        (this.y2 > r.y2) ? this.y2 : r.y2);
    }

    /**
     * Return the intersection of this rectangle with another.
     * I.e. return their overlap.
     **/
    public Rect intersection(Rect r) {
        Rect result =  new Rect((this.x1 > r.x1) ? this.x1 : r.x1,
                                (this.y1 > r.y1) ? this.y1 : r.y1,
                                (this.x2 < r.x2) ? this.x2 : r.x2,
                                (this.y2 < r.y2) ? this.y2 : r.y2);
        if (result.x1 > result.x2) { result.x1 = result.x2 = 0; }
        if (result.y1 > result.y2) { result.y1 = result.y2 = 0; }
        return result;
    }

    /**
     * This is a method of our superclass, Object.  We override it so that
     * Rect objects can be meaningfully converted to strings, can be
     * concatenated to strings with the + operator, and can be passed to
     * methods like System.out.println()
     **/
    public String toString() {
        return "[" + x1 + "," + y1 + "; " + x2 + "," + y2 + "]";
    }
}
```

Testing the Rect Class

Example 2-2 is a standalone program named RectTest that puts the Rect class of Example 2-1 through its paces. Note the use of the new keyword and the Rect() constructor to create new Rect objects. The program uses the . operator to invoke methods of the Rect objects and to access their fields. The test program also relies implicitly on the toString( ) method of Rect when it uses the string concatenation operator (+) to create strings to be displayed to the user.

Example 2-2. RectTest.java

```
package je3.classes;

/** This class demonstrates how you might use the Rect class */
public class RectTest {
    public static void main(String[ ] args) {
        Rect r1 = new Rect(1, 1, 4, 4);      // Create Rect objects
        Rect r2 = new Rect(2, 3, 5, 6);
        Rect u = r1.union(r2);               // Invoke Rect methods
        Rect i = r2.intersection(r1);

        if (u.isInside(r2.x1, r2.y1))    // Use Rect fields and invoke a method
            System.out.println("(" + r2.x1 + "," + r2.y1 +
                               ") is inside the union");

        // These lines implicitly call the Rect.toString( ) method
        System.out.println(r1 + " union " + r2 + " = " + u);
        System.out.println(r1 + " intersect " + r2 + " = " + i);
    }
}
```

A Rect Subclass

Example 2-3 is a simple subclass of the Rect class of Example 2-1. This DrawableRect class inherits the fields and methods of Rect and adds its own method, draw( ), that draws a rectangle using a specified java.awt.Graphics object. (We'll see more of the Graphics object in Chapter 12.) DrawableRect also defines a constructor that simply uses the super keyword to pass its arguments up to the corresponding Rect constructor. Note the use of the extends keyword to indicate that Rect is the superclass of DrawableRect.

Example 2-3. DrawableRect.java

```
package je3.classes;
/**
 * This is a subclass of Rect that allows itself to be drawn on a screen.
 * It inherits all the fields and methods of Rect
 * It relies on the java.awt.Graphics object to perform the drawing.
 **/
public class DrawableRect extends Rect {
    /** The DrawableRect constructor just invokes the Rect() constructor */
    public DrawableRect(int x1, int y1, int x2, int y2) { super(x1,y1,x2,y2); }

    /** This is the new method defined by DrawableRect */
    public void draw(java.awt.Graphics g) {
        g.drawRect(x1, y1, (x2 - x1), (y2-y1));
    }
}
```

Another Subclass

Example 2-4 shows another subclass. ColoredRect is a subclass of DrawableRect (see Example 2-3), which makes it a sub-subclass of Rect (see Example 2-1). This class inherits the fields and methods of DrawableRect and of Rect (and of Object, which is the implicit superclass of Rect). ColoredRect adds two new fields that specify the border color and fill color of the rectangle when it is drawn. (These fields are of type java.awt.Color, which we'll learn about in Chapter 12.) The class also defines a new constructor that allows these fields to be initialized. Finally, ColoredRect overrides the draw( ) method of the DrawableRect class. The draw( ) method defined by ColoredRect draws a rectangle using the specified colors, rather than simply using the default colors as the method in DrawableRect did.

Example 2-4. ColoredRect.java

```
package je3.classes;
import java.awt.*;

/**
 * This class subclasses DrawableRect and adds colors to the rectangle it draws
 **/
public class ColoredRect extends DrawableRect {
    // These are new fields defined by this class.
    // x1, y1, x2, and y2 are inherited from our super-superclass, Rect.
    protected Color border, fill;

    /**
     * This constructor uses super() to invoke the superclass constructor, and
     * also does some initialization of its own.
     **/
    public ColoredRect(int x1, int y1, int x2, int y2,
                    Color border, Color fill)
    {
        super(x1, y1, x2, y2);
        this.border = border;
        this.fill = fill;
    }

    /**
     * This method overrides the draw() method of our superclass so that it
     * can make use of the colors that have been specified.
     **/
    public void draw(Graphics g) {
        g.setColor(fill);
        g.fillRect(x1, y1, (x2-x1), (y2-y1));
        g.setColor(border);
        g.drawRect(x1, y1, (x2-x1), (y2-y1));
    }
}
```

Complex Numbers

Example 2-5 shows the definition of a class that represents complex numbers. You may recall from algebra class that a complex number is the sum of a real number and an imaginary number. The imaginary number *i* is the square root of -1. This ComplexNumber class defines two double fields, which represent the real and imaginary parts of the number. These fields are declared private, which means they can be used only within the body of the class; they are inaccessible outside the class. Because the fields are inaccessible, the class defines two accessor methods, real( ) and imaginary( ), that simply return their values. This technique of making fields private and defining accessor methods is called *encapsulation*. Encapsulation hides the implementation of a class from its users, which means that you can change the implementation without it affecting the users.

Notice that the ComplexNumber class doesn't define any methods, other than the constructor, that set the values of its fields. Once a ComplexNumber object is created, the number it represents can never be changed. This property is known as *immutability*; it is often useful to design objects that are immutable like this.

ComplexNumber defines two add( ) methods and two multiply( ) methods that perform addition and multiplication of complex numbers. The difference between the two versions of each method is that one is an instance method and one is a class, or static, method. Consider the add( ) methods, for example. The instance method adds the value of the current instance of ComplexNumber to another specified ComplexNumber object. The class method doesn't have a current instance; it simply adds the values of two specified ComplexNumber objects. The instance method is invoked through an instance of the class, like this:

```
ComplexNumber sum = a.add(b);
```

The class method, however, is invoked through the class itself, rather than through an instance:

```
ComplexNumber sum = ComplexNumber.add(a, b);
```

Example 2-5. ComplexNumber.java

```
package je3.classes;

/**
 * This class represents complex numbers, and defines methods for performing
 * arithmetic on complex numbers.
 **/
public class ComplexNumber {
    // These are the instance variables.  Each ComplexNumber object holds
    // two double values, known as x and y.  They are private, so they are
    // not accessible from outside this class.  Instead, they are available
    // through the real() and imaginary() methods below.
    private double x, y;
```

Example 2-5. ComplexNumber.java (continued)

```java
/** This is the constructor.  It initializes the x and y variables */
public ComplexNumber(double real, double imaginary) {
    this.x = real;
    this.y = imaginary;
}

/**
 * An accessor method.  Returns the real part of the complex number.
 * Note that there is no setReal() method to set the real part.  This means
 * that the ComplexNumber class is "immutable".
 **/
public double real() { return x; }

/** An accessor method. Returns the imaginary part of the complex number */
public double imaginary() { return y; }

/** Compute the magnitude of a complex number */
public double magnitude() { return Math.sqrt(x*x + y*y); }

/**
 * This method converts a ComplexNumber to a string.  This is a method of
 * Object that we override so that complex numbers can be meaningfully
 * converted to strings, and so they can conveniently be printed out with
 * System.out.println() and related methods
 **/
public String toString() { return "{" + x + "," + y + "}"; }

/**
 * This is a static class method.  It takes two complex numbers, adds
 * them, and returns the result as a third number.  Because it is static,
 * there is no "current instance" or "this" object.  Use it like this:
 * ComplexNumber c = ComplexNumber.add(a, b);
 **/
public static ComplexNumber add(ComplexNumber a, ComplexNumber b) {
    return new ComplexNumber(a.x + b.x, a.y + b.y);
}

/**
 * This is a non-static instance method by the same name.  It adds the
 * specified complex number to the current complex number.  Use it like
 * this:
 * ComplexNumber c = a.add(b);
 **/
public ComplexNumber add(ComplexNumber a) {
    return new ComplexNumber(this.x + a.x, this.y+a.y);
}

/** A static class method to multiply complex numbers */
public static ComplexNumber multiply(ComplexNumber a, ComplexNumber b) {
    return new ComplexNumber(a.x*b.x - a.y*b.y, a.x*b.y + a.y*b.x);
}
```

Example 2-5. ComplexNumber.java (continued)

```
/** An instance method to multiply complex numbers */
public ComplexNumber multiply(ComplexNumber a) {
    return new ComplexNumber(x*a.x - y*a.y, x*a.y + y*a.x);
}
}
```

Computing Statistics

So far, the classes we've defined have modeled mathematical abstractions like rectangles and complex numbers. It is easy to imagine other objects that model things like a mailing address or a record in a database. This is not a requirement, however: classes do not have to model "things." They merely have to hold some state (i.e., define some fields) and optionally define methods to manipulate that state. Example 2-6 is just this kind of class: it computes simple statistics about a series of numbers. As numbers are passed to the addDatum( ) method, the Averager class updates its internal state so that its other methods can easily return the average and standard deviation of the numbers that have been passed to it so far. Although this Averager class does not model any "thing," we've followed the Java naming convention of giving classes names that are nouns (although, in this case, we had to use a noun that does not appear in any dictionary).

Example 2-6. Averager.java

```
package je3.classes;
/**
 * A class to compute the running average of numbers passed to it
 **/
public class Averager {
    // Private fields to hold the current state.
    private int n = 0;
    private double sum = 0.0, sumOfSquares = 0.0;

    /**
     * This method adds a new datum into the average.
     **/
    public void addDatum(double x) {
        n++;
        sum += x;
        sumOfSquares += x * x;
    }

    /** This method returns the average of all numbers passed to addDatum( ) */
    public double getAverage() { return sum / n; }

    /** This method returns the standard deviation of the data */
    public double getStandardDeviation() {
        return Math.sqrt(((sumOfSquares - sum*sum/n)/n));
    }

    /** This method returns the number of numbers passed to addDatum( ) */
    public double getNum() { return n; }
```

Example 2-6. Averager.java (continued)

```java
/** This method returns the sum of all numbers passed to addDatum( ) */
public double getSum( ) { return sum; }

/** This method returns the sum of the squares of all numbers. */
public double getSumOfSquares( ) { return sumOfSquares; }

/** This method resets the Averager object to begin from scratch */
public void reset( ) { n = 0; sum = 0.0; sumOfSquares = 0.0; }

/**
 * This nested class is a simple test program we can use to check that
 * our code works okay.
 **/
public static class Test {
    public static void main(String args[ ]) {
        Averager a = new Averager( );
        for(int i = 1; i <= 100; i++) a.addDatum(i);
        System.out.println("Average: " + a.getAverage( ));
        System.out.println("Standard Deviation: " +
                           a.getStandardDeviation( ));
        System.out.println("N: " + a.getNum( ));
        System.out.println("Sum: " + a.getSum( ));
        System.out.println("Sum of squares: " + a.getSumOfSquares( ));
    }
}
}
```

Example 2-6 introduces an important new feature. The Averager class defines a static inner class named Test. This class, Averager.Test, contains a main( ) method and is thus a standalone program suitable for testing the Averager class. When you compile the *Averager.java* file, you get two class files, *Averager.class* and *Averager$Test.class*. Running this nested Averager.Test class is a little tricky. You *ought* to be able to do so like this:

```
% java je3.classes.Averager.Test
```

However, current versions of the Java SDK don't correctly map from the class name Averager.Test to the class file *Averager$Test.class*. So, to run the test program, you must invoke the Java interpreter using a $ character instead of a . character in the class name:

```
% java je3.classes.Averager$Test
```

On a Unix system, however, you should be aware that the $ character has special significance and must be escaped. Therefore, on such a system, you have to type:

```
% java je3.classes.Averager\$Test
```

or:

```
% java 'je3.classes.Averager$Test'
```

You must use this technique whenever you need to run a Java program that is defined as an inner class.

An Integer List

Example 2-7 is a class that implements a list or growable array of int values. This IntList class is like the java.util.ArrayList class, but it works with primitive int values rather than objects. When you need to store int values and do not know the number of values in advance (i.e., you can't use an array), IntList is much more efficient than using an ArrayList because there is no need to wrap your int values in Integer objects. The interesting thing about this example is not its efficiency, however, but the fact that it is a real-world example: the code is nontrivial but easy to understand, and the class actually serves a useful purpose.

Also interesting is the fact that this class overrides a number of methods inherited from Object in order to provide meaningful implementations. Like the ComplexNumber class of Example 2-5, this class defines a toString() method to convert its state to a textual representation that can be displayed in log messages, debugging statements, and elsewhere. Additionally, it overrides the equals() method to determine if two IntList objects are equal. It also overrides the hashCode() method to provide a compatible implementation that ensures that IntList objects that are equal have the same hash code. This enables IntList objects to be used as keys in hashtables such as the java.util.HashMap class.

The Object class also defines the clone() or finalize() methods, but neither method is recommend for general use, and IntList does not override either one. The requirements for the clone() method are ill-defined, and it is hard to implement this method correctly. Instead of providing a clone() method, IntList defines a "copy constructor" to create a new IntList that is an exact copy of the old one.

In addition to methods inherited from Object, the IntList class implements the Comparable interface and its compareTo() method. This method defines an ordering for IntList objects, allowing them to be compared and sorted.

The book *Effective Java Programming Language Guide*, by Joshua Bloch (Addison-Wesley), contains a particularly helpful discussion about implementing the toString(), equals(), hashCode(), compareTo(), clone(), and finalize() methods.

One final feature to note about the IntList example is that the nonpublic setCapacity() method uses an assert statement to verify that it has been called correctly. assert was added to the Java language in Java 1.4, and for backward compatibility, this code will compile only if you use the -source 1.4 option to *javac*:

```
javac -source 1.4 IntList.java
```

If you are using Java 1.3 or before, just comment out the assert keyword to make the class compile. The Java interpreter does not test assertions by default. If you develop a program that uses the IntList class, you should enable assertions during your development and testing process by passing the -ea option to the *java* command:

```
java -ea MyIntListTestProgram
```

If you do this, then each time it is called, the setCapacity( ) method will verify that it is not being asked to set the list capacity to less than the list size (which would mean a loss of data). We'll see test programs that use the IntList class in Chapter 10.

Example 2-7. IntList.java

```java
package je3.classes;

/**
 * A growable array of primitive int values.  It is more efficient than
 * ArrayList or Vector because Integer objects are not used.
 **/
public class IntList implements Comparable {
    // These are the fields of this class.
    // They are protected so that subclasses can access them directly.
    protected int[ ] data;    // This array holds the integers
    protected int size;       // This is how many it currently holds

    // Static final values are constants.  This one is private.
    private static final int DEFAULT_CAPACITY = 8;

    // This no-argument constructor creates an IntList with a default capacity
    public IntList( ) { this(DEFAULT_CAPACITY); }

    // This constructor allows us to specify the initial size.  Useful when
    // we have an approximate idea of how big the list will need to be.
    public IntList(int initialCapacity) {
        // We don't have to set size to zero because newly created objects
        // automatically have their fields set to zero, false, and null.
        data = new int[initialCapacity];   // Allocate the array
    }

    // This constructor returns a copy of an existing IntList.
    public IntList(IntList original) {
        // All arrays are Cloneable, and their clone( ) method is an easy way
        // to copy them. Cloneable is ill-defined and hard to implement
        // correctly, however, so it is not usually worth making your classes
        // cloneable.  A copy constructor like this one is a good alternative.
        this.data = (int[ ]) original.data.clone( );
        this.size = original.size;
    }

    // Return the number of ints stored in the list
    public int size( ) { return size; }

    // Return the int stored at the specified index
    public int get(int index) {
        if (index < 0 || index >= size) // Check that argument is legitimate
            throw new IndexOutOfBoundsException(String.valueOf(index));
        return data[index];
    }
```

Example 2-7. IntList.java (continued)

```java
// Append a new value to the list, reallocating if necessary
public void add(int value) {
    if (size == data.length) setCapacity(size*2); // realloc if necessary
    data[size++] = value;                          // add value to list
}

// Set the value at the specified index
public void set(int index, int value) {
    if (index < 0 || index >= size)
        throw new IndexOutOfBoundsException(String.valueOf(index));
    data[index] = value;
}

// Shrink the list so that its capacity is the same as its size.
// This is useful to free up unneeded memory when we know the list
// will not have any new values added to it.
public void trim() { setCapacity(size); }

// Remove all elements from the list
public void clear() { size = 0; }

// Copy the contents of the list into a new array and return that array
public int[ ] toArray() {
    int[ ] copy = new int[size];
    System.arraycopy(data, 0, copy, 0, size);
    return copy;
}

// This is a very useful method, especially for logging and debugging.
// Consider overriding it in every class you write.
public String toString() {
    // Repetitive string contatenation with the + operator is inefficient.
    // It is much better to use a StringBuffer here.  In Java 1.5, use
    // StringBuilder instead.
    StringBuffer b = new StringBuffer(size*7); // Guess string length
    b.append('[');                             // Start the array
    for(int i = 0; i < size; i++) {            // Loop through list elements
        if (i > 0) {                           // If not the first element
            b.append(", ");                    // put a comma before it
            if (i%8 == 0) b.append('\n');      // newline every 8 elements
        }
        b.append(data[i]);                     // append a number
    }
    b.append(']');                             // end the array.
    return b.toString();                       // Return as a string
}


// Does this object contain the same values as the object o?
// This is an Object method that we override.  Note that we must also
// override hashCode() to match this.
public boolean equals(Object o) {
```

Example 2-7. IntList.java (continued)

```java
        // If o is the same object as this, then they are equal
        if (o == this) return true;

        // If o is null or of the wrong type, it is not equal
        if (!(o instanceof IntList)) return false;

        // It is an IntList, so we can cast it, and compare this to that.
        IntList that = (IntList) o;

        // If the lists have different sizes, they are not equal
        // Note that equal lists may have different array lengths.
        if (this.size != that.size) return false;

        // If any of their elements differ, then they are not equal
        for(int i = 0; i < this.size; i++)
            if (this.data[i] != that.data[i]) return false;

        // If we get here, then the two lists contain exactly the same values
        // in the same positions, so they are equal
        return true;
    }

    // Map this object to an integer hash code used for hashtable data
    // structures.  Objects that are equal() must have the same hashCode(), so
    // we always override this method when we override equals().
    // Note that non-equal objects may have the same hashCode(), but we strive
    // to minimize that possibility.
    public int hashCode() {
        // It would be legal to just add the values up and return that as
        // the hash code, but then the list [1,2,3] would have the same hash
        // code as [3,2,1] and [3,3], which is not desired behavior.  Using
        // multiplication and addition here makes the result dependent on
        // order, and spreads codes out across the full range of ints.
        int code = 1; // non-zero to hash [0] and [] to distinct values
        for(int i = 0; i < size; i++)
            code = code*997 + data[i];  // ignore overflow
        return code;
    }

    /**
     * The compareTo() method is defined by the Comparable interface.
     * It defines an ordering for IntList objects and allows them to be sorted.
     *
     * Return a negative value if this object is "less than" the argument.
     * Return a postive value if this object is "greater than" the argument.
     * Return zero if the two objects are equal.
     * The first list value that differs is used to determine ordering.
     * If one list is a prefix of the other, then the longer list is greater.
     */
    public int compareTo(Object o) {
        // Cast the argument to an IntList. This will correctly throw
        // CastClassException if the wrong type is passed
        IntList that = (IntList) o;
```

Example 2-7. IntList.java (continued)

```
        int n = Math.min(this.size, that.size);  // get length of shorter list
        // Compare elements of the two lists, looking for one that differs
        for(int i = 0; i < n; i++) {
            if (this.data[i] < that.data[i]) return -1;
            if (this.data[i] > that.data[i]) return 1;
        }

        // If we get here, then the lists are equal, or one is a prefix
        // of the other.
        return this.size - that.size;
    }

    // Reallocate the data array to enlarge or shrink it.
    // This is a non-public method used internally to grow or trim( ) the array.
    protected void setCapacity(int n) {
        // We use a Java 1.4 assertion to make sure the class is calling
        // this private method correctly.  Compile with "-source 1.4" to make
        // the compiler recognize this statement and run with "-ea" to make
        // the VM actually test the assertion.
        // Syntax: assert <condition> : <error message>
        assert (n >= size) : (n + "<" +size);

        if (n == data.length) return;              // Check size
        int[ ] newdata = new int[n];               // Allocate the new array
        System.arraycopy(data, 0, newdata, 0, size); // Copy data into it
        data = newdata;                            // Replace old array
    }
}
```

Tokenizing Text

We end this chapter with an extended (and more complex) example in three parts. Example 2-8 is a listing of *Tokenizer.java*. This Tokenizer interface defines an API for tokenizing text. *Tokenizing* simply means breaking into chunks; tokenizers are also known as lexers or scanners, and are commonly used when writing parsers. This Tokenizer interface is intended to provide an alternative to java. util.StringTokenizer, which is too simple for many uses, and java.io. StreamTokenizer, which is complex and poorly documented.

As an interface, Tokenizer doesn't do anything itself. But Example 2-8 is followed by an implementation in Examples 2-9 and 2-10. Following a pattern that you'll also see frequently in Java platform APIs, the implementation is broken into two classes: AbstractTokenizer, an abstract class that implements Tokenizer and implements its methods in terms of a small number of abstract methods, followed by CharSequenceTokenizer, a concrete subclass for tokenizing String and StringBuffer (or any CharSequence) objects. To demonstrate the flexibility of this implementation scheme, we'll see other Tokenizer implementations based on AbstractTokenizer throughout this book. ReaderTokenizer (for tokenizing character streams) is defined in Example 3-7, ChannelTokenizer (for tokenizing text read from high-performance "channels" of the New I/O API) is defined in Example 6-8, and MappedFileTokenizer (for tokenizing memory-mapped files) is defined in Example 6-7.

In addition to demonstrating the use of interfaces, abstract implementation classes, and concrete subclasses, Examples 2-8 through 2-10 are interesting because their public and protected members are fully documented using javadoc comments and javadoc tags. Space limitations prevent the use of this verbose documentation style elsewhere in the book, but these three classes provide a fully fleshed-out example of proper javadoc documentation. You can produce HTML javadoc documentation for these classes with the *javadoc* tool, using commands like the following:

```
cd ~/Examples/je3/classes
javadoc -source 1.4 -d api Tokenizer.java AbstractTokenizer.java \
    CharSequenceTokenizer.java
```

The Tokenizer Interface

Example 2-8 is the file *Tokenizer.java*. Because it contains complete javadoc comments, it is self-documenting. The documentation is a little hard to read in source-code form because it contains unformatted javadoc and HTML tags, but with a careful reading, you'll be able to understand the Tokenizer API. (And you should make sure you do understand it before moving on to the implementations that follow.) To get started, note the following things about the API:

- tokenType( ) returns the type of the current token, and tokenText( ) returns the characters that comprise the token.

- Token types are integers. Negative values represent special tokens, such as words and numbers. Most positive values are character codes that represent single-character tokens, such as punctuation characters. Positive values that match an opening quote character represent quote tokens instead.

- next( ) reads the next token, making it the current token, and returns its type.

- When a Tokenizer is first created, it returns every input character as a separate token. You must call various configuration methods to tell the tokenizer what kind of tokens (words, numbers, spaces, keywords, quotes) you are interested in.

Example 2-8. Tokenizer.java

```
package je3.classes;
import java.io.IOException;

/**
 * This interface defines basic character sequence tokenizing capabilities.
 * It can serve as the underpinnings of simple parsers.
 * <p>
 * The methods of this class fall into three categories:
 * <ul>
 * <li>methods to configure the tokenizer, such as {@link #skipSpaces} and
 *     {@link #tokenizeWords}.
 * <li>methods to read a token: {@link #next}, {@link #nextChar}, and
 *     {@link #scan(char,boolean,boolean,boolean)}.
 * <li>methods to query the current token, such as {@link #tokenType},
 *     {@link #tokenText} and {@link #tokenKeyword}.
 * </ul>
```

Example 2-8. Tokenizer.java (continued)

```
 * <p>
 * In its default state, a Tokenizer performs no tokenization at all:
 * {@link #next} returns each input character as an individual token.
 * You must call one or more configuration methods to specify the type of
 * tokenization to be performed.  Note that the configuration methods all
 * return the Tokenizer object so that repeated method calls can be chained.
 * For example:
 * <pre>
 * Tokenizer t;
 * t.skipSpaces( ).tokenizeNumbers( ).tokenizeWords( ).quotes("'#","'\n");
 * </pre>
 * <p>
 * One particularly important configuration method is
 * {@link #maximumTokenLength}
 * which is used to specify the maximum token length in the input.  A
 * Tokenizer implementation must ensure that it can handle tokens at least
 * this long, typically by allocating a buffer at least that long.
 * <p>
 * The constant fields of this interface are token type constants.
 * Note that their values are all negative. Non-negative token types
 * always represent Unicode characters.
 * <p>
 * A tokenizer may be in one of three states: <ol>
 * <li>Before any tokens have been read.  In this state, {@link #tokenType}
 * always returns (@link #BOF}, and {@link #tokenLine} always returns 0.
 * {@link #maximumTokenLength} and {@link #trackPosition} may only be called
 * in this state.
 * <li>During tokenization.  In this state, {@link #next}, {@link #nextChar},
 * and {@link #scan(char,boolean,boolean,boolean)} are being called to tokenize
 * input characters, but none of these methods has yet returned {@link #EOF}.
 * Configuration methods other than those listed above may be called from this
 * state to dynamically change tokenizing behavior.
 * <li>End-of-file.  Once one of the tokenizing methods have returned EOF,
 * the tokenizer has reached the end of its input.  Any subsequent calls to
 * the tokenizing methods or to {@link #tokenType} will return EOF. Most
 * methods may still be called from this state, although it is not useful
 * to do so.
 * </ol>
 * @author David Flanagan
 */
public interface Tokenizer {
    // The following are token type constants.
    /** End-of-file.  Returned when there are no more characters to tokenize */
    public static final int EOF = -1;
    /** The token is a run of whitespace. @see #tokenizeSpaces( ) */
    public static final int SPACE = -2;
    /** The token is a run of digits. @see #tokenizeNumbers( ) */
    public static final int NUMBER = -3;
    /** The token is a run of word characters. @see #tokenizeWords( ) */
    public static final int WORD = -4;
    /** The token is a keyword. @see #keywords( ) */
    public static final int KEYWORD = -5;
```

Example 2-8. Tokenizer.java (continued)

```java
/**
 * The token is arbitrary text returned by
 * {@link #scan(char,boolean,boolean,boolean)}.
 */
public static final int TEXT = -6;
/**
 * Beginning-of-file. This is the value returned by {@link #tokenType}
 * when it is called before tokenization begins.
 */
public static final int BOF = -7;
/** Special return value for {@link #scan(char,boolean,boolean,boolean)}.*/
public static final int OVERFLOW = -8; // internal buffer overflow

/**
 * Specify whether to skip spaces or return them.
 * @param skip If false (the default), then return whitespace characters
 *             or tokens.  If true, then next() never returns whitespace.
 * @return this Tokenizer object for method chaining.
 * @see #tokenizeSpaces
 */
public Tokenizer skipSpaces(boolean skip);

/**
 * Specify whether adjacent whitespace characters should be coalesced
 * into a single SPACE token.  This has no effect if spaces are being
 * skipped.  The default is false.
 * @param tokenize whether {@link #next} should colaesce adjacent
 *     whitespace into a single {@link #SPACE} token.
 * @return this Tokenizer object for method chaining.
 * @see #skipSpaces
 */
public Tokenizer tokenizeSpaces(boolean tokenize);

/**
 * Specify whether adjacent digit characters should be coalesced into
 * a single token.  The default is false.
 * @param tokenize whether {@link #next} should colaesce adjacent digits
 *     into a single {@link #NUMBER} token.
 * @return this Tokenizer object for method chaining.
 */
public Tokenizer tokenizeNumbers(boolean tokenize);

/**
 * Specify whether adjacent word characters should be coalesced into
 * a single token.  The default is false. Word characters are defined by
 * a {@link WordRecognizer}.
 * @param tokenize whether {@link #next} should colaesce adjacent word
 *     characters into a single {@link #WORD} token.
 * @return this Tokenizer object for method chaining.
 * @see #wordRecognizer
 */
public Tokenizer tokenizeWords(boolean tokenize);
```

Example 2-8. Tokenizer.java (continued)

```
/**
 * Specify a {@link Tokenizer.WordRecognizer} to define what constitues a
 * word. If set to null (the default), then words are defined by
 * {@link Character#isJavaIdentifierStart} and
 * {@link Character#isJavaIdentifierPart}.
 * This has no effect if word tokenizing has not been enabled.
 * @param wordRecognizer the {@link Tokenizer.WordRecognizer} to use.
 * @return this Tokenizer object for method chaining.
 * @see #tokenizeWords
 */
public Tokenizer wordRecognizer(WordRecognizer wordRecognizer);

/**
 * Specify keywords to receive special recognition.
 * If a {@link #WORD} token matches one of these keywords, then the token
 * type will be set to {@link #KEYWORD}, and {@link #tokenKeyword} will
 * return the index of the keyword in the specified array.
 * @param keywords an array of words to be treated as keywords, or null
 *                  (the default) for no keywords.
 * @return this Tokenizer object for method chaining.
 * @see #tokenizeWords
 */
public Tokenizer keywords(String[ ] keywords);

/**
 * Specify whether the tokenizer should keep track of the line number
 * and column number for each returned token.  The default is false.
 * If set to true, then tokenLine( ) and tokenColumn( ) return the
 * line and column numbers of the current token.
 * @param track whether to track the line and column numbers for each
 *         token.
 * @return this Tokenizer object for method chaining.
 * @throws java.lang.IllegalStateException
 *         if invoked after tokenizing begins
 * @see #tokenizeWords
 */
public Tokenizer trackPosition(boolean track);

/**
 * Specify pairs of token delimiters.  If the tokenizer encounters
 * any character in <tt>openquotes</tt>, then it will scan until it
 * encounters the corresponding character in <tt>closequotes</tt>.
 * When such a token is tokenized, {@link #tokenType} returns the character
 * from <tt>openquotes</tt> that was recognized and {@link #tokenText}
 * returns the characters between, but not including the delimiters.
 * Note that no escape characters are recognized. Quote tokenization occurs
 * after other types of tokenization so <tt>openquotes</tt> should not
 * include whitespace, number or word characters, if spaces, numbers, or
 * words are being tokenized.
 * <p>
 * Quote tokenization is useful for tokens other than quoted strings.
 * For example to recognize single-quoted strings and single-line
```

Example 2-8. Tokenizer.java (continued)

```
 * comments, you might call this method like this:
 * <code>quotes("'#", "'\n");</code>
 *
 * @param openquotes The string of characters that can begin a quote,
 * @param closequotes The string of characters that end a quote
 * @return this Tokenizer object for method chaining.
 * @throws java.lang.NullPointerException if either argument is null
 * @throws java.lang.IllegalArgumentException if <tt>openquotes</tt> and
 *          <tt>closequotes</tt> have different lengths.
 * @see #scan(char,boolean,boolean,boolean)
 */
public Tokenizer quotes(String openquotes, String closequotes);

/**
 * Specify the maximum token length that the Tokenizer is required to
 * accommodate. If presented with an input token longer than the specified
 * size, a Tokenizer behavior is undefined. Implementations must typically
 * allocate an internal buffer at least this large, but may use a smaller
 * buffer if they know that the total length of the input is smaller.
 * Implementations should document their default value, and are encouraged
 * to define constructors that take the token length as an argument.
 *
 * @param size maximum token length the tokenizer must handle. Must be > 0.
 * @return this Tokenizer object for method chaining.
 * @throws java.lang.IllegalArgumentException if <tt>size</tt> < 1.
 * @throws java.lang.IllegalStateException
 *          if invoked after tokenizing begins
 */
public Tokenizer maximumTokenLength(int size);

/**
 * This nested interface defines what a "word" is.
 * @see Tokenizer#tokenizeWords
 * @see Tokenizer#wordRecognizer
 */
public static interface WordRecognizer {
    /**
     * Determine whether <tt>c</tt> is a valid word start character.
     * @param c the character to test
     * @return true if a word may begin with the character <tt>c</tt>.
     */
    public boolean isWordStart(char c);

    /**
     * Determine whether a word that begins with <tt>firstChar</tt> may
     * contain <tt>c</tt>.
     * @param c the character to test.
     * @param firstChar the character that started this word
     * @return true if a word that begins with <tt>firstChar</tt> may
     *          contain the character <tt>c</tt>
     */
    public boolean isWordPart(char c, char firstChar);
}
```

Example 2-8. Tokenizer.java (continued)

```java
/**
 * Get the type of the current token. Valid token types are the token
 * type constants (all negative values) defined by this interface, and all
 * Unicode characters.  Positive return values typically represent
 * punctuation characters or other single characters that were not
 * tokenized.  But see {@link #quotes} for an exception.
 * @return the type of the current token, or {@link #BOF} if no tokens
 *      have been read yet, or {@link #EOF} if no more tokens are available.
 */
public int tokenType( );

/**
 * Get the text of the current token.
 * @return the text of the current token as a String, or null, when
 *    {@link #tokenType} returns {@link #BOF} or {@link #EOF}.
 *    Tokens delimited by quote characters (see {@link #quotes}) do not
 *    include the opening and closing delimiters, so this method may return
 *    the empty string when an empty quote is tokenized.  The same is
 *    possible after a call to {@link #scan(char,boolean,boolean,boolean)}.
 */
public String tokenText( );

/**
 * Get the index of the tokenized keyword.
 * @return the index into the keywords array of the tokenized word or
 *    -1 if the current token type is not {@link #KEYWORD}.
 * @see #keywords
 */
public int tokenKeyword( );

/**
 * Get the line number of the current token.
 * @return The line number of the start of the current token. Lines
 * are numbered from 1, not 0. This method returns 0 if the tokenizer is
 * not tracking token position or if tokenizing has not started yet, or if
 * the current token is {@link #EOF}.
 * @see #trackPosition
 */
public int tokenLine( );

/**
 * Get the column number of the current token.
 * @return The column of the start of the current token. Columns
 * are numbered from 1, not 0. This method returns 0 if the tokenizer is
 * not tracking token position or if tokenizing has not started yet, or if
 * the current token is {@link #EOF}.
 * @see #trackPosition
 */
public int tokenColumn( );

/**
 * Make the next token of input the current token, and return its type.
```

Example 2-8. Tokenizer.java (continued)

```
 * Implementations must tokenize input using the following algorithm, and
 * must perform each step in the order listed. <ol>
 *
 * <li>If there are no more input characters, set the current token to
 * {@link #EOF} and return that value.
 *
 * <li>If configured to skip or tokenize spaces, and the current character
 * is whitespace, coalesce any subsequent whitespace characters into a
 * token.  If spaces are being skipped, start tokenizing a new token;
 * otherwise, make the spaces the current token and return {@link #SPACE}.
 * See {@link #skipSpaces}, {@link #tokenizeSpaces}, and
 * {@link Character#isWhitespace}.
 *
 * <li>If configured to tokenize numbers and the current character is a
 * digit, coalesce all adjacent digits into a single token, make it the
 * current token, and return {@link #NUMBER}. See {@link #tokenizeNumbers}
 * and {@link Character#isDigit}
 *
 * <li>If configured to tokenize words, and the current character is a
 * word character, coalesce all adjacent word characters into a single
 * token, and make it the current token. If the word matches a registered
 * keyword, determine the keyword index and return {@link #KEYWORD}.
 * Otherwise return {@link #WORD}. Determine whether a character is a
 * word character using the registered {@link WordRecognizer}, if any,
 * or with {@link Character#isJavaIdentifierStart} and
 * {@link Character#isJavaIdentifierPart}.  See also
 * {@link #tokenizeWords} and {@link #wordRecognizer}.
 *
 * <li>If configured to tokenize quotes or other delimited tokens, and the
 * current character appears in the string of opening delimiters, then
 * scan until the character at the same position in the string of closing
 * delimiters is encountered or until there is no more input or the
 * maximum token size is reached.  Coalesce the characters between (but
 * not including) the delimiters into a single token, set the token type
 * to the opening delimiter, and return this character.
 * See {@link #quotes}.
 *
 * <li>If none of the steps above has returned a token, then make the
 * current character the current token, and return the current character.
 * </ol>
 *
 * @return the type of the next token, or {@link #EOF} if there are
 *         no more tokens to be read.
 * @see #nextChar @see #scan(char,boolean,boolean,boolean) */
public int next( ) throws IOException;

/**
 * Make the next character of input the current token, and return it.
 * @return the next character or {@link #EOF} if there are no more.
 * @see #next @see #scan(char,boolean,boolean,boolean)
 */
public int nextChar( ) throws IOException;
```

Example 2-8. Tokenizer.java (continued)

```
    /**
     * Scan until the first occurrence of the specified delimiter character.
     * Because a token scanned in this way may contain arbitrary characters,
     * the current token type is set to {@link #TEXT}.
     * @param delimiter the character to scan until.
     * @param extendCurrentToken if true, the scanned characters extend the
     *    current token. Otherwise, they are a token of their own.
     * @param includeDelimiter if true, then the delimiter character is
     *    included at the token. If false, then see skipDelimiter.
     * @param skipDelimiter if <tt>includeDelimiter</tt> is false, then this
     *    parameter specifies whether to skip the delimiter or return it in
     *    the next token.
     * @return the token type {@link #TEXT} if the delimiter character is
     *    successfully found. If the delimiter is not found, the return value
     *    is {@link #EOF} if all input was read, or {@link #OVERFLOW} if the
     *    maximum token length was exceeded. Note that even when this method
     *    does not return {@link #TEXT}, {@link #tokenType} does still return
     *    that value, and {@link #tokenText} returns as much of the token
     *    as could be read.
     * @see #scan(java.lang.String,boolean,boolean,boolean,boolean)
     * @see #next @see #nextChar
     */
    public int scan(char delimiter, boolean extendCurrentToken,
                    boolean includeDelimiter, boolean skipDelimiter)
        throws IOException;


    /**
     * This method is just {@link #scan(char,boolean,boolean,boolean)} except
     * that it uses a String delimiter, possibly containing more than one
     * character.
     * @param delimiter the string of characters that will terminate the scan.
     *    This argument must not be null, and must be of length 1 or greater.
     * @param matchall true if all characters of the delimiter must be matched
     *    sequentially. False if any one character in the string will do.
     * @param extendCurrentToken add scanned text to current token if true.
     * @param includeDelimiter include delimiter text in token if true.
     * @param skipDelimiter if <tt>includeDelimiter</tt> is false, then this
     *    parameter specifies whether to skip the delimiter or return it in
     *    the next token.
     * @return {@link #TEXT}, {@link #EOF}, or {@link #OVERFLOW}. See
     *    {@link #scan(char,boolean,boolean,boolean)} for details.
     * @throws java.lang.NullPointerException if delimiter is null.
     * @throws java.lang.IllegalArgumentException if delimiter is empty.
     * @throws java.lang.IllegalArgumentException if matchall is true and
     *    includeDelimiter and skipDelimiter are both false.
     * @see #scan(char,boolean,boolean,boolean)
     */
    public int scan(String delimiter, boolean matchAll,
                    boolean extendCurrentToken, boolean includeDelimiter,
                    boolean skipDelimiter)
        throws IOException;
}
```

The AbstractTokenizer Implementation

Example 2-9 defines the AbstractTokenizer class. As its name implies, this class implements the Tokenizer interface but is abstract, so it cannot be instantiated. The class begins by declaring a number of protected fields that hold its state. It then declares two abstract methods that subclasses must implement. The javadoc comments for these methods describe exactly what their implementations must do, and how those implementations should modify the protected fields of AbstractTokenizer. The rest of the class is a Tokenizer implementation that uses those protected fields and methods. This is the relatively complex code that does the actual tokenizing. Note that it tokenizes text stored in a character array named text. text is one of the protected fields defined by AbstractTokenizer. It is allocated and filled by concrete subclasses of AbstractTokenizer.

Example 2-9. AbstractTokenizer.java

```
package je3.classes;
import java.util.*;
import java.io.IOException;

/**
 * This class implements all the methods of the Tokenizer interface, and
 * defines two new abstract methods, {@link #createBuffer} and
 * {@link #fillBuffer} which all concrete subclasses must implement.
 * By default, instances of this class can handle tokens of up to 16*1024
 * characters in length.
 * @author David Flanagan
 */
public abstract class AbstractTokenizer implements Tokenizer {
    boolean skipSpaces;
    boolean tokenizeSpaces;
    boolean tokenizeNumbers;
    boolean tokenizeWords;
    boolean testquotes;
    Tokenizer.WordRecognizer wordRecognizer;
    Map keywordMap;
    String openquotes, closequotes;
    boolean trackPosition;

    int maximumTokenLength = 16 * 1024;

    int tokenType = BOF;
    int tokenLine = 0;
    int tokenColumn = 0;
    int tokenKeyword = -1;

    int line=0, column=0;  // The line and column numbers of text[p]

    // The name of this field is a little misleading. If eof is true, it
    // means that no more characters are available. But tokenType and tokenText
    // may still be valid until the next call to next(), nextChar(), or scan().
    boolean eof;           // Set to the return value of fillBuffer()
```

Example 2-9. AbstractTokenizer.java (continued)

```
// The following fields keep track of the tokenizer's state
// Invariant:  tokenStart <= tokenEnd <= p <= numChars <= text.length

/**
 * The start of the current token in {@link #text}.
 * Subclasses may need to update this field in {@link #fillBuffer}.
 */
protected int tokenStart = 0;

/**
 * The index in {@link #text} of the first character after the current
 * token. Subclasses may need to update this field in {@link #fillBuffer}.
 */
protected int tokenEnd = 0;

/**
 * The position of the first untokenized character in {@link #text}.
 * Subclasses may need to update this field in {@link #fillBuffer}.
 */
protected int p = 0;

/**
 * The number of valid characters of input text stored in {@link #text}.
 * Subclasses must implement {@link #createBuffer} and {@link #fillBuffer}
 * to set this value appropriately.
 */
protected int numChars = 0;

/**
 * A buffer holding the text we're parsing.  Subclasses must implement
 * {@link #createBuffer} to set this field to a character array, and
 * {@link #fillBuffer} to refill the array.
 */
protected char[ ] text = null;

/**
 * Create the {@link #text} buffer to use for parsing.  This method may
 * put text in the buffer, but it is not required to.  In either case, it
 * should set {@link #numChars} appropriately.  This method will be called
 * once, before tokenizing begins.
 *
 * @param bufferSize the minimum size of the created array, unless the
 * subclass knows in advance that the input text is smaller than this, in
 * which case, the input text size may be used instead.
 * @see #fillBuffer
 */
protected abstract void createBuffer(int bufferSize);

/**
 * Fill or refill the {@link #text} buffer and adjust related fields.
 * This method will be called when the tokenizer needs more characters to
 * tokenize. Concrete subclasses must implement this method to put
```

Example 2-9. AbstractTokenizer.java (continued)

```
 * characters into the @{link #text} buffer, blocking if necessary to wait
 * for characters to become available.  This method may make room in the
 * buffer by shifting the contents down to remove any characters before
 * tokenStart.  It must preserve any characters after {@link #tokenStart}
 * and before {@link #numChars}, however.  After such a shift, it must
 * adjust {@link #tokenStart}, {@link #tokenEnd} and {@link #p}
 * appropriately.  After the optional shift, the method should add as many
 * new characters as possible to {@link #text} (and always at least 1) and
 * adjust {@link #numChars} appropriately.
 *
 * @return false if no more characters are available; true otherwise.
 * @see #createBuffer
 */
protected abstract boolean fillBuffer() throws IOException;

public Tokenizer skipSpaces(boolean skip) {
    skipSpaces = skip;
    return this;
}

public Tokenizer tokenizeSpaces(boolean tokenize) {
    tokenizeSpaces = tokenize;
    return this;
}

public Tokenizer tokenizeNumbers(boolean tokenize) {
    tokenizeNumbers = tokenize;
    return this;
}

public Tokenizer tokenizeWords(boolean tokenize) {
    tokenizeWords = tokenize;
    return this;
}

public Tokenizer wordRecognizer(Tokenizer.WordRecognizer wordRecognizer) {
    this.wordRecognizer = wordRecognizer;
    return this;
}

public Tokenizer quotes(String openquotes, String closequotes) {
    if (openquotes == null || closequotes == null)
        throw new NullPointerException("arguments must be non-null");
    if (openquotes.length() != closequotes.length())
        throw new IllegalArgumentException("argument lengths differ");
    this.openquotes = openquotes;
    this.closequotes = closequotes;
    this.testquotes = openquotes.length() > 0;
    return this;
}

public Tokenizer trackPosition(boolean track) {
    if (text != null) throw new IllegalStateException();
```

Example 2-9. AbstractTokenizer.java (continued)

```
        trackPosition = track;
        return this;
    }

    public Tokenizer keywords(String[ ] keywords) {
        if (keywords != null) {
            keywordMap = new HashMap(keywords.length);
            for(int i = 0; i < keywords.length; i++)
                keywordMap.put(keywords[i], new Integer(i));
        }
        else keywordMap = null;
        return this;
    }

    public Tokenizer maximumTokenLength(int size) {
        if (size < 1) throw new IllegalArgumentException( );
        if (text != null) throw new IllegalStateException( );
        maximumTokenLength = size;
        return this;
    }

    public int tokenType( ) { return tokenType; }

    public String tokenText( ) {
        if (text == null || tokenStart >= numChars) return null;
        return new String(text, tokenStart, tokenEnd-tokenStart);
    }

    public int tokenLine( ) {
        if (trackPosition && tokenStart < numChars) return tokenLine;
        else return 0;
    }

    public int tokenColumn( ) {
        if (trackPosition && tokenStart < numChars) return tokenColumn;
        else return 0;
    }

    public int tokenKeyword( ) {
        if (tokenType == KEYWORD) return tokenKeyword;
        else return -1;
    }

    public int next( ) throws IOException {
        int quoteindex;
        beginNewToken( );
        if (eof) return tokenType = EOF;

        char c = text[p];

        if ((skipSpaces||tokenizeSpaces) && Character.isWhitespace(c)) {
            tokenType = SPACE;
```

Example 2-9. AbstractTokenizer.java (continued)

```
            do {
                        ckPosition) updatePosition(text[p]);

                        = numChars) eof = !fillBuffer();
                    of && Character.isWhitespace(text[p]));

        // If we don't return space tokens, then recursively call
        // this method to find another token. Note that the next character
        // is not space, so we will not get into infinite recursion
        if (skipSpaces) return next();
        tokenEnd = p;
    }
    else if (tokenizeNumbers && Character.isDigit(c)) {
        tokenType = NUMBER;
        do {
            if (trackPosition) column++;
            p++;
            if (p >= numChars) eof = !fillBuffer();
        } while(!eof && Character.isDigit(text[p]));
        tokenEnd = p;
    }
    else if (tokenizeWords &&
            (wordRecognizer!=null
                ?wordRecognizer.isWordStart(c)
                :Character.isJavaIdentifierStart(c))) {
        tokenType = WORD;
        do {
            if (trackPosition) column++;
            p++;
            if (p >= numChars) eof = !fillBuffer();
        } while(!eof &&
            (wordRecognizer!=null
                ?wordRecognizer.isWordPart(text[p], c)
                :Character.isJavaIdentifierPart(text[p])));

        if (keywordMap != null) {
            String ident = new String(text,tokenStart,p-tokenStart);
            Integer index = (Integer) keywordMap.get(ident);
            if (index != null) {
                tokenType = KEYWORD;
                tokenKeyword = index.intValue();
            }
        }
        tokenEnd = p;
    }
    else if (testquotes && (quoteindex = openquotes.indexOf(c)) != -1) {
        // Notes: we do not recognize any escape characters.
        // We do not include the opening or closing quote.
        // We do not report an error on EOF or OVERFLOW.
        if (trackPosition) column++;
        p++;
        // Scan until we find a matching quote, but do not include
        // the opening or closing quote.  Set the token type to the
```

Example 2-9. AbstractTokenizer.java (continued)

```
            // opening delimiter
            char closequote = closequotes.charAt(quoteindex);
            scan(closequote, false, false, true);
            tokenType = c;
            // the call to scan set tokenEnd, so we don't have to
        }
        else {
            // Otherwise, the character itself is the token
            if (trackPosition) updatePosition(text[p]);
            tokenType = text[p];
            p++;
            tokenEnd = p;
        }

        // Check the invariants before returning
        assert text != null && 0 <= tokenStart && tokenStart <= tokenEnd &&
            tokenEnd <= p && p <= numChars && numChars <= text.length;
        return tokenType;
    }

    public int nextChar( ) throws IOException {
        beginNewToken( );
        if (eof) return tokenType = EOF;
        tokenType = text[p];
        if (trackPosition) updatePosition(text[p]);
        tokenEnd = ++p;
        // Check the invariants before returning
        assert text != null && 0 <= tokenStart && tokenStart <= tokenEnd &&
            tokenEnd <= p && p <= numChars && numChars <= text.length;
        return tokenType;
    }

    public int scan(char delimiter, boolean extendCurrentToken,
                    boolean includeDelimiter, boolean skipDelimiter)
        throws IOException
    {
        return scan(new char[ ] { delimiter }, false,
                    extendCurrentToken, includeDelimiter, skipDelimiter);
    }

    public int scan(String delimiter, boolean matchall,
                    boolean extendCurrentToken,
                    boolean includeDelimiter, boolean skipDelimiter)
        throws IOException
    {
        return scan(delimiter.toCharArray( ), matchall,
                    extendCurrentToken, includeDelimiter, skipDelimiter);
    }

    protected int scan(char[ ] delimiter,
                       boolean matchall, boolean extendCurrentToken,
                       boolean includeDelimiter, boolean skipDelimiter)
        throws IOException
```

Example 2-9. AbstractTokenizer.java (continued)

```
{
    if (matchall && !includeDelimiter && !skipDelimiter)
        throw new IllegalArgumentException("must include or skip " +
                                    "delimiter when matchall is true");

    if (extendCurrentToken) ensureChars();
    else beginNewToken();

    tokenType = TEXT; // Even if return value differs
    if (eof) return EOF;

    int delimiterMatchIndex = 0;
    String delimString = null;
    if (!matchall && delimiter.length > 0)
        delimString = new String(delimiter);

    while(!eof) {
        // See if we've found the delimiter.  There are 3 cases here:
        // 1) single-character delimiter
        // 2) multi-char delimiter, and all must be matched sequentially
        // 3) multi-char delimiter, must match any one of them.
        if (delimiter.length == 1) {
            if (text[p] == delimiter[0]) break;
        }
        else if (matchall) {
            if (text[p] == delimiter[delimiterMatchIndex]) {
                delimiterMatchIndex++;
                if (delimiterMatchIndex == delimiter.length) break;
            }
            else delimiterMatchIndex = 0;
        }
        else {
            if (delimString.indexOf(text[p]) != -1) break;
        }

        if (trackPosition) updatePosition(text[p]);
        p++;
        if (p >= numChars) {      // Do we need more text?
            if (tokenStart > 0)      // Do we have room for more?
                eof = !fillBuffer(); // Yes, so go get some
            else {                   // No room for more characters
                tokenEnd = p;        // so report an overflow
                return OVERFLOW;
            }
        }
    }

    if (eof) {
        tokenEnd = p;
        return EOF;
    }

    if (includeDelimiter) {
```

Example 2-9. AbstractTokenizer.java (continued)

```
            if (trackPosition) updatePosition(text[p]);
            p++;
            tokenEnd = p;
        }
        else if (skipDelimiter) {
            if (trackPosition) updatePosition(text[p]);
            p++;
            if (matchall) tokenEnd = p - delimiter.length;
            else tokenEnd = p - 1;
        }
        else {
            // we know the delimiter length is 1 in this case
            tokenEnd = p;
        }

        // Check the invariants before returning
        assert text != null && 0 <= tokenStart && tokenStart <= tokenEnd &&
            tokenEnd <= p && p <= numChars && numChars <= text.length;
        return TEXT;
    }

    private void ensureChars() throws IOException {
        if (text == null) {
            createBuffer(maximumTokenLength);  // create text[], set numChars
            p = tokenStart = tokenEnd = 0;     // initialize other state
            if (trackPosition) line = column = 1;
        }
        if (!eof && p >= numChars) // Fill the text[] buffer if needed
            eof = !fillBuffer();

        // Make sure our class invariants hold true before we start a token
        assert text != null && 0 <= tokenStart && tokenStart <= tokenEnd &&
            tokenEnd <= p && (p < numChars || (p == numChars && eof)) &&
            numChars <= text.length;
    }

    private void beginNewToken() throws IOException {
        ensureChars();
        if (!eof) {
            tokenStart = p;
            tokenColumn = column;
            tokenLine = line;
        }
    }

    private void updatePosition(char c) {
        if (c == '\n') {
            line++;
            column = 1;
        }
        else column++;
    }
}
```

A Concrete CharSequenceTokenizer

Example 2-10 is a concrete implementation of the Tokenizer interface that subclasses AbstractTokenizer to tokenize any CharSequence (i.e., any String, StringBuffer, or java.nio.CharBuffer object). The code is refreshingly simple, which shows the power of the three-way interface/abstract class/concrete class design. The class includes an inner class named Test that tokenizes its command-line arguments.

Example 2-10. CharSequenceTokenizer.java

```
package je3.classes;

/**
 * This trivial subclass of AbstractTokenizer is suitable for tokenizing input
 * stored in a String, StringBuffer, CharBuffer, or any other class that
 * implements CharSequence.  Because CharSequence instances may be mutable,
 * the construtor makes an internal copy of the character sequence.  This means
 * that any subsequent changes to the character sequence will not be seen
 * during tokenizing.
 *
 * @author David Flanagan
 */
public class CharSequenceTokenizer extends AbstractTokenizer {
    char[] buffer;  // a copy of the characters in the sequence

    /**
     * Construct a new CharSequenceTokenizer to tokenize <tt>sequence</tt>.
     * This constructor makes an internal copy of the characters in the
     * specified sequence.
     * @param sequence the character sequence to be tokenized.
     */
    public CharSequenceTokenizer(CharSequence sequence) {
        buffer = sequence.toString().toCharArray();
    }

    /**
     * Set the inherited {@link #text} and {@link #numChars} fields.
     * This class knows the complete length of the input text, so it ignores
     * the <tt>bufferSize</tt> argument and uses the complete input sequence.
     * @param bufferSize ignored in this implementation
     */
    protected void createBuffer(int bufferSize) {
        assert text == null;        // verify that we're only called once
        text = buffer;
        numChars = buffer.length;
    }

    /**
     * Return false to indicate no more input is available.
     * {@link #createBuffer} fills the buffer with the complete input sequence,
     * so this method returns false to indicate that no more text is available.
     * @return always returns false.
     */
```

Example 2-10. CharSequenceTokenizer.java (continued)

```java
    protected boolean fillBuffer() { return false; }

    public static class Test {
        public static void main(String[] args) throws java.io.IOException {
            StringBuffer text = new StringBuffer();
            for(int i = 0; i < args.length; i++) text.append(args[i]+" ");
            CharSequenceTokenizer t=new CharSequenceTokenizer(text.toString());
            t.tokenizeWords(true).quotes("'&","';").skipSpaces(true);
            while(t.next() != Tokenizer.EOF)
                System.out.println(t.tokenText());
        }
    }
}
```

Exercises

Exercise 2-1. Write a Circle class that is similar to the Rect class. Define a move( ) method and an isInside( ) method. (Recall that a circle is defined as all points within a given radius from the center. Test for insideness by using the Pythagorean theorem to compute the distance between a point and the center of the circle.) Also, define a boundingBox( ) method that returns the smallest Rect that encloses the complete Circle. Write a simple program to test the methods you've implemented.

Exercise 2-2. Write a class that represents a person's mailing address. It should have separate fields for the name, street address, city, state, and ZIP code. Define a toString( ) method that produces nicely formatted output.

Exercise 2-3. Modify the ComplexNumber class of Example 2-5 to override the equals( ) and hashCode( ) methods inherited from Object. Use the IntList class of Example 2-7 as a model.

Exercise 2-4. Modify Example 2-5 again to implement Comparable as Example 2-7 does. Note that this is not as straightforward as its seems, since there is not an unambiguous ordering for complex numbers. One possible way to order complex numbers is by their magnitude. Although this ordering is suitable for some applications, note that it is not compatible with the equals( ) method. That is, a compareTo( ) method based on magnitude will return 0 (equality) for numbers that are nonequal according to the equals( ) method.

Exercise 2-5. Modify the IntList class of Example 2-7 to create a sort( ) method that rearranges the list elements into sorted order. You can use the sorting algorithm from the SortNumbers class of Example 1-14, or you may prefer to research and implement a more advanced sorting algorithm, such as quicksort or mergesort.

Exercise 2-6. The IntList class implements the Comparable interface, which means that IntList objects can be compared to each other. Write a program that initializes an array of IntList objects, sorts those objects, and then prints the lists in their new order (IntList overrides toString( ), so printing the lists is easy).

II

Core Java APIs

Part II contains examples that demonstrate basic Java functionality and essential Java APIs. These examples correspond to the portion of Java that is covered in *Java in a Nutshell*.

Chapter 3, *Input/Output*
Chapter 4, *Threads*
Chapter 5, *Networking*
Chapter 6, *New I/O*
Chapter 7, *Security and Cryptography*
Chapter 8, *Internationalization*
Chapter 9, *Reflection*
Chapter 10, *Object Serialization*

3

Input/Output

A computer program isn't much good unless it can communicate with the outside world, and input/output (I/O) capabilities are a fundamental feature of any programming platform. In Java, I/O is done with the classes and interfaces of the java.io package and, in Java 1.4, with the "New IO" package java.nio and its subpackages. This chapter demonstrates the input/output capabilities of java.io. The New I/O API is covered in Chapter 6. The examples here demonstrate how to:

- Read and write files
- List directories and obtain file size and date information
- Use various Java stream classes
- Define customized stream subclasses

The techniques introduced in this chapter are also used in other places in this book. We'll see many examples that use streams for input and output in Chapter 5, and we'll see a specialized kind of I/O in Chapter 10.

Files and Streams

One of the commonly used classes in the java.io package is File. This class is somewhat misleadingly named, as it represents a filename (or directory name), rather than a file itself. Because files (and directories) have different naming conventions under different operating systems, Java provides the File class to try to hide some of those differences. The File class also defines various methods for operating on files as a whole: deleting files, creating directories, listing directories, querying the size and modification time of a file, and so on.

While the File class provides methods to manipulate directories and the files within those directories, it doesn't provide any methods that manipulate the contents of the files. In other words, it doesn't provide any way to read or write the bytes or characters that are contained in files. In Java, sequential file I/O is performed through a stream abstraction. (Random-access file I/O is performed with the RandomAccessFile class, but sequential I/O is much more common.)

A *stream* is simply an object from which data can be read sequentially or to which data can be written sequentially. The bulk of the java.io package consists of stream classes: there are 40 of them. InputStream and OutputStream and their respective subclasses are objects for reading and writing streams of bytes, whereas Reader and Writer and their subclasses are objects for reading and writing streams of Unicode characters. In addition to these stream classes, the java.util.zip package defines another eight input and output byte streams for data compression and decompression. Tables 3-1 through 3-4 summarize the stream classes available in java.io and java.util.zip.

Table 3-1. Byte input streams

Byte input stream	Description
BufferedInputStream	Reads a buffer of bytes from an InputStream, and then returns bytes from the buffer, making small reads more efficient.
ByteArrayInputStream	Reads bytes sequentially from an array.
CheckedInputStream	This java.util.zip class computes a checksum of the bytes it reads from an InputStream.
DataInputStream	Reads binary representations of Java primitive types from an InputStream.
FileInputStream	Reads bytes sequentially from a file.
FilterInputStream	The superclass of byte input stream filter classes.
GZIPInputStream	This java.util.zip class uncompresses GZIP-compressed bytes it reads from an InputStream.
InflaterInputStream	The superclass of GZIPInputStream and ZipInputStream.
InputStream	The superclass of all byte input streams.
LineNumberInputStream	This class is deprecated as of Java 1.1; use LineNumberReader instead.
ObjectInputStream	Reads binary representations of Java objects and primitive values from a byte stream. This class is used for the deserialization of objects.
PipedInputStream	Reads bytes written to the PipedOutputStream to which it is connected. Used in multithreaded programs.
PushbackInputStream	Adds a fixed-size pushback buffer to an input stream, so that bytes can be unread. Useful with some parsers.
SequenceInputStream	Reads bytes sequentially from two or more input streams, as if they were a single stream.
StringBufferInputStream	This class is deprecated as of Java 1.1; use StringReader instead.
ZipInputStream	This java.util.zip class uncompresses entries in a ZIP file.

Table 3-2. Character input streams

Character input stream	Description
BufferedReader	Reads a buffer of characters from a Reader, and then returns characters from the buffer, making small reads more efficient.
CharArrayReader	Reads characters sequentially from an array.
FileReader	Reads characters sequentially from a file. An InputStreamReader subclass that reads from an automatically created FileInputStream.
FilterReader	The superclass of character input stream filter classes.

Table 3-2. Character input streams (continued)

Character input stream	Description
InputStreamReader	Reads characters from a byte input stream. Converts bytes to characters using the encoding of the default locale, or a specified encoding.
LineNumberReader	Reads lines of text and keeps track of how many have been read.
PipedReader	Reads characters written to the PipedWriter to which it is connected. Used in multithreaded programs.
PushbackReader	Adds a fixed-size pushback buffer to a Reader, so that characters can be unread. Useful with some parsers.
Reader	The superclass of all character input streams.
StringReader	Reads characters sequentially from a string.

Table 3-3. Byte output streams

Byte output stream	Description
BufferedOutputStream	Buffers byte output for efficiency; writes to an OutputStream only when the buffer fills up.
ByteArrayOutputStream	Writes bytes sequentially into an array.
CheckedOutputStream	This java.util.zip class computes a checksum of the bytes it writes to an OutputStream.
DataOutputStream	Writes binary representations of Java primitive types to an OutputStream.
DeflaterOutputStream	The superclass of GZIPOutputStream and ZipOutputStream.
FileOutputStream	Writes bytes sequentially to a file.
FilterOutputStream	The superclass of all byte output stream filters.
GZIPOutputStream	This java.util.zip class outputs a GZIP-compressed version of the bytes written to it.
ObjectOutputStream	Writes binary representations of Java objects and primitive values to an OutputStream. Used for the serialization of objects.
OutputStream	The superclass of all byte output streams.
PipedOutputStream	Writes bytes to the PipedInputStream to which it is connected. Used in multithreaded programs.
PrintStream	Writes a textual representation of Java objects and primitive values. Deprecated except for use by the standard output stream System.out as of Java 1.1. In other contexts, use PrintWriter instead.
ZipOutputStream	This java.util.zip class compresses entries in a ZIP file.

Table 3-4. Character output streams

Character output stream	Description
BufferedWriter	Buffers output for efficiency; writes characters to a Writer only when the buffer fills up.
CharArrayWriter	Writes characters sequentially into an array.
FileWriter	Writes characters sequentially to a file. A subclass of OutputStreamWriter that automatically creates a FileOutputStream.
FilterWriter	The superclass of all character output stream filters.
OutputStreamWriter	Writes characters to a byte output stream. Converts characters to bytes using the encoding of the default locale, or a specified encoding.

Table 3-4. Character output streams (continued)

Character output stream	Description
PipedWriter	Writes characters to the PipedReader to which it is connected. Used in multithreaded programs.
PrintWriter	Writes textual representations of Java objects and primitive values to a Writer.
StringWriter	Writes characters sequentially into an internally created StringBuffer.
Writer	The superclass of all character output streams.

Working with Files

Example 3-1 is a relatively short program that deletes a file or directory specified on the command line. Before it does the actual deletion, it performs several checks to ensure that the specified file exists, that it is writable, and, if it is a directory, that it is empty. If any of the tests fail, the program throws an exception explaining why the file cannot be deleted. These tests demonstrate some of the important features of the File class, and are necessary because the File.delete( ) method does not have useful failure diagnostics: instead of throwing an informative IOException on failure, it simply returns false. Thus, if we want to know why a file could not be deleted, we must test its deleteability before calling File.delete( ). Other useful File methods (worth looking up) include getParent( ), length( ), mkdir( ), and renameTo( ).

Example 3-1. Delete.java

```java
package je3.io;
import java.io.*;

/**
 * This class is a static method delete() and a standalone program that
 * deletes a specified file or directory.
 **/
public class Delete {
    /**
     * This is the main() method of the standalone program.  After checking
     * it arguments, it invokes the Delete.delete() method to do the deletion
     **/
    public static void main(String[] args) {
        if (args.length != 1) {    // Check command-line arguments
            System.err.println("Usage: java Delete <file or directory>");
            System.exit(0);
        }
        // Call delete() and display any error messages it throws.
        try { delete(args[0]); }
        catch (IllegalArgumentException e) {
            System.err.println(e.getMessage());
        }
    }

    /**
     * The static method that does the deletion.  Invoked by main(), and
```

Example 3-1. Delete.java (continued)

```
 * designed for use by other programs as well.  It first makes sure that
 * the specified file or directory is deleteable before attempting to
 * delete it.  If there is a problem, it throws an
 * IllegalArgumentException.
 **/
public static void delete(String filename) {
    // Create a File object to represent the filename
    File f = new File(filename);

    // Make sure the file or directory exists and isn't write protected
    if (!f.exists()) fail("Delete: no such file or directory: " +filename);
    if (!f.canWrite()) fail("Delete: write protected: " + filename);

    // If it is a directory, make sure it is empty
    if (f.isDirectory()) {
        String[ ] files = f.list();
        if (files.length > 0)
            fail("Delete: directory not empty: " + filename);
    }

    // If we passed all the tests, then attempt to delete it
    boolean success = f.delete();

    // And throw an exception if it didn't work for some (unknown) reason.
    // For example, because of a bug with Java 1.1.1 on Linux,
    // directory deletion always fails
    if (!success) fail("Delete: deletion failed");
}

/** A convenience method to throw an exception */
protected static void fail(String msg) throws IllegalArgumentException {
    throw new IllegalArgumentException(msg);
}
}
```

Copying File Contents

Example 3-2 shows a program that copies the contents of a specified file to another file. This example uses the File class, much as Example 3-1 did, to check that the source file exists, that the destination is writable, and so on. But it also introduces the use of streams to work with the contents of files. It uses a FileInputStream to read the bytes of the source file and a FileOutputStream to copy those bytes to the destination file.

The copy( ) method implements the functionality of the program. This method is heavily commented, so that you can follow the steps it takes. First, it performs a surprisingly large number of checks to verify that the copy request is a legitimate one. If all those tests succeed, it then creates a FileInputStream to read bytes from the source and a FileOutputStream to write those bytes to the destination. Notice the use of a byte array buffer to store bytes during the copy. Pay particular attention to the short while loop that actually performs the copy. The combination of assignment and testing in the condition of the while loop is a useful idiom that occurs frequently in I/O programming. Also notice the finally statement that ensures the streams are properly closed before the program exits.

In addition to using streams to read from and write to files, this program also uses streams to read from and write to the console. Before overwriting an existing file, this example asks for user confirmation. It demonstrates how to read lines of text with a BufferedReader that reads individual characters from an InputStreamReader, which in turn reads bytes from System.in (an InputStream), which reads keystrokes from the user's keyboard. Additionally, the program displays textual output with System.out and System.err, which are both instances of PrintStream.

The static FileCopy.copy( ) method can be called directly by any program. The FileCopy class also provides a main( ) method, however, so that it can be used as a standalone program.

Example 3-2. FileCopy.java

```
package je3.io;
import java.io.*;

/**
 * This class is a standalone program to copy a file, and also defines a
 * static copy() method that other programs can use to copy files.
 **/
public class FileCopy {
    /** The main() method of the standalone program.  Calls copy(). */
    public static void main(String[] args) {
        if (args.length != 2)      // Check arguments
            System.err.println("Usage: java FileCopy <source> <destination>");
        else {
            // Call copy() to do the copy; display any error messages
            try { copy(args[0], args[1]); }
            catch (IOException e) { System.err.println(e.getMessage()); }
        }
    }

    /**
     * The static method that actually performs the file copy.
     * Before copying the file, however, it performs a lot of tests to make
     * sure everything is as it should be.
     */
    public static void copy(String from_name, String to_name)
        throws IOException
    {
        File from_file = new File(from_name);  // Get File objects from Strings
        File to_file = new File(to_name);

        // First make sure the source file exists, is a file, and is readable.
        // These tests are also performed by the FileInputStream constructor,
        // which throws a FileNotFoundException if they fail.
        if (!from_file.exists())
            abort("no such source file: " + from_name);
        if (!from_file.isFile())
            abort("can't copy directory: " + from_name);
```

Example 3-2. FileCopy.java (continued)

```java
    if (!from_file.canRead( ))
        abort("source file is unreadable: " + from_name);

    // If the destination is a directory, use the source file name
    // as the destination file name
    if (to_file.isDirectory( ))
        to_file = new File(to_file, from_file.getName( ));

    // If the destination exists, make sure it is a writeable file
    // and ask before overwriting it.  If the destination doesn't
    // exist, make sure the directory exists and is writeable.
    if (to_file.exists( )) {
        if (!to_file.canWrite( ))
            abort("destination file is unwriteable: " + to_name);
        // Ask whether to overwrite it
        System.out.print("Overwrite existing file " + to_file.getName( ) +
                        "? (Y/N): ");
        System.out.flush( );
        // Get the user's response.
        BufferedReader in=
            new BufferedReader(new InputStreamReader(System.in));
        String response = in.readLine( );
        // Check the response.  If not a Yes, abort the copy.
        if (!response.equals("Y") && !response.equals("y"))
            abort("existing file was not overwritten.");
    }
    else {
        // If file doesn't exist, check if directory exists and is
        // writeable.  If getParent( ) returns null, then the directory is
        // the current dir.  so look up the user.dir system property to
        // find out what that is.
        String parent = to_file.getParent( );  // The destination directory
        if (parent ==== null)      // If none, use the current directory
            parent = System.getProperty("user.dir");
        File dir = new File(parent);            // Convert it to a file.
        if (!dir.exists( ))
            abort("destination directory doesn't exist: "+parent);
        if (dir.isFile( ))
            abort("destination is not a directory: " + parent);
        if (!dir.canWrite( ))
            abort("destination directory is unwriteable: " + parent);
    }

    // If we've gotten this far, then everything is okay.
    // So we copy the file, a buffer of bytes at a time.
    FileInputStream from = null;  // Stream to read from source
    FileOutputStream to = null;   // Stream to write to destination
    try {
        from = new FileInputStream(from_file);  // Create input stream
        to = new FileOutputStream(to_file);     // Create output stream
        byte[ ] buffer = new byte[4096];        // To hold file contents
        int bytes_read;                         // How many bytes in buffer
```

Example 3-2. FileCopy.java (continued)

```
            // Read a chunk of bytes into the buffer, then write them out,
            // looping until we reach the end of the file (when read( ) returns
            // -1).  Note the combination of assignment and comparison in this
            // while loop.  This is a common I/O programming idiom.
            while((bytes_read = from.read(buffer)) != -1) // Read until EOF
                to.write(buffer, 0, bytes_read);              // write
        }
        // Always close the streams, even if exceptions were thrown
        finally {
            if (from != null) try { from.close( ); } catch (IOException e) { ; }
            if (to != null) try { to.close( ); } catch (IOException e) { ; }
        }
    }

    /** A convenience method to throw an exception */
    private static void abort(String msg) throws IOException {
        throw new IOException("FileCopy: " + msg);
    }
}
```

Reading and Displaying Text Files

Example 3-3 shows the FileViewer class. It combines the use of the File class and I/O streams to read the contents of a text file with GUI techniques to display those contents. FileViewer uses a java.awt.TextArea component to display file contents, as shown in Figure 3-1. Example 3-3 uses graphical user interface techniques that are introduced in Chapter 11. If you have not yet read that chapter or do not already have AWT programming experience, you probably won't understand all the code in the example. That's okay; just concentrate on the I/O code, which is the main focus of this chapter.

The FileViewer constructor concerns itself mainly with the mechanics of setting up the necessary GUI. There are some interesting uses of the File object at the end of this constructor, however. The heart of this example is the setFile( ) method. This is where the file contents are loaded and displayed. Because the file contents are to be displayed in a TextArea component, the legitimate assumption is that the file contains characters. Thus, we use a character input stream, a FileReader, instead of the byte input stream used in the FileCopy program of Example 3-2. Once again, use a finally clause to ensure that the FileReader stream is properly closed.

The actionPerformed( ) method handles GUI events. If the user clicks on the **Open File** button, this method creates a FileDialog object to prompt for a new file to display. Note how the default directory is set before the dialog is displayed and then retrieved after the user makes a selection. This is possible because the show( ) method actually blocks until the user selects a file and dismisses the dialog.

The FileViewer class is designed to be used by other classes. It also has its own main( ) method, however, so that it can be run as a standalone program.

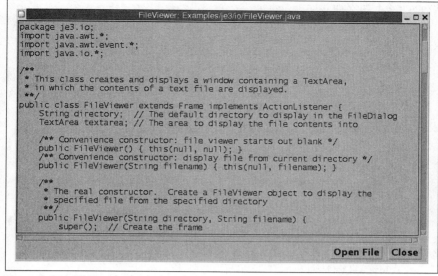

```
FileViewer: Examples/je3/io/FileViewer.java      _ □ X
package je3.io;
import java.awt.*;
import java.awt.event.*;
import java.io.*;

/**
 * This class creates and displays a window containing a TextArea,
 * in which the contents of a text file are displayed.
 **/
public class FileViewer extends Frame implements ActionListener {
    String directory;  // The default directory to display in the FileDialog
    TextArea textarea; // The area to display the file contents into

    /** Convenience constructor: file viewer starts out blank */
    public FileViewer() { this(null, null); }
    /** Convenience constructor: display file from current directory */
    public FileViewer(String filename) { this(null, filename); }

    /**
     * The real constructor.  Create a FileViewer object to display the
     * specified file from the specified directory
     **/
    public FileViewer(String directory, String filename) {
        super(); // Create the frame
                                                    Open File   Close
```

Figure 3-1. A FileViewer window

Example 3-3. FileViewer.java

```java
package je3.io;
import java.awt.*;
import java.awt.event.*;
import java.io.*;

/**
 * This class creates and displays a window containing a TextArea,
 * in which the contents of a text file are displayed.
 **/
public class FileViewer extends Frame implements ActionListener {
    String directory;  // The default directory to display in the FileDialog
    TextArea textarea; // The area to display the file contents into

    /** Convenience constructor: file viewer starts out blank */
    public FileViewer() { this(null, null); }
    /** Convenience constructor: display file from current directory */
    public FileViewer(String filename) { this(null, filename); }

    /**
     * The real constructor.  Create a FileViewer object to display the
     * specified file from the specified directory
     **/
    public FileViewer(String directory, String filename) {
        super();  // Create the frame

        // Destroy the window when the user requests it
        addWindowListener(new WindowAdapter() {
                public void windowClosing(WindowEvent e) { dispose(); }
            });
```

Example 3-3. FileViewer.java (continued)

```
        // Create a TextArea to display the contents of the file in
        textarea = new TextArea("", 24, 80);
        textarea.setFont(new Font("MonoSpaced", Font.PLAIN, 12));
        textarea.setEditable(false);
        this.add("Center", textarea);

        // Create a bottom panel to hold a couple of buttons in
        Panel p = new Panel();
        p.setLayout(new FlowLayout(FlowLayout.RIGHT, 10, 5));
        this.add(p, "South");

        // Create the buttons and arrange to handle button clicks
        Font font = new Font("SansSerif", Font.BOLD, 14);
        Button openfile = new Button("Open File");
        Button close = new Button("Close");
        openfile.addActionListener(this);
        openfile.setActionCommand("open");
        openfile.setFont(font);
        close.addActionListener(this);
        close.setActionCommand("close");
        close.setFont(font);
        p.add(openfile);
        p.add(close);

        this.pack();

        // Figure out the directory, from filename or current dir, if necessary
        if (directory == null) {
            File f;
            if ((filename != null)&& (f = new File(filename)).isAbsolute()) {
                directory = f.getParent();
                filename = f.getName();
            }
            else directory = System.getProperty("user.dir");
        }

        this.directory = directory;    // Remember the directory, for FileDialog
        setFile(directory, filename); // Now load and display the file
    }

    /**
     * Load and display the specified file from the specified directory
     **/
    public void setFile(String directory, String filename) {
        if ((filename == null) || (filename.length() == 0)) return;
        File f;
        FileReader in = null;
        // Read and display the file contents.  Since we're reading text, we
        // use a FileReader instead of a FileInputStream.
        try {
            f = new File(directory, filename); // Create a file object
            in = new FileReader(f);            // And a char stream to read  it
```

Example 3-3. FileViewer.java (continued)

```java
        char[ ] buffer = new char[4096];    // Read 4K characters at a time
        int len;                            // How many chars read each time
        textarea.setText("");               // Clear the text area
        while((len = in.read(buffer)) != -1) { // Read a batch of chars
            String s = new String(buffer, 0, len); // Convert to a string
            textarea.append(s);             // And display them
        }
        this.setTitle("FileViewer: " + filename);  // Set the window title
        textarea.setCaretPosition(0);       // Go to start of file
    }
    // Display messages if something goes wrong
    catch (IOException e) {
        textarea.setText(e.getClass().getName() + ": " + e.getMessage());
        this.setTitle("FileViewer: " + filename + ": I/O Exception");
    }
    // Always be sure to close the input stream!
    finally { try { if (in!=null) in.close(); } catch (IOException e) {} }
}

/**
 * Handle button clicks
 **/
public void actionPerformed(ActionEvent e) {
    String cmd = e.getActionCommand();
    if (cmd.equals("open")) {               // If user clicked "Open" button
        // Create a file dialog box to prompt for a new file to display
        FileDialog f = new FileDialog(this, "Open File", FileDialog.LOAD);
        f.setDirectory(directory);          // Set the default directory

        // Display the dialog and wait for the user's response
        f.show();

        directory = f.getDirectory();       // Remember new default directory
        setFile(directory, f.getFile());    // Load and display selection
        f.dispose();                        // Get rid of the dialog box
    }
    else if (cmd.equals("close"))           // If user clicked "Close" button,
        this.dispose();                     //    then close the window
}

/**
 * The FileViewer can be used by other classes, or it can be
 * used standalone with this main() method.
 **/
static public void main(String[ ] args) throws IOException {
    // Create a FileViewer object
    Frame f = new FileViewer((args.length == 1)?args[0]:null);
    // Arrange to exit when the FileViewer window closes
    f.addWindowListener(new WindowAdapter() {
        public void windowClosed(WindowEvent e) { System.exit(0); }
    });
```

Example 3-3. FileViewer.java (continued)

```
        // And pop the window up
        f.show( );
    }
}
```

Listing Directory and File Information

Just as the FileViewer class of Example 3-3 displays the contents of a file in a TextArea component, the FileLister class, shown in Example 3-4, displays the contents of a directory in a java.awt.List component. When you select a file or directory name from the list, the program displays information (size, modification date, etc.) about the file or directory in a TextField component. When you double-click on a directory, the contents of that directory are displayed. When you double-click on a file, it displays the contents of the file in a FileViewer object. Figure 3-2 shows a FileLister window. Again, if you are not already familiar with GUI programming in Java, don't expect to understand all of the code until you've read Chapter 11; instead, just pay attention to the various uses of the File object that are demonstrated in this example.

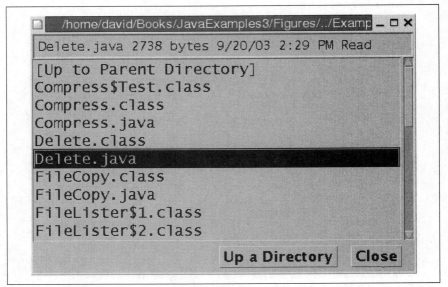

Figure 3-2. A FileLister window

The GUI mechanics of making the FileLister work form a large part of this example. The listDirectory( ) method lists the contents of a directory, using an optionally specified FilenameFilter object passed to the FileLister( ) constructor. This object defines an accept( ) method that is called for every entry in a directory to determine whether it should be listed.

The itemStateChanged( ) method is invoked when an item in the list is selected. It obtains information about the file or directory and displays it. The actionPerformed( ) method is another event listener method. This one is invoked when the user clicks either of the Button objects or double-clicks on an item in the list. If the user double-clicks on a directory, the program lists the contents of that directory. If the user double-clicks on a file, however, it creates and displays a FileViewer window to list the contents of the file.

Like the FileViewer class, the FileLister can be used by other classes, or it can be invoked as a standalone program. If you invoke it standalone, it lists the contents of the current directory. You can also invoke it with an optional directory name to see the contents of that directory. Using the optional -e flag followed by a file extension causes the program to filter the list of files and displays only the ones that have the specified extension. Note how the main( ) method parses the command-line arguments and uses an anonymous class to implement the FilenameFilter interface.

Example 3-4. FileLister.java

```
package je3.io;
import java.awt.*;
import java.awt.event.*;
import java.io.*;
import java.text.DateFormat;
import java.util.Date;


/**
 * This class creates and displays a window containing a list of
 * files and sub-directories in a specified directory.  Clicking on an
 * entry in the list displays more information about it. Double-clicking
 * on an entry displays it, if a file, or lists it if a directory.
 * An optionally-specified FilenameFilter filters the displayed list.
 **/
public class FileLister extends Frame implements ActionListener, ItemListener {
    private List list;                      // To display the directory contents in
    private TextField details;              // To display detail info in
    private Panel buttons;                  // Holds the buttons
    private Button up, close;               // The Up and Close buttons
    private File currentDir;                // The directory currently listed
    private FilenameFilter filter;          // An optional filter for the directory
    private String[ ] files;                // The directory contents
    private DateFormat dateFormatter =      // To display dates and time correctly
        DateFormat.getDateTimeInstance(DateFormat.SHORT, DateFormat.SHORT);

    /**
     * Constructor: create the GUI, and list the initial directory.
     **/
    public FileLister(String directory, FilenameFilter filter) {
        super("File Lister");               // Create the window
        this.filter = filter;               // Save the filter, if any

        // Destroy the window when the user requests it
        addWindowListener(new WindowAdapter( ) {
                public void windowClosing(WindowEvent e) { dispose( ); }
            });
```

Example 3-4. FileLister.java (continued)

```java
        list = new List(12, false);        // Set up the list
        list.setFont(new Font("MonoSpaced", Font.PLAIN, 14));
        list.addActionListener(this);
        list.addItemListener(this);

        details = new TextField();          // Set up the details area
        details.setFont(new Font("MonoSpaced", Font.PLAIN, 12));
        details.setEditable(false);

        buttons = new Panel();              // Set up the button box
        buttons.setLayout(new FlowLayout(FlowLayout.RIGHT, 15, 5));
        buttons.setFont(new Font("SansSerif", Font.BOLD, 14));

        up = new Button("Up a Directory"); // Set up the two buttons
        close = new Button("Close");
        up.addActionListener(this);
        close.addActionListener(this);

        buttons.add(up);                   // Add buttons to button box
        buttons.add(close);

        this.add(list, "Center");          // Add stuff to the window
        this.add(details, "North");
        this.add(buttons, "South");
        this.setSize(500, 350);

        listDirectory(directory);          // And now list initial directory.
    }

    /**
     * This method uses the list() method to get all entries in a directory
     * and then displays them in the List component.
     **/
    public void listDirectory(String directory) {
        // Convert the string to a File object, and check that the dir exists
        File dir = new File(directory);
        if (!dir.isDirectory())
            throw new IllegalArgumentException("FileLister: no such directory");

        // Get the (filtered) directory entries
        files = dir.list(filter);

        // Sort the list of filenames.
        java.util.Arrays.sort(files);

        // Remove any old entries in the list, and add the new ones
        list.removeAll();
        list.add("[Up to Parent Directory]"); // A special case entry
        for(int i = 0; i < files.length; i++) list.add(files[i]);
```

Example 3-4. FileLister.java (continued)

```java
        // Display directory name in window titlebar and in the details box
        this.setTitle(directory);
        details.setText(directory);

        // Remember this directory for later.
        currentDir = dir;
    }

    /**
     * This ItemListener method uses various File methods to obtain information
     * about a file or directory. Then it displays that info.
     **/
    public void itemStateChanged(ItemEvent e) {
        int i = list.getSelectedIndex() - 1;  // minus 1 for Up To Parent entry
        if (i < 0) return;
        String filename = files[i];                 // Get the selected entry
        File f = new File(currentDir, filename);  // Convert to a File
        if (!f.exists())                            // Confirm that it exists
            throw new IllegalArgumentException("FileLister: " +
                                               "no such file or directory");

        // Get the details about the file or directory, concatenate to a string
        String info = filename;
        if (f.isDirectory()) info += File.separator;
        info += " " + f.length() + " bytes ";
        info += dateFormatter.format(new java.util.Date(f.lastModified()));
        if (f.canRead()) info += " Read";
        if (f.canWrite()) info += " Write";

        // And display the details string
        details.setText(info);
    }

    /**
     * This ActionListener method is invoked when the user double-clicks on an
     * entry or clicks on one of the buttons. If they double-click on a file,
     * create a FileViewer to display that file. If they double-click on a
     * directory, call the listDirectory() method to display that directory
     **/
    public void actionPerformed(ActionEvent e) {
        if (e.getSource() == close) this.dispose();
        else if (e.getSource() == up) { up(); }
        else if (e.getSource() == list) {  // Double-click on an item
            int i = list.getSelectedIndex(); // Check which item
            if (i == 0) up();                       // Handle first Up To Parent item
            else {                                  // Otherwise, get filename
                String name = files[i-1];
                File f = new File(currentDir, name);   // Convert to a File
                String fullname = f.getAbsolutePath();
                if (f.isDirectory()) listDirectory(fullname);  // List dir
```

Example 3-4. FileLister.java (continued)

```
            else new FileViewer(fullname).show( );            // display file
        }
    }
}

/** A convenience method to display the contents of the parent directory */
protected void up( ) {
    String parent = currentDir.getParent( );
    if (parent == null) return;
    listDirectory(parent);
}

/** A convenience method used by main( ) */
public static void usage( ) {
    System.out.println("Usage: java FileLister [directory_name] " +
                       "[-e file_extension]");
    System.exit(0);
}

/**
 * A main( ) method so FileLister can be run standalone.
 * Parse command-line arguments and create the FileLister object.
 * If an extension is specified, create a FilenameFilter for it.
 * If no directory is specified, use the current directory.
 **/
public static void main(String args[ ]) throws IOException {
    FileLister f;
    FilenameFilter filter = null;  // The filter, if any
    String directory = null;       // The specified dir, or the current dir

    // Loop through args array, parsing arguments
    for(int i = 0; i < args.length; i++) {
        if (args[i].equals("-e")) {
            if (++i >= args.length) usage( );
            final String suffix = args[i];  // final for anon. class below

            // This class is a simple FilenameFilter.  It defines the
            // accept( ) method required to determine whether a specified
            // file should be listed.  A file will be listed if its name
            // ends with the specified extension, or if it is a directory.
            filter = new FilenameFilter( ) {
                    public boolean accept(File dir, String name) {
                        if (name.endsWith(suffix)) return true;
                        else return (new File(dir, name)).isDirectory( );
                    }
                };
        }
        else {
            if (directory != null) usage( );  // If already specified, fail.
            else directory = args[i];
        }
    }
```

Example 3-4. FileLister.java (continued)

```
        // if no directory specified, use the current directory
        if (directory == null) directory = System.getProperty("user.dir");
        // Create the FileLister object, with directory and filter specified.
        f = new FileLister(directory, filter);
        // Arrange for the application to exit when the window is closed
        f.addWindowListener(new WindowAdapter( ) {
            public void windowClosed(WindowEvent e) { System.exit(0); }
        });
        // Finally, pop the window up.
        f.show( );
    }
}
```

Compressing Files and Directories

Example 3-5 demonstrates an interesting application of stream classes: compressing files and directories. The classes of interest in this example are not actually part of the java.io package, but instead part of the java.util.zip package. The Compress class defines two static methods, gzipFile( ), which compresses a file using GZIP compression format, and zipDirectory( ), which compresses the files (but not directories) in a directory using the ZIP archive and compression format. gzipFile( ) uses the GZIPOutputStream class, while zipDirectory( ) uses the ZipOutputStream and ZipEntry classes, all from java.util.zip.

This example demonstrates the versatility of the stream classes and shows again how streams can be wrapped around one another so that the output of one stream becomes the input of another. This technique makes it possible to achieve a great variety of effects. Notice again the while loop in both methods that does the actual copying of data from source file to compressed file. These methods do not attempt to handle exceptions; instead they just pass them on to the caller, which is often exactly the right thing to do.

Compress is meant to be used as a utility class by other programs, so it doesn't itself include a main( ) method. The example does include an inner Compress.Test class, however, which has a main( ) method that can test the gzipFile( ) and zipDirectory( ) methods.

Example 3-5. Compress.java

```
package je3.io;
import java.io.*;
import java.util.zip.*;

/**
 * This class defines two static methods for gzipping files and zipping
 * directories.  It also defines a demonstration program as a nested class.
 **/
public class Compress {
    /** Gzip the contents of the from file and save in the to file. */
    public static void gzipFile(String from, String to) throws IOException {
        // Create stream to read from the from file
        FileInputStream in = new FileInputStream(from);
```

Example 3-5. Compress.java (continued)

```java
    // Create stream to compress data and write it to the to file.
    GZIPOutputStream out = new GZIPOutputStream(new FileOutputStream(to));
    // Copy bytes from one stream to the other
    byte[] buffer = new byte[4096];
    int bytes_read;
    while((bytes_read = in.read(buffer)) != -1)
        out.write(buffer, 0, bytes_read);
    // And close the streams
    in.close();
    out.close();
}

/** Zip the contents of the directory, and save it in the zipfile */
public static void zipDirectory(String dir, String zipfile)
    throws IOException, IllegalArgumentException {
    // Check that the directory is a directory, and get its contents
    File d = new File(dir);
    if (!d.isDirectory())
        throw new IllegalArgumentException("Compress: not a directory:  " +
                                            dir);
    String[] entries = d.list();
    byte[] buffer = new byte[4096];  // Create a buffer for copying
    int bytes_read;

    // Create a stream to compress data and write it to the zipfile
    ZipOutputStream out =
        new ZipOutputStream(new FileOutputStream(zipfile));

    // Loop through all entries in the directory
    for(int i = 0; i < entries.length; i++) {
        File f = new File(d, entries[i]);
        if (f.isDirectory()) continue;          // Don't zip sub-directories
        FileInputStream in = new FileInputStream(f); // Stream to read file
        ZipEntry entry = new ZipEntry(f.getPath());  // Make a ZipEntry
        out.putNextEntry(entry);                      // Store entry
        while((bytes_read = in.read(buffer)) != -1)  // Copy bytes
            out.write(buffer, 0, bytes_read);
        in.close();                              // Close input stream
    }
    // When we're done with the whole loop, close the output stream
    out.close();
}

/**
 * This nested class is a test program that demonstrates the use of the
 * static methods defined above.
 **/
public static class Test {
    /**
     * Compress a specified file or directory.  If no destination name is
     * specified, append .gz to a file name or .zip to a directory name
     **/
```

Example 3-5. Compress.java (continued)

```
    public static void main(String args[ ]) throws IOException {
        if ((args.length != 1)&& (args.length != 2)) {   // check arguments
            System.err.println("Usage: java Compress$Test <from> [<to>]");
            System.exit(0);
        }
        String from = args[0], to;
        File f = new File(from);
        boolean directory = f.isDirectory( );   // Is it a file or directory?
        if (args.length == 2) to = args[1];
        else {                                    // If destination not specified
            if (directory) to = from + ".zip";   //    use a .zip suffix
            else to = from + ".gz";               //    or a .gz suffix
        }

        if ((new File(to)).exists( )) { // Make sure not to overwrite
            System.err.println("Compress: won't overwrite existing file: "+
                                to);
            System.exit(0);
        }

        // Finally, call one of the methods defined above to do the work.
        if (directory) Compress.zipDirectory(from, to);
        else Compress.gzipFile(from, to);
    }
  }
}
```

Filtering Character Streams

FilterReader is an abstract class that defines a null filter; it reads characters from a specified Reader and returns them with no modification. In other words, FilterReader defines no-op implementations of all the Reader methods. A subclass must override at least the two read( ) methods to perform whatever sort of filtering is necessary. Some subclasses may override other methods as well. Example 3-6 shows RemoveHTMLReader, which is a custom subclass of FilterReader that reads HTML text from a stream and filters out all of the HTML tags from the text it returns.

In the example, we implement the HTML tag filtration in the three-argument version of read( ), and then implement the no-argument version in terms of that more complicated version. The example includes an inner Test class with a main( ) method that shows how you might use the RemoveHTMLReader class.

Note that we could also define a RemoveHTMLWriter class by performing the same filtration in a FilterWriter subclass. Or, to filter a byte stream instead of a character stream, we could subclass FilterInputStream and FilterOutputStream. RemoveHTMLReader is only one example of a filter stream. Other possibilities include streams that count the number of characters or bytes processed, convert characters to uppercase, extract URLs, perform search-and-replace operations, convert Unix-style LF line terminators to Windows-style CRLF line terminators, and so on.

Example 3-6. RemoveHTMLReader.java

```java
package je3.io;
import java.io.*;

/**
 * A simple FilterReader that strips HTML tags (or anything between
 * pairs of angle brackets) out of a stream of characters.
 **/
public class RemoveHTMLReader extends FilterReader {
    /** A trivial constructor.  Just initialize our superclass */
    public RemoveHTMLReader(Reader in) { super(in); }

    boolean intag = false;     // Used to remember whether we are "inside" a tag

    /**
     * This is the implementation of the no-op read() method of FilterReader.
     * It calls in.read() to get a buffer full of characters, then strips
     * out the HTML tags.  (in is a protected field of the superclass).
     **/
    public int read(char[] buf, int from, int len) throws IOException {
        int numchars = 0;         // how many characters have been read
        // Loop, because we might read a bunch of characters, then strip them
        // all out, leaving us with zero characters to return.
        while (numchars == 0) {
            numchars = in.read(buf, from, len); // Read characters
            if (numchars == -1) return -1;      // Check for EOF and handle it.

            // Loop through the characters we read, stripping out HTML tags.
            // Characters not in tags are copied over previous tags
            int last = from;                    // Index of last non-HTML char
            for(int i = from; i < from + numchars; i++) {
                if (!intag) {                   // If not in an HTML tag
                    if (buf[i] == '<') intag = true; // check for tag start
                    else buf[last++] = buf[i];       // and copy the character
                }
                else if (buf[i] == '>') intag = false; // check for end of tag
            }
            numchars = last - from; // Figure out how many characters remain
        }                           // And if it is more than zero characters
        return numchars;            // Then return that number.
    }

    /**
     * This is another no-op read() method we have to implement.  We
     * implement it in terms of the method above.  Our superclass implements
     * the remaining read() methods in terms of these two.
     **/
    public int read() throws IOException {
        char[] buf = new char[1];
        int result = read(buf, 0, 1);
        if (result == -1) return -1;
        else return (int)buf[0];
    }
```

Example 3-6. RemoveHTMLReader.java (continued)

```java
/** This class defines a main( ) method to test the RemoveHTMLReader */
public static class Test {
    /** The test program: read a text file, strip HTML, print to console */
    public static void main(String[ ] args) {
        try {
            if (args.length != 1)
                throw new IllegalArgumentException("Wrong number of args");
            // Create a stream to read from the file and strip tags from it
            BufferedReader in = new BufferedReader(
                        new RemoveHTMLReader(new FileReader(args[0])));
            // Read line by line, printing lines to the console
            String line;
            while((line = in.readLine( )) != null)
                System.out.println(line);
            in.close( );  // Close the stream.
        }
        catch(Exception e) {
            System.err.println(e);
            System.err.println("Usage: java RemoveHTMLReader$Test" +
                                " <filename>");
        }
    }
}
}
```

Tokenizing a Character Stream

Example 3-6 was a Reader implementation wrapped around another Reader.
ReaderTokenizer (Example 3-7) is a Tokenizer implementation wrapped around a
Reader. The Tokenizer interface was shown in Example 2-8, and the
ReaderTokenizer class shown here is a subclass of the AbstractTokenizer class of
Example 2-9.

As its name implies, ReaderTokenizer tokenizes the text it reads from a Reader
stream. The class implements the abstract createBuffer( ) and fillBuffer( )
methods of its superclass, and you may want to reread Example 2-9 to refresh
your memory about the interactions between ReaderTokenizer and
AbstractTokenizer.

Example 3-7 includes an inner class named Test that reads and tokenizes characters from a FileReader, listing the tokens read on the standard output. It also
writes the text of each token to a FileWriter, producing a copy of the input file
and demonstrating that the tokenizer accounts for every character of the input file
(as long as it is not configured to discard spaces, that is). Like its superclass,
ReaderTokenizer uses the assert keyword, and must be compiled with the -source
1.4 option to *javac*.

Example 3-7. ReaderTokenizer.java

```java
package je3.io;
import je3.classes.Tokenizer;
import je3.classes.AbstractTokenizer;
```

Example 3-7. ReaderTokenizer.java (continued)

```java
import java.io.*;

/**
 * This Tokenizer implementation extends AbstractTokenizer to tokenize a stream
 * of text read from a java.io.Reader.  It implements the createBuffer() and
 * fillBuffer() methods required by AbstractTokenizer.  See that class for
 * details on how these methods must behave.  Note that a buffer size may
 * be selected, and that this buffer size also determines the maximum token
 * length.  The Test class is a simple test that tokenizes a file and uses
 * the tokens to produce a copy of the file
 **/
public class ReaderTokenizer extends AbstractTokenizer {
    Reader in;

    // Create a ReaderTokenizer with a default buffer size of 16K characters
    public ReaderTokenizer(Reader in) { this(in, 16*1024); }

    public ReaderTokenizer(Reader in, int bufferSize) {
        this.in = in;  // Remember the reader to read input from
        // Tell our superclass about the selected buffer size.
        // The superclass will pass this number to createBuffer()
        maximumTokenLength(bufferSize);
    }

    // Create a buffer to tokenize.
    protected void createBuffer(int bufferSize) {
        // Make sure AbstractTokenizer only calls this method once
        assert text == null;
        this.text = new char[bufferSize];  // the new buffer
        this.numChars = 0;                  // how much text it contains
    }

    // Fill or refill the buffer.
    // See AbstractTokenizer.fillBuffer() for what this method must do.
    protected boolean fillBuffer() throws IOException {
        // Make sure AbstractTokenizer is upholding its end of the bargain
        assert text!=null && 0 <= tokenStart && tokenStart <= tokenEnd &&
            tokenEnd <= p && p <= numChars && numChars <= text.length;

        // First, shift already tokenized characters out of the buffer
        if (tokenStart > 0) {
            // Shift array contents
            System.arraycopy(text, tokenStart, text, 0, numChars-tokenStart);
            // And update buffer indexes
            tokenEnd -= tokenStart;
            p -= tokenStart;
            numChars -= tokenStart;
            tokenStart = 0;
        }

        // Now try to read more characters into the buffer
        int numread = in.read(text, numChars, text.length-numChars);
```

Example 3-7. ReaderTokenizer.java (continued)

```
        // If there are no more characters, return false
        if (numread == -1) return false;
        // Otherwise, adjust the number of valid characters in the buffer
        numChars += numread;
        return true;
    }

    // This test class tokenizes a file, reporting the tokens to standard out
    // and creating a copy of the file to demonstrate that every input
    // character is accounted for (since spaces are not skipped).
    public static class Test {
        public static void main(String[ ] args) throws java.io.IOException {
            Reader in = new FileReader(args[0]);
            PrintWriter out = new PrintWriter(new FileWriter(args[0]+".copy"));
            ReaderTokenizer t = new ReaderTokenizer(in);
            t.tokenizeWords(true).tokenizeNumbers(true).tokenizeSpaces(true);
            while(t.next( ) != Tokenizer.EOF) {
                switch(t.tokenType( )) {
                case Tokenizer.EOF:
                    System.out.println("EOF"); break;
                case Tokenizer.WORD:
                    System.out.println("WORD: " + t.tokenText( )); break;
                case Tokenizer.NUMBER:
                    System.out.println("NUMBER: " + t.tokenText( )); break;
                case Tokenizer.SPACE:
                    System.out.println("SPACE"); break;
                default:
                    System.out.println((char)t.tokenType( ));
                }
                out.print(t.tokenText( ));  // Copy token to the file
            }
            out.close( );
        }
    }
}
```

Random Access to Files

The examples we've seen so far have all read or written file content using streams. Streams provide sequential access to data and are particularly useful for network applications, which are often stream-oriented. Files stored on modern hard disks (as opposed to streaming tape drives) need not be accessed sequentially, and Java provides random access to files with the RandomAccessFile class. Example 3-8 demonstrates the use of random-access files by defining a list of strings stored in a file, along with an index to the position of each string. Note the use of writeInt( ), writeLong( ), and writeUTF( ) to write integers, longs, and strings, and the use of readInt( ), readLong( ), and readUTF( ) to read the corresponding values back. These methods are defined by the DataOutput and DataInput interfaces, which are also implemented by the DataOutputStream and DataInputStream classes. Note also the use of the seek( ) method to set the file position of a RandomAccessFile and the getFilePosition( ) method for querying the current position. Finally, don't forget that, like streams, random-access files must be closed when they are no longer needed.

Example 3-8. WordList.java

```java
package je3.io;
import java.io.*;

/**
 * This class represents a list of strings saved persistently to a file,
 * along with an index that allows random access to any string in the list.
 * The static method writeWords() creates such an indexed list in a file.
 * The class demostrates the use of java.io.RandomAccessFile
 */
public class WordList {
    // This is a simple test method
    public static void main(String args[]) throws IOException {
        // Write command-line arguments to a WordList file named "words.data"
        writeWords("words.data", args);

        // Now create a WordList based on that file
        WordList list = new WordList("words.data");
        // And iterate through the elements of the list backward
        // This would be very inefficient with sequential-access streams
        for(int i = list.size()-1; i >= 0; i--)
            System.out.println(list.get(i));
        // Tell the list we're done with it.
        list.close();
    }

    // This static method creates a WordList file
    public static void writeWords(String filename, String[] words)
        throws IOException
    {
        // Open the file for read/write access ("rw").  We only need to write,
        // but have to request read access as well
        RandomAccessFile f = new RandomAccessFile(filename, "rw");

        // This array will hold the positions of each word in the file
        long wordPositions[] = new long[words.length];

        // Reserve space at the start of the file for the wordPositions array
        // and the length of that array. 4 bytes for length plus 8 bytes for
        // each long value in the array.
        f.seek(4L + (8 * words.length));

        // Now, loop through the words and write them out to the file,
        // recording the start position of each word.  Note that the
        // text is written in the UTF-8 encoding, which uses 1, 2, or 3 bytes
        // per character, so we can't assume that the string length equals
        // the string size on the disk.  Also note that the writeUTF() method
        // records the length of the string so it can be read by  readUTF().
        for(int i = 0; i < words.length; i++) {
```

Example 3-8. WordList.java (continued)

```
            wordPositions[i] = f.getFilePointer(); // record file position
            f.writeUTF(words[i]);                  // write word
        }

        // Now go back to the beginning of the file and write the positions
        f.seek(0L);                                // Start at beginning
        f.writeInt(wordPositions.length);          // Write array length
        for(int i = 0; i < wordPositions.length; i++) // Loop through array
            f.writeLong(wordPositions[i]);         // Write array element
        f.close();   // Close the file when done.
    }

    // These are the instance fields of the WordList class
    RandomAccessFile f;  // the file to read words from
    long[] positions;    // the index that gives the position of each word

    // Create a WordList object based on the named file
    public WordList(String filename) throws IOException {
        // Open the random access file for read-only access
        f = new RandomAccessFile(filename, "r");

        // Now read the array of file positions from it
        int numwords = f.readInt();                // Read array length
        positions = new long[numwords];            // Allocate array
        for(int i = 0; i < numwords; i++)          // Read array contents
            positions[i] = f.readLong();
    }

    // Call this method when the WordList is no longer needed.
    public void close() throws IOException {
        if (f != null) f.close();  // close file
        f = null;                  // remember that it is closed
        positions = null;
    }

    // Return the number of words in the WordList
    public int size() {
        // Make sure we haven't closed the file already
        if (f == null) throw new IllegalStateException("already closed");
        return positions.length;
    }

    // Return the string at the specified position in the WordList
    // Throws IllegalStateException if already closed, and throws
    // ArrayIndexOutOfBounds if i is negative or >= size()
    public String get(int i) throws IOException {
        // Make sure close() hasn't already been called.
        if (f == null) throw new IllegalStateException("already closed");
        f.seek(positions[i]);  // Move to the word position in the file.
        return f.readUTF();     // Read and return the string at that position.
    }
}
```

Exercises

Exercise 3-1. Write a program named Head that prints out the first 10 lines of each file specified on the command line.

Exercise 3-2. Write a corresponding program named Tail that prints out the last 10 lines of each file specified on the command line.

Exercise 3-3. Write a program that counts and reports the number of lines, words, and characters in a specified file. Use static methods of the java.lang. Character class to determine whether a given character is a space (and therefore the boundary between two words).

Exercise 3-4. Write a program that adds up and reports the size of all files in a specified directory. It should recursively scan any subdirectories, summing and reporting the size of the files that they contain, and incorporate those directory sizes into its final output.

Exercise 3-5. Write a program that lists all of the files and subdirectories in a specified directory, along with their sizes and modification dates. By default, the output should be sorted by name. If invoked with the -s option, however, output should be sorted by size, from largest to smallest. If invoked with the -d option, output should be sorted by date, from most recent to least. Use the sort( ) method of java.util.Collections to help with the sorting.

Exercise 3-6. Modify the Compress program of Example 3-5 to make it recursively zip the contents of directories.

Exercise 3-7. Write a program named Uncompress that uncompresses files and directories compressed by the Compress example in this chapter.

Exercise 3-8. Write a subclass of OutputStream named TeeOutputStream that acts like a T joint in a pipe; the stream sends its output to two different output streams, specified when the TeeOutputStream is created. Write a simple test program that uses two TeeOutputStream objects to send text read from System.in to System.out and to two different test files.

Exercise 3-9. The WordList class of Example 3-8 uses a long to store the position of each word in the file. It uses a long because this is the data type used by the getFilePosition( ) and seek( ) methods of RandomAccessFile. It is inefficient to store the entire 8 bytes of the long to the disk file, however, since the strings are written sequentially and the positions in the position[ ] array are strictly increasing. Modify the example to store the differences between adjacent positions instead of the positions themselves. This should cut the index size in half (or more, if you choose to limit the length of individual strings).

Assume that most (but not all) strings stored in a WordList will be short and require less than 256 bytes of storage, meaning that the offsets between adjacent strings will typically fit into one byte. Design and implement a compression scheme that will further compress the size of the positions[ ] array on disk by using a variable number of bytes to store the position offset values. Note that because the length of the position table is no longer fixed, it can no longer be stored at the start of the WordList. Instead, you'll need to save the positions at the end of the file, and simply store the location of the positions at the start of the file.

4

Threads

A *thread* is a unit of program execution that runs independently from other threads. Java programs may consist of multiple threads of execution that behave as if they were running on independent CPUs, even when the host computer actually has only a single CPU. In many programming languages, multithreading capabilities are added on as an afterthought. In Java, however, they are integrated tightly with the language and its core packages:

- The java.lang.Runnable interface defines a run( ) method that serves as the block of code a thread executes. When that method exits, the thread stops running.

- The java.lang.Thread class represents a thread; it defines methods for setting and querying thread properties (such as execution priority level) and for starting the execution of a thread.

- The synchronized statement and modifier can be used to write blocks of code or entire methods that require a thread to obtain a lock before executing the block or the method. This mechanism ensures that two threads can't run the block or method at the same time, to avoid problems with different threads putting shared data in an inconsistent state.

- The wait( ) and notify( ) methods of java.lang.Object can be used to suspend threads and wake them up again.

The use of threads is common in Java programming; it is not possible to confine a discussion of them to just one chapter. We'll start with some simple examples in this chapter. We'll see threads again in Chapter 5, where they are quite useful for writing network server programs that can respond to multiple client requests simultaneously. Threads also appear in Chapter 12, and then again in Chapter 16, where they are used to produce animation effects.

Thread Basics

Example 4-1 is a simple program that demonstrates how to define, manipulate, and run threads. The bulk of the program is the main( ) method; it is run by the initial thread created by the Java interpreter. This main( ) method defines two additional threads, sets their priorities, and starts them running. The two threads are defined using two different techniques: the first is defined by subclassing the Thread class, while the second implements the Runnable interface and passes a Runnable object to the Thread( ) constructor. The example also demonstrates how you might use the important sleep( ), yield( ), and join( ) methods. Finally, Example 4-1 demonstrates the java.lang.ThreadLocal class, which has been added as of Java 1.2.

Example 4-1. ThreadDemo.java

```java
package je3.thread;

/**
 * This class demonstrates the use of threads.  The main() method is the
 * initial method invoked by the interpreter.  It defines and starts two
 * more threads and the three threads run at the same time.  Note that this
 * class extends Thread and overrides its run() method.  That method provides
 * the body of one of the threads started by the main() method
 **/
public class ThreadDemo extends Thread {
    /**
     * This method overrides the run() method of Thread.  It provides
     * the body for this thread.
     **/
    public void run() { for(int i = 0; i < 5; i++) compute(); }

    /**
     * This main method creates and starts two threads in addition to the
     * initial thread that the interpreter creates to invoke the main() method.
     **/
    public static void main(String[ ] args) {
        // Create the first thread: an instance of this class.  Its body is
        // the run() method above
        ThreadDemo thread1 = new ThreadDemo();

        // Create the second thread by passing a Runnable object to the
        // Thread() construtor.  The body of this thread is the run() method
        // of the anonymous Runnable object below.
        Thread thread2 = new Thread(new Runnable() {
                public void run() { for(int i = 0; i < 5; i++) compute(); }
            });

        // Set the priorities of these two threads, if any are specified
        if (args.length >= 1) thread1.setPriority(Integer.parseInt(args[0]));
        if (args.length >= 2) thread2.setPriority(Integer.parseInt(args[1]));
```

Example 4-1. ThreadDemo.java (continued)

```java
        // Start the two threads running
        thread1.start();
        thread2.start();

        // This main() method is run by the initial thread created by the
        // Java interpreter.  Now that thread does some stuff, too.
        for(int i = 0; i < 5; i++) compute();

        // We could wait for the threads to stop running with these lines
        // But they aren't necessary here, so we don't bother.
        // try {
        //     thread1.join();
        //     thread2.join();
        // } catch (InterruptedException e) { }

        // The Java VM exits only when the main() method returns, and when all
        // threads stop running (except for daemon threads--see setDaemon()).
    }

    // ThreadLocal objects respresent a value accessed with get() and set().
    // But they maintain a different value for each thread.  This object keeps
    // track of how many times each thread has called compute().
    static ThreadLocal numcalls = new ThreadLocal();

    /** This is the dummy method our threads all call */
    static synchronized void compute() {
        // Figure out how many times we've been called by the current thread
        Integer n = (Integer) numcalls.get();
        if (n == null) n = new Integer(1);
        else n = new Integer(n.intValue() + 1);
        numcalls.set(n);

        // Display the name of the thread, and the number of times called
        System.out.println(Thread.currentThread().getName() + ": " + n);

        // Do a long computation, simulating a "compute-bound" thread
        for(int i = 0, j=0; i < 1000000; i++) j += i;

        // Alternatively, we can simulate a thread subject to network or I/O
        // delays by causing it to sleep for a random amount of time:
        try {
            // Stop running for a random number of milliseconds
            Thread.sleep((int)(Math.random()*100+1));
        }
        catch (InterruptedException e) { }

        // Each thread politely offers the other threads a chance to run.
        // This is important so that a compute-bound thread does not "starve"
        // other threads of equal priority.
        Thread.yield();
    }
}
```

Thread-Safe Classes

When designing a class that may be used for concurrent programming—that is, a class whose instances may be used by more than one thread at a time—it is imperative that you make sure the class is "thread-safe." Consider the IntList class of Example 2-7. This class is not thread safe. Imagine what could happen if one thread called clear( ) while another thread was calling add( ). If the clear( ) method sets the list size to 0 after add( ) has read the list size but before it has stored the incremented list size back into the size field of the IntList, it may appear as if the call to clear( ) never happened! In general, a thread-safe class ensures that no thread can ever observe its instances in an inconsistent state.

There are several approaches to thread safety. A particularly simple one is to design immutable classes: if the state of an object can never change, then no thread can ever observe the object in an inconsistent state. Some classes, such as IntList, must be mutable, however. To make these classes thread-safe, you must prevent concurrent access to the internal state of an instance by more than one thread. Because Java was designed with threads in mind, the language provides the synchronized modifier, which does just that. When an instance method is declared synchronized, a thread must obtain a lock on the instance before it calls the method. If the lock is already held by another thread, the thread blocks until it can obtain the lock it needs. This ensures that only one thread may call any of the synchronized methods of the instance at a time.

Example 4-2 is a simplified version of the IntList class of Example 2-7 whose methods have been declared synchronized. This prevents two threads from calling the add( ) method at the same time, and also prevents a thread from calling clear( ) while another thread is calling add( ). The synchronized keyword can also be applied to arbitrary blocks of code within a method, simply by specifying the object to be locked before the code is executed. The ThreadSafeIntList( ) copy constructor uses this technique to synchronize access to the internal state of the object it is copying.

Note that it is not good design to declare every method of every class synchronized. Calling a synchronized method is substantially slower than calling a nonsynchronized one because of the overhead of object locking. The java.util.Vector class that shipped with the original version of Java has synchronized methods to guarantee thread safety. But most applications do not require thread safety, and Java 1.2 provided the more efficient unsynchronized alternative java.util.ArrayList.

Example 4-2. ThreadSafeIntList.java

```java
package je3.thread;

/**
 * A growable array of int values, suitable for use with multiple threads.
 **/
public class ThreadSafeIntList {
    protected int[] data;    // This array holds the integers
    protected int size;      // This is how many it current holds

    // Static final values are constants.  This one is private.
    private static final int DEFAULT_CAPACITY = 8;
```

Example 4-2. ThreadSafeIntList.java (continued)

```java
    // Create a ThreadSafeIntList with a default capacity
    public ThreadSafeIntList( ) {
        // We don't have to set size to zero because newly created objects
        // automatically have their fields set to zero, false, and null.
        data = new int[DEFAULT_CAPACITY];  // Allocate the array
    }

    // This constructor returns a copy of an existing ThreadSafeIntList.
    // Note that it synchronizes its access to the original list.
    public ThreadSafeIntList(ThreadSafeIntList original) {
        synchronized(original) {
            this.data = (int[ ]) original.data.clone( );
            this.size = original.size;
        }
    }

    // Return the number of ints stored in the list
    public synchronized int size( ) { return size; }

    // Return the int stored at the specified index
    public synchronized int get(int index) {
        if (index < 0 || index >= size) // Check that argument is legitimate
            throw new IndexOutOfBoundsException(String.valueOf(index));
        return data[index];
    }

    // Append a new value to the list, reallocating if necessary
    public synchronized void add(int value) {
        if (size == data.length) setCapacity(size*2); // realloc if necessary
        data[size++] = value;                         // add value to list
    }

    // Remove all elements from the list
    public synchronized void clear( ) { size = 0; }

    // Copy the contents of the list into a new array and return that array
    public synchronized int[ ] toArray( ) {
        int[ ] copy = new int[size];
        System.arraycopy(data, 0, copy, 0, size);
        return copy;
    }

    // Reallocate the data array to enlarge or shrink it.
    // Not synchronized, because it is always called from synchronized methods.
    protected void setCapacity(int n) {
        if (n == data.length) return;                  // Check size
        int[ ] newdata = new int[n];                   // Allocate the new array
        System.arraycopy(data, 0, newdata, 0, size);  // Copy data into it
        data = newdata;                                // Replace old array
    }
}
```

Threads and Thread Groups

Every Java Thread belongs to some ThreadGroup and may be constrained and controlled through the methods of that ThreadGroup. Similarly, every ThreadGroup is itself contained in some parent ThreadGroup. Thus, there is a hierarchy of thread groups and the threads they contain. Example 4-3 shows a ThreadLister class, with a public listAllThreads() method that displays this hierarchy by listing all threads and thread groups currently running on the Java interpreter. This method displays the name and priority of each thread, as well as other information about threads and thread groups. The example defines a main() method that creates a simple Swing user interface and uses it to display a listing of its own threads. Figure 4-1 shows such a listing.

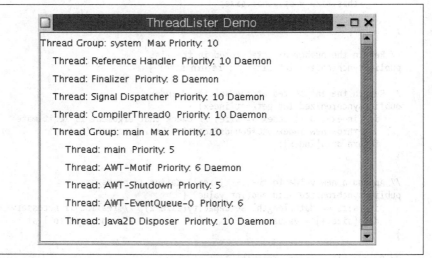

Figure 4-1. The threads and thread groups of a Swing application

The listAllThreads() method uses the static Thread method currentThread() to obtain the current thread and then calls getThreadGroup() to find the thread group of that thread. The method then uses the ThreadGroup.getParent() method to move up through the thread-group hierarchy until it finds the root thread group, the thread group that contains all other threads and thread groups.

Now listAllThreads() calls the private ThreadLister.printGroupInfo() method to display the contents of the root thread group and then recursively display the contents of all the thread groups it contains. printGroupInfo(), and the printThreadInfo() method it calls, use various Thread and ThreadGroup methods to obtain information about the threads and their groups. Note that the isDaemon() method returns, regardless of whether a thread is a daemon thread. Daemon threads are background threads that are not expected to exit. The Java interpreter exits when all nondaemon threads have quit.

The ThreadLister class has a main() method, so it can be run as a standalone program. It is more interesting, of course, to invoke the listAllThreads() method from within another program; it can also help you to diagnose problems you are having with threads.

Example 4-3. ThreadLister.java

```java
package je3.thread;
import java.io.*;
import java.awt.*;      // AWT classes for the demo program
import javax.swing.*;   // Swing GUI classes for the demo

/**
 * This class contains a useful static method for listing all threads
 * and threadgroups in the VM.  It also has a simple main( ) method so it
 * can be run as a standalone program.
 **/
public class ThreadLister {
    /** Display information about a thread. */
    private static void printThreadInfo(PrintWriter out, Thread t,
                                        String indent) {
        if (t == null) return;
        out.println(indent + "Thread: " + t.getName() +
                    " Priority: " + t.getPriority() +
                    (t.isDaemon()?" Daemon":"") +
                    (t.isAlive()?"":" Not Alive"));
    }

    /** Display info about a thread group and its threads and groups */
    private static void printGroupInfo(PrintWriter out, ThreadGroup g,
                                       String indent) {
        if (g == null) return;
        int num_threads = g.activeCount();
        int num_groups = g.activeGroupCount();
        Thread[ ] threads = new Thread[num_threads];
        ThreadGroup[ ] groups = new ThreadGroup[num_groups];

        g.enumerate(threads, false);
        g.enumerate(groups, false);

        out.println(indent + "Thread Group: " + g.getName() +
                    " Max Priority: " + g.getMaxPriority() +
                    (g.isDaemon()?" Daemon":""));

        for(int i = 0; i < num_threads; i++)
            printThreadInfo(out, threads[i], indent + "    ");
        for(int i = 0; i < num_groups; i++)
            printGroupInfo(out, groups[i], indent + "    ");
    }

    /** Find the root thread group and list it recursively */
    public static void listAllThreads(PrintWriter out) {
        ThreadGroup current_thread_group;
        ThreadGroup root_thread_group;
        ThreadGroup parent;
```

Example 4-3. ThreadLister.java (continued)

```
        // Get the current thread group
        current_thread_group = Thread.currentThread( ).getThreadGroup( );

        // Now go find the root thread group
        root_thread_group = current_thread_group;
        parent = root_thread_group.getParent( );
        while(parent != null) {
            root_thread_group = parent;
            parent = parent.getParent( );
        }

        // And list it, recursively
        printGroupInfo(out, root_thread_group, "");
    }

    /**
     * The main( ) method creates a simple graphical user interface to display
     * the threads in.  This allows us to see the "event dispatch thread" used
     * by AWT and Swing.
     **/
    public static void main(String[ ] args) {
        // Create a simple Swing GUI
        JFrame frame = new JFrame("ThreadLister Demo");
        JTextArea textarea = new JTextArea( );
        frame.getContentPane( ).add(new JScrollPane(textarea),
                                    BorderLayout.CENTER);
        frame.setSize(500, 400);
        frame.setVisible(true);

        // Get the threadlisting as a string using a StringWriter stream
        StringWriter sout = new StringWriter( );  // To capture the listing
        PrintWriter out = new PrintWriter(sout);
        ThreadLister.listAllThreads(out);          // List threads to stream
        out.close( );
        String threadListing = sout.toString( );  // Get listing as a string

        // Finally, display the thread listing in the GUI
        textarea.setText(threadListing);
    }
}
```

Deadlock

Multithreaded programming requires a programmer to take special care in several areas. For example, if multiple threads can be changing the state of an object at the same time, you typically must use synchronized methods or the synchronized statement to ensure that only one thread changes the object's state at a time. If you do not, two threads could end up overwriting each other's edits, leaving the object in an inconsistent state.

Unfortunately, using synchronization can itself cause problems. Thread synchronization involves acquiring an exclusive lock. Only the one thread that currently holds the lock can execute the synchronized code. When a program uses more than one lock, however, a situation known as deadlock can arise. Deadlock occurs when two or more threads are all waiting to acquire a lock that is currently held by one of the other waiting threads. Because each thread is waiting to acquire a lock, none ever releases the lock or locks it already holds, which means that none of the waiting threads ever acquires the lock it is waiting for. The situation is a total impasse; all the threads involved come to a halt, and the program can't continue.

Example 4-4 is a simple program that creates a deadlock situation in which two threads attempt to acquire locks on two different resources. It is pretty easy to see how deadlock can arise in this simple program. It might not be as clear, however, if there were synchronized methods involved, instead of a simple symmetrical set of synchronized statements. More complicated situations also arise with multiple threads and multiple resources. In general, the problem of deadlock is a deep and nasty one. One good technique for preventing it, however, is for all threads always to acquire all the locks they need in the same order.

Example 4-4. Deadlock.java

```
package je3.thread;

/**
 * This is a demonstration of how NOT to write multi-threaded programs.
 * It is a program that purposely causes deadlock between two threads that
 * are both trying to acquire locks for the same two resources.
 * To avoid this sort of deadlock when locking multiple resources, all threads
 * should always acquire their locks in the same order.
 **/
public class Deadlock {
    public static void main(String[] args) {
        // These are the two resource objects we'll try to get locks for
        final Object resource1 = "resource1";
        final Object resource2 = "resource2";
        // Here's the first thread.  It tries to lock resource1 then resource2
        Thread t1 = new Thread( ) {
            public void run( ) {
                // Lock resource 1
                synchronized(resource1) {
                    System.out.println("Thread 1: locked resource 1");

                    // Pause for a bit, simulating some file I/O or
                    // something.  Basically, we just want to give the
                    // other thread a chance to run.  Threads and deadlock
                    // are asynchronous things, but we're trying to force
                    // deadlock to happen here...
                    try { Thread.sleep(50); }
                    catch (InterruptedException e) { }
```

Example 4-4. Deadlock.java (continued)

```
            // Now wait 'till we can get a lock on resource 2
            synchronized(resource2) {
                System.out.println("Thread 1: locked resource 2");
            }
        }
    }
};

// Here's the second thread.  It tries to lock resource2 then resource1
Thread t2 = new Thread( ) {
    public void run( ) {
        // This thread locks resource 2 right away
        synchronized(resource2) {
            System.out.println("Thread 2: locked resource 2");

            // Then it pauses, just like the first thread.
            try { Thread.sleep(50); }
            catch (InterruptedException e) { }

            // Then it tries to lock resource1.  But wait!  Thread
            // 1 locked resource1, and won't release it 'till it
            // gets a lock on resource2.  This thread holds the
            // lock on resource2, and won't release it 'till it
            // gets resource1.  We're at an impasse. Neither
            // thread can run, and the program freezes up.
            synchronized(resource1) {
                System.out.println("Thread 2: locked resource 1");
            }
        }
    }
};

// Start the two threads. If all goes as planned, deadlock will occur,
// and the program will never exit.
t1.start( );
t2.start( );
}
}
```

Timers

Java 1.3 introduced the java.util.Timer class and the abstract java.util.
TimerTask class. If you subclass TimerTask and implement its run( ) method, you
can then use a Timer object to schedule invocations of that run( ) method at a
specified time or at multiple times at a specified interval. One Timer object can
schedule and invoke many TimerTask objects. Timer is quite useful, as it simplifies
many programs that would otherwise have to create their own threads to provide
the same functionality. Note that java.util.Timer is not at all the same as the Java
1.2 class javax.swing.Timer.

Examples 4-5 and 4-6 are simple implementations of the TimerTask and Timer classes that can be used prior to Java 1.3. They implement the same API as the Java 1.3 classes, except that they are in the je3.thread package instead of the java.util package. These implementations are not intended to be as robust as the official implementations in Java 1.3, but they are useful for simple tasks and are a good example of a nontrivial use of threads. Note in particular the use of wait( ) and notify( ) in Example 4-6. After studying these examples, you may be interested to compare them to the implementations that come with Java 1.3.[*]

Example 4-5. TimerTask.java

```
package je3.thread;

/**
 * This class implements the same API as the Java 1.3 java.util.TimerTask.
 * Note that a TimerTask can only be scheduled on one Timer at a time, but
 * that this implementation does not enforce that constraint.
 **/
public abstract class TimerTask implements Runnable {
    boolean cancelled = false;   // Has it been cancelled?
    long nextTime = -1;          // When is it next scheduled?
    long period;                 // What is the execution interval?
    boolean fixedRate;           // Fixed-rate execution?

    protected TimerTask( ) { }

    /**
     * Cancel the execution of the task.  Return true if it was actually
     * running, or false if it was already cancelled or never scheduled.
     **/
    public boolean cancel( ) {
        if (cancelled) return false;        // Already cancelled;
        cancelled = true;                   // Cancel it
        if (nextTime == -1) return false;   // Never scheduled;
        return true;
    }

    /**
     * When it the timer scheduled to execute? The run( ) method can use this
     * to see whether it was invoked when it was supposed to be
     **/
    public long scheduledExecutionTime( ) { return nextTime; }

    /**
     * Subclasses must override this to provide that code that is to be run.
     * The Timer class will invoke this from its internal thread.
     **/
    public abstract void run( );
```

---

[*] If you have the Java SDK™ from Sun, look in the *src.jar* archive that comes with it.

Example 4-5. TimerTask.java (continued)

```
    // This method is used by Timer to tell the Task how it is scheduled.
    void schedule(long nextTime, long period, boolean fixedRate) {
        this.nextTime = nextTime;
        this.period = period;
        this.fixedRate = fixedRate;
    }

    // This will be called by Timer after Timer calls the run method.
    boolean reschedule( ) {
        if (period == 0 || cancelled) return false; // Don't run it again
        if (fixedRate) nextTime += period;
        else nextTime = System.currentTimeMillis( ) + period;
        return true;
    }
}
```

Example 4-6. Timer.java

```
package je3.thread;
import java.util.Date;
import java.util.SortedSet;
import java.util.TreeSet;
import java.util.Comparator;

/**
 * This class is a simple implementation of the Java 1.3 java.util.Timer API
 **/
public class Timer {

    // This sorted set stores the tasks that this Timer is responsible for.
    // It uses a comparator to sort the tasks by scheduled execution time.
    SortedSet tasks = new TreeSet(new Comparator( ) {
            public int compare(Object a, Object b) {
                return (int)(((TimerTask)a).nextTime-((TimerTask)b).nextTime);
            }
            public boolean equals(Object o) { return this == o; }
        });

    // This is the thread the timer uses to execute the tasks.
    // The TimerThread class is defined below.
    TimerThread timer;

    /** This constructor creates a Timer that does not use a daemon thread */
    public Timer( ) { this(false); }

    /** The main constructor: the internal thread is a daemon if specified */
    public Timer(boolean isDaemon) {
        timer = new TimerThread(isDaemon);  // TimerThread is defined below
        timer.start( );                      // Start the thread running
    }
```

Example 4-6. Timer.java (continued)

```java
/** Stop the timer thread, and discard all scheduled tasks */
public void cancel( ) {
    synchronized(tasks) {       // Only one thread at a time!
        timer.pleaseStop( );    // Set a flag asking the thread to stop
        tasks.clear( );         // Discard all tasks
        tasks.notify( );        // Wake up the thread if it is in wait( ).
    }
}

/** Schedule a single execution after delay milliseconds */
public void schedule(TimerTask task, long delay) {
    task.schedule(System.currentTimeMillis( ) + delay, 0, false);
    schedule(task);
}

/** Schedule a single execution at the specified time */
public void schedule(TimerTask task, Date time) {
    task.schedule(time.getTime( ), 0, false);
    schedule(task);
}

/** Schedule a periodic execution starting at the specified time */
public void schedule(TimerTask task, Date firstTime, long period) {
    task.schedule(firstTime.getTime( ), period, false);
    schedule(task);
}

/** Schedule a periodic execution starting after the specified delay */
public void schedule(TimerTask task, long delay, long period) {
    task.schedule(System.currentTimeMillis( ) + delay, period, false);
    schedule(task);
}

/**
 * Schedule a periodic execution starting after the specified delay.
 * Schedule fixed-rate executions period ms after the start of the last.
 * Instead of fixed-interval executions measured from the end of the last.
 **/
public void scheduleAtFixedRate(TimerTask task, long delay, long period) {
    task.schedule(System.currentTimeMillis( ) + delay, period, true);
    schedule(task);
}

/** Schedule a periodic execution starting after the specified time */
public void scheduleAtFixedRate(TimerTask task, Date firstTime,
                                long period)
{
    task.schedule(firstTime.getTime( ), period, true);
    schedule(task);
}
```

Example 4-6. Timer.java (continued)

```
    // This internal method adds a task to the sorted set of tasks
    void schedule(TimerTask task) {
        synchronized(tasks) {  // Only one thread can modify tasks at a time!
            tasks.add(task);   // Add the task to the sorted set of tasks
            tasks.notify();    // Wake up the thread if it is waiting
        }
    }

    /**
     * This inner class defines the thread that runs each of the tasks at their
     * scheduled times
     **/
    class TimerThread extends Thread {
        // This flag will be set true to tell the thread to stop running.
        // Note that it is declared volatile, which means that it may be
        // changed asynchronously by another thread, so threads must always
        // read its current value, and not used a cached version.
        volatile boolean stopped = false;

        // The constructor
        TimerThread(boolean isDaemon) { setDaemon(isDaemon); }

        // Ask the thread to stop by setting the flag above
        void pleaseStop() { stopped = true; }

        // This is the body of the thread
        public void run() {
            TimerTask readyToRun = null;  // Is there a task to run right now?

            // The thread loops until the stopped flag is set to true.
            while(!stopped) {
                // If there is a task that is ready to run, then run it!
                if (readyToRun != null) {
                    if (readyToRun.cancelled) {  // If it was cancelled, skip.
                        readyToRun = null;
                        continue;
                    }
                    // Run the task.
                    readyToRun.run();
                    // Ask it to reschedule itself, and if it wants to run
                    // again, then insert it back into the set of tasks.
                    if (readyToRun.reschedule())
                        schedule(readyToRun);
                    // We've run it, so there is nothing to run now
                    readyToRun = null;
                    // Go back to top of the loop to see if we've been stopped
                    continue;
                }

                // Now acquire a lock on the set of tasks
                synchronized(tasks) {
                    long timeout;  // how many ms 'till the next execution?
```

Example 4-6. Timer.java (continued)

```
                    if (tasks.isEmpty()) {   // If there aren't any tasks
                        timeout = 0;  // Wait 'till notified of a new task
                    }
                    else {
                        // If there are scheduled tasks, then get the first one
                        // Since the set is sorted, this is the next one.
                        TimerTask t = (TimerTask) tasks.first();
                        // How long 'till it is next run?
                        timeout = t.nextTime - System.currentTimeMillis();
                        // Check whether it needs to run now
                        if (timeout <= 0) {
                            readyToRun = t;   // Save it as ready to run
                            tasks.remove(t); // Remove it from the set
                            // Break out of the synchronized section before
                            // we run the task
                            continue;
                        }
                    }

                    // If we get here, there is nothing ready to run now,
                    // so wait for time to run out, or wait 'till notify() is
                    // called when something new is added to the set of tasks.
                    try { tasks.wait(timeout); }
                    catch (InterruptedException e) {}

                    // When we wake up, go back up to the top of the while loop
                }
            }
        }
    }

    /** This inner class defines a test program */
    public static class Test {
        public static void main(String[] args) {
            final TimerTask t1 = new TimerTask() { // Task 1: print "boom"
                public void run() { System.out.println("boom"); }
            };
            final TimerTask t2 = new TimerTask() { // Task 2: print "BOOM"
                public void run() { System.out.println("\tBOOM"); }
            };
            final TimerTask t3 = new TimerTask() { // Task 3: cancel the tasks
                public void run() { t1.cancel(); t2.cancel(); }
            };

            // Create a timer, and schedule some tasks
            final Timer timer = new Timer();
            timer.schedule(t1, 0, 500);        // boom every .5sec starting now
            timer.schedule(t2, 2000, 2000); // BOOM every 2s, starting in 2s
            timer.schedule(t3, 5000);          // Stop them after 5 seconds

            // Schedule a final task: starting in 5 seconds, count
            // down from 5, then destroy the timer, which, since it is
```

Example 4-6. Timer.java (continued)

```
            // the only remaining thread, will cause the program to exit.
            timer.scheduleAtFixedRate(new TimerTask( ) {
                    public int times = 5;
                    public void run( ) {
                        System.out.println(times--);
                        if (times == 0) timer.cancel( );
                    }
                },
                                        5000,500);

        }
    }
}
```

Exercises

Exercise 4-1. Write a Java program that takes a list of filenames on the command line and prints out the number of lines in each file. The program should create one thread for each file and use these threads to count the lines in all the files at the same time. Use `java.io.LineNumberReader` to help you count lines. You'll probably want to define a `LineCounter` class that extends `Thread` or implements `Runnable`. Now write a variant of your program that uses your `LineCounter` class to read the files sequentially, rather than at the same time. Compare the performance of the multithreaded and single-threaded programs, using `System.currentTimeMills( )` to determine elapsed time. Compare the performance of the two programs for two, five, and ten files.

Exercise 4-2. The `ThreadSafeIntList` class of Example 4-2 is a simplified version of Example 2-7 with synchronized methods. Another approach to synchronizing data structures is to write a wrapper class with synchronized methods that delegate to an instance of the original class. See, for example, the `synchronizedList( )` and related methods of `java.util.Collections`. Modify the original `IntList` class (Example 2-7) to use this approach. Add a static factory method named `synchronizedIntList( )` that takes an `IntList` as its argument and returns an `IntList` object that has thread-safe behavior. You'll need to implement the wrapper class as a subclass of `IntList`, overriding its public methods to make them synchronized and make them delegate to the specified `IntList` instance.

Exercise 4-3. Example 4-4 demonstrates how deadlock can occur when two threads each attempt to obtain a lock held by the other. Modify the example to create deadlock among three threads, where each thread is trying to acquire a lock held by one of the other threads.

Exercise 4-4. Example 4-4 uses the synchronized statement to demonstrate deadlock. Write a similar program that causes two threads to deadlock, but use synchronized methods instead of the synchronized statement. This sort of deadlock is a little more subtle and harder to detect.

Exercise 4-5. Example 4-6 shows an implementation of the Java 1.3 `java.util.Timer` API. Java 1.2 introduced another `Timer` class, the `javax.swing.Timer` class, which has a similar purpose but a different API. It invokes the actionPerformed( ) method of any number of registered ActionListener objects one or more times after a specified delay and at a specified interval. Read the documentation for this Timer class, then create your own implementation of it. If you've read Chapter 11, you know that the methods of event listeners, such as the actionPerformed( ) method, are supposed to be invoked only by the event dispatch thread. Therefore, your implementation of the Timer class should not invoke actionPerformed( ) directly, but should instead use java.awt.EventQueue.invokeLater( ) or javax.swing.SwingUtilities. invokeLater( ) to tell the event dispatch thread to invoke the method.

Exercise 4-6. Once you have read Chapter 5, you may want to come back to this chapter to try this exercise. The Server class of Chapter 5 is a multithreaded, multiservice network server. It demonstrates important networking techniques, but it also makes heavy use of threads. One particular feature of this program is that it creates a ThreadGroup to contain all the threads it creates. Modify Server so that in addition to creating this one master thread group, it also creates a nested thread group for each of the individual services it provides. Place the thread for each individual client connection within the thread group for its service. Also, modify the program so that each service can have a thread priority specified and use this priority value when creating connection threads. You will probably want to store the thread group and priority for each service as fields of the nested Listener class.

5

Networking

Sun Microsystems has long used the slogan "The Network Is The Computer." It's no surprise, therefore, that they designed Java to be a network-centric language. The java.net package provides powerful and easy-to-use networking capabilities. The examples in this chapter demonstrate those capabilities at a number of different levels of abstraction. They show you how to:

- Use the URL class to parse URLs and download the network resources specified by a URL
- Use the URLConnection class to gain more control over the downloading of network resources
- Write client programs that use the Socket class to communicate over the network
- Use the Socket and ServerSocket classes to write servers
- Send and receive low-overhead datagram packets

Java 1.4 introduced the New I/O API of java.nio and its subpackages. This new API is channel-based instead of stream-based, and can be used for local file I/O as well as network I/O. java.nio is particularly suited to high-performance servers, and does not make the java.net package obsolete. The New I/O API is covered in Chapter 6.

Downloading the Contents of a URL

Example 5-1 shows how you can download the network resource referred to by a URL using the URL class. This class serves mainly to represent and parse URLs but also has several important methods for downloading URLs. The most high-level of these methods is getContent( ), which downloads the content of a URL, parses it, and returns the parsed object. This method relies on special content handlers having been installed to perform the parsing. By default, the Java SDK has content handlers for plain text and for several common image formats. When you call the getContent( ) method of a URL object that refers to a plain text or GIF or JPEG image file, the method returns a String or Image object. More commonly, when getContent( ) doesn't know how to handle the data type, it simply returns an InputStream so that you can read and parse the data yourself.

Example 5-1 doesn't use the getContent( ) method. Instead, it calls openStream( ) to return an InputStream from which the contents of the URL can be downloaded. This InputStream is connected, through the network, to the remote resource named by the URL, but the URL class hides all the details of setting up this connection. (In fact, the connection is set up by a protocol handler class; the Java SDK has default handlers for the most common network protocols, including *http:, ftp:, mailto:* and *file:*.)

Example 5-1 is a simple standalone program that downloads the contents of a specified URL and saves it in a file or writes it to the console. You'll note that most of this program looks like it belongs in Chapter 3. In fact, as we'll see in this and other examples in this chapter, almost all networking involves the use of the stream-based I/O techniques we learned about in that chapter.

Example 5-1. GetURL.java

```
package je3.net;
import java.io.*;
import java.net.*;

/**
 * This simple program uses the URL class and its openStream( ) method to
 * download the contents of a URL and copy them to a file or to the console.
 **/
public class GetURL {
    public static void main(String[] args) {
        InputStream in = null;
        OutputStream out = null;
        try {
            // Check the arguments
            if ((args.length != 1)&& (args.length != 2))
                throw new IllegalArgumentException("Wrong number of args");

            // Set up the streams
            URL url = new URL(args[0]);    // Create the URL
            in = url.openStream( );        // Open a stream to it
            if (args.length == 2)          // Get an appropriate output stream
                out = new FileOutputStream(args[1]);
            else out = System.out;

            // Now copy bytes from the URL to the output stream
            byte[ ] buffer = new byte[4096];
            int bytes_read;
            while((bytes_read = in.read(buffer)) != -1)
                out.write(buffer, 0, bytes_read);
        }
        // On exceptions, print error message and usage message.
        catch (Exception e) {
            System.err.println(e);
```

Example 5-1. GetURL.java (continued)

```
            System.err.println("Usage: java GetURL <URL> [<filename>]");
        }
        finally {  // Always close the streams, no matter what.
            try { in.close();  out.close(); } catch (Exception e) {}
        }
    }
}
```

Using a URLConnection

The URLConnection class establishes a connection to a URL. The openStream() method of URL we used in Example 5-1 is merely a convenience method that creates a URLConnection object and calls its getInputStream() method. By using a URLConnection object directly instead of relying on openStream(), you have much more control over the process of downloading the contents of a URL.

Example 5-2 is a simple program that shows how to use a URLConnection to obtain the content type, size, last-modified date, and other information about the resource referred to by a URL. If the URL uses the HTTP protocol, it also demonstrates how to use the HttpURLConnection subclass to obtain additional information about the connection.

Note the use of the java.util.Date class to convert a timestamp (a long that contains the number of milliseconds since midnight, January 1, 1970 GMT) to a human-readable date and time string.

Example 5-2. GetURLInfo.java

```java
package je3.net;
import java.net.*;
import java.io.*;
import java.util.Date;

/**
 * A class that displays information about a URL.
 **/
public class GetURLInfo {
    /** Use the URLConnection class to get info about the URL */
    public static void printinfo(URL url) throws IOException {
        URLConnection c = url.openConnection();  // Get URLConnection from URL
        c.connect();                             // Open a connection to URL

        // Display some information about the URL contents
        System.out.println("  Content Type: " + c.getContentType());
        System.out.println("  Content Encoding: " + c.getContentEncoding());
        System.out.println("  Content Length: " + c.getContentLength());
        System.out.println("  Date: " + new Date(c.getDate()));
        System.out.println("  Last Modified: " +new Date(c.getLastModified()));
        System.out.println("  Expiration: " + new Date(c.getExpiration()));

        // If it is an HTTP connection, display some additional information.
        if (c instanceof HttpURLConnection) {
            HttpURLConnection h = (HttpURLConnection) c;
```

Example 5-2. GetURLInfo.java (continued)

```
            System.out.println("  Request Method: " + h.getRequestMethod());
            System.out.println("  Response Message: " +h.getResponseMessage());
            System.out.println("  Response Code: " + h.getResponseCode());
        }
    }

    /** Create a URL, call printinfo() to display information about it. */
    public static void main(String[] args) {
        try { printinfo(new URL(args[0])); }
        catch (Exception e) {
            System.err.println(e);
            System.err.println("Usage: java GetURLInfo <url>");
        }
    }
}
```

Sending Email Through a URLConnection

As mentioned earlier, Java includes support for different URL protocols through protocol handlers that are implemented internally to the Java SDK. These handlers include support for the *mailto:* protocol. Example 5-3 shows a program that uses a *mailto:* URL to send email. The program prompts the user to enter the sender, recipient or recipients, subject, and body of the message, and then creates an appropriate *mailto:* URL and obtains a URLConnection object for it. The program uses the setDoInput() and setDoOutput() methods to specify that it is writing data to the URLConnection. It obtains the appropriate stream with getOutputStream() and then writes the message headers and body to that stream, closing the stream when the message body is complete. The program uses the user.name system property and the InetAddress class to attempt to create a valid return address for the sender of the email, though this doesn't actually work correctly on all platforms.

In order for the *mailto:* protocol handler to send mail, it must know what computer, or mailhost, to send it to. By default, it attempts to send it to the machine on which it is running. Some computers, particularly Unix machines on intranets, work as mailhosts, so this works fine. Other computers, such as PCs connected to the Internet by a dialup connection, have to specify a mailhost explicitly on the command line. For example, if your Internet service provider has the domain name *isp.net*, the appropriate mailhost is often *mail.isp.net* or *smtp.isp.net*. If you specify a mailhost, it is stored in the system property mail.host, which is read by the internal *mailto:* protocol handler.

Note that Example 5-3 uses the println() method to display messages to the console but uses the print() method and explicit "\r\n" line terminator characters to send text over the network. Different operating systems use different line terminators, and println() uses whatever terminator is expected on the local system. The standard line terminator for network services, however, is the two-character sequence "\r\n". We use it explicitly here, so that this client program works correctly regardless of the platform-specific line terminator.

Example 5-3. SendMail.java

```java
package je3.net;
import java.io.*;
import java.net.*;

/**
 * This program sends e-mail using a mailto: URL
 **/
public class SendMail {
    public static void main(String[ ] args) {
        try {
            // If the user specified a mailhost, tell the system about it.
            if (args.length >= 1)
                System.getProperties( ).put("mail.host", args[0]);

            // A Reader stream to read from the console
            BufferedReader in =
                new BufferedReader(new InputStreamReader(System.in));

            // Ask the user for the from, to, and subject lines
            System.out.print("From: ");
            String from = in.readLine( );
            System.out.print("To: ");
            String to = in.readLine( );
            System.out.print("Subject: ");
            String subject = in.readLine( );

            // Establish a network connection for sending mail
            URL u = new URL("mailto:" + to);           // Create a mailto: URL
            URLConnection c = u.openConnection( );      // Create its URLConnection
            c.setDoInput(false);                        // Specify no input from it
            c.setDoOutput(true);                        // Specify we'll do output
            System.out.println("Connecting...");        // Tell the user
            System.out.flush( );                        // Tell them right now
            c.connect( );                               // Connect to mail host
            PrintWriter out =                           // Get output stream to host
                new PrintWriter(new OutputStreamWriter(c.getOutputStream( )));

            // We're talking to the SMTP server now.
            // Write out mail headers.  Don't let users fake the From address
            out.print("From: \"" + from + "\" <" +
                    System.getProperty("user.name") + "@" +
                    InetAddress.getLocalHost( ).getHostName( ) + ">\r\n");
            out.print("To: " + to + "\r\n");
            out.print("Subject: " + subject + "\r\n");
            out.print("\r\n");  // blank line to end the list of headers

            // Now ask the user to enter the body of the message
            System.out.println("Enter the message. " +
                            "End with a '.' on a line by itself.");
            // Read message line by line and send it out.
            String line;
            for(;;) {
                line = in.readLine( );
```

Example 5-3. SendMail.java (continued)

```
                    if ((line == null) || line.equals(".")) break;
                    out.print(line + "\r\n");
                }

                // Close (and flush) the stream to terminate the message
                out.close();
                // Tell the user it was successfully sent.
                System.out.println("Message sent.");
            }
            catch (Exception e) {  // Handle any exceptions, print error message.
                System.err.println(e);
                System.err.println("Usage: java SendMail [<mailhost>]");
            }
        }
    }
}
```

A Simple Network Client

Example 5-4 is a simple network client program that does not use the URL class. Instead, it uses java.net.Socket to connect to server. It sends a line of text to the server, and then reads and prints out the server's response. The main point of interest in this example is the introduction of the Socket class, which creates a stream-based network connection between a client and a server. To create a network connection to another host, you simply create a Socket, specifying the desired host and port. If there is a program (a server) running on the specified host and listening for connections on the specified port, the Socket( ) constructor returns a Socket object you can use to communicate with the server. (If there is not a server listening on the specified host and port, or if anything goes wrong— and many things can go wrong with networking—the Socket( ) constructor throws an exception.)

If you are not familiar with hosts and ports, think of the host as a post office and the port as a post-office box. Just as a post office has many different post-office boxes, any host on the network can run many different servers at a time. Different servers use different ports for their addresses. To establish a connection, you must specify both the correct host and the correct port. Many services have standard default ports. Web servers run on port 80, POP email servers run on port 110, and so on.

Once you have a Socket object, you are connected, across the network, to a server. The getInputStream( ) method of the socket returns an InputStream you can use to read bytes from the server, and getOutputStream( ) returns an OutputStream you can use to write bytes to the server. This is exactly what this Connect program does.

Despite its simplicity, our simple Connect client is actually useful in conjunction with simple network servers like "daytime" (port 13) and "finger" (port 79). For example, here is how you can use the program to find out the current time (daytime) and to find out who is logged on to a server (finger):

```
java je3.net.Connect time-a.nist.gov 13
java je3.net.Connect rtfm.mit.edu 79
```

Example 5-4. Connect.java

```java
package je3.net;
import java.io.*;
import java.net.*;

/**
 * A simple network client that establishes a network connection to a specified
 * port on a specified host, sends an optional message across the connection,
 * reads the response from the server, and exits.  A suitable client for simple
 * network services like the daytime or finger.
 **/
public class Connect {
    public static void main(String[ ] args) {
        try {  // Handle exceptions below
            // Get our command-line arguments
            String hostname = args[0];
            int port = Integer.parseInt(args[1]);
            String message = "";
            if (args.length > 2)
                for(int i = 2; i < args.length; i++) message += args[i] + " ";

            // Create a Socket connected to the specified host and port.
            Socket s = new Socket(hostname, port);

            // Get the socket output stream and wrap a PrintWriter around it
            PrintWriter out = new PrintWriter(s.getOutputStream( ));

            // Send the specified message through the socket to the server.
            out.print(message + "\r\n");
            out.flush( );  // Send it now.

            // Get an input stream from the socket and wrap a BufferedReader
            // around it, so we can read lines of text from the server.
            BufferedReader in =
                new BufferedReader(new InputStreamReader(s.getInputStream( )));

            // Before we start reading the server's response, tell the socket
            // that we don't want to wait more than 3 seconds
            s.setSoTimeout(3000);

            // Now read lines from the server until the server closes the
            // connection (and we get a null return indicating EOF) or until
            // the server is silent for 3 seconds.
            try {
                String line;
                while((line = in.readLine( )) != null) // If we get a line
                    System.out.println(line);          // print it out.
            }
            catch(SocketTimeoutException e) {
                // We end up here if readLine( ) times out.
                System.err.println("Timeout; no response from server.");
            }
```

Example 5-4. Connect.java (continued)

```
                out.close( );  // Close the output stream
                in.close( );   // Close the input stream
                s.close( );    // Close the socket
        }
        catch(IOException e) {  // Handle IO and network exceptions here
                System.err.println(e);
        }
        catch(NumberFormatException e) {  // Bad port number
                System.err.println("You must specify the port as a number");
        }
        catch(ArrayIndexOutOfBoundsException e) {  // wrong # of args
                System.err.println("Usage: Connect <hostname> <port> message...");
        }
    }
}
```

A Generic Client

The Connect class of Example 5-4 was a useful first example of the Socket class, but it is too simple to use with most network protocols. Example 5-5 defines a class, GenericClient, that can serve as a client for a variety of text-based services. When you run this program, it connects to the host and port you have specified on the command line. From that point on, it simply sends the text you type to the server and then outputs the text the server sends in response to the console.

You can use GenericClient to download files from a web server by sending HTTP GET commands, for example. (We'll see what that protocol looks like in Example 5-6.) For big files, however, the server's output scrolls by too quickly for this to be useful. GenericClient is more useful for text-based interactive protocols. The Post Office Protocol (POP) is such a protocol. You can use GenericClient to preview any email you have waiting for you at your ISP (or elsewhere). An interaction, using GenericClient, with a POP server might look as follows. The lines in bold are those typed by the user:

```
oxymoron% java je3.net.GenericClient mail.isp.net 110
Connected to mail.isp.net/208.99.99.251:110
+OK QUALCOMM Pop server derived from UCB (version 2.1.4-R3) at mail.isp.net
starting.
USER david
+OK Password required for david.
PASS notrealpassword
+OK david has 3 message(s) (2861 octets).
RETR 3
+OK 363 octets
Received: from obsidian.oreilly.com (obsidian.oreilly.com [207.144.66.251])
        by mail.isp.net (8.8.5/8.8.5) with SMTP id RAA11654
        for david@isp.net; Wed, 21 Jun 2999 17:01:50 -0400 (EDT)
Date: Wed, 25 Jun 1997 17:01:50 -0400 (EDT)
Message-Id: <199706252101.RAA11654@mail.isp.net>
From: "Brett McLaughlin" <bmc@oreilly.com>
To: david@isp.net
Subject: schedule!
```

Networking

```
Aren't you done with that book yet?
.
DELE 3
+OK Message 3 has been deleted.
QUIT
+OK Pop server at mail.isp.net signing off.
Connection closed by server.
oxymoron%
```

The GenericClient class uses two threads. The main thread reads input from the
console and sends it to the server. This thread spends most of its time blocked
while waiting for input from the user. The second thread is implemented by an
anonymous inner class. This second thread reads data from the server and prints
it out to the console. It spends most of its time blocked while waiting to read from
the server. Two threads are required because there are two read methods that
must both block at the same time! The java.net package does not support
nonblocking streams, and it is common for networking code (particularly server
code) to require two or more threads. (This is the reason I placed the "Threads"
chapter of this book between the chapter on I/O and this chapter on networking.)
In Java 1.4, the java.nio package and its subpackages allow multiple nonblocking
channels to be "multiplexed" in a single thread, which greatly enhances the scalability of Java servers. We'll learn about this in Chapter 6.

Example 5-5. GenericClient.java

```java
package je3.net;
import java.io.*;
import java.net.*;

/**
 * This program connects to a server at a specified host and port.
 * It reads text from the console and sends it to the server.
 * It reads text from the server and sends it to the console.
 **/
public class GenericClient {
    public static void main(String[] args) throws IOException {
        try {
            // Check the number of arguments
            if (args.length != 2)
                throw new IllegalArgumentException("Wrong number of args");

            // Parse the host and port specifications
            String host = args[0];
            int port = Integer.parseInt(args[1]);

            // Connect to the specified host and port
            Socket s = new Socket(host, port);

            // Set up streams for reading from and writing to the server.
            // The from_server stream is final for use in the inner class below
            final Reader from_server=new InputStreamReader(s.getInputStream());
            PrintWriter to_server = new PrintWriter(s.getOutputStream());
```

Example 5-5. GenericClient.java (continued)

```java
        // Set up streams for reading from and writing to the console
        // The to_user stream is final for use in the anonymous class below
        BufferedReader from_user =
            new BufferedReader(new InputStreamReader(System.in));
        // Pass true for auto-flush on println()
        final PrintWriter to_user = new PrintWriter(System.out, true);

        // Tell the user that we've connected
        to_user.println("Connected to " + s.getInetAddress() +
                        ":" + s.getPort());

        // Create a thread that gets output from the server and displays
        // it to the user.  We use a separate thread for this so that we
        // can receive asynchronous output
        Thread t = new Thread() {
            public void run() {
                char[] buffer = new char[1024];
                int chars_read;
                try {
                    // Read characters from the server until the
                    // stream closes, and write them to the console
                    while((chars_read = from_server.read(buffer)) != -1) {
                        to_user.write(buffer, 0, chars_read);
                        to_user.flush();
                    }
                }
                catch (IOException e) { to_user.println(e); }

                // When the server closes the connection, the loop above
                // will end.  Tell the user what happened, and call
                // System.exit(), causing the main thread to exit along
                // with this one.
                to_user.println("Connection closed by server.");
                System.exit(0);
            }
        };

        // Now start the server-to-user thread
        t.start();

        // In parallel, read the user's input and pass it on to the server.
        String line;
        while((line = from_user.readLine()) != null) {
            to_server.print(line + "\r\n");
            to_server.flush();
        }

        // If the user types a Ctrl-D (Unix) or Ctrl-Z (Windows) to end
        // their input, we'll get an EOF, and the loop above will exit.
        // When this happens, we stop the server-to-user thread and close
        // the socket.
```

Example 5-5. GenericClient.java (continued)

```
            s.close( );
            to_user.println("Connection closed by client.");
            System.exit(0);
        }
        // If anything goes wrong, print an error message
        catch (Exception e) {
            System.err.println(e);
            System.err.println("Usage: java GenericClient <hostname> <port>");
        }
    }
}
```

An HTTP Client

Example 5-6 shows a program, HttpClient, that downloads the contents of a URL from a web server and writes it to a file. It behaves like the GetURL program from Example 5-1. Despite the similarity in behavior, however, the implementation of these two programs is entirely different. Whereas GetURL relies on the URL class and its protocol handlers to handle protocol details, HttpClient connects directly to a web server and communicates with it using the HTTP protocol. As a consequence, HttpClient is restricted to downloading URLs that use the *http:* or *https:* protocol. It can't handle *ftp:* or other network protocols.

At its heart, HttpClient is much like the Connect program of Example 5-4: it connects to a server, sends some text, and reads the response. This example is more complex, however, for three main reasons. First, it supports the https: protocol in addition to plain HTTP, demonstrating how to do networking with SSL secure sockets (a feature new in Java 1.4). Second, it sends an HTTP request to the server, which is more complex than the single line sent by Connect. Third, it doesn't just read and print the server's response; instead, it parses it to separate the HTTP response headers from the document content that follows.

A feature to note in Example 5-6 is its use of the java.net.URI class to parse the HTTP URL it is given. URI is new in Java 1.4. It has more powerful URL parsing features than the URL class we've already seen, but has none of the networking capabilities that URL does.

Example 5-6. HttpClient.java

```
package je3.net;
import java.io.*;
import java.net.*;
import javax.net.*;
import javax.net.ssl.*;
import java.security.cert.*;

/**
 * This program connects to a web server and downloads the specified URL
 * from it.  It uses the HTTP protocol directly and can also handle HTTPS
 **/
public class HttpClient {
```

Example 5-6. HttpClient.java (continued)

```java
public static void main(String[] args) {
    try {
        // Check the arguments
        if (args.length != 2)
            throw new IllegalArgumentException("Wrong number of args");

        // Get an output stream to write the URL contents to
        OutputStream to_file = new FileOutputStream(args[1]);

        // Now use the URI class to parse the user-specified URL into
        // its various parts.  java.net.URI is new in Java 1.4; it is like
        // URL, but has more powerful parsing, and does not have built-in
        // networking capability.
        URI uri = new URI(args[0]);
        String protocol = uri.getScheme();
        String host = uri.getHost();
        int port = uri.getPort();
        String path = uri.getRawPath();
        if (path == null || path.length() == 0) path = "/";
        String query = uri.getRawQuery();
        if (query != null && query.length() > 0)
            path += "?" + query;

        Socket socket; // The socket we'll use to communicate

        if (protocol.equals("http")) {
            // This is a normal http protocol, create a normal socket
            if (port == -1) port = 80;  // Default http port
            socket = new Socket(host, port);
        }
        else if (protocol.equals("https")) {
            // For HTTPS we need to create a secure socket
            if (port == -1) port = 443;
            SocketFactory factory = SSLSocketFactory.getDefault();
            SSLSocket ssock = (SSLSocket) factory.createSocket(host, port);

            // Get the server's certificate
            SSLSession session = ssock.getSession();
            X509Certificate cert = null;
            try {
                cert = (X509Certificate)session.getPeerCertificates()[0];
            }
            catch(SSLPeerUnverifiedException e) {
                // This means there was no certificate, or the certificate
                // was not valid.
                System.err.println(session.getPeerHost() +
                                " did not present a valid certificate");
                System.exit(1);
            }

            // Print certificate details
            System.out.println(session.getPeerHost() +
                    " has presented a certificate belonging to:\t" +
```

Example 5-6. HttpClient.java (continued)

```
                        "[" + cert.getSubjectDN( ) + "]\n" +
                        "The certificate was issued by: \t" +
                        "[" + cert.getIssuerDN( ) + "]");

                // We could ask the user here to confirm that they trust
                // the certificate owner and issuer before proceeding...
                socket = ssock;
            }
            else {
                throw new IllegalArgumentException("URL must use http: or " +
                                                  "https: protocol");
            }

            /*
             * We now have a regular socket or an SSL socket.  HTTP and HTTPS
             * are the same from here on.
             */

            // Get input and output streams for the socket
            InputStream from_server = socket.getInputStream( );
            PrintWriter to_server = new PrintWriter(socket.getOutputStream( ));

            // Send the HTTP GET command to the web server, specifying the file
            // We specify HTTP 1.0 instead of 1.1 because we don't know how
            // to handle Transfer-Encoding: chunked in the response
            to_server.print("GET " + path + " HTTP/1.0\r\n" +
                            "Host: " + host + "\r\n" +
                            "Connection: close\r\n\r\n");
            to_server.flush( );  // Send it right now!

            // Here is a buffer we use for reading from the server
            byte[ ] buffer = new byte[8 * 1024];
            int bytes_read;

            // Now read the HTTP headers the server returns, and print these
            // to the console.  Read from the server until we've got at
            // least 4K bytes or until we get EOF.  Assume that we'll find
            // the end of the headers somewhere in the first 4K bytes.
            int numbytes = 0;
            while(true) {
                bytes_read = from_server.read(buffer, numbytes,
                                              buffer.length-numbytes);
                if (bytes_read == -1) break;
                numbytes += bytes_read;
                if (numbytes >= 4 * 1024) break;
            }

            // Loop through the bytes, looking for the \r\n\r\n pattern
            // (13, 10, 13, 10) that marks the end of the headers
            int i = 0;
            while(i <= numbytes-4) {
                if (buffer[i++] == 13 && buffer[i++] == 10 &&
```

Example 5-6. HttpClient.java (continued)

```
                    buffer[i++] == 13 && buffer[i++] == 10) break;
            }
            // If we didn't find the end of the headers, abort
            if (i > numbytes-4) {
                throw new IOException("End of headers not found in first " +
                                      numbytes + " bytes");
            }

            // Now convert the headers to a Latin-1 string (omitting the final
            // blank line) and then print them out to the console
            String headers = new String(buffer, 0, i-2, "ISO-8859-1");
            System.out.print(headers);

            // Any bytes we read after the headers get written to the file.
            to_file.write(buffer, i, numbytes-i);

            // Now read the rest of the bytes and write to the file
            while((bytes_read = from_server.read(buffer)) != -1)
                to_file.write(buffer, 0, bytes_read);

            // When the server closes the connection, we close our stuff, too
            socket.close( );
            to_file.close( );
        }
        catch (Exception e) {      // Report any errors that arise
            System.err.println(e);
            System.err.println("Usage: java HttpClient <URL> [<filename>]");
        }
    }
}
```

A POP Client

Example 5-7 is a useful network client that connects to a POP3 mailbox and lists or deletes messages there based on their size and optionally their Subject lines. I wrote this program in response to a particularly virulent Internet virus that was sending hundreds of infected messages each day. At the peak of the viral outbreak, my mailbox was filling up with 50 megabytes of junk overnight. This program allowed me to delete the bogus messages without having to download them first.

The networking code in this example is straightforward, but the example is valuable because it is the most real-world one we've seen so far. The details of the POP3 protocol encoded in the example are also quite interesting. Please note that this example deletes messages from your mailbox—be sure you understand exactly what it does before trying to use it. One new feature demonstrated by this example is the Java 1.4 regular expression matching capability of the java.util. regex package. Look up the Pattern and Matcher classes of that package for details. Regular expressions are defined as part of the New I/O API, and we'll see more examples of their use in Chapter 6.

Example 5-7. PopClean.java

```java
package je3.net;
import java.io.*;
import java.net.*;
import java.util.*;
import java.util.regex.*;

/**
 * A simple utility program for deleting messages from a POP3 mailbox based on
 * message size and Subject line. Don't run this program unless you understand
 * what it is doing.  It deletes e-mail without downloading it:
 * YOU MAY PERMANENTLY LOSE DATA!
 *
 * Typical usage:
 * 1) Look at the subject lines for the big messages you've got
 *        java PopClean -host host -user user -pass pass -size 100000
 *
 * 2) Create a regular expression to match viral subject lines, and use it
 *    to delete large matching messages
 *        java PopClean -host h -user u -pass p -delete -size 100000 \
 *            -subject 'Thank you!|Re: Your application'
 *    This will ask for confirmation before proceeding.
 *
 * 3) If you're confident that all big messages are virus-infected, then
 *    you can skip the -subject argument and delete on size alone
 *        java PopClean -host h -user u -pass p -delete -size 100000
 *    This will ask for confirmation before proceeding.
 */
public class PopClean {
    static Socket s = null;            // The connection to the server
    static BufferedReader in = null;   // To read lines from the server
    static PrintWriter out = null;     // To write to the server
    static boolean debug = false;      // Are we in debug mode?

    public static void main(String args[]) {
        try {
            String hostname = null, username = null, password = null;
            int port = 110;
            int sizelimit = -1;
            String subjectPattern = null;
            Pattern pattern = null;
            Matcher matcher = null;
            boolean delete = false;
            boolean confirm = true;

            // Handle command-line arguments
            for(int i = 0; i < args.length; i++) {
                if (args[i].equals("-user"))
                    username = args[++i];
                else if (args[i].equals("-pass"))
                    password = args[++i];
                else if (args[i].equals("-host"))
                    hostname = args[++i];
```

Example 5-7. PopClean.java (continued)

```
            else if (args[i].equals("-port"))
                port = Integer.parseInt(args[++i]);
            else if (args[i].equals("-size"))
                sizelimit = Integer.parseInt(args[++i]);
            else if (args[i].equals("-subject"))
                subjectPattern = args[++i];
            else if (args[i].equals("-debug"))
                debug = true;
            else if (args[i].equals("-delete"))
                delete = true;
            else if (args[i].equals("-force"))  // don't confirm
                confirm = false;
        }

        // Verify them
        if (hostname == null || username == null || password == null ||
            sizelimit == -1)
            usage();

        // Make sure the pattern is a valid regexp
        if (subjectPattern != null) {
            pattern = Pattern.compile(subjectPattern);
            matcher = pattern.matcher("");
        }

        // Say what we are going to do
        System.out.println("Connecting to " + hostname + " on port " +
                           port + " with username " + username + ".");
        if (delete) {
            System.out.println("Will delete all messages longer than "+
                               sizelimit + " bytes");
            if (subjectPattern != null)
                System.out.println("that have a subject matching: [" +
                                   subjectPattern + "]");
        }
        else {
            System.out.println("Will list subject lines for messages " +
                               "longer than " + sizelimit + " bytes");
            if (subjectPattern != null)
                System.out.println("that have a subject matching: [" +
                                   subjectPattern + "]");
        }

        // If asked to delete, ask for confirmation unless -force is given
        if (delete && confirm) {
            System.out.println();
            System.out.print("Do you want to proceed (y/n) [n]: ");
            System.out.flush();
            BufferedReader console =
                new BufferedReader(new InputStreamReader(System.in));
            String response = console.readLine();
```

Example 5-7. PopClean.java (continued)

```
                if (!response.equals("y")) {
                    System.out.println("No messages deleted.");
                    System.exit(0);
                }
            }

            // Connect to the server, and set up streams
            s = new Socket(hostname, port);
            in = new BufferedReader(new InputStreamReader(s.getInputStream( )));
            out = new PrintWriter(new OutputStreamWriter(s.getOutputStream( )));

            // Read the welcome message from the server, confirming it is OK.
            System.out.println("Connected: " + checkResponse( ));

            // Now log in
            send("USER " + username);    // Send username, wait for response
            send("PASS " + password);    // Send password, wait for response
            System.out.println("Logged in");

            // Check how many messages are waiting, and report it
            String stat = send("STAT");
            StringTokenizer t = new StringTokenizer(stat);
            System.out.println(t.nextToken( ) + " messages in mailbox.");
            System.out.println("Total size: " + t.nextToken( ));

            // Get a list of message numbers and sizes
            send("LIST");  // Send LIST command, wait for OK response.
            // Now read lines from the server until we get . by itself
            List msgs = new ArrayList( );
            String line;
            for(;;) {
                line = in.readLine( );
                if (line == null) throw new IOException("Unexpected EOF");
                if (line.equals(".")) break;
                msgs.add(line);
            }

            // Now loop through the lines we read one at a time.
            // Each line should specify the message number and its size.
            int nummsgs = msgs.size( );
            for(int i = 0; i < nummsgs; i++) {
                String m = (String) msgs.get(i);
                StringTokenizer st = new StringTokenizer(m);
                int msgnum = Integer.parseInt(st.nextToken( ));
                int msgsize = Integer.parseInt(st.nextToken( ));

                // If the message is too small, ignore it.
                if (msgsize <= sizelimit) continue;

                // If we're listing messages or matching subject lines,
                // find the subject line for this message
                String subject = null;
```

Example 5-7. PopClean.java (continued)

```
                    if (!delete || pattern != null) {
                        subject = getSubject(msgnum);  // get the subject line

                        // If we couldn't find a subject, skip the message
                        if (subject == null) continue;

                        // If this subject does not match the pattern, then
                        // skip the message
                        if (pattern != null) {
                            matcher.reset(subject);
                            if (!matcher.matches()) continue;
                        }

                        // If we are listing, list this message
                        if (!delete) {
                            System.out.println("Subject " + msgnum + ": " +
                                               subject);
                            continue;  // so we never delete it
                        }
                    }

                    // If we were asked to delete, then delete the message
                    if (delete) {
                        send("DELE " + msgnum);
                        if (pattern == null)
                            System.out.println("Deleted message " + msgnum);
                        else
                            System.out.println("Deleted message " + msgnum +
                                               ": " + subject);
                    }
                }

                // When we're done, log out and shut down the connection
                shutdown();
            }
            catch(Exception e) {
                // If anything goes wrong, print exception and show usage
                System.err.println(e);
                usage();
                // Always try to shut down nicely so the server doesn't hang on us
                shutdown();
            }
        }

    // Explain how to use the program
    public static void usage() {
        System.err.println("java PopClean <options>");
        System.err.println(
"Options are:\n" +
"-host <hostname>  # Required\n" +
"-port <port>      # Optional; default is 110\n" +
"-user <username>  # Required\n" +
```

Example 5-7. PopClean.java (continued)

```
"-pass <password>  # Required and sent as cleartext; APOP not supported\n" +
"-size <limit>     # Message size in bytes. Shorter messages are ignored.\n" +
"-subject <regexp> # Optional java.util.regex.Pattern regular expression\n" +
"                  # only messages with a matching Subject line are deleted\n"+
"-delete           # Delete messages; the default is just to list them\n" +
"-force            # Don't ask for confirmation before deleting\n" +
"-debug            # Display POP3 protocol requests and responses\n");

        System.exit(1);
    }

    // Send a POP3 command to the server and return its response
    public static String send(String cmd) throws IOException {
        if (debug) System.out.println(">>>" + cmd);
        out.print(cmd);          // Send command
        out.print("\r\n");       // and line terminator.
        out.flush();             // Send it now!
        String response = checkResponse();  // Get the response.
        if (debug) System.out.println("<<<+OK " + response);
        return response;
    }

    // Wait for a response and make sure it is an "OK" response.
    public static String checkResponse() throws IOException {
        String response;
        for(;;) {
            response = in.readLine();
            if (response == null)
                throw new IOException("Server unexpectedly closed connection");
            else if (response.startsWith("-ERR"))
                throw new IOException("Error from server: " + response);
            else if (response.startsWith("+OK"))
                return response.substring(3);
        }
    }

    // Ask the server to send the headers of the numbered message.
    // Look through them for the Subject header and return its content.
    public static String getSubject(int msgnum) throws IOException {
        send("TOP " + msgnum + " 0");
        String subject = null, line;
        for(;;) {
            line = in.readLine();
            if (line == null) throw new IOException("Unexpected EOF");
            if (line.startsWith("Subject: ")) subject = line.substring(9);
            if (line.equals(".")) break;
        }
        return subject;
    }

    // Disconnect nicely from the POP server.
    // This method is called for normal termination and exceptions.
    public static void shutdown() {
```

Example 5-7. PopClean.java (continued)

```
        try {
            if (out != null) {
                send("QUIT");
                out.close( );
            }
            if (in != null) in.close( );
            if (s != null) s.close( );
        }
        catch(IOException e) { }
    }
}
```

A Simple Web Server

Example 5-8 shows a very simple web server, HttpMirror. Instead of returning a requested file, however, this server simply "mirrors" the request back to the client as its reply. This can be useful when debugging web clients and can be interesting if you are just curious about the details of HTTP client requests. To run the program, specify the port that it should listen on as an argument. For example, I can run the server like this:

```
oxymoron% java je3.net.HttpMirror 4444
```

Then, in my web browser, I can load *http://localhost:4444/testing.html*. The server ignores the request for the file *testing.html*, but it echoes back the request that my web browser sent. It might look something like this:

```
GET /testing.html HTTP/1.1
Host: localhost:4444
User-Agent: Mozilla/5.0 (X11; U; Linux i686; en-US; rv:1.3) Gecko/20030312
Accept-Language: en-us,en;q=0.5
Accept-Encoding: gzip,deflate,compress;q=0.9
Accept-Charset: ISO-8859-1,utf-8;q=0.7,*;q=0.7
Keep-Alive: 300
Connection: keep-alive
```

The main new feature introduced in Example 5-8 is the ServerSocket class. This class is used by a server, or any other program, that wants to sit and wait for a connection request from a client. When you create a ServerSocket, you specify the port to listen on. To connect to a client, call the accept( ) method of the ServerSocket. This method blocks until a client attempts to connect to the port that the ServerSocket is listening on. When such a connection attempt occurs, the ServerSocket establishes a connection to the client and returns a Socket object that can communicate with the client. Your code can then call the getInputStream( ) and getOutputStream( ) methods of the socket to get streams for reading bytes from the client and for writing bytes to the client.

Note that the ServerSocket is not used for communication between the server and its client; it is used only to wait for and establish the connection to the client. Typically, a single ServerSocket object is used over and over again to establish connections to any number of clients.

Example 5-8 is quite straightforward. It creates a ServerSocket and calls its accept( ) method, as outlined previously. When a client connects, it sets up the streams and then sends some HTTP headers to the client, telling it that the request has been received successfully and that the reply is text/plain data. Next, it reads all the HTTP headers of the client's request and sends them back to the client as the body of its reply. When it reads a blank line from the client, this indicates the end of the client's headers, so it closes the connection.

Note that the body of the HttpMirror program is a big infinite loop. It connects to a client, handles the request, and then loops and waits for another client connection. Although this simple server works perfectly well for the testing purposes for which it is designed, there is a flaw in it: it is a single-threaded server and can talk to only one client at a time. Later in this chapter, we'll see examples of servers that use multiple threads and can maintain connections to any number of clients.

Example 5-8. HttpMirror.java

```
package je3.net;
import java.io.*;
import java.net.*;

/**
 * This program is a very simple web server.  When it receives a HTTP request
 * it sends the request back as the reply.  This can be of interest when
 * you want to see just what a web client is requesting, or what data is
 * being sent when a form is submitted, for example.
 **/
public class HttpMirror {
    public static void main(String args[ ]) {
        try {
            // Get the port to listen on
            int port = Integer.parseInt(args[0]);
            // Create a ServerSocket to listen on that port.
            ServerSocket ss = new ServerSocket(port);
            // Now enter an infinite loop, waiting for & handling connections.
            for(;;) {
                // Wait for a client to connect.  The method will block;
                // when it returns the socket will be connected to the client
                Socket client = ss.accept( );

                // Get input and output streams to talk to the client
                BufferedReader in = new BufferedReader(
                        new InputStreamReader(client.getInputStream( )));
                PrintWriter out = new PrintWriter(client.getOutputStream( ));

                // Start sending our reply, using the HTTP 1.1 protocol
                out.print("HTTP/1.1 200 \r\n");        // Version & status code
                out.print("Content-Type: text/plain\r\n"); // The type of data
                out.print("Connection: close\r\n");     // Will close stream
                out.print("\r\n");                      // End of headers

                // Now, read the HTTP request from the client, and send it
                // right back to the client as part of the body of our
                // response.  The client doesn't disconnect, so we never get
```

Example 5-8. HttpMirror.java (continued)

```
                    // an EOF.  It does sends an empty line at the end of the
                    // headers, though.  So when we see the empty line, we stop
                    // reading.  This means we don't mirror the contents of POST
                    // requests, for example.  Note that the readLine( ) method
                    // works with Unix, Windows, and Mac line terminators.
                    String line;
                    while((line = in.readLine( )) != null) {
                        if (line.length( ) == 0) break;
                        out.print(line + "\r\n");
                    }

                    // Close socket, breaking the connection to the client, and
                    // closing the input and output streams
                    out.close( );      // Flush and close the output stream
                    in.close( );       // Close the input stream
                    client.close( );   // Close the socket itself
                } // Now loop again, waiting for the next connection
            }
            // If anything goes wrong, print an error message
            catch (Exception e) {
                System.err.println(e);
                System.err.println("Usage: java HttpMirror <port>");
            }
        }
    }
```

A Proxy Server

Example 5-9 shows another network server: a simple, single-threaded proxy server. A proxy server is one that acts as a proxy for some other real server. When a client connects to a proxy server, the proxy forwards the client's requests to the real server, and then forwards the server's responses to the client. To the client, the proxy looks like the server. To the real server, the proxy looks like a client. This program allows you to create fake services on your machine that are just proxies for real services running somewhere else. (Note that this program is not the same as an HTTP proxy server, which parses a client's HTTP request and redirects to the appropriate server; this program is a proxy for one specific server, and treats client requests and server responses as opaque streams of bytes.)

There are not any major new networking features in Example 5-9. It is an interesting example because it combines the features of both client and server into one program. When studying this code, remember that the proxy server mediates the connection between a client and a server. It acts like a server to the client and like a client to the server. SimpleProxyServer is a single-threaded server; it can only handle one client connection at a time. Nevertheless, you'll notice that it does use a thread (implemented in an anonymous inner class) so that one thread can block while waiting for input from the server, while the other thread blocks while waiting for input from the client. In this example, the main thread reads bytes from the server and sends them to the client. A separate thread reads bytes from the client and sends them to the server.

Example 5-9. SimpleProxyServer.java

```java
package je3.net;
import java.io.*;
import java.net.*;

/**
 * This class implements a simple single-threaded proxy server.
 **/
public class SimpleProxyServer {
    /** The main method parses arguments and passes them to runServer */
    public static void main(String[ ] args) throws IOException {
        try {
            // Check the number of arguments
            if (args.length != 3)
                throw new IllegalArgumentException("Wrong number of args.");

            // Get the command-line arguments: the host and port we are proxy
            // for and the local port that we listen for connections on.
            String host = args[0];
            int remoteport = Integer.parseInt(args[1]);
            int localport = Integer.parseInt(args[2]);
            // Print a start-up message
            System.out.println("Starting proxy for " + host + ":" +
                               remoteport + " on port " + localport);
            // And start running the server
            runServer(host, remoteport, localport);   // never returns
        }
        catch (Exception e) {
            System.err.println(e);
            System.err.println("Usage: java SimpleProxyServer " +
                               "<host> <remoteport> <localport>");
        }
    }

    /**
     * This method runs a single-threaded proxy server for
     * host:remoteport on the specified local port.  It never returns.
     **/
    public static void runServer(String host, int remoteport, int localport)
            throws IOException {
        // Create a ServerSocket to listen for connections with
        ServerSocket ss = new ServerSocket(localport);

        // Create buffers for client-to-server and server-to-client transfer.
        // We make one final so it can be used in an anonymous class below.
        // Note the assumptions about the volume of traffic in each direction.
        final byte[ ] request = new byte[1024];
        byte[ ] reply = new byte[4096];

        // This is a server that never returns, so enter an infinite loop.
        while(true) {
            // Variables to hold the sockets to the client and to the server.
            Socket client = null, server = null;
            try {
```

Example 5-9. SimpleProxyServer.java (continued)

```
// Wait for a connection on the local port
client = ss.accept();

// Get client streams.  Make them final so they can
// be used in the anonymous thread below.
final InputStream from_client = client.getInputStream();
final OutputStream to_client = client.getOutputStream();

// Make a connection to the real server.
// If we cannot connect to the server, send an error to the
// client, disconnect, and continue waiting for connections.
try { server = new Socket(host, remoteport); }
catch (IOException e) {
    PrintWriter out = new PrintWriter(to_client);
    out.print("Proxy server cannot connect to " + host + ":"+
            remoteport + ":\n" + e + "\n");
    out.flush();
    client.close();
    continue;
}

// Get server streams.
final InputStream from_server = server.getInputStream();
final OutputStream to_server = server.getOutputStream();

// Make a thread to read the client's requests and pass them
// to the server.  We have to use a separate thread because
// requests and responses may be asynchronous.
Thread t = new Thread() {
    public void run() {
        int bytes_read;
        try {
            while((bytes_read=from_client.read(request))!=-1) {
                to_server.write(request, 0, bytes_read);
                to_server.flush();
            }
        }
        catch (IOException e) { }

        // the client closed the connection to us, so close our
        // connection to the server.  This will also cause the
        // server-to-client loop in the main thread exit.
        try {to_server.close();} catch (IOException e) { }
    }
};

// Start the client-to-server request thread running
t.start();

// Meanwhile, in the main thread, read the server's responses
// and pass them back to the client.  This will be done in
// parallel with the client-to-server request thread above.
int bytes_read;
```

Example 5-9. SimpleProxyServer.java (continued)

```
                    try {
                        while((bytes_read = from_server.read(reply)) != -1) {
                            to_client.write(reply, 0, bytes_read);
                            to_client.flush();
                        }
                    }
                    catch(IOException e) { }

                    // The server closed its connection to us, so we close our
                    // connection to our client.
                    // This will make the other thread exit.
                    to_client.close();
                }
                catch (IOException e) { System.err.println(e); }
                finally {  // Close the sockets no matter what happens.
                    try {
                        if (server != null) server.close();
                        if (client != null) client.close();
                    }
                    catch(IOException e) { }
                }
            }
        }
    }
}
```

A Generic Multithreaded Server

Example 5-10 is a long and fairly complex example. The Server class it defines is a multithreaded server that provides services defined by implementations of a nested Server.Service interface. It can provide multiple services (defined by multiple Service objects) on multiple ports, and it has the ability to dynamically load and instantiate Service classes and add (and remove) new services at runtime. It logs its actions (to a stream, or, in Java 1.4, to a Logger) and limits the number of concurrent connections to a specified maximum.

The Server class uses a number of inner classes. The Server.Listener class is a thread that waits for connections on a given port. There is one Listener object for each service the Server is providing. The Server.ConnectionManager class manages the list of current connections to all services. There is one ConnectionManager shared by all services. When a Listener gets a connection from a client, it passes it to the ConnectionManager, which rejects it if the connection limit has been reached. If the ConnectionManager doesn't reject a client, it creates a Server.Connection object to handle the connection. Connection is a Thread subclass, so each service can handle multiple connections at a time, making this a multithreaded server. Each Connection object is passed a Service object and invokes its serve() method, which is what actually provides the service.

The Service interface is a nested member of the Server class; Server includes a number of implementations of this interface. Many of these implementations are trivial demonstration services. The Control class, however, is a nontrivial Service. This service provides password-protected runtime access to the server, allowing a remote administrator to add and remove services, check the server status, and change the current connection limit.

Finally, the main( ) method of Server is a standalone program that creates and runs a Server. By specifying the -control argument on the command line, you can tell this program to create an instance of the Control service so that the server can be administered at runtime. Other arguments to this program specify the names of Service classes to be run and the ports that they should use. For example, you could start the server with a command like this:

```
% java je3.net.Server -control secret 3000 \
        je3.net.Server\$Time 3001 \
        je3.net.Server\$Reverse 3002
```

This command starts the Control service on port 3000 with the password "secret", the Server.Time service on port 3001, and the Server.Reverse service on port 3002. Once you have started the server program, you can use GenericClient (see Example 5-5) to connect to each of the services it provides. Using the Control service is the most interesting, of course, and you can use it to add (and remove) other services.

The main( ) method sets up the Server to send logging messages to a java.util. logging.Logger object. In most implementations, the logging messages will appear on your console. If not, you can modify the main( ) method to construct a Server that logs to System.out. You can also change the way Logger messages are handled by editing the jre/lib/logging.properties file in your Java installation or by specifying an alternate logging properties file with the -Djava.util.logging.config. file switch to the *java* interpreter. See the discussion of Example 6-14 for more details on configuring logging output.

The best way to understand the Server class and its inner classes and interfaces is to dive in and study the code. It is heavily commented. I recommend that you skim it, reading comments first, and then go back through and study each class in detail.

Example 5-10. Server.java

```
package je3.net;
import java.io.*;
import java.net.*;
import java.util.*;
import java.util.logging.*;

/**
 * This class is a generic framework for a flexible, multi-threaded server.
 * It listens on any number of specified ports, and, when it receives a
 * connection on a port, passes input and output streams to a specified Service
 * object which provides the actual service.  It can limit the number of
 * concurrent connections, and logs activity to a specified stream.
 **/
public class Server {
    /**
     * A main() method for running the server as a standalone program.  The
     * command-line arguments to the program should be pairs of servicenames
     * and port numbers.  For each pair, the program will dynamically load the
```

Example 5-10. Server.java (continued)

```
    * named Service class, instantiate it, and tell the server to provide
    * that Service on the specified port.  The special -control argument
    * should be followed by a password and port, and will start special
    * server control service running on the specified port, protected by the
    * specified password.
    **/
    public static void main(String[ ] args) {
        try {
            if (args.length < 2)  // Check number of arguments
                throw new IllegalArgumentException("Must specify a service");

            // Create a server object that has a limit of 10 concurrent
            // connections, and logs to a Logger at the Level.INFO level
            // Prior to Java 1.4 we did this: new Server(System.out, 10);
            Server s = new Server(Logger.getLogger(Server.class.getName( )),
                                  Level.INFO, 10);

            // Parse the argument list
            int i = 0;
            while(i < args.length) {
                if (args[i].equals("-control")) {  // Handle the -control arg
                    i++;
                    String password = args[i++];
                    int port = Integer.parseInt(args[i++]);
                    // add control service
                    s.addService(new Control(s, password), port);
                }
                else {
                    // Otherwise start a named service on the specified port.
                    // Dynamically load and instantiate a Service class
                    String serviceName = args[i++];
                    Class serviceClass = Class.forName(serviceName);
                    Service service = (Service)serviceClass.newInstance( );
                    int port = Integer.parseInt(args[i++]);
                    s.addService(service, port);
                }
            }
        }
        catch (Exception e) { // Display a message if anything goes wrong
            System.err.println("Server: " + e);
            System.err.println("Usage: java Server " +
                               "[-control <password> <port>] " +
                               "[<servicename> <port> ... ]");
            System.exit(1);
        }
    }

    // This is the state for the server
    Map services;                 // Hashtable mapping ports to Listeners
    Set connections;              // The set of current connections
    int maxConnections;           // The concurrent connection limit
    ThreadGroup threadGroup;      // The threadgroup for all our threads
```

Example 5-10. Server.java (continued)

```java
    // This class was originally written to send logging output to a stream.
    // It has been retrofitted to also support the java.util.logging API of
    // Java 1.4.  You can use either, neither, or both.
    PrintWriter logStream;              // Where we send our logging output to
    Logger logger;                      // A Java 1.4 logging destination
    Level logLevel;                     // the level to log messages at

    /**
     * This is the Server( ) constructor.  It must be passed a stream
     * to send log output to (may be null), and the limit on the number of
     * concurrent connections.
     **/
    public Server(OutputStream logStream, int maxConnections) {
        this(maxConnections);
        setLogStream(logStream);
        log("Starting server");
    }

    /**
     * This constructor added to support logging with the Java 1.4 Logger class
     **/
    public Server(Logger logger, Level logLevel, int maxConnections) {
        this(maxConnections);
        setLogger(logger, logLevel);
        log("Starting server");
    }

    /**
     * This constructor supports no logging
     **/
    public Server(int maxConnections) {
        threadGroup = new ThreadGroup(Server.class.getName( ));
        this.maxConnections = maxConnections;
        services = new HashMap( );
        connections = new HashSet(maxConnections);
    }

    /**
     * A public method to set the current logging stream.  Pass null
     * to turn logging off.
     **/
    public synchronized void setLogStream(OutputStream out) {
        if (out != null) logStream = new PrintWriter(out);
        else logStream = null;
    }

    /**
     * Set the current Logger and logging level. Pass null to turn logging off.
     **/
    public synchronized void setLogger(Logger logger, Level level) {
        this.logger = logger;
        this.logLevel = level;
    }
```

Example 5-10. Server.java (continued)

```java
/** Write the specified string to the log */
protected synchronized void log(String s) {
    if (logger != null) logger.log(logLevel, s);
    if (logStream != null) {
        logStream.println("[" + new Date() + "] " + s);
        logStream.flush();
    }
}
/** Write the specified object to the log */
protected void log(Object o) { log(o.toString()); }

/**
 * This method makes the server start providing a new service.
 * It runs the specified Service object on the specified port.
 **/
public synchronized void addService(Service service, int port)
    throws IOException
{
    Integer key = new Integer(port);  // the hashtable key
    // Check whether a service is already on that port
    if (services.get(key) != null)
        throw new IllegalArgumentException("Port " + port +
                                           " already in use.");
    // Create a Listener object to listen for connections on the port
    Listener listener = new Listener(threadGroup, port, service);
    // Store it in the hashtable
    services.put(key, listener);
    // Log it
    log("Starting service " + service.getClass().getName() +
        " on port " + port);
    // Start the listener running.
    listener.start();
}

/**
 * This method makes the server stop providing a service on a port.
 * It does not terminate any pending connections to that service, merely
 * causes the server to stop accepting new connections
 **/
public synchronized void removeService(int port) {
    Integer key = new Integer(port);  // hashtable key
    // Look up the Listener object for the port in the hashtable
    final Listener listener = (Listener) services.get(key);
    if (listener == null) return;
    // Ask the listener to stop
    listener.pleaseStop();
    // Remove it from the hashtable
    services.remove(key);
    // And log it.
    log("Stopping service " + listener.service.getClass().getName() +
        " on port " + port);
}
```

Example 5-10. Server.java (continued)

```java
/**
 * This nested Thread subclass is a "listener".  It listens for
 * connections on a specified port (using a ServerSocket) and when it gets
 * a connection request, it calls the server's addConnection() method to
 * accept (or reject) the connection.  There is one Listener for each
 * Service being provided by the Server.
 **/
public class Listener extends Thread {
    ServerSocket listen_socket;    // The socket to listen for connections
    int port;                      // The port we're listening on
    Service service;               // The service to provide on that port
    volatile boolean stop = false; // Whether we've been asked to stop

    /**
     * The Listener constructor creates a thread for itself in the
     * threadgroup.  It creates a ServerSocket to listen for connections
     * on the specified port.  It arranges for the ServerSocket to be
     * interruptible, so that services can be removed from the server.
     **/
    public Listener(ThreadGroup group, int port, Service service)
        throws IOException
    {
        super(group, "Listener:" + port);
        listen_socket = new ServerSocket(port);
        // give it a non-zero timeout so accept() can be interrupted
        listen_socket.setSoTimeout(5000);
        this.port = port;
        this.service = service;
    }

    /**
     * This is the polite way to get a Listener to stop accepting
     * connections
     ***/
    public void pleaseStop() {
        this.stop = true;                  // Set the stop flag
        this.interrupt();                  // Stop blocking in accept()
        try { listen_socket.close(); } // Stop listening.
        catch(IOException e) {}
    }

    /**
     * A Listener is a Thread, and this is its body.
     * Wait for connection requests, accept them, and pass the socket on
     * to the addConnection method of the server.
     **/
    public void run() {
        while(!stop) {        // loop until we're asked to stop.
            try {
                Socket client = listen_socket.accept();
                addConnection(client, service);
            }
```

Networking

Example 5-10. Server.java (continued)

```
                catch (InterruptedIOException e) { }
                catch (IOException e) {log(e);}
            }
        }
    }

    /**
     * This is the method that Listener objects call when they accept a
     * connection from a client.  It either creates a Connection object
     * for the connection and adds it to the list of current connections,
     * or, if the limit on connections has been reached, it closes the
     * connection.
     **/
    protected synchronized void addConnection(Socket s, Service service) {
        // If the connection limit has been reached
        if (connections.size() >= maxConnections) {
            try {
                // Then tell the client it is being rejected.
                PrintWriter out = new PrintWriter(s.getOutputStream());
                out.print("Connection refused; " +
                          "the server is busy; please try again later.\r\n");
                out.flush();
                // And close the connection to the rejected client.
                s.close();
                // And log it, of course
                log("Connection refused to " +
                    s.getInetAddress().getHostAddress() +
                    ":" + s.getPort() + ": max connections reached.");
            } catch (IOException e) {log(e);}
        }
        else { // Otherwise, if the limit has not been reached
            // Create a Connection thread to handle this connection
            Connection c = new Connection(s, service);
            // Add it to the list of current connections
            connections.add(c);
            // Log this new connection
            log("Connected to " + s.getInetAddress().getHostAddress() +
                ":" + s.getPort() + " on port " + s.getLocalPort() +
                " for service " + service.getClass().getName());
            // And start the Connection thread to provide the service
            c.start();
        }
    }

    /**
     * A Connection thread calls this method just before it exits.  It removes
     * the specified Connection from the set of connections.
     **/
    protected synchronized void endConnection(Connection c) {
        connections.remove(c);
        log("Connection to " + c.client.getInetAddress().getHostAddress() +
```

Example 5-10. Server.java (continued)

```
            ":" + c.client.getPort( ) + " closed.");
    }

    /** Change the current connection limit */
    public synchronized void setMaxConnections(int max) {
        maxConnections = max;
    }

    /**
     * This method displays status information about the server on the
     * specified stream.  It can be used for debugging, and is used by the
     * Control service later in this example.
     **/
    public synchronized void displayStatus(PrintWriter out) {
        // Display a list of all Services that are being provided
        Iterator keys = services.keySet().iterator( );
        while(keys.hasNext( )) {
            Integer port = (Integer) keys.next( );
            Listener listener = (Listener) services.get(port);
            out.print("SERVICE " + listener.service.getClass( ).getName( )
                    + " ON PORT " + port + "\r\n");
        }

        // Display the current connection limit
        out.print("MAX CONNECTIONS: " + maxConnections + "\r\n");

        // Display a list of all current connections
        Iterator conns = connections.iterator( );
        while(conns.hasNext( )) {
            Connection c = (Connection)conns.next( );
            out.print("CONNECTED TO " +
                    c.client.getInetAddress( ).getHostAddress( ) +
                    ":" + c.client.getPort( ) + " ON PORT " +
                    c.client.getLocalPort( ) + " FOR SERVICE " +
                    c.service.getClass( ).getName( ) + "\r\n");
        }
    }

    /**
     * This class is a subclass of Thread that handles an individual
     * connection between a client and a Service provided by this server.
     * Because each such connection has a thread of its own, each Service can
     * have multiple connections pending at once.  Despite all the other
     * threads in use, this is the key feature that makes this a
     * multi-threaded server implementation.
     **/
    public class Connection extends Thread {
        Socket client;     // The socket to talk to the client through
        Service service;   // The service being provided to that client
```

Example 5-10. Server.java (continued)

```
    /**
     * This constructor just saves some state and calls the superclass
     * constructor to create a thread to handle the connection.  Connection
     * objects are created by Listener threads.  These threads are part of
     * the server's ThreadGroup, so all Connection threads are part of that
     * group, too.
     **/
    public Connection(Socket client, Service service) {
        super("Server.Connection:" +
            client.getInetAddress().getHostAddress() +
            ":" + client.getPort());
        this.client = client;
        this.service = service;
    }

    /**
     * This is the body of each and every Connection thread.
     * All it does is pass the client input and output streams to the
     * serve() method of the specified Service object.  That method is
     * responsible for reading from and writing to those streams to
     * provide the actual service.  Recall that the Service object has
     * been passed from the Server.addService() method to a Listener
     * object to the addConnection() method to this Connection object, and
     * is now finally being used to provide the service.  Note that just
     * before this thread exits it always calls the endConnection() method
     * to remove itself from the set of connections
     **/
    public void run() {
        try {
            InputStream in = client.getInputStream();
            OutputStream out = client.getOutputStream();
            service.serve(in, out);
        }
        catch (IOException e) {log(e);}
        finally { endConnection(this); }
    }
}

/**
 * Here is the Service interface that we have seen so much of.  It defines
 * only a single method which is invoked to provide the service.  serve()
 * will be passed an input stream and an output stream to the client.  It
 * should do whatever it wants with them, and should close them before
 * returning.
 *
 * All connections through the same port to this service share a single
 * Service object.  Thus, any state local to an individual connection must
 * be stored in local variables within the serve() method.  State that
 * should be global to all connections on the same port should be stored
 * in instance variables of the Service class.  If the same Service is
 * running on more than one port, there will typically be different
```

Example 5-10. Server.java (continued)

```
 * Service instances for each port.  Data that should be global to all
 * connections on any port should be stored in static variables.
 *
 * Note that implementations of this interface must have a no-argument
 * constructor if they are to be dynamically instantiated by the main()
 * method of the Server class.
 **/
public interface Service {
    public void serve(InputStream in, OutputStream out) throws IOException;
}

/**
 * A very simple service.  It displays the current time on the server
 * to the client, and closes the connection.
 **/
public static class Time implements Service {
    public void serve(InputStream i, OutputStream o) throws IOException {
        PrintWriter out = new PrintWriter(o);
        out.print(new Date() + "\r\n");
        out.close();
        i.close();
    }
}

/**
 * This is another example service.  It reads lines of input from the
 * client, and sends them back, reversed.  It also displays a welcome
 * message and instructions, and closes the connection when the user
 * enters a '.' on a line by itself.
 **/
public static class Reverse implements Service {
    public void serve(InputStream i, OutputStream o) throws IOException {
        BufferedReader in = new BufferedReader(new InputStreamReader(i));
        PrintWriter out =
            new PrintWriter(new BufferedWriter(new OutputStreamWriter(o)));
        out.print("Welcome to the line reversal server.\r\n");
        out.print("Enter lines.  End with a '.' on a line by itself.\r\n");
        for(;;) {
            out.print("> ");
            out.flush();
            String line = in.readLine();
            if ((line == null) || line.equals(".")) break;
            for(int j = line.length()-1; j >= 0; j--)
                out.print(line.charAt(j));
            out.print("\r\n");
        }
        out.close();
        in.close();
    }
}
```

Example 5-10. Server.java (continued)

```java
/**
 * This service is an HTTP mirror, just like the HttpMirror class
 * implemented earlier in this chapter.  It echoes back the client's
 * HTTP request
 **/
public static class HTTPMirror implements Service {
    public void serve(InputStream i, OutputStream o) throws IOException {
        BufferedReader in = new BufferedReader(new InputStreamReader(i));
        PrintWriter out = new PrintWriter(o);
        out.print("HTTP/1.0 200\r\n");
        out.print("Content-Type: text/plain\r\n\r\n");
        String line;
        while((line = in.readLine()) != null) {
            if (line.length() == 0) break;
            out.print(line + "\r\n");
        }
        out.close();
        in.close();
    }
}

/**
 * This service demonstrates how to maintain state across connections by
 * saving it in instance variables and using synchronized access to those
 * variables.  It maintains a count of how many clients have connected and
 * tells each client what number it is
 **/
public static class UniqueID implements Service {
    public int id=0;
    public synchronized int nextId() { return id++; }
    public void serve(InputStream i, OutputStream o) throws IOException {
        PrintWriter out = new PrintWriter(o);
        out.print("You are client #: " + nextId() + "\r\n");
        out.close();
        i.close();
    }
}

/**
 * This is a non-trivial service.  It implements a command-based protocol
 * that gives password-protected runtime control over the operation of the
 * server.  See the main() method of the Server class to see how this
 * service is started.
 *
 * The recognized commands are:
 *   password: give password; authorization is required for most commands
 *   add:      dynamically add a named service on a specified port
 *   remove:   dynamically remove the service running on a specified port
 *   max:      change the current maximum connection limit.
 *   status:   display current services, connections, and connection limit
 *   help:     display a help message
 *   quit:     disconnect
 *
```

Example 5-10. Server.java (continued)

```
 * This service displays a prompt, and sends all of its output to the user
 * in capital letters.  Only one client is allowed to connect to this
 * service at a time.
 **/
public static class Control implements Service {
    Server server;              // The server we control
    String password;            // The password we require
    boolean connected = false; // Whether a client is already connected

    /**
     * Create a new Control service.  It will control the specified Server
     * object, and will require the specified password for authorization
     * Note that this Service does not have a no-argument constructor,
     * which means that it cannot be dynamically instantiated and added as
     * the other, generic services above can be.
     **/
    public Control(Server server, String password) {
        this.server = server;
        this.password = password;
    }

    /**
     * This is the serve method that provides the service.  It reads a
     * line from the client, and uses java.util.StringTokenizer to parse it
     * into commands and arguments.  It does various things depending on
     * the command.
     **/
    public void serve(InputStream i, OutputStream o) throws IOException {
        // Set up the streams
        BufferedReader in = new BufferedReader(new InputStreamReader(i));
        PrintWriter out = new PrintWriter(o);
        String line;  // For reading client input lines
        // Has the user given the password yet?
        boolean authorized = false;

        // If there is already a client connected to this service, display
        // a message to this client and close the connection.  We use a
        // synchronized block to prevent a race condition.
        synchronized(this) {
            if (connected) {
                out.print("ONLY ONE CONTROL CONNECTION ALLOWED.\r\n");
                out.close();
                return;
            }
            else connected = true;
        }

        // This is the main loop: read a command, parse it, and handle it
        for(;;) {  // infinite loop
            out.print("> ");           // Display a prompt
            out.flush();               // Make it appear right away
            line = in.readLine();      // Get the user's input
            if (line == null) break;   // Quit if we get EOF.
```

Example 5-10. Server.java (continued)

```
try {
    // Use a StringTokenizer to parse the user's command
    StringTokenizer t = new StringTokenizer(line);
    if (!t.hasMoreTokens()) continue;  // if input was empty
    // Get first word of the input and convert to lowercase
    String command = t.nextToken().toLowerCase();
    // Now compare to each of the possible commands, doing the
    // appropriate thing for each command
    if (command.equals("password")) {  // Password command
        String p = t.nextToken();        // Get the next word
        if (p.equals(this.password)) {  // Is it the password?
            out.print("OK\r\n");          // Say so
            authorized = true;            // Grant authorization
        }
        else out.print("INVALID PASSWORD\r\n");
    }
    else if (command.equals("add")) {  // Add Service command
        // Check whether password has been given
        if (!authorized) out.print("PASSWORD REQUIRED\r\n");
        else {
            // Get the name of the service and try to
            // dynamically load and instantiate it.
            // Exceptions will be handled below
            String serviceName = t.nextToken();
            Class serviceClass = Class.forName(serviceName);
            Service service;
            try {
                service = (Service)serviceClass.newInstance();
            }
            catch (NoSuchMethodError e) {
                throw new IllegalArgumentException(
                            "Service must have a " +
                            "no-argument constructor");
            }
            int port = Integer.parseInt(t.nextToken());
            // If no exceptions occurred, add the service
            server.addService(service, port);
            out.print("SERVICE ADDED\r\n");    // acknowledge
        }
    }
    else if (command.equals("remove")) { // Remove service
        if (!authorized) out.print("PASSWORD REQUIRED\r\n");
        else {
            int port = Integer.parseInt(t.nextToken());
            server.removeService(port); // remove the service
            out.print("SERVICE REMOVED\r\n"); // acknowledge
        }
    }
    else if (command.equals("max")) { // Set connection limit
        if (!authorized) out.print("PASSWORD REQUIRED\r\n");
        else {
            int max = Integer.parseInt(t.nextToken());
            server.setMaxConnections(max);
```

Example 5-10. Server.java (continued)

```
                        out.print("MAX CONNECTIONS CHANGED\r\n");
                    }
                }
                else if (command.equals("status")) { // Status Display
                    if (!authorized) out.print("PASSWORD REQUIRED\r\n");
                    else server.displayStatus(out);
                }
                else if (command.equals("help")) {  // Help command
                    // Display command syntax.  Password not required
                    out.print("COMMANDS:\r\n" +
                              "\tpassword <password>\r\n" +
                              "\tadd <service> <port>\r\n" +
                              "\tremove <port>\r\n" +
                              "\tmax <max-connections>\r\n" +
                              "\tstatus\r\n" +
                              "\thelp\r\n" +
                              "\tquit\r\n");
                }
                else if (command.equals("quit")) break; // Quit command.
                else out.print("UNRECOGNIZED COMMAND\r\n"); // Error
            }
            catch (Exception e) {
                // If an exception occurred during the command, print an
                // error message, then output details of the exception.
                out.print("ERROR WHILE PARSING OR EXECUTING COMMAND:\r\n" +
                          e + "\r\n");
            }
        }
        // Finally, when the command loop ends, close the streams and
        // set our connected flag to false so that other clients can
        // now connect.
        connected = false;
        out.close();
        in.close();
    }
  }
}
```

Sending Datagrams

Now that we've thoroughly covered the possibilities of networking with sockets and streams, let's examine how low-level networking can be done using datagrams and packets. Examples 5-11 and 5-12 show how you can implement simple network communication using datagrams. Datagram communication is sometimes called UDP, for Unreliable Datagram Protocol. Sending datagrams is fast, but the trade-off is that they are not guaranteed to reach their destination. In addition, multiple datagrams are not guaranteed to travel to their destination by the same route or to arrive at their destination in the order in which they were sent. Datagrams are useful when you want low-overhead communication of noncritical data and when a stream model of communication is not necessary. For example, you might implement a multiuser chat server for a local area network using datagrams.

To send and receive datagrams, you use the `DatagramPacket` and `DatagramSocket` classes. These objects are created and initialized differently, depending on whether they send or receive datagrams. Example 5-11 shows how to send a datagram; Example 5-12 shows how to receive a datagram and how to find who sent it.

To send a datagram, you first create a `DatagramPacket`, specifying the data to be sent, the length of the data, the host to send it to, and the port on that host where it is to be sent. You then use the `send( )` method of a `DatagramSocket` to send the packet. The `DatagramSocket` is a generic one, created with no arguments. It can be reused to send any packet to any address and port.

Example 5-11. UDPSend.java

```java
package je3.net;
import java.io.*;
import java.net.*;

/**
 * This class sends the specified text or file as a datagram to the
 * specified port of the specified host.
 **/
public class UDPSend {
    public static final String usage =
        "Usage: java UDPSend <hostname> <port> <msg>...\n" +
        "   or: java UDPSend <hostname> <port> -f <file>";

    public static void main(String args[ ]) {
        try {
            // Check the number of arguments
            if (args.length < 3)
                throw new IllegalArgumentException("Wrong number of args");

            // Parse the arguments
            String host = args[0];
            int port = Integer.parseInt(args[1]);

            // Figure out the message to send.
            // If the third argument is -f, then send the contents of the file
            // specified as the fourth argument.  Otherwise, concatenate the
            // third and all remaining arguments and send that.
            byte[ ] message;
            if (args[2].equals("-f")) {
                File f = new File(args[3]);
                int len = (int)f.length( );     // figure out how big the file is
                message = new byte[len];        // create a buffer big enough
                FileInputStream in = new FileInputStream(f);
                int bytes_read = 0, n;
                do {                            // loop until we've read it all
                    n = in.read(message, bytes_read, len-bytes_read);
                    bytes_read += n;
                } while((bytes_read < len)&& (n != -1));
            }
            else { // Otherwise, just combine all the remaining arguments.
                String msg = args[2];
                for (int i = 3; i < args.length; i++) msg += " " + args[i];
```

Example 5-11. UDPSend.java (continued)

```
                // Convert the message to bytes using UTF-8 encoding
                message = msg.getBytes("UTF-8");
            }

            // Get the internet address of the specified host
            InetAddress address = InetAddress.getByName(host);

            // Initialize a datagram packet with data and address
            DatagramPacket packet = new DatagramPacket(message, message.length,
                                                       address, port);

            // Create a datagram socket, send the packet through it, close it.
            DatagramSocket dsocket = new DatagramSocket();
            dsocket.send(packet);
            dsocket.close();
        }
        catch (Exception e) {
            System.err.println(e);
            System.err.println(usage);
        }
    }
}
```

Receiving Datagrams

Example 5-12 is a program that sits and waits to receive datagrams. When it receives one, it prints out the contents of the datagram and the name of the host that sent it.

To receive a datagram, you must first create a DatagramSocket that listens on a particular port of the local host. This socket can receive only those packets sent to that particular port. Then, you must create a DatagramPacket with a byte buffer into which datagram data is stored. Finally, you call the DatagramSocket.receive() method to wait for a datagram to arrive on the specified port. When it does, the data it contains is transferred into the specified buffer, and receive() returns. If the datagram contains more bytes than fit into the specified buffer, the extra bytes are discarded. When a datagram arrives, receive() also stores the host and port that the datagram was sent from into the packet.

Example 5-12. UDPReceive.java

```
package je3.net;
import java.io.*;
import java.net.*;

/**
 * This program waits to receive datagrams sent to the specified port.
 * When it receives one, it displays the sending host and prints the
 * contents of the datagram as a string.  Then it loops and waits again.
 **/
public class UDPReceive {
    public static final String usage = "Usage: java UDPReceive <port>";
```

Networking

Example 5-12. UDPReceive.java (continued)

```java
public static void main(String args[ ]) {
    try {
        if (args.length != 1)
            throw new IllegalArgumentException("Wrong number of args");

        // Get the port from the command line
        int port = Integer.parseInt(args[0]);

        // Create a socket to listen on the port.
        DatagramSocket dsocket = new DatagramSocket(port);

        // Create a buffer to read datagrams into.  If anyone sends us a
        // packet containing more than will fit into this buffer, the
        // excess will simply be discarded!
        byte[ ] buffer = new byte[2048];

        // Create a packet to receive data into the buffer
        DatagramPacket packet = new DatagramPacket(buffer, buffer.length);

        // Now loop forever, waiting to receive packets and printing them.
        for(;;) {
            // Wait to receive a datagram
            dsocket.receive(packet);

            // Decode the bytes of the packet to characters, using the
            // UTF-8 encoding, and then display those characters.
            String msg = new String(buffer, 0, packet.getLength(),"UTF-8");
            System.out.println(packet.getAddress().getHostName() +
                               ": " + msg);

            // Reset the length of the packet before reusing it.
            // Prior to Java 1.1, we'd just create a new packet each time.
            packet.setLength(buffer.length);
        }
    }
    catch (Exception e) {
        System.err.println(e);
        System.err.println(usage);
    }
}
}
```

Exercises

Exercise 5-1. Using the URLConnection techniques demonstrated in Example 5-2, write a program that prints the modification date of a specified URL.

Exercise 5-2. Write a simple server that reports the current time (in textual form) to any client that connects. Use Example 5-8, HttpMirror, as a framework for your server. This server should simply output the current time and close the connection, without reading anything from the client. You need to choose a

---

port number that your service listens on. Use the `Connect` or `GenericClient` programs of Examples 5-4 and 5-5 to connect to this port and test your program.

Exercise 5-3. Write a program that connects to a POP3 mailbox and displays the Subject and From lines of the messages held there. Base your program on the `PopClean` program of Example 5-7, but be sure to never send the `DELE` command to delete any messages. A shortcoming of the `PopClean` program is that it requires you to type your password on the command line, where it can be observed by others in the room. Solve this problem by storing username, password, hostname, and port in an external configuration file that the program reads. See `java.util.Properties.load( )` for an easy way to read and parse a configuration file. Alternatively, create a Swing GUI for your program, and use `JPasswordField` to get the user's password without displaying the characters on the screen.

Exercise 5-4. Write a simple web server that responds to `GET` requests for local files. You may want to use Example 5-8, `HttpMirror`, as a framework for your server. Alternatively, you can implement your server as a `Service` subclass for use with the `Server` program developed in Example 5-10.

The web server you write should be started with a directory specified on the command line, and it should serve files relative to this directory. When a client requests a file in or beneath the directory, the server should return the contents of the file, but should first output Content-Type, Content-Length, and Last-Modified header lines. For this exercise, assume that files with an extension of *.html* or *.htm* have a content type of text/html, and that all other files are text/plain. If a client requests a file that doesn't exist, your server should return an appropriate error code and message.

You may want to use the `HttpMirror` example to see what a typical HTTP request from a web browser looks like, as your server must be able to handle this kind of request. And you may want to use the `HttpClient` or `GenericClient` example to see how existing web servers respond to requests for existing and nonexistent files, since your server should be able to send responses of this sort. Strict conformance to all the details of the HTTP protocol is not a requirement for this exercise, but successful interaction with web browsers and the `HttpClient` example is.

Exercise 5-5. Modify the `UDPSend` and `UDPReceive` programs of Examples 5-11 and 5-12 so that `UDPReceive` sends an acknowledgment when it receives a datagram, and so that `UDPSend` doesn't exit until it receives the acknowledgment. The acknowledgment should itself be a datagram, and can contain any data you desire. (You could use the checksum classes of the `java.util.zip` package, for example, to compute a checksum of the received data and then send this back in the acknowledgment packet.) Use the `setSoTimeout( )` method of `DatagramSocket` so that `UDPSend` doesn't wait for more than a few seconds to receive the acknowledgment. If the acknowledgment packet is not received before the timeout, `UDPSend` should assume that the original packet got lost and was not received. Your modified `UDPSend` should try to resend the packet once or twice, and if it still doesn't receive an acknowledgment, it should exit with an error message.

6

New I/O

One of the major new features of Java 1.4 is a new Input/Output (I/O) architecture, intended for servers and other applications that require high-performance I/O. Features of this New I/O API include:

- Network channels (the New I/O version of sockets) can be placed in nonblocking mode.
- Multiple nonblocking channels can be multiplexed with a Selector object. This means that it is no longer necessary to create a new thread to monitor each network connection.
- Files can be memory mapped.
- Files, and sections of files, can be locked to prevent concurrent read and write access.
- The new Charset class and related classes give better control over character-to-byte encoding and byte-to-character decoding.
- The java.util.regex package supports text matching with Perl 5–style regular expressions. Although regular expressions are not directly related to I/O, they were developed under the umbrella of the same Java Specification Request (JSR) and are often considered to be part of the New I/O API.

This chapter demonstrates all of these features. To understand the examples, an overview of the New I/O API is in order. Except for the java.util.regex package already mentioned, the bulk of the New I/O is in java.nio and its subpackages. java.nio defines the Buffer class and various concrete subclasses, such as ByteBuffer and CharBuffer for holding sequences of bytes, characters, and other primitive types. All actual I/O is done with byte buffers, but values of other primitive types can be inserted into byte buffers, and byte buffers and their subranges can be viewed as buffers of other types, such as IntBuffer or FloatBuffer.

While the original java.io architecture is based on a stream abstraction (InputStream, OutputStream, Reader, and Writer), the new I/O architecture is based on the Channel abstraction defined in java.nio.channels. A ReadableByteChannel transfers bytes from some source (such as a socket or a file) into a ByteBuffer. A WritableByteChannel transfers bytes from a ByteBuffer to some destination (such as a socket or file). All channels are byte-oriented: there is no such interface as WritableCharChannel, for example.

Because channels work exclusively with bytes, any I/O or networking code that involves character data requires the writer to encode characters into bytes and the reader to decode those bytes back into characters. The java.nio.charset package defines a Charset class to represent a character encoding. Charset and related classes define methods for converting bytes in a ByteBuffer to characters in a CharBuffer and vice versa.

A FileChannel is a read/write conduit to a file, which provides random-access, memory-mapping, locking, and bulk-transfer facilities. A SocketChannel is a read/write channel built on top of a java.net.Socket. ServerSocketChannel provides the Channel abstraction on top of java.net.ServerSocket. The important thing about SocketChannel and ServerSocketChannel is that they are "selectable": they can be placed in nonblocking mode and multiplexed with a Selector object. This allows a single thread to block until activity occurs on any one of the channels it is interested in. This is a basic feature of most operating systems, which, until Java 1.4, has been absent from the Java API. It dramatically improves the scalability of servers written in Java because it no longer requires a new thread to block on each client socket. SocketChannel and ServerSocketChannel perform stream-based networking. For UDP datagram-based networking, java.nio.channels provides the DatagramChannel, which, like the socket channel classes, may be multiplexed with a Selector.

In addition to file and socket channels, java.nio.channels also includes the Pipe class and its inner channel classes, Pipe.SourceChannel and Pipe.SinkChannel, for interthread communication. Like the socket channels, these channel types can be multiplexed with a Selector. Their use is similar to other channels, but they are not demonstrated in this chapter.

The new channel-based I/O architecture is more efficient and powerful, but also more complicated, than the original stream-based API. High-performance servers need the new API, but many other applications can and should continue to use the simpler streams of the java.io and java.net packages. The New I/O API is also valuable to applications that need regular expressions or want to take advantage of the advanced file features of the FileChannel class, such as file locking. This chapter begins by demonstrating basic file and regular expression capabilities. It then creates a Tokenizer implementation (see Example 2-8) for arbitrary channels, and demonstrates advanced byte-to-character conversion with java.nio.charset. Finally, it moves on to networking, demonstrating client and server applications using SocketChannel and ServerSocketChannel. The networking examples include simple programs and more advanced programs that multiplex channels with a Selector.

New I/O

Locking Files

In addition to enabling high-performance I/O, the FileChannel class also enables file locking, a feature that is not available through the java.io package. Example 6-1 demonstrates how it can be used to prevent two instances of the same application from running at the same time. When the program starts, it attempts to obtain an exclusive write lock on a temporary file. If it succeeds, it just sleeps for 10 seconds to simulate a real application. If it fails, it prints a message saying that another instance of the application is running.

The example also demonstrates simple write and read operations on the file using a ByteBuffer. If the program obtains a write lock on the file, it writes a timestamp 10 seconds in the future into the file (this is the approximate time when the program will stop sleeping and exit). If the program does not obtain a lock on the file, it attempts to read the file anyway. If the underlying operating system enforces locking, this read attempt will fail because another instance of the application holds the lock. Many operating systems, however, provide only advisory locking in which all applications must cooperatively use file-locking calls in order to prevent concurrent access. On an operating system, or Java implementation that performs only advisory locking, the program will be allowed to read the file contents even if another instance of the program has an exclusive lock. In this case, the application reads the timestamp written by the original instance of the application and lets the user know how much longer the original instance will continue to run. Note that if two instances of the program are started at the same time, it is possible for one to read the timestamp file before the other has finished writing it. This would cause corrupt data to be read and could cause spurious output. Since the output is only in an informative error message, we are willing to accept this possibility in this example.

One important thing to understand about file locking with FileChannel is that the locks are held on a per-VM basis, not a per-thread basis. This means that if multiple threads want to access the same file, you must use some other mechanism to prevent concurrent access.

The code for writing and reading the files in this example is relatively simple. We'll see many more detailed examples later in the chapter. The FileChannel has write( ) and read( ) methods that write data from a ByteBuffer and read data into a ByteBuffer. In addition to these methods, you should also note the allocate( ) factory method, used to allocate the ByteBuffer objects, and the putLong( ) and getLong( ) methods for storing and retrieving a long timestamp into and from a ByteBuffer. Finally, note that when a buffer is first allocated, it is empty and is ready to receive data via calls like putLong( ) or read( ). Once data is in the buffer, it is then extracted by calls like write( ) or getLong( ). Every buffer has a current position, and when our code stops filling the buffer and gets ready to drain it, it must call the flip( ) method to reset that current position to the beginning of the buffer. Read the javadoc documentation of the java.nio.Buffer class for complete details.

Example 6-1. Lock.java

```java
package je3.nio;
import java.io.*;
import java.nio.*;
import java.nio.channels.*;

/**
 * Lock.java: this class demonstrates file locking and simple file read and
 * write operations using java.nio.channels.FileChannel.  It uses file locking
 * to prevent two instances of the program from running at the same time.
 */
public class Lock {
    public static void main(String args[ ])
        throws IOException, InterruptedException
    {
        RandomAccessFile file = null; // The file we'll lock
        FileChannel f = null;         // The channel to the file
        FileLock lock = null;         // The lock object we hold

        try {    // The finally clause closes the channel and releases the lock
            // We use a temporary file as the lock file.
            String tmpdir = System.getProperty("java.io.tmpdir");
            String filename = Lock.class.getName( )+ ".lock";
            File lockfile = new File(tmpdir, filename);

            // Create a FileChannel that can read and write that file.
            // Note that we rely on the java.io package to open the file,
            // in read/write mode, and then just get a channel from it.
            // This will create the file if it doesn't exit.  We'll arrange
            // for it to be deleted below, if we succeed in locking it.
            file = new RandomAccessFile(lockfile, "rw");
            f = file.getChannel( );

            // Try to get an exclusive lock on the file.
            // This method will return a lock or null, but will not block.
            // See also FileChannel.lock( ) for a blocking variant.
            lock = f.tryLock( );

            if (lock != null) {
                // We obtained the lock, so arrange to delete the file when
                // we're done, and then write the approximate time at which
                // we'll relinquish the lock on the file.
                lockfile.deleteOnExit( );  // Just a temporary file

                // First, we need a buffer to hold the timestamp
                ByteBuffer bytes = ByteBuffer.allocate(8); // a long is 8 bytes

                // Put the time in the buffer and flip to prepare for writing
                // Note that many Buffer methods can be "chained" like this.
                bytes.putLong(System.currentTimeMillis( ) + 10000).flip( );

                f.write(bytes); // Write the buffer contents to the channel
                f.force(false); // Force them out to the disk
            }
```

Example 6-1. Lock.java (continued)

```
            else {
                // We didn't get the lock, which means another instance is
                // running.  First, let the user know this.
                System.out.println("Another instance is already running");

                // Next, we attempt to read the file to figure out how much
                // longer the other instance will be running.  Since we don't
                // have a lock, the read may fail or return inconsistent data.
                try {
                    ByteBuffer bytes = ByteBuffer.allocate(8);
                    f.read(bytes);   // Read 8 bytes from the file
                    bytes.flip();    // Flip buffer before extracting bytes
                    long exittime = bytes.getLong(); // Read bytes as a long
                    // Figure out how long that time is from now and round
                    // it to the nearest second.
                    long secs = (exittime-System.currentTimeMillis()+500)/1000;
                    // And tell the user about it.
                    System.out.println("Try again in about "+secs+" seconds");
                }
                catch(IOException e) {
                    // This probably means that locking is enforced by the OS
                    // and we were prevented from reading the file.
                }

                // This is an abnormal exit, so set an exit code.
                System.exit(1);
            }


            // Simulate a real application by sleeping for 10 seconds.
            System.out.println("Starting...");
            Thread.sleep(10000);
            System.out.println("Exiting.");
        }
        finally {
            // Always release the lock and close the file
            // Closing the RandomAccessFile also closes its FileChannel.
            if (lock != null && lock.isValid()) lock.release();
            if (file != null) file.close();
        }
    }
}
```

Copying Files

Example 6-2 is a New I/O version of the FileCopy class of Example 3-2. It copies the file named in its first command-line argument to the file named second or, if there is no second argument, to standard output. This example demonstrates a special bulk-transfer method that is unique to the FileChannel class: the transferTo() method copies the entire contents of the file to the specified channel without the need for any explicitly allocated ByteBuffer objects. This method is particularly useful for web servers and other applications that transfer file contents. The transferFrom( ) method performs the reverse operation and can be useful for programs such as FTP clients.

Note that this example omits the safety features of the original FileCopy program and can overwrite existing files, so be careful when using it.

Example 6-2. FileCopy2.java

```java
package je3.nio;
import java.io.*;
import java.nio.channels.*;

/**
 * FileCopy2.java: this program copies the file named in its first argument
 * to the file named in its second argument, or to standard output if there
 * is no second argument.
 **/
public class FileCopy2 {
    public static void main(String[ ] args) {
        FileInputStream fin = null;   // Streams to the two files.
        FileOutputStream fout = null; // These are closed in the finally block.
        try {
            // Open a stream to the input file and get a channel from it
            fin = new FileInputStream(args[0]);
            FileChannel in = fin.getChannel( );

            // Now get the output channel
            WritableByteChannel out;
            if (args.length > 1) { // If there is a second filename
                fout = new FileOutputStream(args[1]);  // open file stream
                out = fout.getChannel( );              // get its channel
            }
            else { // There is no destination filename
                out = Channels.newChannel(System.out); // wrap stdout stream
            }

            // Query the size of the input file
            long numbytes = in.size( );

            // Bulk-transfer all bytes from one channel to the other.
            // This is a special feature of FileChannel channels.
            // See also FileChannel.transferFrom( )
            in.transferTo(0, numbytes, out);
        }
        catch(IOException e) {
            // IOExceptions usually have useful informative messages.
            // Display the message if anything goes wrong.
            System.out.println(e);
        }
        finally {
            // Always close input and output streams.  Doing this closes
            // the channels associated with them as well.
            try {
                if (fin != null) fin.close( );
```

New I/O

Example 6-2. FileCopy2.java (continued)

```
            if (fout != null) fout.close( );
        }
        catch(IOException e) { }
    }
}
}
```

Regular Expressions and Character Decoding

Example 6-3 demonstrates the text-matching capabilities of the `java.util.regex` package. This `BGrep` class is a variant of the Unix "grep" command for searching files for text that matches a given regular expression. Unlike Unix *grep*, which is line-oriented, `BGrep` is block-oriented: the matched text can span multiple lines, and its location in the file is indicated by character number rather than line number. Invoke `BGrep` with the regular expression to search for and one or more filenames. Use `-i` to specify case-insensitive matching. If the files contain characters in some encoding other than UTF-8, use the `-e` option to specify the encoding. For example, you could use this command to search a bunch of Java source files for occurrences of "ByteBuffer", "CharBuffer", and the like.

```
java je3.nio.BGrep '[A-Z][a-z]*Buffer' *.java
```

The `java.util.regex` package uses a regular expression syntax that is much like that of Perl 5. Look up `java.util.regex.Pattern` in Sun's javadocs or in *Java in a Nutshell* for a summary of this syntax, and look up the `Matcher` class in the same package for details on how to use `Pattern` objects to match character sequences. If you are not already familiar with regular expressions, you can find complete details in the book *Mastering Regular Expressions*, by Jeffrey Friedl (O'Reilly).

This program also demonstrates an easy way to read the contents of a file: simply use the memory-mapping capabilities of `FileChannel` to map the contents of the entire file into a `ByteBuffer`. In order to perform pattern matching on the characters in a file, the bytes of the file must be decoded into characters; this example uses a simple `Charset` method to decode a complete `ByteBuffer` into a newly allocated `CharBuffer` all at once. This `CharBuffer` is then used with a `java.util.regex. Matcher` object to look for pattern matches. Later examples in this chapter will illustrate lower-level character decoding techniques.

Example 6-3. BGrep.java

```
package je3.nio;
import java.io.*;
import java.nio.*;
import java.nio.charset.*;
import java.nio.channels.*;
import java.util.regex.*;

/**
 * BGrep: a regular expression search utility, like Unix grep, but
 * block-oriented instead of line-oriented.  For any match found, the
 * filename and character position within the file (note: not the line
```

Example 6-3. BGrep.java (continued)

```
 * number) are printed along with the text that matched.
 *
 * Usage:
 *   java je3.nio.BGrep [options] <pattern> <files>...
 *
 * Options:
 *   -e <encoding> specifies and encoding. UTF-8 is the default
 *   -i enables case-insensitive matching.  Use -s also for non-ASCII text
 *   -s enables strict (but slower) processing of non-ASCII characters
 *
 * This program requires that each file to be searched fits into main
 * memory, and so does not work with extremely large files.
 **/
public class BGrep {
    public static void main(String[ ] args) {
        String encodingName = "UTF-8"; // Default to UTF-8 encoding
        int flags = Pattern.MULTILINE; // Default regexp flags

        try { // Fatal exceptions are handled after this try block
            // First, process any options
            int nextarg = 0;
            while(args[nextarg].charAt(0) == '-') {
                String option = args[nextarg++];
                if (option.equals("-e")) {
                    encodingName = args[nextarg++];
                }
                else if (option.equals("-i")) {  // case-insensitive matching
                    flags |= Pattern.CASE_INSENSITIVE;
                }
                else if (option.equals("-s")) { // Strict Unicode processing
                    flags |= Pattern.UNICODE_CASE; // case-insensitive Unicode
                    flags |= Pattern.CANON_EQ;     // canonicalize Unicode
                }
                else {
                    System.err.println("Unknown option: " + option);
                    usage();
                }
            }

            // Get the Charset for converting bytes to chars
            Charset charset = Charset.forName(encodingName);

            // Next argument must be a regexp. Compile it to a Pattern object
            Pattern pattern = Pattern.compile(args[nextarg++], flags);

            // Require that at least one file is specified
            if (nextarg == args.length) usage();

            // Loop through each of the specified filenames
            while(nextarg < args.length) {
                String filename = args[nextarg++];
                CharBuffer chars;  // This will hold complete text of the file
                try {  // Handle per-file errors locally
```

New I/O

Example 6-3. BGrep.java (continued)

```java
                        // Open a FileChannel to the named file
                        FileInputStream stream = new FileInputStream(filename);
                        FileChannel f = stream.getChannel();

                        // Memory-map the file into one big ByteBuffer.  This is
                        // easy but may be somewhat inefficient for short files.
                        ByteBuffer bytes = f.map(FileChannel.MapMode.READ_ONLY,
                                                 0, f.size());

                        // We can close the file once it is is mapped into memory.
                        // Closing the stream closes the channel, too.
                        stream.close();

                        // Decode the entire ByteBuffer into one big CharBuffer
                        chars = charset.decode(bytes);
                    }
                    catch(IOException e) { // File not found or other problem
                        System.err.println(e);   // Print error message
                        continue;                 // and move on to the next file
                    }

                    // This is the basic regexp loop for finding all matches in a
                    // CharSequence. Note that CharBuffer implements CharSequence.
                    // A Matcher holds state for a given Pattern and text.
                    Matcher matcher = pattern.matcher(chars);
                    while(matcher.find()) { // While there are more matches
                        // Print out details of the match
                        System.out.println(filename + ":" +      // file name
                                           matcher.start()+": "+ // character pos
                                           matcher.group());      // matching text
                    }
                }
            }
            // These are the things that can go wrong in the code above
            catch(UnsupportedCharsetException e) {     // Bad encoding name
                System.err.println("Unknown encoding: " + encodingName);
            }
            catch(PatternSyntaxException e) {          // Bad pattern
                System.err.println("Syntax error in search pattern:\n" +
                                   e.getMessage());
            }
            catch(ArrayIndexOutOfBoundsException e) { // Wrong number of arguments
                usage();
            }
        }

        /** A utility method to display invocation syntax and exit. */
        public static void usage() {
            System.err.println("Usage: java BGrep [-e <encoding>] [-i] [-s]" +
                               " <pattern> <filename>...");
            System.exit(1);
        }
    }
```

File Copying with Buffers

Example 6-4 is another file copying program. Instead of using the shortcut FileChannel.transferTo( ) method, this example defines a generic copy( ) method for copying bytes from one channel to another and demonstrates the basic java. nio I/O loop, described here:

1. The buffer is filled with bytes from one channel.

2. The buffer is flipped, making it ready to be drained. See Buffer and Buffer. flip( ) for details.

3. The buffer is drained by writing bytes from it to another channel.

4. The buffer is compacted, discarding bytes that have been drained from it and shifting remaining bytes to the beginning of the buffer. As part of this process, the current position of the buffer is reset to point to the first available byte in the buffer, making the buffer ready to be filled again. See ByteBuffer.compact( ) for details. If the call to write( ) completely drained the buffer, then clear( ) can be used instead of compact( ).

This loop continues until the input channel indicates that there are no more bytes to read (its read( ) method returns -1) and the buffer is empty.

Variants on this basic loop appear in most programs that use the New I/O API, so it is important to understand it. For clarity, Example 6-4 omits exception-handling and stream-closing code so that you can focus on the basic loop.

Example 6-4. FileCopy3.java

```
package je3.nio;
import java.io.*;
import java.nio.*;
import java.nio.channels.*;

public class FileCopy3 {
    public static void main(String[] args) throws IOException {
        // Open file streams and get channels for them.
        ReadableByteChannel in = new FileInputStream(args[0]).getChannel();
        WritableByteChannel out;
        if (args.length > 1) out = new FileOutputStream(args[1]).getChannel();
        else out = Channels.newChannel(System.out);

        // Do the copy
        copy(in, out);

        // Exception-handling and stream-closing code has been omitted.
    }

    // Read all available bytes from one channel and copy them to the other.
    public static void copy(ReadableByteChannel in, WritableByteChannel out)
        throws IOException
    {
        // First, we need a buffer to hold blocks of copied bytes.
        ByteBuffer buffer = ByteBuffer.allocateDirect(32 * 1024);
```

Example 6-4. FileCopy3.java (continued)

```
                  // Now loop until no more bytes to read and the buffer is empty
                  while(in.read(buffer) != -1 || buffer.position( ) > 0) {
                      // The read( ) call leaves the buffer in "fill mode".  To prepare
                      // to write bytes from the buffer, we have to put it in "drain mode"
                      // by flipping it: setting limit to position and position to zero
                      buffer.flip( );

                      // Now write some or all of the bytes out to the output channel
                      out.write(buffer);

                      // Compact the buffer by discarding bytes that were written
                      // and shifting any remaining bytes.  This method also
                      // prepares the buffer for the next call to read( ) by setting the
                      // position to the limit and the limit to the buffer capacity.
                      buffer.compact( );
                  }
              }
          }
```

Loop Alternatives

The code shown in Example 6-4 isn't the only way to express the basic java.nio channel copying loop. Following are two variants from the book *Java NIO*, by Ron Hitchens (O'Reilly). The first variant simplifies the exit condition for the loop, by adding a second loop to drain the buffer when the first loop reaches end-of-file:

```
      public static void copy1(ReadableByteChannel in, WritableByteChannel out)
          throws IOException
      {
          ByteBuffer buffer = ByteBuffer.allocateDirect(16 * 1024);

          while(in.read(buffer) != -1) {
              // Prepare the buffer to be drained
              buffer.flip( );

              // Write to the channel; may block
              out.write(buffer);

              // If partial transfer, shift remainder down
              // If buffer is empty, same as doing clear( )
              buffer.compact( );
          }

          // EOF will leave buffer in fill state
          buffer.flip( );

          // Make sure that the buffer is fully drained
          while (buffer.hasRemaining( )) {
              out.write(buffer);
          }
      }
```

The second variant of the loop ensures that the buffer is fully drained on each iteration, so that the call to compact( ) is no longer necessary:

```
public static void copy2(ReadableByteChannel in, WritableByteChannel out)
    throws IOException
{
    ByteBuffer buffer = ByteBuffer.allocateDirect(16 * 1024);

    while(in.read(buffer) != -1) {
        // Prepare the buffer to be drained
        buffer.flip( );

        // Make sure that the buffer was fully drained
        while (buffer.hasRemaining( )) {
            out.write(buffer);
        }

        // Make the buffer empty, ready for filling
        buffer.clear( );
    }
}
```

Advanced Byte-to-Character Conversion

In Example 6-4 we saw a basic loop for copying bytes from one channel to another. Another commonly seen loop in programs that use the New I/O API is one that combines reading or writing bytes with decoding bytes to characters, or encoding characters to bytes. In Example 6-3 we saw the Charset.decode( ) method for decoding a buffer of bytes into a buffer of characters. This is actually a high-level convenience method, and we'll see similar convenience methods elsewhere in this chapter. For better streaming performance, however, you can use the lower-level CharsetDecoder and CharsetEncoder classes, as is done in Example 6-5. This example is the ChannelToWriter class, which defines a single static copy( ) method. This method reads bytes from a specified channel, decodes them to characters using the specified Charset, and then writes them to the specified Writer. (Note that this is not the same function performed by Channels.newReader( ), Channels.newWriter( ), or Channels.newChannel( ). The factory methods of the Channels class allow you to wrap a channel around a stream or a stream around a channel, but do not perform a copy.)

The read/decode/write loop shown in this example is a common one in java.nio code, but is more complex than you might expect. One reason for the complexity is that in many character encodings, there is not a one-to-one correspondence between bytes and characters. This means that there is no guarantee that all bytes in a buffer can be decoded into characters each time through the loop—one or more bytes at the end of the buffer might not encode a complete character. Note also that before entering the loop, we tell the CharsetDecoder to ignore bad input. If we don't do this, we must examine the return value of each decode( ) call to ensure that it was successful.

Example 6-5. ChannelToWriter.java

```java
package je3.nio;
import java.io.*;
import java.nio.*;
import java.nio.charset.*;
import java.nio.channels.*;

public class ChannelToWriter {
    /**
     * Read bytes from the specified channel, decode them using the specified
     * Charset, and write the resulting characters to the specified writer
     */
    public static void copy(ReadableByteChannel channel, Writer writer,
                            Charset charset)
        throws IOException
    {
        // Get and configure the CharsetDecoder we'll use
        CharsetDecoder decoder = charset.newDecoder();
        decoder.onMalformedInput(CodingErrorAction.IGNORE);
        decoder.onUnmappableCharacter(CodingErrorAction.IGNORE);

        // Get the buffers we'll use and the backing array for the CharBuffer.
        ByteBuffer bytes = ByteBuffer.allocateDirect(2*1024);
        CharBuffer chars = CharBuffer.allocate(2*1024);
        char[] array = chars.array();

        while(channel.read(bytes) != -1) { // Read from channel until EOF
            bytes.flip();                  // Switch to drain mode for decoding
            // Decode the byte buffer into the char buffer.
            // Pass false to indicate that we're not done.
            decoder.decode(bytes, chars, false);

            // Put the char buffer into drain mode, and write its contents
            // to the Writer, reading them from the backing array.
            chars.flip();
            writer.write(array, chars.position(), chars.remaining());

            // Discard all bytes we decoded, and put the byte buffer back into
            // fill mode.  Since all characters were output, clear that buffer.
            bytes.compact();           // Discard decoded bytes
            chars.clear();             // Clear the character buffer
        }

        // At this point there may still be some bytes in the buffer to decode
        // So put the buffer into drain mode, call decode() a final time, and
        // finish with a flush().
        bytes.flip();
        decoder.decode(bytes, chars, true);  // True means final call
        decoder.flush(chars);                // Flush any buffered chars
        // Write these final chars (if any) to the writer.
        chars.flip();
        writer.write(array, chars.position(), chars.remaining());
        writer.flush();
    }
}
```

Example 6-5. ChannelToWriter.java (continued)

```
    // A test method: copy a UTF-8 file to standard out
    public static void main(String[] args) throws IOException {
        FileChannel c = new FileInputStream(args[0]).getChannel();
        OutputStreamWriter w = new OutputStreamWriter(System.out);
        Charset utf8 = Charset.forName("UTF-8");
        ChannelToWriter.copy(c, w, utf8);
        c.close();
        w.close();
    }
}
```

Tokenizing Byte Buffers

In this section we present an abstract Tokenizer implementation (see Example 2-8) for tokenizing the contents of a ByteBuffer. The subsections that follow include concrete subclasses for tokenizing characters read from a memory-mapped file or an arbitrary Channel. The ByteBufferTokenizer class in Example 6-6 extends the AbstractTokenizer class of Example 2-9. You may want to reread that example before starting in on this one.

As you recall, the AbstractTokenizer class has abstract methods it calls when it needs more characters to tokenize. The ByteBufferTokenizer class implements these methods to get more characters by using a CharsetDecoder to decode bytes from a ByteBuffer, but it defines and calls new abstract methods when it needs to get more bytes into the ByteBuffer.

As with AbstractTokenizer, the code for this class is a little dense; it is intended as a moderately advanced example. The most interesting thing to note about this example is the use of the CharsetDecoder. Notice how it is obtained from the Charset object, how its error behavior is configured, how the decode() method is called, and how the return values of that method are handled. It is useful to compare the use of the CharsetDecoder in this example with the decoding loop of Example 6-5.

Example 6-6. ByteBufferTokenizer.java

```
package je3.nio;
import java.nio.*;
import java.nio.charset.*;
import java.io.IOException;
import je3.classes.AbstractTokenizer;

/**
 * This is an abstract Tokenizer implementation for tokenizing ByteBuffers.
 * It implements the two abstract methods of AbstractTokenizer, but defines
 * two new abstract methods that subclasses must implement.  This class
 * provides byte-to-character decoding but leaves it up to concrete subclasses
 * to provide the ByteBuffers to decode
 */
public abstract class ByteBufferTokenizer extends AbstractTokenizer {
    CharsetDecoder decoder;    // For converting bytes to characters
```

Example 6-6. ByteBufferTokenizer.java (continued)

```
    CharBuffer chars;          // The characters we're working on
    ByteBuffer bytes;          // The bytes supplied by our subclass.

    // Initialize a decoder for the specified Charset, and tell our superclass
    // how big our buffer is (and thus what size tokens we can handle).
    protected ByteBufferTokenizer(Charset charset, int charBufferSize) {
        maximumTokenLength(charBufferSize);
        decoder = charset.newDecoder();
        decoder.onMalformedInput(CodingErrorAction.IGNORE);
        decoder.onUnmappableCharacter(CodingErrorAction.IGNORE);
    }

    // Create the text[] array and set numChars.
    // These two fields are defined by the superclass.
    // Our superclass needs characters in the text[] array. We're going to
    // decode bytes into characters in a CharBuffer. So we create a CharBuffer
    // that uses text[] as its backing array.
    protected void createBuffer(int bufferSize) {
        // Make sure AbstractTokenizer calls this method only once
        assert text == null;

        text = new char[bufferSize];   // Create the new buffer.
        chars = CharBuffer.wrap(text); // Wrap a char buffer around it.
        numChars = 0;                  // Say how much text it contains.
    }

    // Fill or refill the buffer.
    // See AbstractTokenizer.fillBuffer() for what this method must do.
    protected boolean fillBuffer() throws IOException {
        // Make sure AbstractTokenizer is upholding its end of the bargain
        assert text!=null && 0 <= tokenStart && tokenStart <= tokenEnd &&
            tokenEnd <= p && p <= numChars && numChars <= text.length;

        // First, shift already tokenized characters out of the buffer
        if (tokenStart > 0) {
            // Shift array contents in the text[] array.
            System.arraycopy(text, tokenStart, text, 0, numChars-tokenStart);
            // And update buffer indexes. These fields defined in superclass.
            tokenEnd -= tokenStart;
            p -= tokenStart;
            numChars -= tokenStart;
            tokenStart = 0;

            // Keep the CharBuffer in sync with the changes we made above.
            chars.position(p);
        }

        // If there is still no space in the char buffer, then we've
        // encountered a token too large for our buffer size.
        // We could try to recover by creating a larger buffer, but
        // instead, we just throw an exception
        if (chars.remaining() == 0)
```

Example 6-6. ByteBufferTokenizer.java (continued)

```
                throw new IOException("Token too long at " + tokenLine() + ":" +
                                      tokenColumn());

        // Get more bytes if we don't have a buffer or if the buffer
        // has been emptied
        if ((bytes == null || bytes.remaining()==0) && hasMoreBytes())
            bytes = getMoreBytes();

        // Now that we have room in the chars buffer and data in the bytes
        // buffer, we can decode some bytes into chars
        CoderResult result = decoder.decode(bytes, chars, !hasMoreBytes());

        // Get the index of the last valid character plus one.
        numChars = chars.position();

        if (result == CoderResult.OVERFLOW) {
            // We've filled up the char buffer.  It wasn't full before, so
            // we know we got at least one new character.
            return true;
        }
        else if (result == CoderResult.UNDERFLOW) {
            // This means that we decoded all the bytes and have room left
            // in the char buffer.  Normally, this is fine.  But there is
            // a possibility that we didn't actually get any characters.
            if (numChars > p) return true;
            else { // We didn't get any new characters.  Figure out why.
                if (!hasMoreBytes()) {
                    // If there are no more bytes to read, then we're at EOF
                    return false;
                }
                else {
                    // If there are still bytes remaining to read, then
                    // we probably got part of a multi-byte sequence, and need
                    // more bytes before we can decode a character from it.
                    // Try again (recursively) to get some more bytes.
                    return fillBuffer();
                }
            }
        }
        else {
            // We used CodingErrorAction.IGNORE for the CharsetDecoder, so
            // the decoding result should always be one of the above two.
            assert false : "Unexpected CoderResult: " + result;
            return false;
        }
    }

    /**
     * Determine if more bytes are available.
     * @return true if and only if more bytes are available for reading.
     */
    protected abstract boolean hasMoreBytes();
```

Example 6-6. ByteBufferTokenizer.java (continued)

```
    /**
     * Get a buffer of bytes for decoding and tokenizing.
     * Repeated calls to this method may create a new ByteBuffer,
     * or may refill and return the same buffer each time.
     * @return a ByteBuffer with its position set to the first new byte, and
     *          its limit set to the index of the last new byte plus 1.
     *          The return value should never be null.  If no more bytes are
     *          available, return an empty buffer (with limit == position).
     */
    protected abstract ByteBuffer getMoreBytes() throws IOException;
}
```

Tokenizing Memory Mapped Files

Example 6-7 is a concrete subclass of Example 6-6. MappedFileTokenizer extends
ByteBufferTokenizer to tokenize the contents of a given file, as represented by a
FileChannel object. The implementation is particularly simple because refilling the
byte buffer is simply a matter of memory mapping a new section of the file.

Example 6-7. MappedFileTokenizer.java

```
package je3.nio;
import java.io.*;
import java.nio.*;
import java.nio.channels.*;
import java.nio.charset.*;

/**
 * This class implements the Tokenizer interface for a FileChannel and Charset.
 * It extends ByteBufferTokenizer and uses FileChannel.map() to memory map the
 * contents of the file into a ByteBuffer.
 */
public class MappedFileTokenizer extends ByteBufferTokenizer {
    static final int DEFAULT_BUFFER_SIZE = 32*1024;
    FileChannel channel;      // The file we want to tokenize
    int byteBufferSize;       // What size chunks to map at a time
    long filesize;            // How big the file is
    long fileposition;        // Starting position of the next chunk

    // Construct a tokenizer for the specified FileChannel, assuming the
    // file contains text encoded using the specified Charset.
    public MappedFileTokenizer(FileChannel channel, Charset charset)
        throws IOException
    {
        this(channel, charset, DEFAULT_BUFFER_SIZE, DEFAULT_BUFFER_SIZE);
    }

    // Construct a tokenizer for the specified file and charset, additionally
    // specifying the size of the byte and character buffers to use.
    public MappedFileTokenizer(FileChannel channel, Charset charset,
                               int charBufferSize, int byteBufferSize)
        throws IOException
```

Example 6-7. MappedFileTokenizer.java (continued)

```
    {
        super(charset, charBufferSize); // Superclass handles charset and size
        this.channel = channel;
        this.byteBufferSize = byteBufferSize;
        filesize = channel.size();      // Get the length of the file
        fileposition = 0;               // And start at the beginning
    }

    // Return true if there are more bytes for us to return
    protected boolean hasMoreBytes() { return fileposition < filesize; }

    // Read the next chunk of bytes and return them.
    protected ByteBuffer getMoreBytes() throws IOException {
        // Return byteBufferSize bytes, or the number remaining in the file
        // if that is less
        long length = byteBufferSize;
        if (fileposition + length > filesize) length = filesize-fileposition;

        // Memory map the bytes into a buffer
        ByteBuffer buffer =
            channel.map(FileChannel.MapMode.READ_ONLY, fileposition, length);
        // Store the position of the next chunk
        fileposition += length;
        // And return the memory-mapped buffer of bytes.
        return buffer;
    }
}
```

Tokenizing Channels

Example 6-8 is another subclass of Example 6-6. ChannelTokenizer extends
ByteBufferTokenizer to fill the byte buffer from an arbitrary ReadableByteChannel.
The implementation is straightforward.

Example 6-8. ChannelTokenizer.java

```
package je3.nio;
import java.io.*;
import java.nio.*;
import java.nio.channels.*;
import java.nio.charset.*;

public class ChannelTokenizer extends ByteBufferTokenizer {
    static final int DEFAULT_BUFFER_SIZE = 32*1024;
    ReadableByteChannel channel; // Where the bytes come from
    ByteBuffer buffer;           // Where we put those bytes
    boolean hasMoreBytes;        // Whether there are any more

    // Construct a ChannelTokenizer to tokenize the specified channel,
    // decoding its bytes using the specified charset.
    public ChannelTokenizer(ReadableByteChannel channel, Charset charset) {
        this(channel, charset, DEFAULT_BUFFER_SIZE, DEFAULT_BUFFER_SIZE);
    }
```

Example 6-8. ChannelTokenizer.java (continued)

```
    // Construct a ChannelTokenizer for the channel and charset, additionally
    // specifying the character and byte buffer sizes to use.
    public ChannelTokenizer(ReadableByteChannel channel, Charset charset,
                            int charBufferSize, int byteBufferSize)
    {
        super(charset, charBufferSize); // Superclass handles charset and size
        this.channel = channel;         // Remember the channel
        this.hasMoreBytes = true;       // Assume some bytes in the channel
        // Allocate the buffer we'll use to store bytes
        buffer = ByteBuffer.allocateDirect(byteBufferSize);
    }

    // Return false when we're at EOF and have returned all bytes.
    protected boolean hasMoreBytes( ) { return hasMoreBytes; }

    // Refill the buffer and return it
    protected ByteBuffer getMoreBytes( ) throws IOException {
        buffer.clear( );  // Clear the buffer; prepare to fill it.
        // Read a chunk of bytes
        int bytesRead = channel.read(buffer);
        // If we are at EOF, remember that for hasMoreBytes( )
        if (bytesRead == -1) hasMoreBytes = false;
        // Prepare the buffer to be drained and return it
        buffer.flip( );   // Set limit to position and position to 0
        return buffer;    // And return it.
    }
}
```

A Simple HTTP Client

With Example 6-9, we move away from file-based New I/O examples and move into networking examples. HttpGet is a program that performs an HTTP GET request to download a file from a web server. It uses a SocketChannel object for communication with the server, and a FileChannel to store the downloaded data into a file. (Or, if no filename is specified on the command line, it uses the Channels utility class to obtain a WritableByteChannel wrapper around the System. out standard output stream.)

HttpGet uses some networking classes that are new in Java 1.4, but are not part of java.nio. java.net.URI is the most important: it has more powerful URL parsing capabilities than java.net.URL, but does not have the built-in networking capability of the URL class. The other important new class is InetSocketAddress, which encapsulates a hostname and a port.

The HTTP request that is sent to the web server is first built as a String, then wrapped in a CharBuffer, which is encoded into a Charset object. The resulting ByteBuffer is then sent to the server using the write( ) method of the SocketChannel. Once the request is sent, the program enters a loop to read response data from the server and copy that data into the destination file (or standard output channel). The basic loop is essentially the same as the one in Example 6-4, but is complicated by code that extracts the HTTP status code from the response and scans for the byte sequence that identifies the end of the HTTP headers and the beginning of the actual data. You may find it interesting to compare this example to Example 5-6, which performs similarly but is implemented using java.net and java.io instead of java.nio.

Note that HttpGet does not implement the complete HTTP 1.1 protocol. Shortcomings include the inability to handle the server response "100 Continue" (which, if properly implemented, would ignore it and continue to read) or the response codes 301, 302, 303, and 305 (which should redirect to a new URL). Also, the code does not know how to handle a Transfer-Encoding: chunked header in the response.

Example 6-9. HttpGet.java

```java
package je3.nio;
import java.io.*;
import java.net.*;
import java.nio.*;
import java.nio.channels.*;
import java.nio.charset.*;

public class HttpGet {
    public static void main(String[] args) {
        SocketChannel server = null;        // Channel for reading from server
        FileOutputStream outputStream = null;  // Stream to destination file
        WritableByteChannel destination;        // Channel to write to it

        try { // Exception-handling and channel-closing code follows this block

            // Parse the URL. Note we use the new java.net.URI, not URL here.
            URI uri = new URI(args[0]);

            // Now query and verify the various parts of the URI
            String scheme = uri.getScheme();
            if (scheme == null || !scheme.equals("http"))
                throw new IllegalArgumentException("Must use 'http:' protocol");

            String hostname = uri.getHost();

            int port = uri.getPort();
            if (port == -1) port = 80; // Use default port if none specified

            String path = uri.getRawPath();
            if (path == null || path.length() == 0) path = "/";

            String query = uri.getRawQuery();
            query = (query == null)?"":'?'+query;

            // Combine the hostname and port into a single address object.
            // java.net.SocketAddress and InetSocketAddress are new in Java 1.4
            SocketAddress serverAddress=new InetSocketAddress(hostname, port);

            // Open a SocketChannel to the server
            server = SocketChannel.open(serverAddress);
```

New I/O

Example 6-9. HttpGet.java (continued)

```
                // Put together the HTTP request we'll send to the server.
                String request =
                    "GET " + path + query + " HTTP/1.1\r\n" +  // The request
                    "Host: " + hostname + "\r\n" +    // Required in HTTP 1.1
                    "Connection: close\r\n" +          // Don't keep connection open
                    "User-Agent: " + HttpGet.class.getName() + "\r\n" +
                    "\r\n";  // Blank line indicates end of request headers

                // Now wrap a CharBuffer around that request string
                CharBuffer requestChars = CharBuffer.wrap(request);

                // Get a Charset object to encode the char buffer into bytes
                Charset charset = Charset.forName("ISO-8859-1");

                // Use the charset to encode the request into a byte buffer
                ByteBuffer requestBytes = charset.encode(requestChars);

                // Finally, we can send this HTTP request to the server.
                server.write(requestBytes);

                // Set up an output channel to send the output to.
                if (args.length > 1) {    // Use a specified filename
                    outputStream = new FileOutputStream(args[1]);
                    destination = outputStream.getChannel();
                }
                else                      // Or wrap a channel around standard out
                    destination = Channels.newChannel(System.out);

                // Allocate a 32 Kilobyte byte buffer for reading the response.
                // Hopefully we'll get a low-level "direct" buffer
                ByteBuffer data = ByteBuffer.allocateDirect(32 * 1024);

                // Have we discarded the HTTP response headers yet?
                boolean skippedHeaders = false;
                // The code sent by the server
                int responseCode = -1;

                // Now loop, reading data from the server channel and writing it
                // to the destination channel until the server indicates that it
                // has no more data.
                while(server.read(data) != -1) {  // Read data, and check for end
                    data.flip();        // Prepare to extract data from buffer

                    // All HTTP reponses begin with a set of HTTP headers, which
                    // we need to discard.  The headers end with the string
                    // "\r\n\r\n" or the bytes 13,10,13,10.  If we haven't already
                    // skipped them, then do so now.
                    if (!skippedHeaders) {
                        // First, though, read the HTTP response code.
                        // Assume that we get the complete first line of the
                        // response when the first read() call returns. Assume also
                        // that the first 9 bytes are the ASCII characters
```

Example 6-9. HttpGet.java (continued)

```
                        // "HTTP/1.1 ", and that the response code is the ASCII
                        // characters in the following three bytes.
                        if (responseCode == -1) {
                            responseCode =
                                100 * (data.get(9)-'0') +
                                10 * (data.get(10)-'0') +
                                1 * (data.get(11)-'0');

                            // If there was an error, report it and quit
                            // Note that we do not handle redirect responses.
                            if (responseCode < 200 || responseCode >= 300) {
                                System.err.println("HTTP Error: " + responseCode);
                                System.exit(1);
                            }
                        }

                        // Now skip the rest of the headers.
                        try {
                            for(;;) {
                                if ((data.get( ) == 13) && (data.get( ) == 10) &&
                                    (data.get( ) == 13) && (data.get( ) == 10)) {
                                    skippedHeaders = true;
                                    break;
                                }
                            }
                        }
                        catch (BufferUnderflowException e) {
                            // If we arrive here, it means we reached the end of
                            // the buffer and didn't find the end of the headers.
                            // There is a chance that the last 1, 2, or 3 bytes in
                            // the buffer were the beginning of the \r\n\r\n
                            // sequence, so back up a bit.
                            data.position(data.position( )-3);
                            // Now discard the headers we have read
                            data.compact( );
                            // And go read more data from the server.
                            continue;
                        }
                    }

                    // Write the data out; drain the buffer fully.
                    while(data.hasRemaining( )) destination.write(data);

                    // Now that the buffer is drained, put it into fill mode
                    // in preparation for reading more data into it.
                    data.clear( );          // data.compact( ) also works here
                }
            }
            catch (Exception e) {      // Report any errors that arise
                System.err.println(e);
                System.err.println("Usage: java HttpGet <URL> [<filename>]");
            }
```

Example 6-9. HttpGet.java (continued)

```
        finally { // Close the channels and output file stream, if needed
            try {
                if (server != null && server.isOpen()) server.close();
                if (outputStream != null) outputStream.close();
            }
            catch(IOException e) { }
        }
    }
}
```

The Daytime Service

daytime is an ancient (by Internet standards) network service that simply sends the current local day and time as an ASCII string to any client that connects to port 13, via either TCP or UDP. Example 6-10 is a simple daytime server that accepts TCP connections using a ServerSocketChannel and sends responses to the client with a SocketChannel. This simple program is followed by Example 6-11, a more robust implementation that handles TCP and UDP connections, and includes exception handling and error logging. This more advanced server demonstrates ServerSocketChannel and DatagramChannel, and shows how a program can wait for activity on both channels simultaneously using a Selector object. This section concludes with Example 6-12, a simple datagram-based client of the daytime service, suitable for testing Example 6-11.

SimpleDaytimeServer is, as its name implies, a simple program. It first creates a ServerSocketChannel, and then binds it to port 13 or some other port specified on the command line. Binding the channel to a port is done by querying the underlying java.net.ServerSocket object and using its bind() method. It obtains a CharsetEncoder object that it will use later to encode the characters of the daytime string into ASCII bytes.

Next, the server enters an infinite loop to service clients. This loop is made particularly simple by the fact that there is no need to read or parse client requests: the server sends a date and time string to every client that connects. The server first calls the channel's accept(), which blocks until a client initiates a connection to the server. The return value of accept() is a SocketChannel connected to the client. Next, the server gets the current time, converts it to a string using the local time zone, wraps the string in a CharBuffer, and encodes that CharBuffer to create a ByteBuffer. Finally, it sends the contents of that buffer to the client, using the SocketChannel returned by accept(), and then closes the connection. The loop then repeats and the server blocks in a call to accept() again.

Example 6-10. SimpleDaytimeServer.java

```
package je3.nio;
import java.nio.*;
import java.nio.channels.*;
import java.nio.charset.*;
import java.net.*;
```

Example 6-10. SimpleDaytimeServer.java (continued)

```java
/**
 * A simple TCP server for the daytime service.  See RFC867 for details.
 * This implementation lacks meaningful exception handling and cannot
 * handle UDP connections.
 **/
public class SimpleDaytimeServer {
    public static void main(String args[ ]) throws java.io.IOException {
        // RFC867 specifies port 13 for this service.  On Unix platforms,
        // you need to be running as root to use that port, so we allow
        // this service to use other ports for testing.
        int port = 13;
        if (args.length > 0) port = Integer.parseInt(args[0]);

        // Create a channel to listen for connections on.
        ServerSocketChannel server = ServerSocketChannel.open( );

        // Bind the channel to a local port.  Note that we do this by obtaining
        // the underlying java.net.ServerSocket and binding that socket.
        server.socket( ).bind(new InetSocketAddress(port));

        // Get an encoder for converting strings to bytes
        CharsetEncoder encoder = Charset.forName("US-ASCII").newEncoder( );

        for(;;) {  // Loop forever, processing client connections
            // Wait for a client to connect
            SocketChannel client = server.accept( );

            // Build response string, wrap, and encode to bytes
            String date = new java.util.Date( ).toString( ) + "\r\n";
            ByteBuffer response = encoder.encode(CharBuffer.wrap(date));

            // Send the response to the client and disconnect.
            client.write(response);
            client.close( );
        }
    }
}
```

Listening for TCP and UDP Connections

Example 6-11 is an improved version of the SimpleDaytimeServer class. This DaytimeServer class adds the exception handling that was missing from the previous example, and uses the java.util.logging package (new in Java 1.4) to log errors. (We'll discuss logging in more detail when we consider Example 6-14.) Most importantly, it provides the daytime service using UDP datagrams as well as TCP connections. It uses the DatagramChannel class to receive and send datagrams, and also demonstrates how to multiplex the ServerSocketChannel and the DatagramChannel.

If we were using the java.io and java.net architecture instead of the java.nio architecture, the server would have to use two threads. One of these threads would block in an accept( ) method of the ServerSocketChannel while waiting for a TCP client to connect; the other thread would block in the receive( ) method of the DatagramChannel while waiting for a UDP client to send a datagram. Instead, our New I/O server places both channels in nonblocking mode and uses a single thread that blocks in the select( ) method of the Selector class. The Selector monitors both channels, and select( ) returns when there is activity of interest (i.e., a connection ready to accept or a datagram ready to receive) on either one.

Example 6-11. DaytimeServer.java

```java
package je3.nio;
import java.nio.*;
import java.nio.channels.*;
import java.nio.charset.*;
import java.net.*;
import java.util.logging.*;
import java.util.*;

/**
 * A more robust daytime service that handles TCP and UDP connections and
 * provides exception handling and error logging.
 **/
public class DaytimeServer {
    public static void main(String args[ ]) {
        try {      // Handle startup exceptions at the end of this block
            // Get an encoder for converting strings to bytes
            CharsetEncoder encoder = Charset.forName("US-ASCII").newEncoder( );

            // Allow an alternative port for testing with non-root accounts
            int port = 13;   // RFC867 specifies this port.
            if (args.length > 0) port = Integer.parseInt(args[0]);

            // The port we'll listen on
            SocketAddress localport = new InetSocketAddress(port);

            // Create and bind a TCP channel to listen for connections on.
            ServerSocketChannel tcpserver = ServerSocketChannel.open( );
            tcpserver.socket( ).bind(localport);

            // Also create and bind a DatagramChannel to listen on.
            DatagramChannel udpserver = DatagramChannel.open( );
            udpserver.socket( ).bind(localport);

            // Specify non-blocking mode for both channels, since our
            // Selector object will be doing the blocking for us.
            tcpserver.configureBlocking(false);
            udpserver.configureBlocking(false);

            // The Selector object is what allows us to block while waiting
            // for activity on either of the two channels.
            Selector selector = Selector.open( );

            // Register the channels with the selector, and specify what
            // conditions (a connection ready to accept, a datagram ready
```

Example 6-11. DaytimeServer.java (continued)

```
        // to read) we'd like the Selector to wake up for.
        // These methods return SelectionKey objects, which we don't
        // need to retain in this example.
        tcpserver.register(selector, SelectionKey.OP_ACCEPT);
        udpserver.register(selector, SelectionKey.OP_READ);

        // This is an empty byte buffer to receive empty datagrams with.
        // If a datagram overflows the receive buffer size, the extra bytes
        // are automatically discarded, so we don't have to worry about
        // buffer overflow attacks here.
        ByteBuffer receiveBuffer = ByteBuffer.allocate(0);

        // Now loop forever, processing client connections
        for(;;) {
            try { // Handle per-connection problems below
                // Wait for a client to connect
                selector.select();

                // If we get here, a client has probably connected, so
                // put our response into a ByteBuffer.
                String date = new java.util.Date().toString() + "\r\n";
                ByteBuffer response=encoder.encode(CharBuffer.wrap(date));

                // Get the SelectionKey objects for the channels that have
                // activity on them. These are the keys returned by the
                // register() methods above. They are returned in a
                // java.util.Set.
                Set keys = selector.selectedKeys();

                // Iterate through the Set of keys.
                for(Iterator i = keys.iterator(); i.hasNext(); ) {
                    // Get a key from the set, and remove it from the set
                    SelectionKey key = (SelectionKey)i.next();
                    i.remove();

                    // Get the channel associated with the key
                    Channel c = (Channel) key.channel();

                    // Now test the key and the channel to find out
                    // whether something happened on the TCP or UDP channel
                    if (key.isAcceptable() && c == tcpserver) {
                        // A client has attempted to connect via TCP.
                        // Accept the connection now.
                        SocketChannel client = tcpserver.accept();
                        // If we accepted the connection successfully,
                        // then send our response back to the client.
                        if (client != null) {
                            client.write(response);  // send response
                            client.close();          // close connection
                        }
                    }
                    else if (key.isReadable() && c == udpserver) {
```

Example 6-11. DaytimeServer.java (continued)

```
                        // A UDP datagram is waiting.  Receive it now,
                        // noting the address it was sent from.
                        SocketAddress clientAddress =
                            udpserver.receive(receiveBuffer);
                        // If we got the datagram successfully, send
                        // the date and time in a response packet.
                        if (clientAddress != null)
                            udpserver.send(response, clientAddress);
                    }
                }
            }
            catch(java.io.IOException e) {
                // This is a (hopefully transient) problem with a single
                // connection: we log the error, but continue running.
                // We use our classname for the logger so that a sysadmin
                // can configure logging for this server independently
                // of other programs.
                Logger l = Logger.getLogger(DaytimeServer.class.getName());
                l.log(Level.WARNING, "IOException in DaytimeServer", e);
            }
            catch(Throwable t) {
                // If anything else goes wrong (out of memory, for example),
                // then log the problem and exit.
                Logger l = Logger.getLogger(DaytimeServer.class.getName());
                l.log(Level.SEVERE, "FATAL error in DaytimeServer", t);
                System.exit(1);
            }
        }
    }
    catch(Exception e) {
        // This is a startup error: there is no need to log it;
        // just print a message and exit
        System.err.println(e);
        System.exit(1);
    }
  }
}
```

A Daytime Client

Example 6-12 is a simple UDP client for testing the UDP portion of DaytimeServer.
It uses java.net.DatagramSocket instead of java.nio.channels.DatagramChannel
because DatagramChannel does not honor calls to setSoTimeout( ) on its underlying
DatagramSocket. The program does simple datagram networking, and the code is
easy to figure out. The most interesting feature of this program is that it specifies a
timeout (so that it doesn't hang forever if the server is down) and retries the
connection three times before giving up (because UDP is an unreliable protocol
and a server's response could be lost in the network).

Example 6-12. DaytimeClient.java

```
package je3.nio;
import java.net.*;
```

Example 6-12. DaytimeClient.java (continued)

```java
/**
 * Connect to a daytime server using the UDP protocol.
 * We use java.net instead of java.nio because DatagramChannel doesn't honor
 * the setSoTimeout( ) method on the underlying DatagramSocket
 */
public class DaytimeClient {
    public static void main(String args[ ]) throws java.io.IOException {
        // Figure out the host and port we're going to talk to
        String host = args[0];
        int port = 13;
        if (args.length > 1) port = Integer.parseInt(args[1]);

        // Create a socket to use
        DatagramSocket socket = new DatagramSocket( );

        // Specify a 1-second timeout so that receive( ) does not block forever.
        socket.setSoTimeout(1000);

        // This buffer will hold the response.  On overflow, extra bytes are
        // discarded: there is no possibility of a buffer overflow attack here.
        byte[ ] buffer = new byte[512];
        DatagramPacket packet = new DatagramPacket(buffer, buffer.length,
                                        new InetSocketAddress(host,port));

        // Try three times before giving up
        for(int i = 0; i < 3; i++) {
            try {
                // Send an empty datagram to the specified host (and port)
                packet.setLength(0);  // make the packet empty
                socket.send(packet);  // send it out

                // Wait for a response (or time out after 1 second)
                packet.setLength(buffer.length); // make room for the response
                socket.receive(packet);          // wait for the response

                // Decode and print the response
                System.out.print(new String(buffer, 0, packet.getLength( ),
                                    "US-ASCII"));
                // We were successful, so break out of the retry loop
                break;
            }
            catch(SocketTimeoutException e) {
                // If the receive call timed out, print error and retry
                System.out.println("No response");
            }
        }

        // We're done with the channel now
        socket.close( );
    }
}
```

A Multiplexed Server

Example 6-13 is a simple server named PrintServiceWebInterface that responds to HTTP GET requests by sending an HTML document describing available printers. The server obtains information about printers using the javax.print package, which we'll see again in Chapter 13.

More important than the printer-information details is the structure of this example: it is a simple single-threaded server, multiplexed using a Selector object so that it can handle requests from multiple clients concurrently. The code is well-commented and should be easy to understand. The Selector monitors the ServerSocketChannel used to accept client connections and also monitors any SocketChannel objects that represent currently active clients. When a new connection is accepted, the new SocketChannel is registered with the Selector. When that channel becomes readable, the server reads the client's request (in this case it ignores the details of the request), sends a response, and then (in this case, since HTTP is a stateless protocol) closes SocketChannel and cancels its registration with the Selector so that it will no longer be monitored. This basic architecture is adaptable to a variety of server implementations.

One interesting feature of this class is that it uses the write( ) method of the GatheringByteChannel interface. This method takes an array of ByteBuffer objects and writes their contents sequentially, which allows us to separate the fixed content of the HTTP headers from the variable content of the HTML document. The ScatteringByteChannel interface has a multibuffer read( ) method that can be useful when reading data that is logically divided into segments of known length.

Example 6-13. PrintServiceWebInterface.java

```java
package je3.nio;
import java.io.*;
import java.net.*;
import java.nio.*;
import java.nio.channels.*;
import java.nio.charset.*;
import java.util.*;           // For Set and Iterator
import javax.print.*;
import javax.print.attribute.*;

/**
 * PrintServiceWebInterface:
 * A simple HTTP server that displays information about all accessible
 * printers on the network.
 */
public class PrintServiceWebInterface {
    public static void main(String[ ] args) throws IOException {
        // Get the character encoders and decoders we'll need
        Charset charset = Charset.forName("ISO-8859-1");
        CharsetEncoder encoder = charset.newEncoder( );

        // The HTTP headers we send back to the client are fixed
        String headers =
            "HTTP/1.1 200 OK\r\n" +
```

Example 6-13. PrintServiceWebInterface.java (continued)

```
            "Content-type: text/html\r\n" +
            "Connection: close\r\n" +
            "\r\n";

    // We'll use two buffers in our response.  One holds the fixed
    // headers, and the other holds the variable body of the response.
    ByteBuffer[ ] buffers = new ByteBuffer[2];
    buffers[0] = encoder.encode(CharBuffer.wrap(headers));
    ByteBuffer body = ByteBuffer.allocateDirect(16*1024);
    buffers[1] = body;

    // Find all available PrintService objects to describe
    PrintService[ ] services =
        PrintServiceLookup.lookupPrintServices(null,null);

    // All of the channels we use in this code will be in non-blocking
    // mode. So we create a Selector object that will block while
    // monitoring all of the channels and will stop blocking only when
    // one or more of the channels is ready for I/O of some sort.
    Selector selector = Selector.open( );

    // Create a new ServerSocketChannel, and bind it to port 8000.
    // Note that we have to do this using the underlying ServerSocket.
    ServerSocketChannel server = ServerSocketChannel.open( );
    server.socket( ).bind(new java.net.InetSocketAddress(8000));

    // Put the ServerSocketChannel into non-blocking mode
    server.configureBlocking(false);

    // Now register the channel with the Selector.  The SelectionKey
    // represents the registration of this channel with this Selector.
    SelectionKey serverkey = server.register(selector,
                                         SelectionKey.OP_ACCEPT);

    for(;;) {  // The main server loop.  The server runs forever.
        // This call blocks until there is activity on one of the
        // registered channels. This is the key method in non-blocking I/O.
        selector.select( );

        // Get a java.util.Set containing the SelectionKey objects for
        // all channels that are ready for I/O.
        Set keys = selector.selectedKeys( );

        // Use a java.util.Iterator to loop through the selected keys
        for(Iterator i = keys.iterator( ); i.hasNext( ); ) {
            // Get the next SelectionKey in the set, and then remove it
            // from the set.  It must be removed explicitly, or it will
            // be returned again by the next call to select( ).
            SelectionKey key = (SelectionKey) i.next( );
            i.remove( );
```

Example 6-13. PrintServiceWebInterface.java (continued)

```
                // Check whether this key is the SelectionKey we got when
                // we registered the ServerSocketChannel.
                if (key == serverkey) {
                    // Activity on the ServerSocketChannel means a client
                    // is trying to connect to the server.
                    if (key.isAcceptable()) {
                        // Accept the client connection, and obtain a
                        // SocketChannel to communicate with the client.
                        SocketChannel client = server.accept();

                        // Make sure we actually got a connection
                        if (client == null) continue;

                        // Put the client channel in non-blocking mode.
                        client.configureBlocking(false);

                        // Now register the client channel with the Selector,
                        // specifying that we'd like to know when there is
                        // data ready to read on the channel.
                        SelectionKey clientkey =
                            client.register(selector, SelectionKey.OP_READ);
                    }
                }
                else {
                    // If the key we got from the Set of keys is not the
                    // ServerSocketChannel key, then it must be a key
                    // representing one of the client connections.
                    // Get the channel from the key.
                    SocketChannel client = (SocketChannel) key.channel();

                    // If we got here, it should mean that there is data to
                    // be read from the channel, but we double-check here.
                    if (!key.isReadable()) continue;

                    // Now read bytes from the client.  We assume that
                    // we get all the client's bytes in one read operation
                    client.read(body);

                    // The data we read should be some kind of HTTP GET
                    // request. We don't bother checking it however since
                    // there is only one page of data we know how to return.
                    body.clear();

                    // Build an HTML document as our reponse.
                    // The body of the document contains PrintService details
                    StringBuffer response = new StringBuffer();
                    response.append(
                        "<html><head><title>Printer Status</title></head>" +
                        "<body><h1>Printer Status</h1>");
                    for(int s = 0; s < services.length; s++) {
                        PrintService service = services[s];
                        response.append("<h2>")
                            .append(service.getName()).append("</h2><table>");
```

Example 6-13. PrintServiceWebInterface.java (continued)

```
                    Attribute[ ] attrs = service.getAttributes( ).toArray( );
                    for(int a = 0; a < attrs.length; a++) {
                        Attribute attr = attrs[a];
                        response.append("<tr><td>").append(attr.getName( )).
                            append("</td><td>").append(attr).
                            append("</tr>");
                    }
                    response.append("</table>");
                }
                response.append("</body></html>\r\n");

                // Encode the response into the body ByteBuffer
                encoder.reset( );
                encoder.encode(CharBuffer.wrap(response), body, true);
                encoder.flush(body);

                body.flip( );    // Prepare the body buffer to be drained
                // While there are bytes left to write
                while(body.hasRemaining( )) {
                    // Write both header and body buffers
                    client.write(buffers);
                }
                buffers[0].flip( );  // Prepare header buffer for next write
                body.clear( );       // Prepare body buffer for next read

                // Once we've sent our response, we have no more interest
                // in the client channel or its SelectionKey
                client.close( );  // Close the channel.
                key.cancel( );    // Tell Selector to stop monitoring it.
            }
        }
    }
}
```

A Multiplexed Network Client

We end this chapter with Example 6-14, a complex class named
HttpDownloadManager. As its name implies, this class is a client-side utility that
manages any number of concurrent HTTP downloads on a background thread.
To download something, just call the download( ) method, passing a java.net.
URI and an optional Listener object to be notified when the download is
complete or has aborted with an error. download( ) does not block: it returns a
Download object immediately, and you can monitor the status of the download
by polling the methods of this object. The data that is downloaded is not saved
to a file, but is available from the getData( ) method of the Download object.

The Listener and Download interfaces are defined as inner classes of
HttpDownloadManager. The Status class is another inner class: it is a type-safe
enumeration of download states returned by Download.getStatus( ). Two other
inner classes used in this example are DownloadImpl, the package-private concrete

implementation of the Download interface, and Test, a simple test program that demonstrates the usage of the HttpDownloadManager.

HttpDownloadManager extends Thread, and the downloads are handled in this background thread. Multiple downloads can be handled concurrently (this is useful when the client has more bandwidth available than the servers which are being downloaded from) because the thread uses a Selector to multiplex the SocketChannel objects from which data is being read: the select( ) call wakes up whenever data is ready to be read from one of the pending downloads. Most of the interesting code is found in the run( ) method, which is the body of the background thread.

We've seen basic channel multiplexing code with Selector.select( ) in previous examples. This one demonstrates three new features. The first is the call to wakeup( ) in the download( ) method. A new channel cannot be registered with a Selector while that selector is blocked in a select( ) call in the background thread. So the download( ) method creates a DownloadImpl object containing all the information about the download, places this object in a synchronized list of pending downloads, and then calls wakeup( ) and returns the Download object to the caller. The wakeup( ) call in download( ) causes the background thread to stop blocking in select( ). In other examples, we've immediately checked the selectedKeys( ) of a Selector when its select( ) method returns. In this case, we first look at the pendingDownloads list and create and register a SocketChannel for any DownloadImpl objects found there.

The second new feature of interest in this example is that it performs asynchronous connection. Before an HTTP GET request can be sent to a web server, the client must connect to the server. Establishing a TCP connection over the Internet can sometimes take a second or two, and we don't want the background thread to block while this connection is set up. So when the thread detects a pending download, it creates a SocketChannel in an unconnected state. It then puts the channel into nonblocking mode and registers it with the Selector object, indicating that the Selector should monitor the channel for readiness to connect as well as readiness to read. Only after registering the channel does the thread call the connect( ) method and supply the address and port to connect to. Since the channel is nonblocking, connect( ) returns immediately. When the connection is ready, select( ) wakes up and the thread calls finishConnect( ) on the channel to complete the connection. (After completing the connection, the thread immediately sends the HTTP GET request across the channel. It assumes that the channel is writable and that the complete text of the request can be written quickly; if this assumption fails, the thread will end up busy-waiting while it repeatedly attempts to send the request to the server.)

The third new feature demonstrated by this example is that when it registers a SocketChannel with the Selector, it uses a three-argument version of the register( ) call to associate the DownloadImpl object with the SelectionKey for the channel. Then, when the key becomes connectable or readable, the background thread can retrieve the channel and the state object associated with the key.

Finally, this example also demonstrates the logging API of java.util.logging. We'll discuss logging in the subsection that follows the example code.

Example 6-14. HttpDownloadManager.java

```java
package je3.nio;
import java.io.*;
import java.nio.*;
import java.nio.channels.*;
import java.nio.charset.*;
import java.net.*;
import java.util.*;
import java.util.logging.*;

/**
 * This class manages asynchronous HTTP GET downloads and demonstrates
 * non-blocking I/O with SocketChannel and Selector and also demonstrates
 * logging with the java.util.logging package.  This example uses a number
 * of inner classes and interfaces.
 *
 * Call download() for each HTTP GET request you want to issue.  You may
 * optionally pass a Listener object that will be notified when the download
 * terminates or encounters an exception.  download() returns a Download object
 * which holds the downloaded bytes (including HTTP headers) and which allows
 * you to poll the Status of the download.  Call release() when there are
 * no more downloads.
 */
public class HttpDownloadManager extends Thread {
    // An enumerated type.  Values are returned by Download.getStatus()
    public static class Status {
        // We haven't connected to the server yet
        public static final Status UNCONNECTED = new Status("Unconnected");
        // We're connected to the server, sending request or receiving response
        public static final Status CONNECTED = new Status("Connected");
        // Response has been received.  Response may have been an HTTP error
        public static final Status DONE = new Status("Done");
        // Something went wrong: bad hostname, for example.
        public static final Status ERROR = new Status("Error");

        private final String name;
        private Status(String name) { this.name = name; }
        public String toString() { return name; }
    }

    // Everything you need to know about a pending download
    public interface Download {
        public String getHost();      // Hostname we're downloading from
        public int getPort();         // Defaults to port 80
        public String getPath();      // includes query string as well
        public Status getStatus();    // Status of the download
        public byte[] getData();      // Download data, including response headers
        public int getHttpStatus();   // Only call when status is DONE
    }

    // Implement this interface if you want to know when a download completes
    public interface Listener {
        public void done(Download download);
```

Example 6-14. HttpDownloadManager.java (continued)

```java
    public void error(Download download, Throwable throwable);
}

Selector selector;              // For multiplexing non-blocking I/O.
ByteBuffer buffer;              // A shared buffer for downloads
List pendingDownloads;          // Downloads that don't have a Channel yet
boolean released = false;       // Set when the release() method is called.
Logger log;                     // Logging output goes here

// The HTTP protocol uses this character encoding
static final Charset LATIN1 = Charset.forName("ISO-8859-1");

public HttpDownloadManager(Logger log) throws IOException {
    if (log == null) log = Logger.getLogger(this.getClass().getName());
    this.log = log;
    selector = Selector.open();                 // create Selector
    buffer = ByteBuffer.allocateDirect(64*1024); // allocate buffer
    pendingDownloads = Collections.synchronizedList(new ArrayList());
    this.start();                               // start thread
}

// Ask the HttpDownloadManager to begin a download.  Returns a Download
// object that can be used to poll the progress of the download.  The
// optional Listener object will be notified when the download completes
// or aborts.
public Download download(URI uri, Listener l)
        throws IOException
{
    if (released)
        throw new IllegalStateException("Can't download() after release()");

    // Get info from the URI
    String scheme = uri.getScheme();
    if (scheme == null || !scheme.equals("http"))
        throw new IllegalArgumentException("Must use 'http:' protocol");
    String hostname = uri.getHost();
    int port = uri.getPort();
    if (port == -1) port = 80; // Use default port if none specified
    String path = uri.getRawPath();
    if (path == null || path.length() == 0) path = "/";
    String query = uri.getRawQuery();
    if (query != null) path += "?" + query;

    // Create a Download object with the pieces of the URL
    Download download = new DownloadImpl(hostname, port, path, l);

    // Add it to the list of pending downloads. This is a synchronized list
    pendingDownloads.add(download);

    // And ask the thread to stop blocking in the select() call so that
    // it will notice and process this new pending Download object.
    selector.wakeup();
```

Example 6-14. HttpDownloadManager.java (continued)

```
    // Return the Download so that the caller can monitor it if desired.
    return download;
}

public void release( ) {
    released = true; // The thread will terminate when it notices the flag.
    try { selector.close( ); } // This will wake the thread up
    catch(IOException e) {
        log.log(Level.SEVERE, "Error closing selector", e);
    }
}

public void run( ) {
    log.info("HttpDownloadManager thread starting.");

    // The download thread runs until release( ) is called
    while(!released) {
        // The thread blocks here waiting for something to happen
        try { selector.select( ); }
        catch(IOException e) {
            // This should never happen.
            log.log(Level.SEVERE, "Error in select( )", e);
            return;
        }

        // If release( ) was called, the thread should exit.
        if (released) break;

        // If any new Download objects are pending, deal with them first
        if (!pendingDownloads.isEmpty( )) {
            // Although pendingDownloads is a synchronized list, we still
            // need to use a synchronized block to iterate through its
            // elements to prevent a concurrent call to download( ).
            synchronized(pendingDownloads) {
                Iterator iter = pendingDownloads.iterator( );
                while(iter.hasNext( )) {
                    // Get the pending download object from the list
                    DownloadImpl download = (DownloadImpl)iter.next( );
                    iter.remove( );  // And remove it.

                    // Now begin an asynchronous connection to the
                    // specified host and port.  We don't block while
                    // waiting to connect.
                    SelectionKey key = null;
                    SocketChannel channel = null;
                    try {
                        // Open an unconnected channel
                        channel = SocketChannel.open( );
                        // Put it in non-blocking mode
                        channel.configureBlocking(false);
```

Example 6-14. HttpDownloadManager.java (continued)

```
                        // Register it with the selector, specifying that
                        // we want to know when it is ready to connect
                        // and when it is ready to read.
                        key = channel.register(selector,
                                            SelectionKey.OP_READ |
                                            SelectionKey.OP_CONNECT,
                                            download);
                        // Create the web server address
                        SocketAddress address =
                            new InetSocketAddress(download.host,
                                                download.port);
                        // Ask the channel to start connecting
                        // Note that we don't send the HTTP request yet.
                        // We'll do that when the connection completes.
                        channel.connect(address);
                    }
                    catch(Exception e) {
                        handleError(download, channel, key, e);
                    }
                }
            }
        }

        // Now get the set of keys that are ready for connecting or reading
        Set keys = selector.selectedKeys();
        if (keys == null) continue; // bug workaround; should not be needed
        // Loop through the keys in the set
        for(Iterator i = keys.iterator(); i.hasNext(); ) {
            SelectionKey key = (SelectionKey)i.next();
            i.remove();  // Remove the key from the set before handling

            // Get the Download object we attached to the key
            DownloadImpl download = (DownloadImpl) key.attachment();
            // Get the channel associated with the key.
            SocketChannel channel = (SocketChannel)key.channel();

            try {
                if (key.isConnectable()) {
                    // If the channel is ready to connect, complete the
                    // connection and then send the HTTP GET request to it.
                    if (channel.finishConnect()) {
                        download.status = Status.CONNECTED;
                        // This is the HTTP request we send
                        String request =
                        "GET " + download.path + " HTTP/1.1\r\n" +
                        "Host: " + download.host + "\r\n" +
                        "Connection: close\r\n" +
                        "\r\n";
                        // Wrap in a CharBuffer and encode to a ByteBuffer
                        ByteBuffer requestBytes =
                            LATIN1.encode(CharBuffer.wrap(request));
```

Example 6-14. HttpDownloadManager.java (continued)

```
                                // Send the request to the server.  If the bytes
                                // aren't all written in one call, we busy loop!
                                while(requestBytes.hasRemaining())
                                    channel.write(requestBytes);

                                log.info("Sent HTTP request: " + download.host +
                                        ":" + download.port + ": " + request);
                            }
                        }
                        if (key.isReadable()) {
                            // If the key indicates that there is data to be read,
                            // then read it and store it in the Download object.
                            int numbytes = channel.read(buffer);

                            // If we read some bytes, store them, otherwise
                            // the download is complete and we need to note this
                            if (numbytes != -1) {
                                buffer.flip();  // Prepare to drain the buffer
                                download.addData(buffer); // Store the data
                                buffer.clear(); // Prepare for another read
                                log.info("Read " + numbytes + " bytes from " +
                                        download.host + ":" + download.port);
                            }
                            else {
                                // If there are no more bytes to read
                                key.cancel();      // We're done with the key
                                channel.close();  // And with the channel.
                                download.status = Status.DONE;
                                if (download.listener != null)  // notify listener
                                    download.listener.done(download);
                                log.info("Download complete from " +
                                        download.host + ":" + download.port);
                            }
                        }
                    }
                    catch (Exception e) {
                        handleError(download, channel, key, e);
                    }
                }
            }
        }
        log.info("HttpDownloadManager thread exiting.");
    }

    // Error-handling code used by the run() method:
    // set status, close channel, cancel key, log error, notify listener.
    void handleError(DownloadImpl download, SocketChannel channel,
                    SelectionKey key, Throwable throwable)
    {
        download.status = Status.ERROR;
        try {if (channel != null) channel.close();} catch(IOException e) { }
        if (key != null) key.cancel();
        log.log(Level.WARNING,
```

Example 6-14. HttpDownloadManager.java (continued)

```
            "Error connecting to or downloading from " + download.host +
            ":" + download.port,
            throwable);
        if (download.listener != null)
            download.listener.error(download, throwable);
    }

    // This is the Download implementation we use internally.
    static class DownloadImpl implements Download {
        final String host;      // Final fields are immutable for thread-safety
        final int port;
        final String path;
        final Listener listener;
        volatile Status status; // Volatile fields may be changed concurrently
        volatile byte[] data = new byte[0];

        DownloadImpl(String host, int port, String path, Listener listener) {
            this.host = host;
            this.port = port;
            this.path = path;
            this.listener = listener;
            this.status = Status.UNCONNECTED;  // Set initial status
        }

        // These are the basic getter methods
        public String getHost() { return host; }
        public int getPort() { return port; }
        public String getPath() { return path; }
        public Status getStatus() { return status; }
        public byte[] getData() { return data; }

        /**
         * Return the HTTP status code for the download.
         * Throws IllegalStateException if status is not Status.DONE
         */
        public int getHttpStatus() {
            if (status != Status.DONE) throw new IllegalStateException();
            // In HTTP 1.1, the return code is in ASCII bytes 10-12.
            return
                (data[9] - '0') * 100 +
                (data[10]- '0') * 10 +
                (data[11]- '0') * 1;
        }

        // Used internally when we read more data.
        // This should use a larger buffer to prevent frequent re-allocation.
        void addData(ByteBuffer buffer) {
            assert status == Status.CONNECTED;  // only called during download
            int oldlen = data.length;           // How many existing bytes
            int numbytes = buffer.remaining();  // How many new bytes
            int newlen = oldlen + numbytes;
            byte[] newdata = new byte[newlen];  // Create new array
```

Example 6-14. HttpDownloadManager.java (continued)

```
            System.arraycopy(data, 0, newdata, 0, oldlen); // Copy old bytes
            buffer.get(newdata, oldlen, numbytes);          // Copy new bytes
            data = newdata;                                 // Save new array
        }
    }

    // This class demonstrates a simple use of HttpDownloadManager.
    public static class Test {
        static int completedDownloads = 0;

        public static void main(String args[ ])
            throws IOException, URISyntaxException
        {
            // With a -v argument, our logger will display lots of messages
            final boolean verbose = args[0].equals("-v");
            int firstarg = 0;
            Logger logger = Logger.getLogger(Test.class.getName( ));

            if (verbose) {
                firstarg = 1;
                logger.setLevel(Level.INFO);
            }
            else                    // regular output
                logger.setLevel(Level.WARNING);

            // How many URLs are on the command line?
            final int numDownloads = args.length - firstarg;
            // Create the download manager
            final HttpDownloadManager dm = new HttpDownloadManager(logger);
            // Now loop through URLs and call download( ) for each one
            // passing a listener object to receive notifications
            for(int i = firstarg; i < args.length; i++) {
                URI uri = new URI(args[i]);
                dm.download(uri,
                    new Listener( ) {
                        public void done(Download d) {
                            System.err.println("DONE: " + d.getHost( ) +
                                              ": " + d.getHttpStatus( ));
                            // If all downloads are complete, we're done
                            // with the HttpDownloadManager thread.
                            if (++completedDownloads == numDownloads)
                                dm.release( );
                        }
                        public void error(Download d, Throwable t) {
                            System.err.println(d.getHost( ) + ": " + t);
                            if (++completedDownloads == numDownloads)
                                dm.release( );
                        }
                    });
            }
        }
    }
}
```

New I/O

Logging in HttpDownloadManager

HttpDownloadManager uses a Logger object to log informational and error messages. It demonstrates the info( ) and log( ) methods of Logger; see the Logger documentation for descriptions of many other logging methods. HttpDownloadManager can use a Logger passed to it, or it can obtain its own. There are examples of obtaining a Logger object in both the constructor method and the inner Test class. The Test class also implements a -v "verbose" switch to demonstrate how to set the logging threshold of a Logger. Informational logging messages will be discarded unless the -v option is specified.

The java.util.logging package allows flexible runtime configuration of how logging is done. In most installations, the default is to print logging messages to the console. See the file *jre/lib/logging.properties* for the default configuration on your installation. You can override this default configuration with your own properties file: define the property java.util.logging.config.file with the -D option when you start the Java VM. For example, to run the HttpDownloadManager test program using a logging configuration specified in a file named *log.props*, you'd use a command line like this one (it has been word wrapped to fit on the page; you'd type it on one line):

```
java -Djava.util.logging.config.file=log.props
je3.nio.HttpDownloadManager\$Test -v ...urls here...
```

Note that we use the -v switch so that the program actually generates log messages. Without this switch, you'd have to purposely specify bad URLs so that the program would log some errors. The following listing is a sample logging configuration file, which you'll find, along with the HttpDownloadManager source code, in a file named *log.props*:

```
#
# A logging properties file for the HttpDownloadManager example
# See also jre/lib/logging.properties in your Java installation.
# Use this file by specifying it as the value of a property named
# java.util.logging.config.file.  For example:
#
# java -Djava.util.logging.config.file je3.nio.Http...
#

# This property specifies the default logging level for log messages
# sent by our program.  Note, however, that if you run the
# HttpDownloadManager\$Test class, this property will be overridden by
# the presence or absence of the -v option.
je3.nio.HttpDownloadManager.level: INFO

# This property says where output should go.  The default configuration
# is for it to go to the console.  This property sends log messages to
# a FileHandler configured below instead
handlers=java.util.logging.FileHandler

# These properties configure the FileHandler
# See java.util.logging.FileHandler for other available properties
java.util.logging.FileHandler.pattern = %h/java%u.log
java.util.logging.FileHandler.formatter = java.util.logging.XMLFormatter
```

Exercises

Exercise 6-1. The `FileCopy3` program in Example 6-4 omits exception-handling and channel-closing code for simplicity. Make this program more robust by adding that code, using Example 6-2, or other examples, as a model.

Exercise 6-2. The `ChannelToWriter.copy()` method of Example 6-5 reads bytes from a `ReadableByteChannel`, decodes them using a `CharsetDecoder`, and writes the resulting characters to a `Writer`. Write a method that does the reverse: reads characters from a `Reader`, encodes them using a `CharsetEncoder`, and writes the resulting bytes to a `WritableByteChannel`. Use a low-level encoding loop based on the decoding loop of Example 6-5.

Exercise 6-3. The `BGrep` class of Example 6-3 is a block-oriented rather than line-oriented regular-expression matcher. Modify the program to search a line at a time, rather than searching an entire file at a time. The easiest way to do this is probably to abandon the `java.nio` package and use `java.io.BufferedReader` to read lines. An alternative is to use the `scan()` method of the `ChannelTokenizer` class (see Examples 6-8 and 2-8).

Exercise 6-4. The `HttpGet` program in Example 6-9 discards HTTP headers. Modify it with a `-h` command-line option, which, when present, causes it to print out the headers it receives.

Exercise 6-5. A shortcoming of the `HttpGet` program of Example 6-9 is that it does not understand and follow HTTP redirects. Some servers use these HTTP response codes to distribute load, and `HttpGet` is unable to download pages from such servers. Modify the program so that if the response code is in the 300–399 range, it parses the HTTP headers, looking for one that begins "Location:". If it finds such a header, it prints a message and attempts to fetch the URL that follows it. If you don't want to write a full-featured HTTP header parser, note that you can convert the headers to a string, and then simply use string methods to search for "\nLocation:" within that string.

Exercise 6-6. The `PrintServiceWebInterface` class of Example 6-13 uses the `GatheringByteChannel` interface to send response data from a `ByteBuffer` array. It divides its response up into a set of fixed headers and a variable body. In fact, however, the first part of the body is also fixed. Additionally, a more robust implementation would include a "Content-Length:" header that specifies the (variable) length, in bytes, of the body. Modify the program to address these two issues by using an array of four buffers instead of two. The first buffer would hold the fixed part of the headers. The second would hold the variable Content-Length header and the header-terminating blank line. The third buffer would hold the fixed part of the document body, and the fourth would hold the variable part of the body. This fourth buffer would be filled, and its length measured, before the second buffer was filled. If you added a "print headers" option to `HttpGet` in the previous exercise, you can use that modified version to test your Content-Length implementation here.

Exercise 6-7. The `PrintServiceWebInterface` class of Example 6-13 demonstrated a simple framework for a multiplexing server. Modify this framework to create a generic server framework, like that of Example 5-10. With the New I/O

API, you should need only a single thread to do this. You'll probably want to create a per-client state object and associate it with each SelectionKey you use.

Exercise 6-8. Study the HttpDownloadManager class of Example 6-14. Analyze it for weaknesses, and remedy them. For example:

- The DownloadImpl.addData( ) method inefficiently reallocates its array every time it is called.

- The Listener interface provides notification only when the download completes or aborts; it does not provide the information a web browser would need to monitor the progress of a download, such as notification of connection establishment and data read.

- It does not parse HTTP response headers, so, for example, it cannot follow redirects and cannot tell the caller how many bytes to expect based on the Content-Length headers.

7

Security and Cryptography

Security is one of the key features that has made Java as successful as it has been. The Java security architecture includes access control mechanisms that allow untrusted programs, such as applets, to be executed safely, without fear that they will cause malicious damage, steal company secrets, or otherwise wreak havoc. The access control mechanisms used by Java have changed substantially between Java 1.0 and 1.2; we'll discuss the Java 1.2 mechanisms in this chapter.

Access control is only one half of the Java security architecture, however. The other half is authentication. The java.security package and its subpackages allow you to create and verify cryptographic checksums and digital signatures, to prove whether a Java class file (or any other file) is authentic, that is, whether it truly comes from the source that it purports to be from. The authentication API has also changed as Java has evolved, and I cover the Java 1.2 API here.

The access control and authentication aspects of the Java security architecture are closely coupled. Access control is about granting privileges only to trusted code. But what code should you trust? If you know which people and organizations to trust (which is ultimately a social, not technological, problem), you can use authentication technologies such as digital signatures to allow you to trust the Java class files from those people and organizations.

Cryptography is closely related to, but not part of, the Java security architecture. Java uses cryptographic techniques such as digital signatures for authentication, but the Java security architecture does not perform any actual encryption or decryption. That is the job of the javax.crypto package and its subpackages. In Java 1.4, these packages are part of the core Java platform. Prior to Java 1.4, they are available as the Java Cryptography Extension™ (JCE).

This chapter contains examples that show how you can use the access control, authentication, and cryptographic APIs.

Running Untrusted Code

Recall the Server example of Chapter 5. That generic server class dynamically loaded and ran Service implementations. Suppose that you are a system administrator in charge of the Server program, and that you don't trust the programmers who are developing the Service implementations; you're afraid that they'll accidentally (or maliciously) include damaging code in their Service classes. Java makes it easy to run these untrusted classes with access-control mechanisms in place, to prevent them from doing anything they shouldn't.

Access control in Java is performed by the SecurityManager and AccessController classes. When a security manager has been registered, Java checks with it every time it is asked to perform any operation that might be restricted, such as reading or writing a file or establishing a network connection. In Java 1.2 and later, the SecurityManager class uses the AccessController class to perform these access-control checks, and the AccessController in turn refers to a Policy file that describes exactly which Permission objects are granted to what code.

As of Java 1.2, it is quite simple to run code under the watchful eye of a security manager. Simply run the Java interpreter using the -D option to set the java.security.manager property. For example, to run the Server class under a security manager, start it like this:

```
% java -Djava.security.manager je3.net.Server \
-control password 4000
```

When you do this, both the Server class and the control service class it loads are subject to the access-control checks of a security manager that uses the system's default security policy.

If you try running Server using the default security policy shipped by Sun, the server will fail when the first client attempts to connect to it, and you'll see the following message:

```
java.security.AccessControlException:
    access denied (java.net.SocketPermission 127.0.0.1:1170 accept,resolve)
```

This message tells you that the security manager has not allowed your Server class to accept a network connection from the client. The reason is that the default security policy is too restrictive for our server. Fortunately, there is an easy way to allow the server to accept connections. Create a file with the following contents (except replace the directory name with the name of the directory where you have your classes installed) and name it *Server.policy*:

```
// These lines grant permissions to any code loaded from the directory shown.
// Edit the directory to match the installation on your system.
// On Windows systems, change the forward slashes to double backslashes: "\\".
grant codeBase "file:/home/david/Books/JavaExamples2/Examples" {
    // Allow the server to listen for and accept network connections
    // from any host on any port > 1024
    permission java.net.SocketPermission "*:1024-", "listen,accept";
};
```

Once you've created the *Server.policy* file, run the server class again but add another -D option to specify that the interpreter should use this policy file:

```
% java -Djava.security.manager -Djava.security.policy=Server.policy \
je3.net.Server -control password 4000
```

When you use this command line, the Java interpreter takes the default security policy and augments it with the policy specified on the command line. Note that if you use = = instead of = in the command line, the interpreter ignores the default policy and uses only the policy you've specified. Our *Server.policy* file should work either way.

The moral of the story is that if you write a Java application and want people who don't trust you to run it, you should figure out exactly what kind of restricted actions it takes and develop a policy file for it. Then your users can study the policy file to see what permissions the application requires. If they're willing to grant those permissions to your code, they can run your program using the -D options shown earlier, secure in the knowledge that your code can't take any dangerous actions other than those explicitly allowed by your policy file.

To fully understand Java's access control mechanisms, you'll want to read about the java.security.Permission class and its many subclasses. You should also read about the java.security.Policy class. To be able to create policy files of your own, you'll want to read about the *policytool* program that ships with the Java SDK from Sun. See *Java in a Nutshell*. If you want to edit policy files by hand (which is often easiest), see the security documentation that comes with the SDK for details on the file format.

Loading Untrusted Code

Let's continue our Server example. Suppose now that you want to modify the server so that it can load Service classes over the network from an arbitrary URL. Suppose also that you want to give Service classes the ability to read and write files from a "scratch" directory on the local system. You can accomplish this by writing a simple class that uses URLClassLoader to load service classes and pass them to an instance of the Server class. To make it work, however, you also have to develop an appropriate security policy file.

Example 7-1 shows our SafeServer class. Like the original Server class, this one expects a list of Service classes and port numbers on the command line. But the first command-line argument it expects is the URL from which the service classes should be downloaded.

Example 7-1. SafeServer.java

```
package je3.security;
import je3.net.Server;
import java.io.*;
import java.net.*;
import java.security.*;
```

Example 7-1. SafeServer.java (continued)

```java
/**
 * This class is a program that uses the Server class defined in Chapter 5.
 * Server would load arbitrary "Service" classes to provide services.
 * This class is an alternative program to start up a Server in a similar
 * way.  The difference is that this one uses a SecurityManager and a
 * ClassLoader to prevent the Service classes from doing anything damaging
 * or malicious on the local system.  This allows us to safely run Service
 * classes that come from untrusted sources.
 **/
public class SafeServer {
    public static void main(String[] args) {
        try {
            // Install a Security manager if the user didn't already install
            // one with the -Djava.security.manager argument
            if (System.getSecurityManager() == null) {
                System.out.println("Establishing a security manager");
                System.setSecurityManager(new SecurityManager());
            }

            // Create a Server object
            Server server = new Server(null, 5);

            // Create the ClassLoader that we'll use to load Service classes.
            // The classes should be stored in the JAR file or the directory
            // specified as a URL by the first command-line argument
            URL serviceURL = new URL(args[0]);
            ClassLoader loader =
                new java.net.URLClassLoader(new URL[] {serviceURL});

            // Parse the argument list, which should contain Service name/port
            // pairs.  For each pair, load the named Service using the class
            // loader, then instantiate it with newInstance(), then tell the
            // server to start running it.
            int i = 1;
            while(i < args.length) {
                // Dynamically load the Service class using the class loader
                Class serviceClass = loader.loadClass(args[i++]);
                // Dynamically instantiate the class.
                Server.Service service =
                    (Server.Service)serviceClass.newInstance();
                int port = Integer.parseInt(args[i++]);  // Parse the port #
                server.addService(service, port);         // Run service
            }
        }
        catch (Exception e) { // Display a message if anything goes wrong
            System.err.println(e);
            System.err.println("Usage: java " + SafeServer.class.getName() +
                          " <url> <servicename> <port>\n" +
                          "\t[<servicename> <port> ... ]");
            System.exit(1);
        }
    }
}
```

A Policy for SafeServer

The SafeServer class creates and establishes a SecurityManager even if the user doesn't do this with the -Djava.security.manager argument. This means that the program is not able to run without a security policy that grants it the permissions it needs. Example 7-2 shows a policy file you can use to make it work.

There are a couple of things to note about the *SafeServer.policy* file. First, the policy file reads system properties named service.dir and service.tmp. These are not standard system properties; they are properties that you must specify to the Java interpreter when you run the SafeServer program. service.dir specifies the directory from which the service classes are to be loaded. Assume here that they are loaded via a local *file*: URL, not through an *http*: or other network URL. The service.tmp property specifies a directory in which the service classes are allowed to read and write temporary scratch files. *SafeServer.policy* demonstrates a syntax that replaces the name of a system property with the value of that property. In this way, the security policy file can be made somewhat independent of the installation location of the application.

Example 7-2. SafeServer.policy

```
// This file grants the SafeServer class the permissions it needs to load
// Service classes through a URLClassLoader, and grants the Service classes
// permission to read and write files in and beneath the directory specified
// by the service.tmp system property.  Note that you'll need to edit the
// URL that specifies the location of the SafeServer class, and that for
// Windows systems, you'll need to replace "/" with "\\"

// Grant permissions to the SafeServer class.
// Edit the directory for your system.
grant codeBase "file:/home/david/Books/JavaExamples2/Examples" {
    // Allow the server to listen for and accept network connections
    // from any host on any port > 1024
    permission java.net.SocketPermission "*:1024-", "listen,accept";

    // Allow the server to create a class loader to load service classes
    permission java.lang.RuntimePermission "createClassLoader";

    // Give the server permission to read the directory that contains the
    // service classes.  If we were using a network URL instead of a file URL,
    // we'd need to add a SocketPermission instead of a FilePermission
    permission java.io.FilePermission "${service.dir}/-", "read";

    // The server cannot grant permissions to the Service classes unless it
    // has those permissions itself. So we give the server these two Service
    // permissions.
    permission java.util.PropertyPermission "service.tmp", "read";
    permission java.io.FilePermission "${service.tmp}/-", "read,write";
};

// Grant permissions to classes loaded from the directory specified by the
// service.dir system property.  If we were using a network URL instead of a
// local file: URL, this line would have to be different.
```

Example 7-2. SafeServer.policy (continued)

```
grant codeBase "file:${service.dir}" {
    // Services can read the system property "service.tmp"
    permission java.util.PropertyPermission "service.tmp", "read";
    // And they can read and write files in the directory specified by
    // that system property
    permission java.io.FilePermission "${service.tmp}/-", "read,write";
};
```

Testing SafeServer

To demonstrate that SafeServer runs its services safely, you need a demonstration service. Example 7-3 shows one such service that attempts various restricted actions and reports its results. Note that since you're going to load this class with a custom class loader, rather than from the class path, I haven't bothered to give it a package statement.

Example 7-3. SecureService.java

```java
import je3.net.*;  // Note no package statement here.
import java.io.*;

/**
 * This is a demonstration service.  It attempts to do things that may
 * or may not be allowed by the security policy and reports the
 * results of its attempts to the client.
 **/
public class SecureService implements Server.Service {
    public void serve(InputStream i, OutputStream o) throws IOException {
        PrintWriter out = new PrintWriter(o);

        // Try to install our own security manager.  If we can do this,
        // we can defeat any access control.
        out.println("Trying to create and install a security manager...");
        try {
            System.setSecurityManager(new SecurityManager());
            out.println("Success!");
        }
        catch (Exception e) { out.println("Failed: " + e); }

        // Try to make the Server and the Java VM exit.
        // This is a denial of service attack, and it should not succeed!
        out.println();
        out.println("Trying to exit...");
        try { System.exit(-1); }
        catch (Exception e) { out.println("Failed: " + e); }

        // The default system policy allows this property to be read
        out.println();
        out.println("Attempting to find java version...");
        try { out.println(System.getProperty("java.version")); }
        catch (Exception e) { out.println("Failed: " + e); }
```

Example 7-3. SecureService.java (continued)

```
        // The default system policy does not allow this property to be read
        out.println();
        out.println("Attempting to find home directory...");
        try { out.println(System.getProperty("user.home")); }
        catch (Exception e) { out.println("Failed: " + e); }

        // Our custom policy explicitly allows this property to be read
        out.println();
        out.println("Attempting to read service.tmp property...");
        try {
            String tmpdir = System.getProperty("service.tmp");
            out.println(tmpdir);
            File dir = new File(tmpdir);
            File f = new File(dir, "testfile");

            // Check whether we've been given permission to write files to
            // the tmpdir directory
            out.println();
            out.println("Attempting to write a file in " + tmpdir + "...");
            try {
                new FileOutputStream(f);
                out.println("Opened file for writing: " + f);
            }
            catch (Exception e) { out.println("Failed: " + e); }

            // Check whether we've been given permission to read files from
            // the tmpdir directory
            out.println();
            out.println("Attempting to read from " + tmpdir + "...");
            try {
                FileReader in = new FileReader(f);
                out.println("Opened file for reading: " + f);
            }
            catch (Exception e) { out.println("Failed: " + e); }
        }
        catch (Exception e) { out.println("Failed: " + e); }

        // Close the Service sockets
        out.close();
        i.close();
    }
}
```

To test SafeServer with the SecureService class, you have to decide which directories you'll use for storing the service classes and for the scratch directory. In the material that follows, I've used */tmp/services* and */tmp/scratch* as the directory names.

First, compile SecureService using the -d option to tell *javac* where to put the resulting class file:

```
% javac -d /tmp/services SecureService.java
```

It is important that you make sure there isn't a copy of the *SecureService.class* file in the current directory or anywhere else that Java might find it in the local class path. If the URLClassLoader can find the class locally, it won't bother loading it through the URL you specify.

Now, to run the SafeServer class, specify the name of the SecureService class, the URL to load it from, the port to listen for connections on, and four different system properties with -D options:

```
% java -Djava.security.manager -Djava.security.policy=SafeServer.policy \
    -Dservice.dir=/tmp/services -Dservice.tmp=/tmp/scratch \
    je3.security.SafeServer file:/tmp/services/ \
    SecureService 4000
```

This is a complicated command line, but it produces the desired results. When you connect to port 4000, you get the following output from the service:

```
% java je3.net.GenericClient localhost 4000
Connected to localhost/127.0.0.1:4000
Trying to create and install a security manager...
Failed: java.security.AccessControlException: access denied
  (java.lang.RuntimePermission createSecurityManager)

Trying to exit...
Failed: java.security.AccessControlException: access denied
  (java.lang.RuntimePermission exitVM)

Attempting to find java version...
1.3.0

Attempting to find home directory...
Failed: java.security.AccessControlException: access denied
  (java.util.PropertyPermission user.home read)

Attempting to read service.tmp property...
/tmp/scratch

Attempting to write a file in /tmp/scratch...
Opened file for writing: /tmp/scratch/testfile

Attempting to read from /tmp/scratch...
Opened file for reading: /tmp/scratch/testfile
Connection closed by server.
```

Message Digests and Digital Signatures

The authentication portion of the Java Security API includes support for message digests (also known as cryptographic checksums), digital signatures, and simple key management tasks through a "keystore" abstraction. Example 7-4 shows a program named Manifest that demonstrates the use of message digests, digital signatures, and keystores. The Manifest program provides the following functionality:

- When you pass a list of filenames on the command line, the program reads each file, computes a message digest on the contents of the file, and then writes an entry in a manifest file (named *MANIFEST* by default) that specifies each of the filenames and its digest.

- If you use the optional -s flag to specify a signer and the -p flag to specify a password, the program signs the contents of the manifest file and includes a digital signature within the manifest.

- When you invoke the program with the -v option, it verifies an existing manifest file. First, it checks the digital signature, if any. If the signature is valid, it then reads each file named in the manifest and verifies that its digest matches the one specified in the manifest.

Using the Manifest program to create a signed manifest file and then later verify it accomplishes two goals. First, the message digests prove that the named files have not been maliciously or inadvertently modified or corrupted since the digests were computed. And second, the digital signature proves that the manifest file itself has not been modified since it was signed. (Attaching a digital signature to a file is like signing a legal document. By signing a manifest file, you are making the implicit assertion that the contents of the manifest are true and valid, and that you are willing to stake your trustworthiness on it.)

Digital signatures use public-key cryptography technology. A *private key* can create a digital signature, and the corresponding *public key* verifies the signature. The classes of the java.security package rely on a keystore in which they can look up these keys. This database stores keys for various entities, which may be people, corporations, or other computers or programs.

In order to make this example work, you need to generate a public and private key pair for yourself (or for some test entity) and add those keys to the keystore. The Java SDK includes a program named *keytool* you can use to generate keys and perform other operations on a keystore. Use *keytool* as follows to generate a key pair for yourself. Note that the program prompts you for the information, including passwords, that it needs. See *Java in a Nutshell* for documentation on *keytool*.

```
% keytool -genkey -alias david
Enter keystore password:  secret
What is your first and last name?
  [Unknown]:  David Flanagan
What is the name of your organizational unit?
  [Unknown]:
What is the name of your organization?
  [Unknown]:  davidflanagan.com
What is the name of your City or Locality?
  [Unknown]:  Bellingham
What is the name of your State or Province?
  [Unknown]:  WA
What is the two-letter country code for this unit?
  [Unknown]:  US
Is <CN=David Flanagan, OU=Unknown, O=davidflanagan.com, L=Bellingham, ST=WA,
C=US> correct?
  [no]:  yes

Enter key password for <david>
        (RETURN if same as keystore password):  moresecret
```

Example 7-4 uses the MessageDigest and DigestInputStream classes to compute and verify message digests. It uses the Signature class with a PrivateKey to compute digital signatures and uses Signature with a PublicKey to verify digital signatures. The PrivateKey and PublicKey objects are obtained from the KeyStore object. The manifest file itself is created and read by a java.util.Properties object, which is ideal for this purpose. Message digests and digital signatures are stored in the manifest file using a simple hexadecimal encoding implemented by convenience methods that appear at the end of the example. (This is one shortcoming of the java.security package: it doesn't provide an easy way to convert an array of bytes to a portable textual representation.)

Example 7-4. Manifest.java

```java
package je3.security;
import java.security.*;
import java.io.*;
import java.util.*;

/**
 * This program creates a manifest file for the specified files, or verifies
 * an existing manifest file.  By default the manifest file is named
 * MANIFEST, but the -m option can be used to override this.  The -v
 * option specifies that the manifest should be verified.  Verification is
 * also the default option if no files are specified.
 **/
public class Manifest {
    public static void main(String[ ] args) throws Exception {
        // Set the default values of the command-line arguments
        boolean verify = false;                  // Verify manifest or create one?
        String manifestfile = "MANIFEST";        // Manifest file name
        String digestAlgorithm = "MD5";          // Algorithm for message digests
        String signername = null;                // Signer. No sig. by default
        String signatureAlgorithm = "DSA";       // Algorithm for digital sig.
        String password = null;                  // Private keys are protected
        File keystoreFile = null;                // Where are keys stored
        String keystoreType = null;              // What kind of keystore
        String keystorePassword = null;          // How to access keystore
        List filelist = new ArrayList( );        // The files to digest

        // Parse the command-line arguments, overriding the defaults above
        for(int i = 0; i < args.length; i++) {
            if (args[i].equals("-v")) verify = true;
            else if (args[i].equals("-m")) manifestfile = args[++i];
            else if (args[i].equals("-da")&& !verify)
                digestAlgorithm = args[++i];
            else if (args[i].equals("-s")&& !verify)
                signername = args[++i];
            else if (args[i].equals("-sa")&& !verify)
                signatureAlgorithm = args[++i];
            else if (args[i].equals("-p"))
                password = args[++i];
            else if (args[i].equals("-keystore"))
                keystoreFile = new File(args[++i]);
```

Example 7-4. Manifest.java (continued)

```
            else if (args[i].equals("-keystoreType"))
                keystoreType = args[++i];
            else if (args[i].equals("-keystorePassword"))
                keystorePassword = args[++i];

            else if (!verify) filelist.add(args[i]);
            else throw new IllegalArgumentException(args[i]);
        }

        // If certain arguments weren't supplied, get default values.
        if (keystoreFile == null) {
            File dir = new File(System.getProperty("user.home"));
            keystoreFile = new File(dir, ".keystore");
        }
        if (keystoreType == null) keystoreType = KeyStore.getDefaultType( );
        if (keystorePassword == null) keystorePassword = password;

        if (!verify && signername != null && password == null) {
            System.out.println("Use -p to specify a password.");
            return;
        }

        // Get the keystore we'll use for signing or verifying signatures
        // If no password was provided, then assume we won't be dealing with
        // signatures, and skip the keystore.
        KeyStore keystore = null;
        if (keystorePassword != null) {
            keystore = KeyStore.getInstance(keystoreType);
            InputStream in =
                new BufferedInputStream(new FileInputStream(keystoreFile));
            keystore.load(in, keystorePassword.toCharArray( ));
        }

        // If -v was specified or no file were given, verify a manifest
        // Otherwise, create a new manifest for the specified files
        if (verify || (filelist.size( ) == 0)) verify(manifestfile, keystore);
        else create(manifestfile, digestAlgorithm,
                    signername, signatureAlgorithm,
                    keystore, password, filelist);
    }

    /**
     * This method creates a manifest file with the specified name, for
     * the specified vector of files, using the named message digest
     * algorithm.  If signername is non-null, it adds a digital signature
     * to the manifest, using the named signature algorithm.  This method can
     * throw a bunch of exceptions.
     **/
    public static void create(String manifestfile, String digestAlgorithm,
                              String signername, String signatureAlgorithm,
                              KeyStore keystore, String password,
                              List filelist)
```

Example 7-4. Manifest.java (continued)

```java
        throws NoSuchAlgorithmException, InvalidKeyException,
            SignatureException, KeyStoreException,
            UnrecoverableKeyException, IOException
{
    // For computing a signature, we have to process the files in a fixed,
    // repeatable order, so sort them alphabetically.
    Collections.sort(filelist);
    int numfiles = filelist.size();

    Properties manifest = new Properties( ), metadata = new Properties( );
    MessageDigest md = MessageDigest.getInstance(digestAlgorithm);
    Signature signature = null;
    byte[ ] digest;

    // If a signer name was specified, then prepare to sign the manifest
    if (signername != null) {
        // Get a Signature object
        signature = Signature.getInstance(signatureAlgorithm);

        // Look up the private key of the signer from the keystore
        PrivateKey key = (PrivateKey)
            keystore.getKey(signername, password.toCharArray( ));

        // Now prepare to create a signature for the specified signer
        signature.initSign(key);
    }

    // Now, loop through the files, in a well-known alphabetical order
    System.out.print("Computing message digests");
    for(int i = 0; i < numfiles; i++) {
        String filename = (String)filelist.get(i);
        // Compute the digest for each, and skip files that don't exist.
        try { digest = getFileDigest(filename, md); }
        catch (IOException e) {
            System.err.println("\nSkipping " + filename + ": " + e);
            continue;
        }
        // If we're computing a signature, use the bytes of the filename
        // and of the digest as part of the data to sign.
        if (signature != null) {
            signature.update(filename.getBytes( ));
            signature.update(digest);
        }
        // Store the filename and the encoded digest bytes in the manifest
        manifest.put(filename, hexEncode(digest));
        System.out.print('.');
        System.out.flush( );
    }

    // If a signer was specified, compute signature for the manifest
    byte[ ] signaturebytes = null;
    if (signature != null) {
        System.out.print("done\nComputing digital signature...");
```

Example 7-4. Manifest.java (continued)

```
        System.out.flush();

        // Compute the digital signature by encrypting a message digest of
        // all the bytes passed to the update() method using the private
        // key of the signer.  This is a time-consuming operation.
        signaturebytes = signature.sign();
    }

    // Tell the user what comes next
    System.out.print("done\nWriting manifest...");
    System.out.flush();

    // Store some metadata about this manifest, including the name of the
    // message digest algorithm it uses
    metadata.put("__META.DIGESTALGORITHM", digestAlgorithm);
    // If we're signing the manifest, store some more metadata
    if (signername != null) {
        // Store the name of the signer
        metadata.put("__META.SIGNER", signername);
        // Store the name of the algorithm
        metadata.put("__META.SIGNATUREALGORITHM", signatureAlgorithm);
        // And generate the signature, encode it, and store it
        metadata.put("__META.SIGNATURE", hexEncode(signaturebytes));
    }

    // Now, save the manifest data and the metadata to the manifest file
    FileOutputStream f = new FileOutputStream(manifestfile);
    manifest.store(f, "Manifest message digests");
    metadata.store(f, "Manifest metadata");
    System.out.println("done");
}

/**
 * This method verifies the digital signature of the named manifest
 * file, if it has one, and if that verification succeeds, it verifies
 * the message digest of each file in filelist that is also named in the
 * manifest.  This method can throw a bunch of exceptions
 **/
public static void verify(String manifestfile, KeyStore keystore)
    throws NoSuchAlgorithmException, SignatureException,
           InvalidKeyException, KeyStoreException, IOException
{
    Properties manifest = new Properties();
    manifest.load(new FileInputStream(manifestfile));
    String digestAlgorithm =
        manifest.getProperty("__META.DIGESTALGORITHM");
    String signername = manifest.getProperty("__META.SIGNER");
    String signatureAlgorithm =
        manifest.getProperty("__META.SIGNATUREALGORITHM");
    String hexsignature = manifest.getProperty("__META.SIGNATURE");

    // Get a list of filenames in the manifest.
    List files = new ArrayList();
```

Example 7-4. Manifest.java (continued)

```java
Enumeration names = manifest.propertyNames( );
while(names.hasMoreElements( )) {
    String s = (String)names.nextElement( );
    if (!s.startsWith("__META")) files.add(s);
}
int numfiles = files.size( );

// If we've got a signature but no keystore, warn the user
if (signername != null && keystore == null)
    System.out.println("Can't verify digital signature without " +
                       "a keystore.");

// If the manifest contained metadata about a digital signature, then
// verify that signature first
if (signername != null && keystore != null) {
    System.out.print("Verifying digital signature...");
    System.out.flush( );

    // To verify the signature, we must process the files in exactly
    // the same order we did when we created the signature.  We
    // guarantee this order by sorting the filenames.
    Collections.sort(files);

    // Create a Signature object to do signature verification with.
    // Initialize it with the signer's public key from the keystore
    Signature signature = Signature.getInstance(signatureAlgorithm);
    PublicKey publickey =
        keystore.getCertificate(signername).getPublicKey( );
    signature.initVerify(publickey);

    // Now loop through these files in their known sorted order. For
    // each one, send the bytes of the filename and of the digest to
    // the signature object for use in computing the signature.  It is
    // important that this be done in exactly the same order when
    // verifying the signature as it was done when creating the
    // signature.
    for(int i = 0; i < numfiles; i++) {
        String filename = (String) files.get(i);
        signature.update(filename.getBytes( ));
        signature.update(hexDecode(manifest.getProperty(filename)));
    }

    // Now decode the signature read from the manifest file and pass
    // it to the verify( ) method of the signature object.  If the
    // signature is not verified, print an error message and exit.
    if (!signature.verify(hexDecode(hexsignature))) {
        System.out.println("\nManifest has an invalid signature");
        System.exit(0);
    }

    // Tell the user we're done with this lengthy computation
    System.out.println("verified.");
}
```

Example 7-4. Manifest.java (continued)

```java
        // Tell the user we're starting the next phase of verification
        System.out.print("Verifying file message digests");
        System.out.flush( );

        // Get a MessageDigest object to compute digests
        MessageDigest md = MessageDigest.getInstance(digestAlgorithm);
        // Loop through all files
        for(int i = 0; i < numfiles; i++) {
            String filename = (String)files.get(i);
            // Look up the encoded digest from the manifest file
            String hexdigest = manifest.getProperty(filename);
            // Compute the digest for the file.
            byte[ ] digest;
            try { digest = getFileDigest(filename, md); }
            catch (IOException e) {
                System.out.println("\nSkipping " + filename + ": " + e);
                continue;
            }

            // Encode the computed digest and compare it to the encoded digest
            // from the manifest.  If they are not equal, print an error
            // message.
            if (!hexdigest.equals(hexEncode(digest)))
                System.out.println("\nFile '" + filename +
                                   "' failed verification.");

            // Send one dot of output for each file we process.  Since
            // computing message digests takes some time, this lets the user
            // know that the program is functioning and making progress
            System.out.print(".");
            System.out.flush( );
        }
        // And tell the user we're done with verification.
        System.out.println("done.");
    }

    /**
     * This convenience method is used by both create( ) and verify( ).  It
     * reads the contents of a named file and computes a message digest
     * for it, using the specified MessageDigest object.
     **/
    public static byte[ ] getFileDigest(String filename, MessageDigest md)
        throws IOException {
        // Make sure there is nothing left behind in the MessageDigest
        md.reset( );

        // Create a stream to read from the file and compute the digest
        DigestInputStream in =
            new DigestInputStream(new FileInputStream(filename),md);

        // Read to the end of the file, discarding everything we read.
        // The DigestInputStream automatically passes all the bytes read to
```

Example 7-4. Manifest.java (continued)

```java
        // the update( ) method of the MessageDigest
        while(in.read(buffer) != -1) /* do nothing */ ;

        // Finally, compute and return the digest value.
        return md.digest( );
    }

    /** This static buffer is used by getFileDigest( ) above */
    public static byte[ ] buffer = new byte[4096];

    /** This array is used to convert from bytes to hexadecimal numbers */
    static final char[ ] digits = { '0', '1', '2', '3', '4', '5', '6', '7',
                                     '8', '9', 'a', 'b', 'c', 'd', 'e', 'f'};

    /**
     * A convenience method to convert an array of bytes to a String.  We do
     * this simply by converting each byte to two hexadecimal digits.
     * Something like Base 64 encoding is more compact, but harder to encode.
     **/
    public static String hexEncode(byte[ ] bytes) {
        StringBuffer s = new StringBuffer(bytes.length * 2);
        for(int i = 0; i < bytes.length; i++) {
            byte b = bytes[i];
            s.append(digits[(b& 0xf0) >> 4]);
            s.append(digits[b& 0x0f]);
        }
        return s.toString( );
    }

    /**
     * A convenience method to convert in the other direction, from a string
     * of hexadecimal digits to an array of bytes.
     **/
    public static byte[ ] hexDecode(String s) throws IllegalArgumentException {
        try {
            int len = s.length( );
            byte[ ] r = new byte[len/2];
            for(int i = 0; i < r.length; i++) {
                int digit1 = s.charAt(i*2), digit2 = s.charAt(i*2 + 1);
                if ((digit1 >= '0')&& (digit1 <= '9')) digit1 -= '0';
                else if ((digit1 >= 'a')&& (digit1 <= 'f')) digit1 -= 'a' - 10;
                if ((digit2 >= '0')&& (digit2 <= '9')) digit2 -= '0';
                else if ((digit2 >= 'a')&& (digit2 <= 'f')) digit2 -= 'a' - 10;
                r[i] = (byte)((digit1 << 4) + digit2);
            }
            return r;
        }
        catch (Exception e) {
            throw new IllegalArgumentException("hexDecode( ): invalid input");
        }
    }
}
```

Cryptography

Although the message digest and digital signature techniques shown in the previous section use cryptographic techniques, note that they do not actually perform any encryption or decryption. Prior to Java 1.4, strict U.S. export regulations for encryption technology prevented Sun from releasing the Java platform with built-in encryption, and programmers instead had to download and install the separate Java Cryptography Extension (JCE). U.S. regulations have since been relaxed and Java 1.4 now includes the JCE classes in the javax.crypto package and its subpackages.

Example 7-5 is a program that allows you to encrypt and decrypt files using the TripleDES encryption algorithm and to generate TripleDES keys that are stored in files. It uses the JCE classes in javax.crypto and its subpackages. The key classes are Cipher, which represents an encryption or decryption algorithm, and SecretKey, which represents the encryption and decryption key used by the algorithm. You can find an API quick-reference for the JCE classes in *Java in a Nutshell*. You can also learn more about cryptography and the JCE from *Java Cryptography* by Jonathan Knudsen (O'Reilly).

Example 7-5. TripleDES.java

```java
package je3.security;
import javax.crypto.*;
import javax.crypto.spec.*;
import java.security.*;
import java.security.spec.*;
import java.io.*;

/**
 * This class defines methods for encrypting and decrypting using the Triple
 * DES algorithm and for generating, reading, and writing Triple DES keys.
 * It also defines a main( ) method that allows these methods to be used
 * from the command line.
 **/
public class TripleDES {
    /**
     * The program.  The first argument must be -e, -d, or -g to encrypt,
     * decrypt, or generate a key.  The second argument is the name of a file
     * from which the key is read or to which it is written for -g.  The
     * -e and -d arguments cause the program to read from standard input and
     * encrypt or decrypt to standard output.
     **/
    public static void main(String[ ] args) {
        try {
            // Check to see whether there is a provider that can do TripleDES
            // encryption.  If not, explicitly install the SunJCE provider.
            try { Cipher c = Cipher.getInstance("DESede"); }
            catch(Exception e) {
                // An exception here probably means the JCE provider hasn't
                // been permanently installed on this system by listing it
                // in the $JAVA_HOME/jre/lib/security/java.security file.
```

Example 7-5. TripleDES.java (continued)

```java
                // Therefore, we have to install the JCE provider explicitly.
                System.err.println("Installing SunJCE provider.");
                Provider sunjce = new com.sun.crypto.provider.SunJCE();
                Security.addProvider(sunjce);
            }

            // This is where we'll read the key from or write it to
            File keyfile = new File(args[1]);

            // Now check the first arg to see what we're going to do
            if (args[0].equals("-g")) {         // Generate a key
                System.out.print("Generating key. This may take some time...");
                System.out.flush();
                SecretKey key = generateKey();
                writeKey(key, keyfile);
                System.out.println("done.");
                System.out.println("Secret key written to " + args[1] +
                                ". Protect that file carefully!");
            }
            else if (args[0].equals("-e")) {  // Encrypt stdin to stdout
                SecretKey key = readKey(keyfile);
                encrypt(key, System.in, System.out);
            }
            else if (args[0].equals("-d")) {  // Decrypt stdin to stdout
                SecretKey key = readKey(keyfile);
                decrypt(key, System.in, System.out);
            }
        }
        catch(Exception e) {
            System.err.println(e);
            System.err.println("Usage: java " + TripleDES.class.getName() +
                            " -d|-e|-g <keyfile>");
        }
    }

    /** Generate a secret TripleDES encryption/decryption key */
    public static SecretKey generateKey() throws NoSuchAlgorithmException {
        // Get a key generator for Triple DES (a.k.a DESede)
        KeyGenerator keygen = KeyGenerator.getInstance("DESede");
        // Use it to generate a key
        return keygen.generateKey();
    }

    /** Save the specified TripleDES SecretKey to the specified file */
    public static void writeKey(SecretKey key, File f)
        throws IOException, NoSuchAlgorithmException, InvalidKeySpecException
    {
        // Convert the secret key to an array of bytes like this
        SecretKeyFactory keyfactory = SecretKeyFactory.getInstance("DESede");
        DESedeKeySpec keyspec =
            (DESedeKeySpec)keyfactory.getKeySpec(key, DESedeKeySpec.class);
        byte[] rawkey = keyspec.getKey();
```

Example 7-5. TripleDES.java (continued)

```java
    // Write the raw key to the file
    FileOutputStream out = new FileOutputStream(f);
    out.write(rawkey);
    out.close();
}

/** Read a TripleDES secret key from the specified file */
public static SecretKey readKey(File f)
    throws IOException, NoSuchAlgorithmException,
           InvalidKeyException, InvalidKeySpecException
{
    // Read the raw bytes from the keyfile
    DataInputStream in = new DataInputStream(new FileInputStream(f));
    byte[] rawkey = new byte[(int)f.length()];
    in.readFully(rawkey);
    in.close();

    // Convert the raw bytes to a secret key like this
    DESedeKeySpec keyspec = new DESedeKeySpec(rawkey);
    SecretKeyFactory keyfactory = SecretKeyFactory.getInstance("DESede");
    SecretKey key = keyfactory.generateSecret(keyspec);
    return key;
}

/**
 * Use the specified TripleDES key to encrypt bytes from the input stream
 * and write them to the output stream.  This method uses
 * CipherOutputStream to perform the encryption and write bytes at the
 * same time.
 **/
public static void encrypt(SecretKey key, InputStream in, OutputStream out)
    throws NoSuchAlgorithmException, InvalidKeyException,
           NoSuchPaddingException, IOException
{
    // Create and initialize the encryption engine
    Cipher cipher = Cipher.getInstance("DESede");
    cipher.init(Cipher.ENCRYPT_MODE, key);

    // Create a special output stream to do the work for us
    CipherOutputStream cos = new CipherOutputStream(out, cipher);

    // Read from the input and write to the encrypting output stream
    byte[] buffer = new byte[2048];
    int bytesRead;
    while((bytesRead = in.read(buffer)) != -1) {
        cos.write(buffer, 0, bytesRead);
    }
    cos.close();

    // For extra security, don't leave any plaintext hanging around memory.
    java.util.Arrays.fill(buffer, (byte) 0);
}
```

Example 7-5. TripleDES.java (continued)

```java
/**
 * Use the specified TripleDES key to decrypt bytes ready from the input
 * stream and write them to the output stream.  This method
 * uses Cipher directly to show how it can be done without
 * CipherInputStream and CipherOutputStream.
 **/
public static void decrypt(SecretKey key, InputStream in, OutputStream out)
    throws NoSuchAlgorithmException, InvalidKeyException, IOException,
            IllegalBlockSizeException, NoSuchPaddingException,
            BadPaddingException
{
    // Create and initialize the decryption engine
    Cipher cipher = Cipher.getInstance("DESede");
    cipher.init(Cipher.DECRYPT_MODE, key);

    // Read bytes, decrypt, and write them out.
    byte[ ] buffer = new byte[2048];
    int bytesRead;
    while((bytesRead = in.read(buffer)) != -1) {
        out.write(cipher.update(buffer, 0, bytesRead));
    }

    // Write out the final bunch of decrypted bytes
    out.write(cipher.doFinal( ));
    out.flush( );
}
}
```

Exercises

Exercise 7-1. Write a PasswordManager class that associates usernames with passwords and has methods for creating and deleting username/password pairs, changing the password associated with a username, and authenticating a user by verifying a supplied password. PasswordManager should store the usernames and passwords in a file (or in a database if you've already read Chapter 18).

Note, however, that the class should not store the passwords as plain text, as that would allow an intruder who broke into the PasswordManager system to obtain full access to all passwords. To prevent this, it is common to use a one-way function to encrypt passwords. Message digests, such as those used in Example 7-4, provide exactly this kind of a one-way function. Computing a message digest for a password is relatively easy, but going in the opposite direction (from digest to password) is very difficult or impossible.

Design the PasswordManager class so that instead of storing the actual password, it stores only a message digest of the password. To verify a user's password, your class should compute a digest for the supplied password and compare it to the stored digest. If the digests match, you can assume that the passwords also match. (There is actually an infinitesimally small chance that two different passwords will produce the same message digest, but you can disregard this possibility.)

Exercise 7-2. Write a network service and client that allow a user to change her current password that is registered with your `PasswordManager` class. If you've read Chapter 21, modify `PasswordManager` so that it runs as a RMI remote object, and write a client program that uses the remote object to change a password. If you have not read that chapter yet, write the password-changing service to run under the `Server` class developed in Chapter 5, and use the `GenericClient` class from that same chapter to interact with the service. In either case, create a security policy file that defines the set of permissions required by your network service, and use this policy file to enable your service to run with the `-Djava.security.manager` option to the Java interpreter.

Exercise 7-3. The `TripleDES` class of Example 7-5 uses the "DESede" algorithm in the default ECB (electronic code book) mode. This encryption mode is more vulnerable to certain decryption attacks than CBC (cipher block chaining) mode. Modify the example so that it uses CBC mode. You specify the mode as part of the algorithm name: in this case, instead of specifying DESede as the algorithm, specify "DESede/CBC/PKCS5Padding".

To encrypt using CBC mode, the `Cipher` object creates an initialization vector (IV) of random bytes, which is also required when decrypting. Modify the `encrypt( )` method so that it obtains the IV with the `getIV( )` method of the `Cipher` object and writes the bytes (and the length) of the IV array to the output stream before it writes out the encrypted bytes. To do this, you may want to modify `encrypt( )` so that it doesn't use the `CipherOutputStream` but instead works with the `Cipher` class directly, the way `decrypt( )` does. Modify the `decrypt( )` method so that it reads the bytes of the IV and uses them to create a `javax.crypto.spec.IvParameterSpec` object, which it then passes (as an `AlgorithmParameterSpec`) to one of the `init( )` methods of the `Cipher` object.

Exercise 7-4. The `TripleDES` program stores and reads secret keys from unprotected files, which is not a very secure way to work with important keys. Modify the program so that it uses a `KeyStore` object to store (and retrieve) the key in password-protected form. The `KeyStore` class was demonstrated in Example 7-4, where it was used to store `PublicKey` and `PrivateKey` objects for digital signatures. A `KeyStore` can also store `SecretKey` objects, however. Simply pass the `SecretKey` to the `setKeyEntry( )` method, specifying a name for the key and a password to protect it with. Since the key is not a `PrivateKey`, you should pass null for the `Certificate[ ]` argument to this method.

8

Internationalization

Internationalization is the process of making a program flexible enough to run correctly in any locale. The required corollary to internationalization is localization—the process of arranging for a program to run in a specific locale.

There are several distinct steps to the task of internationalization. Java (1.1 and later) addresses these steps with several different mechanisms:

- A program must be able to read, write, and manipulate localized text. Java uses the Unicode character encoding, which by itself is a huge step toward internationalization. In addition, the InputStreamReader and OutputStreamWriter classes convert text from a locale-specific encoding to Unicode and from Unicode to a locale-specific encoding, respectively.

- A program must conform to local customs when displaying dates and times, formatting numbers, and sorting strings. Java addresses these issues with the classes in the java.text package.

- A program must display all user-visible text in the local language. Translating the messages a program displays is always one of the main tasks in localizing a program. A more important task is writing the program so that all user-visible text is fetched at runtime, rather than hardcoded directly into the program. Java facilitates this process with the ResourceBundle class and its subclasses in the java.util package.

This chapter discusses all three aspects of internationalization.

A Word About Locales

A *locale* represents a geographic, political, or cultural region. In Java, locales are represented by the java.util.Locale class. A locale is frequently defined by a language, which is represented by its standard lowercase two-letter code, such as en (English) or fr (French). Sometimes, however, language alone is not sufficient to uniquely specify a locale, and a country is added to the specification. A country is represented by an uppercase two-letter code. For example, the United States English locale (en_US) is distinct from the British English locale (en_GB), and the French spoken in Canada (fr_CA) is different from the French spoken in France (fr_FR). Occasionally, the scope of a locale is further narrowed with the addition of a system-dependent variant string.

The Locale class maintains a static default locale, which can be set and queried with Locale.setDefault( ) and Locale.getDefault( ). Locale-sensitive methods in Java typically come in two forms. One uses the default locale, and the other uses a Locale object that is explicitly specified as an argument. A program can create and use any number of nondefault Locale objects, although it is more common simply to rely on the default locale, which is inherited from the underlying default locale on the native platform. Locale-sensitive classes in Java often provide a method to query the list of locales that they support.

Finally, note that AWT and Swing GUI components (see Chapter 11) have a locale property, so it is possible for different components to use different locales. (Most components, however, are not locale-sensitive; they behave the same in any locale.)

Unicode

Java uses the Unicode character encoding. (Java 1.3 uses Unicode Version 2.1. Support for Unicode 3.0 will be included in Java 1.4 or another future release.) Unicode is a 16-bit character encoding established by the Unicode Consortium, which describes the standard as follows (see *http://unicode.org*):

> The Unicode Standard defines codes for characters used in the major languages written today. Scripts include the European alphabetic scripts, Middle Eastern right-to-left scripts, and scripts of Asia. The Unicode Standard also includes punctuation marks, diacritics, mathematical symbols, technical symbols, arrows, dingbats, etc. ... In all, the Unicode Standard provides codes for 49,194 characters from the world's alphabets, ideograph sets, and symbol collections.

In the canonical form of Unicode encoding, which is what Java char and String types use, every character occupies two bytes. The Unicode characters \u0020 to \u007E are equivalent to the ASCII and ISO8859-1 (Latin-1) characters 0x20 through 0x7E. The Unicode characters \u00A0 to \u00FF are identical to the ISO8859-1 characters 0xA0 to 0xFF. Thus, there is a trivial mapping between Latin-1 and Unicode characters. A number of other portions of the Unicode encoding are based on preexisting standards, such as ISO8859-5 (Cyrillic) and ISO8859-8 (Hebrew), though the mappings between these standards and Unicode may not be as trivial as the Latin-1 mapping.

Note that Unicode support may be limited on many platforms. One of the difficulties with the use of Unicode is the poor availability of fonts to display all the Unicode characters. Figure 8-1 shows some of the characters that are available in the standard fonts that ship with Sun's Java 1.3 SDK for Linux. (Note that these fonts do not ship with the Java JRE, so even if they are available on your development platform, they may not be available on your target platform.) Note the special box glyph that indicates undefined characters.

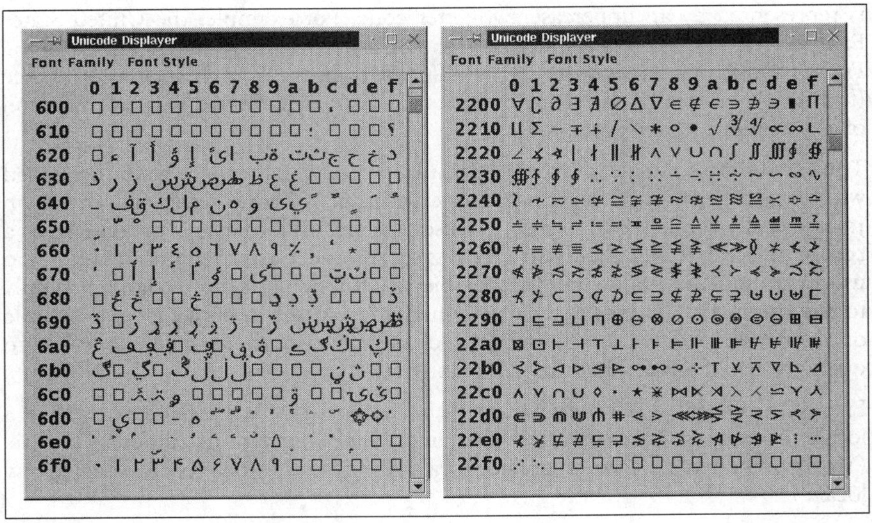

Figure 8-1. Some Unicode characters and their encodings

Example 8-1 lists code used to create the displays of Figure 8-1. Because Unicode characters are integrated so fundamentally into the Java language, this UnicodeDisplay program does not perform any sophisticated internationalization techniques to display Unicode glyphs. Thus, you'll find that Example 8-1 is more of a Swing GUI example rather than an internationalization example. If you haven't read Chapter 11 yet, you may not understand all the code in this example.

Example 8-1. UnicodeDisplay.java

```java
package je3.i18n;
import javax.swing.*;
import java.awt.*;
import java.awt.event.*;

/**
 * This program displays Unicode glyphs using user-specified fonts
 * and font styles.
 **/
public class UnicodeDisplay extends JFrame implements ActionListener {
    int page = 0;
    UnicodePanel p;
    JScrollBar b;
    String fontfamily = "Serif";
    int fontstyle = Font.PLAIN;

    /**
     * This constructor creates the frame, menubar, and scrollbar
     * that work along with the UnicodePanel class, defined below
     **/
    public UnicodeDisplay(String name) {
        super(name);
```

Example 8-1. UnicodeDisplay.java (continued)

```
        p = new UnicodePanel();                 // Create the panel
        p.setBase((char)(page * 0x100));        // Initialize it
        getContentPane().add(p, "Center");      // Center it

        // Create and set up a scrollbar, and put it on the right
        b = new JScrollBar(Scrollbar.VERTICAL, 0, 1, 0, 0xFF);
        b.setUnitIncrement(1);
        b.setBlockIncrement(0x10);
        b.addAdjustmentListener(new AdjustmentListener() {
                public void adjustmentValueChanged(AdjustmentEvent e) {
                    page = e.getValue();
                    p.setBase((char)(page * 0x100));
                }
            });
        getContentPane().add(b, "East");

        // Set things up so we respond to window close requests
        this.addWindowListener(new WindowAdapter() {
                public void windowClosing(WindowEvent e) { System.exit(0); }
            });

        // Handle Page Up and Page Down and the up and down arrow keys
        this.addKeyListener(new KeyAdapter() {
                public void keyPressed(KeyEvent e) {
                    int code = e.getKeyCode();
                    int oldpage = page;
                    if ((code == KeyEvent.VK_PAGE_UP) ||
                        (code == KeyEvent.VK_UP)) {
                        if (e.isShiftDown()) page -= 0x10;
                        else page -= 1;
                        if (page < 0) page = 0;
                    }
                    else if ((code == KeyEvent.VK_PAGE_DOWN) ||
                             (code == KeyEvent.VK_DOWN)) {
                        if (e.isShiftDown()) page += 0x10;
                        else page += 1;
                        if (page > 0xff) page = 0xff;
                    }
                    if (page != oldpage) {       // if anything has changed...
                        p.setBase((char) (page * 0x100)); // update the display
                        b.setValue(page);        // and update scrollbar to match
                    }
                }
            });

        // Set up a menu system to change fonts.  Use a convenience method.
        JMenuBar menubar = new JMenuBar();
        this.setJMenuBar(menubar);
        menubar.add(makemenu("Font Family",
                        new String[] {"Serif", "SansSerif", "Monospaced"},
                        this));
```

Example 8-1. UnicodeDisplay.java (continued)

```java
        menubar.add(makemenu("Font Style",
                             new String[ ]{
                                 "Plain","Italic","Bold","BoldItalic"
                             }, this));
    }

    /** This method handles the items in the menubars */
    public void actionPerformed(ActionEvent e) {
        String cmd = e.getActionCommand();
        if (cmd.equals("Serif")) fontfamily = "Serif";
        else if (cmd.equals("SansSerif")) fontfamily = "SansSerif";
        else if (cmd.equals("Monospaced")) fontfamily = "Monospaced";
        else if (cmd.equals("Plain")) fontstyle = Font.PLAIN;
        else if (cmd.equals("Italic")) fontstyle = Font.ITALIC;
        else if (cmd.equals("Bold")) fontstyle = Font.BOLD;
        else if (cmd.equals("BoldItalic")) fontstyle = Font.BOLD + Font.ITALIC;
        p.setFont(fontfamily, fontstyle);
    }

    /** A convenience method to create a Menu from an array of items */
    private JMenu makemenu(String name, String[ ] itemnames,
                           ActionListener listener)
    {
        JMenu m = new JMenu(name);
        for(int i = 0; i < itemnames.length; i++) {
            JMenuItem item = new JMenuItem(itemnames[i]);
            item.addActionListener(listener);
            item.setActionCommand(itemnames[i]);  // okay here, though
            m.add(item);
        }
        return m;
    }

    /** The main( ) program just creates a window, packs it, and shows it */
    public static void main(String[ ] args) {
        UnicodeDisplay f = new UnicodeDisplay("Unicode Displayer");
        f.pack();
        f.show();
    }

    /**
     * This nested class is the one that displays one "page" of Unicode
     * glyphs at a time.  Each "page" is 256 characters, arranged into 16
     * rows of 16 columns each.
     **/
    public static class UnicodePanel extends JComponent {
        protected char base;  // What character we start the display at
        protected Font font = new Font("serif", Font.PLAIN, 18);
        protected Font headingfont = new Font("monospaced", Font.BOLD, 18);
        static final int lineheight = 25;
        static final int charspacing = 20;
```

Example 8-1. UnicodeDisplay.java (continued)

```java
    static final int x0 = 65;
    static final int y0 = 40;

    /** Specify where to begin displaying, and redisplay */
    public void setBase(char base) { this.base = base; repaint(); }

    /** Set a new font name or style, and redisplay */
    public void setFont(String family, int style) {
        this.font = new Font(family, style, 18);
        repaint();
    }

    /**
     * The paintComponent() method actually draws the page of glyphs
     **/
    public void paintComponent(Graphics g) {
        int start = (int)base & 0xFFF0; // Start on a 16-character boundary

        // Draw the headings in a special font
        g.setFont(headingfont);

        // Draw 0..F on top
        for(int i=0; i < 16; i++) {
            String s = Integer.toString(i, 16);
            g.drawString(s, x0 + i*charspacing, y0-20);
        }

        // Draw column down left.
        for(int i = 0; i < 16; i++) {
            int j = start + i*16;
            String s = Integer.toString(j, 16);
            g.drawString(s, 10, y0+i*lineheight);
        }

        // Now draw the characters
        g.setFont(font);
        char[] c = new char[1];
        for(int i = 0; i < 16; i++) {
            for(int j = 0; j < 16; j++) {
                c[0] = (char)(start + j*16 + i);
                g.drawChars(c, 0, 1, x0 + i*charspacing, y0+j*lineheight);
            }
        }
    }

    /** Custom components like this one should always have this method */
    public Dimension getPreferredSize() {
        return new Dimension(x0 + 16*charspacing,
                             y0 + 16*lineheight);
    }
  }
}
```

Character Encodings

Text representation has traditionally been one of the most difficult problems of internationalization. Java, however, solves this problem quite elegantly and hides the difficult issues. Java uses Unicode internally, so it can represent essentially any character in any commonly used written language. As I noted earlier, the remaining task is to convert Unicode to and from locale-specific encodings. Java includes quite a few internal byte-to-char and char-to-byte converters that handle converting locale-specific character encodings to Unicode and vice versa. Although the converters themselves are not public, they are accessible through the InputStreamReader and OutputStreamWriter classes, which are character streams included in the java.io package.

Any program can automatically handle locale-specific encodings simply by using these character stream classes to do their textual input and output. Note that the FileReader and FileWriter classes use these streams to automatically read and write text files that use the platform's default encoding.

Example 8-2 shows a simple program that works with character encodings. It converts a file from one specified encoding to another by converting from the first encoding to Unicode and then from Unicode to the second encoding. Note that most of the program is taken up with the mechanics of parsing argument lists, handling exceptions, and so on. Only a few lines are required to create the InputStreamReader and OutputStreamWriter classes that perform the two halves of the conversion. Also note that exceptions are handled by calling LocalizedError. display( ). This method is not part of the Java API; it is a custom method shown in Example 8-5 at the end of this chapter.

Example 8-2. ConvertEncoding.java

```
package je3.i18n;
import java.io.*;

/** A program to convert from one character encoding to another */
public class ConvertEncoding {
    public static void main(String[] args) {
        String from = null, to = null;
        String infile = null, outfile = null;
        for(int i = 0; i < args.length; i++) { // Parse command-line arguments.
            if (i == args.length-1) usage( );    // All args require another.
            if (args[i].equals("-from")) from = args[++i];
            else if (args[i].equals("-to")) to = args[++i];
            else if (args[i].equals("-in")) infile = args[++i];
            else if (args[i].equals("-out")) outfile = args[++i];
            else usage( );
        }

        try { convert(infile, outfile, from, to); }  // Attempt conversion.
        catch (Exception e) {                        // Handle exceptions.
            LocalizedError.display(e);  // Defined at the end of this chapter.
            System.exit(1);
```

Example 8-2. ConvertEncoding.java (continued)

```
      }
  }

  public static void usage() {
      System.err.println("Usage: java ConvertEncoding <options>\n" +
                         "Options:\n\t-from <encoding>\n\t" +
                         "-to <encoding>\n\t" +
                         "-in <file>\n\t-out <file>");
      System.exit(1);
  }

  public static void convert(String infile, String outfile,
                             String from, String to)
          throws IOException, UnsupportedEncodingException
  {
      // Set up byte streams.
      InputStream in;
      if (infile != null) in = new FileInputStream(infile);
      else in = System.in;
      OutputStream out;
      if (outfile != null) out = new FileOutputStream(outfile);
      else out = System.out;

      // Use default encoding if no encoding is specified.
      if (from == null) from = System.getProperty("file.encoding");
      if (to == null) to = System.getProperty("file.encoding");

      // Set up character streams.
      Reader r = new BufferedReader(new InputStreamReader(in, from));
      Writer w = new BufferedWriter(new OutputStreamWriter(out, to));

      // Copy characters from input to output.  The InputStreamReader
      // converts from the input encoding to Unicode, and the
      // OutputStreamWriter converts from Unicode to the output encoding.
      // Characters that cannot be represented in the output encoding are
      // output as '?'
      char[] buffer = new char[4096];
      int len;
      while((len = r.read(buffer)) != -1)  // Read a block of input.
          w.write(buffer, 0, len);         // And write it out.
      r.close();                           // Close the input.
      w.close();                           // Flush and close output.
  }
}
```

Handling Local Customs

The second problem of internationalization is the task of following local customs and conventions in areas such as date and time formatting. The java.text package defines classes to help with this duty.

The NumberFormat class formats numbers, monetary amounts, and percentages in a locale-dependent way for display to the user. This is necessary because different locales have different conventions for number formatting. For example, in France, a comma is used as a decimal separator instead of a period, as in many English-speaking countries. A NumberFormat object can use the default locale or any locale you specify. NumberFormat has factory methods for obtaining instances that are suitable for different purposes, such as displaying monetary quantities or percentages. In Java 1.4 and later, the java.util.Currency class can be used with NumberFormat object so that it can correctly print an appropriate currency symbol.

The DateFormat class formats dates and times in a locale-dependent way for display to the user. Different countries have different conventions. Should the month or day be displayed first? Should periods or colons separate fields of the time? What are the names of the months in the language of the locale? A DateFormat object can simply use the default locale, or it can use any locale you specify. The DateFormat class is used in conjunction with the TimeZone and Calendar classes of java.util. The TimeZone object tells the DateFormat what time zone the date should be interpreted in, while the Calendar object specifies how the date itself should be broken down into days, weeks, months, and years. Almost all locales use the standard GregorianCalendar. SimpleDateFormat is a useful subclass of DateFormat: it allows dates to be formatted to or parsed from a date format specified with a simple template string.

The Collator class compares strings in a locale-dependent way. This is necessary because different languages alphabetize strings in different ways (and some languages don't even use alphabets). In traditional Spanish, for example, the letters "ch" are treated as a single character that comes between "c" and "d" for the purposes of sorting. When you need to sort strings or search for a string within Unicode text, you should use a Collator object, either one created to work with the default locale or one created for a specified locale.

The BreakIterator class allows you to locate character, word, line, and sentence boundaries in a locale-dependent way. This is useful when you need to recognize such boundaries in Unicode text, such as when you are implementing a word-wrapping algorithm.

Example 8-3 shows a class that uses the NumberFormat and DateFormat classes to display a hypothetical stock portfolio to the user following local conventions. The program uses various NumberFormat and DateFormat objects to format (using the format( ) method) different types of numbers and dates. These Format objects all operate using the default locale but could have been created with an explicitly specified locale. The program displays information about a hypothetical stock portfolio, formatting dates and numbers and monetary values according to the current or the specified locale. Figure 8-2 shows example output in different locales. The output was produced by running the program in the default locale, with the arguments "en GB" and "ja JP".

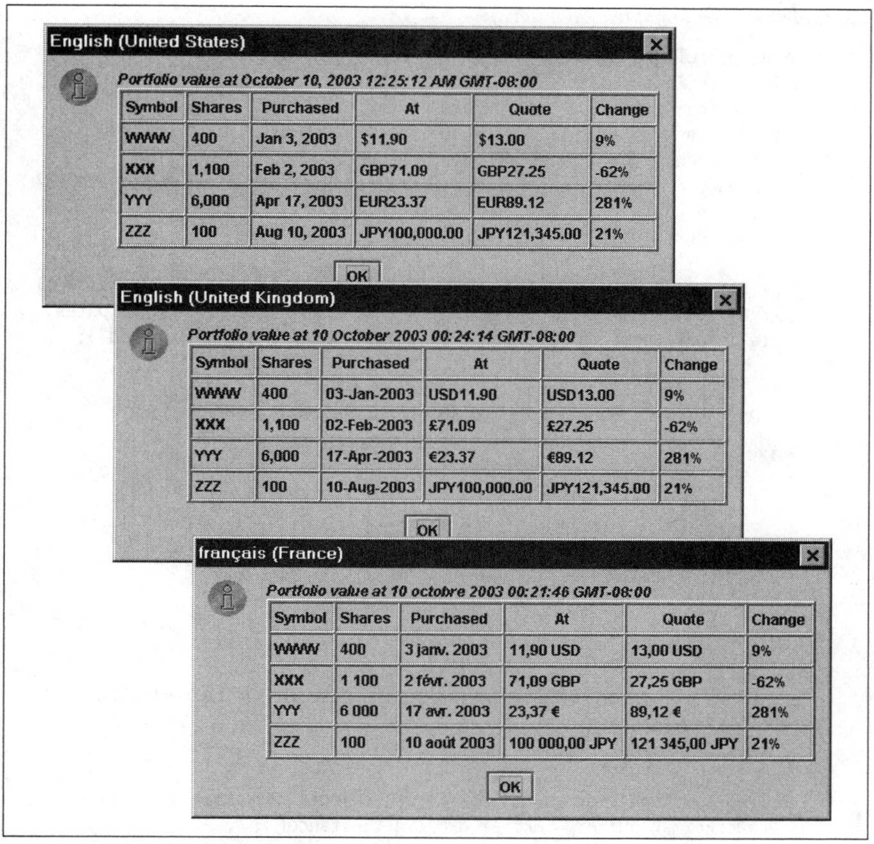

Figure 8-2. Stock portfolios formatted for U.S., British, and French locales

Example 8-3. Portfolio.java

```java
package je3.i18n;
import java.text.*;
import java.util.*;
import java.io.*;

/**
 * A partial implementation of a hypothetical stock portfolio class.
 * We use it only to demonstrate number and date internationalization.
 **/
public class Portfolio {
    EquityPosition[ ] positions;      // The positions in the portfolio
    Date lastQuoteTime = new Date( ); // Time for current quotes

    // Create a Portfolio
    public Portfolio(EquityPosition[ ] positions, Date lastQuoteTime) {
        this.positions = positions;
        this.lastQuoteTime = lastQuoteTime;
    }
```

Example 8-3. Portfolio.java (continued)

```
// A helper class: represents a single stock purchase
static class EquityPosition {
    String name;           // Name of the stock.
    int shares;            // Number of shares held.
    Date purchased;        // When purchased.
    Currency currency;     // What currency are the prices expressed in?
    double bought;         // Purchase price per share
    double current;        // Current price per share

    // Format objects like this one are useful for parsing strings as well
    // as formatting them.  This is for converting date strings to Dates.
    static DateFormat dateParser = new SimpleDateFormat("yyyy-MM-dd");

    EquityPosition(String n, int s, String date, Currency c,
                   double then, double now) throws ParseException
    {
        // Convert the purchased date string to a Date object.
        // The string must be in the format yyyy-mm-dd
        purchased = dateParser.parse(date);
        // And store the rest of the fields, too.
        name = n; shares = s; currency = c;
        bought = then; current = now;
    }
}

// Return a localized HTML-formatted string describing the portfolio
public String toString() {
    StringBuffer b = new StringBuffer();

    // Obtain NumberFormat and DateFormat objects to format our data.
    NumberFormat number = NumberFormat.getInstance();
    NumberFormat price = NumberFormat.getCurrencyInstance();
    NumberFormat percent = NumberFormat.getPercentInstance();
    DateFormat shortdate = DateFormat.getDateInstance(DateFormat.MEDIUM);
    DateFormat fulldate = DateFormat.getDateTimeInstance(DateFormat.LONG,
                                                         DateFormat.LONG);


    // Print some introductory data.
    b.append("<html><body>");
    b.append("<i>Portfolio value at ").
        append(fulldate.format(lastQuoteTime)).append("</i>");
    b.append("<table border=1>");
    b.append("<tr><th>Symbol<th>Shares<th>Purchased<th>At<th>" +
            "Quote<th>Change</tr>");

    // Display the table using the format() methods of the Format objects.
    for(int i = 0; i < positions.length; i++) {
        b.append("<tr><td>");
        b.append(positions[i].name).append("<td>");
        b.append(number.format(positions[i].shares)).append("<td>");
        b.append(shortdate.format(positions[i].purchased)).append("<td>");
```

Example 8-3. Portfolio.java (continued)

```java
            // Set the currency to use when printing the following prices
            price.setCurrency(positions[i].currency);
            b.append(price.format(positions[i].bought)).append("<td>");
            b.append(price.format(positions[i].current)).append("<td>");
            double change =
                (positions[i].current-positions[i].bought)/positions[i].bought;
            b.append(percent.format(change)).append("</tr>");
        }
        b.append("</table></body></html>");
        return b.toString( );
    }


    /**
     * This is a test program that demonstrates the class
     **/
    public static void main(String[ ] args) throws ParseException {
        Currency dollars = Currency.getInstance("USD");
        Currency pounds = Currency.getInstance("GBP");
        Currency euros = Currency.getInstance("EUR");
        Currency yen = Currency.getInstance("JPY");

        // This is the portfolio to display.
        EquityPosition[ ] positions = new EquityPosition[ ] {
            new EquityPosition("WWW", 400, "2003-01-03", dollars, 11.90,13.00),
            new EquityPosition("XXX", 1100, "2003-02-02", pounds, 71.09,27.25),
            new EquityPosition("YYY", 6000, "2003-04-17", euros, 23.37,89.12),
            new EquityPosition("ZZZ", 100, "2003-8-10", yen, 100000,121345)
        };

        // Create the portfolio from these positions
        Portfolio portfolio = new Portfolio(positions, new Date( ));

        // Set the default locale using the language code and country code
        // specified on the command line.
        if (args.length == 2) Locale.setDefault(new Locale(args[0], args[1]));

        // Now display the portfolio.
        // We use a Swing dialog box to display it because the console may
        // not be able to display non-ASCII characters like currency symbols
        // for Pounds, Euros, and Yen.
        javax.swing.JOptionPane.showMessageDialog(null, portfolio,
                            Locale.getDefault( ).getDisplayName( ),
                            javax.swing.JOptionPane.INFORMATION_MESSAGE);

        // The modal dialog starts another thread running, so we have to exit
        // explictly when the user dismisses it.
        System.exit(0);
    }
}
```

Internation-
alization

Setting the Locale

Example 8-3 contains code that explicitly sets the locale using the language code and the country code specified on the command line. If these arguments are not specified, it uses the default locale for your system. When experimenting with internationalization, you may want to change the default locale for the entire platform so you can see what happens. How you do this is platform-dependent. On Unix platforms, you typically set the locale by setting the LANG environment variable. For example, to set the locale for Canadian French, using a Unix *csh*-style shell, use this command:

```
% setenv LANG fr_CA
```

Or, to set the locale to English as spoken in Great Britain when using a Unix *sh*-style shell, use this command:

```
$ export LANG=en_GB
```

To set the locale in Windows, use the Regional Settings control on the Windows Control Panel.

Localizing User-Visible Messages

The third task of internationalization involves ensuring that there are no user-visible strings that are hardcoded in an application; instead, strings should be looked up based on the locale. In Example 8-3, for example, the strings "Portfolio value", "Symbol", "Shares", and others are hardcoded in the application and appear in English, even when the program is run in the French locale. The only way to prevent this is to fetch all user-visible messages at runtime and to translate every message into each language your application must support.

Java helps you handle this task with the ResourceBundle class of the java.util package. This class represents a bundle of resources that can be looked up by name. You define a localized resource bundle for each locale you want to support, and Java loads the correct bundle for the default (or specified) locale. With the correct bundle loaded, you can look up the resources (typically strings) your program needs at runtime.

Working with Resource Bundles

To define a bundle of localized resources, you create a subclass of ResourceBundle and provide definitions for the handleGetObject( ) and getKeys( ) methods. handleGetObject( ) is passed the name of a resource; it should return an appropriate localized version of that resource. getKeys( ) should return an Enumeration object that gives the user a list of all resource names defined in the ResourceBundle. Instead of subclassing ResourceBundle directly, however, it is often easier to subclass ListResourceBundle. You can also simply provide a property file (see the java.util.Properties class) that ResourceBundle.getBundle( ) uses to create an instance of PropertyResourceBundle.

To use localized resources from a ResourceBundle in a program, you should first call the static getBundle() method, which dynamically loads and instantiates a ResourceBundle, as described shortly. The returned ResourceBundle has the name you specify and is appropriate for the specified locale (or for the default locale if no locale is explicitly specified). Once you have obtained a ResourceBundle object with getBundle(), use the getObject() method to look up resources by name. Note that there is a convenience method, getString(), that simply casts the value returned by getObject() to be a String object.

When you call getBundle(), you specify the base name of the desired ResourceBundle and a desired locale (if you don't want to rely on the default locale). Recall that a Locale is specified with a two-letter language code, an optional two-letter country code, and an optional variant string. getBundle() looks for an appropriate ResourceBundle class for the locale by appending this locale information to the base name for the bundle. The method looks for an appropriate class with the following algorithm:

1. Search for a class with the following name:

   basename_language_country_variant

   If no such class is found or no variant string is specified for the locale, it goes to the next step.

2. Search for a class with the following name:

   basename_language_country

   If no such class is found or no country code is specified for the locale, it goes to the next step.

3. Search for a class with the following name:

   basename_language

   If no such class is found, it goes to the final step.

4. Search for a class that has the same name as the basename, or, in other words, search for a class with the following name:

   basename

   This represents a default resource bundle used by any locale that is not explicitly supported.

At each step in this process, getBundle() checks first for a class file with the given name. If no class file is found, it uses the getResourceAsStream() method of ClassLoader to look for a Properties file with the same name as the class and a *.properties* extension. If such a properties file is found, its contents are used to create a Properties object, and getBundle() instantiates and returns a PropertyResourceBundle that exports the properties in the Properties file through the ResourceBundle API.

If getBundle() cannot find a class or properties file for the specified locale in any of the four previous search steps, it repeats the search using the default locale instead of the specified locale. If no appropriate ResourceBundle is found in this search either, getBundle() throws a MissingResourceException.

Any ResourceBundle object can have a parent ResourceBundle specified for it. When you look up a named resource in a ResourceBundle, getObject( ) first looks in the specified bundle, but if the named resource is not defined in that bundle, it recursively looks in the parent bundle. Thus, every ResourceBundle inherits the resources of its parent and may choose to override some, or all, of these resources. (Note that we are using the terms "inherit" and "override" in a different sense than we do when talking about classes that inherit and override methods in their superclass.) What this means is that every ResourceBundle you define does not have to define every resource required by your application. For example, you might define a ResourceBundle of messages to display to French-speaking users. Then you might define a smaller and more specialized ResourceBundle that overrides a few of these messages so that they are appropriate for French-speaking users who live in Canada.

Your application is not required to find and set up the parent objects for the ResourceBundle objects it uses. The getBundle( ) method actually does this for you. When getBundle( ) finds an appropriate class or properties file as described previously, it does not immediately return the ResourceBundle it has found. Instead, it continues through the remaining steps in the previous search process, looking for less-specific class or properties files from which the ResourceBundle may inherit resources. If and when getBundle( ) finds these less-specific resource bundles, it sets them up as the appropriate ancestors of the original bundle. Only once it has checked all possibilities does it return the original ResourceBundle object that it created.

To continue the example begun earlier, when a program runs in Quebec, getBundle( ) might first find a small specialized ResourceBundle class that has only a few specific Quebecois resources. Next, it looks for a more general ResourceBundle that contains French messages, and it sets this bundle as the parent of the original Quebecois bundle. Finally, getBundle( ) looks for (and probably finds) a class that defines a default set of resources, probably written in English (assuming that English is the native tongue of the original programmer). This default bundle is set as the parent of the French bundle (which makes it the grandparent of the Quebecois bundle). When the application looks up a named resource, the Quebecois bundle is searched first. If the resource isn't defined there, the French bundle is searched, and any named resource not found in the French bundle is looked up in the default bundle.

ResourceBundle Example

Examining some code makes this discussion of resource bundles much clearer. Example 8-4 is a convenience routine for creating Swing menu panes. Given a list of menu item names, it looks up labels and menu shortcuts for those named menu items in a resource bundle and creates a localized menu pane. The example has a simple test program attached.

Figure 8-3 shows the menus it creates in the American, British, and French locales. This program cannot run, of course, without localized resource bundles from which the localized menu labels are looked up.

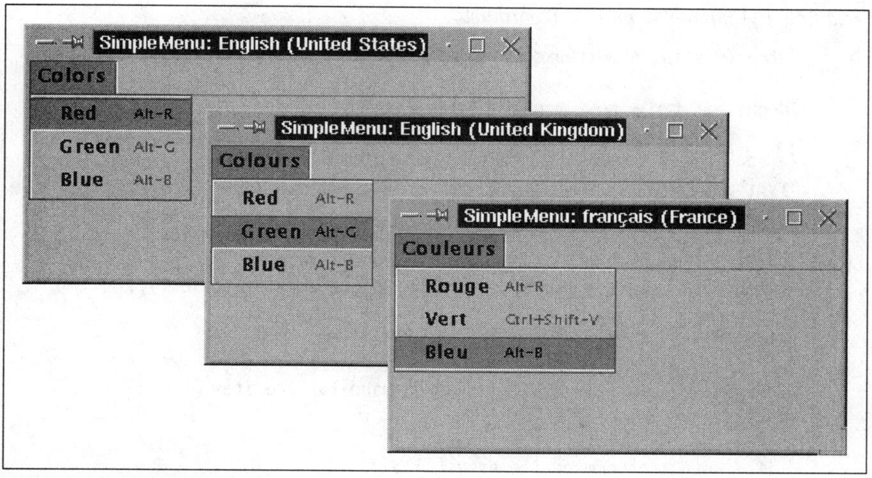

Figure 8-3. Localized menu panes

Example 8-4. SimpleMenu.java

```java
package je3.i18n;
import javax.swing.*;
import java.awt.*;
import java.awt.event.*;
import java.util.Locale;
import java.util.ResourceBundle;
import java.util.MissingResourceException;

/** A convenience class to automatically create localized menu panes */
public class SimpleMenu {
  /** The convenience method that creates menu panes */
  public static JMenu create(ResourceBundle bundle,
               String menuname, String[] itemnames,
               ActionListener listener)
  {
    // Get the menu title from the bundle. Use name as default label.
    String menulabel;
    try { menulabel = bundle.getString(menuname + ".label"); }
    catch(MissingResourceException e) { menulabel = menuname; }

    // Create the menu pane.
    JMenu menu = new JMenu(menulabel);

    // For each named item in the menu.
    for(int i = 0; i < itemnames.length; i++) {
      // Look up the label for the item, using name as default.
      String itemlabel;
      try {
        itemlabel =
          bundle.getString(menuname+"."+itemnames[i]+".label");
      }
```

Example 8-4. SimpleMenu.java (continued)

```
        catch (MissingResourceException e) { itemlabel = itemnames[i]; }

        JMenuItem item = new JMenuItem(itemlabel);

        // Look up an accelerator for the menu item
        try {
          String acceleratorText =
            bundle.getString(menuname+"."+itemnames[i]+".accelerator
bundle.getString(menuname+"."+itemnames[i]+".accelerator");
            item.setAccelerator(KeyStroke.getKeyStroke(acceleratorText));
        }
        catch (MissingResourceException e) {}

        // Register an action listener and command for the item.
        if (listener != null) {
          item.addActionListener(listener);
          item.setActionCommand(itemnames[i]);
        }

        // Add the item to the menu.
        menu.add(item);
      }

      // Return the automatically created localized menu.
      return menu;
  }

  /** A simple test program for the above code */
  public static void main(String[] args) {
      // Get the locale: default, or specified on command-line
      Locale locale;
      if (args.length == 2) locale = new Locale(args[0], args[1]);
      else locale = Locale.getDefault();

      // Get the resource bundle for that Locale. This will throw an
      // (unchecked) MissingResourceException if no bundle is found.
      ResourceBundle bundle =
        ResourceBundle.getBundle("com.davidflanagan.examples.i18n.Menus",
                      locale);

      // Create a simple GUI window to display the menu with
      final JFrame f = new JFrame("SimpleMenu: " + // Window title
              locale.getDisplayName(Locale.getDefault()));
      JMenuBar menubar = new JMenuBar();        // Create a menubar.
      f.setJMenuBar(menubar);              // Add menubar to window

      // Define an action listener that our menu will use.
      ActionListener listener = new ActionListener() {
          public void actionPerformed(ActionEvent e) {
            String s = e.getActionCommand();
            Component c = f.getContentPane();
            if (s.equals("red")) c.setBackground(Color.red);
```

Example 8-4. SimpleMenu.java (continued)

```
        else if (s.equals("green")) c.setBackground(Color.green);
        else if (s.equals("blue")) c.setBackground(Color.blue);
      }
    };

    // Now create a menu using our convenience routine with the resource
    // bundle and action listener we've created
    JMenu menu = SimpleMenu.create(bundle, "colors",
                    new String[] {"red", "green", "blue"},
                    listener);

    // Finally add the menu to the GUI, and pop it up
    menubar.add(menu);        // Add the menu to the menubar
    f.setSize(300, 150);      // Set the window size.
    f.setVisible(true);       // Pop the window up.
  }
}
```

As I've already said, this example does not stand alone. It relies on resource bundles to localize the menu. The following listing shows three property files that serve as resource bundles for this example. Note that this single listing contains the bodies of three separate files:

```
# The file Menus.properties is the default "Menus" resource bundle.
# As an American programmer, I made my own locale the default.
colors.label=Colors
colors.red.label=Red
colors.red.accelerator=alt R
colors.green.label=Green
colors.green.accelerator=alt G
colors.blue.label=Blue
colors.blue.accelerator=alt B

# This is the file Menus_en_GB.properties.  It is the resource bundle for
# British English.  Note that it overrides only a single resource definition
# and simply inherits the rest from the default (American) bundle.
colors.label=Colours

# This is the file Menus_fr.properties.  It is the resource bundle for all
# French-speaking locales.  It overrides most, but not all, of the resources
# in the default bundle.
colors.label=Couleurs
colors.red.label=Rouge
colors.green.label=Vert
colors.green.accelerator=control shift V
colors.blue.label=Bleu
```

Formatted Messages

We've seen that in order to internationalize programs, you must place all user-visible messages into resource bundles. This is straightforward when the text to be localized consists of simple labels such as those on buttons and menu items. It is trickier, however, with messages that are composed partially of static text and partially of dynamic values. For example, a compiler might have to display a message such as "Error at line 5 of file "hello.java"", in which the line number and filename are dynamic and locale-independent, while the rest of the message is static and needs to be localized.

The MessageFormat class of the java.text package helps tremendously with these types of messages. To use it, you store only the static parts of a message in the ResourceBundle and include special characters that indicate where the dynamic parts of the message are to be placed. For example, one resource bundle might contain the message: "Error at line {0} of file {1}". And another resource bundle might contain a "translation" that looks like this: "Erreur: {1}: {0}".

To use such a localized message, you create a MessageFormat object from the static part of the message and then call its format( ) method, passing in an array of the values to be substituted. In this case, the array contains an Integer object that specifies the line number and a String object that specifies the filename. The MessageFormat class knows about other Format classes defined in java.text. It creates and uses NumberFormat objects to format numbers and DateFormat objects to format dates and times. In addition, you can design messages that create ChoiceFormat objects to convert from numbers to strings. This is useful when working with enumerated types, such as numbers that correspond to month names, or when you need to use the singular or plural form of a word based on the value of some number.

Example 8-5 demonstrates this kind of MessageFormat usage. It is a convenience class with a single static method for the localized display of exception and error messages. When invoked, the code attempts to load a ResourceBundle with the basename "Errors". If found, it looks up a message resource using the class name of the exception object that was passed. If such a resource is found, it displays the error message. An array of five values is passed to the format( ) method. The localized error message can include any or all of these arguments.

The LocalizedError.display( ) method defined in this example was used in Example 8-2 at the beginning of this chapter. The default *Errors.properties* resource bundle used in conjunction with this example is shown following the code listing. Error message display for the program is nicely internationalized. Porting the program's error message to a new locale is simply a matter of translating (localizing) the *Errors.properties* file.

Example 8-5. LocalizedError.java

```
package je3.i18n;
import java.text.*;
import java.io.*;
import java.util.*;

/**
 * A convenience class that can display a localized exception message
 * depending on the class of the exception.  It uses a MessageFormat,
 * and passes five arguments that the localized message may include:
 *    {0}: the message included in the exception or error.
 *    {1}: the full class name of the exception or error.
```

Example 8-5. LocalizedError.java (continued)

```
*    {2}: the file the exception occurred in
*    {3}: a line number in that file.
*    {4}: the current date and time.
* Messages are looked up in a ResourceBundle with the basename
* "Errors", using a the full class name of the exception object as
* the resource name.  If no resource is found for a given exception
* class, the superclasses are checked.
**/
public class LocalizedError {
    public static void display(Throwable error) {
        ResourceBundle bundle;
        // Try to get the resource bundle.
        // If none, print the error in a nonlocalized way.
        try {
            String bundleName = "com.davidflanagan.examples.i18n.Errors";
            bundle = ResourceBundle.getBundle(bundleName);
        }
        catch (MissingResourceException e) {
            error.printStackTrace(System.err);
            return;
        }

        // Look up a localized message resource in that bundle, using the
        // classname of the error (or its superclasses) as the resource name.
        // If no resource was found, display the error without localization.
        String message = null;
        Class c = error.getClass();
        while((message == null) && (c != Object.class)) {
            try { message = bundle.getString(c.getName()); }
            catch (MissingResourceException e) { c = c.getSuperclass(); }
        }
        if (message == null) { error.printStackTrace(System.err);   return; }

        // Get the filename and linenumber for the exception
        // In Java 1.4, this is easy, but in prior releases, we had to try
        // parsing the output Throwable.printStackTrace();
        StackTraceElement frame = error.getStackTrace()[0];   // Java 1.4
        String filename = frame.getFileName();
        int linenum = frame.getLineNumber();

        // Set up an array of arguments to use with the message
        String errmsg = error.getMessage();
        Object[] args = {
            ((errmsg!= null)?errmsg:""), error.getClass().getName(),
            filename, new Integer(linenum), new Date()
        };

        // Finally, display the localized error message, using
        // MessageFormat.format() to substitute the arguments into the message.
        System.err.println(MessageFormat.format(message, args));
    }
}
```

Example 8-5. LocalizedError.java (continued)

```
/**
 * This is a simple test program that demonstrates the display( ) method.
 * You can use it to generate and display a FileNotFoundException or an
 * ArrayIndexOutOfBoundsException
 **/
public static void main(String[ ] args) {
    try { FileReader in = new FileReader(args[0]); }
    catch(Exception e) { LocalizedError.display(e); }
}
}
```

The following listing shows the resource bundle properties file used to localize the set of possible error messages that can be thrown by the ConvertEncoding class of Example 8-2:

```
#
# This is the file Errors.properties
# One property for each class of exceptions that our program might
# report.  Note the use of backslashes to continue long lines onto the
# next.  Also note the use of \n and \t for newlines and tabs
#
java.io.FileNotFoundException: \
Error: File "{0}" not found\n\t\
Error occurred at line {3} of file "{2}"\n\tat {4}

java.io.UnsupportedEncodingException: \
Error: Specified encoding not supported\n\t\
Error occurred at line {3} of file "{2}"\n\tat {4,time} on {4,date}

java.io.CharConversionException:\
Error: Character conversion failure.  Input data is not in specified format.

# A generic resource.  Display a message for any error or exception that
# is not handled by a more specific resource.
java.lang.Throwable:\
Error: {1}: {0}\n\t\
Error occurred at line {3} of file "{2}"\n\t{4,time,long} {4,date,long}
```

With a resource bundle like this, ConvertEncoding produces error messages like the following:

```
Error: File "myfile (No such file or directory)" not found
        Error occurred at line 64 of file "FileInputStream.java"
            at 7/9/00 9:28 PM
```

Or, if the current locale is fr_FR:

```
Error: File "myfile (Aucun fichier ou repertoire de ce type)" not found
        Error occurred at line 64 of file "FileInputStream.java"
            at 09/07/00 21:28
```

Exercises

Exercise 8-1. Several internationalization-related classes, such as NumberFormat and DateFormat, have static methods named getAvailableLocales( ) that return an array of the Locale objects they support. You can look up the name of the country of a given Locale object with the getDisplayCountry( ) method. Note that this method has two variants. One takes no arguments and displays the country name as appropriate in the default locale. The other version of getDisplayCountry( ) expects a Locale argument and displays the country name in the language of the specified locale.

Write a program that displays the country names for all locales returned by NumberFormat.getAvailableLocales( ). Using the static locale constants defined by the Locale class, display each country name in English, French, German, and Italian.

Exercise 8-2. Modify the Portfolio class of Example 8-3 to remove all hardcoded display strings. Instead, use the ResourceBundle and MessageFormat classes as demonstrated in Examples 8-4 and 8-5.

Exercise 8-3. Write a multicity digital clock program that displays the current date and time in the cities Washington, London, Paris, Bonn, Beijing, and Tokyo. Display the dates and times using the customary formats for those cities. You'll want to read about the java.util.TimeZone class and the DateFormat.setTimeZone( ) method. Consult a map or search the Internet to determine the time zones for each of the cities. Write the program as an AWT or Swing application or as an applet after you have read Chapters 11 and 16. You may want to base the program on the Clock applet from Example 16-2.

Exercise 8-4. Example 8-4 shows how you can use a ResourceBundle to internationalize the text that appears within menus in your application. One feature of Swing that discourages internationalization is that the JButton, JMenu, and JMenuItem constructors, among others, are passed the labels they are to display. This makes it very tempting for programmers to hardcode these labels into their programs. Create internationalized subclasses of these components, named IButton, IMenu, and IMenuItem, that instead take resource names as their constructor arguments. Each class should look up a resource bundle named "Labels" and use this bundle to look up the button or menu label that corresponds to the resource name passed to the constructor. If the bundle does not exist, or if a given resource is not defined in it, the IButton, IMenu, and IMenuItem classes should default to using the resource names as their labels. Write a simple test program (and some test property files) that demonstrate these new classes under two or three different locales. You'll probably want to read Chapter 11 before working on this exercise.

9

Reflection

The Reflection API allows a Java program to inspect and manipulate itself; it comprises the java.lang.Class class and the java.lang.reflect package, which represents the members of a class with Method, Constructor, and Field objects.

Reflection can obtain information about a class and its members. This is the technique that the JavaBeans™ (see Chapter 15) introspection mechanism uses to determine the properties, events, and methods that are supported by a bean, for example. Reflection can also manipulate objects in Java. You can use the Field class to query and set the values of fields, the Method class to invoke methods, and the Constructor class to create new objects. The examples in this chapter demonstrate both object inspection and manipulation using the Reflection API.

In addition to the examples in this chapter, the Java Reflection API also features prominently in Examples 15-10 and 18-3.

Obtaining Class and Member Information

Example 9-1 shows a program that uses the Class, Constructor, Field, and Method classes to display information about a specified class. The program's output is similar to the class synopses that appear in *Java in a Nutshell*. (You might notice that the names of method arguments are not shown; argument names are not stored in class files, so they are not available through the Reflection API.)

Here is the output from using ShowClass on itself:

```
public class ShowClass extends Object {
  // Constructors
  public ShowClass( );
  // Fields
  // Methods
  public static void main(String[ ]) throws ClassNotFoundException;
  public static String modifiers(int);
  public static void print_class(Class);
  public static String typename(Class);
```

```
        public static void print_field(Field);
        public static void print_method_or_constructor(Member);
    }
```

The code for this example is quite straightforward. It uses the Class.forName( ) method to dynamically load the named class, and then calls various methods of the Class object to look up the superclass, interfaces, and members of the class. The example uses Constructor, Field, and Method objects to obtain information about each member of the class.

Example 9-1. ShowClass.java

```
package je3.reflect;
import java.lang.reflect.*;

/** A program that displays a class synopsis for the named class */
public class ShowClass {
    /** The main method.  Print info about the named class */
    public static void main(String[ ] args) throws ClassNotFoundException {
        Class c = Class.forName(args[0]);
        print_class(c);
    }

    /**
     * Display the modifiers, name, superclass, and interfaces of a class
     * or interface. Then go and list all constructors, fields, and methods.
     **/
    public static void print_class(Class c)
    {
        // Print modifiers, type (class or interface), name, and superclass.
        if (c.isInterface()) {
            // The modifiers will include the "interface" keyword here...
            System.out.print(Modifier.toString(c.getModifiers()) + " " +
                             typename(c));
        }
        else if (c.getSuperclass() != null) {
            System.out.print(Modifier.toString(c.getModifiers()) + " class " +
                             typename(c) +
                             " extends " + typename(c.getSuperclass()));
        }
        else {
            System.out.print(Modifier.toString(c.getModifiers()) + " class " +
                             typename(c));
        }

        // Print interfaces or super-interfaces of the class or interface.
        Class[ ] interfaces = c.getInterfaces();
        if ((interfaces != null)&& (interfaces.length > 0)) {
            if (c.isInterface()) System.out.print(" extends ");
            else System.out.print(" implements ");
            for(int i = 0; i < interfaces.length; i++) {
                if (i > 0) System.out.print(", ");
                System.out.print(typename(interfaces[i]));
            }
        }
```

Example 9-1. ShowClass.java (continued)

```
        System.out.println(" {");                    // Begin class member listing.

        // Now look up and display the members of the class.
        System.out.println("  // Constructors");
        Constructor[ ] constructors = c.getDeclaredConstructors( );
        for(int i = 0; i < constructors.length; i++)    // Display constructors.
            print_method_or_constructor(constructors[i]);

        System.out.println("  // Fields");
        Field[ ] fields = c.getDeclaredFields( );            // Look up fields.
        for(int i = 0; i < fields.length; i++)               // Display them.
            print_field(fields[i]);

        System.out.println("  // Methods");
        Method[ ] methods = c.getDeclaredMethods( );         // Look up methods.
        for(int i = 0; i < methods.length; i++)              // Display them.
            print_method_or_constructor(methods[i]);

        System.out.println("}");                      // End class member listing.
    }

    /** Return the name of an interface or primitive type, handling arrays. */
    public static String typename(Class t) {
        String brackets = "";
        while(t.isArray( )) {
            brackets += "[ ]";
            t = t.getComponentType( );
        }
        String name = t.getName( );
        int pos = name.lastIndexOf('.');
        if (pos != -1) name = name.substring(pos+1);
        return name + brackets;
    }

    /** Return a string version of modifiers, handling spaces nicely. */
    public static String modifiers(int m) {
        if (m == 0) return "";
        else return Modifier.toString(m) + " ";
    }

    /** Print the modifiers, type, and name of a field */
    public static void print_field(Field f) {
        System.out.println("  " + modifiers(f.getModifiers( )) +
                       typename(f.getType( )) + " " + f.getName( ) + ";");
    }

    /**
     * Print the modifiers, return type, name, parameter types, and exception
     * type of a method or constructor.  Note the use of the Member interface
     * to allow this method to work with both Method and Constructor objects
     **/
    public static void print_method_or_constructor(Member member) {
```

Example 9-1. ShowClass.java (continued)

```
        Class returntype=null, parameters[ ], exceptions[ ];
        if (member instanceof Method) {
            Method m = (Method) member;
            returntype = m.getReturnType( );
            parameters = m.getParameterTypes( );
            exceptions = m.getExceptionTypes( );
            System.out.print("   " + modifiers(member.getModifiers( )) +
                             typename(returntype) + " " + member.getName( ) +
                             "(");
        } else {
            Constructor c = (Constructor) member;
            parameters = c.getParameterTypes( );
            exceptions = c.getExceptionTypes( );
            System.out.print("   " + modifiers(member.getModifiers( )) +
                             typename(c.getDeclaringClass( )) + "(");
        }

        for(int i = 0; i < parameters.length; i++) {
            if (i > 0) System.out.print(", ");
            System.out.print(typename(parameters[i]));
        }
        System.out.print(")");
        if (exceptions.length > 0) System.out.print(" throws ");
        for(int i = 0; i < exceptions.length; i++) {
            if (i > 0) System.out.print(", ");
            System.out.print(typename(exceptions[i]));
        }
        System.out.println(";");
    }
}
```

Invoking a Named Method

Example 9-2 defines the Command class, which demonstrates another use of the Reflection API. A Command object encapsulates a Method object, an object on which the method is to be invoked, and an array of arguments to pass to the method. The invoke( ) method invokes the method on the specified object using the specified arguments. The actionPerformed( ) method does the same thing. If you've read Chapter 11, you know that this method implements the java.awt.event. ActionListener interface, which means that Command objects can be used as action listeners to respond to button presses, menu selections, and other events within a graphical user interface (GUI). GUI programs typically create a slew of· ActionListener implementations to handle events. With the Command class, simple action listeners can be defined without creating lots of new classes. (The Command class also implements the InvocationHandler interface, which we'll learn about in the next section.)

The most useful feature (and the most complicated code) in the Command class is the parse( ) method, which parses a string that contains a method name and list of arguments to create a Command object. This is useful because it allows Command objects to be read from configuration files, for example. We'll use this feature of the Command class in Chapter 11. Note that the parse( ) method uses the Tokenizer interface and CharSequenceTokenizer class defined in Chapter 2.

Java does not allow methods to be passed directly as data values, but the Reflection API makes it possible for methods passed by name to be invoked indirectly. Note that this technique is not particularly efficient. For asynchronous event handling in a GUI, though, it is certainly efficient enough: indirect method invocation through the Reflection API is much faster than the response time required by the limits of human perception. Invoking a method by name is not an appropriate technique, however, when repetitive calls are required or when the computer is not waiting for human input. Thus, you should not use this technique for passing a comparison method to a sorting routine or passing a filename filter to a directory listing method, for example. In cases like these, you should use the standard technique of implementing a class that contains the desired method and passing an instance of the class to the appropriate routine.

Example 9-2. Command.java

```java
package je3.reflect;
import java.awt.event.*;
import java.beans.*;
import java.lang.reflect.*;
import java.io.*;
import java.util.*;
import je3.classes.Tokenizer;
import je3.classes.CharSequenceTokenizer;

/**
 * This class represents a Method, the list of arguments to be passed
 * to that method, and the object on which the method is to be invoked.
 * The invoke( ) method invokes the method.  The actionPerformed( ) method
 * does the same thing, allowing this class to implement ActionListener
 * and be used to respond to ActionEvents generated in a GUI or elsewhere.
 * The static parse( ) method parses a string representation of a method
 * and its arguments.
 **/
public class Command implements ActionListener, InvocationHandler {
    Method m;        // The method to be invoked
    Object target;   // The object to invoke it on
    Object[ ] args;  // The arguments to pass to the method

    // An empty array; used for methods with no arguments at all.
    static final Object[ ] nullargs = new Object[ ] { };

    /** This constructor creates a Command object for a no-arg method */
    public Command(Object target, Method m) { this(target, m, nullargs); }

    /**
     * This constructor creates a Command object for a method that takes the
     * specified array of arguments.  Note that the parse( ) method provides
     * another way to create a Command object
     **/
```

Example 9-2. Command.java (continued)

```java
public Command(Object target, Method m, Object[ ] args) {
    this.target = target;
    this.m = m;
    if (args == null) args = nullargs;
    this.args = args;
}

/**
 * This construct specifies the method to call by name.  It looks for a
 * method of the target object with the specified name and specified number
 * of arguments.  It does not attempt to verify the types of the arguments,
 * since wrapper object (Integer, Boolean, etc.) in the args[ ] array could
 * represent reference or primitive arguments.
 */
public Command(Object target, String methodName, Object[ ] args) {
    this.target = target;
    if (args == null) args = nullargs;
    this.args = args;

    Method[ ] methods = target.getClass( ).getMethods( );
    for(int i = 0; i < methods.length; i++) {
        Method m = methods[i];
        if (m.getParameterTypes( ).length == args.length &&
            m.getName( ).equals(methodName)) {
            this.m = m;
            break;
        }
    }

    // If we didn't find a method, throw an exceptoin
    if (this.m == null)
        throw new IllegalArgumentException("Unknown method " + methodName);

}

/**
 * Invoke the Command by calling the method on its target and passing
 * the arguments.  See also actionPerformed( ), which does not throw the
 * checked exceptions that this method does.
 **/
public void invoke( )
    throws IllegalAccessException, InvocationTargetException
{
    m.invoke(target, args);  // Use reflection to invoke the method
}

/**
 * This method implements the ActionListener interface.  It is like
 * invoke( ) except that it catches the exceptions thrown by that method
 * and rethrows them as an unchecked RuntimeException
 **/
public void actionPerformed(ActionEvent e) {
```

Reflection

Example 9-2. Command.java (continued)

```
        try {
            invoke( );                              // Call the invoke method
        }
        catch (InvocationTargetException ex) { // But convert to unchecked
            throw new RuntimeException(ex);      // exceptions.  Note that we
        }                                        // chain to the original
        catch (IllegalAccessException ex) {      // exception.
            throw new RuntimeException(ex);
        }
    }

    /**
     * This method implements the InvocationHandler interface, so that a
     * Command object can be used with Proxy objects.  Note that it simply
     * calls the no-argument invoke( ) method, ignoring its arguments and
     * returning null. This means that it is only useful for proxying
     * interfaces that define a single no-arg void method.
     **/
    public Object invoke(Object p, Method m, Object[ ] a) throws Throwable {
        invoke( );
        return null;
    }

    /**
     * This static method creates a Command using the specified target object
     * and the specified string.  The string should contain the method name
     * followed by an optional parenthesized comma-separated argument list and
     * a semicolon.  The arguments may be boolean, integer or double literals,
     * or double-quoted strings.  The parser is lenient about missing commas,
     * semicolons, and quotes, but throws an IOException if it cannot parse the
     * string.
     **/
    public static Command parse(Object target, String text) throws IOException
    {
        String methodname;                      // The name of the method
        ArrayList args = new ArrayList( );  // Hold arguments as we parse them.
        ArrayList types = new ArrayList( ); // Hold argument types.

        Tokenizer t = new CharSequenceTokenizer(text);
        t.skipSpaces(true).tokenizeWords(true).tokenizeNumbers(true);
        t.quotes("\"'", "\"'");

        if (t.next( ) != Tokenizer.WORD)
            throw new IOException("Missing method name for command");
        methodname = t.tokenText( );
        t.next( );
        if (t.tokenType( ) == '(') {
            t.next( );
            for(;;) { // Loop through all arguments
                int c = t.tokenType( );
                if (c == ')') {
                    // Consume closing paren
                    t.next( );
```

Example 9-2. Command.java (continued)

```
                break;  // and break out of list
            }

            if (c == Tokenizer.WORD) {
                String word = t.tokenText();
                if (word.equals("true")) {
                    args.add(Boolean.TRUE);
                    types.add(boolean.class);
                }
                else if (word.equals("false")) {
                    args.add(Boolean.FALSE);
                    types.add(boolean.class);
                }
                else {  // Treat unquoted identifiers as strings...
                    args.add(word);
                    types.add(String.class);
                }
            }
            else if (c == '"') {  // double-quoted string
                args.add(t.tokenText());
                types.add(String.class);
            }
            else if (c == '\'') { // single-quoted character
                args.add(new Character(t.tokenText().charAt(0)));
                types.add(char.class);
            }
            else if (c == Tokenizer.NUMBER) {  // An integer
                args.add(new Integer(Integer.parseInt(t.tokenText())));
                types.add(int.class);
            }
            else {  // Anything else is a syntax error
                throw new IOException("Unexpected token " + t.tokenText() +
                                      " in argument list of " +
                                      methodname + "().");
            }

            // Consume the token we just parsed, and then consume an
            // optional comma.
            if (t.next() == ',') t.next();
        }
    }

    // Consume optional semicolon after method name or argument list
    if (t.tokenType() == ';') t.next();


    // We've parsed the argument list.
    // Next, convert the lists of argument values and types to arrays
    Object[] argValues = args.toArray();
    Class[] argtypes = (Class[])types.toArray(new Class[argValues.length]);

    // At this point, we've got a method name and arrays of argument
    // values and types.  Use reflection on the class of the target object
```

Example 9-2. Command.java (continued)

```
    // to find a method with the given name and argument types.  Throw
    // an exception if we can't find the named method.
    Method method;
    try { method = target.getClass().getMethod(methodname, argtypes); }
    catch (Exception e) {
        throw new IOException("No such method found, or wrong argument " +
                              "types: " + methodname);
    }

    // Finally, create and return a Command object, using the target object
    // passed to this method, the Method object we obtained above, and
    // the array of argument values we parsed from the string.
    return new Command(target, method, argValues);
}


/**
 * This simple program demonstrates how a Command object can be parsed from
 * a string and used as an ActionListener object in a Swing application.
 **/
static class Test {
    public static void main(String[] args) throws IOException {
        javax.swing.JFrame f = new javax.swing.JFrame("Command Test");
        javax.swing.JButton b1 = new javax.swing.JButton("Tick");
        javax.swing.JButton b2 = new javax.swing.JButton("Tock");
        javax.swing.JLabel label = new javax.swing.JLabel("Hello world");
        java.awt.Container pane = f.getContentPane();

        pane.add(b1, java.awt.BorderLayout.WEST);
        pane.add(b2, java.awt.BorderLayout.EAST);
        pane.add(label, java.awt.BorderLayout.NORTH);

        b1.addActionListener(Command.parse(label, "setText(\"tick\");"));
        b2.addActionListener(Command.parse(label, "setText(\"tock\");"));

        f.pack();
        f.show();
    }
}
}
```

Proxy Objects

Java 1.3 added the Proxy class and InvocationHandler interface to the java.lang.
reflect package. This pair allows the creation of synthetic "proxy objects":
objects that implement one or more specified interfaces, with method invocations
handled by an InvocationHandler object. The key method is Proxy.
newProxyInstance(). This is an advanced reflection feature, and it is not
commonly needed in day-to-day Java programming. It is quite useful for certain
tasks, however, such as integrating scripting languages with Java.

Example 9-3 builds on the Command class. The static create( ) method returns a newly created proxy object that invokes a specified interface using a Map that associates Command objects with method names. The inner class Test provides a GUI-based demonstration like that included with the Command example.

Example 9-3. CommandProxy.java

```java
package je3.reflect;
import java.lang.reflect.*;
import java.util.*;
import javax.swing.*;
import java.awt.event.*;

/**
 * This class is an InvocationHandler based on a Map of method names to Command
 * objects.  When the invoke() method is called, the name of the method to be
 * invoked is looked up in the map, and the associated Command, if any, is
 * invoked.  Arguments passed to invoke() are always ignored.  Note that there
 * is no public constructor for this class.  Instead, there is a static factory
 * method for creating Proxy objects that use an instance of this class.
 * Pass the interface to be implemented and a Map of name/Command pairs.
 **/
public class CommandProxy implements InvocationHandler {
    Map methodMap;  // Maps method names to Command objects that implement

    // private constructor
    private CommandProxy(Map methodMap) { this.methodMap = methodMap; }

    // This method implements InvocationHandler, and invokes the Command,
    // if any associated with the name of Method m.  It ignores args[] and
    // always returns null.
    public Object invoke(Object p, Method m, Object[] args) throws Throwable {
        String methodName = m.getName();
        Command command = (Command) methodMap.get(methodName);
        if (command != null) command.invoke();
        return null;
    }

    // Return an object that implements the specified interface, using the
    // name-to-Command map as the implementation of the interface methods.
    public static Object create(Class iface, Map methodMap) {
        InvocationHandler handler = new CommandProxy(methodMap);
        ClassLoader loader = handler.getClass().getClassLoader();
        return Proxy.newProxyInstance(loader, new Class[] { iface }, handler);
    }

    // This is a test class to demonstrate the use of CommandProxy.
    static class Test {
        public static void main(String[] args)  throws java.io.IOException {
            // Set up a simple GUI
            javax.swing.JFrame f = new javax.swing.JFrame("Command Test");
            javax.swing.JButton b = new javax.swing.JButton("Hello World");
            f.getContentPane().add(b, java.awt.BorderLayout.CENTER);
```

Example 9-3. CommandProxy.java (continued)

```
            f.pack( );
            f.show( );

            // Set up the Map of method names to Command objects
            Map methodMap = new HashMap( );
            methodMap.put("focusGained",Command.parse(b,"setText(\"hello\")"));
            methodMap.put("focusLost",Command.parse(b,"setText(\"goodbye\")"));

            // Use CommandProxy.create( ) to create a proxy FocusListener
            FocusListener l =
                (FocusListener)CommandProxy.create(FocusListener.class,
                                                   methodMap);

            // Use the synthetic FocusListener
            b.addFocusListener(l);
        }
    }
}
```

Exercises

Exercise 9-1. Write a program that takes the name of a Java class as a command-line argument and uses the Class class to print out all the superclasses of that class. For example, if invoked with the argument "java.awt.Applet", the program prints the following: java.lang.Object java.awt.Component java. awt.Container java.awt.Panel.

Exercise 9-2. Modify the program you wrote in Exercise 8-1 so that it prints out all interfaces implemented by a specified class or by any of its superclasses. Check for the case of classes that implement interfaces that extend other interfaces. For example, if a class implements java.awt.LayoutManager2, the LayoutManager2 interface and LayoutManager, its superinterface, should be listed.

Exercise 9-3. Define a class named Assignment that is modeled on the Command class shown in Example 9-2. Instead of invoking a named method, as Command does, Assignment should assign a value to a named field of an object. Give your class a constructor with the following signature:

```
    public Assignment(Object target, Field field, Object value)
```

Also give it an assign( ) method that, when invoked, assigns the specified value to the specified field of the specified object. Assignment should implement ActionListener and define an actionPerformed( ) method that also performs the assignment. Write a static parse( ) method for Assignment that is similar to the parse( ) method of Command. It should parse strings of the form *fieldname=value* and should be able to parse boolean, numeric, and string values.

10

Object Serialization

To *serialize* an object means to write its complete internal state (including its private state) to a byte stream in such a way that a copy of the object can be reconstituted at some later time. When an object is serialized, the entire object graph of all the objects it refers to are serialized along with it. This means it's possible to serialize complex data structures such as binary trees. It's also possible to serialize applets and complete GUI component hierarchies. Serialization is a critical piece of Remote Method Invocation (see Chapter 21) because it allows objects (as long as they are Serializable) to be passed across the network. Serialization also provides a convenient way to produce a "deep clone" of an object graph. Serialization can also be used as a trivial technique for saving application state: just serialize the data structures to disk. This requires care, however, because the serialization file format is sensitive to implementation changes in your classes. In Java 1.4, the java.beans package (see Chapter 15) provides a JavaBeans-based persistence mechanism that is often a better alternative for long-term persistence.

This chapter shows how to serialize and deserialize objects, and how to write serializable classes that make simple use of the serialization mechanism. Serialization is actually a surprisingly complex problem, and the serialization mechanism has been updated with each release of Java. This chapter does not attempt to cover any of the complex details. Joshua Bloch's book *Effective Java Programming Language Guide* (Addison-Wesley) includes an excellent discussion of serialization that goes as deep as most of us ever need to go. If you do need to understand the gory details, see the *Java Object Serialization Specification* that is shipped as part of the documentation bundle for the Java SDK.

Simple Serialization

Despite the power and importance of serialization, it is performed using a simple API that forms part of the java.io package: an object is serialized by the writeObject() method of the ObjectOutputStream class and deserialized by the readObject( ) method of the ObjectInputStream class. These classes are byte streams like the various other streams we saw in Chapter 3. They implement the ObjectOutput and ObjectInput interfaces, respectively, and these interfaces extend the DataOutput and DataInput interfaces. This means that ObjectOutputStream defines the same methods as DataOutputStream for writing primitive values, while ObjectInputStream defines the same methods as DataInputStream for reading primitive values. The methods we're interested in here, however, are writeObject( ) and readObject( ), which write and read objects.

Only objects that implement the java.io.Serializable interface may be serialized. Serializable is a marker interface; it doesn't define any methods that need to be implemented. Nevertheless, for security reasons, some classes don't want their private state to be exposed by the serialization mechanism. Therefore, a class must explicitly declare itself to be serializable by implementing this interface.

An object is serialized by passing it to the writeObject( ) method of an ObjectOutputStream. This writes out the values of all of its fields, including private fields and fields inherited from superclasses. The values of primitive fields are simply written to the stream as they would be with a DataOutputStream. When a field in an object refers to another object, an array, or a string, however, the writeObject( ) method is invoked recursively to serialize that object as well. If that object (or an array element) refers to another object, writeObject( ) is again invoked recursively. Thus, a single call to writeObject( ) may result in an entire object graph being serialized. When two or more objects each refer to the other, the serialization algorithm is careful to output each object only once; writeObject( ) can't enter infinite recursion.

Deserializing an object simply follows the reverse of this process. An object is read from a stream of data by calling the readObject( ) method of an ObjectInputStream. This creates a copy of the object in the state it was in when serialized. If the object refers to other objects, they are recursively deserialized as well.

Example 10-1 demonstrates the basics of serialization. The example defines generic methods that can store and retrieve any serializable object's state to and from a file. It also includes an interesting deepclone( ) method that uses serialization to copy an object graph. The example includes a Serializable inner class and a test class that demonstrates the methods at work.

Example 10-1. Serializer.java

```
package je3.serialization;
import java.io.*;

/**
 * This class defines utility routines that use Java serialization.
 **/
public class Serializer {
    /**
     * Serialize the object o (and any Serializable objects it refers to) and
     * store its serialized state in File f.
     **/
    static void store(Serializable o, File f) throws IOException {
```

Example 10-1. Serializer.java (continued)

```
        ObjectOutputStream out =    // The class for serialization
            new ObjectOutputStream(new FileOutputStream(f));
        out.writeObject(o);         // This method serializes an object graph
        out.close();
    }

    /**
     * Deserialize the contents of File f and return the resulting object
     **/
    static Object load(File f) throws IOException, ClassNotFoundException {
        ObjectInputStream in =      // The class for deserialization
            new ObjectInputStream(new FileInputStream(f));
        return in.readObject();     // This method deserializes an object graph
    }

    /**
     * Use object serialization to make a "deep clone" of the object o.
     * This method serializes o and all objects it refers to, and then
     * deserializes that graph of objects, which means that everything is
     * copied.  This differs from the clone() method of an object, which is
     * usually implemented to produce a "shallow" clone that copies references
     * to other objects, instead of copying all referenced objects.
     **/
    static Object deepclone(final Serializable o)
        throws IOException, ClassNotFoundException
    {
        // Create a connected pair of "piped" streams.
        // We'll write bytes to one, and then from the other one.
        final PipedOutputStream pipeout = new PipedOutputStream();
        PipedInputStream pipein = new PipedInputStream(pipeout);

        // Now define an independent thread to serialize the object and write
        // its bytes to the PipedOutputStream
        Thread writer = new Thread() {
                public void run() {
                    ObjectOutputStream out = null;
                    try {
                        out = new ObjectOutputStream(pipeout);
                        out.writeObject(o);
                    }
                    catch(IOException e) {}
                    finally {
                        try { out.close(); } catch (Exception e) {}
                    }
                }
            };
        writer.start();  // Make the thread start serializing and writing

        // Meanwhile, in this thread, read and deserialize from the piped
        // input stream.  The resulting object is a deep clone of the original.
        ObjectInputStream in = new ObjectInputStream(pipein);
        return in.readObject();
    }
```

Example 10-1. Serializer.java (continued)

```java
/**
 * This is a simple serializable data structure that we use below for
 * testing the methods above
 **/
public static class DataStructure implements Serializable {
    String message;
    int[ ] data;
    DataStructure other;
    public String toString( ) {
        String s = message;
        for(int i = 0; i < data.length; i++)
            s += " " + data[i];
        if (other != null) s += "\n\t" + other.toString( );
        return s;
    }
}

/** This class defines a main( ) method for testing */
public static class Test {
    public static void main(String[ ] args)
        throws IOException, ClassNotFoundException
    {
        // Create a simple object graph
        DataStructure ds = new DataStructure( );
        ds.message = "hello world";
        ds.data = new int[ ] { 1, 2, 3, 4 };
        ds.other = new DataStructure( );
        ds.other.message = "nested structure";
        ds.other.data = new int[ ] { 9, 8, 7 };

        // Display the original object graph
        System.out.println("Original data structure: " + ds);

        // Output it to a file
        File f = new File("datastructure.ser");
        System.out.println("Storing to a file...");
        Serializer.store(ds, f);

        // Read it back from the file, and display it again
        ds = (DataStructure) Serializer.load(f);
        System.out.println("Read from the file: " + ds);

        // Create a deep clone and display that.  After making the copy,
        // modify the original to prove that the clone is "deep".
        DataStructure ds2 = (DataStructure) Serializer.deepclone(ds);
        ds.other.message = null; ds.other.data = null; // Change original
        System.out.println("Deep clone: " + ds2);
    }
}
}
```

Custom Serialization

Not every piece of program state can, or should be, serialized. Such things as
`FileDescriptor` objects are inherently platform-specific or virtual machine–dependent. If a `FileDescriptor` were serialized, for example, it would have no meaning
when deserialized in a different virtual machine. For this reason, and also for the
important security reasons described earlier, not all objects can be serialized.

Even when an object is serializable, it may not make sense for it to serialize all its
state. Some fields may be "scratch" fields that can hold temporary or precomputed values but don't actually hold state needed to restore a serialized object.
Consider a GUI component. It may define fields that store the coordinates of the
last mouse click it received. This information is never of interest when the component is deserialized, so there's no need to bother saving the values of these fields
as part of the component's state. To tell the serialization mechanism that a field
shouldn't be saved, simply declare it `transient`:

```
protected transient short last_x, last_y; // Temporary fields for mouse pos
```

There are also situations where a field is not transient (i.e., it does contain an
important part of an object's state), but for some reason it can't be successfully
serialized. Consider another GUI component that computes its preferred size
based on the size of the text it displays. Because fonts have slight size variations
from platform to platform, this precomputed preferred size isn't valid if the
component is serialized on one type of platform and deserialized on another.
Since the preferred size fields will not be reliable when deserialized, they should
be declared `transient` so that they don't take up space in the serialized object. But
in this case, their values must be recomputed when the object is deserialized.

A class can define custom serialization and deserialization behavior (such as
recomputing a preferred size) for its objects by implementing `writeObject()` and
`readObject()` methods. Surprisingly, these methods are not defined by any interface, and they must be declared `private`. If a class defines these methods, the
appropriate one is invoked by the `ObjectOutputStream` or `ObjectInputStream` when
an object is serialized or deserialized.

For example, a GUI component might define a `readObject()` method to give it an
opportunity to recompute its preferred size upon deserialization. The method
might look like this:

```
private void readObject(ObjectInputStream in)
        throws IOException, ClassNotFoundException
{
    in.defaultReadObject();      // Deserialize the component in the usual way.
    this.computePreferredSize(); // But then go recompute its size.
}
```

This method calls the `defaultReadObject()` method of the `ObjectInputStream` to
deserialize the object as normal and then takes care of the postprocessing it needs
to perform.

Example 10-2 is a more complete example of custom serialization. It shows a class
that implements a growable array of integers, like the `IntList` class of
Example 2-7. This version of the class is declared `Serializable` and defines a

writeObject( ) method to do some preprocessing before being serialized and a readObject( ) method to do postprocessing after deserialization. Note that the size field is declared transient. The example also overrides equals( ) so that serialization can be tested, and overrides hashCode( ) to match.

Example 10-2. SerialIntList.java

```java
package com.davidflanagan.examples.serialization;
import java.io.*;

/**
 * A simple class that implements a growable array of ints, and knows
 * how to serialize itself as efficiently as a nongrowable array.
 **/
public class SerialIntList implements Serializable {
    // These are the fields of this class.  By default the serialization
    // mechanism would just write them out.  But we've declared size to be
    // transient, which means it will not be serialized.  And we've
    // provided writeObject( ) and readObject( ) methods below to customize
    // the serialization process.
    protected int[ ] data = new int[8]; // An array to store the numbers.
    protected transient int size = 0;   // Index of next unused element of array

    /** Return an element of the array */
    public int get(int index) {
        if (index >= size) throw new ArrayIndexOutOfBoundsException(index);
        else return data[index];
    }

    /** Add an int to the array, growing the array if necessary */
    public void add(int x) {
        if (data.length==size) resize(data.length*2); // Grow array if needed.
        data[size++] = x;                             // Store the int in it.
    }

    /** An internal method to change the allocated size of the array */
    protected void resize(int newsize) {
        int[ ] newdata = new int[newsize];         // Create a new array
        System.arraycopy(data, 0, newdata, 0, size); // Copy array elements.
        data = newdata;                            // Replace old array
    }

    /**
     * Get rid of unused array elements before serializing the array.  This
     * may reduce the number of array elements to serialize.  It also makes
     * data.length == size, so there is no need to safe the (transient) size
     * field. The serialization mechanism will automatically call this method
     * when serializing an object of this class.  Note that this must be
     * declared private.
     */
    private void writeObject(ObjectOutputStream out) throws IOException {
        if (data.length > size) resize(size);  // Compact the array.
        out.defaultWriteObject();              // Then write it out normally.
    }
```

Example 10-2. SerialIntList.java (continued)

```java
    /**
     * Restore the transient size field after deserializing the array.
     * The serialization mechanism automatically calls this method.
     */
    private void readObject(ObjectInputStream in)
        throws IOException, ClassNotFoundException
    {
        in.defaultReadObject();             // Read the array normally.
        size = data.length;                 // Restore the transient field.
    }

    /**
     * Does this object contain the same values as the object o?
     * We override this Object method so we can test the class.
     **/
    public boolean equals(Object o) {
        if (!(o instanceof IntList)) return false;
        IntList that = (IntList) o;
        if (this.size != that.size) return false;
        for(int i = 0; i < this.size; i++)
            if (this.data[i] != that.data[i]) return false;
        return true;
    }

    /** We must override this method when we override equals(). */
    public int hashCode() {
        int code = 1; // non-zero to hash [0] and [] to distinct values
        for(int i = 0; i < size; i++)
            code = code*997 + data[i];   // ignore overflow
        return code;
    }

    /** A main() method to prove that it works */
    public static void main(String[] args) throws Exception {
        IntList list = new IntList();
        for(int i = 0; i < 100; i++) list.add((int)(Math.random()*40000));
        IntList copy = (IntList)Serializer.deepclone(list);
        if (list.equals(copy)) System.out.println("equal copies");
        Serializer.store(list, new File("intlist.ser"));
    }
}
```

Externalizable Classes

The Externalizable interface extends Serializable and defines the writeExternal() and readExternal() methods. An Externalizable object may be serialized as other Serializable objects are, but the serialization mechanism calls writeExternal() and readExternal() to perform the serialization and deserialization. Unlike the readObject() and writeObject() methods in Example 10-2, the readExternal() and writeExternal() methods can't call the defaultReadObject( ) and defaultWriteObject( ) methods: they must read and write the complete state of the object by themselves.

It is useful to declare an object Externalizable when the object already has an existing file format or when you want to accomplish something that is simply not possible with the standard serialization methods. Example 10-3 defines the CompactIntList class, an Externalizable subclass of the IntList class of Example 2-7. CompactIntList makes the assumption that it is typically used to store small integers that fit in two bytes instead of four; it implements Externalizable so it can define a serialized form that is more compact than the format used by ObjectOutputStream and ObjectInputStream.

Example 10-3. CompactIntList.java

```java
package je3.serialization;
import je3.classes.IntList;
import java.io.*;

/**
 * This subclass of IntList assumes that most of the integers it contains are
 * less than 32,000.  It implements Externalizable so that it can define a
 * compact serialization format that takes advantage of this fact.
 **/
public class CompactIntList extends IntList implements Externalizable {
    /**
     * This version number is here in case a later revision of this class wants
     * to modify the externalization format, but still retain compatibility
     * with externalized objects written by this version
     **/
    static final byte version = 1;

    /**
     * This method from the Externalizable interface is responsible for saving
     * the complete state of the object to the specified stream.  It can write
     * anything it wants as long as readExternal( ) can read it.
     **/
    public void writeExternal(ObjectOutput out) throws IOException {
        trim( );  // Compact the list to its current size

        out.writeByte(version);  // Start with our version number.
        out.writeInt(size);      // Output the number of array elements
        for(int i = 0; i < size; i++) {  // Now loop through the array
            int n = data[i];             // The array element to write
            if ((n <= Short.MAX_VALUE) && (n > Short.MIN_VALUE)) {
                // If n fits in a short and is not Short.MIN_VALUE, then write
                // it out as a short, saving ourselves two bytes
                out.writeShort(n);
            }
            else {
                // Otherwise write out the special value Short.MIN_VALUE to
                // signal that the number does not fit in a short, and then
                // output the number using a full 4 bytes, for 6 bytes total
                out.writeShort(Short.MIN_VALUE);
                out.writeInt(n);
```

Example 10-3. CompactIntList.java (continued)

```
            }
        }
    }

    /**
     * This Externalizable method is responsible for completely restoring the
     * state of the object.  A no-arg constructor will be called to recreate
     * the object, and this method must read the state written by
     * writeExternal( ) to restore the object's state.
     **/
    public void readExternal(ObjectInput in)
        throws IOException, ClassNotFoundException
    {
        // Start by reading and verifying the version number.
        byte v = in.readByte( );
        if (v != version)
            throw new IOException("CompactIntList: unknown version number");

        // Read the number of array elements, and make array that big
        int newsize = in.readInt( );
        setCapacity(newsize);  // A protected method inherited from IntList
        this.size = newsize;   // Save this size.

        // Now read that many values from the stream
        for(int i = 0; i < newsize; i++) {
            short n = in.readShort( );
            if (n != Short.MIN_VALUE) data[i] = n;
            else data[i] = in.readInt( );
        }
    }

    /** A main( ) method to prove that it works */
    public static void main(String[ ] args) throws Exception {
        CompactIntList list = new CompactIntList( );
        for(int i = 0; i < 100; i++) list.add((int)(Math.random( )*40000));
        CompactIntList copy = (CompactIntList)Serializer.deepclone(list);
        if (list.equals(copy)) System.out.println("equal copies");
        Serializer.store(list, new File("compactintlist.ser"));
    }
}
```

Serialization and Class Versioning

One of the features of Example 10-3 is that it includes a version number in the serialization stream it writes. This is useful if the class evolves in the future and needs to use a new serialization format. The version number allows future versions of the class to recognize serialized objects written by this version of the class.

For Serializable objects that are not Externalizable, the Serialization API handles versioning itself. When an object is serialized, some information about the object's class must obviously be serialized with it, so that the correct class file can be loaded when the object is deserialized. This information about the class is represented by the java.io.ObjectStreamClass class. It contains the fully qualified name of the class and a version number for the class. The version number is very important because an early version of a class may not be able to deserialize a serialized instance created by a later version of the same class. The version number for a class is a long value. By default, the serialization mechanism creates a unique version number by computing a hash of the name of the class, the name of its superclass and any interfaces it implements, the name and type of its fields, and the name and type of its nonprivate methods. Thus, whenever you add a new method, change the name of a field, or make even minor modifications to the API or implementation of a class, its computed version number changes. When an object is serialized by one version of a class, it can't be deserialized by a version that has a different version number.

Thus, when you make changes to a serializable class, even minor changes that don't affect the serialization format, you break serialization compatibility between versions. For example, our SerialIntList class really ought to have a set( ) method that sets the value of a specified element of the list. But if you add this method, the new version of the class can't deserialize objects serialized by the old version. The way to prevent this problem is to explicitly declare a version number for your class. You do this by giving the class a constant field named serialVersionUID.

The value of this field doesn't matter; it must simply be the same for all versions of the class that have a compatible serialization format. Since the SerialIntList class shown in Example 10-2 doesn't have a serialVersionUID field, its version number was implicitly computed based on the API of the class. In order to give an updated version of SerialIntList a version number that matches the original version, use the *serialver* command that comes with the Java SDK:

```
% serialver je3.serialization.SerialIntList
SerialIntList:    static final long serialVersionUID = 2952055272471088220L;
```

If you run this program on the original version of the class, it prints a field definition suitable for inclusion in the modified version of the class. By including this constant field in the modified class, you retain serialization compatibility between it and the original version.

Advanced Versioning

Sometimes you make changes to a class that alter the way the class stores its state. Imagine a Rectangle class that represents the rectangle as the coordinate of the upper-left corner, plus a width and a height. Now suppose that the class is reimplemented so that it maintains exactly the same public API, but the rectangle is now represented by two points: the coordinates of the upper-left corner and the lower-right corner. The internal private fields of the class have changed, so it would appear that serialization compatibility between the two implementations of the class is simply not possible.

One solution is to make the new version of the class Externalizable, taking full control over the data format, and using that to write the new implementation fields in the old format. In Java 1.2 and later, however, the serialization mechanism has been updated to allow the serialization format of Serializable classes to be totally decoupled from the fields used by a particular implementation or version of the class. A class can now declare a private field named serialPersistentFields that refers to an array of java.io.ObjectStreamField objects. Each of these objects defines a field name and a field type. These fields need not have any relationship to the fields implemented by the class; they are the fields of the serialized form of the class. By defining this array of ObjectStreamField objects, the class is specifying its serialization format. When a new version of the class is defined, that new version must be able to save and restore its state in the format defined by the serialPersistentFields array.

The techniques for reading and writing the serialization fields declared by the serialPersistentFields array are beyond the scope of this chapter. For more information, check the putFields( ) and writeFields( ) methods of ObjectOutputStream and the readFields( ) method of ObjectInputStream. See also the advanced serialization examples supplied as part of the Java SDK documentation.

Exercises

Exercise 10-1. The java.util.Properties class is essentially a hashtable that maps string keys to string values. It defines store( ) and load( ) methods that save and load its contents to and from a byte stream. These methods save the Properties object in a human-readable text format despite the fact that they use byte streams. Properties inherits the Serializable interface from its superclass, java.util.Hashtable. Define a subclass of Properties that implements storeBinary( ) and loadBinary( ) methods that use object serialization to save and load the contents of the Properties object in binary form. You may also want to use java.util.zip.GZIPOutputStream and java.util.zip.GZIPInputStream in your methods to make the binary format particularly compact. Use the *serialver* program to obtain a serialVersionUID value for your class.

Exercise 10-2. As noted in the previous exercise, the Properties object has store( ) and load( ) methods that allow it to save and restore its state. Define an Externalizable subclass of Properties that uses these store( ) and load( ) methods as the basis for its writeExternal( ) and readExternal( ) methods. In order to make this work, the writeExternal( ) method needs to determine the number of bytes written by the store( ) method and write this value into the stream before writing the bytes themselves. This allows the readExternal( ) method to know when to stop reading. Also include a version number in the externalizable data format you use.

III

Desktop Java APIs

Part III contains client-side Java programs that demonstrate the graphics, graphical user interface, sound, and related APIs of the Java platform. The APIs demonstrated in this section are documented in detail in *Java Foundation Classes in a Nutshell*.

11

Graphical User Interfaces

Graphical user interfaces, or GUIs, represent an excellent example of software modularity and reuse. GUIs are almost always assembled from libraries of predefined building blocks. To Motif programmers on Unix systems, these GUI building blocks are known as *widgets*. To Windows programmers, they are known as *controls*. In Java, they are known by the generic term *components*, because they are all subclasses of java.awt.Component.*

In Java 1.0 and 1.1, the standard library of GUI components was AWT—the package java.awt and its subpackages. There is debate as to what the letter A stands for in this acronym, but "WT" stands for "windowing toolkit." In practice, it is always called AWT. In addition to GUI components, the AWT includes facilities for drawing graphics, performing cut-and-paste–style data transfer, and other related operations. On most platforms, AWT components are implemented using the operating-system's native GUI system. That is, AWT components are implemented on top of Windows controls on Windows operating systems, on top of Motif widgets on Unix systems, and so on. This implementation style led to a least-common-denominator toolkit, and, as a result, the AWT API is not as complete and full featured as it should be.

Java 1.2 introduced a new library of GUI components known as Swing. Swing consists of the javax.swing package and its subpackages. Unlike the AWT, Swing has a platform-independent implementation and a state-of-the-art set of features. Although Swing first became a core part of the Java platform in Java 1.2, a version of Swing is available for use with Java 1.1 platforms. Swing has largely replaced the AWT for the creation of GUIs, so we'll focus on Swing in this chapter. Note that Swing defines a new, more powerful set of GUI components but retains the same underlying GUI programming model used by the AWT. Thus, if you learn

---

* Except for menu-related AWT components, which are all subclasses of java.awt.MenuComponent.

to create GUIs with Swing components, you can do the same with AWT components.

There are four basic steps to creating a GUI in Java:

1. *Create and configure the components*

   You create a GUI component just like any other object in Java, by calling the constructor. You'll need to consult the documentation for individual components to determine what arguments a constructor expects. For example, to create a Swing JButton component that displays the label "Quit", simply write:

   ```
   JButton quit = new JButton("Quit");
   ```

   Once you have created a component, you may want to configure it by setting one or more properties. For example, to specify the font a JButton component should use, you can write:

   ```
   quit.setFont(new Font("sansserif", Font.BOLD, 18));
   ```

   Again, consult the documentation for the component you are using to determine what methods you can use to configure the component.

2. *Add the components to a container*

   All components must be placed within a *container*. Containers in Java are all subclasses of java.awt.Container. Commonly used containers include JFrame and JDialog classes, which represent top-level windows and dialog boxes, respectively. The java.applet.Applet class, which is subclassed to create applets, is also a container and can therefore contain and display GUI components. A container is a type of component, so containers can be, and commonly are, nested within other containers. JPanel is a container that is often used in this manner. In developing a GUI, you are really creating a containment hierarchy: the top-level window or applet contains containers that may contain other containers, which in turn contain components. To add a component to a container, you simply pass the component to the add( ) method of the container. For example, you can add a quit button to a "button box" container with code like the following:

   ```
   buttonbox.add(quit);
   ```

3. *Arrange, or lay out, the components*

   In addition to specifying which components are placed inside of which containers, you must also specify the position and size of each component within its container, so that the GUI has a pleasing appearance. While it is possible to hardcode the position and size of each component, it is more common to use a LayoutManager object to lay out the components of a container automatically according to certain layout rules defined by the particular LayoutManager you have chosen. We'll learn more about layout management later in this chapter.

4. *Handle the events generated by the components*

   The steps described so far are sufficient to create a GUI that looks good on the screen, but our graphical "user interface" is not complete, because it does not yet respond to the user. As the user interacts with the components that make up your GUI using the keyboard and mouse, those components generate, or fire, events. An *event* is simply an object that contains information about a user interaction. The final step in GUI creation is the addition of *event listeners*—objects that are notified when an event is generated and respond to the event in an appropriate way. For example, the **Quit** button needs an event listener that causes the application to exit.

We'll look at each of these topics in more detail in the first few sections of this chapter. Then we'll move on to more advanced GUI examples that highlight particular Swing components or specific GUI programming techniques. As usual, you'll want to have access to AWT and Swing reference material as you study the examples. One such reference is *Java Foundation Classes in a Nutshell*. You may also find it helpful to read this chapter in conjunction with Chapters 2 and 3 of that book.

Components

As we've just discussed, the first step in creating a GUI is to create and configure the components that comprise it. To do this, you need to be familiar with the components that are available to you and their methods. Chapter 2 of *Java Foundation Classes in a Nutshell* contains tables that list the available AWT and Swing components. You can also find this information by looking at a listing of the classes in the java.awt and javax.swing packages; it is particularly easy to identify Swing components, since their names all begin with the letter J.

Every component defines a set of properties you can use to configure it. A *property* is a named attribute of a component whose value you can set. Typical component properties have such names as font, background, and alignment. You set a property value with a *setter* method and query it with a *getter* method. Setter and getter methods are collectively called *property accessor methods*, and their names usually begin with the words "set" and "get". The notion of component properties is formally defined by the JavaBeans specification; we'll see more about them in Chapter 15. For now, however, an informal understanding will suffice: components can be configured by invoking various methods whose names begin with "set". Remember that components inherit many methods from their superclasses, notably java.awt.Component and javax.swing.JComponent, so just because a component class does not define a setter method directly does not mean that the component does not support a particular property.

Swing includes a large number of components, and it is not feasible to include examples of each one in this chapter. Later in the chapter, we'll see examples that highlight particularly powerful components for displaying tables, trees, and formatted text, and there are examples of more commonplace components—such as buttons, checkboxes, and menus—throughout the chapter. Instead of providing a guided tour to the complete set of Swing components, I instead invite you to conduct your own, using the ShowBean program developed later in this chapter (and also in Chapter 15).

As its name implies, ShowBean is a program for viewing "JavaBeans components." All Swing and AWT components are beans, so you can use it to view and experiment with these components and their properties. Invoke ShowBean with the name of one or more component classes on the command line. Each class name may be followed by zero or more property specifications of the form *name=value*. The program creates an instance of each named class and configures it by setting the specified properties to the given values. The program then displays the components using a Swing JTabbedPane container within a JFrame window. For example, to create the window displayed in Figure 11-1, I invoked ShowBean as follows (this is one long command line that has been wrapped onto multiple lines):

```
% java je3.gui.ShowBean javax.swing.JButton 'text=Hello World!'
    font=helvetica-bold-48 javax.swing.JRadioButton 'text=pick me'
    java.awt.Button label=Hello javax.swing.JSlider
```

Figure 11-1. Components displayed by ShowBean

In addition to the ability to set property values from the command line, the **Properties** menu allows you to view and set the values of certain properties. Similarly, the **Commands** menu allows you to invoke certain methods on the component. This is useful for experimenting with no-argument methods, such as the cut( ) and paste( ) methods inherited by JTextField. The **Properties** menu is most useful if ShowBean has access to "bean info" for the Swing components viewed with the program; in this case, it can display tooltips that give a short description of each property in the menu. BeanInfo classes for Swing components are contained in the file *lib/dt.jar* in Sun's Java SDK. Put this file in your classpath before running ShowBean, or copy it to the *jre/lib/ext/* directory to make it permanently available to all programs. "dt" stands for "design time"—the files in *dt.jar* provide design-time enhancements for GUI builders and programs like ShowBean, but are not required by any of the components at runtime.

One of the powerful features of the Swing component library is its use of a pluggable look-and-feel architecture, which enables an entire GUI to change its appearance. The default appearance, known as the "Metal" look-and-feel, is the same across all platforms. However, a program can choose any installed look-and-feel, including ones that simulate the appearance of native OS applications. One of the interesting features of the ShowBean program is its pull-down menu labeled **Look and Feel**. It allows you to choose from any of the installed look-and-feels.*

Many examples in this chapter (as well as some examples in subsequent chapters) take the form of component subclasses rather than complete programs with a

---

* Although the Windows look-and-feel comes standard with the Java distribution, legal issues prevent its use on any OS other than Windows. So, although this choice may appear in the menu, you can't use it if you are not using a Microsoft operating system.

main( ) method. In addition to using the ShowBean program as a way to experiment with predefined Swing and AWT components, we'll also use it as a viewer for other examples.

Containers

The second step in creating a GUI is to place the components you have created and configured into appropriate containers. Chapter 2 of *Java Foundation Classes in a Nutshell* contains tables that list the container classes available in the AWT and Swing packages. Many of these container classes have specialized uses. JFrame is a top-level window, for example, and JTabbedPane displays the components it contains in individual tabbed panes (like those pictured in Figure 11-1) but Swing and the AWT also define generic container classes, such as JPanel.

Example 11-1 is a listing of *Containers.java*. This class is a subclass of JPanel. Its constructor method creates a number of other nested JPanel instances, as well as a number of JButton objects contained by those JPanel classes. Example 11-1 illustrates the concept of the containment hierarchy of a GUI, using color to represent the nesting depth of the hierarchy. Figure 11-2 shows what the Containers class looks like when displayed with the ShowBean program as follows:

```
% java je3.gui.ShowBean je3.gui.Containers
```

Figure 11-2. Nested containers

Example 11-1. Containers.java

```
package je3.gui;
import javax.swing.*;
import java.awt.*;

/**
 * A component subclass that demonstrates nested containers and components.
 * It creates the hierarchy shown below, and uses different colors to
 * distinguish the different nesting levels of the containers
 *
 * Containers---panel1----button1
 *        |          |---panel2----button2
 *        |          |      |----panel3----button3
 *        |          |------panel4----button4
 *        |                 |----button5
```

Example 11-1. Containers.java (continued)

```
*         |---button6
*/
public class Containers extends JPanel {
    public Containers( ) {
        this.setBackground(Color.white);            // This component is white
        this.setFont(new Font("Dialog", Font.BOLD, 24));

        JPanel p1 = new JPanel( );
        p1.setBackground(new Color(200, 200, 200)); // Panel1 is darker
        this.add(p1);                   // p1 is contained by this component
        p1.add(new JButton("#1"));      // Button 1 is contained in p1

        JPanel p2 = new JPanel( );
        p2.setBackground(new Color(150, 150, 150)); // p2 is darker than p2
        p1.add(p2);                     // p2 is contained in p1
        p2.add(new JButton("#2"));      // Button 2 is contained in p2

        JPanel p3 = new JPanel( );
        p3.setBackground(new Color(100, 100, 100)); // p3 is darker than p2
        p2.add(p3);                     // p3 is contained in p2
        p3.add(new JButton("#3"));      // Button 3 is contained in p3

        JPanel p4 = new JPanel( );
        p4.setBackground(new Color(150, 150, 150)); // p4 is darker than p1
        p1.add(p4);                     // p4 is contained in p1
        p4.add(new JButton("#4"));      // Button4 is contained in p4
        p4.add(new JButton("#5"));      // Button5 is also contained in p4

        this.add(new JButton("#6")); // Button6 is contained in this component
    }
}
```

Layout Management

Once you have created your components and added them to containers, the next step is to arrange those components within the container. This is called *layout management* and is almost always performed by a special object known as a *layout manager*. Layout managers are implementations of the java.awt.LayoutManager interface or its LayoutManager2 subinterface. Each particular LayoutManager implementation enforces a specific layout policy and automatically arranges the components within a container according to that policy. The sections that follow demonstrate the use of each of the AWT and Swing layout managers. Note that BoxLayout is the only layout manager defined by Swing. Although Swing defines many new components, Swing GUIs typically rely on AWT layout managers.

You create a layout manager as you would any other object. Different layout manager classes take different constructor arguments to specify the parameters of their layout policy. Once you create a layout manager, you do not usually invoke its methods. Instead, you pass the layout manager object to the setLayout( ) method of the container that is to be managed; the container invokes the various LayoutManager methods when necessary. Once you have set the layout manager, you can usually forget about it.

As you'll see in the following sections, most of the predefined AWT layout managers have fairly simple layout policies that may not seem like much use on their own. Their power becomes apparent when combined, however. For example, you can use a GridLayout to arrange 10 buttons into two columns within a container, and then use a BorderLayout to position those two columns against the left edge of another container.

The following sections demonstrate all the important layout managers, using a short example and a screen shot of the layout produced by the example. The figures are produced using the ShowBean class from Example 11-30; you can use this program to experiment with the examples yourself. Pay particular attention to the way the layouts change when you resize the window.

FlowLayout

The FlowLayout layout manager arranges its children like words on a page: from left to right in a row and top to bottom. When there is not enough space remaining in the current row for the next component, the FlowLayout "wraps" and places the component in a new row. When you create a FlowLayout, you can specify whether the rows should be left-justified, centered, or right-justified. You can also specify the amount of horizontal and vertical space the layout manager leaves between components. FlowLayout makes no attempt to fit its components into the container; it leaves each component at its preferred size. If there is extra space, FlowLayout leaves it blank. If there is not enough room in the container, some components simply do not appear. Note that FlowLayout is the default layout manager for JPanel containers. If you do not specify a different layout manager, a panel uses a FlowLayout that centers its rows and leaves five pixels between components, both horizontally and vertically.

Example 11-2 is a short program that arranges buttons using a FlowLayout layout manager; Figure 11-3 shows the resulting output.

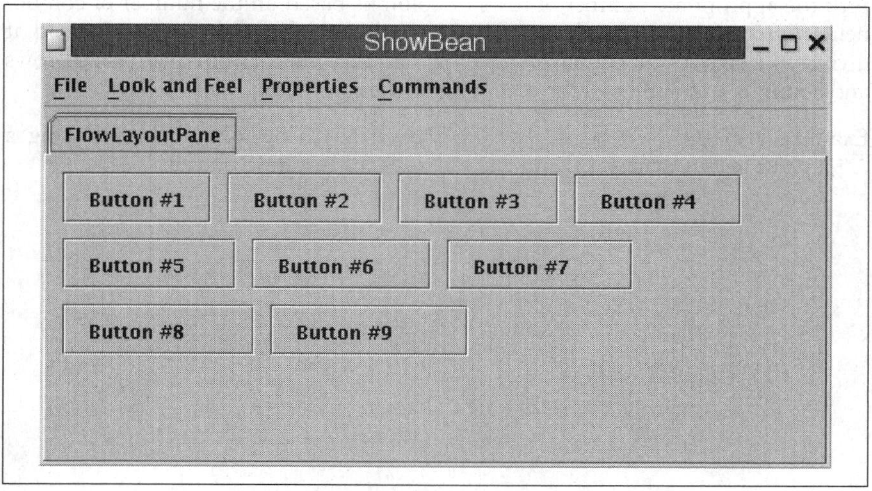

Figure 11-3. Components laid out with a FlowLayout

Example 11-2. FlowLayoutPane.java

```java
package je3.gui;
import java.awt.*;
import javax.swing.*;

public class FlowLayoutPane extends JPanel {
    public FlowLayoutPane( ) {
        // Use a FlowLayout layout manager.  Left justify rows.
        // Leave 10 pixels of horizontal and vertical space between components.
        this.setLayout(new FlowLayout(FlowLayout.LEFT, 10, 10));

        // Add some buttons to demonstrate the layout.
        String spaces = "";  // Used to make the buttons different
        for(int i = 1; i <= 9; i++) {
            this.add(new JButton("Button #" + i + spaces));
            spaces += " ";
        }

        // Give ourselves a default size
        this.setPreferredSize(new Dimension(500, 200));
    }
}
```

GridLayout

GridLayout is a heavy-handed layout manager that arranges components left to right and top to bottom in an evenly spaced grid of specified dimensions. When you create a GridLayout, you can specify the number of rows and columns in the grid, as well as the horizontal and vertical space the GridLayout should leave between the components. Typically, you specify only the desired number of rows or columns, leaving the other dimension set to 0. This allows the GridLayout to pick the appropriate number of rows or columns based on the number of components. GridLayout does not honor the preferred sizes of its components. Instead, it divides the size of the container into the specified number of equally sized rows and columns and makes all the components the same size.

Example 11-3 shows a short program that arranges buttons in a grid using a GridLayout layout manager. Figure 11-4 shows the resulting output.

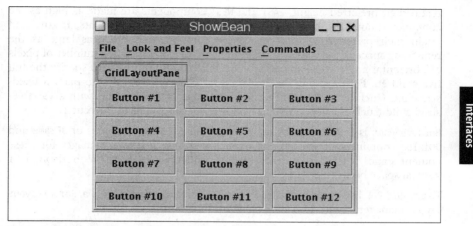

Figure 11-4. Components laid out with a GridLayout

Example 11-3. GridLayoutPane.java

```java
package je3.gui;
import java.awt.*;
import javax.swing.*;

public class GridLayoutPane extends JPanel {
  public GridLayoutPane() {
    // Lay out components into a grid three columns wide, with the number
    // of rows depending on the number of components.  Leave 10 pixels
    // of horizontal and vertical space between components
    this.setLayout(new GridLayout(0, 3, 10, 10));
    // Add some components
    for(int i = 1; i <= 12; i++) this.add(new JButton("Button #" + i));
  }
}
```

BorderLayout

The BorderLayout layout manager arranges up to five components within a container. Four of the components are laid out against specific edges of the container, and one is placed in the center. When you add a component to a container that is managed by BorderLayout, you must specify where you want the component placed. You do this with the two-argument version of add( ), passing one of the constants NORTH, EAST, SOUTH, WEST, or CENTER defined by BorderLayout as the second argument. These constants are called *layout constraints*; you use them with code like the following:

```java
this.add(b, BorderLayout.SOUTH);
```

Remember that BorderLayout can lay out only one component in each of these positions.

BorderLayout does not honor the preferred sizes of the components it manages. Components specified as NORTH or SOUTH are made as wide as the container and retain their preferred height. EAST and WEST components are made as high as the container (minus the heights of the top and bottom components, if any) and retain their preferred width. The CENTER component is made as large as the remaining space in the center of the container, after the specified number of pixels of horizontal and vertical space are allocated. You do not have to specify the full five children. For example, the BorderLayout class is often used to place a fixed-size child (such as a JToolBar) against one edge of a container, with a variable-sized child (such as a JTextArea) in whatever space remains in the center.

BorderLayout is the default layout manager for the content panes of JFrame and JDialog containers. If you do not explicitly specify a layout manager for these content panes, they use a BorderLayout configured to leave no horizontal or vertical space between components.

Example 11-4 lists a program that arranges five buttons using a BorderLayout layout manager; Figure 11-5 shows the resulting output.

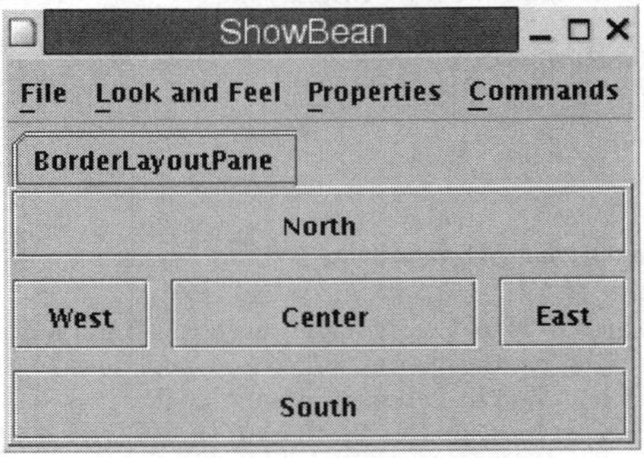

Figure 11-5. Components laid out with a BorderLayout

Example 11-4. BorderLayoutPane.java

```java
package je3.gui;
import java.awt.*;
import javax.swing.*;

public class BorderLayoutPane extends JPanel {
    String[ ] borders = {
        BorderLayout.NORTH, BorderLayout.EAST, BorderLayout.SOUTH,
        BorderLayout.WEST, BorderLayout.CENTER
    };
    public BorderLayoutPane( ) {
        // Use a BorderLayout with 10-pixel margins between components
        this.setLayout(new BorderLayout(10, 10));
        for(int i = 0; i < 5; i++) {          // Add children to the pane
            this.add(new JButton(borders[i]),   // Add this component
                    borders[i]);                // Using this constraint
        }
    }
}
```

Box and BoxLayout

javax.swing.BoxLayout is a simple but versatile layout manager that arranges its children into a row or a column. The javax.swing.Box container uses BoxLayout; it is much more common to work with the Box class than to use BoxLayout directly. What gives Box containers their versatility is the ability to add stretchy space (*glue*) and rigid space (*struts*) to the layout. The Box class defines static methods that make it particularly easy to create rows, columns, glue, and struts.

Example 11-5 creates several Box containers that demonstrate the capabilities of BoxLayout. The various boxes are themselves laid out using a BorderLayout. The program output is shown in Figure 11-6. To keep you on your toes, Example 11-5 also demonstrates the use of Swing borders to add margins and decorations around the outside of certain containers. Note that these borders can be added around any Swing component or container; they are part of the javax.swing. border package and have nothing to do with the BorderLayout layout manager. See javax.swing.border.Border and the setBorder( ) method of JComponent.

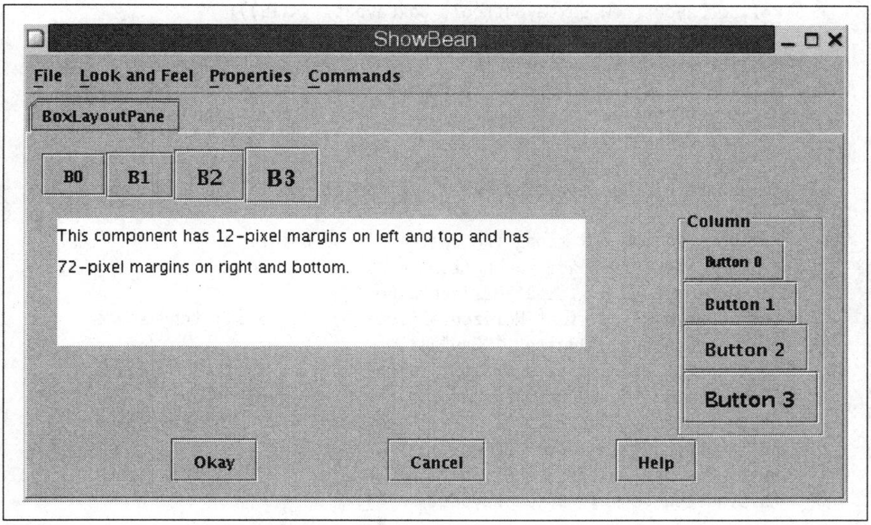

Figure 11-6. Components laid out with a BoxLayout

Example 11-5. BoxLayoutPane.java

```
package je3.gui;
import java.awt.*;
import javax.swing.*;
import javax.swing.border.*;

public class BoxLayoutPane extends JPanel {
    public BoxLayoutPane( ) {
        // Use a BorderLayout layout manager to arrange various Box components
        this.setLayout(new BorderLayout( ));
```

Example 11-5. BoxLayoutPane.java (continued)

```java
        // Give the entire panel a margin by adding an empty border
        // We could also do this by overriding getInsets()
        this.setBorder(new EmptyBorder(10,10,10,10));

        // Add a plain row of buttons along the top of the pane
        Box row = Box.createHorizontalBox();
        for(int i = 0; i < 4; i++) {
            JButton b = new JButton("B" + i);
            b.setFont(new Font("serif", Font.BOLD, 12+i*2));
            row.add(b);
        }
        this.add(row, BorderLayout.NORTH);

        // Add a plain column of buttons along the right edge
        // Use BoxLayout with a different kind of Swing container
        // Give the column a border: can't do this with the Box class
        JPanel col = new JPanel();
        col.setLayout(new BoxLayout(col, BoxLayout.Y_AXIS));
        col.setBorder(new TitledBorder(new EtchedBorder(), "Column"));
        for(int i = 0; i < 4; i++) {
            JButton b = new JButton("Button " + i);
            b.setFont(new Font("sanserif", Font.BOLD, 10+i*2));
            col.add(b);
        }
        this.add(col, BorderLayout.EAST); // Add column to right of panel

        // Add a button box along the bottom of the panel.
        // Use "Glue" to space the buttons evenly
        Box buttonbox = Box.createHorizontalBox();
        buttonbox.add(Box.createHorizontalGlue());      // stretchy space
        buttonbox.add(new JButton("Okay"));
        buttonbox.add(Box.createHorizontalGlue());      // stretchy space
        buttonbox.add(new JButton("Cancel"));
        buttonbox.add(Box.createHorizontalGlue());      // stretchy space
        buttonbox.add(new JButton("Help"));
        buttonbox.add(Box.createHorizontalGlue());      // stretchy space
        this.add(buttonbox, BorderLayout.SOUTH);

        // Create a component to display in the center of the panel
        JTextArea textarea = new JTextArea();
        textarea.setText("This component has 12-pixel margins on left and top"+
                    " and has 72-pixel margins on right and bottom.");
        textarea.setLineWrap(true);
        textarea.setWrapStyleWord(true);

        // Use Box objects to give the JTextArea an unusual spacing
        // First, create a column with 3 kids.  The first and last kids
        // are rigid spaces.  The middle kid is the text area
        Box fixedcol = Box.createVerticalBox();
        fixedcol.add(Box.createVerticalStrut(12));  // 12 rigid pixels
        fixedcol.add(textarea);                  // Component fills in the rest
        fixedcol.add(Box.createVerticalStrut(72));  // 72 rigid pixels
```

Example 11-5. BoxLayoutPane.java (continued)

```
        // Now create a row.  Give it rigid spaces on the left and right,
        // and put the column from above in the middle.
        Box fixedrow = Box.createHorizontalBox( );
        fixedrow.add(Box.createHorizontalStrut(12));
        fixedrow.add(fixedcol);
        fixedrow.add(Box.createHorizontalStrut(72));

        // Now add the JTextArea in the column in the row to the panel
        this.add(fixedrow, BorderLayout.CENTER);
    }
}
```

GridBagLayout

GridBagLayout is the most flexible and powerful of the AWT layout managers but is also the most complicated, and sometimes the most frustrating. It arranges components according to a number of constraints, which are stored in a GridBagConstraints object. BorderLayout is also a constraint-based layout manager, but in that case, the constraint is a simple constant, like BorderLayout. CENTER. GridBagLayout is more complex: it uses a GridBagConstraints object to hold a variety of constraints for each component you add to the container. As with BorderLayout, you pass the GridBagConstraints constraint object as the second argument to the add( ) method of the container, along with the component to be added.

The basic GridBagLayout layout policy is to arrange components at specified positions in a grid. The grid may be of arbitrary size, and the rows and columns of the grid may be of arbitrary heights and widths. A component laid out in this grid may occupy more than one row or column. The gridx and gridy fields of GridBagConstraints specify the position of the component in the grid, and the gridwidth and gridheight fields specify the number of columns and rows, respectively, that the component occupies in the grid. The insets field specifies the margins that should be left around each individual component, while fill specifies whether and how a component should grow when there is more space available for it than it needs for its default size. The anchor field specifies how a component should be positioned when there is more space available than it uses. GridBagConstraints defines a number of constants that are legal values for these last two fields. Finally, weightx and weighty specify how extra horizontal and vertical space should be distributed among the components when the container is resized. Consult reference material on GridBagConstraints for more details.

Example 11-6 shows a short program that uses a GridBagLayout layout manager to produce the layout pictured in Figure 11-7. Note that the program reuses a single GridBagConstraints object, which is perfectly legal.

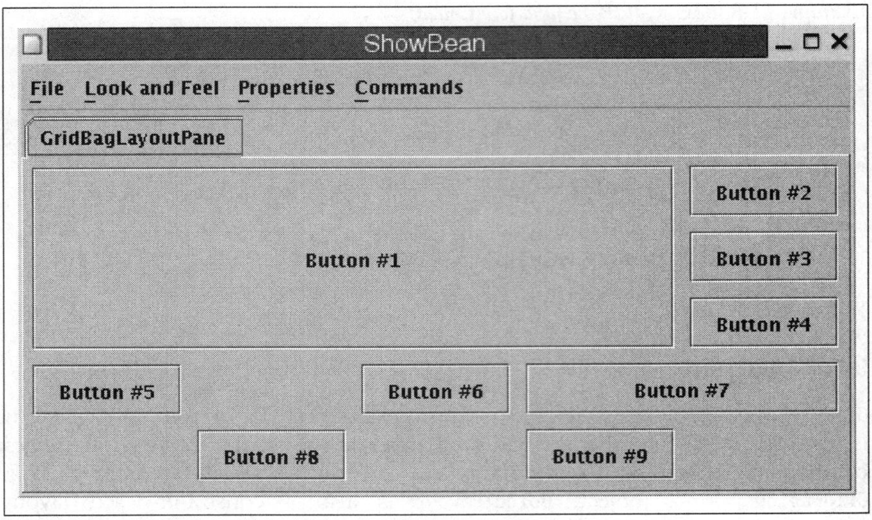

Figure 11-7. Components laid out with a GridBagLayout

Example 11-6. GridBagLayoutPane.java

```java
package je3.gui;
import java.awt.*;
import javax.swing.*;

public class GridBagLayoutPane extends JPanel {
    public GridBagLayoutPane() {
        // Create and specify a layout manager
        this.setLayout(new GridBagLayout());

        // Create a constraints object, and specify some default values
        GridBagConstraints c = new GridBagConstraints();
        c.fill = GridBagConstraints.BOTH; // components grow in both dimensions
        c.insets = new Insets(5,5,5,5);    // 5-pixel margins on all sides

        // Create and add a bunch of buttons, specifying different grid
        // position and size for each.
        // Give the first button a resize weight of 1.0 and all others
        // a weight of 0.0.  The first button will get all extra space.
        c.gridx = 0; c.gridy = 0; c.gridwidth = 4; c.gridheight=4;
        c.weightx = c.weighty = 1.0;
        this.add(new JButton("Button #1"), c);

        c.gridx = 4; c.gridy = 0; c.gridwidth = 1; c.gridheight=1;
        c.weightx = c.weighty = 0.0;
        this.add(new JButton("Button #2"), c);

        c.gridx = 4; c.gridy = 1; c.gridwidth = 1; c.gridheight=1;
        this.add(new JButton("Button #3"), c);
```

Example 11-6. GridBagLayoutPane.java (continued)

```
    c.gridx = 4; c.gridy = 2; c.gridwidth = 1; c.gridheight=2;
    this.add(new JButton("Button #4"), c);

    c.gridx = 0; c.gridy = 4; c.gridwidth = 1; c.gridheight=1;
    this.add(new JButton("Button #5"), c);

    c.gridx = 2; c.gridy = 4; c.gridwidth = 1; c.gridheight=1;
    this.add(new JButton("Button #6"), c);

    c.gridx = 3; c.gridy = 4; c.gridwidth = 2; c.gridheight=1;
    this.add(new JButton("Button #7"), c);

    c.gridx = 1; c.gridy = 5; c.gridwidth = 1; c.gridheight=1;
    this.add(new JButton("Button #8"), c);

    c.gridx = 3; c.gridy = 5; c.gridwidth = 1; c.gridheight=1;
    this.add(new JButton("Button #9"), c);
    }
}
```

Hardcoded Layout

All AWT and Swing containers have a default layout manager. If you set this manager to null, however, you can arrange components within a container however you like. You do this by calling the setBounds( ) method of each component. Note that this technique does not work if any layout manager is specified because the layout manager resizes and repositions all the components in a container.

Before using this technique, you should understand that there are a number of good reasons not to hardcode component sizes and positions. First, since components can have a platform-dependent look-and-feel, they may have different sizes on different platforms. Similarly, fonts differ somewhat from platform to platform, and this can affect the sizes of components. And finally, hardcoding component sizes and positions doesn't allow for customization (using the user's preferred font, for example) or internationalization (translating text in your GUI into other languages).

Nevertheless, there may be times when layout management becomes frustrating enough that you resort to hardcoded component sizes and positions. Example 11-7 is a simple program that does this; the layout it produces is shown in Figure 11-8. Note that this example overrides the getPreferredSize( ) method to report the preferred size of the container. This functionality is usually provided by the layout manager, but in the absence of a manager, you must determine the preferred size of the container yourself. Since a Swing container is being used, overriding getPreferredSize( ) isn't strictly necessary; try calling setPreferredSize( ) instead.

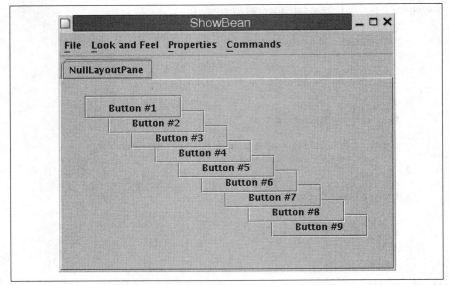

Figure 11-8. Hardcoded component positions

Example 11-7. NullLayoutPane.java

```java
package je3.gui;
import java.awt.*;
import javax.swing.*;

public class NullLayoutPane extends JPanel {
    public NullLayoutPane( ) {
        // Get rid of the default layout manager.
        // We'll arrange the components ourselves.
        this.setLayout(null);

        // Create some buttons and set their sizes and positions explicitly
        for(int i = 1; i <= 9; i++) {
            JButton b = new JButton("Button #" + i);
            b.setBounds(i*30, i*20, 125, 30); // use reshape( ) in Java 1.0
            this.add(b);
        }
    }

    // Specify how big the panel should be.
    public Dimension getPreferredSize( ) { return new Dimension(425, 250); }
}
```

Creating Custom Layout Managers

When none of the predefined AWT layout managers is appropriate for the GUI you want to implement, you have the option of writing your own custom layout manager by implementing LayoutManager or LayoutManager2. This is actually easier to do that it might seem. The primary method of interest is layoutContainer( ), which the container calls when it wants the components it contains to be laid out. This method should loop through the components contained in that container and set the size and position of each one, using setBounds( ). layoutContainer( ) can call preferredSize( ) on each component to determine the size it would like to be.

The other important method is preferredLayoutSize( ). This method should return the preferred size of the container. Typically this is the size required to arrange all the components at their preferred sizes. The minimumLayoutSize( ) method is similar, in that it should return the minimum allowable size for the container. Finally, if your layout manager is interested in constraints specified when the add( ) method is called to add a component to a container, it can define the addLayoutComponent( ) method.

Example 11-8 shows a listing of *ColumnLayout.java*, an implementation of the LayoutManager2 interface that arranges components in a column. ColumnLayout differs from BoxLayout in that it allows a horizontal alignment to be specified for the components in the column. Example 11-9 is a simple program that uses ColumnLayout to produce the output shown in Figure 11-9.

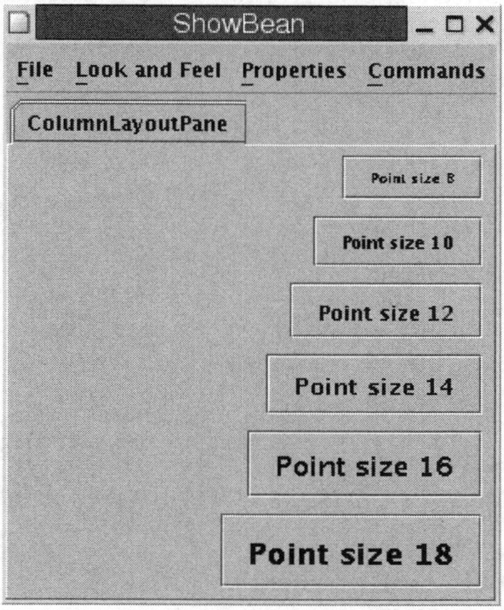

Figure 11-9. Component laid out with a custom layout manager

Example 11-8. ColumnLayout.java

```
package je3.gui;
import java.awt.*;

/**
 * This LayoutManager arranges the components into a column.
 * Components are always given their preferred size.
 *
```

Example 11-8. ColumnLayout.java (continued)

```
 * When you create a ColumnLayout, you may specify four values:
 *    margin_height -- how much space to leave on top and bottom
 *    margin_width -- how much space to leave on left and right
 *    spacing -- how much vertical space to leave between items
 *    alignment -- the horizontal position of the components:
 *       ColumnLayout.LEFT -- left-justify the components
 *       ColumnLayout.CENTER -- horizontally center the components
 *       ColumnLayout.RIGHT -- right-justify the components
 *
 * You never call the methods of a ColumnLayout object.  Just create one
 * and make it the layout manager for your container by passing it to
 * the addLayout( ) method of the Container object.
 */
public class ColumnLayout implements LayoutManager2 {
    protected int margin_height;
    protected int margin_width;
    protected int spacing;
    protected int alignment;

    // Constants for the alignment argument to the constructor.
    public static final int LEFT = 0;
    public static final int CENTER = 1;
    public static final int RIGHT = 2;

    /** The constructor.  See comment above for meanings of these arguments */
    public ColumnLayout(int margin_height, int margin_width,
                        int spacing, int alignment)  {
        this.margin_height = margin_height;
        this.margin_width = margin_width;
        this.spacing = spacing;
        this.alignment = alignment;
    }

    /**
     * A default constructor that creates a ColumnLayout using 5-pixel
     * margin width and height, 5-pixel spacing, and left alignment
     **/
    public ColumnLayout( ) { this(5, 5, 5, LEFT); }

    /**
     * The method that actually performs the layout.
     * Called by the Container
     **/
    public void layoutContainer(Container parent) {
        Insets insets = parent.getInsets( );
        Dimension parent_size = parent.getSize( );
        Component kid;
        int nkids = parent.getComponentCount( );
        int x0 = insets.left + margin_width;   // The base X position
        int x;
        int y = insets.top + margin_height;    // Start at the top of the column
```

Example 11-8. ColumnLayout.java (continued)

```
    for(int i = 0; i < nkids; i++) {      // Loop through the kids
        kid = parent.getComponent(i);     // Get the kid
        if (!kid.isVisible()) continue;   // Skip hidden ones
        Dimension pref = kid.getPreferredSize();  // How big is it?
        switch(alignment) {               // Compute X coordinate
        default:
        case LEFT:   x = x0; break;
        case CENTER: x = (parent_size.width - pref.width)/2; break;
        case RIGHT:
            x = parent_size.width-insets.right-margin_width-pref.width;
            break;
        }
        // Set the size and position of this kid
        kid.setBounds(x, y, pref.width, pref.height);
        y += pref.height + spacing;       // Get Y position of the next one
    }
}

/** The Container calls this to find out how big the layout should be */
public Dimension preferredLayoutSize(Container parent) {
    return layoutSize(parent, 1);
}
/** The Container calls this to find out how big the layout must be */
public Dimension minimumLayoutSize(Container parent) {
    return layoutSize(parent, 2);
}
/** The Container calls this to find out how big the layout can be */
public Dimension maximumLayoutSize(Container parent) {
    return layoutSize(parent, 3);
}

// Compute min, max, or preferred size of all the visible children
protected Dimension layoutSize(Container parent, int sizetype) {
    int nkids = parent.getComponentCount();
    Dimension size = new Dimension(0,0);
    Insets insets = parent.getInsets();
    int num_visible_kids = 0;

    // Compute maximum width and total height of all visible kids
    for(int i = 0; i < nkids; i++) {
        Component kid = parent.getComponent(i);
        Dimension d;
        if (!kid.isVisible()) continue;
        num_visible_kids++;
        if (sizetype == 1) d = kid.getPreferredSize();
        else if (sizetype == 2) d = kid.getMinimumSize();
        else d = kid.getMaximumSize();
        if (d.width > size.width) size.width = d.width;
        size.height += d.height;
    }
```

Example 11-8. ColumnLayout.java (continued)

```
        // Now add in margins and stuff
        size.width += insets.left + insets.right + 2*margin_width;
        size.height += insets.top + insets.bottom + 2*margin_height;
        if (num_visible_kids > 1)
            size.height += (num_visible_kids - 1) * spacing;
        return size;
    }

    // Other LayoutManager(2) methods that are unused by this class
    public void addLayoutComponent(String constraint, Component comp) { }
    public void addLayoutComponent(Component comp, Object constraint) { }
    public void removeLayoutComponent(Component comp) { }
    public void invalidateLayout(Container parent) { }
    public float getLayoutAlignmentX(Container parent) { return 0.5f; }
    public float getLayoutAlignmentY(Container parent) { return 0.5f; }
}
```

Example 11-9. ColumnLayoutPane.java

```
package je3.gui;
import java.awt.*;
import javax.swing.*;

public class ColumnLayoutPane extends JPanel {
    public ColumnLayoutPane( ) {
        // Specify a ColumnLayout LayoutManager, with right alignment
        this.setLayout(new ColumnLayout(5, 5, 10, ColumnLayout.RIGHT));

        // Create some buttons and set their sizes and positions explicitly
        for(int i = 0; i < 6; i++) {
            int pointsize = 8 + i*2;
            JButton b = new JButton("Point size " + pointsize);
            b.setFont(new Font("helvetica", Font.BOLD, pointsize));
            this.add(b);
        }
    }
}
```

Event Handling

In the previous section on layout management, there were a number of examples
that arranged JButton components in interesting ways. If you ran the examples,
however, you probably noticed that nothing interesting happened when you
clicked on the buttons. The fourth step in creating a GUI is hooking up the event
handling that makes components respond to user input. As of Java 1.1 and later,
AWT and Swing components use the event-handling API defined by the Java-
Beans component model. Prior to Java 1.1, the AWT used a different API that is
not covered in this chapter. We'll see some examples of event handling using the
old model when we study applets (see Chapter 16), where this model is still sometimes used for backward compatibility with old web browsers.

In Java 1.1 and later, the event-handling API is based on events and event listeners. Like everything else in Java, events are objects. An event object is an instance of a class that extends java.util.EventObject. The java.awt.event package defines a number of event classes commonly used by AWT and Swing components. The javax.swing.event package defines additional events used by Swing components, but not by AWT components. And the java.beans package defines a couple of JavaBeans event classes also used by Swing components. Event classes usually define methods (or fields) that provide details about the event that occurred. For example, the java.awt.event.MouseEvent class defines a getX() method that returns the X coordinate of the location of the mouse when the event occurred.

An EventListener is an object that is interested in being notified when an event of a particular type occurs. An object that generates events (an *event source*, such as a JButton component) maintains a list of listeners and provides methods that allow listeners to be added to or removed from this list. When an event of the appropriate type occurs, the event source notifies all registered event listeners. To notify the listeners, it first creates an event object that describes the event and then passes that event object to a method defined by the event listeners. The particular method that is invoked depends on the type of event; different event listener types define different methods.

All event listener types are interfaces that extend the java.util.EventListener interface. This is a marker interface; it does not define any methods of its own, but exists so that you can use the instanceof operator to distinguish event listeners from other object types. The java.awt.event, javax.swing.event, and java.beans packages define a number of event listener interfaces that extend the generic EventListener interface. Each listener is specific to a particular type of event and defines one or more methods that are invoked in particular circumstances (e.g., java.awt.MouseListener). The only special feature of an event listener method is that it always takes an event object as its single argument.

Note that the java.awt.event and javax.swing.event packages define only event listener *interfaces*, not event listener *classes*. A GUI must define its own custom implementation of an event listener, as it is this implementation that provides the actual Java code executed in response to an event. These packages do define some Java classes, however: event adapter classes. An *event adapter* is an implementation of an event listener interface that consists entirely of empty methods. Many listener interfaces define multiple methods, but often you are interested in using only one of these methods at a time. In this case, it is easier to subclass an adapter, overriding only the method you are interested in, instead of implementing the interface directly and having to define all its methods.

Every AWT and Swing application has an automatically created thread, called the *event dispatch thread*, that invokes the methods of event listeners. When an application starts, the main thread builds the GUI, and then it often exits. From then on, everything that happens takes place in the event dispatch thread, in response to the invocation of event listener methods. Note that AWT and Swing components are not thread-safe, for performance reasons. Thus, if you are writing a multithreaded program, you must be careful to call component methods only from the event dispatch thread. Calling component methods from other threads may cause intermittent and difficult-to-diagnose bugs. If you need to perform some kind of animation or repetitive task with Swing, use a `javax.swing.Timer` instead of using a separate thread. If another thread really needs to interact with a Swing component, use the `java.awt.EventQueue invokeLater( )` and `invokeAndWait( )` methods.

Chapter 2 of *Java Foundation Classes in a Nutshell* describes the event-handling API in more detail and also contains tables that list the various types of AWT and Swing event listeners, their methods, and the components that use those listener interfaces. The following sections contain some simple examples that illustrate different ways of using the Java event-handling API, as well as a more robust example that demonstrates an API for handling certain types of input events using a lower-level API.

Handling Mouse Events

Example 11-10 is a listing of *ScribblePane1.java*, a simple `JPanel` subclass that implements the `MouseListener` and a `MouseMotionListener` interfaces in order to receive mouse-click and mouse-drag events. It responds to these events by drawing lines, allowing the user to "scribble" in the pane. Figure 11-10 shows the `ScribblePane1` example (and a sample scribble) running within the `ShowBean` program developed in this chapter.

Figure 11-10. A scribble in ScribblePane1

Note that the `ScribblePane1` class is both the source of mouse events (they are generated by the `java.awt.Component` superclass) and the event listener. This can be seen most clearly in the constructor method where the component passes itself to its own `addMouseListener( )` and `addMouseMotionListener( )` methods. The `mouseDragged( )` method is the key to scribbling: it uses the `drawLine( )` method of the `Graphics` object to draw a line from the previous mouse position to the current mouse position.

ScribblePane1 does not save the coordinates of the mouse events, and therefore cannot redraw the scribble (after it is obscured by one of the ShowPane menus, for example). ScribblePane1 demonstrates event handling, but it is not a good example of a custom component because it does not implement a paintComponent( ) method to redraw the component as needed. Examples 11-11 and 11-12 also contain this flaw, which is finally remedied in Example 11-13.

Example 11-10. ScribblePane1.java

```java
package je3.gui;
import javax.swing.*;      // For JPanel component
import java.awt.*;         // For Graphics object
import java.awt.event.*;   // For Event and Listener objects

/**
 * A simple JPanel subclass that uses event listeners to allow the user
 * to scribble with the mouse.  Note that scribbles are not saved or redrawn.
 **/
public class ScribblePane1 extends JPanel
    implements MouseListener, MouseMotionListener {
    protected int last_x, last_y;  // Previous mouse coordinates

    public ScribblePane1( ) {
        // This component registers itself as an event listener for
        // mouse events and mouse motion events.
        this.addMouseListener(this);
        this.addMouseMotionListener(this);

        // Give the component a preferred size
        setPreferredSize(new Dimension(450,200));
    }

    // A method from the MouseListener interface.  Invoked when the
    // user presses a mouse button.
    public void mousePressed(MouseEvent e) {
        last_x = e.getX( );  // remember the coordinates of the click
        last_y = e.getY( );
    }

    // A method from the MouseMotionListener interface.  Invoked when the
    // user drags the mouse with a button pressed.
    public void mouseDragged(MouseEvent e) {
        int x = e.getX( );    // Get the current mouse position
        int y = e.getY( );
        // Draw a line from the saved coordinates to the current position
        this.getGraphics( ).drawLine(last_x, last_y, x, y);
        last_x = x;           // Remember the current position
        last_y = y;
    }

    // The other, unused methods of the MouseListener interface.
    public void mouseReleased(MouseEvent e) { }
```

Example 11-10. ScribblePane1.java (continued)

```
    public void mouseClicked(MouseEvent e) { }
    public void mouseEntered(MouseEvent e) { }
    public void mouseExited(MouseEvent e) { }

    // The other, unused, method of the MouseMotionListener interface.
    public void mouseMoved(MouseEvent e) { }
}
```

More Mouse Events

Example 11-11 shows a listing of *ScribblePane2.java,* which is much like
ScribblePane1 except that it uses anonymous inner classes to define its event
listeners. This is a common GUI programming idiom in Java, and, in fact, it was
one of the motivating factors for adding anonymous inner classes to the language.
Note that the inner classes subclass event adapter classes, rather than implement
the event listeners directly; this means that unused methods don't have to be
implemented.

ScribblePane2 also includes a KeyListener that clears the scribble when the user
types the C key, and defines a color property (with setColor( ) and getColor( ) as
its property accessor methods) that specifies the color in which to scribble. Recall
that the ShowBean program allows you to specify property values. It understands
colors specified using hexadecimal RGB notation, so to use this example to
scribble with blue lines, you can use a command like this:

```
    % java je3.gui.ShowBean \
      je3.gui.ScribblePane2 color=#0000ff
```

A final point to note about this example is that the scribbling functionality has
been cleaned up and placed into moveto( ), lineto( ), and clear( ) methods. This
allows the methods to be invoked by other components and allows the component to be subclassed more cleanly. You can invoke the clear( ) method from the
Commands menu of ShowBean.

Example 11-11. ScribblePane2.java

```
package je3.gui;
import javax.swing.*;        // For JPanel component
import java.awt.*;           // For Graphics object
import java.awt.event.*;     // For Event and Listener objects

/**
 * A simple JPanel subclass that uses event listeners to allow the user
 * to scribble with the mouse.  Note that scribbles are not saved or redrawn.
 **/
public class ScribblePane2 extends JPanel {
    public ScribblePane2( ) {
        // Give the component a preferred size
        setPreferredSize(new Dimension(450,200));

        // Register a mouse event handler defined as an inner class
        // Note the call to requestFocus( ).  This is required in order for
```

Example 11-11. ScribblePane2.java (continued)

```
        // the component to receive key events.
        addMouseListener(new MouseAdapter() {
                public void mousePressed(MouseEvent e) {
                    moveto(e.getX(), e.getY());  // Move to click position
                    requestFocus();              // Take keyboard focus
                }
        });

        // Register a mouse motion event handler defined as an inner class.
        // By subclassing MouseMotionAdapter rather than implementing
        // MouseMotionListener, we only override the method we're interested
        // in and inherit default (empty) implementations of the other methods.
        addMouseMotionListener(new MouseMotionAdapter() {
                public void mouseDragged(MouseEvent e) {
                    lineto(e.getX(), e.getY());  // Draw to mouse position
                }
        });

        // Add a keyboard event handler to clear the screen on key 'C'
        addKeyListener(new KeyAdapter() {
                public void keyPressed(KeyEvent e) {
                    if (e.getKeyCode() == KeyEvent.VK_C) clear();
                }
        });
    }

    /** These are the coordinates of the the previous mouse position */
    protected int last_x, last_y;

    /** Remember the specified point */
    public void moveto(int x, int y) {
        last_x = x;
        last_y = y;
    }

    /** Draw from the last point to this point, then remember new point */
    public void lineto(int x, int y) {
        Graphics g = getGraphics();             // Get the object to draw with
        g.setColor(color);                      // Tell it what color to use
        g.drawLine(last_x, last_y, x, y);       // Tell it what to draw
        moveto(x, y);                           // Save the current point
    }

    /**
     * Clear the drawing area, using the component background color.  This
     * method works by requesting that the component be redrawn.  Since this
     * component does not have a paintComponent() method, nothing will be
     * drawn.  However, other parts of the component, such as borders or
     * subcomponents, will be drawn correctly.
     **/
    public void clear() { repaint(); }
```

Example 11-11. ScribblePane2.java (continued)

```
/** This field holds the current drawing color property */
Color color = Color.black;
/** This is the property "setter" method for the color property */
public void setColor(Color color) { this.color = color; }
/** This is the property "getter" method for the color property */
public Color getColor() { return color; }
```

}

Handling Component Events

The two previous examples have shown how to handle mouse and keyboard events. These are low-level input events generated by the system and reported to event listeners by code in the java.awt.Component class. Usually, when you are building a GUI, you do not handle these low-level events yourself; instead, you use predefined components to interpret the raw input events and generate higher-level semantic events. For example, when the JButton component detects a low-level mouse click and mouse release, it generates a higher-level java.awt.event. ActionEvent to notify any interested listeners that the user clicked on the button to activate it. Similarly, the JList component generates a javax.swing.event. ListSelectionEvent when the user makes a selection from the list.

Example 11-12 is a listing of *ScribblePane3.java*. This example extends ScribblePane2 and adds a JButton and a JList to its user interface. The user can clear the screen by clicking on the button and change the drawing color by selecting from the list. You can see these new components in Figure 11-11 (which also demonstrates that the lack of a proper paintComponent() method allows ScribblePane3 to scribble on top of its children). The example demonstrates implementing the ActionListener and ListSelectionListener interfaces to respond to the high-level events generated by these Swing components.

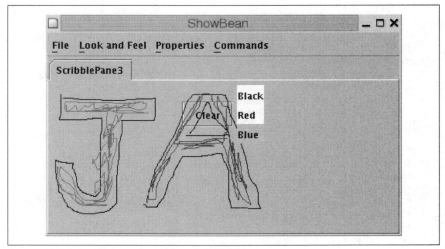

Figure 11-11. Swing components in ScribblePane3

Example 11-12. ScribblePane3.java

```java
package je3.gui;
import java.awt.*;           // For Graphics object and colors
import javax.swing.*;        // For JPanel component
import java.awt.event.*;     // For ActionListener interface
import javax.swing.event.*;  // For ListSelectionListener interface

/**
 * This scribble component includes a JButton to clear the screen, and
 * a JList that lets the user select a drawing color.  It uses
 * event listener objects to handle events from those subcomponents.
 **/
public class ScribblePane3 extends ScribblePane2 {
    // These are colors the user can choose from
    Color[] colors = new Color[] { Color.black, Color.red, Color.blue };
    // These are names for those colors
    String[] colorNames = new String[] { "Black", "Red", "Blue" };

    // Add JButton and JList components to the panel.
    public ScribblePane3() {
        // Implicit super() call here invokes the superclass constructor

        // Add a "Clear" button to the panel.
        // Handle button events with an action listener
        JButton clear = new JButton("Clear");
        clear.addActionListener(new ActionListener() {
                public void actionPerformed(ActionEvent e) { clear(); }
            });
        this.add(clear);

        // Add a JList to allow color choices.
        // Handle list selection events with a ListSelectionListener.
        final JList colorList = new JList(colorNames);
        colorList.addListSelectionListener(new ListSelectionListener() {
                public void valueChanged(ListSelectionEvent e) {
                    setColor(colors[colorList.getSelectedIndex()]);
                }
            });
        this.add(colorList);
    }
}
```

Low-Level Event Handling

As we just discussed, graphical user interfaces do not usually concern themselves with the details of low-level mouse and keyboard events. Instead, they use predefined components to interpret these events for them. By the same token, predefined components that handle frequent mouse and keyboard events do not usually use the high-level event listener API to handle these low-level events.

Example 11-13 shows a listing of *ScribblePane.java*, a final reimplementation of our scribble component. This version does not use event listeners at all, but instead overrides the processMouseEvent( ), and processMouseMotionEvent( ), methods defined by its java.awt.Component superclass.* Event objects are passed to these methods directly, without any requirement to register event listeners. What is required, however, is that the constructor call enableEvents( ) to specify the kinds of events in which it is interested. If the constructor does not do this, the system will not deliver events of those types, and the various event processing methods will never be invoked. Note that the event processing methods invoke the superclass' implementation for any events they do not handle themselves. This allows the superclass to dispatch these events to any listener objects that may have been registered.

This ScribblePane class also fixes the problem that afflicted the previous three versions: it remembers the user's scribble and implements a paintComponent( ) method to redraw that scribble when necessary. (An application never needs to invoke paintComponent( ): the AWT and Swing infrastructure invoke it as appropriate.) Another enhancement is that ScribblePane uses the Java2D API of Java 1.2 and later to draw wide lines. The lines are drawn using the color specified on the foreground property inherited from JComponent, and you can use ShowBean to experiment with this property.

Example 11-13. ScribblePane.java

```
package je3.gui;
import java.awt.*;
import java.awt.event.*;
import javax.swing.*;
import java.util.List;   // Disambiguate from java.awt.List
import java.util.ArrayList;
import je3.graphics.PolyLine;

/**
 * This custom component allows the user to scribble, and retains the scribbles
 * so that they can be redrawn when needed.  It uses the PolyLine custom Shape
 * implementation defined elsewhere in this book, and demonstrates event
 * handling with low-level event processing methods.
 */
public class ScribblePane extends JComponent {
    List lines;            // The PolyLines that comprise this scribble
    PolyLine currentLine;  // The PolyLine currently being drawn
    Stroke stroke;         // How to draw the lines

    public ScribblePane() {
        setPreferredSize(new Dimension(450,200)); // We need a default size
        lines = new ArrayList();                  // Initialize a list of lines
        stroke = new BasicStroke(3.0f);           // Lines are 3 pixels wide

        // Register interest in mouse button and mouse motion events, so
        // that processMouseEvent() and processMouseMotionEvent() will be
        // invoked, even if no event listeners are registered.
```

---

* This same technique can be used with the processKeyEvent( ), processFocusEvent( ), processComponentEvent( ), and processWindowEvent( ) methods of Component.

Example 11-13. ScribblePane.java (continued)

```
        enableEvents(AWTEvent.MOUSE_EVENT_MASK |
                     AWTEvent.MOUSE_MOTION_EVENT_MASK);
    }

    /** We override this method to draw ourselves. */
    public void paintComponent(Graphics g) {
        // Let the superclass do its painting first
        super.paintComponent(g);

        // Make a copy of the Graphics context so we can modify it
        // We cast it at the same time so we can use Java2D graphics
        Graphics2D g2 = (Graphics2D) (g.create());

        // Our superclass doesn't paint the background, so do this ourselves.
        g2.setColor(getBackground());
        g2.fillRect(0, 0, getWidth(), getHeight());

        // Set the line width and color to use for the foreground
        g2.setStroke(stroke);
        g2.setColor(this.getForeground());

        // Now loop through the PolyLine shapes and draw them all
        int numlines = lines.size();
        for(int i = 0; i < numlines; i++)
            g2.draw((PolyLine)lines.get(i));
    }

    /**
     * Erase all lines and repaint.  This method is for the convenience of
     * programs that use this component.
     */
    public void clear() {
        lines.clear();
        repaint();
    }

    /**
     * We override this method to receive notification of mouse button events.
     * See also the enableEvents() call in the constructor method.
     */
    public void processMouseEvent(MouseEvent e) {
        // If the type and button are correct, then process it.
        if (e.getButton() == MouseEvent.BUTTON1) {
            if (e.getID() == MouseEvent.MOUSE_PRESSED) {
                // Start a new line on mouse down
                currentLine = new PolyLine(e.getX(), e.getY());
                lines.add(currentLine);
                e.consume();
            }
            else if (e.getID() == MouseEvent.MOUSE_RELEASED) {
```

Example 11-13. ScribblePane.java (continued)

```
                // End the line on mouse up
                currentLine = null;
                e.consume( );
            }
        }

        // The superclass method dispatches to registered event listeners
        super.processMouseEvent(e);
    }

    /**
     * We override this method to receive notification of mouse motion events.
     */
    public void processMouseMotionEvent(MouseEvent e) {
        if (e.getID( ) == MouseEvent.MOUSE_DRAGGED &&  // If we're dragging
            currentLine != null) {                      // and a line exists
            currentLine.addSegment(e.getX( ), e.getY( ));  // Add a line segment
            e.consume( );

            // Redraw the whole component.
            // Exercise: optimize this by passing the bounding box
            // of the region that needs redrawing to the repaint( ) method.
            // Don't forget to take line width into account, however.
            repaint( );
        }

        super.processMouseMotionEvent(e);
    }
}
```

Custom Events and Event Listeners

Although Swing and the AWT define quite a few event classes and event listener interfaces, there is no reason you cannot define custom event and listener types of your own. The class shown in Example 11-14 does exactly that: it defines its own custom event and listener types using inner classes.

The Swing component set provides a number of ways to allow the user to select an item from a list of items. You can present such a choice with a JList component, a JComboBox component, or a group of cooperating JRadioButton components. The APIs for creating, manipulating, and responding to events with these components differ substantially. Example 11-14 is a listing of an ItemChooser class that abstracts away the differences between these three presentation types. When you create an ItemChooser component, you specify the name of the choice being presented, a list of items to be chosen among, the currently chosen item, and a presentation type. The presentation type determines how the choice is presented to the user, but the API you use to work with the ItemChooser component is independent of the presentation.

The ItemChooser class includes an inner class named Demo. ItemChooser.Demo has a main( ) method that demonstrates the ItemChooser component, as shown in

Figure 11-12. The demo program gets the choice labels from command-line arguments, so you can run it with a command like the following:

```
% java je3.gui.ItemChooser\$Demo Fourscore and twenty \
    years ago
```

Note that on Unix systems, you have to escape the $ in the inner class name with a backslash. On Windows systems, the backslash is not necessary. We'll see another use of ItemChooser in Example 11-17.

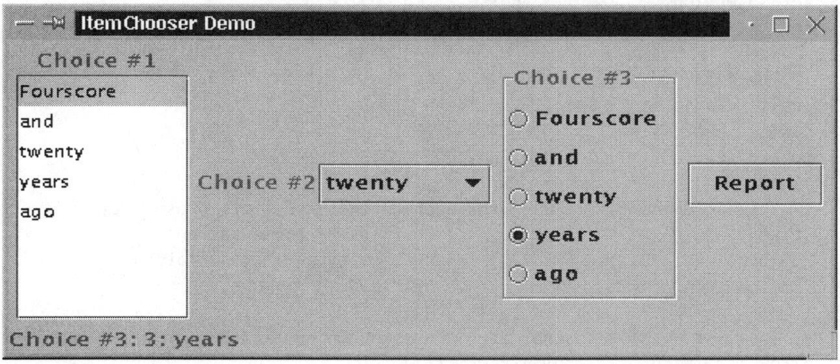

Figure 11-12. A demonstration of the ItemChooser component

The interesting thing about ItemChooser is that it defines its own event and event listener types as inner classes. You should pay attention to the definitions of these types and study how they are used within the ItemChooser Demo classes, as this example demonstrates both sides of the event architecture: event generation and event handling. This example shows you how to work with JList, JComboBox, and JRadioButton components; it is particularly interesting because it listens for and responds to the events generated by those internal components and translates those internal events into its own event type. Once you understand how ItemChooser works, you'll have a thorough understanding of the AWT and Swing event architecture.

Example 11-14. ItemChooser.java

```java
package je3.gui;
import java.awt.*;
import java.awt.event.*;
import javax.swing.*;
import javax.swing.event.*;
import javax.swing.border.*;
import java.util.*;

/**
 * This class is a Swing component that presents a choice to the user.  It
 * allows the choice to be presented in a JList, in a JComboBox, or with a
 * bordered group of JRadioButton components.  Additionally, it displays the
 * name of the choice with a JLabel.  It allows an arbitrary value to be
```

Example 11-14. ItemChooser.java (continued)

```java
 * associated with each possible choice.  Note that this component only allows
 * one item to be selected at a time.  Multiple selections are not supported.
 **/
public class ItemChooser extends JPanel {
    // These fields hold property values for this component
    String name;            // The overall name of the choice
    String[] labels;        // The text for each choice option
    Object[] values;        // Arbitrary values associated with each option
    int selection;          // The selected choice
    int presentation;       // How the choice is presented

    // These are the legal values for the presentation field
    public static final int LIST = 1;
    public static final int COMBOBOX = 2;
    public static final int RADIOBUTTONS = 3;

    // These components are used for each of the 3 possible presentations
    JList list;                       // One type of presentation
    JComboBox combobox;               // Another type of presentation
    JRadioButton[] radiobuttons;      // Yet another type

    // The list of objects that are interested in our state
    ArrayList listeners = new ArrayList();

    // The constructor method sets everything up
    public ItemChooser(String name, String[] labels, Object[] values,
                       int defaultSelection, int presentation)
    {
        // Copy the constructor arguments to instance fields
        this.name = name;
        this.labels = labels;
        this.values = values;
        this.selection = defaultSelection;
        this.presentation = presentation;

        // If no values were supplied, use the labels
        if (values == null) this.values = labels;

        // Now create content and event handlers based on presentation type
        switch(presentation) {
        case LIST: initList(); break;
        case COMBOBOX: initComboBox(); break;
        case RADIOBUTTONS: initRadioButtons(); break;
        }
    }

    // Initialization for JList presentation
    void initList() {
        list = new JList(labels);          // Create the list
        list.setSelectedIndex(selection);  // Set initial state
```

Example 11-14. ItemChooser.java (continued)

```java
        // Handle state changes
        list.addListSelectionListener(new ListSelectionListener( ) {
                public void valueChanged(ListSelectionEvent e) {
                    ItemChooser.this.select(list.getSelectedIndex( ));
                }
            });

        // Lay out list and name label vertically
        this.setLayout(new BoxLayout(this, BoxLayout.Y_AXIS)); // vertical
        this.add(new JLabel(name));         // Display choice name
        this.add(new JScrollPane(list));    // Add the JList
    }

    // Initialization for JComboBox presentation
    void initComboBox( ) {
        combobox = new JComboBox(labels);          // Create the combo box
        combobox.setSelectedIndex(selection);      // Set initial state

        // Handle changes to the state
        combobox.addItemListener(new ItemListener( ) {
                public void itemStateChanged(ItemEvent e) {
                    ItemChooser.this.select(combobox.getSelectedIndex( ));
                }
            });

        // Lay out combo box and name label horizontally
        this.setLayout(new BoxLayout(this, BoxLayout.X_AXIS));
        this.add(new JLabel(name));
        this.add(combobox);
    }

    // Initialization for JRadioButton presentation
    void initRadioButtons( ) {
        // Create an array of mutually exclusive radio buttons
        radiobuttons = new JRadioButton[labels.length];    // the array
        ButtonGroup radioButtonGroup = new ButtonGroup( ); // used for exclusion
        ChangeListener listener = new ChangeListener( ) {  // A shared listener
                public void stateChanged(ChangeEvent e) {
                    JRadioButton b = (JRadioButton)e.getSource( );
                    if (b.isSelected( )) {
                        // If we received this event because a button was
                        // selected, then loop through the list of buttons to
                        // figure out the index of the selected one.
                        for(int i = 0; i < radiobuttons.length; i++) {
                            if (radiobuttons[i] == b) {
                                ItemChooser.this.select(i);
                                return;
                            }
                        }
                    }
                }
            };
```

Example 11-14. ItemChooser.java (continued)

```java
        // Display the choice name in a border around the buttons
        this.setBorder(new TitledBorder(new EtchedBorder( ), name));
        this.setLayout(new BoxLayout(this, BoxLayout.Y_AXIS));

        // Create the buttons, add them to the button group, and specify
        // the event listener for each one.
        for(int i = 0; i < labels.length; i++) {
            radiobuttons[i] = new JRadioButton(labels[i]);
            if (i == selection) radiobuttons[i].setSelected(true);
            radiobuttons[i].addChangeListener(listener);
            radioButtonGroup.add(radiobuttons[i]);
            this.add(radiobuttons[i]);
        }
    }

    // These simple property accessor methods just return field values
    // These are read-only properties.  The values are set by the constructor
    // and may not be changed.
    public String getName( ) { return name; }
    public int getPresentation( ) { return presentation; }
    public String[ ] getLabels( ) { return labels; }
    public Object[ ] getValues( ) { return values; }

    /** Return the index of the selected item */
    public int getSelectedIndex( ) { return selection; }

    /** Return the object associated with the selected item */
    public Object getSelectedValue( ) { return values[selection]; }

    /**
     * Set the selected item by specifying its index.  Calling this
     * method changes the on-screen display but does not generate events.
     **/
    public void setSelectedIndex(int selection) {
        switch(presentation) {
        case LIST: list.setSelectedIndex(selection); break;
        case COMBOBOX: combobox.setSelectedIndex(selection); break;
        case RADIOBUTTONS: radiobuttons[selection].setSelected(true); break;
        }
        this.selection = selection;
    }

    /**
     * This internal method is called when the selection changes.  It stores
     * the new selected index, and fires events to any registered listeners.
     * The event listeners registered on the JList, JComboBox, or JRadioButtons
     * all call this method.
     **/
    protected void select(int selection) {
        this.selection = selection;  // Store the new selected index
        if (!listeners.isEmpty( )) {  // If there are any listeners registered
```

Example 11-14. ItemChooser.java (continued)

```
          // Create an event object to describe the selection
          ItemChooser.Event e =
              new ItemChooser.Event(this, selection, values[selection]);
          // Loop through the listeners using an Iterator
          for(Iterator i = listeners.iterator(); i.hasNext();) {
              ItemChooser.Listener l = (ItemChooser.Listener)i.next();
              l.itemChosen(e);  // Notify each listener of the selection
          }
      }
  }
}

// These methods are for event listener registration and deregistration
public void addItemChooserListener(ItemChooser.Listener l) {
    listeners.add(l);
}
public void removeItemChooserListener(ItemChooser.Listener l) {
    listeners.remove(l);
}

/**
 * This inner class defines the event type generated by ItemChooser objects
 * The inner class name is Event, so the full name is ItemChooser.Event
 **/
public static class Event extends java.util.EventObject {
    int selectedIndex;      // index of the selected item
    Object selectedValue;   // the value associated with it
    public Event(ItemChooser source,
                 int selectedIndex, Object selectedValue) {
        super(source);
        this.selectedIndex = selectedIndex;
        this.selectedValue = selectedValue;
    }

    public ItemChooser getItemChooser() { return (ItemChooser)getSource();}
    public int getSelectedIndex() { return selectedIndex; }
    public Object getSelectedValue() { return selectedValue; }
}

/**
 * This inner interface must be implemented by any object that wants to be
 * notified when the current selection in an ItemChooser component changes.
 **/
public interface Listener extends java.util.EventListener {
    public void itemChosen(ItemChooser.Event e);
}

/**
 * This inner class is a simple demonstration of the ItemChooser component
 * It uses command-line arguments as ItemChooser labels and values.
 **/
public static class Demo {
    public static void main(String[] args) {
```

Example 11-14. ItemChooser.java (continued)

```
// Create a window, arrange to handle close requests
final JFrame frame = new JFrame("ItemChooser Demo");
frame.addWindowListener(new WindowAdapter() {
        public void windowClosing(WindowEvent e) {System.exit(0);}
    });

// A "message line" to display results in
final JLabel msgline = new JLabel(" ");

// Create a panel holding three ItemChooser components
JPanel chooserPanel = new JPanel();
final ItemChooser c1 = new ItemChooser("Choice #1", args, null, 0,
                                        ItemChooser.LIST);
final ItemChooser c2 = new ItemChooser("Choice #2", args, null, 0,
                                        ItemChooser.COMBOBOX);
final ItemChooser c3 = new ItemChooser("Choice #3", args, null, 0,
                                        ItemChooser.RADIOBUTTONS);

// An event listener that displays changes on the message line
ItemChooser.Listener l = new ItemChooser.Listener() {
        public void itemChosen(ItemChooser.Event e) {
            msgline.setText(e.getItemChooser().getName() + ": " +
                            e.getSelectedIndex() + ": " +
                            e.getSelectedValue());
        }
    };
c1.addItemChooserListener(l);
c2.addItemChooserListener(l);
c3.addItemChooserListener(l);

// Instead of tracking every change with an ItemChooser.Listener,
// applications can also just query the current state when
// they need it.  Here's a button that does that.
JButton report = new JButton("Report");
report.addActionListener(new ActionListener() {
        public void actionPerformed(ActionEvent e) {
            // Note the use of multiline italic HTML text
            // with the JOptionPane message dialog box.
            String msg = "<html><i>" +
               c1.getName() + ": " + c1.getSelectedValue() + "<br>"+
               c2.getName() + ": " + c2.getSelectedValue() + "<br>"+
               c3.getName() + ": " + c3.getSelectedValue() + "</i>";
            JOptionPane.showMessageDialog(frame, msg);
        }
    });

// Add the 3 ItemChooser objects, and the Button to the panel
chooserPanel.add(c1);
chooserPanel.add(c2);
chooserPanel.add(c3);
chooserPanel.add(report);
```

Example 11-14. ItemChooser.java (continued)

```
        // Add the panel and the message line to the window
        Container contentPane = frame.getContentPane( );
        contentPane.add(chooserPanel, BorderLayout.CENTER);
        contentPane.add(msgline, BorderLayout.SOUTH);

        // Set the window size and pop it up.
        frame.pack( );
        frame.show( );
    }
  }
}
```

A Complete GUI

We've looked separately at components, containers, layout management, and event handling, so now it is time to tie these pieces together and add the additional details required to create a complete graphical user interface. Example 11-15 lists *ScribbleApp.java*, a simple paint-style application, pictured in Figure 11-13.

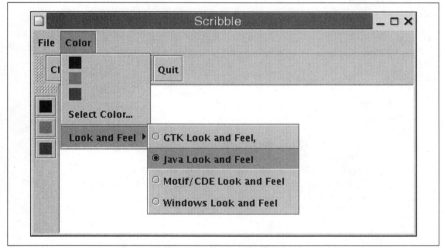

Figure 11-13. The ScribbleApp application

This application relies on the scribbling capabilities of the ScribblePane class of Example 11-13. It places a ScribblePane instance within a JFrame container to create the main application window and then adds a JMenuBar and two JToolBar components to allow the user to control the application. ScribbleApp uses a JColorChooser to let the user select a drawing color and a JOptionPane to display a confirmation dialog when the user asks to quit. You should pay particular attention to how these five Swing components are used; most full-featured applications use them in similar ways. Note that Example 11-15 is a complete application; it is designed to be run standalone, not to be viewed using the ShowBean program. However, the ScribbleApp class is designed as a subclass of JFrame, so that other applications can instantiate ScribbleApp windows of their own if they so choose.

This example also introduces the javax.swing.Action interface, which is a subinterface of java.awt.event.ActionListener. Any Action object can be used as an ActionListener to respond to an ActionEvent generated by a component. What the Action interface adds to the ActionListener interface is the ability to associate arbitrary properties with an Action object. The Action interface also defines standard property names that can specify the name, icon, and description of the action performed by the listener. Action objects are particularly convenient to use because they can be added directly to JMenu and JToolBar components; the components use the action name and/or icon to automatically create appropriate menu items or toolbar buttons to represent the action. (In Java 1.3, Action objects can also be passed directly to the constructor methods of components such as JButton.) Action objects can also be enabled or disabled. When an action is disabled, any component that has been created to represent it is also disabled, preventing the user from attempting to perform the action.

Example 11-15. ScribbleApp.java

```
package je3.gui;
import java.awt.*;
import java.awt.event.*;
import javax.swing.*;
import javax.swing.border.*;

/**
 * This JFrame subclass is a simple "paint" application.
 **/
public class ScribbleApp extends JFrame {
    /**
     * The main method instantiates an instance of the class, sets it size,
     * and makes it visible on the screen
     **/
    public static void main(String[ ] args) {
        // Set the look-and-feel for the application.
        // LookAndFeelPrefs is defined elsewhere in this package.
        LookAndFeelPrefs.setPreferredLookAndFeel(ScribbleApp.class);

        ScribbleApp scribble = new ScribbleApp( );

        // Handle window close requests
        scribble.addWindowListener(new WindowAdapter( ) {
                public void windowClosing(WindowEvent e) { System.exit(0); }
            });

        // Set the window size and make it visible.
        scribble.setSize(500, 300);
        scribble.setVisible(true);
    }

    // The scribble application relies on the ScribblePane component developed
    // earlier.  This field holds the ScribblePane instance it uses.
    ScribblePane scribblePane;
```

Example 11-15. ScribbleApp.java (continued)

```
/**
 * This constructor creates the GUI for this application.
 **/
public ScribbleApp( ) {
    super("Scribble");  // Call superclass constructor and set window title

    // All content of a JFrame (except for the menubar) goes in the
    // Frame's internal "content pane", not in the frame itself.
    // The same is true for JDialog and similar top-level containers.
    Container contentPane = this.getContentPane( );

    // Specify a layout manager for the content pane
    contentPane.setLayout(new BorderLayout( ));

    // Create the main scribble pane component, give it a border and
    // a background color, and add it to the content pane
    scribblePane = new ScribblePane( );
    scribblePane.setBorder(new BevelBorder(BevelBorder.LOWERED));
    scribblePane.setBackground(Color.white);
    contentPane.add(scribblePane, BorderLayout.CENTER);

    // Create a menubar and add it to this window.  Note that JFrame
    // handles menus specially and has a special method for adding them
    // outside of the content pane.
    JMenuBar menubar = new JMenuBar( );  // Create a menubar
    this.setJMenuBar(menubar);           // Display it in the JFrame

    // Create menus and add to the menubar
    JMenu filemenu = new JMenu("File");
    JMenu colormenu = new JMenu("Color");
    menubar.add(filemenu);
    menubar.add(colormenu);

    // Create some Action objects for use in the menus and toolbars.
    // An Action combines a menu title and/or icon with an ActionListener.
    // These Action classes are defined as inner classes below.
    Action clear = new ClearAction( );
    Action quit = new QuitAction( );
    Action black = new ColorAction(Color.black);
    Action red = new ColorAction(Color.red);
    Action blue = new ColorAction(Color.blue);
    Action select = new SelectColorAction( );

    // Populate the menus using Action objects
    filemenu.add(clear);
    filemenu.add(quit);
    colormenu.add(black);
    colormenu.add(red);
    colormenu.add(blue);
    colormenu.add(select);
```

Example 11-15. ScribbleApp.java (continued)

```java
        // Add a submenu for selecting a look-and-feel.
        // The LookAndFeelPrefs utility class is later in the chapter.
        colormenu.add(new JSeparator());
        colormenu.add(LookAndFeelPrefs.createLookAndFeelMenu(ScribbleApp.class,
                new ActionListener() {
                    public void actionPerformed(ActionEvent e) {
                        SwingUtilities.updateComponentTreeUI(ScribbleApp.this);
                    }
                }));

        // Now create a toolbar, add actions to it, and add it to the
        // top of the frame (where it appears underneath the menubar)
        JToolBar toolbar = new JToolBar();
        toolbar.add(clear);
        toolbar.add(select);
        toolbar.add(quit);
        contentPane.add(toolbar, BorderLayout.NORTH);

        // Create another toolbar for use as a color palette, and add to
        // the left side of the window.
        JToolBar palette = new JToolBar();
        palette.add(black);
        palette.add(red);
        palette.add(blue);
        palette.setOrientation(SwingConstants.VERTICAL);
        contentPane.add(palette, BorderLayout.WEST);
    }

    /** This inner class defines the "clear" action that clears the scribble */
    class ClearAction extends AbstractAction {
        public ClearAction() {
            super("Clear");  // Specify the name of the action
        }
        public void actionPerformed(ActionEvent e) { scribblePane.clear(); }
    }

    /** This inner class defines the "quit" action to quit the program */
    class QuitAction extends AbstractAction {
        public QuitAction() { super("Quit"); }
        public void actionPerformed(ActionEvent e) {
            // Use JOptionPane to confirm that the user really wants to quit
            int response =
                JOptionPane.showConfirmDialog(ScribbleApp.this,"Really Quit?");
            if (response == JOptionPane.YES_OPTION) System.exit(0);
        }
    }

    /**
     * This inner class defines an Action that sets the current drawing color
     * of the ScribblePane2 component.  Note that actions of this type have
     * icons rather than labels
     **/
```

Example 11-15. ScribbleApp.java (continued)

```
class ColorAction extends AbstractAction {
    Color color;
    public ColorAction(Color color) {
        this.color = color;
        putValue(Action.SMALL_ICON, new ColorIcon(color)); // specify icon
    }
    public void actionPerformed(ActionEvent e) {
        scribblePane.setForeground(color);  // Set current drawing color
    }
}

/**
 * This inner class implements Icon to draw a solid 16x16 block of the
 * specified color.  Most icons are instances of ImageIcon, but since
 * we're only using solid colors here, it is easier to implement this
 * custom Icon type
 **/
static class ColorIcon implements Icon {
    Color color;
    public ColorIcon(Color color) { this.color = color; }
    // These two methods specify the size of the icon
    public int getIconHeight( ) { return 16; }
    public int getIconWidth( ) { return 16; }
    // This method draws the icon
    public void paintIcon(Component c, Graphics g, int x, int y) {
        g.setColor(color);
        g.fillRect(x, y, 16, 16);
    }
}

/**
 * This inner class defines an Action that uses JColorChooser to allow
 * the user to select a drawing color
 **/
class SelectColorAction extends AbstractAction {
    public SelectColorAction( ) { super("Select Color..."); }
    public void actionPerformed(ActionEvent e) {
        Color color = JColorChooser.showDialog(ScribbleApp.this,
                                        "Select Drawing Color",
                                        scribblePane.getForeground(
));
        if (color != null) scribblePane.setForeground(color);
    }
}
}
```

Actions and Reflection

Example 11-15 demonstrated the use of Action objects, which allow an application's command set to be easily presented to the user in menubars, toolbars, and so on. The awkward part about working with Action objects, however, is that each one must usually be defined as a class of its own. If you are willing to use the

Java Reflection API, however, there is an easier alternative. In Example 9-2 we saw the Command class—a class that encapsulates a java.lang.reflect.Method object, an array of arguments for the method, and the object upon which the method is to be invoked. Calling the invoke( ) method of a Command object invokes the method. The most powerful feature of the Command class, however, is its static parse( ) method, which can create a Command by parsing a textual representation of the method name and argument list.

The Command class implements the ActionListener interface, so Command objects can be used as simple action listeners. But a Command is not an Action. Example 11-16 addresses this; it is a listing of *CommandAction.java*, a subclass of AbstractAction that uses a Command object to perform the action. Since the Command class does the hard work, the code for CommandAction is relatively simple.

Example 11-16. CommandAction.java

```
package je3.gui;
import je3.reflect.*;
import javax.swing.*;
import java.awt.event.*;

public class CommandAction extends AbstractAction {
    Command command;  // The command to execute in response to an ActionEvent

    /**
     * Create an Action object that has the various specified attributes,
     * and invokes the specified Command object in response to ActionEvents
     **/
    public CommandAction(Command command, String label,
                         Icon icon, String tooltip,
                         KeyStroke accelerator, int mnemonic,
                         boolean enabled)
    {
        this.command = command;  // Remember the command to invoke

        // Set the various action attributes with putValue()
        if (label != null) putValue(NAME, label);
        if (icon != null) putValue(SMALL_ICON, icon);
        if (tooltip != null) putValue(SHORT_DESCRIPTION, tooltip);
        if (accelerator != null) putValue(ACCELERATOR_KEY, accelerator);
        if (mnemonic != KeyEvent.VK_UNDEFINED)
            putValue(MNEMONIC_KEY, new Integer(mnemonic));

        // Tell the action whether it is currently enabled or not
        setEnabled(enabled);
    }

    /**
     * This method implements ActionListener, which is a superinterface of
     * Action.  When a component generates an ActionEvent, it is passed to
     * this method.  This method simply passes it on to the Command object,
     * which is also an ActionListener object
     **/
```

Example 11-16. CommandAction.java (continued)

```
    public void actionPerformed(ActionEvent e) { command.actionPerformed(e); }

    // These constants are defined by Action in Java 1.3.
    // For compatibility with Java 1.2, we redefine them here.
    public static final String ACCELERATOR_KEY = "AcceleratorKey";
    public static final String MNEMONIC_KEY = "MnemonicKey";
}
```

Custom Dialogs

The `ScribbleApp` program of Example 11-15 displayed two kinds of dialogs: a confirmation dialog created by `JOptionPane` and a color selection dialog created by `JColorChooser`. These Swing components support many basic dialog box needs. The `JOptionPane` class makes it easy to display simple (and not-so-simple) information, confirmation, and selection dialogs, while `JColorChooser` and `JFileChooser` provide color and file selection capabilities. Most nontrivial applications, however, need to create custom dialogs that go beyond these standard components. This is easy to do with the `JDialog` component.

Example 11-17 shows the `FontChooser` class. It subclasses `JDialog` and uses the `ItemChooser` class developed in Example 11-14 to display font families, styles, and sizes to the user. A `FontChooser` dialog is pictured in Figure 11-14. The inner class `FontChooser.Demo` is a simple demonstration application you can use to experiment with the `FontChooser` dialog.

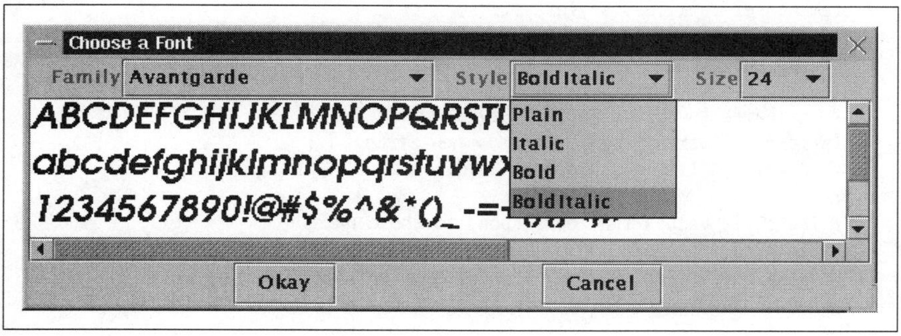

Figure 11-14. The FontChooser dialog

`JDialog` is a `RootPaneContainer`, like `JFrame`, which means you can't add children to it directly. You must instead add them to the container returned by `getContentPane()`. `FontChooser` creates a modal dialog, which means that the `show()` method blocks and does not return to the caller until the user dismisses the dialog. Finally, `FontChooser` is implemented as a subclass of `JDialog`, so that it can be reused by many applications. When you need to create a custom dialog specific to a single application, you can simply create a `JDialog` instance and populate it with whatever child components you need; in other words, you do not need to write a custom subclass to define a new dialog.

Example 11-17. FontChooser.java

```java
package je3.gui;
import java.awt.*;
import java.awt.event.*;
import javax.swing.*;
import javax.swing.event.*;
import je3.gui.ItemChooser;

/**
 * This is a JDialog subclass that allows the user to select a font, in any
 * style and size, from the list of available fonts on the system.  The
 * dialog is modal. Display it with show(); this method does not return
 * until the user dismisses the dialog.  When show() returns, call
 * getSelectedFont() to obtain the user's selection.  If the user clicked the
 * dialog's "Cancel" button, getSelectedFont() will return null.
 **/
public class FontChooser extends JDialog {
    // These fields define the component properties
    String family;           // The name of the font family
    int style;               // The font style
    int size;                // The font size
    Font selectedFont;       // The Font they correspond to

    // This is the list of all font families on the system
    String[] fontFamilies;

    // The various Swing components used in the dialog
    ItemChooser families, styles, sizes;
    JTextArea preview;
    JButton okay, cancel;

    // The names to appear in the "Style" menu
    static final String[] styleNames = new String[] {
        "Plain", "Italic", "Bold", "BoldItalic"
    };
    // The style values that correspond to those names
    static final Integer[] styleValues = new Integer[] {
        new Integer(Font.PLAIN), new Integer(Font.ITALIC),
        new Integer(Font.BOLD), new Integer(Font.BOLD+Font.ITALIC)
    };
    // The size "names" to appear in the size menu
    static final String[] sizeNames = new String[] {
        "8", "10", "12", "14", "18", "20", "24", "28", "32",
        "40", "48", "56", "64", "72"
    };

    // This is the default preview string displayed in the dialog box
    static final String defaultPreviewString =
        "ABCDEFGHIJKLMNOPQRSTUVWXYZ\n" +
        "abcdefghijklmnopqrstuvwxyz\n" +
        "1234567890!@#$%^&*()_-=+[ ]{ }<,.>\n" +
        "The quick brown fox jumps over the lazy dog";
```

Example 11-17. FontChooser.java (continued)

```java
/** Create a font chooser dialog for the specified frame. */
public FontChooser(Frame owner) {
    super(owner, "Choose a Font");  // Set dialog frame and title

    // This dialog must be used as a modal dialog.  In order to be used
    // as a modeless dialog, it would have to fire a PropertyChangeEvent
    // whenever the selected font changed, so that applications could be
    // notified of the user's selections.
    setModal(true);

    // Figure out what fonts are available on the system
    GraphicsEnvironment env =
        GraphicsEnvironment.getLocalGraphicsEnvironment();
    fontFamilies = env.getAvailableFontFamilyNames();

    // Set initial values for the properties
    family = fontFamilies[0];
    style = Font.PLAIN;
    size = 18;
    selectedFont = new Font(family, style, size);

    // Create ItemChooser objects that allow the user to select font
    // family, style, and size.
    families = new ItemChooser("Family", fontFamilies, null, 0,
                               ItemChooser.COMBOBOX);
    styles = new ItemChooser("Style", styleNames, styleValues, 0,
                             ItemChooser.COMBOBOX);
    sizes = new ItemChooser("Size", sizeNames,null,4,ItemChooser.COMBOBOX);

    // Now register event listeners to handle selections
    families.addItemChooserListener(new ItemChooser.Listener() {
            public void itemChosen(ItemChooser.Event e) {
                setFontFamily((String)e.getSelectedValue());
            }
        });
    styles.addItemChooserListener(new ItemChooser.Listener() {
            public void itemChosen(ItemChooser.Event e) {
                setFontStyle(((Integer)e.getSelectedValue()).intValue());
            }
        });
    sizes.addItemChooserListener(new ItemChooser.Listener() {
            public void itemChosen(ItemChooser.Event e) {
                setFontSize(Integer.parseInt((String)e.getSelectedValue()));
            }
        });

    // Create a component to preview the font.
    preview = new JTextArea(defaultPreviewString, 5, 40);
    preview.setFont(selectedFont);

    // Create buttons to dismiss the dialog, and set handlers on them
    okay = new JButton("Okay");
    cancel = new JButton("Cancel");
```

Example 11-17. FontChooser.java (continued)

```java
        okay.addActionListener(new ActionListener( ) {
                public void actionPerformed(ActionEvent e) { hide( ); }
            });
        cancel.addActionListener(new ActionListener( ) {
                public void actionPerformed(ActionEvent e) {
                    selectedFont = null;
                    hide( );
                }
            });

        // Put the ItemChoosers in a Box
        Box choosersBox = Box.createHorizontalBox( );
        choosersBox.add(Box.createHorizontalStrut(15));
        choosersBox.add(families);
        choosersBox.add(Box.createHorizontalStrut(15));
        choosersBox.add(styles);
        choosersBox.add(Box.createHorizontalStrut(15));
        choosersBox.add(sizes);
        choosersBox.add(Box.createHorizontalStrut(15));
        choosersBox.add(Box.createGlue( ));

        // Put the dismiss buttons in another box
        Box buttonBox = Box.createHorizontalBox( );
        buttonBox.add(Box.createGlue( ));
        buttonBox.add(okay);
        buttonBox.add(Box.createGlue( ));
        buttonBox.add(cancel);
        buttonBox.add(Box.createGlue( ));

        // Put the choosers at the top, the buttons at the bottom, and
        // the preview in the middle.
        Container contentPane = getContentPane( );
        contentPane.add(new JScrollPane(preview), BorderLayout.CENTER);
        contentPane.add(choosersBox, BorderLayout.NORTH);
        contentPane.add(buttonBox, BorderLayout.SOUTH);

        // Set the dialog size based on the component size.
        pack( );
    }

    /**
     * Call this method after show( ) to obtain the user's selection.  If the
     * user used the "Cancel" button, this will return null
     **/
    public Font getSelectedFont( ) { return selectedFont; }


    // These are other property getter methods
    public String getFontFamily( ) { return family; }
    public int getFontStyle( ) { return style; }
    public int getFontSize( ) { return size; }
```

Example 11-17. FontChooser.java (continued)

```java
    // The property setter methods are a little more complicated.
    // Note that none of these setter methods update the corresponding
    // ItemChooser components as they ought to.
    public void setFontFamily(String name) {
        family = name;
        changeFont();
    }
    public void setFontStyle(int style) {
        this.style = style;
        changeFont();
    }
    public void setFontSize(int size) {
        this.size = size;
        changeFont();
    }
    public void setSelectedFont(Font font) {
        selectedFont = font;
        family = font.getFamily();
        style = font.getStyle();
        size = font.getSize();
        preview.setFont(font);
    }

    // This method is called when the family, style, or size changes
    protected void changeFont() {
        selectedFont = new Font(family, style, size);
        preview.setFont(selectedFont);
    }

    // Override this inherited method to prevent anyone from making us modeless
    public boolean isModal() { return true; }

    /** This inner class demonstrates the use of FontChooser */
    public static class Demo {
        public static void main(String[] args) {
            // Create some components and a FontChooser dialog
            final JFrame frame = new JFrame("demo");
            final JButton button = new JButton("Push Me!");
            final FontChooser chooser = new FontChooser(frame);

            // Handle button clicks
            button.addActionListener(new ActionListener() {
                    public void actionPerformed(ActionEvent e) {
                        // Pop up the dialog
                        chooser.show();
                        // Get the user's selection
                        Font font = chooser.getSelectedFont();
                        // If not cancelled, set the button font
                        if (font != null) button.setFont(font);
                    }
                });
```

Example 11-17. FontChooser.java (continued)

```
            // Display the demo
            frame.getContentPane( ).add(button);
            frame.setSize(200, 100);
            frame.show( );
        }
    }
}
```

An Error Handler Dialog

Example 11-18 is another example of a custom dialog. This dialog is designed for use when an unrecoverable or unexpected exception occurs in a program. Instead of just printing a stack trace and exiting, as Java programs do by default, the static method ErrorHandler.displayThrowable( ) displays the exception detail message to the user. One of the buttons in the dialog allows the user to view the complete stack trace for the exception, and another button allows the user to report the exception to the program's developer (by POSTing a serialized copy of the exception object to a web server).

One of the interesting features of this example is that the dialog can change its layout and size. As illustrated in Figure 11-15, the dialog includes a **Show Details** button that expands the display to include a stack trace. Similarly, if the **Send Report** button is clicked, the dialog changes to display the text sent by the web server in response to the error report.

The displayThrowable( ) method is assisted by two other static convenience methods that may also be useful on their own. First, getHTMLDetails( ) returns an HTML-formatted string describing the stack trace of a Throwable object. It illustrates two methods of Throwable that are new in Java 1.4. getStackTrace( ) returns an array of StackTraceElement objects (also new in Java 1.4) that provide programmatic access to the stack trace. getCause( ) is used with chained exceptions to obtain the Throwable that caused the current Exception.

The second static convenience method used by displayThrowable( ) is reportThrowable( ), which serializes the Throwable object and reports it to a web server, using an HTTP POST request. It does this with a java.net.URLConnection object, which was introduced and demonstrated in Chapter 5.

The dialog itself is implemented using a JOptionPane. This example is an advanced use of JOptionPane, however, and does not use one of the JOptionPane static methods for displaying a canned dialog. Instead, it uses a custom JLabel component to display the error message (and optional stack trace details). It also uses two custom JButton objects to implement the **Show Details** and **Send Report** buttons. The **Exit** button, however, is left to the JOptionPane itself. Because we use the JOptionPane( ) constructor rather than one of its static dialog display methods, we end up with a JOptionPane component, which needs to be placed within a JDialog in order to be displayed. Conveniently, the createDialog( ) method of JOptionPane creates a suitable JDialog object.

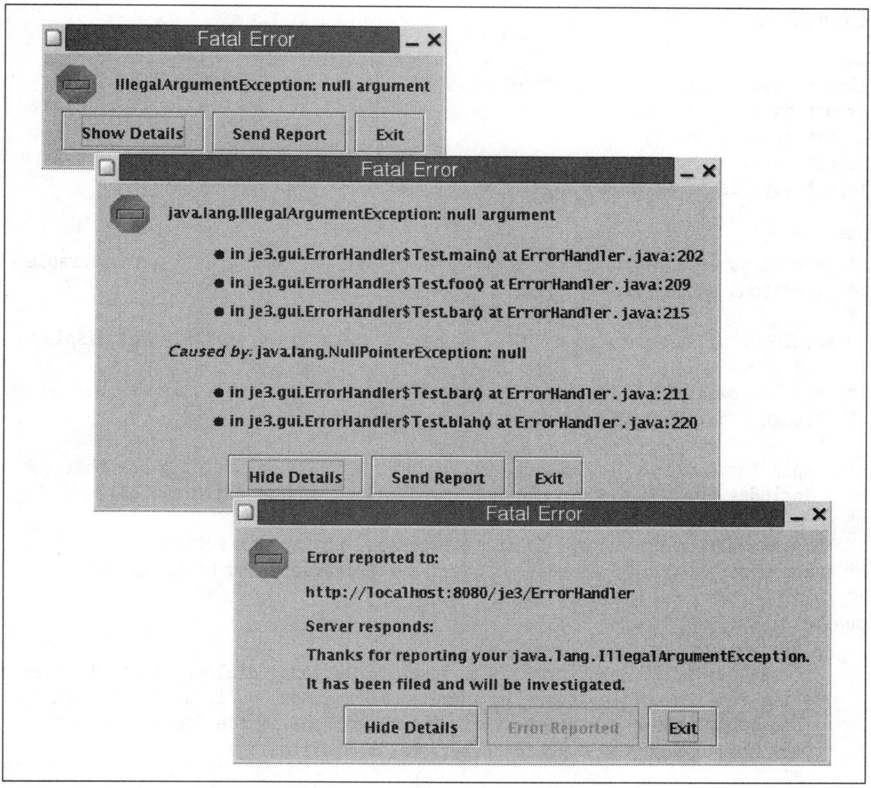

Figure 11-15. An ErrorHandler dialog, in three different states

Example 11-18 includes an inner class named Test that purposely causes an exception (and uses Throwable.initCause( ) to chain the exception to another one) in order to demonstrate the error handling dialog. If you want to test the exception reporting feature, specify the URL to report it to on the command line. Note, however, that you cannot just use the URL of a regular static web page here—you'll probably get an HTTP 405 error message from the web server because static web pages can't be retrieved with a POST request. Instead, your URL must refer to a server-side script or servlet of some kind. Example 20-2 is a Java servlet designed to work hand-in-hand with this class. If you are not already familiar with servlets, however, don't feel that you have to go read Chapter 20 right now. If you have a PHP-enabled web server, the following simple PHP script will do. It does not decode or save the reported exception, but it does count the number of bytes in it and return a response.

```
$len = strlen($HTTP_RAW_POST_DATA);
echo "Thanks for reporting the error<br>" .
    "$len bytes received";
```

Simply place this PHP file on your web server somewhere and pass its URL to the ErrorHandler.Test program.

Example 11-18. ErrorHandler.java

```java
package je3.gui;
import java.awt.*;
import java.awt.event.*;
import javax.swing.*;
import java.net.*;
import java.io.*;

/**
 * This class defines three static methods useful for coping with unrecoverable
 * exceptions and errors.
 *
 * getHTMLDetails( ) returns an HTML-formatted stack trace suitable for display.
 *
 * reportThrowable( ) serializes the exception and POSTs it to a web server
 * through a java.net.URLConnection.
 *
 * displayThrowable( ) displays the exception's message in a dialog box that
 *    includes buttons that invoke getHTMLDetails( ) and reportThrowable( ).
 *
 * This example demonstrates: StackTraceElement, chained exceptions,
 * Swing dialogs with JOptionPane, object serialization, and URLConnection.
 */
public class ErrorHandler {
    /**
     * Display details about throwable in a simple modal dialog.  Title is the
     * title of the dialog box.  If submissionURL is not null, allow the user
     * to report the exception to that URL.  Component is the "owner" of the
     * dialog, and may be null for nongraphical applications.
     **/
    public static void displayThrowable(final Throwable throwable,
                                        String title,
                                        final String submissionURL,
                                        Component component)
    {
        // Get throwable class name minus the package name
        String className = throwable.getClass( ).getName( );
        className = className.substring(className.lastIndexOf('.')+1);

        // Basic error message is className plus exception message if any.
        String msg = throwable.getMessage( );
        final String basicMessage = className + ((msg != null)?(": "+msg):"");

        // Here is a JLabel to display the message.  We create the component
        // explicitly so we can manipulate it with the buttons.  Note final
        final JLabel messageLabel = new JLabel(basicMessage);

        // Here are buttons for the dialog.  They are final for use in
        // the event listeners below.  The "Send Report" button is only
        // enabled if we have a URL to send a bug report to.
        final JButton detailsButton = new JButton("Show Details");
        final JButton reportButton = new JButton("Send Report");
        reportButton.setEnabled(submissionURL != null);
```

Example 11-18. ErrorHandler.java (continued)

```
        // Our dialog will display a JOptionPane.  Note that we don't
        // have to create the "Exit" button ourselves.  JOptionPane will
        // create it for us, and will cause it to close the dialog.
        JOptionPane pane =
            new JOptionPane(messageLabel, JOptionPane.ERROR_MESSAGE,
                            JOptionPane.YES_NO_OPTION, null,
                            new Object[ ] {detailsButton,reportButton,"Exit"});

        // This is the dialog box containing the pane.
        final JDialog dialog = pane.createDialog(component, title);

        // Add an event handler for the Details button
        detailsButton.addActionListener(new ActionListener( ) {
                public void actionPerformed(ActionEvent event) {
                    // Show or hide error details based on state of button.
                    String label = detailsButton.getText( );
                    if (label.startsWith("Show")) {
                        // JLabel can display simple HTML text
                        messageLabel.setText(getHTMLDetails(throwable));
                        detailsButton.setText("Hide Details");
                        dialog.pack( );  // Make dialog resize to fit details
                    }
                    else {
                        messageLabel.setText(basicMessage);
                        detailsButton.setText("Show Details");
                        dialog.pack( );
                    }
                }
            });


        // Event handler for the "Report" button.
        reportButton.addActionListener(new ActionListener( ) {
            public void actionPerformed(ActionEvent event) {
                try {
                    // Report the error, get response.  See below.
                    String response=reportThrowable(throwable, submissionURL);
                    // Tell the user about the report
                    messageLabel.setText("<html>Error reported to:<pre>" +
                                        submissionURL +
                                        "</pre>Server responds:<p>" +
                                        response + "</html>");
                    dialog.pack( );  // Resize dialog to fit new message
                    // Don't allow it to be reported again
                    reportButton.setText("Error Reported");
                    reportButton.setEnabled(false);
                }
                catch (IOException e) {  // If error reporting fails
                    messageLabel.setText("Error not reported: " + e);
                    dialog.pack( );
                }
            }
        });
```

Example 11-18. ErrorHandler.java (continued)

```
            // Display the dialog modally.  This method will return only when the
            // user clicks the "Exit" button of the JOptionPane.
            dialog.show( );
    }


    /**
     * Return an HTML-formatted stack trace for the specified Throwable,
     * including any exceptions chained to the exception.  Note the use of
     * the Java 1.4 StackTraceElement to get stack details.  The returned
     * string begins with "<html>" and is therefore suitable for display in
     * Swing components such as JLabel.
     */
    public static String getHTMLDetails(Throwable throwable) {
        StringBuffer b = new StringBuffer("<html>");
        int lengthOfLastTrace = 1;  // initial value

        // Start with the specified throwable and loop through the chain of
        // causality for the throwable.
        while(throwable != null) {
            // Output Exception name and message, and begin a list
            b.append("<b>" + throwable.getClass( ).getName( ) + "</b>: " +
                    throwable.getMessage( ) + "<ul>");
            // Get the stack trace and output each frame.
            // Be careful not to repeat stack frames that were already reported
            // for the exception that this one caused.
            StackTraceElement[ ] stack = throwable.getStackTrace( );
            for(int i = stack.length-lengthOfLastTrace; i >= 0; i--) {
                b.append("<li> in " +stack[i].getClassName( ) + ".<b>" +
                        stack[i].getMethodName( ) + "</b>( ) at <tt>"+
                        stack[i].getFileName( ) + ":" +
                        stack[i].getLineNumber( ) + "</tt>");
            }
            b.append("</ul>");  // end list
            // See if there is a cause for this exception
            throwable = throwable.getCause( );
            if (throwable != null) {
                // If so, output a header
                b.append("<i>Caused by: </i>");
                // And remember how many frames to skip in the stack trace
                // of the cause exception
                lengthOfLastTrace = stack.length;
            }
        }
        b.append("</html>");
        return b.toString( );
    }


    /**
     * Serialize the specified Throwable, and use an HttpURLConnection to POST
     * it to the specified URL.  Return the response of the web server.
     */
    public static String reportThrowable(Throwable throwable,
                                         String submissionURL)
```

Example 11-18. ErrorHandler.java (continued)

```java
    throws IOException
{

    URL url = new URL(submissionURL);         // Parse the URL
    URLConnection c = url.openConnection();    // Open unconnected Connection
    c.setDoOutput(true);
    c.setDoInput(true);
    // Tell the server what kind of data we're sending
    c.addRequestProperty("Content-type",
                         "application/x-java-serialized-object");

    // This code might work for other URL protocols, but it is intended
    // for HTTP.  We use a POST request to send data with the request.
    if (c instanceof HttpURLConnection)
        ((HttpURLConnection)c).setRequestMethod("POST");

    c.connect();  // Now connect to the server

    // Get a stream to write to the server from the URLConnection.
    // Wrap an ObjectOutputStream around it and serialize the Throwable.
    ObjectOutputStream out =
        new ObjectOutputStream(c.getOutputStream());
    out.writeObject(throwable);
    out.close();

    // Now get the response from the URLConnection.  We expect it to be
    // an InputStream from which we read the server's response.
    Object response = c.getContent();
    StringBuffer message = new StringBuffer();
    if (response instanceof InputStream) {
        BufferedReader in =
          new BufferedReader(new InputStreamReader((InputStream)response));
        String line;
        while((line = in.readLine()) != null) message.append(line);
    }
    return message.toString();
}

// A test program to demonstrate the class
public static class Test {
    public static void main(String[] args) {
        String url = (args.length > 0)?args[0]:null;
        try { foo(); }
        catch(Throwable e) {
            ErrorHandler.displayThrowable(e, "Fatal Error", url, null);
            System.exit(1);
        }
    }
    // These methods purposely throw an exception
    public static void foo() { bar(null); }
    public static void bar(Object o) {
        try { blah(o); }
        catch(NullPointerException e) {
```

Example 11-18. ErrorHandler.java (continued)

```
            // Catch the null pointer exception and throw a new exception
            // that has the NPE specified as its cause.
            throw (IllegalArgumentException)
                new IllegalArgumentException("null argument").initCause(e);
        }
    }
    public static void blah(Object o) {
        Class c = o.getClass();  // throws NPE if o is null
    }
}
}
```

Displaying Tables

Now that we've seen how to assemble a prototypical Swing GUI, we can move on and start studying some more advanced Swing programming topics. We'll start with examples of some of the more powerful, and therefore complicated, components. The JTable class displays tabular data. It is particularly easy to use if your data happens to be organized into arrays of arrays. If this is not the case, however, you must implement the javax.swing.table.TableModel interface to serve as a translator between your data and the JTable component.

Example 11-19, which is a listing of *PropertyTable.java*, does exactly this. PropertyTable is a subclass of JTable that uses a custom TableModel implementation to display a table of the properties defined by a specified JavaBeans class (it uses the java.beans package, which we'll see more of in Chapter 15). The example includes a main() method so you can run it as a standalone application. Figure 11-16 shows the PropertyTable class in action. When studying this example, pay particular attention to the TableModel implementation: the TableModel is the key to working with the JTable component. Also note the PropertyTable constructor method that uses the TableColumnModel to modify the default appearance of the columns in the table.

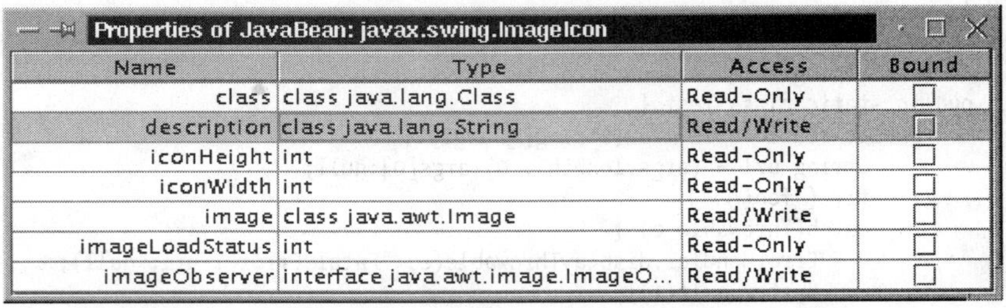

Name	Type	Access	Bound
class	class java.lang.Class	Read-Only	☐
description	class java.lang.String	Read/Write	☑
iconHeight	int	Read-Only	☐
iconWidth	int	Read-Only	☐
image	class java.awt.Image	Read/Write	☐
imageLoadStatus	int	Read-Only	☐
imageObserver	interface java.awt.image.ImageO...	Read/Write	☐

Figure 11-16. The PropertyTable application

Example 11-19. PropertyTable.java

```
package je3.gui;
import java.awt.*;
import javax.swing.*;
```

Example 11-19. PropertyTable.java (continued)

```java
import javax.swing.table.*;    // TableModel and other JTable-related classes
import java.beans.*;           // For JavaBean introspection
import java.util.*;            // For array sorting

/**
 * This class is a JTable subclass that displays a table of the JavaBeans
 * properties of any specified class.
 **/
public class PropertyTable extends JTable {
    /** This main method allows the class to be demonstrated  standalone */
    public static void main(String[ ] args) {
        // Specify the name of the class as a command-line argument
        Class beanClass = null;
        try {
            // Use reflection to get the Class from the classname
            beanClass = Class.forName(args[0]);
        }
        catch (Exception e) {   // Report errors
            System.out.println("Can't find specified class: "+e.getMessage( ));
            System.out.println("Usage: java PropertyTable <bean class name>");
            System.exit(0);
        }

        // Create a table to display the properties of the specified class
        JTable table = new PropertyTable(beanClass);

        // Then put the table in a scrolling window, put the scrolling
        // window into a frame, and pop it all up on to the screen
        JScrollPane scrollpane = new JScrollPane(table);
        JFrame frame = new JFrame("Properties of JavaBean: " + args[0]);
        frame.getContentPane( ).add(scrollpane);
        frame.setSize(500, 400);
        frame.setVisible(true);
    }

    /**
     * This constructor method specifies what data the table will display
     * (the table model) and uses the TableColumnModel to customize the
     * way that the table displays it.  The hard work is done by the
     * TableModel implementation below.
     **/
    public PropertyTable(Class beanClass) {
        // Set the data model for this table
        try {
            setModel(new JavaBeanPropertyTableModel(beanClass));
        }
        catch (IntrospectionException e) {
            System.err.println("WARNING: can't introspect: " + beanClass);
        }

        // Tweak the appearance of the table by manipulating its column model
        TableColumnModel colmodel = getColumnModel( );
```

Example 11-19. PropertyTable.java (continued)

```
        // Set column widths
        colmodel.getColumn(0).setPreferredWidth(125);
        colmodel.getColumn(1).setPreferredWidth(200);
        colmodel.getColumn(2).setPreferredWidth(75);
        colmodel.getColumn(3).setPreferredWidth(50);

        // Right justify the text in the first column
        TableColumn namecol = colmodel.getColumn(0);
        DefaultTableCellRenderer renderer = new DefaultTableCellRenderer();
        renderer.setHorizontalAlignment(SwingConstants.RIGHT);
        namecol.setCellRenderer(renderer);
    }

    /**
     * This class implements TableModel and represents JavaBeans property data
     * in a way that the JTable component can display.  If you've got some
     * type of tabular data to display, implement a TableModel class to
     * describe that data, and the JTable component will be able to display it.
     **/
    static class JavaBeanPropertyTableModel extends AbstractTableModel {
        PropertyDescriptor[] properties;  // The properties to display

        /**
         * The constructor: use the JavaBeans introspector mechanism to get
         * information about all the properties of a bean.  Once we've got
         * this information, the other methods will interpret it for JTable.
         **/
        public JavaBeanPropertyTableModel(Class beanClass)
            throws java.beans.IntrospectionException
        {
            // Use the introspector class to get "bean info" about the class.
            BeanInfo beaninfo = Introspector.getBeanInfo(beanClass);
            // Get the property descriptors from that BeanInfo class
            properties = beaninfo.getPropertyDescriptors();
            // Now do a case-insensitive sort by property name
            // The anonymous Comparator implementation specifies how to
            // sort PropertyDescriptor objects by name
            Arrays.sort(properties, new Comparator() {
                    public int compare(Object p, Object q) {
                        PropertyDescriptor a = (PropertyDescriptor) p;
                        PropertyDescriptor b = (PropertyDescriptor) q;
                        return a.getName().compareToIgnoreCase(b.getName());
                    }
                    public boolean equals(Object o) { return o == this; }
                });
        }

        // These are the names of the columns represented by this TableModel
        static final String[] columnNames = new String[] {
            "Name", "Type", "Access", "Bound"
        };
```

Example 11-19. PropertyTable.java (continued)

```
    // These are the types of the columns represented by this TableModel
    static final Class[ ] columnTypes = new Class[ ] {
        String.class, Class.class, String.class, Boolean.class
    };

    // These simple methods return basic information about the table
    public int getColumnCount( ) { return columnNames.length; }
    public int getRowCount( ) { return properties.length; }
    public String getColumnName(int column) { return columnNames[column]; }
    public Class getColumnClass(int column) { return columnTypes[column]; }

    /**
     * This method returns the value that appears at the specified row and
     * column of the table
     **/
    public Object getValueAt(int row, int column) {
        PropertyDescriptor prop = properties[row];
        switch(column) {
        case 0: return prop.getName( );
        case 1: return prop.getPropertyType( );
        case 2: return getAccessType(prop);
        case 3: return new Boolean(prop.isBound( ));
        default: return null;
        }
    }

    // A helper method called from getValueAt( ) above
    String getAccessType(PropertyDescriptor prop) {
        java.lang.reflect.Method reader = prop.getReadMethod( );
        java.lang.reflect.Method writer = prop.getWriteMethod( );
        if ((reader != null) && (writer != null)) return "Read/Write";
        else if (reader != null) return "Read-Only";
        else if (writer != null) return "Write-Only";
        else return "No Access";  // should never happen
    }
    }
}
```

Displaying Trees

The JTree component is used to display tree-structured data. If your data is in the form of nested arrays, vectors, or hashtables, you can simply pass the root node of the data structure to the JTree constructor, and it displays it. Tree data is not typically in this form, however. In order to display data that is in another form, you must implement the javax.swing.Tree.TreeModel interface to interpret the data in a way the JTree component can use it.

Example 11-20 shows a listing of *ComponentTree.java*, a JTree subclass that uses a custom TreeModel implementation to display the containment hierarchy of an AWT or Swing GUI in tree form. The class includes a main( ) method that uses the ComponentTree class to display its own component hierarchy, as shown in

Figure 11-17. As with the previous JTable example, the key to this example is the TreeModel implementation. The main( ) method also illustrates a technique for responding to tree node selection events.

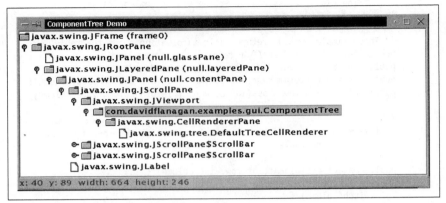

Figure 11-17. The ComponentTree application

Example 11-20. ComponentTree.java

```
package je3.gui;
import java.awt.*;
import java.awt.event.*;
import javax.swing.*;
import javax.swing.event.*;
import javax.swing.tree.*;

/**
 * This class is a JTree subclass that displays the tree of AWT or Swing
 * component that make up a GUI.
 **/
public class ComponentTree extends JTree {
    /**
     * All this constructor method has to do is set the TreeModel and
     * TreeCellRenderer objects for the tree.  It is these classes (defined
     * below) that do all the real work.
     **/
    public ComponentTree(Component c) {
        super(new ComponentTreeModel(c));
        setCellRenderer(new ComponentCellRenderer(getCellRenderer( )));
    }

    /**
     * The TreeModel class puts hierarchical data in a form that the JTree
     * can display.  This implementation interprets the containment hierarchy
     * of a Component for display by the ComponentTree class.  Note that any
     * kind of Object can be a node in the tree, as long as the TreeModel knows
     * how to handle it.
     **/
    static class ComponentTreeModel implements TreeModel {
        Component root;    // The root object of the tree
```

Example 11-20. ComponentTree.java (continued)

```java
// Constructor: just remember the root object
public ComponentTreeModel(Component root) { this.root = root; }

// Return the root of the tree
public Object getRoot() { return root; }

// Is this node a leaf? (Leaf nodes are displayed differently by JTree)
// Any node that isn't a container is a leaf, since they cannot have
// children.  We also define containers with no children as leaves.
public boolean isLeaf(Object node) {
    if (!(node instanceof Container)) return true;
    Container c = (Container) node;
    return c.getComponentCount() == 0;
}

// How many children does this node have?
public int getChildCount(Object node) {
    if (node instanceof Container) {
        Container c = (Container) node;
        return c.getComponentCount();
    }
    return 0;
}

// Return the specified child of a parent node.
public Object getChild(Object parent, int index) {
    if (parent instanceof Container) {
        Container c = (Container) parent;
        return c.getComponent(index);
    }
    return null;
}

// Return the index of the child node in the parent node
public int getIndexOfChild(Object parent, Object child) {
    if (!(parent instanceof Container)) return -1;
    Container c = (Container) parent;
    Component[] children = c.getComponents();
    if (children == null) return -1;
    for(int i = 0; i < children.length; i++) {
        if (children[i] == child) return i;
    }
    return -1;
}

// This method is only required for editable trees, so it is not
// implemented here.
public void valueForPathChanged(TreePath path, Object newvalue) { }

// This TreeModel never fires any events (since it is not editable)
// so event listener registration methods are left unimplemented
public void addTreeModelListener(TreeModelListener l) { }
```

Example 11-20. ComponentTree.java (continued)

```
        public void removeTreeModelListener(TreeModelListener l) { }
    }


    /**
     * A TreeCellRenderer displays each node of a tree.  The default renderer
     * displays arbitrary Object nodes by calling their toString( ) method.
     * The Component.toString( ) method returns long strings with extraneous
     * information.  Therefore, we use this "wrapper" implementation of
     * TreeCellRenderer to convert nodes from Component objects to useful
     * String values before passing those String values on to the default
     * renderer.
     **/
    static class ComponentCellRenderer implements TreeCellRenderer {
        TreeCellRenderer renderer;  // The renderer we are a wrapper for
        // Constructor: just remember the renderer
        public ComponentCellRenderer(TreeCellRenderer renderer) {
            this.renderer = renderer;
        }

        // This is the only TreeCellRenderer method.
        // Compute the string to display, and pass it to the wrapped renderer
        public Component getTreeCellRendererComponent(JTree tree, Object value,
                                                      boolean selected,
                                                      boolean expanded,
                                                      boolean leaf, int row,
                                                      boolean hasFocus) {
            String newvalue = value.getClass( ).getName( );    // Component type
            String name = ((Component)value).getName( );       // Component name
            if (name != null) newvalue += " (" + name + ")"; // unless null
            // Use the wrapped renderer object to do the real work
            return renderer.getTreeCellRendererComponent(tree, newvalue,
                                                         selected, expanded,
                                                         leaf, row, hasFocus);
        }
    }


    /**
     * This main( ) method demonstrates the use of the ComponentTree class: it
     * puts a ComponentTree component in a Frame, and uses the ComponentTree
     * to display its own GUI hierarchy.  It also adds a TreeSelectionListener
     * to display additional information about each component as it is selected
     **/
    public static void main(String[ ] args) {
        // Create a frame for the demo, and handle window close requests
        JFrame frame = new JFrame("ComponentTree Demo");
        frame.addWindowListener(new WindowAdapter( ) {
            public void windowClosing(WindowEvent e) { System.exit(0); }
        });

        // Create a scroll pane and a "message line" and add them to the
        // center and bottom of the frame.
        JScrollPane scrollpane = new JScrollPane( );
```

Example 11-20. ComponentTree.java (continued)

```
        final JLabel msgline = new JLabel(" ");
        frame.getContentPane( ).add(scrollpane, BorderLayout.CENTER);
        frame.getContentPane( ).add(msgline, BorderLayout.SOUTH);

        // Now create the ComponentTree object, specifying the frame as the
        // component whose tree is to be displayed.  Also set the tree's font.
        JTree tree = new ComponentTree(frame);
        tree.setFont(new Font("SansSerif", Font.BOLD, 12));

        // Only allow a single item in the tree to be selected at once
        tree.getSelectionModel( ).setSelectionMode(
                        TreeSelectionModel.SINGLE_TREE_SELECTION);

        // Add an event listener for notifications when
        // the tree selection state changes.
        tree.addTreeSelectionListener(new TreeSelectionListener( ) {
                public void valueChanged(TreeSelectionEvent e) {
                    // Tree selections are referred to by "path"
                    // We only care about the last node in the path
                    TreePath path = e.getPath( );
                    Component c = (Component) path.getLastPathComponent( );
                    // Now we know what component was selected, so
                    // display some information about it in the message line
                    if (c.isShowing( )) {
                        Point p = c.getLocationOnScreen( );
                        msgline.setText("x: " + p.x + "  y: " + p.y +
                                        " width: " + c.getWidth( ) +
                                        " height: " + c.getHeight( ));
                    }
                    else {
                        msgline.setText("component is not showing");
                    }
                }
            });

        // Now that we've set up the tree, add it to the scrollpane
        scrollpane.setViewportView(tree);

        // Finally, set the size of the main window, and pop it up.
        frame.setSize(600, 400);
        frame.setVisible(true);
    }
}
```

A Simple Web Browser

The two previous examples have shown us the powerful JTable and JTree components. A third powerful Swing component is javax.swing.text.JTextComponent and its various subclasses, which include JTextField, JTextArea, and JEditorPane. JEditorPane is a particularly interesting component that makes it easy to display (or edit) HTML text.

As an aside, it is worth noting here that you do not have to create a JEditorPane to display static HTML text. In Java 1.2.2 and later, the JLabel, JButton, and other similar components can all display multiline, multifont formatted HTML labels. The trick is to begin the label with the string "<html>". This tells the component to treat the rest of the label string as formatted HTML text and display it (using an internal JTextComponent) in that way. You can experiment with the feature using the ShowBean program; use it to create a JButton component and set the text property to a value that begins with "<html>".

Example 11-21 is a listing of *WebBrowser.java*, a JFrame subclass that implements the simple web browser shown in Figure 11-18. The WebBrowser class uses the power of the java.net.URL class to download HTML documents from the Web and the JEditorPane component to display the contents of those documents. Although defined as a reusable component, the WebBrowser class includes a main( ) method so that it can be run as a standalone application.

Figure 11-18. The WebBrowser component

Example 11-21 is intended as a demonstration of the power of the JEditorPane component. The truth is, however, that using JEditorPane is quite trivial: simply pass a URL to the setPage( ) method or a string of HTML text to the setText( ) method. So, when you study the code for this example, don't focus too much on the JEditorPane. You should instead look at WebBrowser as an example of pulling together many Swing components and programming techniques to create a fairly substantial GUI. Points of interest include the enabling and disabling of Action objects and the use of the JFileChooser component. The example also uses a JLabel as an application message line, with a javax.swing.Timer that performs a simple text-based animation in that message line.

Another thing to notice about this example is that it demonstrates several other example classes that are developed later in this chapter. GUIResourceBundle, which is developed in Example 11-22, is the primary one. This class allows common GUI resources (such as colors and fonts) to be read from textual descriptions stored in a properties file, which therefore allows the resources to be customized and localized. When GUIResourceBundle is extended with ResourceParser implementations, it can parse more complex "resources," such as entire JMenuBar and JToolBar components. WebBrowser defers the creation of its menus and toolbars to GUIResourceBundle.

The WebBrowser class uses the default Metal look-and-feel, but it allows the user to select a "theme" (a color and font combination) for use within that look-and-feel. This functionality is provided by the ThemeManager class, which is developed in Example 11-28.

Example 11-21. WebBrowser.java

```java
package je3.gui;
import java.awt.*;              // LayoutManager stuff
import javax.swing.*;           // Swing components
import java.awt.event.*;        // AWT event handlers
import javax.swing.event.*;     // Swing event handlers
import java.beans.*;            // JavaBeans event handlers
import java.io.*;               // Input/output
import java.net.*;              // Networking with URLs
import java.util.*;             // Hashtables and other utilities
// Import this class by name.  JFileChooser uses it, and its name conflicts
// with java.io.FileFilter
import javax.swing.filechooser.FileFilter;

/**
 * This class implements a simple web browser using the HTML
 * display capabilities of the JEditorPane component.
 **/
public class WebBrowser extends JFrame
    implements HyperlinkListener, PropertyChangeListener
{
    /**
     * A simple main( ) method that allows the WebBrowser class to be used
     * as a standalone application.
     **/
    public static void main(String[ ] args) throws IOException {
        // End the program when there are no more open browser windows
        WebBrowser.setExitWhenLastWindowClosed(true);
        WebBrowser browser = new WebBrowser( );  // Create a browser window
        browser.setSize(800, 600);               // Set its size
        browser.setVisible(true);                // Make it visible.
```

Example 11-21. WebBrowser.java (continued)

```java
        // Tell the browser what to display.  This method is defined below.
        browser.displayPage((args.length > 0) ? args[0] : browser.getHome());
    }

    // This class uses GUIResourceBundle to create its menubar and toolbar
    // This static initializer performs one-time registration of the
    // required ResourceParser classes.
    static {
        GUIResourceBundle.registerResourceParser(new MenuBarParser());
        GUIResourceBundle.registerResourceParser(new MenuParser());
        GUIResourceBundle.registerResourceParser(new ActionParser());
        GUIResourceBundle.registerResourceParser(new CommandParser());
        GUIResourceBundle.registerResourceParser(new ToolBarParser());
    }

    // These are the Swing components that the browser uses
    JEditorPane textPane;       // Where the HTML is displayed
    JLabel messageLine;         // Displays one-line messages
    JTextField urlField;        // Displays and edits the current URL
    JFileChooser fileChooser;   // Allows the user to select a local file

    // These are Actions that are used in the menubar and toolbar.
    // We obtain explicit references to them from the GUIResourceBundle
    // so we can enable and disable them.
    Action backAction, forwardAction;

    // These fields are used to maintain the browsing history of the window
    java.util.List history = new ArrayList();   // The history list
    int currentHistoryPage = -1;                // Current location in it
    public static final int MAX_HISTORY = 50;   // Trim list when over this size

    // These static fields control the behavior of the close() action
    static int numBrowserWindows = 0;
    static boolean exitWhenLastWindowClosed = false;

    // This is where the "home()" method takes us.  See also setHome()
    String home = "http://www.davidflanagan.com";  // A default value

    /** Create and initialize a new WebBrowser window */
    public WebBrowser() {
        super("WebBrowser");                // Chain to JFrame constructor

        textPane = new JEditorPane();       // Create HTML window
        textPane.setEditable(false);        // Don't allow the user to edit it

        // Register action listeners.  The first is to handle hyperlinks.
        // The second is to receive property change notifications, which tell
        // us when a document is done loading.  This class implements these
        // EventListener interfaces, and the methods are defined below
        textPane.addHyperlinkListener(this);
        textPane.addPropertyChangeListener(this);
```

Example 11-21. WebBrowser.java (continued)

```
// Put the text pane in a JScrollPane in the center of the window
this.getContentPane( ).add(new JScrollPane(textPane),
                          BorderLayout.CENTER);

// Now create a message line and place it at the bottom of the window
messageLine = new JLabel(" ");
this.getContentPane( ).add(messageLine, BorderLayout.SOUTH);

// Read the file WebBrowserResources.properties (and any localized
// variants appropriate for the current Locale) to create a
// GUIResourceBundle from which we'll get our menubar and toolbar.
GUIResourceBundle resources =
    new GUIResourceBundle(this,"je3.gui." +
                          "WebBrowserResources");

// Read a menubar from the resource bundle and display it
JMenuBar menubar = (JMenuBar) resources.getResource("menubar",
                                                     JMenuBar.class);
this.setJMenuBar(menubar);

// Read a toolbar from the resource bundle.  Don't display it yet.
JToolBar toolbar =
    (JToolBar) resources.getResource("toolbar", JToolBar.class);

// Create a text field that the user can enter a URL in.
// Set up an action listener to respond to the ENTER key in that field
urlField = new JTextField( );
urlField.addActionListener(new ActionListener( ) {
        public void actionPerformed(ActionEvent e) {
            displayPage(urlField.getText( ));
        }
    });

// Add the URL field and a label for it to the end of the toolbar
toolbar.add(new JLabel("        URL:"));
toolbar.add(urlField);

// And add the toolbar to the top of the window
this.getContentPane( ).add(toolbar, BorderLayout.NORTH);

// Read cached copies of two Action objects from the resource bundle
// These actions are used by the menubar and toolbar, and enabling and
// disabling them enables and disables the menu and toolbar items.
backAction = (Action)resources.getResource("action.back",Action.class);
forwardAction =
    (Action)resources.getResource("action.forward", Action.class);

// Start off with both actions disabled
backAction.setEnabled(false);
forwardAction.setEnabled(false);
```

Example 11-21. WebBrowser.java (continued)

```java
            // Create a ThemeManager for this frame,
            // and add a Theme menu to the menubar
            ThemeManager themes = new ThemeManager(this, resources);
            menubar.add(themes.getThemeMenu( ));

            // Keep track of how many web browser windows are open
            WebBrowser.numBrowserWindows++;
        }

        /** Set the static property that controls the behavior of close( ) */
        public static void setExitWhenLastWindowClosed(boolean b) {
            exitWhenLastWindowClosed = b;
        }

        /** These are accessor methods for the home property. */
        public void setHome(String home) { this.home = home; }
        public String getHome( ) { return home; }

        /**
         * This internal method attempts to load and display the specified URL.
         * It is called from various places throughout the class.
         **/
        boolean visit(URL url) {
            try {
                String href = url.toString( );
                // Start animating.  Animation is stopped in propertyChanged( )
                startAnimation("Loading " + href + "...");
                textPane.setPage(url);      // Load and display the URL
                this.setTitle(href);        // Display URL in window titlebar
                urlField.setText(href);     // Display URL in text input field
                return true;                // Return success
            }
            catch (IOException ex) {        // If page loading fails
                stopAnimation( );
                messageLine.setText("Can't load page: " + ex.getMessage( ));
                return false;               // Return failure
            }
        }

        /**
         * Ask the browser to display the specified URL, and put it in the
         * history list.
         **/
        public void displayPage(URL url) {
            if (visit(url)) {       // go to the specified url, and if we succeed:
                history.add(url);           // Add the url to the history list
                int numentries = history.size( );
                if (numentries > MAX_HISTORY+10) {  // Trim history when too large
                    history = history.subList(numentries-MAX_HISTORY, numentries);
                    numentries = MAX_HISTORY;
                }
                currentHistoryPage = numentries-1;  // Set current history page
```

Example 11-21. WebBrowser.java (continued)

```
                // If we can go back, then enable the Back action
                if (currentHistoryPage > 0) backAction.setEnabled(true);
        }
    }

    /** Like displayPage(URL), but takes a string instead */
    public void displayPage(String href) {
        try {
            displayPage(new URL(href));
        }
        catch (MalformedURLException ex) {
            messageLine.setText("Bad URL: " + href);
        }
    }

    /** Allow the user to choose a local file, and display it */
    public void openPage( ) {
        // Lazy creation: don't create the JFileChooser until it is needed
        if (fileChooser == null) {
            fileChooser = new JFileChooser( );
            // This javax.swing.filechooser.FileFilter displays only HTML files
            FileFilter filter = new FileFilter( ) {
                    public boolean accept(File f) {
                        String fn = f.getName( );
                        if (fn.endsWith(".html") || fn.endsWith(".htm"))
                            return true;
                        else return false;
                    }
                    public String getDescription( ) { return "HTML Files"; }
                };
            fileChooser.setFileFilter(filter);
            fileChooser.addChoosableFileFilter(filter);
        }

        // Ask the user to choose a file.
        int result = fileChooser.showOpenDialog(this);
        if (result == JFileChooser.APPROVE_OPTION) {
            // If they didn't click "Cancel", then try to display the file.
            File selectedFile = fileChooser.getSelectedFile( );
            String url = "file://" + selectedFile.getAbsolutePath( );
            displayPage(url);
        }
    }

    /** Go back to the previously displayed page. */
    public void back( ) {
        if (currentHistoryPage > 0)  // go back, if we can
            visit((URL)history.get(--currentHistoryPage));
        // Enable or disable actions as appropriate
        backAction.setEnabled((currentHistoryPage > 0));
        forwardAction.setEnabled((currentHistoryPage < history.size( )-1));
    }
```

Example 11-21. WebBrowser.java (continued)

```
/** Go forward to the next page in the history list */
public void forward() {
    if (currentHistoryPage < history.size()-1)  // go forward, if we can
        visit((URL)history.get(++currentHistoryPage));
    // Enable or disable actions as appropriate
    backAction.setEnabled((currentHistoryPage > 0));
    forwardAction.setEnabled((currentHistoryPage < history.size()-1));
}

/** Reload the current page in the history list */
public void reload() {
    if (currentHistoryPage != -1) {
        // We can't reload the current document, so display a blank page
        textPane.setDocument(new javax.swing.text.html.HTMLDocument());
        // Now re-visit the current URL
        visit((URL)history.get(currentHistoryPage));
    }
}

/** Display the page specified by the "home" property */
public void home() { displayPage(getHome()); }

/** Open a new browser window */
public void newBrowser() {
    WebBrowser b = new WebBrowser();
    b.setSize(this.getWidth(), this.getHeight());
    b.setVisible(true);
}

/**
 * Close this browser window.  If this was the only open window,
 * and exitWhenLastBrowserClosed is true, then exit the VM
 **/
public void close() {
    this.setVisible(false);            // Hide the window
    this.dispose();                    // Destroy the window
    synchronized(WebBrowser.class) {   // Synchronize for thread-safety
        WebBrowser.numBrowserWindows--; // There is one window fewer now
        if ((numBrowserWindows==0) && exitWhenLastWindowClosed)
            System.exit(0);            // Exit if it was the last one
    }
}

/**
 * Exit the VM.  If confirm is true, ask the user if they are sure.
 * Note that showConfirmDialog() displays a dialog, waits for the user,
 * and returns the user's response (i.e. the button the user selected).
 **/
public void exit(boolean confirm) {
    if (!confirm ||
        (JOptionPane.showConfirmDialog(this, // dialog parent
            /* message to display */ "Are you sure you want to quit?",
```

Example 11-21. WebBrowser.java (continued)

```
                    /* dialog title */        "Really Quit?",
                    /* dialog buttons */      JOptionPane.YES_NO_OPTION) ==
              JOptionPane.YES_OPTION))  // If Yes button was clicked
          System.exit(0);
    }

    /**
     * This method implements HyperlinkListener.  It is invoked when the user
     * clicks on a hyperlink or moves the mouse onto or off of a link
     **/
    public void hyperlinkUpdate(HyperlinkEvent e) {
        HyperlinkEvent.EventType type = e.getEventType();  // what happened?
        if (type == HyperlinkEvent.EventType.ACTIVATED) {     // Click!
            displayPage(e.getURL());    // Follow the link; display new page
        }
        else if (type == HyperlinkEvent.EventType.ENTERED) {  // Mouse over!
            // When mouse goes over a link, display it in the message line
            messageLine.setText(e.getURL().toString());
        }
        else if (type == HyperlinkEvent.EventType.EXITED) {   // Mouse out!
            messageLine.setText(" ");  // Clear the message line
        }
    }

    /**
     * This method implements java.beans.PropertyChangeListener.  It is
     * invoked whenever a bound property changes in the JEditorPane object.
     * The property we are interested in is the "page" property, because it
     * tells us when a page has finished loading.
     **/
    public void propertyChange(PropertyChangeEvent e) {
        if (e.getPropertyName().equals("page")) // If the page property changed
            stopAnimation();                     // Then stop the loading... animation
    }

    /**
     * The fields and methods below implement a simple animation in the
     * web browser message line; they are used to provide user feedback
     * while web pages are loading.
     **/
    String animationMessage;  // The "loading..." message to display
    int animationFrame = 0;   // What "frame" of the animation are we on
    String[] animationFrames = new String[] {  // The content of each "frame"
        "-", "\\", "|", "/", "-", "\\", "|", "/",
        ",", ".", "o", "0", "O", "#", "*", "+"
    };

    /** This object calls the animate() method 8 times a second */
    javax.swing.Timer animator =
        new javax.swing.Timer(125, new ActionListener() {
                public void actionPerformed(ActionEvent e) { animate(); }
            });
```

Example 11-21. WebBrowser.java (continued)

```
/** Display the next frame. Called by the animator timer */
void animate( ) {
    String frame = animationFrames[animationFrame++];    // Get next frame
    messageLine.setText(animationMessage + " " + frame); // Update msgline
    animationFrame = animationFrame % animationFrames.length;
}

/** Start the animation.  Called by the visit( ) method. */
void startAnimation(String msg) {
    animationMessage = msg;     // Save the message to display
    animationFrame = 0;         // Start with frame 0 of the animation
    animator.start( );          // Tell the timer to start firing.
}

/** Stop the animation.  Called by propertyChanged( ) method. */
void stopAnimation( ) {
    animator.stop( );           // Tell the timer to stop firing events
    messageLine.setText(" ");   // Clear the message line
}
}
```

Describing GUIs with Properties

At its core, the task of specifying a graphical user interface is a descriptive one. This descriptive task does not map well onto a procedural and algorithm-based programming language such as Java. You end up writing lots of code that creates components, sets properties, and adds components to containers. Instead of simply describing the structure of the GUI you want, you must write the step-by-step code to build the GUI.

One way to avoid writing this tedious GUI construction code is to create a GUI-description language of some sort, then write code that can read that language and automatically create the described GUI. One common approach is to describe a GUI using an XML grammar. In this chapter, we'll rely on the simpler syntax of Java properties files as used by the ResourceBundle class. (See Chapter 8 for examples using java.util.ResourceBundle.)

A java.util.Properties object is a hashtable that maps string keys to string values. The Properties class can read and write a simple text file format in which each *name:value* line defines a single property. Furthermore, a Properties object can have a parent Properties object. When you look up the value of a property that does not exist in the child Properties object, the parent Properties object is searched (and this continues recursively). The ResourceBundle class provides an internationalization layer around properties files that allows properties to be customized for use in different locales. Internationalization is an important consideration for GUI-based applications, which makes the ResourceBundle class useful for describing GUI resources.

Handling Basic GUI Resources

Because properties files are text-based, one limitation to working with ResourceBundle objects that are based on properties files is that they support only String resources. The GUIResourceBundle class, presented in Example 11-22, is a subclass of ResourceBundle that adds additional methods for reading string resources and converting them to objects of the types commonly used in GUI programming, such as Color and Font.

The GUIResourceBundle code is straightforward. The ResourceParser interface provides an extension mechanism; we'll look at that next. Note that the MalformedResourceException class used in this example is not a standard Java class; it is a custom subclass of MissingResourceException that was developed for this example. Because it is a trivial subclass, its code is not shown here, but you'll find the code in the online example archive.

Example 11-22. GUIResourceBundle.java

```
package je3.gui;
import java.io.*;
import java.util.*;
import java.awt.*;

/**
 * This class extends ResourceBundle and adds methods to retrieve types of
 * resources commonly used in GUIs.  Additionally, it adds extensibility
 * by allowing ResourceParser objects to be registered to parse other
 * resource types.
 **/
public class GUIResourceBundle extends ResourceBundle {
    // The root object.  Required to parse certain resource types like Commands
    Object root;

    // The resource bundle that actually contains the textual resources
    // This class is a wrapper around this bundle
    ResourceBundle bundle;

    /** Create a GUIResourceBundle wrapper around a specified bundle */
    public GUIResourceBundle(Object root, ResourceBundle bundle) {
        this.root = root;
        this.bundle = bundle;
    }

    /**
     * Load a named bundle and create a GUIResourceBundle around it.  This
     * constructor takes advantage of the internationalization features of
     * the ResourceBundle.getBundle( ) method.
     **/
    public GUIResourceBundle(Object root, String bundleName)
        throws MissingResourceException
    {
        this.root = root;
        this.bundle = ResourceBundle.getBundle(bundleName);
    }
```

Example 11-22. GUIResourceBundle.java (continued)

```java
/**
 * Create a PropertyResourceBundle from the specified stream and then
 * create a GUIResourceBundle wrapper for it
 **/
public GUIResourceBundle(Object root, InputStream propertiesStream)
    throws IOException
{
    this.root = root;
    this.bundle = new PropertyResourceBundle(propertiesStream);
}

/**
 * Create a PropertyResourceBundle from the specified properties file and
 * then create a GUIResourceBundle wrapper for it.
 **/
public GUIResourceBundle(Object root, File propertiesFile)
    throws IOException
{
    this(root, new FileInputStream(propertiesFile));
}

/** This is one of the abstract methods of ResourceBundle */
public Enumeration getKeys() { return bundle.getKeys(); }

/** This is the other abstract method of ResourceBundle */
protected Object handleGetObject(String key)
    throws MissingResourceException
{
    return bundle.getObject(key);  // simply defer to the wrapped bundle
}

/** This is a property accessor method for our root object */
public Object getRoot() { return root; }

/**
 * This method is like the inherited getString() method, except that
 * when the named resource is not found, it returns the specified default
 * instead of throwing an exception
 **/
public String getString(String key, String defaultValue) {
    try { return bundle.getString(key); }
    catch(MissingResourceException e) { return defaultValue; }
}

/**
 * Look up the named resource and parse it as a list of strings separated
 * by spaces, tabs, or commas.
 **/
public java.util.List getStringList(String key)
    throws MissingResourceException
{
    String s = getString(key);
    StringTokenizer t = new StringTokenizer(s, ", \t", false);
```

Example 11-22. GUIResourceBundle.java (continued)

```
        ArrayList list = new ArrayList();
        while(t.hasMoreTokens()) list.add(t.nextToken());
        return list;
    }

    /** Like above, but return a default instead of throwing an exception */
    public java.util.List getStringList(String key,
                                        java.util.List defaultValue) {
        try { return getStringList(key); }
        catch(MissingResourceException e) { return defaultValue; }
    }

    /** Look up the named resource and try to interpret it as a boolean. */
    public boolean getBoolean(String key) throws MissingResourceException {
        String s = bundle.getString(key);
        s = s.toLowerCase();
        if (s.equals("true")) return true;
        else if (s.equals("false")) return false;
        else if (s.equals("yes")) return true;
        else if (s.equals("no")) return false;
        else if (s.equals("on")) return true;
        else if (s.equals("off")) return false;
        else {
            throw new MalformedResourceException("boolean", key);
        }
    }

    /** As above, but return the default instead of throwing an exception */
    public boolean getBoolean(String key, boolean defaultValue) {
        try { return getBoolean(key); }
        catch(MissingResourceException e) {
            if (e instanceof MalformedResourceException)
                System.err.println("WARNING: " + e.getMessage());
            return defaultValue;
        }
    }

    /** Like getBoolean(), but for integers */
    public int getInt(String key) throws MissingResourceException {
        String s = bundle.getString(key);

        try {
            // Use decode() instead of parseInt() so we support octal
            // and hexadecimal numbers
            return Integer.decode(s).intValue();
        } catch (NumberFormatException e) {
            throw new MalformedResourceException("int", key);
        }
    }

    /** As above, but with a default value */
    public int getInt(String key, int defaultValue) {
        try { return getInt(key); }
```

Example 11-22. GUIResourceBundle.java (continued)

```java
            catch(MissingResourceException e) {
                if (e instanceof MalformedResourceException)
                    System.err.println("WARNING: " + e.getMessage());
                return defaultValue;
            }
        }

        /** Return a resource of type double */
        public double getDouble(String key) throws MissingResourceException {
            String s = bundle.getString(key);

            try {
                return Double.parseDouble(s);
            } catch (NumberFormatException e) {
                throw new MalformedResourceException("double", key);
            }
        }

        /** As above, but with a default value */
        public double getDouble(String key, double defaultValue) {
            try { return getDouble(key); }
            catch(MissingResourceException e) {
                if (e instanceof MalformedResourceException)
                    System.err.println("WARNING: " + e.getMessage());
                return defaultValue;
            }
        }

        /** Look up the named resource and convert to a Font */
        public Font getFont(String key) throws MissingResourceException {
            // Font.decode() always returns a Font object, so we can't check
            // whether the resource value was well-formed or not.
            return Font.decode(bundle.getString(key));
        }

        /** As above, but with a default value */
        public Font getFont(String key, Font defaultValue) {
            try { return getFont(key); }
            catch (MissingResourceException e) { return defaultValue; }
        }

        /** Look up the named resource, and convert to a Color */
        public Color getColor(String key) throws MissingResourceException {
            try {
                return Color.decode(bundle.getString(key));
            }
            catch (NumberFormatException e) {
                // It would be useful to try to parse color names here as well
                // as numeric color specifications
                throw new MalformedResourceException("Color", key);
            }
        }
```

Example 11-22. GUIResourceBundle.java (continued)

```
/** As above, but with a default value */
public Color getColor(String key, Color defaultValue) {
    try { return getColor(key); }
    catch(MissingResourceException e) {
        if (e instanceof MalformedResourceException)
            System.err.println("WARNING: " + e.getMessage( ));
        return defaultValue;
    }
}

/** A hashtable for mapping resource types to resource parsers */
static HashMap parsers = new HashMap( );

/** An extension mechanism: register a parser for new resource types */
public static void registerResourceParser(ResourceParser parser) {
    // Ask the ResourceParser what types it can parse
    Class[ ] supportedTypes = parser.getResourceTypes( );
    // Register it in the hashtable for each of those types
    for(int i = 0; i < supportedTypes.length; i++)
        parsers.put(supportedTypes[i], parser);
}

/** Look up a ResourceParser for the specified resource type */
public static ResourceParser getResourceParser(Class type) {
    return (ResourceParser) parsers.get(type);
}

/**
 * Look for a ResourceParser for the named type, and if one is found,
 * ask it to parse and return the named resource
 **/
public Object getResource(String key, Class type)
    throws MissingResourceException
{
    // Get a parser for the specified type
    ResourceParser parser = (ResourceParser)parsers.get(type);
    if (parser == null)
        throw new MissingResourceException(
                "No ResourceParser registered for " +
                type.getName( ) + " resources",
                type.getName( ), key);

    try {  // Ask the parser to parse the resource
        return parser.parse(this, key, type);
    }
    catch(MissingResourceException e) {
        throw e;  // Rethrow MissingResourceException exceptions
    }
    catch(Exception e) {
        // If any other type of exception occurs, convert it to
        // a MalformedResourceException
        String msg = "Malformed " + type.getName( ) + " resource: " +
```

Example 11-22. GUIResourceBundle.java (continued)

```
                    key + ": " + e.getMessage( );
            throw new MalformedResourceException(msg, type.getName( ), key);
        }
    }

    /**
     * Like the 2-argument version of getResource, but return a default value
     * instead of throwing a MissingResourceException
     **/
    public Object getResource(String key, Class type, Object defaultValue) {
        try {  return getResource(key, type); }
        catch (MissingResourceException e) {
            if (e instanceof MalformedResourceException)
                System.err.println("WARNING: " + e.getMessage( ));
            return defaultValue;
        }
    }
}
```

An Extension Mechanism for Complex Resources

As we just saw, Example 11-22 uses the ResourceParser interface to provide an extension mechanism that allows it to handle more complex resource types. Example 11-23 is a listing of this simple interface. We'll see some interesting implementations of the interface in the sections that follow.

Example 11-23. ResourceParser.java

```
package je3.gui;

/**
 * This interface defines an extension mechanism that allows GUIResourceBundle
 * to parse arbitrary resource types
 **/
public interface ResourceParser {
    /**
     * Return an array of classes that specify what kind of resources
     * this parser can handle
     **/
    public Class[ ] getResourceTypes( );

    /**
     * Read the property named by key from the specified bundle, convert
     * it to the specified type, and return it.  For complex resources,
     * the parser may need to read more than one property from the bundle;
     * typically it may be a number of properties whose names begin with the
     * specified key.
     **/
    public Object parse(GUIResourceBundle bundle, String key, Class type)
        throws Exception;
}
```

Parsing Commands and Actions

For our first ResourceParser implementation, we'll add the ability to parse Action objects. As we've seen, Action objects are commonly used in GUIs; an Action includes a number of attributes—such as a description, an icon, and a tooltip—that may need to be localized. Our ActionParser implementation is based on the CommandAction class shown in Example 11-16, which in turn relies on the reflection capabilities of the Command class shown in Example 9-2.

In order to implement the ActionParser class, you need to parse Command objects from a properties file. So let's start with the CommandParser class, shown in Example 11-24. This class is quite simple because it relies on the parsing capabilities of the Command class. The ActionParser listing follows in Example 11-25.

To help you understand how these parser classes work, consider the following properties, excerpted from the *WebBrowserResources.properties* file used by the WebBrowser class of Example 11-21:

```
action.home: home( );
action.home.label: Home
action.home.description: Go to home page
action.oreilly: displayPage("http://www.oreilly.com");
action.oreilly.label: O'Reilly
action.oreilly.description: O'Reilly & Associates home page
```

These properties describe two actions, one named by the key "action.home" and the other by "action.oreilly".

Example 11-24. CommandParser.java

```java
package je3.gui;
import je3.reflect.Command;

/**
 * This class parses a Command object from a GUIResourceBundle.  It uses
 * the Command.parse( ) method to perform all the actual parsing work.
 **/
public class CommandParser implements ResourceParser {
    static final Class[] supportedTypes = new Class[] { Command.class };
    public Class[] getResourceTypes() { return supportedTypes;}

    public Object parse(GUIResourceBundle bundle, String key, Class type)
        throws java.util.MissingResourceException, java.io.IOException
    {
        String value = bundle.getString(key);  // look up the command text
        return Command.parse(bundle.getRoot( ), value);  // parse it!
    }
}
```

Example 11-25. ActionParser.java

```java
package je3.gui;
import je3.reflect.*;
import java.awt.event.*;
```

Example 11-25. ActionParser.java (continued)

```java
import javax.swing.*;
import java.util.*;

/**
 * This class parses an Action object from a GUIResourceBundle.
 * The specified key is used to look up the Command string for the action.
 * The key is also used as a prefix for other resource names that specify
 * other attributes (such as the label and icon) associated with the Action.
 * An action named "zoomOut" might be specified like this:
 *
 *      zoomOut: zoom(0.5);
 *      zoomOut.label: Zoom Out
 *      zoomOut.description: Zoom out by a factor of 2
 *
 * Because Action objects are often reused by an application (for example,
 * in a toolbar and a menu system, this ResourceParser caches the Action
 * objects it returns.  By sharing Action objects, you can disable and enable
 * an action and that change will affect the entire GUI.
 **/
public class ActionParser implements ResourceParser {
    static final Class[] supportedTypes = new Class[] { Action.class };
    public Class[] getResourceTypes() { return supportedTypes; }

    HashMap bundleToCacheMap = new HashMap();

    public Object parse(GUIResourceBundle bundle, String key, Class type)
        throws java.util.MissingResourceException
    {
        // Look up the Action cache associated with this bundle
        HashMap cache = (HashMap) bundleToCacheMap.get(bundle);
        if (cache == null) {  // If there isn't one, create one and save it
            cache = new HashMap();
            bundleToCacheMap.put(bundle, cache);
        }
        // Now look up the Action associated with the key in the cache.
        Action action = (Action) cache.get(key);
        // If we found a cached action, return it.
        if (action != null) return action;

        // If there was no cached action, create one.  The command is
        // the only required resource.  It will throw an exception if
        // missing or malformed.
        Command command = (Command) bundle.getResource(key, Command.class);

        // The remaining calls all supply default values, so they will not
        // throw exceptions, even if ResourceParsers haven't been registered
        // for types like Icon and KeyStroke
        String label = bundle.getString(key + ".label", null);
        Icon icon = (Icon) bundle.getResource(key + ".icon", Icon.class, null);
        String tooltip = bundle.getString(key + ".description", null);
        KeyStroke accelerator =
            (KeyStroke) bundle.getResource(key + ".accelerator",
                                           KeyStroke.class, null);
```

Example 11-25. ActionParser.java (continued)

```
        int mnemonic = bundle.getInt(key + ".mnemonic", KeyEvent.VK_UNDEFINED);
        boolean enabled = bundle.getBoolean(key + ".enabled", true);

        // Create a CommandAction object with these values
        action = new CommandAction(command, label, icon, tooltip,
                                   accelerator, mnemonic, enabled);

        // Save it in the cache, then return it
        cache.put(key, action);
        return action;
    }
}
```

Parsing Menus

We've seen that the GUIResourceBundle class makes it easy to read simple GUI resources, such as colors and fonts, from a properties file. We've also seen how to extend GUIResourceBundle to parse more complex resources, such as Action objects. Fonts, colors, and actions are resources that are used by the components that make up a GUI. With a small conceptual leap, however, we can start to think of GUI components themselves as resources to be used by the larger application.

Examples 11-26 and 11-27 show how this can work. These examples list the MenuBarParser and MenuParser classes, which read JMenuBar and JMenu objects, respectively, from a properties file. MenuBarParser relies on MenuParser to obtain the JMenu objects that populate the menubar, and MenuParser relies on the ActionParser class listed previously to obtain the Action objects that represent the individual menu items in each JMenu.

MenuParser and MenuBarParser read menu descriptions from properties files using a simple grammar illustrated by the following lines from the *WebBrowserResource. properties* file:

```
# The menubar contains two menus, named "menu.file" and "menu.go"
menubar: menu.file menu.go

# The "menu.file" menu has the label "File".  It contains five items
# specified as action objects, and these items are separated into two
# groups by a separator
menu.file: File: action.new action.open - action.close action.exit

# The "menu.go" menu has the label "Go", and contains four items
menu.go: Go: action.back action.forward action.reload action.home
```

These lines describe a menubar with the property name "menubar" and all its submenus. Note that I've omitted the properties that define the actions contained by the individual menu panes.

As you can see, the menubar grammar is quite simple: it is just a list of the property names of the menus contained by the menubar. For this reason, the MenuBarParser code in Example 11-26 is quite simple. The grammar that describes menus is somewhat more complicated, which is reflected in Example 11-27.

You may recall that the WebBrowser example also uses the GUIResourceBundle to read a JToolBar from the properties file. This is done using a ToolBarParser class. The code for that class is quite similar to the code for MenuBarParser and is not listed here. It is available in the online example archive, however.

Example 11-26. MenuBarParser.java

```java
package je3.gui;
import javax.swing.*;
import java.util.*;

/**
 * Parse a JMenuBar from a ResourceBundle.  A menubar is represented
 * simply as a list of menu property names.  E.g.:
 *      menubar: menu.file menu.edit menu.view menu.help
 **/
public class MenuBarParser implements ResourceParser {
    static final Class[] supportedTypes = new Class[] { JMenuBar.class };
    public Class[] getResourceTypes() { return supportedTypes; }

    public Object parse(GUIResourceBundle bundle, String key, Class type)
        throws java.util.MissingResourceException
    {
        // Get the value of the key as a list of strings
        List menuList = bundle.getStringList(key);

        // Create a MenuBar
        JMenuBar menubar = new JMenuBar();

        // Create a JMenu for each of the menu property names,
        // and add it to the bar
        int nummenus = menuList.size();
        for(int i = 0; i < nummenus; i++) {
            menubar.add((JMenu) bundle.getResource((String)menuList.get(i),
                                                    JMenu.class));
        }

        return menubar;
    }
}
```

Example 11-27. MenuParser.java

```java
package je3.gui;
import je3.reflect.*;
import java.awt.event.*;
import javax.swing.*;
import java.util.StringTokenizer;

/**
 * This class parses a JMenu or JPopupMenu from textual descriptions found in
 * a GUIResourceBundle.  The grammar is straightforward: the menu label
 * followed by a colon and a list of menu items.  Menu items that begin with
 * a '>' character are submenus.  Menu items that begin with a '-' character
```

Example 11-27. MenuParser.java (continued)

```
* are separators.  All other items are action names.
**/
public class MenuParser implements ResourceParser {
    static final Class[] supportedTypes = new Class[] {
        JMenu.class, JPopupMenu.class  // This class handles two resource types
    };

    public Class[] getResourceTypes() { return supportedTypes; }

    public Object parse(GUIResourceBundle bundle, String key, Class type)
        throws java.util.MissingResourceException
    {
        // Get the string value of the key
        String menudef = bundle.getString(key);

        // Break it up into words, ignoring whitespace, colons, and commas
        StringTokenizer st = new StringTokenizer(menudef, " \t:,");

        // The first word is the label of the menu
        String menuLabel = st.nextToken();

        // Create either a JMenu or JPopupMenu
        JMenu menu = null;
        JPopupMenu popup = null;
        if (type == JMenu.class) menu = new JMenu(menuLabel);
        else popup = new JPopupMenu(menuLabel);

        // Then loop through the rest of the words, creating a JMenuItem
        // for each one.  Accumulate these items in a list
        while(st.hasMoreTokens()) {
            String item = st.nextToken();      // the next word
            char firstchar = item.charAt(0);   // determines type of menu item
            switch(firstchar) {
            case '-':    // words beginning with - add a separator to the menu
                if (menu != null) menu.addSeparator();
                else popup.addSeparator();
                break;
            case '>':    // words beginning with > are submenu names
                // strip off the > character, and recurse to parse the submenu
                item = item.substring(1);
                // Parse a submenu and add it to the list of items
                JMenu submenu = (JMenu)parse(bundle, item, JMenu.class);
                if (menu != null) menu.add(submenu);
                else popup.add(submenu);
                break;
            case '!': // words beginning with ! are action names
                item = item.substring(1);   // strip off the ! character
                /* falls through */         // fall through to the next case
            default:  // By default all other words are taken as action names
                // Look up the named action and add it to the menu
                Action action = (Action)bundle.getResource(item, Action.class);
                if (menu != null) menu.add(action);
```

Example 11-27. MenuParser.java (continued)

```
                else popup.add(action);
                break;
            }
        }

        // Finally, return the menu or the popup menu
        if (menu != null) return menu;
        else return popup;
    }
}
```

Themes and the Metal Look-and-Feel

The default platform-independent look-and-feel for Swing applications is known as the Metal look-and-feel. One of the powerful but little-known features of Metal is that the fonts and colors it uses are easily customizable. All you have to do is pass a MetalTheme object to the static setCurrentTheme( ) method of MetalLookAndFeel. (These classes are defined in the infrequently used javax.swing.plaf.metal package.)

The MetalTheme class is abstract, so, in practice, you work with DefaultMetalTheme. This class has six methods that return the basic theme colors (really three shades each of a primary and a secondary color) and four methods that return the basic theme fonts. To define a new theme, all you have to do is subclass DefaultMetalTheme and override these methods to return the fonts and colors you want. (If you want more customizability than this, you have to subclass MetalTheme directly.)

Example 11-28 is a listing of *ThemeManager.java*. This example includes a subclass of DefaultMetalTheme, but defines it as an inner class of ThemeManager. The ThemeManager class provides the ability to read theme definitions (i.e., color and font specifications) from a GUIResourceBundle and defines methods for reading the name of a default theme and a list of names of all available themes from the bundle. Finally, ThemeManager can return a JMenu component that displays a list of available themes to the user and switches the current theme based on the user's selection.

ThemeManager also demonstrates a feature unrelated to DefaultMetalTheme: it includes the ability to tell Swing whether it should provide audio feedback for all, some, or none of the user actions for which Swing is capable of playing sounds. It does this by setting an undocumented property[*] with the UIManager.put( ) method.

ThemeManager, and the JMenu component it creates, were used in the WebBrowser class of Example 11-21. Before you examine the ThemeManager code, take a look at

---

[*] The properties are not documented within the javadoc API, but you can find out more by searching the web for the string "AuditoryCues.playList".

the following lines excerpted from the `WebBrowserResources.properties` file, which define the set of available themes for the web browser:

```
# This property defines the property names of all available themes.
themelist: theme.metal theme.rose, theme.lime, theme.primary, theme.bigfont
# This property defines the name of the default property
defaultTheme: theme.metal

# This theme only has a name.  All font and color values are unchanged from
# the default Metal theme
theme.metal.name: Default Metal

# This theme uses shades of red/pink
theme.rose.name: Rose
theme.rose.primary: #905050
theme.rose.secondary: #906050
theme.rose.sounds: all

# This theme uses lime green colors
theme.lime.name: Lime
theme.lime.primary: #509050
theme.lime.secondary: #506060
theme.lime.sounds: none

# This theme uses bright primary colors
theme.primary.name: Primary Colors
theme.primary.primary: #202090
theme.primary.secondary: #209020
theme.primary.sounds: default

# This theme uses big fonts and the default colors
theme.bigfont.name: Big Fonts
theme.bigfont.controlFont: sansserif-bold-18
theme.bigfont.menuFont: sansserif-bold-18
theme.bigfont.smallFont: sansserif-plain-14
theme.bigfont.systemFont: sansserif-plain-14
theme.bigfont.userFont: sansserif-plain-14
theme.bigfont.titleFont: sansserif-bold-18
```

With these theme definitions, you should have no trouble understanding the resource-parsing code of `ThemeManager`. `getThemeMenu()` creates a `JMenu` populated by `JRadioButtonMenuItem` objects, rather than `JMenuItem` or `Action` objects, as we've seen earlier in this chapter. This emphasizes the fact that only one theme can be selected at a time. When the theme is changed, the `setTheme()` method uses a `SwingUtilities` method to propagate the change to all components within the frame. Finally, note that the `Theme` inner class doesn't use `Font` and `Color` objects, but uses `FontUIResource` and `ColorUIResource` objects instead. These classes are part of the `javax.swing.plaf` package and are trivial subclasses of `Font` and `Color` that implement the `UIResource` marker interface. This interface allows components to distinguish between property values assigned by the look-and-feel, which all implement `UIResource`, and property values assigned by the application. Based on this distinction, application settings can override look-and-feel settings, even when the look-and-feel (or theme) changes while the application is running.

Example 11-28. ThemeManager.java

```
package je3.gui;
import java.awt.*;
import java.awt.event.*;
import javax.swing.*;
import javax.swing.plaf.*;
import javax.swing.plaf.metal.MetalLookAndFeel;
import javax.swing.plaf.metal.DefaultMetalTheme;

/**
 * This class reads theme descriptions from a GUIResourceBundle and uses them
 * to specify colors and fonts for the Metal look-and-feel.  It also
 * demonstrates an undocumented feature for turning Swing notification sounds
 * on and off.
 **/
public class ThemeManager {
    JFrame frame;                      // The frame which themes are applied to
    GUIResourceBundle resources;       // Properties describing the themes

    /**
     * Build a ThemeManager for the frame and resource bundle.  If there
     * is a default theme specified, apply it to the frame
     **/
    public ThemeManager(JFrame frame, GUIResourceBundle resources) {
        this.frame = frame;
        this.resources = resources;
        String defaultName = getDefaultThemeName( );
        if (defaultName != null) setTheme(defaultName);
    }

    /** Look up the named theme, and apply it to the frame */
    public void setTheme(String themeName) {
        // Look up the theme in the resource bundle
        Theme theme = new Theme(resources, themeName);

        // Make it the current theme
        MetalLookAndFeel.setCurrentTheme(theme);

        // Reapply the Metal look-and-feel to install new theme
        try { UIManager.setLookAndFeel(new MetalLookAndFeel( )); }
        catch(UnsupportedLookAndFeelException e) { }

        // If the theme has an audio playlist, then set it
        if (theme.playlist != null)
            UIManager.put("AuditoryCues.playList", theme.playlist);

        // Propagate the new l&f across the entire component tree of the frame
        SwingUtilities.updateComponentTreeUI(frame);
    }

    /** Get the "display name" or label of the named theme */
    public String getDisplayName(String themeName) {
        return resources.getString(themeName + ".name", null);
    }
```

Example 11-28. ThemeManager.java (continued)

```java
/** Get the name of the default theme, or null */
public String getDefaultThemeName( ) {
    return resources.getString("defaultTheme", null);
}

/**
 * Get the list of all known theme names.  The returned values are
 * theme property names, not theme display names.
 **/
public String[ ] getAllThemeNames( ) {
    java.util.List names = resources.getStringList("themelist");
    return (String[ ]) names.toArray(new String[names.size( )]);
}

/**
 * Get a JMenu that lists all known themes by display name and
 * installs any selected theme.
 **/
public JMenu getThemeMenu( ) {
    String[ ] names = getAllThemeNames( );
    String defaultName = getDefaultThemeName( );
    JMenu menu = new JMenu("Themes");
    ButtonGroup buttongroup = new ButtonGroup( );
    for(int i = 0; i < names.length; i++) {
        final String themeName = names[i];
        String displayName = getDisplayName(themeName);
        JMenuItem item = menu.add(new JRadioButtonMenuItem(displayName));
        buttongroup.add(item);
        if (themeName.equals(defaultName)) item.setSelected(true);
        item.addActionListener(new ActionListener( ) {
                public void actionPerformed(ActionEvent event) {
                    setTheme(themeName);
                }
            });
    }
    return menu;
}

/**
 * This class extends the DefaultMetalTheme class to return Color and
 * Font values read from a GUIResourceBundle
 **/
public static class Theme extends DefaultMetalTheme {
    // These fields are the values returned by this Theme
    String displayName;
    FontUIResource controlFont, menuFont, smallFont;
    FontUIResource systemFont, userFont, titleFont;
    ColorUIResource primary1, primary2, primary3;
    ColorUIResource secondary1, secondary2, secondary3;
    Object playlist;  // auditory cues
```

Example 11-28. ThemeManager.java (continued)

```
/**
 * This constructor reads all the values it needs from the
 * GUIResourceBundle.  It uses intelligent defaults if properties
 * are not specified.
 **/
public Theme(GUIResourceBundle resources, String name) {
    // Use this theme object to get default font values from
    DefaultMetalTheme defaultTheme = new DefaultMetalTheme();

    // Look up the display name of the theme
    displayName = resources.getString(name + ".name", null);

    // Look up the fonts for the theme
    Font control = resources.getFont(name + ".controlFont", null);
    Font menu = resources.getFont(name + ".menuFont", null);
    Font small = resources.getFont(name + ".smallFont", null);
    Font system = resources.getFont(name + ".systemFont", null);
    Font user = resources.getFont(name + ".userFont", null);
    Font title = resources.getFont(name + ".titleFont", null);

    // Convert fonts to FontUIResource, or get defaults
    if (control != null) controlFont = new FontUIResource(control);
    else controlFont = defaultTheme.getControlTextFont();
    if (menu != null) menuFont = new FontUIResource(menu);
    else menuFont = defaultTheme.getMenuTextFont();
    if (small != null) smallFont = new FontUIResource(small);
    else smallFont = defaultTheme.getSubTextFont();
    if (system != null) systemFont = new FontUIResource(system);
    else systemFont = defaultTheme.getSystemTextFont();
    if (user != null) userFont = new FontUIResource(user);
    else userFont = defaultTheme.getUserTextFont();
    if (title != null) titleFont = new FontUIResource(title);
    else titleFont = defaultTheme.getWindowTitleFont();

    // Look up primary and secondary colors
    Color primary = resources.getColor(name + ".primary", null);
    Color secondary = resources.getColor(name + ".secondary", null);

    // Derive all six colors from these two, using defaults if needed
    if (primary != null) primary1 = new ColorUIResource(primary);
    else primary1 = new ColorUIResource(102, 102, 153);
    primary2 = new ColorUIResource(primary1.brighter());
    primary3 = new ColorUIResource(primary2.brighter());
    if (secondary != null) secondary1 = new ColorUIResource(secondary);
    else secondary1 = new ColorUIResource(102, 102, 102);
    secondary2 = new ColorUIResource(secondary1.brighter());
    secondary3 = new ColorUIResource(secondary2.brighter());

    // Look up what type of sound is desired.  This property should
    // be one of the strings "all", "none", or "default".  These map to
    // undocumented UIManager properties.  playlist is an array of
    // strings, but we keep it as an opaque object.
```

Example 11-28. ThemeManager.java (continued)

```
        String sounds = resources.getString(name + ".sounds", "");
        if (sounds.equals("all"))
            playlist = UIManager.get("AuditoryCues.allAuditoryCues");
        else if (sounds.equals("none"))
            playlist = UIManager.get("AuditoryCues.noAuditoryCues");
        else if (sounds.equals("default"))
            playlist = UIManager.get("AuditoryCues.defaultCueList");
    }

    // These methods override DefaultMetalTheme and return the property
    // values we looked up and computed for this theme
    public String getName() { return displayName; }
    public FontUIResource getControlTextFont() { return controlFont;}
    public FontUIResource getSystemTextFont() { return systemFont;}
    public FontUIResource getUserTextFont() { return userFont;}
    public FontUIResource getMenuTextFont() { return menuFont;}
    public FontUIResource getWindowTitleFont() { return titleFont;}
    public FontUIResource getSubTextFont() { return smallFont;}
    protected ColorUIResource getPrimary1() { return primary1; }
    protected ColorUIResource getPrimary2() { return primary2; }
    protected ColorUIResource getPrimary3() { return primary3; }
    protected ColorUIResource getSecondary1() { return secondary1; }
    protected ColorUIResource getSecondary2() { return secondary2; }
    protected ColorUIResource getSecondary3() { return secondary3; }
    }
}
```

Look-and-Feel Preferences

A number of the examples in this chapter have used the utility class
LookAndFeelPrefs to install the user's preferred look-and-feel and create a JMenu
listing available look-and-feel choices. LookAndFeelPrefs is shown in
Example 11-29. It demonstrates the use of the javax.swing.UIManager class for
querying and setting look-and-feels, and also demonstrates the use of the java.
util.prefs package (new in Java 1.4) for retrieving and storing persistent user
preferences.

LookAndFeelPrefs relies on the list of installed look-and-feel implementations
returned by UIManager.getInstalledLookAndFeels(). By default (in Java 1.4.2, at
least) this method returns three look-and-feels: the Java "Metal" look-and-feel, the
Motif (CDE) look-and-feel, and the Windows look-and-feel. This is true even on
non-Windows platforms for which the Windows look-and-feel is unsupported.
Java 1.4.2 also ships with a GTK look-and-feel, which mimics the Linux GTK
look-and-feel, but getInstalledLookAndFeels() does not know about it. To make
this new look-and-feel available to the LookAndFeelPrefs example, you'll need to
create a *swing.properties* file and place it in the *jre/lib/* directory of your Java SDK.
The contents of the file should look like this:

```
# Add the Mac look-and-feel if your SDK comes with it.
# Delete the Windows look-and-feel if it is not supported on your platform.
swing.installedlafs = gtk,metal,motif,win
```

```
swing.installedlaf.gtk.name = GTK Look and Feel,
swing.installedlaf.gtk.class = com.sun.java.swing.plaf.gtk.GTKLookAndFeel
swing.installedlaf.metal.name = Java Look and Feel
swing.installedlaf.metal.class = javax.swing.plaf.metal.MetalLookAndFeel
swing.installedlaf.motif.name = Motif/CDE Look and Feel
swing.installedlaf.motif.class = com.sun.java.swing.plaf.motif.
MotifLookAndFeel
swing.installedlaf.win.name = Windows Look and Feel
swing.installedlaf.win.class = com.sun.java.swing.plaf.windows.
WindowsLookAndFeel
```

Example 11-29. LookAndFeelPrefs.java

```java
package je3.gui;
import javax.swing.*;
import java.awt.event.*;
import java.util.prefs.Preferences;

public class LookAndFeelPrefs {
    public static final String PREF_NAME = "preferredLookAndFeelClassName";

    /**
     * Get the desired look-and-feel from a per-user preference.  If
     * the preference doesn't exist or is unavailable, use the
     * default look-and-feel.  The preference is shared by all classes
     * in the same package as prefsClass.
     **/
    public static void setPreferredLookAndFeel(Class prefsClass) {
        Preferences prefs=Preferences.userNodeForPackage(prefsClass);
        String defaultLAF = UIManager.getSystemLookAndFeelClassName();
        String laf = prefs.get(PREF_NAME, defaultLAF);
        try { UIManager.setLookAndFeel(laf); }
        catch (Exception e) { // ClassNotFound or InstantiationException
            // An exception here is probably caused by a bogus preference.
            // Ignore it silently; the user will make do with the default LAF.
        }
    }

    /**
     * Create a menu of radio buttons listing the available Look and Feels.
     * When the user selects one, change the component hierarchy under frame
     * to the new LAF, and store the new selection as the current preference
     * for the package containing class c.
     **/
    public static JMenu createLookAndFeelMenu(final Class prefsClass,
                                              final ActionListener listener)
    {
        // Create the menu
        final JMenu plafmenu = new JMenu("Look and Feel");

        // Create an object used for radio button mutual exclusion
        ButtonGroup radiogroup = new ButtonGroup();

        // Look up the available look-and-feels
        UIManager.LookAndFeelInfo[] plafs=UIManager.getInstalledLookAndFeels();
```

Example 11-29. LookAndFeelPrefs.java (continued)

```
        // Find out which one is currently used
        String currentLAFName=UIManager.getLookAndFeel().getClass().getName();

        // Loop through the plafs, and add a menu item for each one
        for(int i = 0; i < plafs.length; i++) {
            String plafName = plafs[i].getName();
            final String plafClassName = plafs[i].getClassName();

            // Create the menu item
            final JMenuItem item =
                plafmenu.add(new JRadioButtonMenuItem(plafName));
            item.setSelected(plafClassName.equals(currentLAFName));

            // Tell the menu item what to do when it is selected
            item.addActionListener(new ActionListener() {
                public void actionPerformed(ActionEvent event) {
                    // Set the new look-and-feel
                    try { UIManager.setLookAndFeel(plafClassName); }
                    catch(UnsupportedLookAndFeelException e) {
                        // Sometimes a Look-and-Feel is installed but not
                        // supported, as in the Windows LaF on Linux platforms.
                        JOptionPane.showMessageDialog(plafmenu,
                            "The selected Look-and-Feel is " +
                            "not supported on this platform.",
                            "Unsupported Look And Feel",
                            JOptionPane.ERROR_MESSAGE);
                        item.setEnabled(false);
                    }
                    catch (Exception e) { // ClassNotFound or Instantiation
                        item.setEnabled(false);   // shouldn't happen
                    }

                    // Make the selection persistent by storing it in prefs.
                    Preferences p = Preferences.userNodeForPackage(prefsClass);
                    p.put(PREF_NAME, plafClassName);

                    // Invoke the supplied action listener so the calling
                    // application can update its components to the new LAF
                    // Reuse the event that was passed here.
                    listener.actionPerformed(event);
                }
            });

            // Only allow one menu item to be selected at once
            radiogroup.add(item);
        }

        return plafmenu;
    }
}
```

The ShowBean Program

We began this chapter using the ShowBean program to experiment with Swing components, and with the custom components developed as examples. As promised, the implementation is here in Example 11-30. This is another example of a Swing application that uses JFrame, JMenuBar, and so on. It uses the LookAndFeelPrefs utility class from Example 11-29, demonstrates the JTabbedPane component, and shows the use of tooltips in Swing.

ShowBean relies on the Bean class of Example 15-10. This class provides the Java-Beans magic for listing, querying, setting, and invoking bean properties and commands. You'll have to skip ahead to Chapter 15 if you want to see how that piece works.

ShowBean also has a feature that was not mentioned before: in addition to creating beans based on their classname, it can also read beans that have been serialized to a file using the java.io serialization mechanism or the (new in Java 1.4) Java-Beans persistence mechanism. Use the -ser or -xml options on the command line to create a bean from a file. Additionally, the **File** menu contains entries that allow you to save a bean (and its currently set properties) to a file using either serialization or the JavaBeans persistence mechanism.

Example 11-30. ShowBean.java

```
package je3.gui;
import java.awt.*;
import java.awt.event.*;
import javax.swing.*;
import javax.swing.event.*;
import java.beans.*;
import java.lang.reflect.*;
import java.util.List;  // explicit import to disambiguate from java.awt.List
import java.util.*;
import java.io.*;
import je3.beans.Bean;

/**
 * This class is a program that uses reflection and JavaBeans introspection to
 * create a set of named components, set named properties on those components,
 * and display them.  It allows the user to view the components using any
 * installed look-and-feel.  It is intended as a simple way to experiment with
 * AWT and Swing components, and to view a number of the other examples
 * developed in this chapter.  It also demonstrates frames, menus, and the
 * JTabbedPane component.
 **/
public class ShowBean extends JFrame {
    // The main program
    public static void main(String[] args) {
        // Set the look-and-feel for the application.
        // LookAndFeelPrefs is defined elsewhere in this package.
        LookAndFeelPrefs.setPreferredLookAndFeel(ShowBean.class);

        // Process the command line to get the components to display
        List beans = getBeansFromArgs(args);
```

Example 11-30. ShowBean.java (continued)

```
        JFrame frame = new ShowBean(beans);  // Create frame

        // Handle window close requests by exiting the VM
        frame.addWindowListener(new WindowAdapter() { // Anonymous inner class
                public void windowClosing(WindowEvent e) { System.exit(0); }
            });

        frame.setVisible(true);     // Make the frame visible on the screen

        // The main() method exits now, but the Java VM keeps running because
        // all AWT programs automatically start an event-handling thread.
    }

    List beans;
    JMenu propertyMenu, commandMenu;
    JTabbedPane pane;
    JFileChooser fileChooser = new JFileChooser();

    // Most initialization code is in the constructor instead of main()
    public ShowBean(final List beans) {
        super("ShowBean");

        this.beans = beans;  // Save the list of Bean objects

        // Create a menubar
        JMenuBar menubar = new JMenuBar();
        this.setJMenuBar(menubar);                  // Tell the frame to display it

        // Create and populate a File menu
        JMenu filemenu = new JMenu("File");
        filemenu.setMnemonic('F');
        JMenuItem save = new JMenuItem("Save as...");
        save.setMnemonic('S');
        JMenuItem serialize = new JMenuItem("Serialize as...");
        JMenuItem quit = new JMenuItem("Quit");
        quit.setMnemonic('Q');
        menubar.add(filemenu);
        filemenu.add(save);
        filemenu.add(serialize);
        filemenu.add(new JSeparator());
        filemenu.add(quit);

        // Here are event handlers for the Save As and Quit menu items
        save.addActionListener(new ActionListener() {
                public void actionPerformed(ActionEvent e) {
                    saveCurrentPane();
                }
            });
        serialize.addActionListener(new ActionListener() {
                public void actionPerformed(ActionEvent e) {
                    serializeCurrentPane();
                }
            });
```

Example 11-30. ShowBean.java (continued)

```
quit.addActionListener(new ActionListener( ) {
        public void actionPerformed(ActionEvent e) {
            System.exit(0);
        }
    });

// Set up a menu that allows the user to select the look-and-feel of
// the component from a list of installed look-and-feels.
// Remember the selected LAF in a persistent Preferences node.
JMenu plafmenu =
  LookAndFeelPrefs.createLookAndFeelMenu(ShowBean.class,
      new ActionListener( ) {
          public void actionPerformed(ActionEvent event) {
              // When the user selects a new LAF, tell each
              // component to change its look-and-feel
              SwingUtilities.updateComponentTreeUI(ShowBean.this);
              // Then repack the frame to its new preferred size.
              ShowBean.this.pack( );
          }
      });
plafmenu.setMnemonic('L');
menubar.add(plafmenu);                        // Add the menu to the menubar

// Create the Properties and Commands menus, but don't populate them.
// JMenuItems are added each time a new tab is selected.
propertyMenu = new JMenu("Properties");
propertyMenu.setMnemonic('P');
menubar.add(propertyMenu);
commandMenu = new JMenu("Commands");
commandMenu.setMnemonic('C');
menubar.add(commandMenu);

// Some components have many properties, so make the property menu
// three columns wide so that we can see all of the entries.
propertyMenu.getPopupMenu( ).setLayout(new GridLayout(0,3));

// Create a JTabbedPane to display each of the components
pane = new JTabbedPane( );
pane.addChangeListener(new ChangeListener( ) {
        public void stateChanged(ChangeEvent e) {
            populateMenus(pane.getSelectedIndex( ));
        }
    });

// Now add each component as a tab of the tabbed pane
for(int i = 0; i < beans.size( ); i++) {
    Bean b = (Bean) beans.get(i);
    Object o = b.getBean( );
    Component component;
    if (o instanceof Component) component = (Component) o;
    else component = new JLabel("This bean has no Component");
    Image image = b.getIcon( );
```

Example 11-30. ShowBean.java (continued)

```
        Icon icon = null;
        if (image != null) icon = new ImageIcon(image);
        pane.addTab(b.getDisplayName( ),            // text for the tab
                    icon,                           // icon for the tab
                    component,                      // contents of the tab
                    b.getShortDescription( ));      // tooltip for the tab
    }

    // Add the tabbed pane to this frame. Note the call to getContentPane( )
    // This is required for JFrame, but not for most Swing components.
    this.getContentPane( ).add(pane);

    this.pack( );   // Make frame as big as its kids need
}

/**
 * This static method loops through the command-line arguments looking for
 * the names of files that contain XML encoded or serialized components,
 * or for class names of components to instantiate or for name=value
 * property settings for those components. It relies on the Bean class
 * developed elsewhere.
 **/
static List getBeansFromArgs(String[ ] args) {
    List beans = new ArrayList( );      // List of beans to return
    Bean bean = null;                   // The current bean
    boolean expert = false;

    for(int i = 0; i < args.length; i++) {  // Loop through all arguments
        if (args[i].charAt(0) == '-') { // Does it begin with a dash?
            try {
                if (args[i].equals("-expert")) {
                    expert = true;
                }
                else if (args[i].equals("-xml")) { // read from xml
                    if (++i >= args.length) continue;
                    InputStream in = new FileInputStream(args[i]);
                    bean = Bean.fromPersistentStream(in, expert);
                    beans.add(bean);
                    in.close( );
                }
                else if (args[i].equals("-ser")) {  // deserialize a file
                    if (++i >= args.length) continue;
                    ObjectInputStream in =
                        new ObjectInputStream(new FileInputStream(args[i]));
                    bean = Bean.fromSerializedStream(in, expert);
                    beans.add(bean);
                    in.close( );
                }
                else {
                    System.err.println("Unknown option: " + args[i]);
                    continue;
                }
            }
```

Example 11-30. ShowBean.java (continued)

```
            catch(Exception e) {  // In case anything goes wrong
                System.err.println(e);
                System.exit(1);
                continue;
            }
        }
        else if (args[i].indexOf('=') == -1){ // It's a component name
            // If the argument does not contain an equal sign, then it is
            // a component class name.
            try {
                bean = Bean.forClassName(args[i], expert);
                beans.add(bean);
            }
            catch(Exception e) {
                // If any step failed, print an error and exit
                System.out.println("Can't load, instantiate, " +
                                    "or introspect: " + args[i]);
                System.out.println(e);
                System.exit(1);
            }
        }
        else { // The arg is a name=value property specification
            // Break into name and value parts
            int pos = args[i].indexOf('=');
            String name = args[i].substring(0, pos); // property name
            String value = args[i].substring(pos+1); // property value

            // If we don't have a component to set this property on, skip!
            if (bean == null) {
                System.err.println("Property " + name +
                                    " specified before any bean.");
                continue;
            }

            // Now try to set the property
            try { bean.setPropertyValue(name, value); }
            catch(Exception e) {
                // Failure to set a property is not a fatal error;
                // Just display the message and continue
                System.out.println(e);
            }
        }
    }

    return beans;
}

/**
 * Ask the user to select a filename, and then save the contents of
 * the current tab to that file using the JavaBeans persistence mechanism.
 */
```

Example 11-30. ShowBean.java (continued)

```java
public void saveCurrentPane( ) {
    int result = fileChooser.showSaveDialog(this);
    if (result == JFileChooser.APPROVE_OPTION) {
        try {
            File file = fileChooser.getSelectedFile( );
            XMLEncoder encoder=new XMLEncoder(new FileOutputStream(file));
            encoder.writeObject(pane.getSelectedComponent( ));
            encoder.close( );
        }
        catch(IOException e) {
            JOptionPane.showMessageDialog(this, e, e.getClass( ).getName( ),
                                JOptionPane.ERROR_MESSAGE);
        }
    }
}

/**
 * Ask the user to choose a filename, and then save the contents of the
 * current pane to that file using traditional object serialization
 */
public void serializeCurrentPane( ) {
    int result = fileChooser.showSaveDialog(this);
    if (result == JFileChooser.APPROVE_OPTION) {
        try {
            File file = fileChooser.getSelectedFile( );
            ObjectOutputStream out =
                new ObjectOutputStream(new FileOutputStream(file));
            out.writeObject(pane.getSelectedComponent( ));
            out.close( );
        }
        catch(IOException e) {
            JOptionPane.showMessageDialog(this, e, e.getClass( ).getName( ),
                                JOptionPane.ERROR_MESSAGE);
        }
    }
}

/**
 * Create JMenuItem objects in the Properties and Command menus.
 * This method is called whenever a new tab is selected.
 */
void populateMenus(int index) {
    // First, delete the old menu contents
    propertyMenu.removeAll( );
    commandMenu.removeAll( );

    // The Bean object for this tab
    final Bean bean = (Bean) beans.get(index);

    List props = bean.getPropertyNames( );
    for(int i = 0; i < props.size( ); i++) {
        final String name = (String)props.get(i);
```

Graphical User
Interfaces

Example 11-30. ShowBean.java (continued)

```
                // Create a menu item for the command
                JMenuItem item = new JMenuItem(name);
                // If the property has a nontrivial description, make it a tooltip
                String tip = bean.getPropertyDescription(name);
                if (tip != null && !tip.equals(name)) item.setToolTipText(tip);

                item.addActionListener(new ActionListener() {
                        public void actionPerformed(ActionEvent e) {
                            editProperty(bean, name);
                        }
                });

                propertyMenu.add(item);
            }

            List commands = bean.getCommandNames();
            for(int i = 0; i < commands.size(); i++) {
                final String name = (String)commands.get(i);
                // Create a menu item for the command
                JMenuItem item = new JMenuItem(name);
                // If the command has a nontrivial description, make it a tooltip
                String tip = bean.getCommandDescription(name);
                if (tip != null && !name.endsWith(tip)) item.setToolTipText(tip);

                // Invoke the command when the item is selected
                item.addActionListener(new ActionListener() {
                        public void actionPerformed(ActionEvent e) {
                            try { bean.invokeCommand(name); }
                            catch(Exception ex) {
                                getToolkit().beep();
                                JOptionPane.showMessageDialog(ShowBean.this,
                                            ex, ex.getClass().getName(),
                                            JOptionPane.ERROR_MESSAGE);
                            }
                        }
                });
                // Add the item to the menu
                commandMenu.add(item);
            }
        if (commands.size() == 0)
            commandMenu.add("No Commands Available");
    }

    void editProperty(Bean bean, String name) {
        try {
            if (bean.isReadOnly(name)) {
                String value = bean.getPropertyValue(name);
                JOptionPane.showMessageDialog(this, name + " = " + value,
                                "Read-only Property Value",
                                JOptionPane.PLAIN_MESSAGE);
            }
```

Example 11-30. ShowBean.java (continued)

```
      else {
          Component editor = bean.getPropertyEditor(name);
          JOptionPane.showMessageDialog(this,
                                        new Object[ ] { name, editor},
                                        "Edit Property",
                                        JOptionPane.PLAIN_MESSAGE);
      }
    }
    catch(Exception e) {
        getToolkit().beep();
        JOptionPane.showMessageDialog(this, e, e.getClass().getName(),
                                      JOptionPane.ERROR_MESSAGE);
    }
  }
}
```

Exercises

Exercise 11-1. Take a look again at Figure 11-7. Write a class that produces a sample layout like GridBagLayoutPane, without using the GridBagLayout layout manager. You'll probably want to use BorderLayout and the Box container or BoxLayout layout manager.

Exercise 11-2. The ScribblePane class of Example 11-13 draws all of its lines using the foreground property. If this property changes, the color of all lines changes. Modify the class so that it remembers the setting of foreground when each PolyLine was drawn, and uses these retained colors in its paintComponent() method. With this modification, changes to the foreground property will not affect the currently displayed lines, only lines subsequently drawn.

Exercise 11-3. The ItemChooser class allows items to be specified only when the component is created. Add methods that allow items to be added and removed. Make the methods work regardless of the presentation type in use.

Exercise 11-4. The ScribbleApp application defines and uses a ColorAction class to allow the user to select the current drawing color. Add a LineWidthAction class that lets the user select the line width. To accomplish this, give the ScribblePane component a setLineWidth() method so that the line width can be varied.

Exercise 11-5. One shortcoming of the FontChooser class is that when you call setSelectedFont(), the ItemChooser components are not updated to match the current font. Modify FontChooser so that it does update these selections. You'll probably want to modify ItemChooser so that, in addition to its setSelectedIndex() method, it also has setSelectedLabel() and setSelectedValue() methods that specify the selected item by label or by value.

Exercise 11-6. Modify ShowBean so that it has a **Containment Hierarchy...** item in the **File** menu. When the user selects this item, the program should display a ComponentTree component (see Example 11-20) in a separate window, to display the containment hierarchy of the currently displayed bean.

Exercise 11-7. A common feature of web browsers is a **Go** menu that lists the last 10 or 15 URLs that have been visited and provides a quick way to revisit those sites. Add this feature to the WebBrowser class. Note that WebBrowser already tracks its browsing history. You need to add a **Go** menu to the JMenuBar that is read from the GUIResourceBundle. The contents of the **Go** menu depends on the current browsing history. One technique is to change the contents of the menu each time the browser visits a new page. Alternatively, you can use a MenuListener object to receive notification just before the menu is popped up, and then, from the menuSelected( ) method of the listener, add the appropriate items to the menu.

Exercise 11-8. The GUIResourceBundle class and the ResourceParser extension interface provide a powerful mechanism for describing a GUI in a properties file. Implement more ResourceParser classes to support other resource types. In particular, write parsers for the ImageIcon and KeyStroke classes; support for these two types is required to fully support the ActionParser class.

Exercise 11-9. Modify the ShowBean class to use the ThemeManager class (with an appropriate properties file) and the **Themes** menu it can create. Ideally, you should make the **Themes** menu a submenu of the **Look and Feel** menu the program already displays. Modify ThemeManager to retain the user's preferred theme using the java.util.prefs package, like LookAndFeelPrefs does.

12

Graphics

Java 1.0 and 1.1 provided rudimentary graphics capabilities through the java.awt. Graphics class and associated classes, such as java.awt.Color and java.awt.Font. In Java 1.2 and later, the Java 2D API provides state-of-the-art, two-dimensional graphics facilities using the java.awt.Graphics2D class (a subclass of Graphics) and associated classes, such as java.awt.BasicStroke, java.awt.GradientPaint, java. awt.TexturePaint, java.awt.AffineTransform, and java.awt.AlphaComposite.

This chapter demonstrates using all these classes; it shows how you can draw graphics with and without the Java 2D API. The key class for all graphics operations is Graphics (or in the Java 2D API, its subclass, Graphics2D). The purpose of this class is threefold:

It defines the drawing surface
>A Graphics object can represent the on-screen drawing area within an AWT (or Swing) component. It can also represent an off-screen image you can draw into or a piece of paper to be printed on a printer.

It defines drawing methods
>All primitive graphics operations, such as drawing lines, filling shapes, and displaying text, are performed using methods of the Graphics class.

It defines attributes used by the drawing methods
>Various methods of the Graphics class can set the font, color, clipping region, and other attributes used when performing graphics operations, such as drawing lines, filling shapes, and displaying text. The values of these graphical attributes are often instances of AWT classes, such as Color, Font, Stroke, AffineTransform, and so on.

The graphics capabilities of Java are intimately wed with the AWT. As such, the Graphics and Graphics2D classes are part of the java.awt package, as are all the associated classes that define graphical attributes. As we discussed in Chapter 11, the central class of the AWT is java.awt.Component. Component is the basic building block of all graphical user interfaces in Java. A Graphics object represents a drawing surface, but Java doesn't allow you to draw directly to the computer screen. Instead, it restricts you to drawing within the confines of a Component, using a Graphics object that represents the drawing surface of that component. Thus, to do graphics in Java, you must have a Component (or a java.applet.Applet, a Component subclass) to draw into. Drawing is usually done by subclassing a specific component and defining a paint( ) method (or a paintComponent( ) method, for Swing components). The examples in this chapter have been structured to focus on the mechanics of drawing, rather than the mechanics of GUI creation, but you will still see some code that handles GUI-related tasks.

Graphics Before Java 1.2

Prior to the introduction of the Java 2D API in Java 1.2, the java.awt.Graphics class provided only rudimentary graphics capabilities. It allowed you to draw lines, draw and fill simple shapes, display text, and draw images and perform basic image manipulation. You could specify a drawing color, a font, a clipping region, and the location of the origin. Notably missing, however, was the ability to specify a line width or rotate or scale drawings. Example 12-1 is a listing of the GraphicsSampler applet that demonstrates all the pre–Java 1.2 basic drawing primitives and attributes. The output of this applet is shown in Figure 12-1.

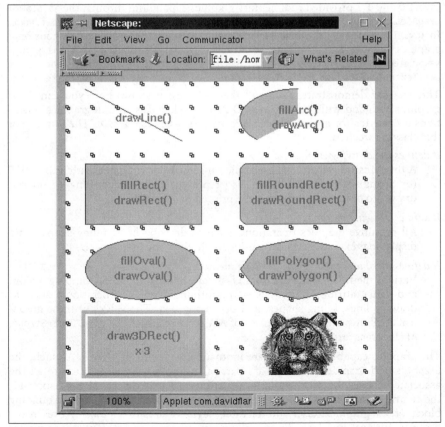

Figure 12-1. A sampling of graphics primitives

If you have read Chapter 16, you should understand the structure of this code. This is a very simple applet, however, so you should be able to understand it even before you read that chapter. The init( ) method is called once, when the applet first starts up, and performs one-time initialization. The paint( ) method displays the content of the applet. The Graphics object passed to this method represents the drawing surface of the applet; it allows you to draw anywhere within the bounds of the Applet object. tile( ) and centerText( ) are utility methods defined for the convenience of the paint( ) method. They demonstrate important graphics drawing techniques, but have nothing to do with the applet API.

It is important to understand that the paint( ) method may be called many times. The drawing done in this method doesn't necessarily persist: if the applet is covered by another window and then uncovered, the graphics contained in the applet may well be lost (whether this actually happens depends on the underlying operating system and other factors). In order to restore the graphics, the system invokes the paint( ) method again. Thus, all drawing should be done in the paint( ) method. If you draw anything in the init( ) method, those graphics may be erased and never reappear. (This is one of the serious shortcomings of Example 11-10 and related examples in Chapter 11.)

Example 12-1. GraphicsSampler.java

```
package je3.graphics;
import java.applet.*;
import java.awt.*;

/**
 * An applet that demonstrates most of the graphics primitives in
 * java.awt.Graphics.
 **/
public class GraphicsSampler extends Applet {
    Color fill, outline, textcolor;  // The various colors we use
    Font font;                       // The font we use for text
    FontMetrics metrics;             // Information about font size
    Image image, background;         // Some images we draw with

    // This method is called when the applet is first created.
    // It performs initialization, such as creating the resources
    // (graphics attribute values) used by the paint( ) method.
    public void init( ) {
        // Initialize color resources.  Note the use of the Color( ) constructor
        // and the use of pre-defined color constants.
        fill = new Color(200, 200, 200); // Equal red, green, and blue == gray
        outline = Color.blue;            // Same as new Color(0, 0, 255)
        textcolor = Color.red;           // Same as new Color(255, 0, 0)

        // Create a font for use in the paint( ) method.  Get its metrics, too.
        font = new Font("sansserif", Font.BOLD, 14);
        metrics = this.getFontMetrics(font);

        // Load some Image objects for use in the paint( ) method.
        image = this.getImage(this.getDocumentBase( ), "tiger.gif");
        background = this.getImage(this.getDocumentBase( ), "background.gif");
```

Graphics

Example 12-1. GraphicsSampler.java (continued)

```
        // Set a property that tells the applet its background color
        this.setBackground(Color.lightGray);
    }

    // This method is called whenever the applet needs to be drawn or redrawn
    public void paint(Graphics g) {
        g.setFont(font);  // Specify the font we'll be using throughout

        // Draw a background by tiling an image. tile() is defined below
        tile(g, this, background);

        // Draw a line
        g.setColor(outline);              // Specify the drawing color
        g.drawLine(25, 10, 150, 80);      // Draw a line from (25,10) to (150,80)
        // Draw some text.  See the centerText() method below.
        centerText("drawLine()", null, g, textcolor, 25, 10, 150, 80);

        // Draw and fill an arc
        g.setColor(fill);
        g.fillArc(225, 10, 150, 80, 90, 135);
        g.setColor(outline);
        g.drawArc(225, 10, 150, 80, 90, 135);
        centerText("fillArc()", "drawArc()", g, textcolor,225,10,150,80);

        // Draw and fill a rectangle
        g.setColor(fill);
        g.fillRect(25, 110, 150, 80);
        g.setColor(outline);
        g.drawRect(25, 110, 150, 80);
        centerText("fillRect()", "drawRect()", g, textcolor, 25, 110, 150, 80);

        // Draw and fill a rounded rectangle
        g.setColor(fill);
        g.fillRoundRect(225, 110, 150, 80, 20, 20);
        g.setColor(outline);
        g.drawRoundRect(225, 110, 150, 80, 20, 20);
        centerText("fillRoundRect()", "drawRoundRect()", g, textcolor,
                   225, 110, 150, 80);

        // Draw and fill an oval
        g.setColor(fill);
        g.fillOval(25, 210, 150, 80);
        g.setColor(outline);
        g.drawOval(25, 210, 150, 80);
        centerText("fillOval()", "drawOval()", g, textcolor, 25, 210, 150, 80);

        // Define an octagon using arrays of X and Y coordinates
        int numpoints = 8;
        int[] xpoints = new int[numpoints+1];
        int[] ypoints = new int[numpoints+1];
```

Example 12-1. GraphicsSampler.java (continued)

```
    for(int i=0; i < numpoints; i++) {
        double angle = 2*Math.PI * i / numpoints;
        xpoints[i] = (int)(300 + 75*Math.cos(angle));
        ypoints[i] = (int)(250 - 40*Math.sin(angle));
    }

    // Draw and fill the polygon
    g.setColor(fill);
    g.fillPolygon(xpoints, ypoints, numpoints);
    g.setColor(outline);
    g.drawPolygon(xpoints, ypoints, numpoints);
    centerText("fillPolygon( )", "drawPolygon( )", g, textcolor,
               225, 210, 150, 80);

    // Draw a 3D rectangle (clear an area for it first)
    g.setColor(fill);
    g.fillRect(20, 305, 160, 90);
    g.draw3DRect(25, 310, 150, 80, true);
    g.draw3DRect(26, 311, 148, 78, true);
    g.draw3DRect(27, 312, 146, 76, true);
    centerText("draw3DRect( )", "x 3", g, textcolor, 25, 310, 150, 80);

    // Draw an image (centered within an area)
    int w = image.getWidth(this);
    int h = image.getHeight(this);
    g.drawImage(image, 225 + (150-w)/2, 310 + (80-h)/2, this);
    centerText("drawImage( )", null, g, textcolor, 225, 310, 150, 80);
}

// Utility method to tile an image on the background of the component
protected void tile(Graphics g, Component c, Image i) {
    // Use bounds( ) instead of getBounds( ) if you want
    // compatibility with Java 1.0 and old browsers like Netscape 3
    Rectangle r = c.getBounds( );           // How big is the component?
    int iw = i.getWidth(c);                 // How big is the image?
    int ih = i.getHeight(c);
    if ((iw <= 0) || (ih <= 0)) return;
    for(int x=0; x < r.width; x += iw)      // Loop horizontally
        for(int y=0; y < r.height; y += ih) // Loop vertically
            g.drawImage(i, x, y, c);        // Draw the image
}

// Utility method to center two lines of text in a rectangle.
// Relies on the FontMetrics obtained in the init( ) method.
protected void centerText(String s1, String s2, Graphics g, Color c,
                          int x, int y, int w, int h)
{
    int height = metrics.getHeight( );  // How tall is the font?
    int ascent = metrics.getAscent( );  // Where is the font baseline?
    int width1=0, width2 = 0, x0=0, x1=0, y0=0, y1=0;
    width1 = metrics.stringWidth(s1);   // How wide are the strings?
```

Example 12-1. GraphicsSampler.java (continued)

```
        if (s2 != null) width2 = metrics.stringWidth(s2);
        x0 = x + (w - width1)/2;              // Center the strings horizontally
        x1 = x + (w - width2)/2;
        if (s2 == null)                       // Center one string vertically
            y0 = y + (h - height)/2 + ascent;
        else {                                // Center two strings vertically
            y0 = y + (h - (int)(height * 2.2))/2 + ascent;
            y1 = y0 + (int)(height * 1.2);
        }
        g.setColor(c);                        // Set the color
        g.drawString(s1, x0, y0);             // Draw the strings
        if (s2 != null) g.drawString(s2, x1, y1);
    }
}
]]>
<?import end_imported_file file=Examples/je3/graphics/GraphicsSampler.java?><!--
RESUME EDITING-->
```

Running the Applet

If you have not yet read Chapter 16, you may not know how to run the applet listed in Example 12-1. All you need to do is include the following <applet> tag in an HTML file, place the file in the same directory as the GraphicsSampler class file, and load the HTML file into a web browser:

```
<applet code="je3/graphics/GraphicsSampler.class" codebase="../../"
        width=400 height=400>
</applet>
```

You'll find this tag in a file named *GraphicsSampler.html* in this book's online example archive.

Note that GraphicsSampler calls the Java 1.1 method getBounds(), so you must use a browser that supports Java 1.1, such as Netscape Navigator 4.0 or later. You can also use the *appletviewer* application that comes with the Java SDK:

```
% appletviewer GraphicsSampler.html
```

Fonts

To enhance cross-platform portability, Java 1.0 and 1.1 defined only a handful of fonts (as we'll see later, Java 1.2 allows you to use any font available on the underlying system). In Java 1.0, these fonts were TimesRoman, Helvetica, and Courier. In Java 1.1, the fonts were given preferred logical names: Serif, SansSerif, and Monospaced. Each font is available in four styles and any number of sizes. Example 12-2 shows the listing of the FontList applet, which displays each of the standard fonts in each of the available styles. Its output is shown in Figure 12-2.

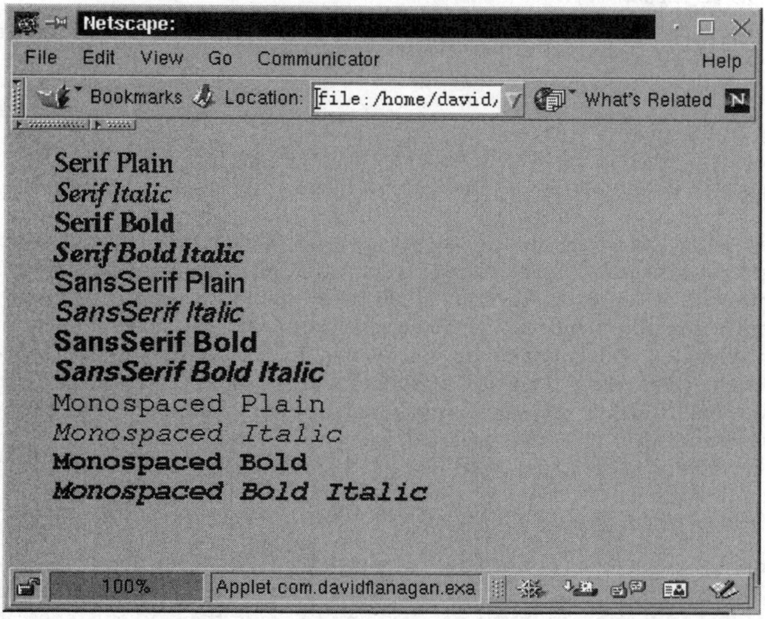

Figure 12-2. The standard fonts and styles

Example 12-2. FontList.java

```java
package je3.graphics;
import java.applet.*;
import java.awt.*;

/**
 * An applet that displays the standard fonts and styles available in Java 1.1
 **/
public class FontList extends Applet {
    // The available font families
    String[] families = {"Serif",           // "TimesRoman" in Java 1.0
                         "SansSerif",        // "Helvetica" in Java 1.0
                         "Monospaced"};      // "Courier" in Java 1.0

    // The available font styles and names for each one
    int[] styles = {Font.PLAIN, Font.ITALIC, Font.BOLD, Font.ITALIC+Font.BOLD};
    String[] stylenames = {"Plain", "Italic", "Bold", "Bold Italic"};

    // Draw the applet.
    public void paint(Graphics g) {
        for(int f=0; f < families.length; f++) {         // for each family
            for(int s = 0; s < styles.length; s++) {         // for each style
                Font font = new Font(families[f],styles[s],18); // create font
                g.setFont(font);                                // set font
                String name = families[f] + " " +stylenames[s]; // create name
```

Example 12-2. FontList.java (continued)

```
                g.drawString(name, 20, (f*4 + s + 1) * 20);      // display name
            }
        }
    }
}
```

Colors

A color in Java is represented by the java.awt.Color class. The Color class defines a number of constants that refer to predefined Color objects for commonly used colors, such as Color.black and Color.white. You can also create your own custom Color object by specifying the red, green, and blue components of the color. These components may be specified as integers between 0 and 255 or as float values between 0.0 and 1.0. Additionally, the static getHSBColor( ) method allows you to create a Color object based on hue, saturation, and brightness values. As of Java 1.1, the java.awt.SystemColor subclass of Color defines a number of constant SystemColor objects that represent standard colors in the system desktop palette. You can use these colors to make your application match the desktop color scheme.

Example 12-3 lists the ColorGradient applet, which uses Color objects to produce the color gradient shown in Figure 12-3. This applet uses applet parameters in the HTML file to specify the starting and ending colors of the gradient. You can use the applet with HTML tags like the following:

```
<applet code="je3/graphics/ColorGradient.class" codebase="../../"
        width=525 height=150>
    <param name="startColor" value="#a06060"> <!-- light red -->
    <param name="endColor" value="#ffffff">   <!-- white -->
</applet>
```

Figure 12-3. A color gradient

Example 12-3. ColorGradient.java

```java
package je3.graphics;
import java.applet.*;
import java.awt.*;

/** An applet that demonstrates the Color class */
public class ColorGradient extends Applet {
    Color startColor, endColor;   // Start and end color of the gradient
    Font bigFont;                 // A font we'll use

    /**
     * Get the gradient start and end colors as applet parameter values, and
     * parse them using Color.decode( ).  If they are malformed, use white.
     **/
    public void init( ) {
        try {
            startColor = Color.decode(getParameter("startColor"));
            endColor = Color.decode(getParameter("endColor"));
        }
        catch (NumberFormatException e) {
            startColor = endColor = Color.white;
        }
        bigFont = new Font("Helvetica", Font.BOLD, 72);
    }

    /** Draw the applet.  The interesting code is in fillGradient( ) below */
    public void paint(Graphics g) {
        fillGradient(this, g, startColor, endColor);  // display the gradient
        g.setFont(bigFont);                           // set a font
        g.setColor(new Color(100, 100, 200));         // light blue
        g.drawString("Colors!", 100, 100);            // draw something interesting
    }

    /**
     * Draw a color gradient from the top of the specified component to the
     * bottom.  Start with the start color and change smoothly to the end
     **/
    public void fillGradient(Component c, Graphics g, Color start, Color end) {
        Rectangle bounds = this.getBounds( );  // How big is the component?
        // Get the red, green, and blue components of the start and end
        // colors as floats between 0.0 and 1.0.  Note that the Color class
        // also works with int values between 0 and 255
        float r1 = start.getRed( )/255.0f;
        float g1 = start.getGreen( )/255.0f;
        float b1 = start.getBlue( )/255.0f;
        float r2 = end.getRed( )/255.0f;
        float g2 = end.getGreen( )/255.0f;
        float b2 = end.getBlue( )/255.0f;
        // Figure out how much each component should change at each y value
        float dr = (r2-r1)/bounds.height;
        float dg = (g2-g1)/bounds.height;
        float db = (b2-b1)/bounds.height;
```

Example 12-3. ColorGradient.java (continued)

```
        // Now loop once for each row of pixels in the component
        for(int y = 0; y < bounds.height; y++) {
            g.setColor(new Color(r1, g1, b1));     // Set the color of the row
            g.drawLine(0, y, bounds.width-1, y);   // Draw the row
            r1 += dr; g1 += dg; b1 += db;          // Increment color components
        }
    }
}
```

Simple Animation

Animation is nothing more than the rapid drawing of a graphic, with small changes between "frames," so the object being drawn appears to move. Example 12-4 shows the listing for an applet that performs a simple animation: it moves a red circle around the screen. The applet uses a Thread object to trigger the redraws. The technique used here is quite simple: when you run the applet, you may notice that it flickers as the ball moves.

Later in this chapter, we'll see another animation example that uses more advanced techniques to prevent flickering and produce smoother animation.

Example 12-4. BouncingCircle.java

```
package je3.graphics;
import java.applet.*;
import java.awt.*;

/** An applet that displays a simple animation */
public class BouncingCircle extends Applet implements Runnable {
    int x = 150, y = 50, r = 50;  // Position and radius of the circle
    int dx = 11, dy = 7;           // Trajectory of circle
    Thread animator;               // The thread that performs the animation
    volatile boolean pleaseStop;   // A flag to ask the thread to stop

    /** This method simply draws the circle at its current position */
    public void paint(Graphics g) {
        g.setColor(Color.red);
        g.fillOval(x-r, y-r, r*2, r*2);
    }

    /**
     * This method moves (and bounces) the circle and then requests a redraw.
     * The animator thread calls this method periodically.
     **/
    public void animate( ) {
        // Bounce if we've hit an edge.
        Rectangle bounds = getBounds();
        if ((x - r + dx < 0) || (x + r + dx > bounds.width)) dx = -dx;
        if ((y - r + dy < 0) || (y + r + dy > bounds.height)) dy = -dy;

        // Move the circle.
        x += dx;  y += dy;
```

Example 12-4. BouncingCircle.java (continued)

```
                // Ask the browser to call our paint( ) method to draw the circle
                // at its new position.
                repaint( );
        }

        /**
         * This method is from the Runnable interface.  It is the body of the
         * thread that performs the animation.  The thread itself is created
         * and started in the start( ) method.
         **/
        public void run( ) {
                while(!pleaseStop) {            // Loop until we're asked to stop
                        animate( );                    // Update and request redraw
                        try { Thread.sleep(100); }      // Wait 100 milliseconds
                        catch(InterruptedException e) { } // Ignore interruptions
                }
        }

        /** Start animating when the browser starts the applet */
        public void start( ) {
                animator = new Thread(this);    // Create a thread
                pleaseStop = false;             // Don't ask it to stop now
                animator.start( );              // Start the thread.
                // The thread that called start now returns to its caller.
                // Meanwhile, the new animator thread has called the run( ) method
        }

        /** Stop animating when the browser stops the applet */
        public void stop( ) {
                // Set the flag that causes the run( ) method to end
                pleaseStop = true;
        }
}
```

The Java 2D API

We now turn to the Java 2D API, which is available in Java 1.2 and later. Features of this API include:

- The Graphics2D class, which is a subclass of Graphics that defines additional graphics primitives and attributes.

- The Shape interface, which Java 2D uses to define many graphics primitives and other operations. The java.awt.geom package contains a number of useful implementations of Shape.

- The Stroke interface, which describes how lines are drawn (or stroked). The BasicStroke class implements this interface and supports the drawing of wide and dashed lines.

- The Paint interface, which describes how shapes are filled. The GradientPaint implementation allows filling with color gradients, while TexturePaint supports tiling with images. Also, as of Java 1.2, the Color class implements the Paint interface, to allow shapes to be filled with a solid color.

- The Composite interface, which defines how colors being drawn are combined with the colors already on the drawing surface. The AlphaComposite class allows colors to be combined based on the rules of alpha transparency. The Color class also has new constructors and methods that support translucent colors.

- The RenderingHints class, which allows an application to request particular types of drawing, such as antialiased drawing. Antialiasing uses transparent colors and compositing to smooth the edges of text and other shapes, preventing "jaggies."

- The java.awt.geom.AffineTransform class, which defines coordinate-system transformations and allows shapes (and entire coordinate systems) to be translated, scaled, rotated, and sheared.

  Because AffineTransform allows coordinate-system transformations, including scaling, the Java 2D API distinguishes between the coordinate system of the device (i.e., device space) and the (possibly) transformed user coordinate system (i.e., user space). Coordinates in user space can be specified using float and double values, and graphics drawn using Java 2D are resolution-independent.

In addition, in Java 1.2 and later, your applications are no longer restricted to using a fixed set of logical fonts; you can now use any font installed on the system. Finally, the Java 2D API also includes easy-to-use image-processing classes.

The rest of this chapter is devoted to examples that demonstrate these features of the Java 2D API. Most of the examples are implementations of the GraphicsExample interface, which is shown in Example 12-5.

Example 12-5. GraphicsExample.java

```java
package je3.graphics;
import java.awt.*;

/**
 * This interface defines the methods that must be implemented by an
 * object that is to be displayed by the GraphicsExampleFrame object
 */
public interface GraphicsExample {
    public String getName();                  // Return the example name
    public int getWidth();                    // Return its width
    public int getHeight();                   // Return its height
    public void draw(Graphics2D g, Component c); // Draw the example
}
```

You can run these examples using the GraphicsExampleFrame frame program, which is shown at the end of the chapter. This program creates a simple GUI, instantiates the classes listed on the command line, and displays them in a window. For example, to display the Shapes example we'll see in the next section, you can use GraphicsExampleFrame as follows:

```
% java je3.graphics.GraphicsExampleFrame Shapes
```

Many of the figures shown in this chapter are drawn at high resolution; they are not typical screenshots of a running program. GraphicsExampleFrame includes the printing functionality that generated these figures. Even though GraphicsExampleFrame doesn't do any graphics drawing of its own and is therefore more of an example of Java's printing capabilities, it is still listed in Example 12-20 in this chapter.

Drawing and Filling Shapes

Example 12-6 lists a GraphicsExample implementation that shows how various Shape objects can be defined, drawn, and filled. The example produces the output shown in Figure 12-4. Although the Java 2D API allows basic shapes to be drawn and filled using the methods demonstrated in Example 12-1, this example uses a different approach. It defines each shape as a Shape object, using various classes, mostly from java.awt.geom.

Each Shape is drawn using the draw( ) method of the Graphics2D class and filled using the fill( ) method. Note that each Shape object is defined with one corner at (or near) the origin, rather than at the location where it is displayed on the screen. This creates position-independent objects that can easily be reused. To draw the shapes at particular locations, the example uses the translate( ) method of Graphics2D to move the origin of the coordinate system. Finally, the call to setStroke( ) specifies that drawing be done with a two-pixel-wide line, while the call to setRenderingHint( ) requests that drawing be done using antialiasing.

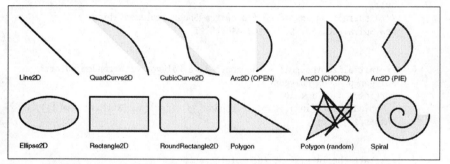

Figure 12-4. Drawing and filling shapes with the Java 2D API

Example 12-6. Shapes.java

```
package je3.graphics;
import java.awt.*;
import java.awt.geom.*;
import java.awt.font.*;
import java.awt.image.*;

/** A demonstration of Java2D shapes */
public class Shapes implements GraphicsExample {
    static final int WIDTH = 725, HEIGHT = 250;    // Size of our example
    public String getName( ) {return "Shapes";}    // From GraphicsExample
```

Example 12-6. Shapes.java (continued)

```java
    public int getWidth( ) { return WIDTH; }          // From GraphicsExample
    public int getHeight( ) { return HEIGHT; }        // From GraphicsExample

    Shape[ ] shapes = new Shape[ ] {
        // A straight line segment
        new Line2D.Float(0, 0, 100, 100),
        // A quadratic bezier curve.  Two end points and one control point
        new QuadCurve2D.Float(0, 0, 80, 15, 100, 100),
        // A cubic bezier curve.  Two end points and two control points
        new CubicCurve2D.Float(0, 0, 80, 15, 10, 90, 100, 100),
        // A 120 degree portion of an ellipse
        new Arc2D.Float(-30, 0, 100, 100, 60, -120, Arc2D.OPEN),
        // A 120 degree portion of an ellipse, closed with a chord
        new Arc2D.Float(-30, 0, 100, 100, 60, -120, Arc2D.CHORD),
        // A 120 degree pie slice of an ellipse
        new Arc2D.Float(-30, 0, 100, 100, 60, -120, Arc2D.PIE),
        // An ellipse
        new Ellipse2D.Float(0, 20, 100, 60),
        // A rectangle
        new Rectangle2D.Float(0, 20, 100, 60),
        // A rectangle with rounded corners
        new RoundRectangle2D.Float(0, 20, 100, 60, 15, 15),
        // A triangle
        new Polygon(new int[ ] { 0, 0, 100 }, new int[ ] {20, 80, 80}, 3),
        // A random polygon, initialized in code below
        null,
        // A spiral: an instance of a custom Shape implementation
        new Spiral(50, 50, 5, 0, 50, 4*Math.PI),
    };

    {   // Initialize the null shape above as a Polygon with random points
        Polygon p = new Polygon( );
        for(int i = 0; i < 10; i++)
            p.addPoint((int)(100*Math.random( )), (int)(100*Math.random( )));
        shapes[10] = p;
    }

    // These are the labels for each of the shapes
    String[ ] labels = new String[ ] {
        "Line2D", "QuadCurve2D", "CubicCurve2D", "Arc2D (OPEN)",
        "Arc2D (CHORD)", "Arc2D (PIE)", "Ellipse2D", "Rectangle2D",
        "RoundRectangle2D", "Polygon", "Polygon (random)", "Spiral"
    };

    /** Draw the example */
    public void draw(Graphics2D g, Component c) {
        // Set basic drawing attributes
        g.setFont(new Font("SansSerif", Font.PLAIN, 10));          // select font
        g.setStroke(new BasicStroke(2.0f));                        // 2 pixel lines
        g.setRenderingHint(RenderingHints.KEY_ANTIALIASING,        // antialiasing
                    RenderingHints.VALUE_ANTIALIAS_ON);
        g.translate(10, 10);                                       // margins
```

Example 12-6. Shapes.java (continued)

```
        // Loop through each shape
        for(int i = 0; i < shapes.length; i++) {
            g.setColor(Color.yellow);              // Set a color
            g.fill(shapes[i]);                     // Fill the shape with it
            g.setColor(Color.black);               // Switch to black
            g.draw(shapes[i]);                     // Outline the shape with it
            g.drawString(labels[i], 0, 110);       // Label the shape
            g.translate(120, 0);                   // Move over for next shape
            if (i % 6  == 5) g.translate(-6*120, 120);  // Move down after 6
        }
    }
}
```

Transforms

The AffineTransform class can transform a shape (or coordinate system) by translating, scaling, rotating, or shearing it, using any combination of these individual transformation types. Figure 12-5 illustrates the results of various types of coordinate-system transformations on the appearance of one shape, drawn multiple times. Example 12-7 shows the Java code that generates the figure.

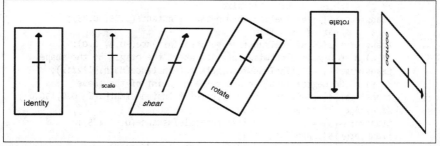

Figure 12-5. Transformed shapes

An *affine transformation* is a linear transformation that has two important properties: all straight lines remain straight, and all parallel lines remain parallel. The AffineTransform class can perform a great variety of transformations, but it can't produce nonlinear effects, such as distorting a figure as through a fisheye lens. That kind of effect can be achieved only with image-processing techniques. For a further discussion of transformations and the linear algebra behind the AffineTransform class, see Chapter 4 of *Java Foundation Classes in a Nutshell*.

Example 12-7. Transforms.java

```
package je3.graphics;
import java.awt.*;
import java.awt.geom.*;

/** A demonstration of Java2D transformations */
public class Transforms implements GraphicsExample {
    public String getName() { return "Transforms"; } // From GraphicsExample
```

Example 12-7. Transforms.java (continued)

```java
    public int getWidth() { return 750; }              // From GraphicsExample
    public int getHeight() { return 250; }             // From GraphicsExample

    Shape shape;                        // The shape to draw
    AffineTransform[] transforms;       // The ways to transform it
    String[] transformLabels;           // Labels for each transform

    /**
     * This constructor sets up the Shape and AffineTransform objects we need
     **/
    public Transforms() {
        GeneralPath path = new GeneralPath();    // Create a shape to draw
        path.append(new Line2D.Float(0.0f, 0.0f, 0.0f, 100.0f), false);
        path.append(new Line2D.Float(-10.0f, 50.0f, 10.0f, 50.0f), false);
        path.append(new Polygon(new int[] { -5, 0, 5 },
                                new int[] { 5, 0, 5 }, 3), false);
        this.shape = path;  // Remember this shape

        // Set up some transforms to alter the shape
        this.transforms = new AffineTransform[6];
        // 1) the identity transform
        transforms[0] = new AffineTransform();
        // 2) A scale tranform: 3/4 size
        transforms[1] = AffineTransform.getScaleInstance(0.75, 0.75);
        // 3) A shearing transform
        transforms[2] = AffineTransform.getShearInstance(-0.4, 0.0);
        // 4) A 30 degree clockwise rotation about the origin of the shape
        transforms[3] = AffineTransform.getRotateInstance(Math.PI*2/12);
        // 5) A 180 degree rotation about the midpoint of the shape
        transforms[4] = AffineTransform.getRotateInstance(Math.PI, 0.0, 50.0);
        // 6) A combination transform
        transforms[5] = AffineTransform.getScaleInstance(0.5, 1.5);
        transforms[5].shear(0.0, 0.4);
        transforms[5].rotate(Math.PI/2, 0.0, 50.0);   // 90 degrees

        // Define names for the transforms
        transformLabels = new String[] {
            "identity", "scale", "shear", "rotate", "rotate", "combo"
        };
    }

    /** Draw the defined shape and label, using each transform */
    public void draw(Graphics2D g, Component c) {
        // Define basic drawing attributes
        g.setColor(Color.black);                                    // black
        g.setStroke(new BasicStroke(2.0f, BasicStroke.CAP_SQUARE,   // 2-pixel
                             BasicStroke.JOIN_BEVEL));
        g.setRenderingHint(RenderingHints.KEY_ANTIALIASING,         // antialias
                     RenderingHints.VALUE_ANTIALIAS_ON);

        // Now draw the shape once using each of the transforms we've defined
        for(int i = 0; i < transforms.length; i++) {
            AffineTransform save = g.getTransform();     // save current state
```

Example 12-7. Transforms.java (continued)

```
        g.translate(i*125 + 50, 50);              // move origin
        g.transform(transforms[i]);               // apply transform
        g.draw(shape);                            // draw shape
        g.drawString(transformLabels[i], -25, 125); // draw label
        g.drawRect(-40, -10, 80, 150);            // draw box
        g.setTransform(save);                     // restore transform
      }
   }
}
```

Line Styles with BasicStroke

In the last couple of examples, we've used the BasicStroke class to draw lines that are wider than the one-pixel lines supported by the Graphics class. Wide lines are more complicated than thin lines, however, so BasicStroke allows you to specify other line attributes as well: the *cap style* of a line specifies how the endpoints of lines look, and the *join style* specifies how the corners, or vertices, of shapes look. These style options for endpoints and vertices are shown in Figure 12-6. The figure also illustrates the use of a dot-dashed patterned line, which is another feature of BasicStroke. The figure was produced using the code listed in Example 12-8, which demonstrates how to use BasicStroke to draw wide lines with a variety of cap and join styles and to draw patterned lines. (The example does not illustrate the use of the "miter limit" line style, which comes into play when two lines with a join style of JOIN_MITER intersect at a small angle; in this case the miter can become very long, and must be limited to some maximum length. See BasicStroke documentation for details.)

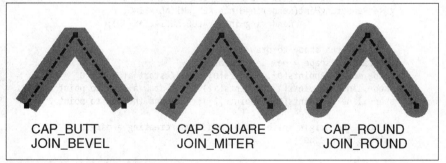

Figure 12-6. Line styles with BasicStroke

Example 12-8. LineStyles.java

```
package je3.graphics;
import java.awt.*;
import java.awt.geom.*;

/** A demonstration of Java2D line styles */
public class LineStyles implements GraphicsExample {
    public String getName() { return "LineStyles"; }  // From GraphicsExample
```

Example 12-8. LineStyles.java (continued)

```java
    public int getWidth( ) { return 450; }          // From GraphicsExample
    public int getHeight( ) { return 180; }         // From GraphicsExample

    int[ ] xpoints = new int[ ] { 0, 50, 100 };  // X coordinates of our shape
    int[ ] ypoints = new int[ ] { 75, 0, 75 };   // Y coordinates of our shape

    // Here are three different line styles we will demonstrate
    // They are thick lines with different cap and join styles
    Stroke[ ] linestyles = new Stroke[ ] {
        new BasicStroke(25.0f, BasicStroke.CAP_BUTT, BasicStroke.JOIN_BEVEL),
        new BasicStroke(25.0f, BasicStroke.CAP_SQUARE, BasicStroke.JOIN_MITER),
        new BasicStroke(25.0f, BasicStroke.CAP_ROUND, BasicStroke.JOIN_ROUND),
    };

    // Another line style: a 2 pixel-wide dot-dashed line
    Stroke thindashed = new BasicStroke(2.0f,  // line width
        /* cap style */                BasicStroke.CAP_BUTT,
        /* join style, miter limit */  BasicStroke.JOIN_BEVEL, 1.0f,
        /* the dash pattern */         new float[ ] {8.0f, 3.0f, 2.0f, 3.0f},
        /* the dash phase */           0.0f);   /* on 8, off 3, on 2, off 3 */

    // Labels to appear in the diagram, and the font to use to display them.
    Font font = new Font("Helvetica", Font.BOLD, 12);
    String[ ] capNames = new String[ ] {"CAP_BUTT", "CAP_SQUARE","CAP_ROUND"};
    String[ ] joinNames = new String[ ] {"JOIN_BEVEL","JOIN_MITER","JOIN_ROUND"};

    /** This method draws the example figure */
    public void draw(Graphics2D g, Component c) {
        // Use anti-aliasing to avoid "jaggies" in the lines
        g.setRenderingHint(RenderingHints.KEY_ANTIALIASING,
                           RenderingHints.VALUE_ANTIALIAS_ON);

        // Define the shape to draw
        GeneralPath shape = new GeneralPath( );
        shape.moveTo(xpoints[0], ypoints[0]);   // start at point 0
        shape.lineTo(xpoints[1], ypoints[1]);   // draw a line to point 1
        shape.lineTo(xpoints[2], ypoints[2]);   // and then on to point 2

        // Move the origin to the right and down, creating a margin
        g.translate(20,40);

        // Now loop, drawing our shape with the three different line styles
        for(int i = 0; i < linestyles.length; i++) {
            g.setColor(Color.gray);            // Draw a gray line
            g.setStroke(linestyles[i]);        // Select the line style to use
            g.draw(shape);                     // Draw the shape

            g.setColor(Color.black);           // Now use black
            g.setStroke(thindashed);           // And the thin dashed line
            g.draw(shape);                     // And draw the shape again.
```

Example 12-8. LineStyles.java (continued)

```
            // Highlight the location of the vertexes of the shape
            // This accentuates the cap and join styles we're demonstrating
            for(int j = 0; j < xpoints.length; j++)
                g.fillRect(xpoints[j]-2, ypoints[j]-2, 5, 5);

            g.drawString(capNames[i], 5, 105);   // Label the cap style
            g.drawString(joinNames[i], 5, 120);  // Label the join style

            g.translate(150, 0); // Move over to the right before looping again
        }
    }
}
```

Stroking Lines

The BasicStroke class is an implementation of the Stroke interface. This interface is responsible for defining how lines are drawn, or stroked, in Java 2D. Filling arbitrary shapes is the fundamental graphics operation defined by Java 2D. The Stroke interface defines the API by which line-drawing operations are transformed into area-filling operations, as illustrated in Figure 12-7. Example 12-9 shows the code used to produce this figure. (Once you understand how the Stroke interface converts a shape to a stroked shape suitable for filling, you can define interesting custom Stroke implementations, as we'll do later in this chapter, in Example 12-17.)

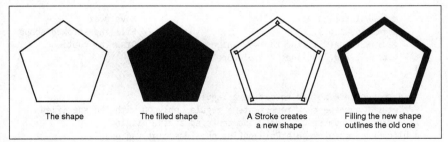

The shape   The filled shape   A Stroke creates a new shape   Filling the new shape outlines the old one

Figure 12-7. How lines are drawn in Java 2D

Example 12-9. Stroking.java

```
package je3.graphics;
import java.awt.*;
import java.awt.geom.*;

/** A demonstration of how Stroke objects work */
public class Stroking implements GraphicsExample {
    static final int WIDTH = 725, HEIGHT = 250;  // Size of our example
    public String getName() {return "Stroking";} // From GraphicsExample
    public int getWidth() { return WIDTH; }      // From GraphicsExample
    public int getHeight() { return HEIGHT; }    // From GraphicsExample
```

Example 12-9. Stroking.java (continued)

```
/** Draw the example */
public void draw(Graphics2D g, Component c) {
    // Create the shape we'll work with.  See convenience method below.
    Shape pentagon = createRegularPolygon(5, 75);

    // Set up basic drawing attributes
    g.setColor(Color.black);                        // Draw in black
    g.setStroke(new BasicStroke(1.0f));             // Use thin lines
    g.setFont(new Font("SansSerif", Font.PLAIN, 12)); // Basic small font

    g.translate(100, 100);                          // Move to position
    g.draw(pentagon);                               // Outline the shape
    g.drawString("The shape", -30, 90);             // Draw the caption

    g.translate(175, 0);                            // Move over
    g.fill(pentagon);                               // Fill the shape
    g.drawString("The filled shape", -50, 90);      // Another caption

    // Now use a Stroke object to create a "stroked shape" for our shape
    BasicStroke wideline = new BasicStroke(10.0f);
    Shape outline = wideline.createStrokedShape(pentagon);

    g.translate(175, 0);                            // Move over
    g.draw(outline);                                // Draw the stroked shape
    g.drawString("A Stroke creates",-50,90);        // Draw the caption
    g.drawString("a new shape", -35, 105);

    g.translate(175,0);                             // Move over
    g.fill(outline);                                // Fill the stroked shape
    g.drawString("Filling the new shape",-65,90);   // Draw the caption
    g.drawString("outlines the old one",-65,105);
}

// A convenience method to define a regular polygon.
// Returns a shape that represents a regular polygon with the specified
// radius and number of sides, and centered at the origin.
public Shape createRegularPolygon(int numsides, int radius) {
    Polygon p = new Polygon();
    double angle = 2 * Math.PI / numsides;   // Angle between vertices
    for(int i = 0; i < numsides; i++)  // Compute location of each vertex
        p.addPoint((int)(radius * Math.sin(angle*i)),
                   (int)(radius * -Math.cos(angle*i)));
    return p;
}
}
```

Filling Shapes with Paint

We've just seen that line drawing in Java 2D is defined in terms of the more funda-mental operation of area filling. In previous examples, we've used the fill( ) method of Graphics2D to fill the interior of a Shape with whatever solid color was previously passed to the setColor( ) method. The Java 2D API generalizes the notion of color, however, and allows you to fill an area using any implementation of the Paint interface. The Paint implementation is responsible for specifying the colors to use in the area-filling (or line-drawing) operation. In Java 1.2 and later, the Color class implements the Paint method, allowing shapes to be filled with solid colors. Java 2D also defines two other Paint implementations: GradientPaint, which fills a shape with a color gradient, and TexturePaint, which fills a shape by tiling an image. These classes can be used to achieve some of the fill effects shown in Figure 12-8.

Figure 12-8. Filling shapes with Paint objects

Example 12-10 shows the code that generates Figure 12-8. In addition to using the GradientPaint and TexturePaint classes, this example demonstrates a variety of other Java 2D capabilities: translucent colors, font glyphs as Shape objects that create "text art," an AffineTransform and a translucent color that produce a shadow effect, and a BufferedImage that performs off-screen drawing. Example 12-10 also illustrates the use of GenericPaint, a custom Paint implementation that we'll see in Example 12-18.

Example 12-10. Paints.java

```java
package je3.graphics;
import java.awt.*;
import java.awt.geom.*;
import java.awt.font.*;
import java.awt.image.*;

/** A demonstration of Java2D transformations */
public class Paints implements GraphicsExample {
    static final int WIDTH = 800, HEIGHT = 375;  // Size of our example

    public String getName() { return "Paints"; } // From GraphicsExample
    public int getWidth() { return WIDTH; }       // From GraphicsExample
    public int getHeight() { return HEIGHT; }     // From GraphicsExample
```

Example 12-10. Paints.java (continued)

```java
/** Draw the example */
public void draw(Graphics2D g, Component c) {
    // Paint the entire background using a GradientPaint.
    // The background color varies diagonally from deep red to pale blue
    g.setPaint(new GradientPaint(0, 0, new Color(150, 0, 0),
                                 WIDTH, HEIGHT, new Color(200, 200, 255)));
    g.fillRect(0, 0, WIDTH, HEIGHT);          // fill the background

    // Use a different GradientPaint to draw a box.
    // This one alternates between deep opaque green and transparent green.
    // Note: the 4th arg to Color() constructor specifies color opacity
    g.setPaint(new GradientPaint(0, 0, new Color(0, 150, 0),
                                 20, 20, new Color(0, 150, 0, 0), true));
    g.setStroke(new BasicStroke(15));          // use wide lines
    g.drawRect(25, 25, WIDTH-50, HEIGHT-50);  // draw the box

    // The glyphs of fonts can be used as Shape objects, which enables
    // us to use Java2D techniques with letters just as we would with
    // any other shape.  Here we get some letter shapes to draw.
    Font font = new Font("Serif", Font.BOLD, 10); // a basic font
    Font bigfont =                             // a scaled up version
        font.deriveFont(AffineTransform.getScaleInstance(30.0, 30.0));
    GlyphVector gv = bigfont.createGlyphVector(g.getFontRenderContext(),
                                               "JAV");
    Shape jshape = gv.getGlyphOutline(0);      // Shape of letter J
    Shape ashape = gv.getGlyphOutline(1);      // Shape of letter A
    Shape vshape = gv.getGlyphOutline(2);      // Shape of letter V

    // We're going to outline the letters with a 5-pixel wide line
    g.setStroke(new BasicStroke(5.0f));

    // We're going to fake shadows for the letters using the
    // following Paint and AffineTransform objects
    Paint shadowPaint = new Color(0, 0, 0, 100);     // Translucent black
    AffineTransform shadowTransform =
        AffineTransform.getShearInstance(-1.0, 0.0); // Shear to the right
    shadowTransform.scale(1.0, 0.5);                 // Scale height by 1/2

    // Move to the baseline of our first letter
    g.translate(65, 270);

    // Draw the shadow of the J shape
    g.setPaint(shadowPaint);
    g.translate(15,20);      // Compensate for the descender of the J
    // transform the J into the shape of its shadow, and fill it
    g.fill(shadowTransform.createTransformedShape(jshape));
    g.translate(-15,-20);    // Undo the translation above

    // Now fill the J shape with a solid (and opaque) color
    g.setPaint(Color.blue);       // Fill with solid, opaque blue
    g.fill(jshape);               // Fill the shape
    g.setPaint(Color.black);      // Switch to solid black
    g.draw(jshape);               // And draw the outline of the J
```

Example 12-10. Paints.java (continued)

```
// Now draw the A shadow
g.translate(75, 0);          // Move to the right
g.setPaint(shadowPaint);     // Set shadow color
g.fill(shadowTransform.createTransformedShape(ashape)); // draw shadow

// Draw the A shape using a solid transparent color
g.setPaint(new Color(0, 255, 0, 125));  // Transparent green as paint
g.fill(ashape);                         // Fill the shape
g.setPaint(Color.black);                // Switch to solid back
g.draw(ashape);                         // Draw the outline

// Move to the right and draw the shadow of the letter V
g.translate(175, 0);
g.setPaint(shadowPaint);
g.fill(shadowTransform.createTransformedShape(vshape));

// We're going to fill the next letter using a TexturePaint, which
// repeatedly tiles an image. The first step is to obtain the image.
// We could load it from an image file, but here we create it
// ourselves by drawing into an off-screen image.  Note that we use
// a GradientPaint to fill the off-screen image, so the fill pattern
// combines features of both Paint classes.
BufferedImage tile =                    // Create an image
    new BufferedImage(50, 50, BufferedImage.TYPE_INT_RGB);
Graphics2D tg = tile.createGraphics( ); // Get its Graphics for drawing
tg.setColor(Color.pink);
tg.fillRect(0, 0, 50, 50);       // Fill tile background with pink
tg.setPaint(new GradientPaint(40, 0, Color.green,  // diagonal gradient
                              0, 40, Color.gray)); // green to gray
tg.fillOval(5, 5, 40, 40);       // Draw a circle with this gradient

// Use this new tile to create a TexturePaint and fill the letter V
g.setPaint(new TexturePaint(tile, new Rectangle(0, 0, 50, 50)));
g.fill(vshape);                         // Fill letter shape
g.setPaint(Color.black);                // Switch to solid black
g.draw(vshape);                         // Draw outline of letter

// Move to the right and draw the shadow of the final A
g.translate(160, 0);
g.setPaint(shadowPaint);
g.fill(shadowTransform.createTransformedShape(ashape));

// For the last letter, use a custom Paint class to fill with a
// complex mathematically defined pattern.  The GenericPaint
// class is defined later in the chapter.
g.setPaint(new GenericPaint( ) {
        public int computeRed(double x, double y) { return 128; }
        public int computeGreen(double x, double y) {
            return (int)((Math.sin(x/7) + Math.cos(y/5) + 2)/4 *255);
        }
        public int computeBlue(double x, double y) {
            return ((int)(x*y))%256;
        }
```

Example 12-10. Paints.java (continued)

```
            public int computeAlpha(double x, double y) {
                return ((int)x%25*8+50) + ((int)y%25*8+50);
            }
        });
    g.fill(ashape);                    // Fill letter A
    g.setPaint(Color.black);           // Revert to solid black
    g.draw(ashape);                    // Draw the outline of the A
    }
}
```

Antialiasing

As we've already seen, you can request that Java 2D perform antialiasing when it draws text and graphics. Antialiasing smooths the edges of shapes (such as text glyphs) and lines and reduces jaggies. Antialiased drawing is necessary because the outline of a shape drawn on a computer monitor can never be perfectly smooth; a mathematically perfect shape can't be mapped precisely onto a grid of discrete pixels. When the shape is drawn, the pixels inside the shape are filled, while the pixels outside are not. The outline of a shape rarely falls on perfect pixel boundaries, however, so approximations are made at the edges. The result is jagged lines that approximate the abstract shape you wish to represent.

Antialiasing is simply a technique for improving these approximations, using translucent colors. For example, if a pixel at the edge of a shape is half covered by the shape, the pixel is filled using a color that is half opaque. If only one-fifth of the pixel is covered, the pixel is one-fifth opaque. This technique works quite well to reduce jaggies. Figure 12-9 illustrates the process of antialiasing: it shows an antialiased figure that has been artificially enlarged to show the translucent colors used at the edges of shapes and text glyphs. The figure is generated by the straightforward code in Example 12-11.

Figure 12-9. Antialiasing enlarged

Example 12-11. AntiAlias.java

```java
package je3.graphics;
import java.awt.*;
import java.awt.geom.*;
import java.awt.image.*;

/** A demonstration of anti-aliasing */
public class AntiAlias implements GraphicsExample {
    static final int WIDTH = 650, HEIGHT = 350;    // Size of our example
    public String getName() {return "AntiAliasing";}  // From GraphicsExample
    public int getWidth() { return WIDTH; }        // From GraphicsExample
    public int getHeight() { return HEIGHT; }      // From GraphicsExample

    /** Draw the example */
    public void draw(Graphics2D g, Component c) {
        BufferedImage image =                      // Create an off-screen image
            new BufferedImage(65, 35, BufferedImage.TYPE_INT_RGB);
        Graphics2D ig = image.createGraphics(); // Get its Graphics for drawing

        // Set the background to a gradient fill.  The varying color of
        // the background helps to demonstrate the anti-aliasing effect
        ig.setPaint(new GradientPaint(0,0,Color.black,65,35,Color.white));
        ig.fillRect(0, 0, 65, 35);

        // Set drawing attributes for the foreground.
        // Most importantly, turn on anti-aliasing.
        ig.setStroke(new BasicStroke(2.0f));                  // 2-pixel lines
        ig.setFont(new Font("Serif", Font.BOLD, 18));         // 18-point font
        ig.setRenderingHint(RenderingHints.KEY_ANTIALIASING,  // Anti-alias!
                        RenderingHints.VALUE_ANTIALIAS_ON);

        // Now draw pure blue text and a pure red oval
        ig.setColor(Color.blue);
        ig.drawString("Java", 9, 22);
        ig.setColor(Color.red);
        ig.drawOval(1, 1, 62, 32);

        // Finally, scale the image by a factor of 10 and display it
        // in the window.  This will allow us to see the anti-aliased pixels
        g.drawImage(image, AffineTransform.getScaleInstance(10, 10), c);

        // Draw the image one more time at its original size, for comparison
        g.drawImage(image, 0, 0, c);
    }
}
```

Combining Colors with AlphaComposite

As we've just seen, antialiasing works by drawing with translucent colors at the edges of a shape. But what exactly does it mean to draw with a translucent color? Take another look at Figure 12-9, or, better yet, run the example using the GraphicsExampleFrame program, so you can see the example in full color. When you draw with a translucent color, whatever color is below it "shows through." In Figure 12-9, the background gray colors show through the pure translucent red and blue colors, resulting in reddish and bluish grays. At the hardware level, of course, there is no such thing as a translucent color; drawing with a translucent color is simulated by combining the drawing color with the existing color beneath it.

Combining colors in this way is called *compositing* and is the job of the Composite interface. You can pass a Composite object to the setComposite( ) method of a Graphics2D object to tell it how to combine a drawing color (the source color) with the colors that are already on the drawing surface (the destination colors). Java 2D defines one implementation of the Composite interface, AlphaComposite, that combines colors based on their alpha transparency values.

The default AlphaComposite object used by Graphics2D is sufficient for most drawing, so you don't often need to create AlphaComposite objects. Still, there are interesting effects you can achieve with AlphaComposite. Example 12-12 demonstrates these effects (and an unrelated clipping effect), which are shown in Figure 12-10.

Figure 12-10. Effects created with AlphaComposite

The example does much of its drawing into an off-screen image, then copies the contents of that image onto the screen. This is because many compositing effects can only be achieved when working with a drawing surface (such as an off-screen image) that has an "alpha channel" and supports transparent colors. Be sure to check out how this off-screen BufferedImage is created.

Example 12-12 also illustrates the type of effects that are possible when you set a clipping region. Java 2D allows any Shape to be used as a clipping region; graphics are displayed only if they fall within this shape. The example uses the java.awt.geom.Area class to define a complex shape, combining two ellipses and a rectangle, and then uses this shape as a clipping region.

Example 12-12. CompositeEffects.java

```
package je3.graphics;
import java.awt.*;
import java.awt.geom.*;
import java.awt.image.*;
```

Example 12-12. CompositeEffects.java (continued)

```java
public class CompositeEffects implements GraphicsExample {
    Image cover;  // The image we'll be displaying, and its size
    static final int COVERWIDTH = 127, COVERHEIGHT = 190;

    /** This constructor loads the cover image */
    public CompositeEffects() {
        java.net.URL imageurl = this.getClass().getResource("cover.gif");
        cover = new javax.swing.ImageIcon(imageurl).getImage();
    }

    // These are basic GraphicsExample methods
    public String getName() {return "Composite Effects";}
    public int getWidth() { return 6*COVERWIDTH + 70; }
    public int getHeight() { return COVERHEIGHT + 35; }

    /** Draw the example */
    public void draw(Graphics2D g, Component c) {
        // fill the background
        g.setPaint(new Color(175, 175, 175));
        g.fillRect(0, 0, getWidth(), getHeight());

        // Set text attributes
        g.setColor(Color.black);
        g.setFont(new Font("SansSerif", Font.BOLD, 12));

        // Draw the unmodified image
        g.translate(10, 10);
        g.drawImage(cover, 0, 0, c);
        g.drawString("SRC_OVER", 0, COVERHEIGHT+15);

        // Draw the cover again, using AlphaComposite to make the opaque
        // colors of the image 50% translucent
        g.translate(COVERWIDTH+10, 0);
        g.setComposite(AlphaComposite.getInstance(AlphaComposite.SRC_OVER,
                                                  0.5f));
        g.drawImage(cover, 0, 0, c);

        // Restore the pre-defined default Composite for the screen, so
        // opaque colors stay opaque.
        g.setComposite(AlphaComposite.SrcOver);
        // Label the effect
        g.drawString("SRC_OVER, 50%", 0, COVERHEIGHT+15);

        // Now get an offscreen image to work with.  In order to achieve
        // certain compositing effects, the drawing surface must support
        // transparency. Onscreen drawing surfaces cannot, so we have to do the
        // compositing in an offscreen image that is specially created to have
        // an "alpha channel", then copy the final result to the screen.
        BufferedImage offscreen =
            new BufferedImage(COVERWIDTH, COVERHEIGHT,
                              BufferedImage.TYPE_INT_ARGB);
```

Example 12-12. CompositeEffects.java (continued)

```java
// First, fill the image with a color gradient background that varies
// left-to-right from opaque to transparent yellow
Graphics2D osg = offscreen.createGraphics();
osg.setPaint(new GradientPaint(0, 0, Color.yellow,
                               COVERWIDTH, 0,
                               new Color(255, 255, 0, 0)));
osg.fillRect(0,0, COVERWIDTH, COVERHEIGHT);

// Now copy the cover image on top of this, but use the DstOver rule
// which draws it "underneath" the existing pixels and allows the
// image to show depending on the transparency of those pixels.
osg.setComposite(AlphaComposite.DstOver);
osg.drawImage(cover, 0, 0, c);

// And display this composited image on the screen. Note that the
// image is opaque and that none of the screen background shows through
g.translate(COVERWIDTH+10, 0);
g.drawImage(offscreen, 0, 0, c);
g.drawString("DST_OVER", 0, COVERHEIGHT+15);

// Now start over and do a new effect with the off-screen image.
// First, fill the offscreen image with a new color gradient. We
// don't care about the colors themselves; we just want the
// translucency of the background to vary. We use opaque black to
// transparent black. Note that since we've already used this offscreen
// image, we set the composite to Src, so we can fill the image and
// ignore anything that is already there.
osg.setComposite(AlphaComposite.Src);
osg.setPaint(new GradientPaint(0, 0, Color.black,
                               COVERWIDTH, COVERHEIGHT,
                               new Color(0, 0, 0, 0)));
osg.fillRect(0,0, COVERWIDTH, COVERHEIGHT);

// Now set the compositing type to SrcIn, so colors come from the
// source, but translucency comes from the destination
osg.setComposite(AlphaComposite.SrcIn);

// Draw our loaded image into the off-screen image, compositing it.
osg.drawImage(cover, 0, 0, c);

// And then copy our off-screen image to the screen. Note that the
// image is translucent and some of the background shows through.
g.translate(COVERWIDTH+10, 0);
g.drawImage(offscreen, 0, 0, c);
g.drawString("SRC_IN", 0, COVERHEIGHT+15);

// If we do the same thing but use SrcOut, then the resulting image
// will have the inverted translucency values of the destination
osg.setComposite(AlphaComposite.Src);
```

Example 12-12. CompositeEffects.java (continued)

```
        osg.setPaint(new GradientPaint(0, 0, Color.black,
                                       COVERWIDTH, COVERHEIGHT,
                                       new Color(0, 0, 0, 0)));
        osg.fillRect(0,0, COVERWIDTH, COVERHEIGHT);
        osg.setComposite(AlphaComposite.SrcOut);
        osg.drawImage(cover, 0, 0, c);
        g.translate(COVERWIDTH+10, 0);
        g.drawImage(offscreen, 0, 0, c);
        g.drawString("SRC_OUT", 0, COVERHEIGHT+15);

        // Here's a cool effect; it has nothing to do with compositing, but
        // uses an arbitrary shape to clip the image.  It uses Area to combine
        // shapes into more complicated ones.
        g.translate(COVERWIDTH+10, 0);
        Shape savedClip = g.getClip();  // Save current clipping region
        // Create a shape to use as the new clipping region.
        // Begin with an ellipse
        Area clip = new Area(new Ellipse2D.Float(0,0,COVERWIDTH,COVERHEIGHT));
        // Intersect with a rectangle, truncating the ellipse.
        clip.intersect(new Area(new Rectangle(5,5,
                                     COVERWIDTH-10,COVERHEIGHT-10)));
        // Then subtract an ellipse from the bottom of the truncated ellipse.
        clip.subtract(new Area(new Ellipse2D.Float(COVERWIDTH/2-40,
                                     COVERHEIGHT-20, 80, 40)));
        // Use the resulting shape as the new clipping region
        g.clip(clip);
        // Then draw the image through this clipping region
        g.drawImage(cover, 0, 0, c);
        // Restore the old clipping region so we can label the effect
        g.setClip(savedClip);
        g.drawString("Clipping", 0, COVERHEIGHT+15);
    }
}
```

Image Processing

Both Java 1.0 and 1.1 included a complex API for filtering images on the fly as they were downloaded over a network connection. Although this API is still available in later versions of Java, it is not commonly used, nor is it demonstrated in this book. Java 2D defines a simpler API based on the BufferedImageOp interface of the java.awt.image package. This package also includes several versatile implementations of the interface that can generate the image-processing effects illustrated in Figure 12-11. Example 12-13 shows the code used to produce Figure 12-11. The code is straightforward: to process a BufferedImage, simply pass it to the filter( ) method of a BufferedImageOp.

Figure 12-11. Image processing with BufferedImageOp

Example 12-13. ImageOps.java

```java
package je3.graphics;
import java.awt.*;
import java.awt.geom.*;
import java.awt.image.*;
import java.awt.color.*;

/** A demonstration of various image processing filters */
public class ImageOps implements GraphicsExample {
    static final int WIDTH = 600, HEIGHT = 675;          // Size of our example
    public String getName() {return "Image Processing";}// From GraphicsExample
    public int getWidth() { return WIDTH; }              // From GraphicsExample
    public int getHeight() { return HEIGHT; }            // From GraphicsExample
```

Example 12-13. ImageOps.java (continued)

```java
Image image;

/** This constructor loads the image we will manipulate */
public ImageOps( ) {
    java.net.URL imageurl = this.getClass( ).getResource("cover.gif");
    image = new javax.swing.ImageIcon(imageurl).getImage( );
}

// These arrays of bytes are used by the LookupImageOp image filters below
static byte[ ] brightenTable = new byte[256];
static byte[ ] thresholdTable = new byte[256];
static {  // Initialize the arrays
    for(int i = 0; i < 256; i++) {
        brightenTable[i] = (byte)(Math.sqrt(i/255.0)*255);
        thresholdTable[i] = (byte)((i < 225)?0:i);
    }
}

// This AffineTransform is used by one of the image filters below
static AffineTransform mirrorTransform;
static {  // Create and initialize the AffineTransform
    mirrorTransform = AffineTransform.getTranslateInstance(127, 0);
    mirrorTransform.scale(-1.0, 1.0);  // flip horizontally
}

// These are the labels we'll display for each of the filtered images
static String[ ] filterNames = new String[ ] {
    "Original", "Gray Scale",  "Negative",  "Brighten (linear)",
    "Brighten (sqrt)", "Threshold", "Blur", "Sharpen",
    "Edge Detect", "Mirror", "Rotate (center)", "Rotate (lower left)"
};

// The following BufferedImageOp image filter objects perform
// different types of image processing operations.
static BufferedImageOp[ ] filters = new BufferedImageOp[ ] {
    // 1) No filter here.  We'll display the original image
    null,
    // 2) Convert to Grayscale color space
    new ColorConvertOp(ColorSpace.getInstance(ColorSpace.CS_GRAY), null),
    // 3) Image negative.  Multiply each color value by -1.0 and add 255
    new RescaleOp(-1.0f, 255f, null),
    // 4) Brighten using a linear formula that increases all color values
    new RescaleOp(1.25f, 0, null),
    // 5) Brighten using the lookup table defined above
    new LookupOp(new ByteLookupTable(0, brightenTable), null),
    // 6) Threshold using the lookup table defined above
    new LookupOp(new ByteLookupTable(0, thresholdTable), null),
    // 7) Blur by "convolving" the image with a matrix
    new ConvolveOp(new Kernel(3, 3, new float[ ] {
        .1111f,.1111f,.1111f,
        .1111f,.1111f,.1111f,
        .1111f,.1111f,.1111f,})),
```

Example 12-13. ImageOps.java (continued)

```
        // 8) Sharpen by using a different matrix
        new ConvolveOp(new Kernel(3, 3, new float[ ] {
            0.0f, -0.75f, 0.0f,
            -0.75f, 4.0f, -0.75f,
            0.0f, -0.75f, 0.0f})),
        // 9) Edge detect using yet another matrix
        new ConvolveOp(new Kernel(3, 3, new float[ ] {
            0.0f,  -0.75f, 0.0f,
            -0.75f, 3.0f, -0.75f,
            0.0f,  -0.75f, 0.0f})),
        // 10) Compute a mirror image using the transform defined above
        new AffineTransformOp(mirrorTransform,AffineTransformOp.TYPE_BILINEAR),
        // 11) Rotate the image 180 degrees about its center point
        new AffineTransformOp(AffineTransform.getRotateInstance(Math.PI,64,95),
                              AffineTransformOp.TYPE_NEAREST_NEIGHBOR),
        // 12) Rotate the image 15 degrees about the bottom left
        new AffineTransformOp(AffineTransform.getRotateInstance(Math.PI/12,
                                                      0, 190),
                              AffineTransformOp.TYPE_NEAREST_NEIGHBOR),
    };

    /** Draw the example */
    public void draw(Graphics2D g, Component c) {
        // Create a BufferedImage big enough to hold the Image loaded
        // in the constructor.  Then copy that image into the new
        // BufferedImage object so that we can process it.
        BufferedImage bimage = new BufferedImage(image.getWidth(c),
                                                 image.getHeight(c),
                                                 BufferedImage.TYPE_INT_RGB);
        Graphics2D ig = bimage.createGraphics( );
        ig.drawImage(image, 0, 0, c);  // copy the image

        // Set some default graphics attributes
        g.setFont(new Font("SansSerif", Font.BOLD, 12));  // 12pt bold text
        g.setColor(Color.green);                           // Draw in green
        g.translate(10, 10);                               // Set some margins

        // Loop through the filters
        for(int i = 0; i < filters.length; i++) {
            // If the filter is null, draw the original image; otherwise,
            // draw the image as processed by the filter
            if (filters[i] == null) g.drawImage(bimage, 0, 0, c);
            else g.drawImage(filters[i].filter(bimage, null), 0, 0, c);
            g.drawString(filterNames[i], 0, 205);       // Label the image
            g.translate(137, 0);                        // Move over
            if (i % 4 == 3) g.translate(-137*4, 215);   // Move down after 4
        }
    }
}
```

Image I/O

Java 1.4 introduced the Image I/O API in the javax.imageio package. This API has many complex features, but at its heart it is a facility for reading and writing image files. Java was previously able to read images, but writing image files was not something it could do. javax.imageio solves that problem, as demonstrated in Example 12-14, a utility program to generate and save PNG images that fade from opaque to transparent: these images make interesting backgrounds for web pages.* Default implementations of javax.imageio can read GIF, JPEG, and PNG images, and can write JPEG and PNG images. The patent covering GIF image creation has expired since Java 1.4 was released, and hopefully future releases will support GIF format as well.

Example 12-14. MakeFades.java

```java
package je3.graphics;
import java.io.*;
import java.awt.*;
import java.awt.image.*;

/*
 * This program creates PNG images of the specified color that fade from fully
 * opaque to fully transparent.  Images of this sort are useful in web design
 * where they can be used as background images and combined with background
 * colors to produce two-color fades. (IE6 does not support PNG transparency.)
 *
 * Images are produced in three sizes and with 8 directions.  The images
 * are written into the current directory and are given names of the form:
 * fade-to-color-speed-direction.png
 *
 *    color:     the color name specified on the command line
 *    speed:     slow (1024px), medium (512px), fast(256px)
 *    direction: a compass point: N, E, S, W, NE, SE, SW, NW
 *
 * Invoke this program with a color name and three floating-point values
 * specifying the red, green, and blue components of the color.
 */
public class MakeFades  {
    // A fast fade is a small image, and a slow fade is a large image
    public static final String[ ] sizeNames = { "fast", "medium", "slow" };
    public static final int[ ] sizes = { 256, 512, 1024 };

    // Direction names and coordinates
    public static final String[ ] directionNames = {
        "N", "E", "S", "W", "NE", "SE", "SW", "NW"
    };
    public static float[ ][ ] directions = {
        new float[ ] { 0f, 1f, 0f, 0f },  // North
```

---

* They are particularly interesting when the transparent background image is combined with a solid background color: it produces a fade from one solid color to another. Unfortunately, PNG transparency is not supported by Internet Explorer 6 on Windows, so you'll need to use a different browser to appreciate the effect.

Example 12-14. MakeFades.java (continued)

```
        new float[ ] { 0f, 0f, 1f, 0f },   // East
        new float[ ] { 0f, 0f, 0f, 1f },   // South
        new float[ ] { 1f, 0f, 0f, 0f },   // West
        new float[ ] { 0f, 1f, 1f, 0f },   // Northeast
        new float[ ] { 0f, 0f, 1f, 1f },   // Southeast
        new float[ ] { 1f, 0f, 0f, 1f },   // Southwest
        new float[ ] { 1f, 1f, 0f, 0f }    // Northwest
};


    public static void main(String[ ] args)
        throws IOException, NumberFormatException
    {
        // Parse the command-line arguments
        String colorname = args[0];
        float red = Float.parseFloat(args[1]);
        float green = Float.parseFloat(args[2]);
        float blue = Float.parseFloat(args[3]);

        // Create from and to colors based on those arguments
        Color from = new Color(red, green, blue, 0.0f);  // transparent
        Color to = new Color(red, green, blue, 1.0f);     // opaque

        // Loop through the sizes and directions, and create an image for each
        for(int s = 0; s < sizes.length; s++) {
            for(int d = 0; d < directions.length; d++) {
                // This is the size of the image
                int size = sizes[s];

                // Create a GradientPaint for this direction and size
                Paint paint = new GradientPaint(directions[d][0]*size,
                                                directions[d][1]*size,
                                                from,
                                                directions[d][2]*size,
                                                directions[d][3]*size,
                                                to);

                // Start with a blank image that supports transparency
                BufferedImage image =
                    new BufferedImage(size, size, BufferedImage.TYPE_INT_ARGB);

                // Now fill the image with our color gradient
                Graphics2D g = image.createGraphics( );
                g.setPaint(paint);
                g.fillRect(0, 0, size, size);

                // This is the name of the file we'll write the image to
                File file = new File("fade-to-" +
                                     colorname + "-" +
                                     sizeNames[s] + "-" +
                                     directionNames[d] + ".png");
```

Example 12-14. MakeFades.java (continued)

```
            // Save the image in PNG format using the javax.imageio API
            javax.imageio.ImageIO.write(image, "png", file);

            // Show the user our progress by printing the filename
            System.out.println(file);
        }
    }
  }
}
```

Custom Shapes

Figure 12-4 showed how Java 2D can be used to draw and fill various types of shapes. One of the shapes shown in that figure is a spiral, which was drawn using the Spiral class, a custom Shape implementation shown in Example 12-15. That example is followed by another custom shape, PolyLine, in Example 12-16. PolyLine represents a series of connect line segments, and is the basis of the ScribblePane class of Example 11-13. PolyLine also features prominently in Chapter 14, where it is used for dragging-and-dropping scribbles.

The Shape interface defines three important methods (some of which have multiple overloaded versions) that all shapes must implement. The contains( ) methods determine whether a shape contains a point or a rectangle; a Shape has to be able to tell its inside from its outside. The intersects( ) methods determine whether any part of the shape intersects a specified rectangle. Since both contains( ) and intersects( ) are difficult to compute exactly for a spiral, the Spiral class approximates the spiral with a circle for the purposes of these methods.

The getPathIterator( ) methods are the heart of any Shape implementation. Each method returns a PathIterator object that describes the outline of the shape in terms of line and curve segments. Java 2D relies on PathIterator objects to draw and fill shapes. The key methods of the SpiralIterator implementation are currentSegment( ), which returns one line segment of the spiral, and next( ), which moves the iterator to the next segment. next( ) uses some hairy mathematics to make sure that the line segment approximation of the spiral is good enough.

Example 12-15. Spiral.java

```java
package je3.graphics;
import java.awt.*;
import java.awt.geom.*;

/** This Shape implementation represents a spiral curve */
public class Spiral implements Shape {
    double centerX, centerY;        // The center of the spiral
    double startRadius, startAngle; // The spiral starting point
    double endRadius, endAngle;     // The spiral ending point
    double outerRadius;             // the bigger of the two radii
    int angleDirection;             // 1 if angle increases, -1 otherwise
```

Example 12-15. Spiral.java (continued)

```java
    // It's hard to do contains( ) and intersects( ) tests on a spiral, so we
    // do them on this circular approximation of the spiral.  This is not an
    // ideal solution, and is only a good approximation for "tight" spirals.
    Shape approximation;

    /**
     * The constructor.  It takes arguments for the center of the shape, the
     * start point, and the end point.  The start and end points are specified
     * in terms of angle and radius.  The spiral curve is formed by varying
     * the angle and radius smoothly between the two end points.
     **/
    public Spiral(double centerX, double centerY,
                  double startRadius, double startAngle,
                  double endRadius, double endAngle)
    {
        // Save the parameters that describe the spiral
        this.centerX = centerX;          this.centerY = centerY;
        this.startRadius = startRadius;  this.startAngle = startAngle;
        this.endRadius = endRadius;      this.endAngle = endAngle;

        // figure out the maximum radius, and the spiral direction
        this.outerRadius = Math.max(startRadius, endRadius);
        if (startAngle < endAngle) angleDirection = 1;
        else angleDirection = -1;

        if ((startRadius < 0) || (endRadius < 0))
            throw new IllegalArgumentException("Spiral radii must be >= 0");

        // Here's how we approximate the inside of the spiral
        approximation = new Ellipse2D.Double(centerX-outerRadius,
                                             centerY-outerRadius,
                                             outerRadius*2, outerRadius*2);
    }

    /**
     * The bounding box of a Spiral is the same as the bounding box of a
     * circle with the same center and the maximum radius
     **/
    public Rectangle getBounds( ) {
        return new Rectangle((int)(centerX-outerRadius),
                             (int)(centerY-outerRadius),
                             (int)(outerRadius*2), (int)(outerRadius*2));
    }

    /** Same as getBounds( ), but with floating-point coordinates */
    public Rectangle2D getBounds2D( ) {
        return new Rectangle2D.Double(centerX-outerRadius, centerY-outerRadius,
                                      outerRadius*2, outerRadius*2);
    }
```

Example 12-15. Spiral.java (continued)

```java
/**
 * These methods use a circle approximation to determine whether a point
 * or rectangle is inside the spiral.  We could be more clever than this.
 **/
public boolean contains(Point2D p) { return approximation.contains(p); }
public boolean contains(Rectangle2D r) { return approximation.contains(r);}
public boolean contains(double x, double y) {
    return approximation.contains(x,y);
}
public boolean contains(double x, double y, double w, double h) {
    return approximation.contains(x, y, w, h);
}

/**
 * These methods determine whether the specified rectangle intersects the
 * spiral. We use our circle approximation.  The Shape interface explicitly
 * allows approximations to be used for these methods.
 **/
public boolean intersects(double x, double y, double w, double h) {
    return approximation.intersects(x, y, w, h);
}
public boolean intersects(Rectangle2D r) {
    return approximation.intersects(r);
}

/**
 * This method is the heart of all Shape implementations.  It returns a
 * PathIterator that describes the shape in terms of the line and curve
 * segments that comprise it.  Our iterator implementation approximates
 * the shape of the spiral using line segments only.  We pass in a
 * "flatness" argument that tells it how good the approximation must be
 * (smaller numbers mean a better approximation).
 */
public PathIterator getPathIterator(AffineTransform at) {
    return new SpiralIterator(at, outerRadius/500.0);
}

/**
 * Return a PathIterator that describes the shape in terms of line
 * segments only, with an approximation quality specified by flatness.
 **/
public PathIterator getPathIterator(AffineTransform at, double flatness) {
    return new SpiralIterator(at, flatness);
}

/**
 * This inner class is the PathIterator for our Spiral shape.  For
 * simplicity, it does not describe the spiral path in terms of Bezier
 * curve segments, but simply approximates it with line segments.  The
```

Example 12-15. Spiral.java (continued)

```
 * flatness property specifies how far the approximation is allowed to
 * deviate from the true curve.
 **/
class SpiralIterator implements PathIterator {
    AffineTransform transform;      // How to transform generated coordinates
    double flatness;                // How close an approximation
    double angle = startAngle;      // Current angle
    double radius = startRadius;    // Current radius
    boolean done = false;           // Are we done yet?

    /** A simple constructor.  Just store the parameters into fields */
    public SpiralIterator(AffineTransform transform, double flatness) {
        this.transform = transform;
        this.flatness = flatness;
    }

    /**
     * All PathIterators have a "winding rule" that helps to specify what
     * is the inside of an area and what is the outside.  If you fill a
     * spiral (which you're not supposed to do) the winding rule returned
     * here yields better results than the alternative, WIND_EVEN_ODD
     **/
    public int getWindingRule() { return WIND_NON_ZERO; }

    /** Returns true if the entire path has been iterated */
    public boolean isDone() { return done; }

    /**
     * Store the coordinates of the current segment of the path into the
     * specified array, and return the type of the segment.  Use
     * trigonometry to compute the coordinates based on the current angle
     * and radius.  If this was the first point, return a MOVETO segment,
     * otherwise return a LINETO segment. Also, check to see if we're done.
     **/
    public int currentSegment(float[] coords) {
        // given the radius and the angle, compute the point coords
        coords[0] = (float)(centerX + radius*Math.cos(angle));
        coords[1] = (float)(centerY - radius*Math.sin(angle));

        // If a transform was specified, use it on the coordinates
        if (transform != null) transform.transform(coords, 0, coords, 0,1);

        // If we've reached the end of the spiral, remember that fact
        if (angle == endAngle) done = true;

        // If this is the first point in the spiral, then move to it
        if (angle == startAngle) return SEG_MOVETO;

        // Otherwise draw a line from the previous point to this one
        return SEG_LINETO;
    }
```

Example 12-15. Spiral.java (continued)

```java
    /** This method is the same as above, except using double values */
    public int currentSegment(double[ ] coords) {
        coords[0] = centerX + radius*Math.cos(angle);
        coords[1] = centerY - radius*Math.sin(angle);
        if (transform != null) transform.transform(coords, 0, coords, 0,1);
        if (angle == endAngle) done = true;
        if (angle == startAngle) return SEG_MOVETO;
        else return SEG_LINETO;
    }

    /**
     * Move on to the next segment of the path.  Compute the angle and
     * radius values for the next point in the spiral.
     **/
    public void next( ) {
        if (done) return;

        // First, figure out how much to increment the angle.  This
        // depends on the required flatness, and also upon the current
        // radius.  When drawing a circle (which we'll use as our
        // approximation) of radius r, we can maintain a flatness f by
        // using angular increments given by this formula:
        //     a = acos(2*(f/r)*(f/r) - 4*(f/r) + 1)
        // Use this formula to figure out how much we can increment the
        // angle for the next segment.  Note that the formula does not
        // work well for very small radii, so we special case those.
        double x = flatness/radius;
        if (Double.isNaN(x) || (x > .1))
            angle += Math.PI/4*angleDirection;
        else {
            double y = 2*x*x - 4*x + 1;
            angle += Math.acos(y)*angleDirection;
        }

        // Check whether we've gone past the end of the spiral
        if ((angle-endAngle)*angleDirection > 0) angle = endAngle;

        // Now that we know the new angle, we can use interpolation to
        // figure out what the corresponding radius is.
        double fractionComplete = (angle-startAngle)/(endAngle-startAngle);
        radius = startRadius + (endRadius-startRadius)*fractionComplete;
    }
}
}
```

Example 12-16. PolyLine.java

```java
package je3.graphics;
import java.awt.geom.*;  // PathIterator, AffineTransform, and related
import java.awt.Shape;
import java.awt.Rectangle;
import java.io.Externalizable;
```

Example 12-16. PolyLine.java (continued)

```java
/**
 * This Shape implementation represents a series of connected line segments.
 * It is like a Polygon, but is not closed.  This class is used by the
 * ScribblePane class of the GUI chapter.  It implements the Cloneable and
 * Externalizable interfaces so it can be used in the Drag-and-Drop examples
 * in the Data Transfer chapter.
 */
public class PolyLine implements Shape, Cloneable, Externalizable {
    float x0, y0;      // The starting point of the polyline.
    float[] coords;    // The x and y coordinates of the end point of each line
                       // segment packed into a single array for simplicity:
                       // [x1,y1,x2,y2,...] Note that these are relative to x0,y0
    int numsegs;       // How many line segments in this PolyLine

    // Coordinates of our bounding box, relative to (x0, y0);
    float xmin=0f, xmax=0f, ymin=0f, ymax=0f;

    // No-arg constructor assumes an origin of (0,0)
    // A no-arg constructor is required for the Externalizable interface
    public PolyLine() { this(0f, 0f); }

    // The constructor.
    public PolyLine(float x0, float y0) {
        setOrigin(x0,y0);      // Record the starting point.
        numsegs = 0;           // Note that we have no line segments, so far
    }

    /** Set the origin of the PolyLine.  Useful when moving it */
    public void setOrigin(float x0, float y0) {
        this.x0 = x0;
        this.y0 = y0;
    }

    /** Add dx and dy to the origin */
    public void translate(float dx, float dy) {
        this.x0 += dx;
        this.y0 += dy;
    }

    /**
     * Add a line segment to the PolyLine.  Note that x and y are absolute
     * coordinates, even though the implementation stores them relative to
     * x0, y0;
     */
    public void addSegment(float x, float y) {
        // Allocate or reallocate the coords[] array when necessary
        if (coords == null) coords = new float[32];
        if (numsegs*2 >= coords.length) {
            float[] newcoords = new float[coords.length * 2];
            System.arraycopy(coords, 0, newcoords, 0, coords.length);
            coords = newcoords;
        }
```

Example 12-16. PolyLine.java (continued)

```
    // Convert from absolute to relative coordinates
    x = x - x0;
    y = y - y0;

    // Store the data
    coords[numsegs*2] = x;
    coords[numsegs*2+1] = y;
    numsegs++;

    // Enlarge the bounding box, if necessary
    if (x > xmax) xmax = x;
    else if (x < xmin) xmin = x;
    if (y > ymax) ymax = y;
    else if (y < ymin) ymin = y;
}

/*----------------- The Shape Interface -------------------- */

// Return floating-point bounding box
public Rectangle2D getBounds2D( ) {
    return new Rectangle2D.Float(x0 + xmin, y0 + ymin,
                                 xmax-xmin, ymax-ymin);
}

// Return integer bounding box, rounded to outermost pixels.
public Rectangle getBounds( ) {
    return new Rectangle((int)(x0 + xmin - 0.5f),      // x0
                         (int)(y0 + ymin - 0.5f),      // y0
                         (int)(xmax - xmin + 0.5f),    // width
                         (int)(ymax - ymin + 0.5f));   // height
}

// PolyLine shapes are open curves, with no interior.
// The Shape interface says that open curves should be implicitly closed
// for the purposes of insideness testing.  For our purposes, however,
// we define PolyLine shapes to have no interior, and the contains( )
// methods always return false.
public boolean contains(Point2D p) { return false; }
public boolean contains(Rectangle2D r) { return false; }
public boolean contains(double x, double y) { return false; }
public boolean contains(double x, double y, double w, double h) {
    return false;
}

// The intersects methods simply test whether any of the line segments
// within a polyline intersects the given rectangle.  Strictly speaking,
// the Shape interface requires us to also check whether the rectangle
// is entirely contained within the shape as well.  But the contains( )
// methods for this class always return false.
// We might improve the efficiency of this method by first checking for
// intersection with the overall bounding box to rule out cases that
// aren't even close.
```

Graphics

Example 12-16. PolyLine.java (continued)

```java
public boolean intersects(Rectangle2D r) {
    if (numsegs < 1) return false;
    float lastx = x0, lasty = y0;
    for(int i = 0; i < numsegs; i++) {  // loop through the segments
        float x = coords[i*2] + x0;
        float y = coords[i*2+1] + y0;
        // See if this line segment intersects the rectangle
        if (r.intersectsLine(x, y, lastx, lasty)) return true;
        // Otherwise move on to the next segment
        lastx = x;
        lasty = y;
    }
    return false;  // No line segment intersected the rectangle
}

// This variant method is just defined in terms of the last.
public boolean intersects(double x, double y, double w, double h) {
    return intersects(new Rectangle2D.Double(x,y,w,h));
}

// This is the key to the Shape interface; it tells Java2D how to draw
// the shape as a series of lines and curves.  We use only lines
public PathIterator getPathIterator(final AffineTransform transform) {
    return new PathIterator() {
            int curseg = -1; // current segment
            // Copy the current segment for thread-safety, so we don't
            // mess up if a segment is added while we're iterating
            int numsegs = PolyLine.this.numsegs;

            public boolean isDone() { return curseg >= numsegs; }

            public void next() { curseg++; }

            // Get coordinates and type of current segment as floats
            public int currentSegment(float[] data) {
                int segtype;
                if (curseg == -1) {         // First time we're called
                    data[0] = x0;           // Data is the origin point
                    data[1] = y0;
                    segtype = SEG_MOVETO; // Returned as a moveto segment
                }
                else { // Otherwise, the data is a segment endpoint
                    data[0] = x0 + coords[curseg*2];
                    data[1] = y0 + coords[curseg*2 + 1];
                    segtype = SEG_LINETO; // Returned as a lineto segment
                }
                // If a tranform was specified, transform point in place
                if (transform != null)
                    transform.transform(data, 0, data, 0, 1);
                return segtype;
            }
```

Example 12-16. PolyLine.java (continued)

```
            // Same as last method, but use doubles
            public int currentSegment(double[ ] data) {
                int segtype;
                if (curseg == -1) {
                    data[0] = x0;
                    data[1] = y0;
                    segtype = SEG_MOVETO;
                }
                else {
                    data[0] = x0 + coords[curseg*2];
                    data[1] = y0 + coords[curseg*2 + 1];
                    segtype = SEG_LINETO;
                }
                if (transform != null)
                    transform.transform(data, 0, data, 0, 1);
                return segtype;
            }

            // This only matters for closed shapes
            public int getWindingRule( ) { return WIND_NON_ZERO; }
        };
    }

    // PolyLines never contain curves, so we can ignore the flatness limit
    // and implement this method in terms of the one above.
    public PathIterator getPathIterator(AffineTransform at, double flatness) {
        return getPathIterator(at);
    }

    /*----------------- Externalizable -------------------- */

    /**
     * The following two methods implement the Externalizable interface.
     * We use Externalizable instead of Seralizable so we have full control
     * over the data format, and only write out the defined coordinates
     */
    public void writeExternal(java.io.ObjectOutput out)
        throws java.io.IOException
    {
        out.writeFloat(x0);
        out.writeFloat(y0);
        out.writeInt(numsegs);
        for(int i=0; i < numsegs*2; i++) out.writeFloat(coords[i]);
    }

    public void readExternal(java.io.ObjectInput in)
        throws java.io.IOException, ClassNotFoundException
    {
        this.x0 = in.readFloat( );
        this.y0 = in.readFloat( );
        this.numsegs = in.readInt( );
        this.coords = new float[numsegs*2];
```

Example 12-16. PolyLine.java (continued)

```
    for(int i=0; i < numsegs*2; i++) coords[i] = in.readFloat( );
}

/*----------------- Cloneable -------------------- */

/**
 * Override the Object.clone( ) method so that the array gets cloned, too.
 */
public Object clone( ) {
    try {
        PolyLine copy = (PolyLine) super.clone( );
        if (coords != null) copy.coords = (float[ ]) this.coords.clone( );
        return copy;
    }
    catch(CloneNotSupportedException e) {
        throw new AssertionError( ); // This should never happen
    }
}
}
```

Custom Strokes

As we saw in Example 12-9, the Stroke class converts a line-drawing operation into an area-filling operation by taking the Shape whose outline is to be drawn and returning a stroked shape that represents the outline itself. Because Stroke is such a simple interface, it is relatively easy to implement custom Stroke classes that perform interesting graphical effects. Example 12-17 includes four custom Stroke implementations that it uses along with a simple BasicStroke object to produce the output shown in Figure 12-12.

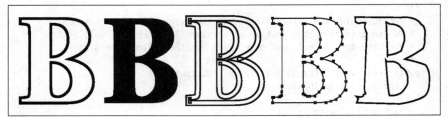

Figure 12-12. Special effects with custom Stroke classes

You should pay particular attention to the ControlPointsStroke and SloppyStroke implementations. These classes are interesting because they use a PathIterator object to break a shape down into its component line and curve segments (just the opposite of what was done in the Spiral class shown in Example 12-15). These two custom Stroke classes also use the GeneralPath class of java.awt.geom to build a custom shape out of arbitrary line and curve segments (which shows how closely linked the GeneralPath class and the PathIterator interface are).

Example 12-17. CustomStrokes.java

```java
package je3.graphics;
import java.awt.*;
import java.awt.geom.*;
import java.awt.font.*;

/** A demonstration of writing custom Stroke classes */
public class CustomStrokes implements GraphicsExample {
    static final int WIDTH = 750, HEIGHT = 200;          // Size of our example
    public String getName() {return "Custom Strokes";}   // From GraphicsExample
    public int getWidth() { return WIDTH; }              // From GraphicsExample
    public int getHeight() { return HEIGHT; }            // From GraphicsExample

    // These are the various stroke objects we'll demonstrate
    Stroke[] strokes = new Stroke[] {
        new BasicStroke(4.0f),            // The standard, predefined stroke
        new NullStroke(),                 // A Stroke that does nothing
        new DoubleStroke(8.0f, 2.0f),     // A Stroke that strokes twice
        new ControlPointsStroke(2.0f),    // Shows the vertices & control points
        new SloppyStroke(2.0f, 3.0f)      // Perturbs the shape before stroking
    };

    /** Draw the example */
    public void draw(Graphics2D g, Component c) {
        // Get a shape to work with.  Here we'll use the letter B
        Font f = new Font("Serif", Font.BOLD, 200);
        GlyphVector gv = f.createGlyphVector(g.getFontRenderContext(), "B");
        Shape shape = gv.getOutline();

        // Set drawing attributes and starting position
        g.setColor(Color.black);
        g.setRenderingHint(RenderingHints.KEY_ANTIALIASING,
                           RenderingHints.VALUE_ANTIALIAS_ON);
        g.translate(10, 175);

        // Draw the shape once with each stroke
        for(int i = 0; i < strokes.length; i++) {
            g.setStroke(strokes[i]);   // set the stroke
            g.draw(shape);             // draw the shape
            g.translate(140,0);        // move to the right
        }
    }
}

/**
 * This Stroke implementation does nothing.  Its createStrokedShape()
 * method returns an unmodified shape.  Thus, drawing a shape with
 * this Stroke is the same as filling that shape!
 **/
class NullStroke implements Stroke {
    public Shape createStrokedShape(Shape s) { return s; }
}
```

Example 12-17. CustomStrokes.java (continued)

```java
/**
 * This Stroke implementation applies a BasicStroke to a shape twice.
 * If you draw with this Stroke, then instead of outlining the shape,
 * you're outlining the outline of the shape.
 **/
class DoubleStroke implements Stroke {
    BasicStroke stroke1, stroke2;   // the two strokes to use
    public DoubleStroke(float width1, float width2) {
        stroke1 = new BasicStroke(width1);   // Constructor arguments specify
        stroke2 = new BasicStroke(width2);   // the line widths for the strokes
    }

    public Shape createStrokedShape(Shape s) {
        // Use the first stroke to create an outline of the shape
        Shape outline = stroke1.createStrokedShape(s);
        // Use the second stroke to create an outline of that outline.
        // It is this outline of the outline that will be filled in
        return stroke2.createStrokedShape(outline);
    }
}


/**
 * This Stroke implementation strokes the shape using a thin line, and
 * also displays the end points and Bezier curve control points of all
 * the line and curve segments that make up the shape.  The radius
 * argument to the constructor specifies the size of the control point
 * markers. Note the use of PathIterator to break the shape down into
 * its segments, and of GeneralPath to build up the stroked shape.
 **/
class ControlPointsStroke implements Stroke {
    float radius;   // how big the control point markers should be
    public ControlPointsStroke(float radius) { this.radius = radius; }

    public Shape createStrokedShape(Shape shape) {
        // Start off by stroking the shape with a thin line.  Store the
        // resulting shape in a GeneralPath object so we can add to it.
        GeneralPath strokedShape =
            new GeneralPath(new BasicStroke(1.0f).createStrokedShape(shape));

        // Use a PathIterator object to iterate through each of the line and
        // curve segments of the shape.  For each one, mark the endpoint and
        // control points (if any) by adding a rectangle to the GeneralPath
        float[ ] coords = new float[6];
        for(PathIterator i=shape.getPathIterator(null); !i.isDone( );i.next( )) {
            int type = i.currentSegment(coords);
            Shape s = null, s2 = null, s3 = null;
            switch(type) {
            case PathIterator.SEG_CUBICTO:
                markPoint(strokedShape, coords[4], coords[5]); // falls through
            case PathIterator.SEG_QUADTO:
                markPoint(strokedShape, coords[2], coords[3]); // falls through
            case PathIterator.SEG_MOVETO:
```

Example 12-17. CustomStrokes.java (continued)

```
            case PathIterator.SEG_LINETO:
                markPoint(strokedShape, coords[0], coords[1]); // falls through
            case PathIterator.SEG_CLOSE:
                break;
            }
        }

        return strokedShape;
    }

    /** Add a small square centered at (x,y) to the specified path */
    void markPoint(GeneralPath path, float x, float y) {
        path.moveTo(x-radius, y-radius);  // Begin a new sub-path
        path.lineTo(x+radius, y-radius);  // Add a line segment to it
        path.lineTo(x+radius, y+radius);  // Add a second line segment
        path.lineTo(x-radius, y+radius);  // And a third
        path.closePath();                 // Go back to last moveTo position
    }
}

/**
 * This Stroke implementation randomly perturbs the line and curve segments
 * that make up a Shape, and then strokes that perturbed shape.  It uses
 * PathIterator to loop through the Shape and GeneralPath to build up the
 * modified shape.  Finally, it uses a BasicStroke to stroke the modified
 * shape.  The result is a "sloppy" looking shape.
 **/
class SloppyStroke implements Stroke {
    BasicStroke stroke;
    float sloppiness;
    public SloppyStroke(float width, float sloppiness) {
        this.stroke = new BasicStroke(width); // Used to stroke modified shape
        this.sloppiness = sloppiness;         // How sloppy should we be?
    }

    public Shape createStrokedShape(Shape shape) {
        GeneralPath newshape = new GeneralPath();  // Start with an empty shape

        // Iterate through the specified shape, perturb its coordinates, and
        // use them to build up the new shape.
        float[] coords = new float[6];
        for(PathIterator i=shape.getPathIterator(null); !i.isDone();i.next()) {
            int type = i.currentSegment(coords);
            switch(type) {
            case PathIterator.SEG_MOVETO:
                perturb(coords, 2);
                newshape.moveTo(coords[0], coords[1]);
                break;
            case PathIterator.SEG_LINETO:
                perturb(coords, 2);
                newshape.lineTo(coords[0], coords[1]);
                break;
```

Example 12-17. CustomStrokes.java (continued)

```java
        case PathIterator.SEG_QUADTO:
            perturb(coords, 4);
            newshape.quadTo(coords[0], coords[1], coords[2], coords[3]);
            break;
        case PathIterator.SEG_CUBICTO:
            perturb(coords, 6);
            newshape.curveTo(coords[0], coords[1], coords[2], coords[3],
                            coords[4], coords[5]);
            break;
        case PathIterator.SEG_CLOSE:
            newshape.closePath( );
            break;
        }
    }

    // Finally, stroke the perturbed shape and return the result
    return stroke.createStrokedShape(newshape);
    }

    // Randomly modify the specified number of coordinates, by an amount
    // specified by the sloppiness field.
    void perturb(float[ ] coords, int numCoords) {
        for(int i = 0; i < numCoords; i++)
            coords[i] += (float)((Math.random( )*2-1.0)*sloppiness);
    }
}
```

Custom Paint

Figure 12-8 showed a variety of shape-filling techniques; it included a large letter A filled with a complex pattern defined by the GenericPaint class. Example 12-18 shows the implementation of this class. You may want to take another look at Example 12-10 to see how the GenericPaint class is used, before you dive into the code listed here.

The GenericPaint class itself is pretty simple: it defines both the abstract color computation methods that subclasses implement and a createContext( ) method that returns a PaintContext. The implementation of PaintContext does all the hard work. This is pretty low-level stuff, so don't be dismayed if you don't understand everything. The code should at least give you a basic idea of how painting works in Java 2D.

Example 12-18. GenericPaint.java

```java
package je3.graphics;
import java.awt.*;
import java.awt.geom.*;
import java.awt.image.*;

/**
 * This is an abstract Paint implementation that computes the color of each
 * point to be painted by passing the coordinates of the point to the calling
```

Example 12-18. GenericPaint.java (continued)

```
 * abstract methods computeRed( ), computeGreen( ), computeBlue( ) and
 * computeAlpha( ).  Subclasses must implement these three methods to perform
 * whatever type of painting is desired.  Note that while this class provides
 * great flexibility, it is not very efficient.
**/
public abstract class GenericPaint implements Paint {
    /** This is the main Paint method;  all it does is return a PaintContext */
    public PaintContext createContext(ColorModel cm,
                                      Rectangle deviceBounds,
                                      Rectangle2D userBounds,
                                      AffineTransform xform,
                                      RenderingHints hints) {
        return new GenericPaintContext(xform);
    }

    /** This paint class allows translucent painting */
    public int getTransparency( ) { return TRANSLUCENT; }

    /**
     * These three methods return the red, green, blue, and alpha values of
     * the pixel that appears at the specified user-space coordinates.  The return
     * value of each method should be between 0 and 255.
    **/
    public abstract int computeRed(double x, double y);
    public abstract int computeGreen(double x, double y);
    public abstract int computeBlue(double x, double y);
    public abstract int computeAlpha(double x, double y);

    /**
     * The PaintContext class does all the work of painting
    **/
    class GenericPaintContext implements PaintContext {
        ColorModel model; // The color model
        Point2D origin, unitVectorX, unitVectorY; // For device-to-user xform

        public GenericPaintContext(AffineTransform userToDevice) {
            // Our color model packs RGB values into a single int
            model = new DirectColorModel(32, 0x00ff0000,0x0000ff00,
                                         0x000000ff, 0xff000000);
            // The specified transform converts user to device pixels
            // We need to figure out the reverse transformation, so we
            // can compute the user space coordinates of each device pixel
            try {
                AffineTransform deviceToUser = userToDevice.createInverse( );
                origin = deviceToUser.transform(new Point(0,0), null);
                unitVectorX = deviceToUser.deltaTransform(new Point(1,0),null);
                unitVectorY = deviceToUser.deltaTransform(new Point(0,1),null);
            }
            catch (NoninvertibleTransformException e) {
                // If we can't invert the transform, just use device space
                origin = new Point(0,0);
                unitVectorX = new Point(1,0);
```

Graphics

Example 12-18. GenericPaint.java (continued)

```
            unitVectorY = new Point(0, 1);
        }
    }

    /** Return the color model used by this Paint implementation */
    public ColorModel getColorModel() { return model; }

    /**
     * This is the main method of PaintContext.  It must return a Raster
     * that contains fill data for the specified rectangle.  It creates a
     * raster of the specified size, and loops through the device pixels.
     * For each one, it converts the coordinates to user space, then calls
     * the computeRed(), computeGreen() and computeBlue() methods to
     * obtain the appropriate color for the device pixel.
     **/
    public Raster getRaster(int x, int y, int w, int h) {
        WritableRaster raster = model.createCompatibleWritableRaster(w,h);
        int[] colorComponents = new int[4];
        for(int j = 0; j < h; j++) {       // Loop through rows of raster
            int deviceY = y + j;
            for(int i = 0; i < w; i++) {  // Loop through columns
                int deviceX = x + i;
                // Convert device coordinate to user-space coordinate
                double userX = origin.getX() +
                    deviceX * unitVectorX.getX() +
                    deviceY * unitVectorY.getX();
                double userY = origin.getY() +
                    deviceX * unitVectorX.getY() +
                    deviceY * unitVectorY.getY();
                // Compute the color components of the pixel
                colorComponents[0] = computeRed(userX, userY);
                colorComponents[1] = computeGreen(userX, userY);
                colorComponents[2] = computeBlue(userX, userY);
                colorComponents[3] = computeAlpha(userX, userY);
                // Set the color of the pixel
                raster.setPixel(i, j, colorComponents);
            }
        }
        return raster;
    }

    /** Called when the PaintContext is no longer needed. */
    public void dispose() { }
    }
}
```

Advanced Animation

Way back in Example 12-4, we saw a simple animation technique that suffered, unfortunately, from flickering. Example 12-19 is a program that performs a more graphics-intensive animation but doesn't flicker, because it uses a technique known as *double-buffering*: it draws each frame of the animation off-screen, then copies the frame onto the screen all at once. This example also has better performance because it requests redraws of only the relatively small portion of the screen that needs to be redrawn.

Another interesting feature of this example is its use of the javax.swing.Timer class to call the actionPerformed( ) method of a specified ActionListener object at specified intervals. The Timer class is used here so that you don't have to create a Thread. (Note that Java 1.3 includes java.util.Timer, a class that is similar to, but quite distinct from, javax.swing.Timer.)

Example 12-19. Hypnosis.java

```java
package je3.graphics;
import java.awt.*;
import java.awt.event.*;
import java.awt.image.*;
import javax.swing.*;
import javax.swing.Timer;  // Import explicitly because of java.util.Timer

/**
 * A Swing component that smoothly animates a spiral in a hypnotic way.
 **/
public class Hypnosis extends JComponent implements ActionListener {
    double x, y;            // The center of the spiral
    double r1, r2;          // The inner and outer radii of the spiral
    double a1, a2;          // The start and end angles of the spiral
    double deltaA;          // How much the angle changes in each frame
    double deltaX, deltaY;  // The trajectory of the center
    float linewidth;        // How wide the lines are
    Timer timer;            // The object that triggers the animation
    BufferedImage buffer;   // The image we use for double-buffering
    Graphics2D osg;         // Graphics2D object for drawing into the buffer

    public Hypnosis(double x, double y, double r1, double r2,
                    double a1, double a2, float linewidth, int delay,
                    double deltaA, double deltaX, double deltaY)
    {
        this.x = x; this.y = y;
        this.r1 = r1; this.r2 = r2;
        this.a1 = a1; this.a2 = a2;
        this.linewidth = linewidth;
        this.deltaA = deltaA;
        this.deltaX = deltaX;
        this.deltaY = deltaY;

        // Set up a timer to call actionPerformed( ) every delay milliseconds
        timer = new Timer(delay, this);

        // Create a buffer for double-buffering
        buffer = new BufferedImage((int)(2*r2+linewidth),
                                   (int)(2*r2+linewidth),
                                   BufferedImage.TYPE_INT_RGB);
```

Example 12-19. Hypnosis.java (continued)

```java
        // Create a Graphics object for the buffer, and set the linewidth
        // and request antialiasing when drawing with it
        osg = buffer.createGraphics();
        osg.setStroke(new BasicStroke(linewidth, BasicStroke.CAP_ROUND,
                                BasicStroke.JOIN_ROUND));
        osg.setRenderingHint(RenderingHints.KEY_ANTIALIASING,
                            RenderingHints.VALUE_ANTIALIAS_ON);
    }

    // Start and stop the animation by starting and stopping the timer
    public void start() { timer.start(); }
    public void stop() { timer.stop(); }

    /**
     * Swing calls this method to ask the component to redraw itself.
     * This method uses double-buffering to make the animation smoother.
     * Swing does double-buffering automatically, so this may not actually
     * make much difference, but it is important to understand the technique.
     **/
    public void paintComponent(Graphics g) {
        // Clear the background of the off-screen image
        osg.setColor(getBackground());
        osg.fillRect(0, 0, buffer.getWidth(), buffer.getHeight());

        // Now draw a black spiral into the off-screen image
        osg.setColor(Color.black);
        osg.draw(new Spiral(r2+linewidth/2, r2+linewidth/2, r1, a1, r2, a2));

        // Now copy that off-screen image onto the screen
        g.drawImage(buffer, (int)(x-r2), (int)(y-r2), this);
    }

    /**
     * This method implements the ActionListener interface.  Our Timer object
     * calls this method periodically.  It updates the position and angles
     * of the spiral and requests a redraw.  Instead of redrawing the entire
     * component, however, this method requests a redraw only for the
     * area that has changed.
     **/
    public void actionPerformed(ActionEvent e) {
        // Ask to have the old bounding box of the spiral redrawn.
        // Nothing else has anything drawn in it, so it doesn't need a redraw
        repaint((int)(x-r2-linewidth), (int)(y-r2-linewidth),
                (int)(2*(r2+linewidth)), (int)(2*(r2+linewidth)));

        // Now animate: update the position and angles of the spiral

        // Bounce if we've hit an edge
        Rectangle bounds = getBounds();
        if ((x - r2 + deltaX < 0) || (x + r2 + deltaX > bounds.width))
            deltaX = -deltaX;
        if ((y - r2 + deltaY < 0) || (y + r2 + deltaY > bounds.height))
            deltaY = -deltaY;
```

Example 12-19. Hypnosis.java (continued)

```
        // Move the center of the spiral
        x += deltaX;
        y += deltaY;

        // Increment the start and end angles;
        a1 += deltaA;
        a2 += deltaA;
        if (a1 > 2*Math.PI) {  // Don't let them get too big
            a1 -= 2*Math.PI;
            a2 -= 2*Math.PI;
        }

        // Now ask to have the new bounding box of the spiral redrawn.  This
        // rectangle will be intersected with the redraw rectangle requested
        // above, and only the combined region will be redrawn
        repaint((int)(x-r2-linewidth), (int)(y-r2-linewidth),
                (int)(2*(r2+linewidth)), (int)(2*(r2+linewidth)));
    }

    /** Tell Swing not to double-buffer for us, since we do our own */
    public boolean isDoubleBuffered( ) { return false; }

    /** This is a main( ) method for testing the component */
    public static void main(String[ ] args) {
        JFrame f = new JFrame("Hypnosis");
        Hypnosis h = new Hypnosis(200, 200, 10, 100, 0, 5*Math.PI, 10, 100,
                                  2*Math.PI/15, 3, 5);
        f.getContentPane( ).add(h, BorderLayout.CENTER);
        f.setSize(400, 400);
        f.show( );
        h.start( );
    }
}
```

Displaying Graphics Examples

Example 12-20 shows the GraphicsExampleFrame class we've been using to display GraphicsExample implementations throughout this chapter. This program mainly demonstrates the Swing and Printing APIs, but is included here for completeness. The paintComponent( ) method of the GraphicsExamplePane inner class is where the draw( ) method of each GraphicsExample object is invoked. Although paintComponent( ) is declared as taking a Graphics object, in Java 1.2 and later it is always passed a Graphics2D object, which can be safely cast to that type.

Example 12-20. GraphicsExampleFrame.java

```
package je3.graphics;
import java.awt.*;
import java.awt.event.*;
import javax.swing.*;
import javax.swing.event.*;
import java.awt.print.*;
```

Example 12-20. GraphicsExampleFrame.java (continued)

```java
/**
 * This class displays one or more GraphicsExample objects in a
 * Swing JFrame and a JTabbedPane
 */
public class GraphicsExampleFrame extends JFrame {
    public GraphicsExampleFrame(final GraphicsExample[] examples) {
        super("GraphicsExampleFrame");

        Container cpane = getContentPane();      // Set up the frame
        cpane.setLayout(new BorderLayout());
        final JTabbedPane tpane = new JTabbedPane(); // And the tabbed pane
        cpane.add(tpane, BorderLayout.CENTER);

        // Add a menubar
        JMenuBar menubar = new JMenuBar();           // Create the menubar
        this.setJMenuBar(menubar);                   // Add it to the frame
        JMenu filemenu = new JMenu("File");          // Create a File menu
        menubar.add(filemenu);                       // Add to the menubar
        JMenuItem print = new JMenuItem("Print");    // Create a Print item
        filemenu.add(print);                         // Add it to the menu
        JMenuItem quit = new JMenuItem("Quit");      // Create a Quit item
        filemenu.add(quit);                          // Add it to the menu

        // Tell the Print menu item what to do when selected
        print.addActionListener(new ActionListener() {
                public void actionPerformed(ActionEvent e) {
                    // Get the currently displayed example, and call
                    // the print method (defined below)
                    print(examples[tpane.getSelectedIndex()]);
                }
        });

        // Tell the Quit menu item what to do when selected
        quit.addActionListener(new ActionListener() {
                public void actionPerformed(ActionEvent e) { System.exit(0); }
        });

        // In addition to the Quit menu item, also handle window close events
        this.addWindowListener(new WindowAdapter() {
                public void windowClosing(WindowEvent e) { System.exit(0); }
        });

        // Insert each of the example objects into the tabbed pane
        for(int i = 0; i < examples.length; i++) {
            GraphicsExample e = examples[i];
            tpane.addTab(e.getName(), new GraphicsExamplePane(e));
        }
    }

    /**
     * This inner class is a custom Swing component that displays
     * a GraphicsExample object.
     */
```

Example 12-20. GraphicsExampleFrame.java (continued)

```java
public class GraphicsExamplePane extends JComponent {
    GraphicsExample example;    // The example to display
    Dimension size;             // How much space it requires

    public GraphicsExamplePane(GraphicsExample example) {
        this.example = example;
        size = new Dimension(example.getWidth( ), example.getHeight( ));
    }

    /** Draw the component and the example it contains */
    public void paintComponent(Graphics g) {
        g.setColor(Color.white);                    // set the background
        g.fillRect(0, 0, size.width, size.height);  // to white
        g.setColor(Color.black);                    // set a default drawing color
        example.draw((Graphics2D) g, this);  // ask example to draw itself
    }

    // These methods specify how big the component must be
    public Dimension getPreferredSize( ) { return size; }
    public Dimension getMinimumSize( ) { return size; }
}

/** This method is invoked by the Print menu item */
public void print(final GraphicsExample example) {
    // Start off by getting a printer job to do the printing
    PrinterJob job = PrinterJob.getPrinterJob( );
    // Wrap the example in a Printable object (defined below)
    // and tell the PrinterJob that we want to print it
    job.setPrintable(new PrintableExample(example));

    // Display the print dialog to the user
    if (job.printDialog( )) {
        // If they didn't cancel it, then tell the job to start printing
        try {
            job.print( );
        }
        catch(PrinterException e) {
            System.out.println("Couldn't print: " + e.getMessage( ));
        }
    }
}

/**
 * This inner class implements the Printable interface in order to print
 * a GraphicsExample object.
 **/
class PrintableExample implements Printable {
    GraphicsExample example;  // The example to print

    // The constructor.  Just remember the example
    public PrintableExample(GraphicsExample example) {
        this.example = example;
    }
```

Graphics

Example 12-20. GraphicsExampleFrame.java (continued)

```java
    /**
     * This method is called by the PrinterJob to print the example
     **/
    public int print(Graphics g, PageFormat pf, int pageIndex) {
        // Tell the PrinterJob that there is only one page
        if (pageIndex != 0) return NO_SUCH_PAGE;

        // The PrinterJob supplies us a Graphics object to draw with.
        // Anything drawn with this object will be sent to the printer.
        // The Graphics object can safely be cast to a Graphics2D object.
        Graphics2D g2 = (Graphics2D)g;

        // Translate to skip the left and top margins.
        g2.translate(pf.getImageableX( ), pf.getImageableY( ));

        // Figure out how big the printable area is, and how big
        // the example is.
        double pageWidth = pf.getImageableWidth( );
        double pageHeight = pf.getImageableHeight( );
        double exampleWidth = example.getWidth( );
        double exampleHeight = example.getHeight( );

        // Scale the example if needed
        double scalex = 1.0, scaley = 1.0;
        if (exampleWidth > pageWidth) scalex = pageWidth/exampleWidth;
        if (exampleHeight > pageHeight) scaley = pageHeight/exampleHeight;
        double scalefactor = Math.min(scalex, scaley);
        if (scalefactor != 1) g2.scale(scalefactor, scalefactor);

        // Finally, call the draw( ) method of the example, passing in
        // the Graphics2D object for the printer
        example.draw(g2, GraphicsExampleFrame.this);

        // Tell the PrinterJob that we successfully printed the page
        return PAGE_EXISTS;
    }
}

/**
 * The main program.  Use Java reflection to load and instantiate
 * the specified GraphicsExample classes, then create a
 * GraphicsExampleFrame to display them.
 **/
public static void main(String[ ] args) {
    GraphicsExample[ ] examples = new GraphicsExample[args.length];

    // Loop through the command line arguments
    for(int i=0; i < args.length; i++) {
        // The class name of the requested example
        String classname = args[i];
```

Example 12-20. GraphicsExampleFrame.java (continued)

```
                // If no package is specified, assume it is in this package
                if (classname.indexOf('.') == -1)
                    classname = "je3.graphics." + args[i];

                // Try to instantiate the named GraphicsExample class
                try {
                    Class exampleClass = Class.forName(classname);
                    examples[i] = (GraphicsExample) exampleClass.newInstance();
                }
                catch (ClassNotFoundException e) {  // unknown class
                    System.err.println("Couldn't find example: " + classname);
                    System.exit(1);
                }
                catch (ClassCastException e) {       // wrong type of class
                    System.err.println("Class " + classname +
                                        " is not a GraphicsExample");
                    System.exit(1);
                }
                catch (Exception e) {  // class doesn't have a public constructor
                    // catch InstantiationException, IllegalAccessException
                    System.err.println("Couldn't instantiate example: " +
                                        classname);
                    System.exit(1);
                }
            }

            // Now create a window to display the examples in, and make it visible
            GraphicsExampleFrame f = new GraphicsExampleFrame(examples);
            f.pack();
            f.setVisible(true);
        }
    }
```

Exercises

Exercise 12-1. Example 12-1 contains a centerText( ) method that centers one or two lines of text within a rectangle. Write a modified version of this method that positions a single line of text according to two new method parameters. One parameter should specify the horizontal positioning: left-, center-, or right-justified. The other parameter should specify the vertical position: at the top of the rectangle, centered, or at the bottom of the rectangle. You can use the FontMetrics class, as Example 12-1 does, or the Java 2D getStringBounds( ) method of the Font class. Write a GraphicsExample class that demonstrates all nine possible positioning types supported by your method.

Exercise 12-2. Use the animation techniques demonstrated in this chapter to write an applet that scrolls a textual message across the screen. The text to scroll and the scrolling speed should be read from applet parameters specified with <PARAM> tags in an HTML file.

Exercise 12-3. Experiment with the graphics capabilities of the Graphics and Graphics2D classes, and write an applet or application that displays some kind of interesting and dynamic graphics. You may want to take your inspiration from one of the many screensaver programs on the market. For example, you might draw filled rectangles on the screen, using random sizes, positions, and colors. (See Math.random( ) and java.util.Random for ways to generate random numbers.) Feel free to use any of the custom Shape, Stroke, or Paint classes developed in this chapter. Be creative!

Exercise 12-4. One of the things that makes graphics so powerful is that it gives us the ability to visualize patterns. Look back at Example 1-15. This program computes prime numbers with the "Sieve of Eratosthenes" algorithm, whereby prime numbers are located by ruling out multiples of all previous prime numbers. As part of this algorithm, you maintain an array that specifies whether a number is prime or not. Write a graphical version of the Sieve program. It should display the array as a 2D matrix; cells in the matrix that represent prime numbers should be displayed in one color, and nonprimes should be displayed in another color. Write your program as a standalone application or as a GraphicsExample implementation, if you prefer.

Now extend your program again. When computing primes, don't simply store a boolean value to indicate whether a number is prime or not. Instead, store an int value that specifies, for nonprime numbers, the prime number that was used to rule this one out. After computing a set of primes, display the contents of your array as a rectangular grid, using a different color to indicate the multiples of each prime. The patterns that emerge look best when viewed in a square grid with a prime number as its height and width. For example, if you compute all the primes up to 361, you can graphically display your results in a square grid with 19 cells per side. Study the patterns you see. Does it give you insight into the workings of the algorithm? Does it help you understand why it is called a "sieve"?

Exercise 12-5. Example 12-10 demonstrates how font glyphs can be used as Shape objects and shows how those Shape objects can be transformed with an arbitrary AffineTransform object. Write a custom Stroke object that is initialized with a Font and a string of text. When this Stroke class is used to draw a shape, it should display the specified text, using the specified font, along the outline of the specified shape. The text should hug the outline of the shape as closely as possible, which means that each font glyph has to be rotated, positioned, and drawn independently of the other glyphs. Use the two-argument version of Shape.getPathIterator( ) to obtain a FlatteningPathIterator that approximates the shape using straight line segments. You'll need to use geometry to compute the slope of each line segment and trigonometry to convert the slope to a rotation angle for each font glyph (you may find Math.atan2( ) helpful). Write a GraphicsExample class that displays some text art that demonstrates your new Stroke object.

13

Printing

The Graphics and Graphics2D objects represent a "drawing surface"; in Chapter 12, we saw examples of using both the screen and an off-screen buffer as drawing surfaces. Printing in Java is simply a matter of obtaining a Graphics object that uses a printer as a drawing surface.* Once you have a Graphics object, you can print text and draw graphics to the printer, just as you do onscreen.

The tricky thing about printing in Java is obtaining the Graphics object that represents the printer. The API for doing this keeps changing:

- Java 1.1 added the first simple printing API using the java.awt.PrintJob class. The major weakness of this API is that it does not support Java 2D graphics.

- Java 1.2 defined a more advanced printing API in the new package java.awt. print. This new API supports Java 2D graphics, includes a Printable interface, and provides the ability to explicitly set printing attributes such as page margins, orientation, and use of color. It also allows print jobs to be initiated without displaying a **Print** dialog to the user.

- Java 1.3 enhanced the Java 1.1 API by adding the ability to define printing attributes with the java.awt.JobAttributes and java.awt.PageAttributes classes. Unfortunately, the API is still limited to drawing with the basic Graphics object, and it cannot use the Java 2D graphics methods defined in Graphics2D.

- Java 1.4 defined a new API in the javax.print package and subpackages. This new API is interoperable with the Java 1.2 API but is substantially new. It is the most complex API yet, introducing the ability to select a printer from a list of available printers based on printer name, capabilities, or location; print to files instead of printers; track the progress of print jobs with event listeners; and spool text and image files directly to a printer without actually drawing them.

---

* Although, as we'll see, Java 1.4 introduces facilities for spooling text and image files directly to a printer without having to draw the text or images to a Graphics object.

As you can tell from this list of API revisions, printing is a difficult topic, and it is hard to get it right. This applies to implementations as well as APIs, and you may find that your Java implementation does not support printing as well as you would like. While the most common cases typically work, you may run into difficulties if you push any of these APIs too hard.

This chapter includes examples of each of these printing APIs, including extended examples of the Java 1.1 and Java 1.4 APIs. It starts by developing a simple Swing component that displays an image. Three revisions of this component illustrate each of the three printing APIs.

Printing with the Java 1.1 API

Example 13-1 is a Swing component that displays a fractal image known as a "Julia set," pictured in Figure 13-1. The image is fascinating, and the mathematics interesting, but the real point of the example is the print( ) method, which demonstrates how to print the Julia set using the Java 1.1 API and the Java 1.3 extensions to that API. The print( ) code is straightforward: it sets some default attribute values, then displays a dialog box to the user, to allow him to modify those attributes or cancel the print request. The dialog box returns a PrintJob object. The print( ) method then obtains a Graphics object from the PrintJob. Next, it draws the Julia set to this Graphics object and, finally, calls the Graphics. dispose( ) method to tell the printer that printing is done. These basic steps are repeated in the next two examples as well: when studying the examples of the Java 1.2 and Java 1.4 APIs, look for the code that sets attributes, displays a dialog, and obtains the Graphics object.

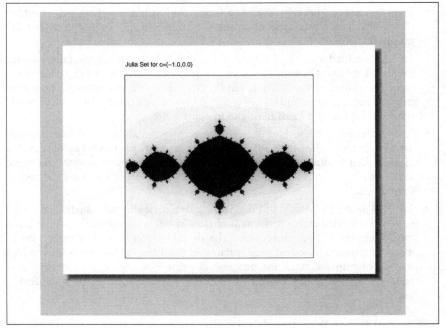

Figure 13-1. A Julia set printed with the Java 1.1 API

Example 13-1 does not include a main( ) method. To display the component, use the ShowBean program from Chapter 11, and then use the **Commands** menu to test the print( ) method:

```
java je3.gui.ShowBean je3.print.JuliaSet1
```

Example 13-1. JuliaSet1.java

```java
package je3.print;
import javax.swing.*;
import java.awt.*;
import java.awt.image.*;

/**
 * This class is a Swing component that computes and displays a fractal image
 * known as a "Julia set".  The print( ) method demonstrates printing with the
 * Java 1.1 printing API, and is the main point of the example.  The code
 * that computes the Julia set uses complex numbers, and you don't need to
 * understand it.
 **/
public class JuliaSet1 extends JComponent {
    // These constants are hard-coded for simplicity
    double x1=-1.5, y1=-1.5, x2=1.5, y2=1.5;  // Region of complex plane
    int width = 400, height = 400;            // Mapped to these pixels
    double cx, cy;  // This complex constant defines the set we display
    BufferedImage image; // The image we compute

    // We compute values between 0 and 63 for each point in the complex plane.
    // This array holds the color values for each of those values.
    static int[] colors;
    static {  // Static initializer for the colors[] array.
        colors = new int[64];
        for(int i = 0; i < colors.length; i++) {
            colors[63-i] = (i*4 << 16) + (i*4 << 8) + i*4; // grayscale
            // (i*4) ^ ((i * 3)<<6) ^ ((i * 7)<<13); // crazy technicolor
        }
    }

    // No-arg constructor with default values for cx, cy.
    public JuliaSet1() { this(-1, 0); }

    // This constructor specifies the {cx,cy} constant.
    // For simplicity, the other constants remain hardcoded.
    public JuliaSet1(double cx, double cy) {
        this.cx = cx;
        this.cy = cy;
        setPreferredSize(new Dimension(width, height));
        computeImage();
    }


    // This method computes a color value for each pixel of the image
    void computeImage() {
        // Create the image
        image = new BufferedImage(width, height, BufferedImage.TYPE_INT_RGB);
```

Example 13-1. JuliaSet1.java (continued)

```java
        // Now loop through the pixels
        int i,j;
        double x, y;
        double dx = (x2 - x1)/width;
        double dy = (y2 - y1)/height;
        for(j = 0, y = y1; j < height; j++, y += dy) {
            for(i = 0, x = x1; i < width; i++, x += dx) {
                // For each pixel, call testPoint( ) to determine a value.
                // Then map that value to a color and set it in the image.
                // If testPoint( ) returns 0, the point is part of the Julia set
                // and is displayed in black.  If it returns 63, the point is
                // displayed in white.  Values in-between are displayed in
                // varying shades of gray.
                image.setRGB(i, j, colors[testPoint(x,y)]);
            }
        }
    }

    // This is the key method for computing Julia sets.  For each point z
    // in the complex plane, we repeatedly compute z = z*z + c using complex
    // arithmetic.  We stop iterating when the magnitude of z exceeds 2 or
    // after 64 iterations.  We return the number of iterations-1.
    public int testPoint(double zx, double zy) {
        for(int i = 0; i < colors.length; i++) {
            // Compute z = z*z + c;
            double newx = zx*zx - zy*zy + cx;
            double newy = 2*zx*zy + cy;
            zx = newx;
            zy = newy;
            // Check magnitude of z and return iteration number
            if (zx*zx + zy*zy > 4) return i;
        }
        return colors.length-1;
    }

    // This method overrides JComponent to display the Julia set.
    // Just scale the image to fit and draw it.
    public void paintComponent(Graphics g) {
        g.drawImage(image,0,0,getWidth( ), getHeight( ),this);
    }

    // This method demonstrates the Java 1.1 java.awt.PrintJob printing API.
    // It also demonstrates the JobAttributes and PageAttributes classes
    // added in Java 1.3.  Display the Julia set with ShowBean and use
    // the Command menu to invoke this print command.
    public void print( ) {
        // Create some attributes objects.  This is Java 1.3 stuff.
        // In Java 1.1, we'd use a java.util.Preferences object instead.
        JobAttributes jattrs = new JobAttributes( );
        PageAttributes pattrs = new PageAttributes( );
```

Example 13-1. JuliaSet1.java (continued)

```java
    // Set some example attributes: monochrome, landscape mode
    pattrs.setColor(PageAttributes.ColorType.MONOCHROME);
    pattrs.setOrientationRequested(
                        PageAttributes.OrientationRequestedType.LANDSCAPE);
    // Print to file by default
    jattrs.setDestination(JobAttributes.DestinationType.FILE);
    jattrs.setFileName("juliaset.ps");

    // Look up the Frame that holds this component
    Component frame = this;
    while(!(frame instanceof Frame)) frame = frame.getParent();

    // Get a PrintJob object to print the Julia set with.
    // The getPrintJob() method displays a print dialog and allows the user
    // to override and modify the default JobAttributes and PageAttributes
    Toolkit toolkit = this.getToolkit();
    PrintJob job = toolkit.getPrintJob((Frame)frame, "JuliaSet1",
                                    jattrs, pattrs);

    // We get a null PrintJob if the user clicked cancel
    if (job == null) return;

    // Get a Graphics object from the PrintJob.
    // We print simply by drawing to this Graphics object.
    Graphics g = job.getGraphics();

    // Center the image on the page
    Dimension pagesize = job.getPageDimension();    // how big is page?
    Dimension panesize = this.getSize();            // how big is image?
    g.translate((pagesize.width-panesize.width)/2,  // center it
                (pagesize.height-panesize.height)/2);

    // Draw a box around the Julia set and label it
    g.drawRect(-1, -1, panesize.width+2, panesize.height+2);
    g.drawString("Julia Set for c={" + cx + "," + cy + "}",
                0, -15);

    // Set a clipping region
    g.setClip(0, 0, panesize.width, panesize.height);

    // Now print the component by calling its paint method
    this.paint(g);

    // Finally tell the printer we're done with the page.
    // No output will be generated if we don't call dispose() here.
    g.dispose();
    }
}
```

Printing with the Java 1.2 API

Example 13-2 is a listing of JuliaSet2. This subclass of Example 13-1 displays a different Julia set (pictured in Figure 13-2) and overrides the print( ) method, to demonstrate printing out the set using the Java 1.2 API. Like its superclass, JuliaSet2 should be tested using the ShowBean program.

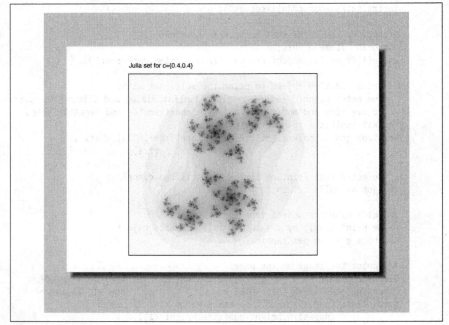

Figure 13-2. A Julia set printed with the Java 1.2 API

The key to this example is the inner class PrintableComponent, which implements the java.awt.print.Printable interface to print a component and a title for that component. Pay attention to the return value of the Printable.print( ) method: the Printable interface can represent multipage documents, and uses its return value to tell the printing system when the last page of the document has been reached.

The java.awt.print package also defines an interface named Pageable, which is useful for defining multipage documents for which the number of pages is known in advance. It allows different pages of the document to be printed using different PageFormat objects, which allows for different margins, orientations, and so forth. Pageable documents are not demonstrated in this chapter.

Example 13-2. JuliaSet2.java

```
package je3.print;
import javax.swing.*;
import java.awt.*;
import java.awt.print.*; // This package is the Java 1.2 printing API
```

Example 13-2. JuliaSet2.java (continued)

```
/**
 * This class extends JuliaSet1 and overrides the print( ) method to demonstrate
 * the Java 1.2 printing API.
 */
public class JuliaSet2 extends JuliaSet1 {
    public JuliaSet2( ) { this(.4, .4); }  // Display a different set by default
    public JuliaSet2(double cx, double cy) { super(cx,cy); }

    // This method demonstrates the Java 1.2 printing API.
    // Test it using the ShowBean program.
    public void print( ) {
        // Java 1.1 used java.awt.PrintJob.
        // In Java 1.2 we use java.awt.print.PrinterJob
        PrinterJob job = PrinterJob.getPrinterJob( );

        // Alter the default page settings to request landscape mode
        PageFormat page = job.defaultPage( );
        page.setOrientation(PageFormat.LANDSCAPE);  // landscape by default

        // Tell the PrinterJob what Printable object we want to print.
        // PrintableComponent is defined as an inner class below
        String title = "Julia set for c={" + cx + "," + cy + "}";
        Printable printable = new PrintableComponent(this, title);
        job.setPrintable(printable, page);

        // Call the printDialog( ) method to give the user a chance to alter
        // the printing attributes or to cancel the printing request.
        if (job.printDialog( )) {
            // If we get here, then the user did not cancel the print job
            // So start printing, displaying a dialog for errors.
            try { job.print( ); }
            catch(PrinterException e) {
                JOptionPane.showMessageDialog(this, e.toString( ),
                                              "PrinterException",
                                              JOptionPane.ERROR_MESSAGE);
            }
        }
    }

    // This inner class implements the Printable interface for an AWT component
    public static class PrintableComponent implements Printable {
        Component c;
        String title;
        public PrintableComponent(Component c, String title) {
            this.c = c;
            this.title = title;
        }

        // This method should print the specified page number to the specified
        // Graphics object, abiding by the specified page format.
        // The printing system will call this method repeatedly to print all
        // pages of the print job.  If pagenum is greater than the last page,
```

Example 13-2. JuliaSet2.java (continued)

```
        // it should return NO_SUCH_PAGE to indicate that it is done.  The
        // printing system may call this method multiple times per page.
        public int print(Graphics g, PageFormat format, int pagenum) {
            // This implemenation is always a single page
            if (pagenum > 0) return Printable.NO_SUCH_PAGE;

            // The Java 1.2 printing API passes us a Graphics object, but we
            // can always cast it to a Graphics2D object
            Graphics2D g2 = (Graphics2D) g;

            // Translate to accomodate the requested top and left margins.
            g2.translate(format.getImageableX( ), format.getImageableY( ));

            // Figure out how big the drawing is, and how big the page
            // (excluding margins) is
            Dimension size = c.getSize( );                   // component size
            double pageWidth = format.getImageableWidth( );   // Page width
            double pageHeight = format.getImageableHeight( );  // Page height

            // If the component is too wide or tall for the page, scale it down
            if (size.width > pageWidth) {
                double factor = pageWidth/size.width; // How much to scale
                g2.scale(factor, factor);             // Adjust coordinate system
                pageWidth /= factor;                  // Adjust page size up
                pageHeight /= factor;
            }
            if (size.height > pageHeight) {   // Do the same thing for height
                double factor = pageHeight/size.height;
                g2.scale(factor, factor);
                pageWidth /= factor;
                pageHeight /= factor;
            }

            // Now we know the component will fit on the page.  Center it by
            // translating as necessary.
            g2.translate((pageWidth-size.width)/2,(pageHeight-size.height)/2);

            // Draw a line around the outside of the drawing area and label it
            g2.drawRect(-1, -1, size.width+2, size.height+2);
            g2.drawString(title, 0, -15);

            // Set a clipping region so the component can't draw outside of
            // its own bounds.
            g2.setClip(0, 0, size.width, size.height);

            // Finally, print the component by calling its paint( ) method.
            // This prints the background, border, and children as well.
            // For Swing components, if you don't want the background, border,
            // and children, then call printComponent( ) instead.
            c.paint(g);
```

Example 13-2. JuliaSet2.java (continued)

```
            // Tell the PrinterJob that the page number was valid
            return Printable.PAGE_EXISTS;
        }
    }
}
```

Printing with the Java 1.4 API

Example 13-3 is a further subclass of our Julia set component, which once again overrides the print( ) method and this time uses the Java 1.4 Printing API to produce the printed output shown in Figure 13-3. In addition, it defines a save( ) method that uses the Java 1.4 Printing API to print the image of the Julia set directly to a PostScript file. The actual printing of the image is done by the PrintableComponent class inherited from the previous example: what is different in this example is the way the Printable object is sent to a printer.

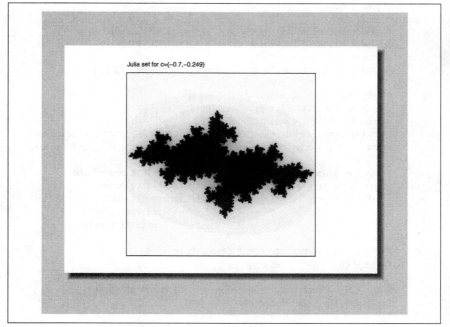

Figure 13-3. A Julia set printed with the Java 1.4 API

The print( ) and save( ) methods start by obtaining an appropriate PrintService object that represents a printer or print engine that can print to a file. Both methods then call the printToService( ) method, which uses the inherited PrintableComponent class to print the Julia set to the PrintService. One interesting feature of this method is its use of a PrintJobListener to monitor the progress of the print job and display its current status in a dialog box.

Example 13-3. JuliaSet3.java

```java
package je3.print;
import javax.swing.*;
import java.awt.print.*;        // Java 1.4 can use the 1.2 Printable API
import javax.print.*;           // Java 1.4 API
import javax.print.event.*;
import javax.print.attribute.*;
import javax.print.attribute.standard.*;
import java.io.*;

/**
 * This class extends JuliaSet2, and its print() and save() methods demonstrate
 * the Java 1.4 printing API.
 **/
public class JuliaSet3 extends JuliaSet2 {
    public JuliaSet3() { super(-.7, -.25); }

    // This method overrides JuliaSet2.print() and demonstrates the javax.print
    // printing API.
    public void print() {
        // Get a list of all printers that can handle Printable objects.
        DocFlavor flavor = DocFlavor.SERVICE_FORMATTED.PRINTABLE;
        PrintService[] services =
            PrintServiceLookup.lookupPrintServices(flavor, null);

        // Set some printing attributes
        PrintRequestAttributeSet printAttributes =
            new HashPrintRequestAttributeSet();
        printAttributes.add(OrientationRequested.LANDSCAPE); // landscape mode
        printAttributes.add(Chromaticity.MONOCHROME);        // print in mono

        // Display a dialog that allows the user to select one of the
        // available printers and to edit the default attributes
        PrintService service = ServiceUI.printDialog(null, 100, 100,
                                                      services, null, null,
                                                      printAttributes);

        // If the user canceled, don't do anything
        if (service == null) return;

        // Now call a method defined below to finish the printing
        printToService(service, printAttributes);
    }

    // This method is like print() above but prints to a PostScript file
    // instead of printing to a printer.
    public void save() throws IOException {
        // Find a factory object for printing Printable objects to PostScript.
        DocFlavor flavor = DocFlavor.SERVICE_FORMATTED.PRINTABLE;
        String format = "application/postscript";
```

Example 13-3. JuliaSet3.java (continued)

```
        StreamPrintServiceFactory factory = StreamPrintServiceFactory.
            lookupStreamPrintServiceFactories(flavor, format)[0];

        // Ask the user to select a file and open the selected file
        JFileChooser chooser = new JFileChooser( );
        if (chooser.showSaveDialog(this)!=JFileChooser.APPROVE_OPTION) return;
        File f = chooser.getSelectedFile( );
        FileOutputStream out = new FileOutputStream(f);

        // Obtain a PrintService that prints to that file
        StreamPrintService service = factory.getPrintService(out);

        // Do the printing with the method below
        printToService(service, null);

        // And close the output file.
        out.close( );
    }

    // Print the Julia set to the sepecifed PrintService using the specified
    // attributes.
    public void printToService(PrintService service,
                               PrintRequestAttributeSet printAttributes)
    {
        // Wrap ourselves in the PrintableComponent class defined by JuliaSet2.
        String title = "Julia set for c={" + cx + "," + cy + "}";
        Printable printable = new PrintableComponent(this, title);

        // Now create a Doc that encapsulates the Printable object and its type
        DocFlavor flavor = DocFlavor.SERVICE_FORMATTED.PRINTABLE;
        Doc doc = new SimpleDoc(printable, flavor, null);

        // Java 1.1 uses PrintJob.
        // Java 1.2 uses PrinterJob.
        // Java 1.4 uses DocPrintJob. Create one from the service
        DocPrintJob job = service.createPrintJob( );

        // Set up a dialog box to  monitor printing status
        final JOptionPane pane = new JOptionPane("Printing...",
                                               JOptionPane.PLAIN_MESSAGE);
        JDialog dialog = pane.createDialog(this, "Print Status");
        // This listener object updates the dialog as the status changes
        job.addPrintJobListener(new PrintJobAdapter( ) {
                public void printJobCompleted(PrintJobEvent e) {
                    pane.setMessage("Printing complete.");
                }
                public void printDataTransferCompleted(PrintJobEvent e) {
                    pane.setMessage("Document transfered to printer.");
                }
```

Example 13-3. JuliaSet3.java (continued)

```
                public void printJobRequiresAttention(PrintJobEvent e) {
                    pane.setMessage("Check printer: out of paper?");
                }
                public void printJobFailed(PrintJobEvent e) {
                    pane.setMessage("Print job failed");
                }
            });

        // Show the dialog, non-modal.
        dialog.setModal(false);
        dialog.show( );

        // Now print the Doc to the DocPrintJob
        try {
            job.print(doc, printAttributes);
        }
        catch(PrintException e) {
            // Display any errors to the dialog box
            pane.setMessage(e.toString( ));
        }
    }
}
```

Printing Multipage Text Documents

The printing examples we've seen so far print GUI components on a single page. Printing multipage documents is more interesting, but also trickier, because we have to decide where to place the page breaks. Example 13-4 shows how this can be done. This HardcopyWriter class is a custom java.io.Writer stream that uses the Java 1.1 Printing API to print the characters sent through it, inserting line breaks and page breaks as necessary.

The HardcopyWriter class includes two demonstration programs as inner classes. The first, PrintFile, reads a specified text file and prints it by sending its contents to a HardcopyWriter stream. The second, Demo, prints a demonstration page that shows off the font and tabbing capabilities of the class, as shown in Figure 13-4.

Example 13-4 is long but worth studying. In addition to demonstrating the Java 1.1 Printing API again, it shows an approach to paginating a text document. It is also a useful example of a custom Writer stream.

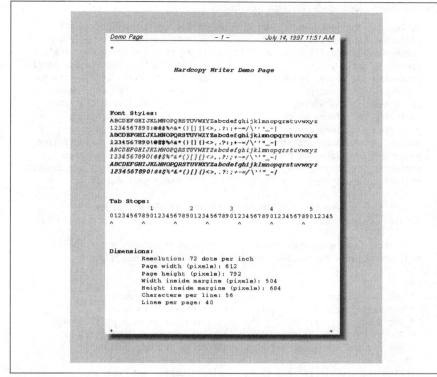

Figure 13-4. Demonstration page printed by HardcopyWriter

Example 13-4. HardcopyWriter.java

```java
package je3.print;
import java.awt.*;
import java.awt.event.*;
import java.io.*;
import java.text.*;
import java.util.*;

/**
 * A character output stream that sends output to a printer.
 **/
public class HardcopyWriter extends Writer {
    // These are the instance variables for the class
    protected PrintJob job;              // The PrintJob object in use
    protected Graphics page;             // Graphics object for current page
    protected String jobname;            // The name of the print job
    protected int fontsize;              // Point size of the font
    protected String time;               // Current time (appears in header)
    protected Dimension pagesize;        // Size of the page (in dots)
    protected int pagedpi;               // Page resolution in dots per inch
```

Example 13-4. HardcopyWriter.java (continued)

```
protected Font font, headerfont;          // Body font and header font
protected FontMetrics metrics;            // Metrics for the body font
protected FontMetrics headermetrics;      // Metrics for the header font
protected int x0, y0;                      // Upper-left corner inside margin
protected int width, height;              // Size (in dots) inside margins
protected int headery;                    // Baseline of the page header
protected int charwidth;                  // The width of each character
protected int lineheight;                 // The height of each line
protected int lineascent;                 // Offset of font baseline
protected int chars_per_line;             // Number of characters per line
protected int lines_per_page;             // Number of lines per page
protected int charnum = 0, linenum = 0;   // Current column and line position
protected int pagenum = 0;                // Current page number

// A field to save state between invocations of the write( ) method
private boolean last_char_was_return = false;

// A static variable that holds user preferences between print jobs
protected static Properties printprops = new Properties( );

/**
 * The constructor for this class has a bunch of arguments:
 * The frame argument is required for all printing in Java.
 * The jobname appears left justified at the top of each printed page.
 * The font size is specified in points, as on-screen font sizes are.
 * The margins are specified in inches (or fractions of inches).
 **/
public HardcopyWriter(Frame frame, String jobname, int fontsize,
                      double leftmargin, double rightmargin,
                      double topmargin, double bottommargin)
    throws HardcopyWriter.PrintCanceledException
{
    // Get the PrintJob object with which we'll do all the printing.
    // The call is synchronized on the static printprops object, which
    // means that only one print dialog can be popped up at a time.
    // If the user clicks Cancel in the print dialog, throw an exception.
    Toolkit toolkit = frame.getToolkit( );   // get Toolkit from Frame
    synchronized(printprops) {
        job = toolkit.getPrintJob(frame, jobname, printprops);
    }
    if (job == null)
        throw new PrintCanceledException("User cancelled print request");

    pagesize = job.getPageDimension( );      // query the page size
    pagedpi = job.getPageResolution( );      // query the page resolution

    // Bug Workaround:
    // On Windows, getPageDimension( ) and getPageResolution don't work, so
    // we've got to fake them.
    if (System.getProperty("os.name").regionMatches(true,0,"windows",0,7)){
        // Use screen dpi, which is what the PrintJob tries to emulate
        pagedpi = toolkit.getScreenResolution( );
```

Example 13-4. HardcopyWriter.java (continued)

```
        // Assume a 8.5" x 11" page size.  A4 paper users must change this.
        pagesize = new Dimension((int)(8.5 * pagedpi), 11*pagedpi);
        // We also have to adjust the fontsize.  It is specified in points,
        // (1 point = 1/72 of an inch) but Windows measures it in pixels.
        fontsize = fontsize * pagedpi / 72;
    }

    // Compute coordinates of the upper-left corner of the page.
    // I.e. the coordinates of (leftmargin, topmargin).  Also compute
    // the width and height inside of the margins.
    x0 = (int)(leftmargin * pagedpi);
    y0 = (int)(topmargin * pagedpi);
    width = pagesize.width - (int)((leftmargin + rightmargin) * pagedpi);
    height = pagesize.height - (int)((topmargin + bottommargin) * pagedpi);

    // Get body font and font size
    font = new Font("Monospaced", Font.PLAIN, fontsize);
    metrics = frame.getFontMetrics(font);
    lineheight = metrics.getHeight();
    lineascent = metrics.getAscent();
    charwidth = metrics.charWidth('0');   // Assumes a monospaced font!

    // Now compute the number of columns and lines
    // that will fit inside the margins
    chars_per_line = width / charwidth;
    lines_per_page = height / lineheight;

    // Get header font information
    // And compute baseline of page header: 1/8" above the top margin
    headerfont = new Font("SansSerif", Font.ITALIC, fontsize);
    headermetrics = frame.getFontMetrics(headerfont);
    headery = y0 - (int)(0.125 * pagedpi) -
        headermetrics.getHeight() + headermetrics.getAscent();

    // Compute the date/time string to display in the page header
    DateFormat df = DateFormat.getDateTimeInstance(DateFormat.LONG,
                                                   DateFormat.SHORT);
    df.setTimeZone(TimeZone.getDefault());
    time = df.format(new Date());

    this.jobname = jobname;             // save name
    this.fontsize = fontsize;           // save font size
}

/**
 * This is the write() method of the stream.  All Writer subclasses
 * implement this.  All other versions of write() are variants of this one
 **/
public void write(char[] buffer, int index, int len) {
    synchronized(this.lock) {  // For thread safety
        // Loop through all the characters passed to us
        for(int i = index; i < index + len; i++) {
```

Example 13-4. HardcopyWriter.java (continued)

```
                    // If we haven't begun a page (or a new page), do that now.
                    if (page == null) newpage();

                    // If the character is a line terminator, then begin new line,
                    // unless it is a \n immediately after a \r.
                    if (buffer[i] == '\n') {
                        if (!last_char_was_return) newline();
                        continue;
                    }
                    if (buffer[i] == '\r') {
                        newline();
                        last_char_was_return = true;
                        continue;
                    }
                    else last_char_was_return = false;

                    // If it's some other non-printing character, ignore it.
                    if (Character.isWhitespace(buffer[i]) &&
                        !Character.isSpaceChar(buffer[i]) && (buffer[i] != '\t'))
                        continue;

                    // If no more characters will fit on the line, start new line.
                    if (charnum >= chars_per_line) {
                        newline();
                        // Also start a new page, if necessary
                        if (page == null) newpage();
                    }

                    // Now print the character:
                    // If it is a space, skip one space, without output.
                    // If it is a tab, skip the necessary number of spaces.
                    // Otherwise, print the character.
                    // It is inefficient to draw only one character at a time, but
                    // because our FontMetrics don't match up exactly to what the
                    // printer uses, we need to position each character individually
                    if (Character.isSpaceChar(buffer[i])) charnum++;
                    else if (buffer[i] == '\t') charnum += 8 - (charnum % 8);
                    else {
                        page.drawChars(buffer, i, 1,
                                       x0 + charnum * charwidth,
                                       y0 + (linenum*lineheight) + lineascent);
                        charnum++;
                    }
                }
            }
        }

    /**
     * This is the flush() method that all Writer subclasses must implement.
     * There is no way to flush a PrintJob without prematurely printing the
     * page, so we don't do anything.
     **/
    public void flush() { /* do nothing */ }
```

Example 13-4. HardcopyWriter.java (continued)

```
/**
 * This is the close( ) method that all Writer subclasses must implement.
 * Print the pending page (if any) and terminate the PrintJob.
 */
public void close( ) {
    synchronized(this.lock) {
        if (page != null) page.dispose( );   // Send page to the printer
        job.end( );                          // Terminate the job
    }
}

/**
 * Set the font style.  The argument should be one of the font style
 * constants defined by the java.awt.Font class.  All subsequent output
 * will be in that style.  This method relies on all styles of the
 * Monospaced font having the same metrics.
 **/
public void setFontStyle(int style) {
    synchronized (this.lock) {
        // Try to set a new font, but restore current one if it fails
        Font current = font;
        try { font = new Font("Monospaced", style, fontsize); }
        catch (Exception e) { font = current; }
        // If a page is pending, set the new font. Otherwise newpage( ) will
        if (page != null) page.setFont(font);
    }
}

/** End the current page.  Subsequent output will be on a new page. */
public void pageBreak( ) { synchronized(this.lock) { newpage( ); } }

/** Return the number of columns of characters that fit on the page */
public int getCharactersPerLine( ) { return this.chars_per_line; }

/** Return the number of lines that fit on a page */
public int getLinesPerPage( ) { return this.lines_per_page; }

/** This internal method begins a new line */
protected void newline( ) {
    charnum = 0;                   // Reset character number to 0
    linenum++;                     // Increment line number
    if (linenum >= lines_per_page) {  // If we've reached the end of page
        page.dispose( );              //  send page to printer
        page = null;                  //  but don't start a new page yet.
    }
}

/** This internal method begins a new page and prints the header. */
protected void newpage( ) {
    page = job.getGraphics( );         // Begin the new page
    linenum = 0; charnum = 0;          // Reset line and char number
    pagenum++;                         // Increment page number
```

Example 13-4. HardcopyWriter.java (continued)

```
        page.setFont(headerfont);                // Set the header font.
        page.drawString(jobname, x0, headery); // Print job name left justified

        String s = "- " + pagenum + " -";       // Print the page # centered.
        int w = headermetrics.stringWidth(s);
        page.drawString(s, x0 + (this.width - w)/2, headery);
        w = headermetrics.stringWidth(time);    // Print date right justified
        page.drawString(time, x0 + width - w, headery);

        // Draw a line beneath the header
        int y = headery + headermetrics.getDescent() + 1;
        page.drawLine(x0, y, x0+width, y);

        // Set the basic monospaced font for the rest of the page.
        page.setFont(font);
    }

    /**
     * This is the exception class that the HardcopyWriter constructor
     * throws when the user clicks "Cancel" in the print dialog box.
     **/
    public static class PrintCanceledException extends Exception {
        public PrintCanceledException(String msg) { super(msg); }
    }

    /**
     * A program that prints the specified file using HardcopyWriter
     **/
    public static class PrintFile {
        public static void main(String[ ] args) {
            try {
                if (args.length != 1)
                    throw new IllegalArgumentException("Wrong # of arguments");
                FileReader in = new FileReader(args[0]);
                HardcopyWriter out = null;
                Frame f = new Frame("PrintFile: " + args[0]);
                f.setSize(200, 50);
                f.show();
                try {
                    out = new HardcopyWriter(f, args[0], 10, .5, .5, .5, .5);
                }
                catch (HardcopyWriter.PrintCanceledException e) {
                    System.exit(0);
                }
                f.setVisible(false);
                char[ ] buffer = new char[4096];
                int numchars;
                while((numchars = in.read(buffer)) != -1)
                    out.write(buffer, 0, numchars);
                in.close();
                out.close();
            }
```

Example 13-4. HardcopyWriter.java (continued)

```
            catch (Exception e) {
                System.err.println(e);
                System.err.println("Usage: " +
                                "java HardcopyWriter$PrintFile <filename>");
                System.exit(1);
            }
            System.exit(0);
        }
    }

    /**
     * A program that prints a demo page using HardcopyWriter
     **/
    public static class Demo extends Frame implements ActionListener {
        /** The main method of the program.  Create a test window */
        public static void main(String[ ] args) {
            Frame f = new Demo( );
            f.show( );
        }
        // Buttons used in this program
        protected Button print, quit;

        /** Constructor for the test program's window. */
        public Demo( ) {
            super("HardcopyWriter Test");        // Call frame constructor
            Panel p = new Panel();                // Add a panel to the frame
            this.add(p, "Center");                // Center it
            p.setFont(new Font("SansSerif",       // Set a default font
                            Font.BOLD, 18));
            print = new Button("Print Test Page"); // Create a Print button
            quit = new Button("Quit");            // Create a Quit button
            print.addActionListener(this);        // Specify that we'll handle
            quit.addActionListener(this);         //    button presses
            p.add(print);                         // Add the buttons to panel
            p.add(quit);
            this.pack( );                         // Set the frame size
        }

        /** Handle the button presses */
        public void actionPerformed(ActionEvent e) {
            Object o = e.getSource();
            if (o == quit) System.exit(0);
            else if (o == print) printDemoPage( );
        }

        /** Print the demo page */
        public void printDemoPage( ) {
            // Create a HardcopyWriter, using a 10 point font and 3/4" margins.
            HardcopyWriter hw;
            try { hw=new HardcopyWriter(this, "Demo Page",10,.75,.75,.75,.75);}
            catch (HardcopyWriter.PrintCanceledException e) { return; }
```

Example 13-4. HardcopyWriter.java (continued)

```java
            // Send output to it through a PrintWriter stream
            PrintWriter out = new PrintWriter(hw);

            // Figure out the size of the page
            int rows = hw.getLinesPerPage( ), cols = hw.getCharactersPerLine( );

            // Mark upper-left and upper-right corners
            out.print("+");                              // upper-left corner
            for(int i=0;i<cols-2;i++) out.print(" ");    // space over
            out.print("+");                              // upper-right corner

            // Display a title
            hw.setFontStyle(Font.BOLD + Font.ITALIC);
            out.println("\n\t\tHardcopy Writer Demo Page\n\n");

            // Demonstrate font styles
            hw.setFontStyle(Font.BOLD);
            out.println("Font Styles:");
            int[ ] styles = { Font.PLAIN, Font.BOLD,
                              Font.ITALIC, Font.ITALIC+Font.BOLD };
            for(int i = 0; i < styles.length; i++) {
                hw.setFontStyle(styles[i]);
                out.println("ABCDEFGHIJKLMNOPQRSTUVWXYZ" +
                            "abcdefghijklmnopqrstuvwxyz");
                out.println("1234567890!@#$%^&*( )[ ]{ }<>,.?:;+-=/\\`'\"_~|");
            }
            hw.setFontStyle(Font.PLAIN);
            out.println("\n");

            // Demonstrate tab stops
            hw.setFontStyle(Font.BOLD);
            out.println("Tab Stops:");
            hw.setFontStyle(Font.PLAIN);
            out.println("         1         2         3         4         5");
            out.println("0123456789012345678901234567890123456789012345678901234567890");
            out.println("^\t^\t^\t^\t^\t^\t^");
            out.println("\n");

            // Output some information about page dimensions and resolution
            hw.setFontStyle(Font.BOLD);
            out.println("Dimensions:");
            hw.setFontStyle(Font.PLAIN);
            out.println("\tResolution: " + hw.pagedpi + " dots per inch");
            out.println("\tPage width (pixels): " + hw.pagesize.width);
            out.println("\tPage height (pixels): " + hw.pagesize.height);
            out.println("\tWidth inside margins (pixels): " + hw.width);
            out.println("\tHeight inside margins (pixels): " + hw.height);
            out.println("\tCharacters per line: " + cols);
            out.println("\tLines per page: " + rows);

            // Skip down to the bottom of the page
            for(int i = 0; i < rows-30; i++) out.println( );
```

Example 13-4. HardcopyWriter.java (continued)

```
            // And mark the lower-left and lower-right
            out.print("+");                             // lower-left
            for(int i=0;i<cols-2;i++) out.print(" ");   // space-over
            out.print("+");                             // lower-right

            // Close the output stream, forcing the page to be printed
            out.close( );
        }
    }
}
```

Advanced Printing with Java 1.4

The Java 1.4 Printing API is substantially more complex than the Java 1.1 and Java 1.2 APIs. It is a command-line utility that can:

- List available printers capable of handling specific printing requests (color printing, collation, stapling, etc.)
- Query the status of a particular named printer
- Spool text or image files directly to a printer
- Convert GIF, JPEG, and PNG image files to PostScript files

Example 13-5 demonstrates some of these advanced features. The example does not create a GUI, and, unlike the other examples in this chapter, it prints without using a Graphics object. The code is well-commented and straightforward; the example is long only because it demonstrates several different features of the Java 1.4 API.

Example 13-5. Print.java

```
package je3.print;
import javax.print.*;
import javax.print.event.*;
import javax.print.attribute.*;
import javax.print.attribute.standard.*;
import java.io.*;

/**
 * This utility program demonstrates the javax.print API and allows you to
 * list available printers, query a named printer, print text and image files
 * to a printer, and print to PostScript files.
 *
 * Usage:
 * java Print -i inputfile [-q] [-p printer] [-ps outputfile] [attributes]
 **/
public class Print {
    public static void main(String[ ] args) throws IOException {
        // These are values we'll set from the command-line arguments
        boolean query = false;
        String printerName = null;
        String inputFileName = null;
```

Example 13-5. Print.java (continued)

```
        String outputFileName = null;
        String outputFileType = null;
        PrintRequestAttributeSet attributes =
            new HashPrintRequestAttributeSet( );

        // Loop through the arguments
        for(int i = 0; i < args.length; i++) {
            if (args[i].equals("-q")) query = true; // Is this a query?
            else if (args[i].equals("-p"))               // Specific printer name
                printerName = args[++i];
            else if (args[i].equals("-i"))               // The file to print
                inputFileName = args[++i];
            else if (args[i].equals("-ps")) {            // Print it to this file
                // Sun's Java 1.4 implementation only supports PostScript
                // output.  Other implementations might offer PDF, for example.
                outputFileName = args[++i];
                outputFileType = "application/postscript";
            }
            // The rest of the arguments represent common printing attributes
            else if (args[i].equals("-color"))          // Request a color printer
                attributes.add(Chromaticity.COLOR);
            else if (args[i].equals("-landscape"))  // Request landscape mode
                attributes.add(OrientationRequested.LANDSCAPE);
            else if (args[i].equals("-letter"))        // US Letter-size paper
                attributes.add(MediaSizeName.NA_LETTER);
            else if (args[i].equals("-a4"))             // European A4 paper
                attributes.add(MediaSizeName.ISO_A4);
            else if (args[i].equals("-staple"))        // Request stapling
                attributes.add(Finishings.STAPLE);
            else if (args[i].equals("-collate"))    // Collate multiple copies
                attributes.add(SheetCollate.COLLATED);
            else if (args[i].equals("-duplex"))        // Request 2-sided
                attributes.add(Sides.DUPLEX);
            else if (args[i].equals("-2"))              // 2 pages to a sheet
                attributes.add(new NumberUp(2));
            else if (args[i].equals("-copies"))        // how many copies
                attributes.add(new Copies(Integer.parseInt(args[++i])));
            else {
                System.out.println("Unknown argument: " + args[i]);
                System.exit(1);
            }
        }

        if (query) {
            // If the -q argument was specified, but no printer was named,
            // then list all available printers that can support the attributes
            if (printerName == null) queryServices(attributes);
            // Otherwise, look for a named printer that can support the
            // attributes and print its status
            else queryPrinter(printerName, attributes);
        }
        else if (outputFileName != null)
```

Example 13-5. Print.java (continued)

```
        // If this is not a query and we have a filename, print to a file
        printToFile(outputFileName, outputFileType,
                        inputFileName, attributes);
    else
        // Otherwise, print to the named printer, or to the default
        // printer otherwise.
        print(printerName, inputFileName, attributes);

    // The main( ) method ends here, but there may be a printing thread
    // operating in the background.  So the program may not terminate
    // until printing completes.
}

// List names of all PrintServices that can support the attributes
public static void queryServices(PrintRequestAttributeSet attributes) {
    // Find all services that can support the specified attributes
    PrintService[ ] services =
        PrintServiceLookup.lookupPrintServices(null, attributes);
    // Loop through available services
    for(int i = 0; i < services.length; i++) {
        // Print service name
        System.out.print(services[i].getName( ));

        // Then query and print the document types it can print
        DocFlavor[ ] flavors = services[i].getSupportedDocFlavors( );
        for(int j = 0; j < flavors.length; j++) {
            // Filter out DocFlavors that have a representation class other
            // than java.io.InputStream.
            String repclass = flavors[j].getRepresentationClassName( );
            if (!repclass.equals("java.io.InputStream"))continue;
            System.out.println("\t" + flavors[j].getMimeType( ));
        }
    }
}

// List details about the named printer
public static void queryPrinter(String printerName,
                                PrintRequestAttributeSet attributes)
{
    // Find the named printer
    PrintService service = getNamedPrinter(printerName, attributes);
    if (service == null) {
        System.out.println(printerName + ": no such printer capable of " +
                        "handling the specified attributes");
        return;
    }

    // Print status and other information about the printer
    System.out.println(printerName + " status:");
    Attribute[ ] attrs = service.getAttributes( ).toArray( );
```

Example 13-5. Print.java (continued)

```
        for(int i = 0; i < attrs.length; i++)
            System.out.println("\t" + attrs[i].getName( ) + ": " + attrs[i]);

    }

    // Print the contents of the named file to the named printer (or to a
    // default printer if printerName is null) requesting the specified
    // attributes.
    public static void print(String printerName, String filename,
                              PrintRequestAttributeSet attributes)
        throws IOException
    {
        // Look for a printer that can support the attributes
        PrintService service = getNamedPrinter(printerName, attributes);
        if (service == null) {
            System.out.println("Can't find a printer " +
                                "with specified attributes");
            return;
        }
        // Print the file to that printer.  See method definition below
        printToService(service, filename, attributes);
        // Let the user know where to pick up their printout
        System.out.println("Printed " + filename + " to " + service.getName( ));
    }

    // Print to an output file instead of a printer
    public static void printToFile(String outputFileName,
                                    String outputFileType,
                                    String inputFileName,
                                    PrintRequestAttributeSet attributes)
        throws IOException
    {

        // Determine whether the system can print to the specified type, and
        // get a factory object if so.
        // The name of this static method is way too long!
        StreamPrintServiceFactory[ ] factories = StreamPrintServiceFactory.
            lookupStreamPrintServiceFactories(null, outputFileType);

        // Error message if we can't print to the specified output type
        if (factories.length == 0) {
            System.out.println("Unable to print files of type: " +
                                outputFileType);
            return;
        }

        // Open the output file
        FileOutputStream out = new FileOutputStream(outputFileName);
        // Get a PrintService object to print to that file
        StreamPrintService service = factories[0].getPrintService(out);
```

Example 13-5. Print.java (continued)

```
        // Print using the method below
        printToService(service, inputFileName, attributes);
        // And remember to close the output file
        out.close( );
    }

    // Print the contents of the named file to the specified PrintService,
    // requesting the specified attributes.
    // This is shared code used by print( ) and printToFile( ) above.
    public static void printToService(PrintService service, String filename,
                                PrintRequestAttributeSet attributes)
        throws IOException
    {
        // Figure out what type of file we're printing
        DocFlavor flavor = getFlavorFromFilename(filename);
        // Open the file
        InputStream in = new FileInputStream(filename);
        // Create a Doc object to print from the file and flavor.
        Doc doc = new SimpleDoc(in, flavor, null);
        // Create a print job from the service
        DocPrintJob job = service.createPrintJob( );

        // Monitor the print job with a listener
        job.addPrintJobListener(new PrintJobAdapter( ) {
                public void printJobCompleted(PrintJobEvent e) {
                    System.out.println("Print job complete");
                    System.exit(0);
                }
                public void printDataTransferCompleted(PrintJobEvent e) {
                    System.out.println("Document transfered to printer");
                }
                public void printJobRequiresAttention(PrintJobEvent e) {
                    System.out.println("Print job requires attention");
                    System.out.println("Check printer: out of paper?");
                }
                public void printJobFailed(PrintJobEvent e) {
                    System.out.println("Print job failed");
                    System.exit(1);
                }
            });

        // Now print the document, catching errors
        try {
            job.print(doc, attributes);
        }
        catch(PrintException e) {
            System.out.println(e);
            System.exit(1);
        }
    }
```

Example 13-5. Print.java (continued)

```java
// A utility method to look up printers that can support the specified
// attributes and return the one that matches the specified name.
public static PrintService getNamedPrinter(String name,
                                           PrintRequestAttributeSet attrs)
{
    PrintService[] services =
        PrintServiceLookup.lookupPrintServices(null, attrs);
    if (services.length > 0) {
        if (name == null) return services[0];
        else {
            for(int i = 0; i < services.length; i++) {
                if (services[i].getName().equals(name)) return services[i];
            }
        }
    }
    return null;
}

// A utility method to return a DocFlavor object matching the
// extension of the filename.
public static DocFlavor getFlavorFromFilename(String filename) {
    String extension = filename.substring(filename.lastIndexOf('.')+1);
    extension = extension.toLowerCase();
    if (extension.equals("gif"))
        return DocFlavor.INPUT_STREAM.GIF;
    else if (extension.equals("jpeg"))
        return DocFlavor.INPUT_STREAM.JPEG;
    else if (extension.equals("jpg"))
        return DocFlavor.INPUT_STREAM.JPEG;
    else if (extension.equals("png"))
        return DocFlavor.INPUT_STREAM.PNG;
    else if (extension.equals("ps"))
        return DocFlavor.INPUT_STREAM.POSTSCRIPT;
    else if (extension.equals("txt"))
        return DocFlavor.INPUT_STREAM.TEXT_PLAIN_HOST;
    // Fallback: try to determine flavor from file content
    else return DocFlavor.INPUT_STREAM.AUTOSENSE;
}
}
```

Exercises

Exercise 13-1. In Java 1.3, java.awt.JobAttributes and java.awt.PageAttributes are new classes that enhance the Java 1.1 Printing API. Read the documentation for these classes, then modify the HardcopyWriter class so that you can pass PageAttributes and JobAttributes objects to the HardcopyWriter constructor. Test your modification by writing a program that prints in landscape mode and uses duplex (two-sided) printing (if you have a printer that supports this feature).

Exercise 13-2. With the Java 1.2 Printing API, the print( ) method of a Printable object may be called multiple times per page to facilitate the printing of high-resolution images and drawings. For this reason, it is not possible to print a character stream with the Java 1.2 API, as is done with the Java 1.1 API in the HardcopyWriter class. Nevertheless, it is still possible to print multipage text documents using the Java 1.2 API. Write a program that reads a plain text file, paginates it, and prints its contents using the Java 1.2 API. If you paginate the entire document in an initial pass, then you can implement the Pageable interface. Otherwise, if you paginate as you print, you'll have to implement the Printable interface. In either case, you should be able to reuse code from HardcopyWriter.

Exercise 13-3. Modify your program from the previous example so that the Printable or Pageable object you implemented is printed with a Java 1.4 javax.print.PrintService object instead of a Java 1.2 java.print.PrinterJob.

Exercise 13-4. Modify your program from the previous exercise again to support "2-up" printing—printing two reduced-size pages side by side in landscape mode. You'll need to use Java 2D scaling and rotation features to accomplish this.

14

Data Transfer

Data transfer is the generic term for GUI mechanisms that allow an end user to transfer text or other data within an application or between applications. The two common data transfer metaphors are cut-and-paste and drag-and-drop. Java's support for data transfer has evolved over several releases:

- In Java 1.1, the java.awt.datatransfer package provided a data transfer infrastructure and support for the cut-and-paste metaphor.
- Java 1.2 extended the data transfer infrastructure with the java.awt.dnd package, and added support for drag-and-drop.
- In Java 1.4, the javax.swing package introduces the TransferHandler class, which simplifies the data transfer infrastructure of previous releases and makes it easier to provide simple drag-and-drop capabilities in a Swing application.

This chapter demonstrates how you can add support for cut-and-paste and drag-and-drop to your AWT and Swing applications. It shows how to use the Swing TransferHandler class for simple cases, and how to use the underlying DataFlavor class and the Transferable interface to permit the transfer of custom data types between applications.

Simple Swing Data Transfer

We begin with an examination of the built-in data transfer capabilities of Swing components and how to perform simple customizations. As a general rule, Swing components that display text and allow it to be selected (JList and JTable, for example, but not JLabel) support Copy and Drag operations. Components that display editable text typically support Cut, Paste, and Drop operations as well. JPasswordField is a special case: it supports Paste and Drop, but because of the sensitivity of password data, does not allow its masked text to be dragged, cut, or copied to the clipboard. Finally, JColorChooser allows colors to be dragged, and JFileChooser allows files to be dragged.

Swing components that support dragging do not enable it by default. To enable drags in a component that supports it, pass true to setDragEnabled( ). Components that do not support dragging at all do not define this setDragEnabled( ) method.

Swing data transfer is enabled by a TransferHandler object. Components that support data transfer by default have a default TransferHandler installed. The TransferHandler( ) constructor method takes a JavaBeans property name as its sole argument. A TransferHandler created in this way is responsible for transferring the value of the named property. In a Cut, Copy, or Drag operation, it reads the value of the named property and makes it available for transfer. In a Paste or Drop operation, it reads the transferred data and then attempts to set the named property to the specified value. If the named property is read-only, the TransferHandler will enable only Copy and Drag operations, not Cut, Paste, or Drop operations. If the data to be transferred is not available through a property, or if you want to support pastes and drops of more than one type of data, you can subclass TransferHandler to add these capabilities.

Example 14-1 illustrates two simple customizations of the default Swing data transfer behavior. First, it registers custom TransferHandler objects to support Drag and Drop of colors. Second, it enables Drag operations from a JLabel component by registering a MouseMotionListener to detect drag gestures and initiate the drag through the TransferHandler. When you run the program, it allows you to drag the foreground color of the first JLabel and drop it on the second JLabel, which will use the dropped color as its background. This example is more interesting if you also display a JColorChooser component at the same time, using the ShowBean program of Chapter 11. To enable drags from the JColorChooser, you must set its dragEnabled property:

```
java je3.gui.ShowBean javax.swing.JColorChooser dragEnabled=true
```

Note that the JColorChooser component does not allow drags from the tiny color swatches in the main part of the window. Instead, you must select a color and then drag it from the sample swatch at the bottom of the window.

Example 14-1. ColorDrag.java

```
package je3.datatransfer;
import javax.swing.*;
import java.awt.*;
import java.awt.event.*;

/**
 * Simple Drag-and-Drop customization: drag the foreground color from the first
 * label and drop it as the background color into the second one.  Try it also
 * using the ShowBean program to display a JColorChooser component with
 * dragEnabled=true.
 */
public class ColorDrag {
    public static void main(String args[]) {
        // Create two JLabel objects
        final JLabel label1 = new JLabel("Drag here");
        JLabel label2 = new JLabel("Drop here");
```

Example 14-1. ColorDrag.java (continued)

```
        // Register TransferHandler objects on them: label1 transfers its
        // foreground color and label2 transfers its background color.
        label1.setTransferHandler(new TransferHandler("foreground"));
        label2.setTransferHandler(new TransferHandler("background"));

        // Give label1 a foreground color other than the default
        // Make label2 opaque so it displays its background color
        label1.setForeground(new Color(100, 100, 200));
        label2.setOpaque(true);

        // Now look for drag gestures over label1.  When one occurs,
        // tell the TransferHandler to begin a drag.
        // Exercise: modify this gesture recognition so that the drag doesn't
        // begin until the mouse has moved 4 pixels.  This helps to keep
        // drags distinct from sloppy clicks.  To do this, you'll need both
        // a MouseListener and a MouseMotionListener.
        label1.addMouseMotionListener(new MouseMotionAdapter( ) {
                public void mouseDragged(MouseEvent e) {
                    TransferHandler handler = label1.getTransferHandler( );
                    handler.exportAsDrag(label1, e, TransferHandler.COPY);
                }
            });

        // Create a window, add the labels, and make it all visible.
        JFrame f = new JFrame("ColorDrag");
        f.getContentPane( ).setLayout(new FlowLayout( ));
        f.getContentPane( ).add(label1);
        f.getContentPane( ).add(label2);
        f.pack( );
        f.setVisible(true);
    }
}
```

A Clock with Drag and Copy Support

Another way to customize Swing drag-and-drop is to subclass a Swing component, define new property accessor methods for it, and then register a TransferHandler to transfer the value of the new property. This is what we do in Example 14-2: we define a custom Swing component that displays the current time and uses a TransferHandler to make the contents of its new time property available. Like Example 14-1, this program uses a MouseMotionListener to detect drags. It also defines a key binding so that **Ctrl-C** copies the time to the clipboard. This example defines a custom component, but not a main( ) method: use the ShowBean program of Chapter 11 to display the component. You may want to run ShowBean again to display a JTextField or similar component, so that you have somewhere to drop or paste the time values you've dragged or copied. Also try dropping or pasting the value into other non-Java applications (such as your text editor) that you have running on your desktop.

Example 14-2 also demonstrates the javax.swing.Timer and java.text.DateFormat classes, and shows how to use the (new in Java 1.4) InputMap and ActionMap Swing classes for associating key bindings with components.

Example 14-2. DigitalClock.java

```
package je3.datatransfer;
import javax.swing.*;
import javax.swing.border.*;
import java.awt.*;
import java.awt.event.*;
import java.awt.datatransfer.*;
import javax.swing.Timer; // disambiguate from java.util.Timer
import java.text.DateFormat;
import java.util.Date;

/**
 * A custom Swing component that displays a simple digital clock.
 * Demonstrates how to add copy and drag support to a Swing component
 * with TransferHandler.
 */
public class DigitalClock extends JLabel {
    DateFormat format;    // How to display the time in string form
    int updateFrequency; // How often to update the time (in milliseconds)
    Timer timer;          // Triggers repeated updates to the clock

    public DigitalClock( ) {
        // Set default values for our properties
        setFormat(DateFormat.getTimeInstance(DateFormat.MEDIUM, getLocale( )));
        setUpdateFrequency(1000);  // Update once a second

        // Specify a Swing TransferHandler object to do the dirty work of
        // copy-and-paste and drag-and-drop for us.  This one will transfer
        // the value of the "time" property.  Since this property is read-only
        // it will allow drags but not drops.
        setTransferHandler(new TransferHandler("time"));

        // Since JLabel does not normally support drag-and-drop, we need an
        // event handler to detect a drag and start the transfer.
        addMouseMotionListener(new MouseMotionAdapter( ) {
                public void mouseDragged(MouseEvent e) {
                    getTransferHandler( ).exportAsDrag(DigitalClock.this, e,
                                                     TransferHandler.COPY);
                }
            });

        // Before we can have a keyboard binding for a Copy command,
        // the component needs to be able to accept keyboard focus.
        setFocusable(true);
        // Request focus when we're clicked on
        addMouseListener(new MouseAdapter( ) {
                public void mouseClicked(MouseEvent e) { requestFocus( ); }
            });
```

Example 14-2. DigitalClock.java (continued)

```java
        // Use a LineBorder to indicate when we've got the keyboard focus
        addFocusListener(new FocusListener() {
                public void focusGained(FocusEvent e) {
                    setBorder(LineBorder.createBlackLineBorder());
                }
                public void focusLost(FocusEvent e) { setBorder(null); }
            });

        // Now bind the Ctrl-C keystroke to a "Copy" command.
        InputMap im = new InputMap();
        im.setParent(getInputMap(WHEN_FOCUSED));
        im.put(KeyStroke.getKeyStroke(KeyEvent.VK_C,InputEvent.CTRL_MASK),
                "Copy");
        setInputMap(WHEN_FOCUSED, im);

        // And bind the "Copy" command to a pre-defined Action that performs
        // a copy using the TransferHandler we've installed.
        ActionMap am = new ActionMap();
        am.setParent(getActionMap());
        am.put("Copy", TransferHandler.getCopyAction());
        setActionMap(am);

        // Create a javax.swing.Timer object that will generate ActionEvents
        // to tell us when to update the displayed time.  Every updateFrequency
        // milliseconds, this timer will cause the actionPerformed() method
        // to be invoked.  (For non-GUI applications, see java.util.Timer.)
        timer = new Timer(updateFrequency, new ActionListener() {
                public void actionPerformed(ActionEvent e) {
                    setText(getTime());  // set label to current time string
                }
            });
        timer.setInitialDelay(0); // Do the first update immediately
        timer.start();            // Start timing now!
    }

    // Return the current time as a String.
    // This is the property accessor method used by the TransferHandler.
    // Since there is a getter, but no setter, the TransferHandler will
    // reject any attempts to drop data on us.
    public String getTime() {
        // Use the DateFormat object to convert current time to a string
        return format.format(new Date());
    }

    // Here are two related property setter methods
    public void setFormat(DateFormat format) { this.format = format; }
    public void setUpdateFrequency(int ms) { this.updateFrequency = ms; }
}
```

When you try out this DigitalClock component, you may notice a shortcoming: the TransferHandler class calls getTime() when the time value is dropped or pasted, not when it is originally dragged or copied. This is counterintuitive, but it is how TransferHandler works.

Data Transfer Architecture

Before we consider any more advanced data transfer examples, it is important that you understand the Java 1.1 `java.awt.datatransfer` infrastructure that the `javax.swing.TransferHandler` mechanism relies upon. The `java.awt.datatransfer.DataFlavor` class is perhaps the most central class; it represents the type of data to be transferred. Every data flavor consists of a human-readable name, a `Class` object that specifies the Java data type of the transferred data, and a MIME type that specifies the encoding used during data transfer. The `DataFlavor` class predefines a couple of commonly used flavors for transferring strings and lists of `File` objects. It also predefines several MIME types used with those flavors. For example, `DataFlavor.stringFlavor` can transfer Java `String` objects as Unicode text. It has a representation class of `java.lang.String` and a MIME type of:

```
application/x-java-serialized-object; class=java.lang.String
```

The `java.awt.datatransfer.Transferable` interface is another important piece of the data transfer picture. This interface specifies three methods that should be implemented by any object that wants to make data available for transfer: `getTransferDataFlavors()`, which returns an array of all the `DataFlavor` types it can use to transfer its data; `isDataFlavorSupported()`, which checks whether the `Transferable` object supports a given flavor; and the most important method, `getTransferData()`, which actually returns the data in a format appropriate for the requested `DataFlavor`.

The data transfer architecture relies on object serialization as one of its means of transferring data between applications, which makes the architecture quite general and flexible. It was designed to allow arbitrary data to be transferred between independent Java virtual machines. Java data transfer can also work between Java applications and native-platform applications. Note, however, that your native operating system doesn't know how to work with serialized Java objects, so if you want to enable data transfer with native applications, you should restrict yourself to using predefined flavors that have well-known mappings to native types, such as `DataFlavor.stringFlavor` and `DataFlavor.javaFileListFlavor`.

Dropping Multiple Datatypes

A limitation of the Swing data transfer mechanism is that, by default, it supports only a single type of data. It is useful, sometimes, to allow a component to accept pastes and drops of more than one type, handling each type in a different way. A `JEditorPane` component might handle dropped text in one way, handle dropped colors another way (by changing the foreground color of the selected text, for example), and handle dropped files yet another way (for example, by inserting the contents of the file). In the previous examples, we've created our own `TransferHandler` instances for simple data transfer customization. For more complex customizations, such as supporting multiple drop types, we need to subclass `TransferHandler`.

Example 14-3 lists the `FileTransferHandler` class. It is a `TransferHandler` subclass that wraps and delegates to some other specified `TransferHandler`, adding the

ability to accept pastes and drops of files using the predefined DataFlavor.
javaFileListFlavor flavor. The example includes an inner class named Test that
demonstrates its use with a JTextArea and a JFileChooser. Depending on how well
integrated your Java implementation is with your operating system's desktop, you
may also be able to drag files from your desktop into the JTextArea.

Example 14-3. FileTransferHandler.java

```java
package je3.datatransfer;
import javax.swing.*;
import java.awt.datatransfer.*;
import java.io.*;
import java.awt.event.InputEvent;
import java.util.List;

/**
 * This TransferHandler subclass wraps another TransferHandler and delegates
 * most of its operations to the wrapped handler.  It adds the ability to
 * to drop or paste files using the predefined DataFlavor.javaFileListFlavor.
 * When a file list is pasted or dropped, it assumes the files are text, reads
 * them in order, concatenates their contents, and then passes the resulting
 * string to the wrapped handler for insertion.
 */
public class FileTransferHandler extends TransferHandler {
    TransferHandler wrappedHandler;      // The handler that we wrap
    // We use this array to test the wrapped handler
    static DataFlavor[] stringFlavorArray =
        new DataFlavor[] { DataFlavor.stringFlavor };

    /** Pass an existing TransferHandler to this constructor */
    public FileTransferHandler(TransferHandler wrappedHandler) {
        if (wrappedHandler == null)            // Fail immediately on null
            throw new NullPointerException();
        this.wrappedHandler = wrappedHandler; // Remember wrapped handler
    }

    /**
     * This method returns true if the TransferHandler knows how to work
     * with one of the specified flavors.  This implementation first checks
     * the superclass, then checks for fileListFlavor support
     */
    public boolean canImport(JComponent c, DataFlavor[] flavors) {
        // If the wrapped handler can import it, we're done
        if (wrappedHandler.canImport(c, flavors)) return true;

        // Otherwise, if the wrapped handler can handle string imports, then
        // see if we are being offered a list of files that we can convert
        // to a string.
        if (wrappedHandler.canImport(c, stringFlavorArray)) {
            for(int i = 0; i < flavors.length; i++)
                if (flavors[i].equals(DataFlavor.javaFileListFlavor))
                    return true;
        }
```

Example 14-3. FileTransferHandler.java (continued)

```
        // Otherwise, we can't import any of the flavors.
        return false;
    }

    /**
     * If the wrapped handler can import strings and the specified Transferable
     * can provide its data as a List of File objects, then we read the
     * files, and pass their contents as a string to the wrapped handler.
     * Otherwise, we offer the Transferable to the wrapped handler to handle
     * on its own.
     */
    public boolean importData(JComponent c, Transferable t) {
        // See if we're offered a java.util.List of java.io.File objects.
        // We handle this case first because the Transferable is likely to
        // also offer the filenames as strings, and we want to import the
        // file contents, not their names!
        if (t.isDataFlavorSupported(DataFlavor.javaFileListFlavor) &&
            wrappedHandler.canImport(c, stringFlavorArray)) {
            try {
                List filelist =
                    (List)t.getTransferData(DataFlavor.javaFileListFlavor);

                // Loop through the files to determine total size
                int numfiles = filelist.size();
                int numbytes = 0;
                for(int i = 0; i < numfiles; i++) {
                    File f = (File)filelist.get(i);
                    numbytes += (int)f.length();
                }

                // There will never be more characters than bytes in the files
                char[] text = new char[numbytes]; // to hold file contents
                int p = 0;            // current position in the text[] array

                // Loop through the files again, reading their content as text
                for(int i = 0; i < numfiles; i++) {
                    File f = (File)filelist.get(i);
                    Reader r = new BufferedReader(new FileReader(f));
                    p += r.read(text, p, (int)f.length());
                }

                // Convert the character array to a string and wrap it
                // in a pre-defined Transferable class for transferring strings
                StringSelection selection =
                    new StringSelection(new String(text, 0, p));

                // Ask the wrapped handler to import the string
                return wrappedHandler.importData(c, selection);
            }
            // If anything goes wrong, just beep to tell the user
            catch(UnsupportedFlavorException e) {
                c.getToolkit().beep(); // audible error
                return false;          // return failure code
```

Example 14-3. FileTransferHandler.java (continued)

```
            }
            catch(IOException e) {
                c.getToolkit( ).beep( ); // audible error
                return false;            // return failure code
            }
        }

        // Otherwise let the wrapped class handle this Transferable itself
        return wrappedHandler.importData(c, t);
    }

    /*
     * The following methods just delegate to the wrapped TransferHandler
     */
    public void exportAsDrag(JComponent c, InputEvent e, int action) {
        wrappedHandler.exportAsDrag(c, e, action);
    }
    public void exportToClipboard(JComponent c, Clipboard clip, int action) {
        wrappedHandler.exportToClipboard(c, clip, action);
    }
    public int getSourceActions(JComponent c) {
        return wrappedHandler.getSourceActions(c);
    }
    public Icon getVisualRepresentation(Transferable t) {
        // This method is not currently (Java 1.4) used by Swing
        return wrappedHandler.getVisualRepresentation(t);
    }

    /**
     * This class demonstrates the FileTransferHandler by installing it on a
     * JTextArea component and providing a JFileChooser to drag and cut files.
     */
    public static class Test {
        public static void main(String[ ] args) {
            // Here's the text area.  Note how we wrap our TransferHandler
            // around the default handler returned by getTransferHandler( )
            JTextArea textarea = new JTextArea( );
            TransferHandler defaultHandler = textarea.getTransferHandler( );
            textarea.setTransferHandler(new FileTransferHandler(defaultHandler));
            // Here's a JFileChooser, with dragging explicitly enabled.
            JFileChooser filechooser = new JFileChooser( );
            filechooser.setDragEnabled(true);

            // Display them both in a window
            JFrame f = new JFrame("File Transfer Handler Test");
            f.getContentPane( ).add(new JScrollPane(textarea), "Center");
            f.getContentPane( ).add(filechooser, "South");
            f.setSize(400, 600);
            f.setVisible(true);
        }
    }
}
```

A Transferable Shape

In order to support data transfer of custom data types, we need to implement the Transferable interface. Example 14-4 does that for the PolyLine class (a java.awt. Shape implementation) defined in Example 12-16. Transferable is a simple interface to implement, and this example is short. Note that the example also defines a DataFlavor for transferring PolyLine objects.

Example 14-4. TransferablePolyLine.java

```java
package je3.datatransfer;
import java.awt.datatransfer.*;
import je3.graphics.PolyLine;

/**
 * This class implements the Transferable interface for PolyLine objects.
 * It also defines a DataFlavor used to describe this data type.
 */
public class TransferablePolyLine implements Transferable {
    public static DataFlavor FLAVOR= new DataFlavor(PolyLine.class,"PolyLine");
    static DataFlavor[ ] FLAVORS = new DataFlavor[ ] { FLAVOR };

    PolyLine line;  // This is the PolyLine we wrap.
    public TransferablePolyLine(PolyLine line) { this.line = line; }

    /** Return the supported flavor */
    public DataFlavor[ ] getTransferDataFlavors() { return FLAVORS; }

    /** Check for the one flavor we support */
    public boolean isDataFlavorSupported(DataFlavor f){return f.equals(FLAVOR);}

    /** Return the wrapped PolyLine, if the flavor is right */
    public Object getTransferData(DataFlavor f)
        throws UnsupportedFlavorException
    {
        if (!f.equals(FLAVOR)) throw new UnsupportedFlavorException(f);
        return line;
    }
}
```

Custom Data Transfer

Example 14-5 is a custom Swing component named TransferableScribblePane. It allows the user to scribble with the mouse and to select one scribble at a time. It defines cut( ), copy( ), and paste( ) methods that operate on the selected line, and also allows the selected line to be dragged and dropped within the component or into another instance of the component. The scribbles are transferred using the TransferablePolyLine class defined in Example 14-4, of course.

This example does not use the high-level Swing TransferHandler class, but instead relies on the underlying data transfer and drag-and-drop architecture of java.awt. datatransfer and java.awt.dnd. The code for performing drag-and-drop is substantially more complex than the code for cut-and-paste. This is because the asynchronous drag-and-drop model requires a number of distinct event listeners and their corresponding event objects. The key interfaces are DragGestureListener, which triggers a new drag, and DragSourceListener and DropTargetListener, which notify the source of a drag and the target of a drop of important events that occur during the drag-and-drop process. The example implements all three interfaces as anonymous inner classes. When studying the example, pay particular attention to the dragGestureRecognized() method of the DragSourceListener and the drop() method of the DropTargetListener. The first is where the drag is initiated, and the second is where the data transfer actually transpires.

To test this component, display two copies of it using the ShowBean program. Draw a line with the mouse, then select the line by shift-clicking on it. Next, drag and drop the selected line while holding down the **Shift** or **Ctrl** keys. Also, use the **Commands** menu of ShowBean to invoke the cut(), copy(), and paste() methods.

Example 14-5. TransferableScribblePane.java

```
package je3.datatransfer;
import java.awt.*;                  // Graphics, Rectangle, Stroke, etc.
import java.awt.datatransfer.*;     // Transferable, DataFlavor
import java.awt.dnd.*;              // Drag-and-drop listeners and events
import java.awt.event.*;            // Mouse events
import javax.swing.*;               // JComponent
import javax.swing.border.*;        // LineBorder and BevelBorder
import java.util.*;                 // ArrayList, etc.
import java.util.List;     // Explicit import to disambiguate from java.awt.List
import je3.graphics.PolyLine; // The Shape of scribbles

/**
 * This rewrite of ScribblePane allows individual PolyLine lines to be
 * selected, cut, copied, pasted, dragged, and dropped.
 */
public class TransferableScribblePane extends JComponent {
    List lines;              // The PolyLines that comprise this scribble
    PolyLine currentLine;    // The line currently being drawn
    PolyLine selectedLine;   // The line that is current selected
    boolean canDragImage;    // Can we drag an image of the line?

    // Lines are 3 pixels wide, and the selected line is drawn dashed
    static Stroke stroke = new BasicStroke(3.0f);
    static Stroke selectedStroke = new BasicStroke(3, BasicStroke.CAP_BUTT,
                                     BasicStroke.JOIN_ROUND, 0f,
                                     new float[] { 3f, 3f, },0f);

    // Different borders indicate receptivity to drops
    static Border normalBorder = new LineBorder(Color.black, 3);
    static Border canDropBorder = new BevelBorder(BevelBorder.LOWERED);

    // The constructor method
    public TransferableScribblePane() {
        setPreferredSize(new Dimension(450,200)); // We need a default size
```

Example 14-5. TransferableScribblePane.java (continued)

```
    setBorder(normalBorder);                    // and a border.
    lines = new ArrayList();   // Start with an empty list of lines

    // Register interest in mouse button and mouse motion events.
    enableEvents(AWTEvent.MOUSE_EVENT_MASK |
                 AWTEvent.MOUSE_MOTION_EVENT_MASK);

    // Enable drag-and-drop by specifying a listener that will be
    // notified when a drag begins.  dragGestureListener is defined later.
    DragSource dragSource = DragSource.getDefaultDragSource();
    dragSource.createDefaultDragGestureRecognizer(this,
                            DnDConstants.ACTION_COPY_OR_MOVE,
                                        dragGestureListener);

    // Enable drops on this component by registering a listener to
    // be notified when something is dragged or dropped over us.
    this.setDropTarget(new DropTarget(this, dropTargetListener));

    // Check whether the system allows us to drag an image of the line
    canDragImage = dragSource.isDragImageSupported();
}

/** We override this method to draw ourselves. */
public void paintComponent(Graphics g) {
    // Let the superclass do its painting first
    super.paintComponent(g);

    // Make a copy of the Graphics context so we can modify it
    Graphics2D g2 = (Graphics2D) (g.create());

    // Our superclass doesn't paint the background, so do this ourselves.
    g2.setColor(getBackground());
    g2.fillRect(0, 0, getWidth(), getHeight());

    // Set the line width and color to use for the foreground
    g2.setStroke(stroke);
    g2.setColor(this.getForeground());

    // Now loop through the PolyLine shapes and draw them all
    int numlines = lines.size();
    for(int i = 0; i < numlines; i++) {
        PolyLine line = (PolyLine)lines.get(i);
        if (line == selectedLine) {        // If it is the selected line
            g2.setStroke(selectedStroke);  // Set dash pattern
            g2.draw(line);                 // Draw the line
            g2.setStroke(stroke);          // Revert to solid lines
        }
        else g2.draw(line);  // Otherwise just draw the line
    }
}
```

Example 14-5. TransferableScribblePane.java (continued)

```java
/**
 * This method is called on mouse button events.  It begins a new line
 * or tries to select an existing line.
 */
public void processMouseEvent(MouseEvent e) {
    if (e.getButton( ) == MouseEvent.BUTTON1) {         // Left mouse button
        if (e.getID( ) == MouseEvent.MOUSE_PRESSED) {   // Pressed down
            if (e.isShiftDown( )) {                     // with Shift key
                // If the shift key is down, try to select a line
                int x = e.getX( );
                int y = e.getY( );

                // Loop through the lines, checking to see if we hit one
                PolyLine selection = null;
                int numlines = lines.size( );
                for(int i = 0; i < numlines; i++) {
                    PolyLine line = (PolyLine)lines.get(i);
                    if (line.intersects(x-2, y-2, 4, 4)) {
                        selection = line;
                        e.consume( );
                        break;
                    }
                }
                // If we found an intersecting line, save it and repaint
                if (selection != selectedLine) { // If selection changed
                    selectedLine = selection; // remember which is selected
                    repaint( );                     // will make selection dashed
                }
            }
            else if (!e.isControlDown( )) {    // no shift key or ctrl key
                // Start a new line on mouse down without shift or ctrl
                currentLine = new PolyLine(e.getX( ), e.getY( ));
                lines.add(currentLine);
                e.consume( );
            }
        }
        else if (e.getID( ) == MouseEvent.MOUSE_RELEASED) {// Left Button Up
            // End the line on mouse up
            if (currentLine != null) {
                currentLine = null;
                e.consume( );
            }
        }
    }

    // The superclass method dispatches to registered event listeners
    super.processMouseEvent(e);
}

/**
 * This method is called for mouse motion events.
 * We don't have to detect gestures that initiate a drag in this method.
```

Example 14-5. TransferableScribblePane.java (continued)

```
    * That is the job of the DragGestureRecognizer we created in the
    * constructor: it will notify the DragGestureListener defined below.
    */
    public void processMouseMotionEvent(MouseEvent e) {
        if (e.getID( ) == MouseEvent.MOUSE_DRAGGED &&      // If we're dragging
            currentLine != null) {                         // and a line exists
            currentLine.addSegment(e.getX( ), e.getY( ));  // Add a line segment
            e.consume( );                                  // Eat the event
            repaint( );                                    // Redisplay all lines
        }
        super.processMouseMotionEvent(e); // Invoke any listeners
    }

    /** Copy the selected line to the clipboard, then delete it */
    public void cut( ) {
        if (selectedLine == null) return; // Only works if a line is selected
        copy( );                          // Do a Copy operation...
        lines.remove(selectedLine);       // and then erase the selected line
        selectedLine = null;
        repaint( );                       // Repaint because a line was removed
    }

    /** Copy the selected line to the clipboard */
    public void copy( ) {
        if (selectedLine == null) return; // Only works if a line is selected
        // Get the system Clipboard object.
        Clipboard c = this.getToolkit( ).getSystemClipboard( );

        // Wrap the selected line in a TransferablePolyLine object
        // and pass it to the clipboard, with an object to receive notification
        // when some other application takes ownership of the clipboard
        c.setContents(new TransferablePolyLine((PolyLine)selectedLine.clone( )),
                      new ClipboardOwner( ) {
                          public void lostOwnership(Clipboard c,Transferable t){
                              // This method is called when something else
                              // is copied to the clipboard.  We could use it
                              // to deselect the selected line, if we wanted.
                          }
                      });
    }

    /** Get a PolyLine from the clipboard, if one exists, and display it */
    public void paste( ) {
        // Get the system Clipboard and ask for its Transferable contents
        Clipboard c = this.getToolkit( ).getSystemClipboard( );
        Transferable t = c.getContents(this);

        // See if we can extract a PolyLine from the Transferable object
        PolyLine line;
        try {
            line = (PolyLine)t.getTransferData(TransferablePolyLine.FLAVOR);
        }
```

Data Transfer

Example 14-5. TransferableScribblePane.java (continued)

```
        catch(Exception e) {  // UnsupportedFlavorException or IOException
            // If we get here, the clipboard doesn't hold a PolyLine we can use
            getToolkit().beep();   // So beep to indicate the error
            return;
        }

        lines.add(line); // We got a line from the clipboard, so add it to list
        repaint();        // And repaint to make the line appear
    }

    /** Erase all lines and repaint. */
    public void clear() {
        lines.clear();
        repaint();
    }

    /**
     * This DragGestureListener is notified when the user initiates a drag.
     * We passed it to the DragGestureRecognizer we created in the constructor.
     */
    public DragGestureListener dragGestureListener = new DragGestureListener(){
        public void dragGestureRecognized(DragGestureEvent e) {
            // Don't start a drag if there isn't a selected line
            if (selectedLine == null) return;

            // Find out where the drag began
            MouseEvent trigger = (MouseEvent)e.getTriggerEvent();
            int x = trigger.getX();
            int y = trigger.getY();

            // Don't do anything if the drag was not near the selected line
            if (!selectedLine.intersects(x-4, y-4, 8, 8)) return;

            // Make a copy of the selected line, adjust the copy so that
            // the point under the mouse is (0,0), and wrap the copy in a
            // Tranferable wrapper.
            PolyLine copy = (PolyLine)selectedLine.clone();
            copy.translate(-x, -y);
            Transferable t = new TransferablePolyLine(copy);

            // If the system allows custom images to be dragged, make
            // an image of the line on a transparent background
            Image dragImage = null;
            Point hotspot = null;
            if (canDragImage) {
                Rectangle box = copy.getBounds();
                dragImage = createImage(box.width, box.height);
                Graphics2D g = (Graphics2D)dragImage.getGraphics();
                g.setColor(new Color(0,0,0,0));   // transparent bg
                g.fillRect(0, 0, box.width, box.height);
                g.setColor(getForeground());
                g.setStroke(selectedStroke);
```

Example 14-5. TransferableScribblePane.java (continued)

```
                    g.translate(-box.x, -box.y);
                    g.draw(copy);
                    hotspot = new Point(-box.x, -box.y);

                }

                // Now begin dragging the line, specifying the listener
                // object to receive notifications about the progress of
                // the operation.  Note: the startDrag() method is defined by
                // the event object, which is unusual.
                e.startDrag(null,           // Use default drag-and-drop cursors
                            dragImage,  // Use the image, if supported
                            hotspot,    // Ditto for the image hotspot
                            t,          // Drag this object
                            dragSourceListener); // Send notifications here
            }
        };

    /**
     * If this component is the source of a drag, then this DragSourceListener
     * will receive notifications about the progress of the drag.  The only
     * one we use here is dragDropEnd() which is called after a drop occurs.
     * We could use the other methods to change cursors or perform other
     * "drag over effects"
     */
    public DragSourceListener dragSourceListener = new DragSourceListener() {
        // Invoked when dragging stops
        public void dragDropEnd(DragSourceDropEvent e) {
            if (!e.getDropSuccess()) return; // Ignore failed drops
            // If the drop was a move, then delete the selected line
            if (e.getDropAction() == DnDConstants.ACTION_MOVE) {
                lines.remove(selectedLine);
                selectedLine = null;
                repaint();
            }
        }
        // The following methods are unused here.  We could implement them
        // to change custom cursors or perform other "drag over effects".
        public void dragEnter(DragSourceDragEvent e) { }
        public void dragExit(DragSourceEvent e) { }
        public void dragOver(DragSourceDragEvent e) { }
        public void dropActionChanged(DragSourceDragEvent e) { }
    };

    /**
     * This DropTargetListener is notified when something is dragged over
     * this component.
     */
    public DropTargetListener dropTargetListener = new DropTargetListener() {
        // This method is called when something is dragged over us.
        // If we understand what is being dragged, then tell the system
        // we can accept it, and change our border to provide extra
```

Example 14-5. TransferableScribblePane.java (continued)

```
        // "drag under" visual feedback to the user to indicate our
        // receptivity to a drop.
        public void dragEnter(DropTargetDragEvent e) {
            if (e.isDataFlavorSupported(TransferablePolyLine.FLAVOR)) {
                e.acceptDrag(e.getDropAction());
                setBorder(canDropBorder);
            }
        }

        // Revert to our normal border if the drag moves off us.
        public void dragExit(DropTargetEvent e) { setBorder(normalBorder); }
        // This method is called when something is dropped on us.
        public void drop(DropTargetDropEvent e) {
            // If a PolyLine is dropped, accept either a COPY or a MOVE
            if (e.isDataFlavorSupported(TransferablePolyLine.FLAVOR))
                e.acceptDrop(e.getDropAction());
            else {  // Otherwise, reject the drop and return
                e.rejectDrop();
                return;
            }

            // Get the dropped object and extract a PolyLine from it
            Transferable t = e.getTransferable();
            PolyLine line;
            try {
                line =
                    (PolyLine)t.getTransferData(TransferablePolyLine.FLAVOR);
            }
            catch(Exception ex) {  // UnsupportedFlavor or IOException
                getToolkit().beep();   // Something went wrong, so beep
                e.dropComplete(false); // Tell the system we failed
                return;
            }

            // Figure out where the drop occurred, and translate so the
            // point that was formerly (0,0) is now at that point.
            Point p = e.getLocation();
            line.translate((float)p.getX(), (float)p.getY());

            // Add the line to our list, and repaint
            lines.add(line);
            repaint();

            // Tell the system that we successfully completed the transfer.
            // This means it is safe for the initiating component to delete
            // its copy of the line
            e.dropComplete(true);
        }

        // We could provide additional drag under effects with this method.
        public void dragOver(DropTargetDragEvent e) {}
```

Example 14-5. TransferableScribblePane.java (continued)

```
        // If we used custom cursors, we would update them here.
        public void dropActionChanged(DropTargetDragEvent e) { }
    };
}
```

Exercises

Exercise 14-1. The DigitalClock class of Example 14-2 uses a MouseMotionListener to initiate a drag when the user drags the mouse. It initiates a drag even when the user meant to click but jiggled the mouse a pixel or two. Modify the example so that a drag is not initiated unless the mouse has actually moved four pixels from where the button was pressed down. You'll need a MouseListener in addition to the MouseMotionListener.

Exercise 14-2. Define a custom Swing component, named ColorSwatch, with a read/write property named "color" that displays a color swatch and allows that color to be dragged. Use a TransferHandler to transfer the value of the "color" property. Next, modify ColorSwatch to add a property named "allowsDrop". If this property is false, then the ColorSwatch should not allow colors to be dropped onto itself. To do this, you'll need to subclass TransferHandler to modify the canImport( ) and importData( ) methods.

Exercise 14-3. The copy( ) method of Example 14-5 defines an anonymous implementation of the ClipboardOwner interface that has an empty lostOwnership( ) method. Provide an implementation of this method to deselect the currently selected line: this provides visual feedback to the user that indicates the line is no longer available for pasting. Test your method by selecting and copying a line in one instance of the component, and then doing the same thing in another instance. Next, modify your method so that it only deselects the selected line if it is the same one that was transferred to the clipboard.

15

JavaBeans

The JavaBeans API provides a framework for defining reusable, embeddable, modular software components. The JavaBeans specification includes the following definition of a bean: "a reusable software component that can be manipulated visually in a builder tool." As you can see, this is a rather loose definition; beans can take a variety of forms. At the simplest level, individual GUI components are all beans, while at a much higher level, an embeddable spreadsheet application might also function as a bean. Most beans, however, probably fall somewhere between these two extremes.

Note that the definition of a Java bean explicitly supposes the existence of a visual GUI builder tool. In this chapter, we'll use the term "beanbox" to refer to any such tool. The name is from an obsolete JavaBeans demonstration tool shipped by Sun with the early releases of JavaBeans. A new tool, called "Bean Builder," has replaced the beanbox, and you can download it from *http://java.sun.com/products/javabeans* if you do not already have a bean-enabled development environment.

One of the goals of the JavaBeans model is interoperability with similar component frameworks. So, for example, a native Windows program can, with an appropriate bridge or wrapper object, use a Java bean as if it were a COM or ActiveX component. The details of this sort of interoperability are beyond the scope of this chapter, however.

Beans can be used at three levels, by three different categories of programmers:

- If you are writing applications that use beans developed by other programmers (perhaps using a beanbox visual development tool to combine those beans into an application), you don't actually need to be familiar with the JavaBeans API. You only need to know how to use your beanbox and be familiar with the documentation for specific beans that you use.

- If you are writing actual beans, you need to be familiar with JavaBeans naming conventions, so that you can follow those conventions when designing your bean's API. You may also use the java.beans API to create auxiliary classes that integrate it more tightly into beanboxes.

- If you are developing GUI editors, application builders, or other "beanbox" tools, you need the JavaBeans API to manipulate beans within these tools. Note that the ShowBean program of Example 11-30 was a simple kind of beanbox.

This chapter explains how to use the JavaBeans API at the second and third levels: how to write beans and their auxiliary classes, and how to write programs that manipulate beans. The emphasis is on writing beans, but Example 15-10 shows the Bean class, which implements the inner workings for the ShowBean beanbox of Chapter 11. Contents of this chapter include:

- Basic bean concepts and terminology
- Requirements for the simplest beans
- Packaging beans in JAR files
- Providing additional information about beans with the BeanInfo class
- Defining property editors to allow custom editing of bean properties
- Defining bean customizers to allow customization of an entire bean
- Instantiating beans, introspecting on them, using property editors to convert property values to and from strings, and using Java reflection to set named properties and invoke named methods

Bean Basics

We begin our discussion of beans with some basic concepts and terminology. Any object that conforms to certain basic rules and naming conventions can be a bean; there is no Bean class that all beans are required to subclass. Many beans are Swing or AWT components, but it is also quite possible, and often useful, to write "invisible" beans that don't have an onscreen appearance. (Just because a bean doesn't have an onscreen appearance in a finished application doesn't mean that it can't be visually manipulated by a beanbox tool, however.)

A bean exports properties, events, and methods. A *property* is a piece of the bean's internal state that can be programmatically set and queried, usually through a standard pair of get and set accessor methods. A bean may generate *events* in the same way that a GUI component, such as a JButton, generates ActionEvent events. The JavaBeans API uses the same event model (in fact, it defines the event model) used by Swing and AWT GUIs in Java 1.1 and later. See Chapter 11 for a full discussion of this model. A bean defines an event by providing methods for adding and removing event listener objects from a list of interested listeners for that event. Finally, the *methods* exported by a bean are simply any public methods defined by the bean, excluding those methods used to get and set property values and register and remove event listeners.

In addition to the regular sort of properties just described, the JavaBeans API also provides support for indexed properties, bound properties, and constrained properties. An *indexed property* is any property that has an array value and for which the bean provides methods to get and set individual elements of the array, as well as methods to get and set the entire array. A *bound property* is one that sends out a notification event when its value changes, while a *constrained property* is one that sends out a notification event when its value changes and allows the change to be vetoed by listeners.

Because Java allows dynamic loading of classes, beanbox programs can load arbitrary beans. The beanbox tool determines the properties, events, and methods a bean supports with an introspection mechanism that is based on the `java.lang.reflect` reflection mechanism for obtaining information about the members of a class. A bean can also provide an auxiliary `BeanInfo` class that supplies additional information about the bean. The `BeanInfo` class provides this additional information in the form of a number of `FeatureDescriptor` objects, each of which describes a single feature of the bean. `FeatureDescriptor` has a number of subclasses: `BeanDescriptor`, `PropertyDescriptor`, `IndexedPropertyDescriptor`, `EventSetDescriptor`, `MethodDescriptor`, and `ParameterDescriptor`.

A primary task of a beanbox application is to allow the user to customize a bean by setting property values. A *beanbox* defines property editors for commonly used property types, such as numbers, strings, fonts, and colors. If a bean has a property of a more complicated type, however, it may need to define a `PropertyEditor` class that enables the beanbox to let the user set values for that property.

In addition, a complex bean may not be satisfied with the property-by-property customization mechanism provided by most beanboxes. Such a bean may want to define a `Customizer` class, which creates a graphical interface that allows the user to configure a bean in some useful way. A particularly complex bean may even define customizers that serve as "wizards" that guide the user step-by-step through the customization process.

A Simple Bean

As noted earlier, Swing and AWT components can all function as beans. When you write a custom GUI component, it is not difficult to make it function as a bean as well. Example 15-1 shows the definition of a custom JavaBeans component, `MultiLineLabel`, that displays one or more lines of static text.

What makes this component a bean is that all its properties have get and set accessor methods. Because `MultiLineLabel` doesn't respond to user input in any way, it doesn't define any events, so no event-listener registration methods are required. `MultiLineLabel` also defines a no-argument constructor, so that it can be easily instantiated by beanboxes.

Example 15-1. MultiLineLabel.java

```
package je3.beans;
import java.awt.*;
import javax.swing.*;
import java.util.StringTokenizer;
```

Example 15-1. MultiLineLabel.java (continued)

```
/**
 * A custom component that displays multiple lines of text with specified
 * margins and alignment.
 **/
public class MultiLineLabel extends JComponent {
    // User-specified properties
    protected String label;                 // The label, not broken into lines
    protected int margin_width;             // Left and right margins
    protected int margin_height;            // Top and bottom margins
    protected Alignment alignment;          // The alignment of the text.

    // Computed state values
    protected int num_lines;                // The number of lines
    protected String[] lines;               // The label, broken into lines
    protected int[] line_widths;            // How wide each line is
    protected int max_width;                // The width of the widest line
    protected int line_height;              // Total height of the font
    protected int line_ascent;              // Font height above baseline
    protected boolean measured = false;     // Have the lines been measured?

    // Here are five versions of the constructor.
    public MultiLineLabel(String label, int margin_width,
                          int margin_height, Alignment alignment) {
        this.label = label;                 // Remember all the properties.
        this.margin_width = margin_width;
        this.margin_height = margin_height;
        this.alignment = alignment;
        newLabel();                         // Break the label up into lines.
    }

    public MultiLineLabel(String label, int margin_width, int margin_height) {
        this(label, margin_width, margin_height, Alignment.LEFT);
    }

    public MultiLineLabel(String label, Alignment alignment) {
        this(label, 10, 10, alignment);
    }

    public MultiLineLabel(String label) { this(label, 10, 10, Alignment.LEFT);}

    public MultiLineLabel() { this(""); }

    // Methods to set and query the various attributes of the component.
    // Note that some query methods are inherited from the superclass.
    public void setLabel(String label) {
        this.label = label;
        newLabel();             // Break the label into lines.
        repaint();              // Request a redraw.
        measured = false;       // Note that we need to measure lines.
        invalidate();           // Tell our containers about this
    }
```

Example 15-1. MultiLineLabel.java (continued)

```java
    public void setAlignment(Alignment a) { alignment = a; repaint(); }
    public void setMarginWidth(int mw) { margin_width = mw; repaint(); }
    public void setMarginHeight(int mh) { margin_height = mh; repaint(); }

    // Override this property setter method because we need to remeasure
    public void setFont(Font f) {
        super.setFont(f);          // Tell our superclass about the new font.
        repaint();                 // Request a redraw.
        measured = false;          // Note that we need to remeasure lines.
        invalidate();              // Tell our containers about new size
    }

    // Property getter methods.
    public String getLabel() { return label; }
    public Alignment getAlignment() { return alignment; }
    public int getMarginWidth() { return margin_width; }
    public int getMarginHeight() { return margin_height; }

    /**
     * This method is called by a layout manager when it wants to
     * know how big we'd like to be.
     */
    public Dimension getPreferredSize() {
        if (!measured) measure();
        return new Dimension(max_width + 2*margin_width,
                             num_lines * line_height + 2*margin_height);
    }

    /**
     * This method is called when the layout manager wants to know
     * the bare minimum amount of space we need to get by.
     */
    public Dimension getMinimumSize() { return getPreferredSize(); }

    /**
     * This method draws the component.
     * Note that it handles the margins and the alignment, but that
     * it doesn't have to worry about the color or font--the superclass
     * takes care of setting those in the Graphics object we're passed.
     **/
    public void paintComponent(Graphics g) {
        int x, y;
        Dimension size = this.getSize();
        if (!measured) measure();
        y = line_ascent + (size.height - num_lines * line_height)/2;
        for(int i = 0; i < num_lines; i++, y += line_height) {
            if (alignment == Alignment.LEFT) x = margin_width;
            else if (alignment == Alignment.CENTER)
                x = (size.width - line_widths[i])/2;
            else x = size.width - margin_width - line_widths[i];
            g.drawString(lines[i], x, y);
        }
    }
}
```

Example 15-1. MultiLineLabel.java (continued)

```java
/**
 * This internal method breaks a specified label up into an array of lines.
 * It uses the StringTokenizer utility class.
 **/
protected synchronized void newLabel() {
    StringTokenizer t = new StringTokenizer(label, "\n");
    num_lines = t.countTokens();
    lines = new String[num_lines];
    line_widths = new int[num_lines];
    for(int i = 0; i < num_lines; i++) lines[i] = t.nextToken();
}

/**
 * This internal method figures out how the font is, and how wide each
 * line of the label is, and how wide the widest line is.
 **/
protected synchronized void measure() {
    FontMetrics fm = this.getFontMetrics(this.getFont());
    line_height = fm.getHeight();
    line_ascent = fm.getAscent();
    max_width = 0;
    for(int i = 0; i < num_lines; i++) {
        line_widths[i] = fm.stringWidth(lines[i]);
        if (line_widths[i] > max_width) max_width = line_widths[i];
    }
    measured = true;
}
}
```

The Alignment Class

MultiLineLabel uses an auxiliary class named Alignment to define three alignment constants. The definition of this class is shown in Example 15-2. The class defines three constants that hold three instances of itself, and declares its constructor private so that no other instances can be created. In this way, Alignment effectively creates an enumerated type. This is a useful technique that is not at all specific to JavaBeans.

Example 15-2. Alignment.java

```java
package je3.beans;

/** This class defines an enumerated type with three values */
public class Alignment {
    /** This private constructor prevents anyone from instantiating us */
    private Alignment() {};
    // The following three constants are the only instances of this class
    public static final Alignment LEFT = new Alignment();
    public static final Alignment CENTER = new Alignment();
    public static final Alignment RIGHT = new Alignment();
}
```

Packaging a Bean

To prepare a bean for use in a beanbox, you must package it in a JAR file, along with any other classes or resource files it requires. (JAR files are "Java archives"; you can read about the *jar* tool in *Java in a Nutshell*.) Because a single bean can have many auxiliary files, and because a JAR file can contain multiple beans, the manifest of the JAR file must define which JAR file entries are beans. You create a JAR file with the c option to the *jar* command. When you use the m option in conjunction with c, it tells *jar* to read a partial manifest file that you specify. *jar* uses the information in your partially specified manifest file when creating the complete manifest for the JAR file. To identify a class file as a bean, you simply add the following line to the file's manifest entry:

```
Java-Bean: true
```

To package the MultiLineLabel class in a JAR file, first create a manifest "stub" file. Create a file, perhaps named *manifest.stub*, with these contents:

```
Name: je3/beans/MultiLineLabel.class
Java-Bean: true
```

Note that the forward slashes in the manifest file shouldn't be changed to backward slashes on Windows systems. The format of the JAR manifest file requires forward slashes to separate directories, regardless of the platform. Having created this partial manifest file, you can now create the JAR file:

```
% jar cfm MultiLineLabel.jar manifest.stub
  je3/beans/MultiLineLabel.class je3/beans/Alignment.class
```

Note that this is a single long command line that has been broken onto two lines. Also, on a Windows system, you do need to replace forward slashes with backslashes in this command line. If this bean required auxiliary files, you would specify them at the end of the *jar* command line, along with the class files for the bean.

Installing a Bean

The procedure for installing a bean depends on the beanbox tool you use. For Sun's demonstration *Bean Builder* tool, for example, use the **Load Jar...** command in the **File** menu to make your beans appear on the palette of available beans. For our own ShowBean tool, you simply need to ensure that the JAR file is in your classpath. In fact, you don't need to create the JAR file at all to use ShowBean: you can just ensure that the bean development directory is in your classpath.

A More Complex Bean

Example 15-3 shows another bean, YesNoPanel. This bean displays a message (using MultiLineLabel) and three buttons to the user. It fires an event when the user clicks on one of the buttons. YesNoPanel is intended for use within dialog boxes, as it provides an ideal way to ask the user yes/no/cancel questions. Figure 15-1 shows a YesNoPanel instance being edited with the ShowBean program.

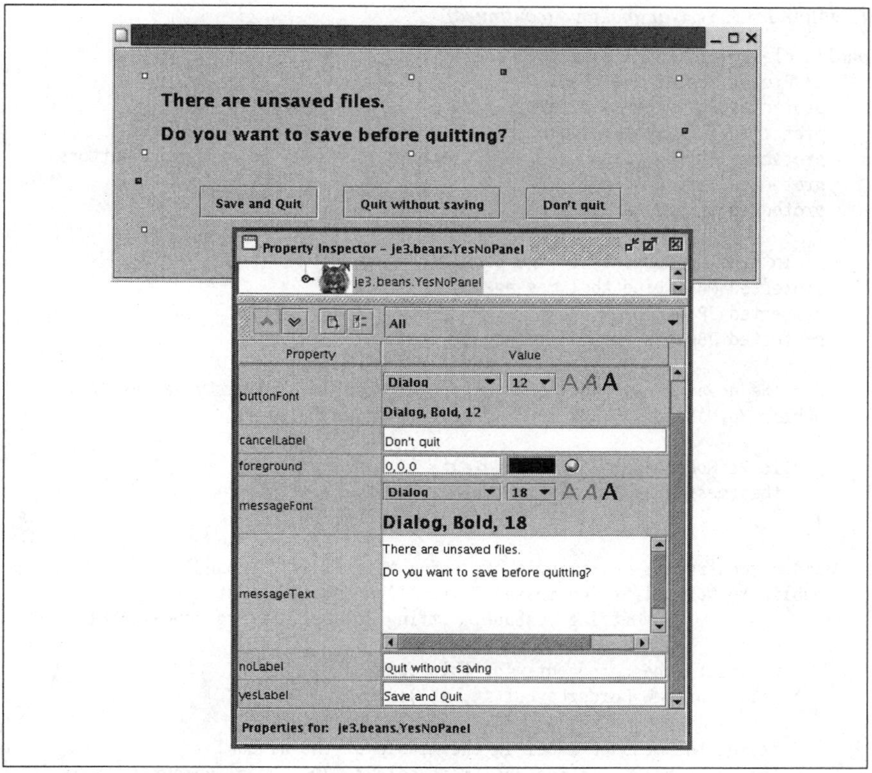

Figure 15-1. The YesNoPanel bean in a beanbox

The YesNoPanel bean uses a custom AnswerEvent type to notify AnswerListener objects when the user has clicked on one of its three buttons. This new event class and listener interface are defined in the next section.

Notice that YesNoPanel doesn't use any classes from the java.beans package. One of the surprising things about beans is that they typically don't have to use any classes from this package. As you'll see later in this chapter, it's the auxiliary classes that are shipped with a bean that make heavy use of that package.

Example 15-3. YesNoPanel.java

```
package je3.beans;
import java.awt.*;
import java.awt.event.*;
import javax.swing.*;
import java.util.List;
import java.util.ArrayList;

/**
 * This JavaBean displays a multi-line message and up to three buttons.  It
 * fires an AnswerEvent when the user clicks on one of the buttons
 **/
```

Example 15-3. YesNoPanel.java (continued)

```java
public class YesNoPanel extends JPanel {
    // Properties of the bean.
    protected String messageText;  // The message to display
    protected Alignment alignment; // The alignment of the message
    protected String yesLabel;     // Text for the yes, no, & cancel buttons
    protected String noLabel;
    protected String cancelLabel;

    // Internal components of the panel
    protected MultiLineLabel message;
    protected JPanel buttonbox;
    protected JButton yes, no, cancel;

    /** The no-argument bean constructor, with default property values */
    public YesNoPanel() { this("Your\nMessage\nHere"); }

    public YesNoPanel(String messageText) {
        this(messageText, Alignment.LEFT, "Yes", "No", "Cancel");
    }

    /** A constructor for programmers using this class "by hand" */
    public YesNoPanel(String messageText, Alignment alignment,
                      String yesLabel, String noLabel, String cancelLabel)
    {
        // Create the components for this panel
        setLayout(new BorderLayout(15, 15));

        // Put the message label in the middle of the window.
        message = new MultiLineLabel(messageText, 20, 20, alignment);
        message.setOpaque(false);  // allow background color to show through
        add(message, BorderLayout.CENTER);

        // Create a panel for the Panel buttons and put it at the bottom
        // of the Panel.  Specify a FlowLayout layout manager for it.
        buttonbox = new JPanel();
        buttonbox.setLayout(new FlowLayout(FlowLayout.CENTER, 25, 15));
        buttonbox.setOpaque(false);  // allow background color to show through
        add(buttonbox, BorderLayout.SOUTH);

        // Create each specified button, specifying the action listener
        // and action command for each, and adding them to the buttonbox
        yes = new JButton();                    // Create buttons
        no = new JButton();
        cancel = new JButton();
        // Add the buttons to the button box
        buttonbox.add(yes);
        buttonbox.add(no);
        buttonbox.add(cancel);

        // Register listeners for each button
        yes.addActionListener(new ActionListener() {
                public void actionPerformed(ActionEvent e) {
```

Example 15-3. YesNoPanel.java (continued)

```
                fireEvent(new AnswerEvent(YesNoPanel.this,
                                          AnswerEvent.YES));
            }
        });

    no.addActionListener(new ActionListener( ) {
            public void actionPerformed(ActionEvent e) {
                fireEvent(new AnswerEvent(YesNoPanel.this,
                                          AnswerEvent.NO));
            }
        });
    cancel.addActionListener(new ActionListener( ) {
            public void actionPerformed(ActionEvent e) {
                fireEvent(new AnswerEvent(YesNoPanel.this,
                                          AnswerEvent.CANCEL));
            }
        });

    // Now call property setter methods to set the message and button
    // components to contain the right text
    setMessageText(messageText);
    setAlignment(alignment);
    setYesLabel(yesLabel);
    setNoLabel(noLabel);
    setCancelLabel(cancelLabel);
}

// Methods to query all of the bean properties.
public String getMessageText( ) { return messageText; }
public Alignment getAlignment( ) { return alignment; }
public String getYesLabel( ) { return yesLabel; }
public String getNoLabel( ) { return noLabel; }
public String getCancelLabel( ) { return cancelLabel; }
public Font getMessageFont( ) { return message.getFont( ); }
public Color getMessageColor( ) { return message.getForeground( ); }
public Font getButtonFont( ) { return yes.getFont( ); }

// Methods to set all of the bean properties.
public void setMessageText(String messageText) {
    this.messageText = messageText;
    message.setLabel(messageText);
}

public void setAlignment(Alignment alignment) {
    this.alignment = alignment;
    message.setAlignment(alignment);
}

public void setYesLabel(String l) {
    yesLabel = l;
    yes.setText(l);
    yes.setVisible((l != null) && (l.length( ) > 0));
}
```

JavaBeans

Example 15-3. YesNoPanel.java (continued)

```java
public void setNoLabel(String l) {
    noLabel = l;
    no.setText(l);
    no.setVisible((l != null) && (l.length( ) > 0));
}

public void setCancelLabel(String l) {
    cancelLabel = l;
    cancel.setText(l);
    cancel.setVisible((l != null) && (l.length( ) > 0));
}

public void setMessageFont(Font f) {
    message.setFont(f);
}

public void setMessageColor(Color c) {
    message.setForeground(c);
}

public void setButtonFont(Font f) {
    yes.setFont(f);
    no.setFont(f);
    cancel.setFont(f);
}

/** This field holds a list of registered ActionListeners. */
protected List listeners = new ArrayList( );

/** Register an action listener to be notified when a button is pressed */
public void addAnswerListener(AnswerListener l) { listeners.add(l); }

/** Remove an Answer listener from our list of interested listeners */
public void removeAnswerListener(AnswerListener l) { listeners.remove(l); }

/** Send an event to all registered listeners */
public void fireEvent(AnswerEvent e) {
    // Make a copy of the list and fire the events using that copy.
    // This means that listeners can be added or removed from the original
    // list in response to this event.
    Object[ ] copy = listeners.toArray( );
    for(int i = 0; i < copy.length; i++) {
        AnswerListener listener = (AnswerListener) copy[i];
        switch(e.getID( )) {
        case AnswerEvent.YES: listener.yes(e); break;
        case AnswerEvent.NO:  listener.no(e); break;
        case AnswerEvent.CANCEL: listener.cancel(e); break;
        }
    }
}
```

Example 15-3. YesNoPanel.java (continued)

```
/** A main method that demonstrates the class */
public static void main(String[ ] args) {
    // Create an instance of YesNoPanel, with title and message specified:
    YesNoPanel p = new YesNoPanel("Do you really want to quit?");

    // Register an action listener for the Panel.  This one just prints
    // the results out to the console.
    p.addAnswerListener(new AnswerListener( ) {
            public void yes(AnswerEvent e) { System.exit(0); }
            public void no(AnswerEvent e) { System.out.println("No"); }
            public void cancel(AnswerEvent e) {
                System.out.println("Cancel");
            }
        });

    JFrame f = new JFrame( );
    f.getContentPane( ).add(p);
    f.pack( );
    f.setVisible(true);
    }
}
```

Custom Events

Beans can use the standard event types defined in the java.awt.event and javax.
swing.event packages, but they don't have to. Our YesNoPanel class defines its
own event type, AnswerEvent. Defining a new event class is really quite simple;
AnswerEvent is shown in Example 15-4.

Example 15-4. AnswerEvent.java

```
package je3.beans;

/**
 * The YesNoPanel class fires an event of this type when the user clicks one
 * of its buttons.  The id field specifies which button the user pressed.
 **/
public class AnswerEvent extends java.util.EventObject {
    public static final int YES = 0, NO = 1, CANCEL = 2;   // Button constants
    protected int id;                                      // Which button was pressed?
    public AnswerEvent(Object source, int id) {
        super(source);
        this.id = id;
    }
    public int getID( ) { return id; }          // Return the button
}
```

Along with the AnswerEvent class, YesNoPanel also defines a new type of event
listener interface, AnswerListener, that defines the methods that must be implemented by any object that wants to receive notification from a YesNoPanel. The
definition of AnswerListener is shown in Example 15-5.

Example 15-5. AnswerListener.java

```
package je3.beans;

/**
 * Classes that want to be notified when the user clicks a button in a
 * YesNoPanel should implement this interface.  The method invoked depends
 * on which button the user clicked.
 **/
public interface AnswerListener extends java.util.EventListener {
    public void yes(AnswerEvent e);
    public void no(AnswerEvent e);
    public void cancel(AnswerEvent e);
}
```

Specifying Bean Information

The YesNoPanel class itself, as well as the MultiLineLabel, Alignment, AnswerEvent, and AnswerListener classes it relies on, are all a required part of our bean. When an application that uses the bean is shipped, it has to include all five class files. There are other kinds of classes, however, that are often bundled with a bean but not intended for use by the application developer. These classes are used at "design time" by the beanbox tool that manipulates the bean. The bean class itself doesn't refer to any of these auxiliary beanbox classes, so it is not dependent on them, and they don't have to be shipped with the bean in finished products.

The first of these optional, auxiliary classes is a BeanInfo class. As explained earlier, a beanbox discovers the properties, events, and methods exported by a bean through introspection based on the Java Reflection API. A bean developer who wants to provide additional information about a bean, or refine the (somewhat rough) information available through introspection, should define a class that implements the BeanInfo interface to provide that information. The ShowBean class, for example, uses the short descriptions it obtained through a BeanInfo as tooltips in its **Properties** menu.

A BeanInfo class typically subclasses SimpleBeanInfo, which provides a no-op implementation of the BeanInfo interface. When you want to override only one or two methods, it is easier to subclass SimpleBeanInfo than to implement BeanInfo directly. Beanbox tools rely on a naming convention in order to find the BeanInfo class for a given bean: a BeanInfo class should have the same name as the bean, with the string "BeanInfo" appended. Example 15-6 shows an implementation of the YesNoPanelBeanInfo class.

This BeanInfo class specifies a number of pieces of information for our bean:

- An icon that represents the bean.
- A BeanDescriptor object, which includes a reference to a Customizer class for the bean. We'll see an implementation of this class later in the chapter.
- A list of the supported properties of the bean, along with a short description of each one. Some beanbox tools (but not Sun's *beanbox*) display these strings to the user in some useful way.

- A method that returns the most commonly customized property of the bean; this is called the "default" property.
- A reference to a `PropertyEditor` class for one of the properties. We'll see the implementation of this property editor class later in the chapter.

Besides specifying this information, a `BeanInfo` class can also provide information about the methods it defines and the events it generates. The various `FeatureDescriptor` objects that provide information about such things as properties and methods can also include other information not provided by `YesNoPanelBeanInfo`, such as a localized display name that is distinct from the programmatic name.

If `YesNoPanelBeanInfo` is available in your classpath when you run `ShowBean` on the `YesNoPanel` bean, you'll see an icon displayed in the `YesNoPanel` tab, and you'll also see tooltips displayed over items in the **Properties** menu. `ShowBean` will also have access to the custom `PropertyEditor` for the `messageText` property. See Figure 15-1. (Similarly, if the *lib/dt.jar* file from your Java SDK is in your classpath or has been copied to the *jre/lib/ext/* directory, you'll see icons and tooltips for Swing components. "dt" stands for "design time," and the *dt.jar* file contains bean info, icons, and other resources required at design time but not at runtime.)

Example 15-6. YesNoPanelBeanInfo.java

```
package je3.beans;
import java.beans.*;
import java.lang.reflect.*;
import java.awt.*;

/**
 * This BeanInfo class provides additional information about the YesNoPanel
 * bean in addition to what can be obtained through  introspection alone.
 **/
public class YesNoPanelBeanInfo extends SimpleBeanInfo {
    /**
     * Return an icon for the bean.  We should really check the kind argument
     * to see what size icon the beanbox wants, but since we only have one
     * icon to offer, we just return it and let the beanbox deal with it
     **/
    public Image getIcon(int kind) { return loadImage("YesNoPanelIcon.gif"); }


    /**
     * Return a descriptor for the bean itself.  It specifies a customizer
     * for the bean class.  We could also add a description string here
     **/
    public BeanDescriptor getBeanDescriptor() {
        return new BeanDescriptor(YesNoPanel.class,
                                  YesNoPanelCustomizer.class);
    }

    /** This is a convenience method for creating PropertyDescriptor objects */
    static PropertyDescriptor prop(String name, String description) {
        try {
```

Example 15-6. YesNoPanelBeanInfo.java (continued)

```
        PropertyDescriptor p =
            new PropertyDescriptor(name, YesNoPanel.class);
        p.setShortDescription(description);
        return p;
    }
    catch(IntrospectionException e) { return null; }
}

// Initialize a static array of PropertyDescriptor objects that provide
// additional information about the properties supported by the bean.
// By explicitly specifying property descriptors, we are able to provide
// simple help strings for each property; these would not be available to
// the beanbox through simple introspection.  We are also able to register
// a special property editor for the messageText property
static PropertyDescriptor[] props = {
    prop("messageText", "The message text that appears in the bean body"),
    prop("alignment", "The alignment of the message text"),
    prop("yesLabel", "The label for the Yes button"),
    prop("noLabel", "The label for the No button"),
    prop("cancelLabel","The label for the Cancel button"),
    prop("messageFont", "The font for the message"),
    prop("messageColor", "The color of the message text"),
    prop("buttonFont", "The font for the buttons"),
    prop("background", "The background color"),
};
static {
    props[0].setPropertyEditorClass(YesNoPanelMessageEditor.class);
}

/** Return the property descriptors for this bean */
public PropertyDescriptor[] getPropertyDescriptors() { return props; }

/** The message property is most often customized; make it the default */
public int getDefaultPropertyIndex() { return 0; }
}
```

Defining a Simple Property Editor

A bean can also provide auxiliary `PropertyEditor` classes for use by a beanbox tool. `PropertyEditor` is a flexible interface that allows a bean to tell a beanbox how to display and edit the values of certain types of properties.

A beanbox tool always provides simple property editors for common property types, such as strings, numbers, fonts, and colors. If your bean has a property of a nonstandard type, however, you should register a property editor for that type. The easiest way to "register" a property editor is through a simple naming convention. If your type is defined by the class *X*, the editor for it should be defined in the class *X*Editor. Alternatively, you can register a property editor by calling the `PropertyEditorManager.registerEditor()` method, probably from the constructor of your `BeanInfo` class. If you call this method from the bean itself, the bean then depends on the property editor class, so the editor has to be bundled with the bean in applications, which is not desirable. Another way to register a property editor is by using a `PropertyDescriptor` object in a `BeanInfo` class to specify the `PropertyEditor` for a specific property. The `YesNoPanelBeanInfo` class does this for the `messageText` property, for example.

The `PropertyEditor` interface can seem confusing at first. Its methods allow you to define three techniques for displaying the value of a property and two techniques for allowing the user to edit the value of a property. The value of a property can be displayed:

As a string

If you define the `getAsText( )` method, a beanbox can convert a property to a string and display that string to the user.

As an enumerated value

If a property can take only on values from a fixed set of values, you can define the `getTags( )` method to allow a beanbox to display a drop-down menu of allowed values for the property.

In a graphical display

If you define `paintValue( )`, a beanbox can ask the property editor to display the value using some natural graphical format, such as a color swatch for colors. You also need to define `isPaintable( )` to specify that a graphical format is supported.

The two editing techniques are:

String editing

If you define the `setAsText( )` method, a beanbox knows it can simply have the user type a value into a text field and pass that value to `setAsText( )`. If your property editor defines `getTags( )`, it should also define `setAsText( )`, so that a beanbox can set the property value using the individual tag values.

Custom editing

If your property editor defines `getCustomEditor( )`, a beanbox can call it to obtain some kind of GUI component that can be displayed in a dialog box and serve as a custom editor for the property. You also need to define `supportsCustomEditor( )` to specify that custom editing is supported.

The `setValue( )` method of a `PropertyEditor` is called to specify the current value of the property. It is this value that should be converted to a string or graphical representation by `getAsText( )` or `paintValue( )`.

A property editor must maintain a list of event listeners that are interested in changes to the value of the property. The `addPropertyChangeListener( )` and `removePropertyChangeListener( )` methods are standard event-listener registration and removal methods. When a property editor changes the value of a property, either through `setAsText( )` or through a custom editor, it must send a `PropertyChangeEvent` to all registered listeners.

`PropertyEditor` defines the `getJavaInitializationString( )` for use by beanbox tools that generate Java code. This method should return a fragment of Java code that can initialize a variable to the current property value.

Finally, a class that implements the PropertyEditor interface must have a no-argument constructor, so it can be dynamically loaded and instantiated by a beanbox.

Most property editors can be much simpler than this detailed description suggests. In many cases, you can subclass PropertyEditorSupport instead of implementing the PropertyEditor interface directly. This useful class provides no-op implementations of most PropertyEditor methods. It also implements the methods for adding and removing event listeners.

A property that has an enumerated value requires a simple property editor. The alignment property of the YesNoPanel bean is an example of this common type of property. The property has only the three legal values defined by the Alignment class. The AlignmentEditor class shown in Example 15-7 is a property editor that tells a beanbox how to display and edit the value of this property. Because AlignmentEditor follows a JavaBeans naming convention, a beanbox automatically uses it for any property of type Alignment.

Example 15-7. AlignmentEditor.java

```java
package je3.beans;
import java.beans.*;
import java.awt.*;

/**
 * This PropertyEditor defines the enumerated values of the alignment property
 * so that a bean box or IDE can present those values to the user for selection
 **/
public class AlignmentEditor extends PropertyEditorSupport {
    /** Return the list of value names for the enumerated type. */
    public String[] getTags() {
        return new String[] { "left", "center", "right" };
    }

    /** Convert each of those value names into the actual value. */
    public void setAsText(String s) {
        if (s.equals("left")) setValue(Alignment.LEFT);
        else if (s.equals("center")) setValue(Alignment.CENTER);
        else if (s.equals("right")) setValue(Alignment.RIGHT);
        else throw new IllegalArgumentException(s);
    }

    /** This is an important method for code generation. */
    public String getJavaInitializationString() {
        Object o = getValue();
        if (o == Alignment.LEFT)
            return "je3.beans.Alignment.LEFT";
        if (o == Alignment.CENTER)
            return "je3.beans.Alignment.CENTER";
        if (o == Alignment.RIGHT)
            return "je3.beans.Alignment.RIGHT";
        return null;
    }
}
```

Defining a Complex Property Editor

There is another YesNoPanel property value that requires a property editor. The messageText property of YesNoPanel can specify a multiline message to be displayed in the panel. This property requires a property editor because simple beanbox programs like ShowBean don't distinguish between single-line and multiline string types; the JTextField object it uses for text input doesn't allow the user to enter multiple lines of text. For this reason, we define the YesNoPanelMessageEditor class and register it with the PropertyDescriptor for the message property, as shown in Example 15-6.

Example 15-8 shows the definition of this property editor. This is a more complex editor that supports the creation of a custom editor component and graphical display of the value. Note that this example implements PropertyEditor directly, which means that it must handle registration and notification of PropertyChangeListener objects. getCustomEditor() returns an editor component for multiline strings. Figure 15-1 shows this custom editor within a dialog box created by the ShowBean program. Note that the **Ok** button in this figure is part of the ShowBean dialog, not part of the property editor itself.

The paintValue() method displays the value of the messageText property. This multiline value doesn't typically fit in the small rectangle of screen space allowed for the property, so paintValue() displays instructions for popping up the custom editor, which allows the user to inspect and edit the property value. ShowBean does not use the paintValue() method, however.

Example 15-8. YesNoPanelMessageEditor.java

```java
package je3.beans;
import java.beans.*;
import java.awt.*;
import javax.swing.*;
import javax.swing.event.*;

/**
 * This class is a custom editor for the messageText property of the
 * YesNoPanel bean.  It is necessary because the default editor for
 * properties of type String does not allow multi-line strings
 * to be entered.
 */
public class YesNoPanelMessageEditor implements PropertyEditor {
    protected String value;  // The value we will be editing.

    public void setValue(Object o) {  value = (String) o; }
    public Object getValue() { return value; }
    public void setAsText(String s) { value = s; }
    public String getAsText() { return value; }
    public String[ ] getTags() { return null; }  // not enumerated; no tags

    // Say that we allow custom editing.
    public boolean supportsCustomEditor() { return true; }
```

Example 15-8. YesNoPanelMessageEditor.java (continued)

```
// Return the custom editor.  This just creates and returns a TextArea
// wrapped in a JScrollPane to edit the multi-line text.
// But it also registers a listener on the text area to update the value
// as the user types and to fire the property change events that property
// editors are required to fire.
public Component getCustomEditor( ) {
    final JTextArea t = new JTextArea(value, 5, 30); // 5 rows, 30 cols
    t.getDocument( ).addDocumentListener(new DocumentListener( ) {
            public void insertUpdate(DocumentEvent e) { update( ); }
            public void changedUpdate(DocumentEvent e) { update( ); }
            public void removeUpdate(DocumentEvent e) { update( ); }
            public void update( ) {
                value = t.getText( );
                listeners.firePropertyChange(null, null, null);
            }
        });

    return new JScrollPane(t);
}

// Visual display of the value, for use with the custom editor.
// Just print some instructions and hope they fit in the box.
// This could be more sophisticated.
public boolean isPaintable( ) { return true; }
public void paintValue(Graphics g, Rectangle r) {
    g.setClip(r);
    g.drawString("Click to edit...", r.x+5, r.y+15);
}

// Important method for code generators.  Note that it really ought to
// escape any quotes or backslashes in value before returning the string.
public String getJavaInitializationString( ) { return "\"" + value + "\""; }

// This code uses the PropertyChangeSupport class to maintain a list of
// listeners interested in the edits we make to the value.
protected PropertyChangeSupport listeners =new PropertyChangeSupport(this);
public void addPropertyChangeListener(PropertyChangeListener l) {
    listeners.addPropertyChangeListener(l);
}
public void removePropertyChangeListener(PropertyChangeListener l) {
    listeners.removePropertyChangeListener(l);
}
}
```

Defining a Bean Customizer

A bean may want to provide some way for the user of a beanbox program to customize its properties other than by setting them one at a time. A bean can do this by creating a Customizer class for itself and registering the customizer class with the BeanDescriptor object returned by its BeanInfo class, as in Example 15-6.

A customizer must be some kind of GUI component that is suitable for display in a dialog box created by the beanbox. In addition, a customizer must implement the `Customizer` interface. This interface consists of methods for adding and removing property change event listeners and a `setObject()` method that the beanbox calls to tell the customizer what bean object it is customizing. Whenever the user makes a change to the bean through the customizer, the customizer sends a `PropertyChangeEvent` to any interested listeners. Finally, like a property editor, a customizer must have a no-argument constructor, so it can easily be instantiated by a beanbox.

Example 15-9 shows a customizer for our `YesNoPanel` bean. This customizer displays a panel that has the same layout as a `YesNoPanel`, but it substitutes a `TextArea` object for the message display and three `TextField` objects for the three buttons that the dialog can display. These text entry areas allow the user to enter values for the `messageText`, `yesLabel`, `noLabel`, and `cancelLabel` properties. Figure 15-2 shows this customizer panel displayed within a dialog box created by a beanbox program. Again, note that the **Done** button is part of the *beanbox* dialog, not part of the customizer itself. `ShowBean` does not support the use of customizers, so this example cannot be demonstrated with that program.

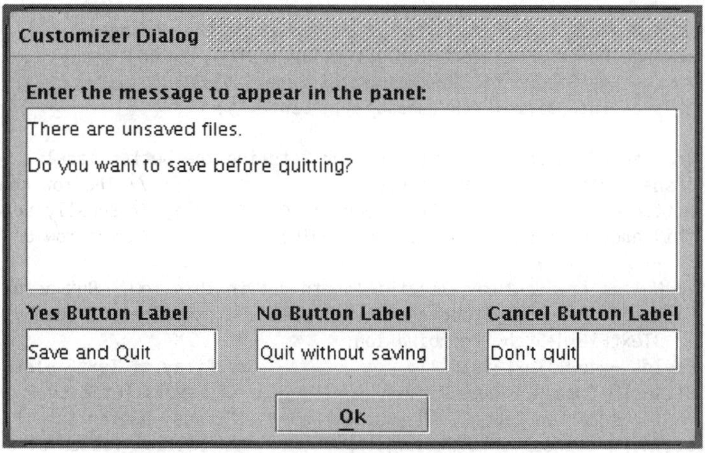

Figure 15-2. The customizer dialog for the YesNoPanel bean

Example 15-9. YesNoPanelCustomizer.java

```
package je3.beans;
import java.awt.*;
import javax.swing.*;
import javax.swing.event.*;
import javax.swing.text.*;
import java.beans.*;

/**
 * This class is a customizer for the YesNoPanel bean.  It displays a
 * JTextArea and three JTextFields where the user can enter the main message
```

Example 15-9. YesNoPanelCustomizer.java (continued)

```
* and the labels for each of the three buttons.  It does not allow the
* alignment property to be set.
**/
public class YesNoPanelCustomizer extends JComponent
    implements Customizer, DocumentListener
{
    protected YesNoPanel bean;      // The bean being customized
    protected JTextArea message;    // For entering the message
    protected JTextField fields[ ]; // For entering button text

    // The bean box calls this method to tell us what object to customize.
    // This method will always be called before the customizer is displayed,
    // so it is safe to create the customizer GUI here.
    public void setObject(Object o) {
        bean = (YesNoPanel)o;    // save the object we're customizing

        // Put a label at the top of the panel.
        this.setLayout(new BorderLayout( ));
        this.add(new JLabel("Enter the message to appear in the panel:"),
                BorderLayout.NORTH);

        // And a big text area below it for entering the message.
        message = new JTextArea(bean.getMessageText( ), 5, 35);
        message.getDocument( ).addDocumentListener(this);
        this.add(new JScrollPane(message), "Center");

        // Then add a row of textfields for entering the button labels.
        JPanel buttonbox = new JPanel( );                        // The row container
        buttonbox.setLayout(new GridLayout(1, 0, 25, 10)); // Equally spaced
        this.add(buttonbox, BorderLayout.SOUTH);                 // Put row on bottom

        // Now go create three JTextFields to put in this row.  But actually
        // position a JLabel above each, so create a container for each
        // JTextField+JLabel combination.
        fields = new JTextField[3];                      // Array of TextFields.
        String[ ] labels = new String[ ] {        // Labels for each.
            "Yes Button Label", "No Button Label", "Cancel Button Label"};
        String[ ] values = new String[ ] {        // Initial values of each.
            bean.getYesLabel( ), bean.getNoLabel( ), bean.getCancelLabel( )};
        for(int i = 0; i < 3; i++) {
            JPanel p = new JPanel( );                      // Create a container.
            p.setLayout(new BorderLayout( ));        // Give it a BorderLayout.
            p.add(new JLabel(labels[i]), "North"); // Put a label on the top.
            fields[i] = new JTextField(values[i]); // Create the text field.
            p.add(fields[i], "Center");              // Put it below the label.
            buttonbox.add(p);                        // Add container to row.
            // register listener for the JTextField
            fields[i].getDocument( ).addDocumentListener(this);
        }
    }
```

Example 15-9. YesNoPanelCustomizer.java (continued)

```
    // Give ourselves some space around the outside of the panel.
    public Insets getInsets() { return new Insets(10, 10, 10, 10); }

    // These are the methods defined by the DocumentListener interface. Whenever
    // the user types a character in the JTextArea or JTextFields, they will be
    // called.  They all just call the internal method update() below.
    public void changedUpdate(DocumentEvent e) { update(e); }
    public void insertUpdate(DocumentEvent e) { update(e); }
    public void removeUpdate(DocumentEvent e) { update(e); }

    // Updates the appropriate property of the bean and fires a
    // property changed event, as all customizers are required to do.
    // Note that we are not required to fire an event for every keystroke.
    void update(DocumentEvent e) {
        Document doc = e.getDocument();       // What document was updated?
        if (doc == message.getDocument())
            bean.setMessageText(message.getText());
        else if (doc == fields[0].getDocument())
            bean.setYesLabel(fields[0].getText());
        else if (doc == fields[1].getDocument())
            bean.setNoLabel(fields[1].getText());
        else if (doc == fields[2].getDocument())
            bean.setCancelLabel(fields[2].getText());
        listeners.firePropertyChange(null, null, null);
    }

    // This code uses the PropertyChangeSupport class to maintain a list of
    // listeners interested in the edits we make to the bean.
    protected PropertyChangeSupport listeners =new PropertyChangeSupport(this);
    public void addPropertyChangeListener(PropertyChangeListener l) {
        listeners.addPropertyChangeListener(l);
    }
    public void removePropertyChangeListener(PropertyChangeListener l) {
        listeners.removePropertyChangeListener(l);
    }
}
```

Manipulating Beans

The ShowBean class of Chapter 11 is a simple beanbox for displaying and experimenting with individual beans. The ShowBean code listed in Example 11-30 is concerned primarily with the creation of a GUI, and the key bean-manipulation methods are handled by a separate Bean class. Now that we've seen how to write a bean and its auxiliary classes, we're ready to tackle this Bean class itself; it is listed in Example 15-10.

An instance of the Bean class represents a single bean and its associated BeanInfo. Bean defines methods for querying and setting bean properties and for querying and invoking bean commands. (It defines a command as a method with no arguments and no return values.) In some ways, Bean can be considered a simplified interface to the BeanInfo class. Note that the java.beans package does not define any class named Bean: JavaBeans are not required to implement any Bean interface or extend any Bean superclass, so we've appropriated this class name for our own use here.

The Bean class has a public constructor that uses the java.beans.Introspector class to obtain BeanInfo for the bean object you pass to it. Bean also defines three static factory methods that you can use to instantiate the bean object instead of creating it yourself: forClassName( ) instantiates a named class to create the bean; fromSerializedStream( ) reads a serialized bean object from a java.io. ObjectInputStream (see Chapter 10); and fromPersistentStream( ) uses the Java-Beans persistence mechanism to read a bean instance from a stream using java. beans.XMLDecoder. XMLDecoder and the corresponding XMLEncoder class (demonstrated in Example 11-30) are new in Java 1.4 and are usually a better choice for saving the persistent state of beans: although the storage format is XML-based, it is usually more compact than the binary serialization format, and it is based on the public API of the bean rather than the private implementation, which is subject to versioning problems.

Pay attention to the ways Bean sets named properties. The setPropertyValue( ) method is passed a property name and value as strings. It checks whether the type of the named property is one that it knows how to convert a string to, and, if so, it converts the string and sets the property. If it does not know the type of the property, it attempts to find and use a PropertyEditor for that type, but this does not work for editors that implement getCustomEditor( ) instead of setAsText( ).

ShowBean uses setPropertyValue( ) to set property values specified on the command line. It does not use this method to set properties from its Properties menu, however; in this case, ShowBean calls getPropertyEditor( ). getPropertyEditor( ) does not return a PropertyEditor object directly—as we noted when implementing property editors, the PropertyEditor interface is confusing and hard to work with. Instead, getPropertyEditor( ) looks for a PropertyEditor for the named property and, if it finds one, returns a Component that is hooked up to the PropertyEditor. The Component is suitable for display in a dialog box or panel: when the user interacts with the returned component, the component interacts with the PropertyEditor to set the property.

Example 15-10. Bean.java

```
package je3.beans;
import java.awt.*;
import java.awt.event.*;
import javax.swing.*;
import javax.swing.event.*;
import java.beans.*;
import java.lang.reflect.*;
import java.util.*;
import java.util.List;  // explicit import to disambiguate from java.awt.List
import java.io.*;

/**
 * This class encapsulates a bean object and its BeanInfo.
 * It is a key part of the ShowBean "beanbox" program, and demonstrates
```

Example 15-10. Bean.java (continued)

```
 * how to instantiate and instrospect beans, and how to use reflection to
 * set properties and invoke methods.  It also illustrates how to work with
 * PropertyEditor classes.
 */
public class Bean {
    Object bean;        // The bean object we encapsulate
    BeanInfo info;      // Information about beans of that type
    Map properties;     // Map property names to PropertyDescriptor objects
    Map commands;       // Map command names to MethodDescriptor objects
    boolean expert;     // Whether to include "expert" properties and commands

    // Utility object used when invoking no-arg methods
    static final Object[ ] NOARGS = new Object[0];

    // This constructor introspects the specified component.
    // Typically you'll use one of the static factory methods instead.
    public Bean(Object bean, boolean expert) throws IntrospectionException {
        this.bean = bean;       // The object to instrospect
        this.expert = expert;   // Is the end-user an expert?

        // Introspect to get BeanInfo for the bean
        info = Introspector.getBeanInfo(bean.getClass( ));

        // Now create a map of property names to PropertyDescriptor objects
        properties = new HashMap( );
        PropertyDescriptor[ ] props = info.getPropertyDescriptors( );
        for(int i = 0; i < props.length; i++) {
            // Skip hidden properties, indexed properties, and expert
            // properties unless the end-user is an expert.
            if (props[i].isHidden( )) continue;
            if (props[i] instanceof IndexedPropertyDescriptor) continue;
            if (!expert && props[i].isExpert( )) continue;
            properties.put(props[i].getDisplayName( ), props[i]);
        }

        // Create a map of command names to MethodDescriptor objects
        // Commands are methods with no arguments and no return value.
        // We skip commands defined in Object, Component, Container, and
        // JComponent because they contain methods that meet this definition
        // but are not intended for end-users.
        commands = new HashMap( );
        MethodDescriptor[ ] methods = info.getMethodDescriptors( );
        for(int i = 0; i < methods.length; i++) {
            // Skip it if it is hidden or expert (unless user is expert)
            if (methods[i].isHidden( )) continue;
            if (!expert && methods[i].isExpert( )) continue;
            Method m = methods[i].getMethod( );
            // Skip it if it has arguments or a return value
            if (m.getParameterTypes( ).length > 0) continue;
            if (m.getReturnType( ) != Void.TYPE) continue;
            // Check the declaring class and skip useless superclasses
            Class c = m.getDeclaringClass( );
```

JavaBeans

Example 15-10. Bean.java (continued)

```
            if (c==JComponent.class || c==Component.class ||
                c==Container.class || c==Object.class)  continue;
            // Get the unqualifed classname to prefix method name with
            String classname = c.getName();
            classname = classname.substring(classname.lastIndexOf('.')+1);
            // Otherwise, this is a valid command, so add it to the list
            commands.put(classname + "." + m.getName(),  methods[i]);
        }
    }

    // Factory method to instantiate a bean from a named class
    public static Bean forClassName(String className, boolean expert)
        throws ClassNotFoundException, InstantiationException,
               IllegalAccessException, IntrospectionException
    {
        // Load the named bean class
        Class c = Class.forName(className);
        // Instantiate it to create the component instance
        Object bean = c.newInstance();

        return new Bean(bean, expert);
    }

    // Factory method to read a serialized bean
    public static Bean fromSerializedStream(ObjectInputStream in,
                                            boolean expert)
        throws IOException, ClassNotFoundException, IntrospectionException
    {
        return new Bean(in.readObject(), expert);
    }

    // Factory method to read a persistent XMLEncoded bean from a stream.
    public static Bean fromPersistentStream(InputStream in, boolean expert)
        throws IntrospectionException
    {
        return new Bean(new XMLDecoder(in).readObject(), expert);
    }

    // Return the bean object itself.
    public Object getBean() { return bean; }

    // Return the name of the bean
    public String getDisplayName() {
        return info.getBeanDescriptor().getDisplayName();
    }

    // Return an icon for the bean
    public Image getIcon() {
        Image icon = info.getIcon(BeanInfo.ICON_COLOR_32x32);
        if (icon != null) return icon;
        else return info.getIcon(BeanInfo.ICON_COLOR_16x16);
    }
```

Example 15-10. Bean.java (continued)

```
    // Return a short description for the bean
    public String getShortDescription( ) {
        return info.getBeanDescriptor( ).getShortDescription( );
    }

    // Return an alphabetized list of property names for the bean
    // Note the elegant use of the Collections Framework
    public List getPropertyNames( ) {
        // Make a List from a Set (from a Map), and sort it before returning.
        List names = new ArrayList(properties.keySet( ));
        Collections.sort(names);
        return names;
    }

    // Return an alphabetized list of command names for the bean.
    public List getCommandNames( ) {
        List names = new ArrayList(commands.keySet( ));
        Collections.sort(names);
        return names;
    }

    // Get a description of a property; useful for tooltips
    public String getPropertyDescription(String name) {
        PropertyDescriptor p = (PropertyDescriptor) properties.get(name);
        if (p == null) throw new IllegalArgumentException(name);
        return p.getShortDescription( );
    }

    // Get a description of a command; useful for tooltips
    public String getCommandDescription(String name) {
        MethodDescriptor m = (MethodDescriptor) commands.get(name);
        if (m == null) throw new IllegalArgumentException(name);
        return m.getShortDescription( );
    }

    // Return true if the named property is read-only
    public boolean isReadOnly(String name) {
        PropertyDescriptor p = (PropertyDescriptor) properties.get(name);
        if (p == null) throw new IllegalArgumentException(name);
        return p.getWriteMethod( ) == null;
    }

    // Invoke the named (no-arg) method of the bean
    public void invokeCommand(String name)
        throws IllegalAccessException, InvocationTargetException
    {
        MethodDescriptor method = (MethodDescriptor) commands.get(name);
        if (method == null) throw new IllegalArgumentException(name);
        Method m = method.getMethod( );
        m.invoke(bean, NOARGS);
    }
```

Example 15-10. Bean.java (continued)

```java
// Return the value of the named property as a string
// This method relies on the toString() method of the returned value.
// A more robust implementation might use a PropertyEditor.
public String getPropertyValue(String name)
    throws IllegalAccessException, InvocationTargetException
{
    PropertyDescriptor p = (PropertyDescriptor) properties.get(name);
    if (p == null) throw new IllegalArgumentException(name);
    Method m = p.getReadMethod();              // property accessor method
    Object value = m.invoke(bean, NOARGS);   // invoke it to get value
    if (value == null) return "null";
    return value.toString();                   // use the toString method()
}

// Set the named property to the named value, if possible.
// This method knows how to convert a handful of well-known types.  It
// attempts to use a PropertyEditor for types it does not know about but
// this only works for editors that have working setAsText() methods.
public void setPropertyValue(String name, String value)
    throws IllegalAccessException, InvocationTargetException
{
    // Get the descriptor for the named property
    PropertyDescriptor p = (PropertyDescriptor) properties.get(name);
    if (p == null || isReadOnly(name))  // Make sure we can set it
        throw new IllegalArgumentException(name);

    Object v;  // Store the converted string value here.
    Class type = p.getPropertyType();

    // Convert common types in well-known ways
    if (type == String.class) v = value;
    else if (type == boolean.class) v = Boolean.valueOf(value);
    else if (type == byte.class) v = Byte.valueOf(value);
    else if (type == char.class) v = new Character(value.charAt(0));
    else if (type == short.class) v = Short.valueOf(value);
    else if (type == int.class) v = Integer.valueOf(value);
    else if (type == long.class) v = Long.valueOf(value);
    else if (type == float.class) v = Float.valueOf(value);
    else if (type == double.class) v = Double.valueOf(value);
    else if (type == Color.class) v = Color.decode(value);
    else if (type == Font.class) v = Font.decode(value);
    else {
        // Try to find a property editor for unknown types
        PropertyEditor editor = PropertyEditorManager.findEditor(type);
        if (editor != null) {
            editor.setAsText(value);
            v = editor.getValue();
        }
        // Otherwise, give up.
        else throw new UnsupportedOperationException("Can't set " +
                                                "properties of type "+
                                                type.getName());
    }
}
```

Example 15-10. Bean.java (continued)

```
        // Now get the Method object for the property setter method and
        // invoke it on the bean object, passing the converted value.
        Method setter = p.getWriteMethod();
        setter.invoke(bean, new Object[] { v });
    }

    // Return a component that allows the user to edit the property value.
    // The component is live and changes the property value in real time;
    // there is no need to call setPropertyValue().
    public Component getPropertyEditor(final String name)
        throws IllegalAccessException, InvocationTargetException,
               InstantiationException
    {
        // Get the descriptor for the named property; final for inner classes.
        final PropertyDescriptor p = (PropertyDescriptor) properties.get(name);
        if (p == null || isReadOnly(name))  // Make sure we can edit it.
            throw new IllegalArgumentException(name);

        // Find a PropertyEditor for the property
        final PropertyEditor editor;  // final for inner class use
        if (p.getPropertyEditorClass() != null) {
            // If there is a custom editor for this property, instantiate one.
            editor = (PropertyEditor)p.getPropertyEditorClass().newInstance();
        }
        else {
            // Otherwise, look up an editor based on the property type
            Class type = p.getPropertyType();
            editor = PropertyEditorManager.findEditor(type);
            // If there is no editor, give up
            if (editor == null)
                throw new UnsupportedOperationException("Can't set " +
                                                "properties of type " +
                                                type.getName());
        }

        // Get the property accessor methods for this property so we can
        // query the initial value and set the edited value
        final Method getter = p.getReadMethod();
        final Method setter = p.getWriteMethod();

        // Use Java reflection to find the current property value. Then tell
        // the property editor about it.
        Object currentValue = getter.invoke(bean, NOARGS);
        editor.setValue(currentValue);

        // If the PropertyEditor has a custom editor, then we'll just return
        // that custom editor component from this method. User changes to the
        // component change the value in the PropertyEditor, which generates
        // a PropertyChangeEvent. We register a listener so that these changes
        // set the property on the bean as well.
        if (editor.supportsCustomEditor()) {
            final Component editComponent = editor.getCustomEditor();
```

Example 15-10. Bean.java (continued)

```
                // Note that we register the listener on the PropertyEditor, not
                // on its custom editor Component.
                editor.addPropertyChangeListener(new PropertyChangeListener( ) {
                        public void propertyChange(PropertyChangeEvent e) {
                            try {
                                // Pass edited value to property setter
                                Object editedValue = editor.getValue( );
                                setter.invoke(bean, new Object[ ] { editedValue});
                            }
                            catch(Exception ex) {
                                JOptionPane.showMessageDialog(editComponent,
                                                ex, ex.getClass( ).getName( ),
                                                JOptionPane.ERROR_MESSAGE);
                            }
                        }
                });
            return editComponent;
        }

        // Otherwise, if the PropertyEditor is for an enumerated type based
        // on a fixed list of possible values, then return a JComboBox
        // component that allows the user to select one of the values.
        final String[ ] tags = editor.getTags( );
        if (tags != null) {
            // Create the component
            final JComboBox combobox = new JComboBox(tags);
            // Use the current value of the property as the currently selected
            // item in the combo box.
            combobox.setSelectedItem(editor.getAsText( ));
            // Add a listener to hook the combo box up to the property. When
            // the user selects an item, set the property value.
            combobox.addItemListener(new ItemListener( ) {
                    public void itemStateChanged(ItemEvent e) {
                        // Ignore deselect events
                        if (e.getStateChange( ) == ItemEvent.DESELECTED) return;
                        try {
                            // Get the user's selected string from combo box
                            String selectedTag =
                                (String)combobox.getSelectedItem( );
                            // Tell the editor about this string value
                            editor.setAsText(selectedTag);
                            // Ask the editor to convert to the property type
                            Object editedValue = editor.getValue( );
                            // Pass this value to the property setter method
                            setter.invoke(bean, new Object[ ] { editedValue });
                        }
                        catch(Exception ex) {
                            JOptionPane.showMessageDialog(combobox,
                                                ex, ex.getClass( ).getName( ),
                                                JOptionPane.ERROR_MESSAGE);
```

Example 15-10. Bean.java (continued)

```
                            }
                        }
                    });
                return combobox;
            }

            // Otherwise, property type is not enumerated, and we use a JTextField
            // to allow the user to enter arbitrary text for conversion by the
            // setAsText( ) method of the PropertyEditor
            final JTextField textfield = new JTextField( );
            // Display the current value of the property in the field
            textfield.setText(editor.getAsText( ));
            // Hook the JTextField up to the PropertyEditor.
            textfield.addActionListener(new ActionListener( ) {
                // This is called when the user strikes the Enter key
                public void actionPerformed(ActionEvent e) {
                    try {
                        // Get the user's input from the text field
                        String newText = textfield.getText( );
                        // Tell the editor about it
                        editor.setAsText(newText);
                        // Ask the editor to convert to the property type
                        Object editedValue = editor.getValue( );
                        // Pass this value to the property setter method
                        setter.invoke(bean, new Object[ ] { editedValue });
                    }
                    catch(Exception ex) {
                        JOptionPane.showMessageDialog(textfield,
                                        ex, ex.getClass( ).getName( ),
                                        JOptionPane.ERROR_MESSAGE);
                    }
                }
            });
        return textfield;
        }
    }
}
```

Exercises

Exercise 15-1. Chapters 10, 12, and 13 contain examples of Swing components that allow the user to scribble with the mouse. Choose one of these classes, rename it to ScribbleBean, and package it in a JAR file (along with any other example classes it may require). Now install it in a beanbox application of your choice, to demonstrate that it works. Give your bean an erase( ) method that erases the scribbles, and use the beanbox to create a push button of some sort that invokes this method.

Exercise 15-2. Modify your ScribbleBean bean so that it has color and line-width properties that specify the color and width of the lines used for the scribbles. Repackage the bean and test the properties in a beanbox.

Exercise 15-3. An application that uses a ScribbleBean bean might want to be notified each time the user completes a single "stroke" of the scribble (i.e., each time the user clicks, drags, and then releases the mouse). For example, an application might make an off-screen copy of the scribble after each stroke, so that it could implement an undo facility. In order to provide this kind of notification, modify your ScribbleBean bean to support a "stroke" event. Define a simple StrokeEvent class and StrokeListener interface. Modify the ScribbleBean bean so that it allows registration and removal of StrokeListener objects, and so that it notifies all registered listeners each time a stroke of the scribble is complete. Regenerate the bean's JAR file so that it includes the StrokeEvent and StrokeListener class files.

Exercise 15-4. Define a BeanInfo subclass for the ScribbleBean bean. This class should provide information about the erase( ) method, the color and width properties, and the stroke event defined by the bean. The BeanInfo class should use the FeatureDescriptor.setShortDescription( ) method to provide simple, descriptive strings for the bean itself and its method, properties, and event.

Exercise 15-5. Modify the Bean class of Example 15-10 so that it can return a customizer object for the bean it represents, if a customizer class exists. Modify the ShowBean class of Example 11-30 to include a **Customize...** button in its **File** menu that displays the customizer. This menu item should be disabled when no customizer exists. Test your changes with the YesNoPanel bean and its customizer class.

16

Applets

An applet, as the name implies, is a kind of mini-application, designed to be run by a web browser or in the context of some other "applet viewer." Java 1.0 was released in the early days of the World Wide Web, and it was applets that drove the adoption of the language. In those days (late 1995 and early 1996) web browsers could not display animated GIFs, much less Flash animations, and client-side scripting languages like JavaScript did not exist yet. At that time, the ability to embed a Java applet on a web page opened up a world of interactive web content that was not possible in any other way. Browser vendors responded by bundling Java with their browsers. Java programming became wildly popular, and programmers put silly animations on their web pages. In the first edition of this book, this chapter on applets was right up front as Chapter 3.

Times have changed. Applets no longer rule the Web. Dynamic web content is usually provided by Flash animations and JavaScript-driven DHTML (see my book *JavaScript: The Definitive Guide* for details). Applets have found a niche in large high-end applications, such as delivering streaming stock quotes, and for providing scientific or mathematical visualizations in online course notes, but they are no longer commonplace. The Java platform has grown too big to bundle with web browsers, and Java support is now relegated to plug-in status. And this chapter has been banished to its relatively obscure present location.

This chapter demonstrates the techniques of applet writing. It proceeds from a trivial "Hello World" applet to more sophisticated applets. Along the way, it explains how to:

- Draw graphics in your applet
- Handle and respond to simple user input
- Read and use values of applet parameters, allowing customization of an applet
- Load and display images and load and play sounds

Introduction to Applets

Applets differ from regular applications in a number of ways. One of the most important is that there are a number of security restrictions on what applets are allowed to do. An applet often consists of untrusted code, so it cannot be allowed access to the local filesystem, for example.

All applets subclass java.applet.Applet, which inherits from java.awt.Panel and java.awt.Component. (In Java 1.2 and later, you can also subclass an applet from the JApplet Swing component.) So creating an applet is more like subclassing a GUI component than it is like writing an application. In particular, an applet does not have a main( ) method or other single entry point from which the program starts running. Instead, to write an applet, you subclass Applet and override a number of standard methods. At appropriate times, under well-defined circumstances, the web browser or applet viewer invokes the methods you have defined. The applet is not in control of the thread of execution; it simply responds when the browser or viewer tells it to. For this reason, the methods you write must take the necessary action and return promptly; they are not allowed to enter time-consuming (or infinite) loops. To perform a time-consuming or repetitive task, such as animation, an applet must create its own thread, over which it does have complete control.

The task of writing an applet, then, comes down to defining the appropriate methods. A number of these methods are defined by the Applet class:

init( )
> Called when the applet is first loaded into the browser or viewer. It typically performs applet initialization, in preference to a constructor method. (An applet is allowed to have a constructor, but it must not require any arguments.)

destroy( )
> Called when the applet is about to be unloaded from the browser or viewer. It should free any resources, other than memory, that the applet has allocated. Applets often do not need to define this.

start( )
> Called when the applet becomes visible and should start doing whatever it does. Often used to start animation threads, for example.

stop( )
> This method tells the applet to stop doing whatever it does. A web browser might invoke this method when an applet is scrolled off the visible region of the web page, for example.

getAppletInfo( )
> Called to get information about the applet. Should return a string suitable for display in a dialog box. Most web browsers never call this method, so most applets don't implement it.

getParameterInfo( )
> Called to obtain information about the parameters the applet responds to. Should return strings describing those parameters. Like getAppletInfo( ), this method is usually not implemented.

In addition to these Applet methods, there are a number of other methods, inherited from superclasses of Applet, that the browser invokes at appropriate times, and which an applet should override. The most obvious of these methods is paint( ) (or paintComponent( ) for Swing-based applets that extend JApplet), which the browser or viewer invokes to ask the applet to draw itself on the screen. A related method is print( ), which an applet should override if it wants to display itself on paper differently than it does on the screen.

The Applet class also defines some methods that are commonly used (but not overridden) by applets:

getImage( )
  Loads an image file from the network and returns a java.awt.Image object.

getAudioClip( )
  Loads a sound clip from the network and returns a java.applet.AudioClip object.

getParameter( )
  Looks up and returns the value of a named parameter, specified in the HTML file that refers to the applet with the <param> tag.

getCodeBase( )
  Returns the base URL from which the applet class file was loaded.

getDocumentBase( )
  Returns the base URL of the HTML file that refers to the applet.

showStatus( )
  Displays a message in the status line of the browser or applet viewer.

getAppletContext( )
  Returns the java.applet.AppletContext object for the applet. AppletContext defines the useful showDocument( ) method that asks the browser to load and display a new web page.

A First Applet

Example 16-1 shows what is probably the simplest possible applet you can write in Java. Figure 16-1 shows the output it produces. This example introduces the paint( ) method, which is invoked by the applet viewer (or web browser) when the applet needs to be drawn. This method should perform graphical output— such as drawing text or lines or displaying images—for your applet. The argument to paint( ) is a java.awt.Graphics object that you use to do the drawing.

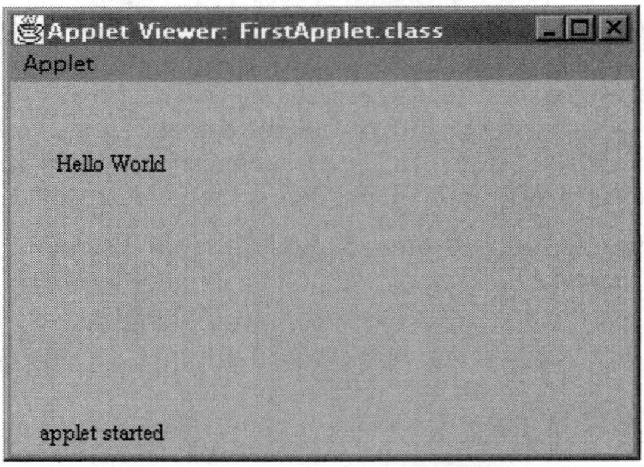

Figure 16-1. A simple applet

Example 16-1. FirstApplet.java

```java
package je3.applet;
import java.applet.*;    // Don't forget this import statement!
import java.awt.*;       // Or this one for the graphics!

/** This applet just says "Hello World" */
public class FirstApplet extends Applet {
    // This method displays the applet.
    public void paint(Graphics g) {
        g.drawString("Hello World", 25, 50);
    }
}
```

To display an applet, you need an HTML file that references it. Here is an HTML fragment that can be used with this first applet:

```
<applet code="je3.applet.FirstApplet.class"
        codebase="../../"
        width=150 height=100>
</applet>
```

With an HTML file that references the applet, you can now view the applet with an applet viewer or web browser. Note that the WIDTH and HEIGHT attributes of this HTML tag are required. For most applet examples in this book, I show only the Java code, not the corresponding HTML file that goes with it. Typically, that HTML file contains a tag as simple as the one shown here.

A Clock Applet

Example 16-2 is an applet that displays the current time, as shown in Figure 16-2, and updates it once every second. Unlike Example 16-1, which defines a paint( ) method and does its own text drawing with Graphics.drawString( ), this example uses a java.awt.Label component to do the drawing. While it is common for applets to do their own drawing with a paint( ) method, it is also important to remember that applets extend java.awt.Panel and can contain any type of GUI components. Clock defines an init( ) method that creates and configures the Label component.

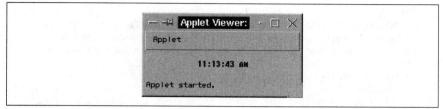

Figure 16-2. A clock applet

In order to update the time every second, Clock implements the Runnable interface and creates a Thread that runs the run( ) method. The applet's start( ) and stop( ) methods are invoked by the browser when the applet becomes visible or is hidden; they start and stop the thread. (Although the example is written to use Java 1.1, it does not rely on the Thread.stop( ) method, which was deprecated in Java 1.2.)

Finally, the Clock applet implements getAppletInfo( ) to provide information about the applet. Sun's *appletviewer* tool is able to display this information, but most web browsers don't.

Example 16-2. Clock.java

```java
package je3.applet;
import java.applet.*;        // Don't forget this import statement!
import java.awt.*;           // Or this one for the graphics!
import java.util.Date;       // To obtain the current time
import java.text.DateFormat; // For displaying the time

/**
 * This applet displays the time, and updates it every second
 **/
public class Clock extends Applet implements Runnable {
    Label time;               // A component to display the time in
    DateFormat timeFormat;    // This object converts the time to a string
    Thread timer;             // The thread that updates the time
    volatile boolean running; // A flag used to stop the thread

    /**
     * The init method is called when the browser first starts the applet.
     * It sets up the Label component and obtains a DateFormat object
     **/
    public void init( ) {
        time = new Label( );
        time.setFont(new Font("helvetica", Font.BOLD, 12));
        time.setAlignment(Label.CENTER);
        setLayout(new BorderLayout( ));
```

Example 16-2. Clock.java (continued)

```java
        add(time, BorderLayout.CENTER);
        timeFormat = DateFormat.getTimeInstance(DateFormat.MEDIUM);
    }

    /**
     * This browser calls this method to tell the applet to start running.
     * Here, we create and start a thread that will update the time each
     * second.  Note that we take care never to have more than one thread
     **/
    public void start() {
        running = true;                    // Set the flag
        if (timer == null) {               // If we don't already have a thread
            timer = new Thread(this);      // Then create one
            timer.start();                 // And start it running
        }
    }

    /**
     * This method implements Runnable.  It is the body of the thread.  Once a
     * second, it updates the text of the Label to display the current time.
     * AWT and Swing components are not, in general, thread-safe, and should
     * typically only be updated from the event-handling thread. We can get
     * away with using a separate thread here because there is no event
     * handling in this applet, and this component will never be modified by
     * any other thread.
     **/
    public void run() {
        while(running) {        // Loop until we're stopped
            // Get current time, convert to a String, and display in the Label
            time.setText(timeFormat.format(new Date()));
            // Now wait 1000 milliseconds
            try { Thread.sleep(1000); }
            catch (InterruptedException e) { }
        }
        // If the thread exits, set it to null so we can create a new one
        // if start() is called again.
        timer = null;
    }

    /**
     * The browser calls this method to tell the applet that it is not visible
     * and should not run.  It sets a flag that tells the run() method to exit
     **/
    public void stop() { running = false; }

    /**
     * Returns information about the applet for display by the applet viewer
     **/
    public String getAppletInfo() {
        return "Clock applet Copyright (c) 2000 by David Flanagan";
    }
}
```

A Timer Applet

Example 16-3 is a full-featured applet named Countdown. As illustrated in Figure 16-3, it displays an amount of remaining time in minutes and seconds and counts backward down to zero. When it reaches zero, it can play an optional sound and also optionally make the web browser load a new page. The applet demonstrates all of the applet methods listed at the beginning of this chapter, including getParameter( ), getImage( ), getAudioClip( ), showStatus( ), and AppletContext.showDocument( ). It also includes event-handling methods to pause the countdown while the mouse is over the timer. Finally, it demonstrates how to write a Swing-based applet by extending JApplet (you may notice an increase in applet start-up time with the switch to Swing and its attendant overhead). Instead of using a Thread as the Clock applet did, this Countdown applet uses the javax.swing.Timer class.

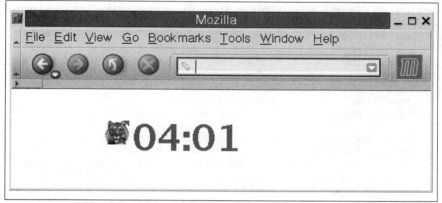

Figure 16-3. The Countdown applet

An important feature of this applet is its configurability: it uses getParameter( ) to read configuration parameters specified in the <param> tags inside the <applet> tag. Invoke the applet with HTML code like this:

```
<applet code="je3/applet/Countdown.class"
        codebase="../../" width=400 height=100>
  <param name="minutes" value="5">           <!-- Count down from 05:00 -->
  <param name="font" value="helvetica-bold-48"> <!-- Use a big bold font -->
  <param name="foreground" value="#0000ff">   <!-- and blue text-->
  <param name="background" value="#ffffff">   <!-- on white -->
  <param name="image" value="clock.gif">      <!-- with an image -->
  <param name="sound" value="beep.au">        <!-- and an alarm bell. -->
  <!-- Where to go when time is up.  Here we just display a dialog box -->
  <param name="newpage" value="javascript:void alert('times up!');">
</applet>
```

Example 16-3. Countdown.java

```
package je3.applet;
import java.applet.*;
import java.awt.*;
import java.awt.event.*;
import javax.swing.*;
import javax.swing.Timer;  // not java.util.Timer
import java.text.NumberFormat;
import java.net.*;

/**
 * An applet that counts down from a specified time. When it reaches 00:00,
 * it optionally plays a sound and optionally moves the browser to a new page.
 * Place the mouse over the applet to pause the count; move it off to resume.
 * This class demonstrates most applet methods and features.
 **/
public class Countdown extends JApplet implements ActionListener, MouseListener
{
    long remaining;       // How many milliseconds remain in the countdown.
    long lastUpdate;      // When count was last updated
    JLabel label;         // Displays the count
    Timer timer;          // Updates the count every second
    NumberFormat format;  // Format minutes:seconds with leading zeros
    Image image;          // Image to display along with the time
    AudioClip sound;      // Sound to play when we reach 00:00

    // Called when the applet is first loaded
    public void init() {
        // Figure out how long to count for by reading the "minutes" parameter
        // defined in a <param> tag inside the <applet> tag.  Convert to ms.
        String minutes = getParameter("minutes");
        if (minutes != null) remaining = Integer.parseInt(minutes) * 60000;
        else remaining = 600000; // 10 minutes by default

        // Create a JLabel to display remaining time, and set some properties.
        label = new JLabel();
        label.setHorizontalAlignment(SwingConstants.CENTER);
        label.setOpaque(true);   // So label draws the background color

        // Read some parameters for this JLabel object
        String font = getParameter("font");
        String foreground = getParameter("foreground");
        String background = getParameter("background");
        String imageURL = getParameter("image");

        // Set label properties based on those parameters
        if (font != null) label.setFont(Font.decode(font));
        if (foreground != null) label.setForeground(Color.decode(foreground));
        if (background != null) label.setBackground(Color.decode(background));
        if (imageURL != null) {
            // Load the image, and save it so we can release it later
            image = getImage(getDocumentBase(), imageURL);
```

Example 16-3. Countdown.java (continued)

```java
        // Now display the image in the JLabel.
        label.setIcon(new ImageIcon(image));
    }

    // Now add the label to the applet. Like JFrame and JDialog, JApplet
    // has a content pane that you add children to
    getContentPane().add(label, BorderLayout.CENTER);

    // Get an optional AudioClip to play when the count expires
    String soundURL = getParameter("sound");
    if (soundURL != null) sound=getAudioClip(getDocumentBase(), soundURL);

    // Obtain a NumberFormat object to convert number of minutes and
    // seconds to strings.  Set it up to produce a leading 0 if necessary
    format = NumberFormat.getNumberInstance();
    format.setMinimumIntegerDigits(2); // pad with 0 if necessary

    // Specify a MouseListener to handle mouse events in the applet.
    // Note that the applet implements this interface itself
    addMouseListener(this);

    // Create a timer to call the actionPerformed() method immediately,
    // and then every 1000 milliseconds. Note we don't start the timer yet.
    timer = new Timer(1000, this);
    timer.setInitialDelay(0);  // First timer is immediate.
}

// Free up any resources we hold; called when the applet is done
public void destroy() { if (image != null) image.flush(); }

// The browser calls this to start the applet running
// The resume() method is defined below.
public void start() { resume(); } // Start displaying updates

// The browser calls this to stop the applet.  It may be restarted later.
// The pause() method is defined below
public void stop() { pause(); }    // Stop displaying updates

// Return information about the applet
public String getAppletInfo() {
    return "Countdown applet Copyright (c) 2003 by David Flanagan";
}

// Return information about the applet parameters
public String[][] getParameterInfo() { return parameterInfo; }

// This is the parameter information.  One array of strings for each
// parameter.  The elements are parameter name, type, and description.
static String[][] parameterInfo = {
    {"minutes", "number", "time, in minutes, to countdown from"},
    {"font", "font", "optional font for the time display"},
    {"foreground", "color", "optional foreground color for the time"},
    {"background", "color", "optional background color"},
```

Example 16-3. Countdown.java (continued)

```
        {"image", "image URL", "optional image to display next to countdown"},
        {"sound", "sound URL", "optional sound to play when we reach 00:00"},
        {"newpage", "document URL", "URL to load when timer expires"},
    };

    // Start or resume the countdown
    void resume( ) {
        // Restore the time we're counting down from and restart the timer.
        lastUpdate = System.currentTimeMillis( );
        timer.start( );  // Start the timer
    }

    // Pause the countdown
    void pause( ) {
        // Subtract elapsed time from the remaining time and stop timing
        long now = System.currentTimeMillis( );
        remaining -= (now - lastUpdate);
        timer.stop( );   // Stop the timer
    }

    // Update the displayed time.  This method is called from actionPerformed( )
    // which is itself invoked by the timer.
    void updateDisplay( ) {
        long now = System.currentTimeMillis( );  // current time in ms
        long elapsed = now - lastUpdate;         // ms elapsed since last update
        remaining -= elapsed;                    // adjust remaining time
        lastUpdate = now;                        // remember this update time

        // Convert remaining milliseconds to mm:ss format and display
        if (remaining < 0) remaining = 0;
        int minutes = (int)(remaining/60000);
        int seconds = (int)((remaining%60000)/1000);
        label.setText(format.format(minutes) + ":" + format.format(seconds));

        // If we've completed the countdown, beep and display new page
        if (remaining == 0) {
            // Stop updating now.
            timer.stop( );
            // If we have an alarm sound clip, play it now.
            if (sound != null) sound.play( );
            // If there is a newpage URL specified, make the browser
            // load that page now.
            String newpage = getParameter("newpage");
            if (newpage != null) {
                try {
                    URL url = new URL(getDocumentBase( ), newpage);
                    getAppletContext( ).showDocument(url);
                }
                catch(MalformedURLException ex) { showStatus(ex.toString( )); }
            }
        }
    }
}
```

Example 16-3. Countdown.java (continued)

```java
    // This method implements the ActionListener interface.
    // It is invoked once a second by the Timer object
    // and updates the JLabel to display minutes and seconds remaining.
    public void actionPerformed(ActionEvent e) { updateDisplay(); }

    // The methods below implement the MouseListener interface.  We use
    // two of them to pause the countdown when the mouse hovers over the timer.
    // Note that we also display a message in the statusline
    public void mouseEntered(MouseEvent e) {
        pause();                     // pause countdown
        showStatus("Paused");        // display statusline message
    }
    public void mouseExited(MouseEvent e) {
        resume();                    // resume countdown
        showStatus("");              // clear statusline
    }
    // These MouseListener methods are unused.
    public void mouseClicked(MouseEvent e) { }
    public void mousePressed(MouseEvent e) { }
    public void mouseReleased(MouseEvent e) { }
}
```

Applets and the Java 1.0 Event Model

The AWT event model changed dramatically between Java 1.0 and 1.1. Chapter 11 described the Java 1.1 event-handling model exclusively, since the Java 1.0 event model is now deprecated. However, because there is still a (dwindling) installed base of web browsers that support only the Java 1.0 event model, applets are sometimes still written using this model. This section briefly describes Java 1.0 event handling and includes an example applet that uses the model.[*]

In Java 1.0, all events are represented by the java.awt.Event class. This class has a number of instance fields that describe the event. One of these fields, id, specifies the type of the event. Event defines a number of constants that are the possible values for the id field. The target field specifies the object (typically a Component) that generated the event, or on which the event occurred (i.e., the source of the event). The other fields may or may not be used, depending on the type of the event. For example, the x and y fields are defined when id is BUTTON_EVENT, but not when it is ACTION_EVENT. The arg field can provide additional type-dependent data.

Java 1.0 events are dispatched first to the handleEvent( ) method of the Component on which they occurred. The default implementation of this method checks the id field of the Event object and dispatches the most commonly used types of events to various type-specific methods, listed in Table 16-1.

[*] Note that this section and its example are excerpted from *Java Foundation Classes in a Nutshell*.

Table 16-1. Java 1.0 event-processing methods of Component

action( )	lostFocus( )	mouseExit( )
gotFocus( )	mouseDown( )	mouseMove( )
keyDown( )	mouseDrag( )	mouseUp( )
keyUp( )	mouseEnter( )	

The methods listed in Table 16-1 are defined by the Component class. One of the primary characteristics of the Java 1.0 event model is that you must override these methods to process events. This means that you must create a subclass to define custom event-handling behavior, which is exactly what you do when you write an applet. Notice, however, that not all the event types are dispatched by handleEvent( ) to more specific methods. So, if you are interested in LIST_SELECT or WINDOW_ICONIFY events, for example, you have to override handleEvent( ) itself, rather than one of the more specific methods. If you do this, you should usually invoke super.handleEvent( ) to continue dispatching events of other types in the default way.

The handleEvent( ) method, and all the type-specific methods, return boolean values. If an event-handling method returns false, as they all do by default, it means that the event was not handled, so it should be passed to the container of the current component to see if that container is interested in processing it. If a method returns true, on the other hand, it is a signal that the event *has* been handled, and no further processing is needed.

The fact that unhandled events are passed up the containment hierarchy is important. It means that you can override the action( ) method (for example) in an applet in order to handle the ACTION_EVENT events that are generated by the buttons within the applet. If they were not propagated up as they are, you would have to create a custom subclass of Button for every button you wanted to add to an interface.

In the Java 1.0 model, there is no de facto way to know what types of events are generated by what GUI components, nor to know what fields of the Event object are filled in for what types of events. You simply have to look up this information in the documentation of individual AWT components.

Many event types use the modifiers field of the Event object to report which keyboard modifier keys were depressed when the event occurred. This field contains a bitmask of the SHIFT_MASK, CTRL_MASK, META_MASK, and ALT_MASK constants defined by the Event class. The shiftDown( ), controlDown( ), and metaDown( ) methods can test for the various modifiers. When a mouse event occurs, the Event class does not have a special field to indicate which mouse button was pressed. Instead, this information is provided by reusing the keyboard modifier constants. This allows such systems as the Macintosh that use a one-button mouse to simulate other mouse buttons by using keyboard modifiers. If the left mouse button is in use, no keyboard modifiers are reported; if the right button is used, the META_MASK bit is set in the modifiers field; and if the middle button is down, the ALT_MASK bit is set.

When a keyboard event occurs, you should check the id field of the Event object to determine what kind of key was pressed. If the event type is KEY_PRESS or KEY_RELEASE, the keyboard key has an ASCII or Unicode representation, and the key field of the event object contains the encoding of the key. On the other hand, if id is KEY_ACTION or KEY_ACTION_RELEASE, the key is a function key of some sort, and the key field contains one of the keyboard constants defined by the Event class, such as Event.F1 or Event.LEFT.

Keep this quick introduction to the Java 1.0 event model in mind as you read over Example 16-4. This applet allows the user to produce simple drawings by scribbling with the mouse. It also allows the user to erase those drawings by clicking on a button or typing the E key. As you'll see, the applet overrides methods to handle mouse events, keyboard events, and action events generated by the Button component. In particular, note the boolean return values of these event-handling methods. This applet does not define a paint( ) method. For simplicity, it does its drawing directly in response to the events it receives and does not store the coordinates. This means that it cannot regenerate the user's drawing if it is scrolled off the screen and then scrolled back on. Since the Java 1.0 event model is deprecated, you'll see deprecation warnings when you compile this example.

Example 16-4. Scribble.java

```java
package je3.applet;
import java.applet.*;
import java.awt.*;

/**
 * This applet lets the user scribble with the mouse.
 * It demonstrates the Java 1.0 event model.
 **/
public class Scribble extends Applet {
    private int lastx, lasty;      // Remember last mouse coordinates.
    Button erase_button;           // The Erase button.

    /** Initialize the erase button, ask for keyboard focus */
    public void init( ) {
        erase_button = new Button("Erase");
        this.add(erase_button);
        this.setBackground(Color.white);  // Set background color for scribble
        this.requestFocus( );  // Ask for keyboard focus so we get key events
    }

    /** Respond to mouse clicks */
    public boolean mouseDown(Event e, int x, int y) {
        lastx = x; lasty = y;              // Remember where the click was
        return true;
    }

    /** Respond to mouse drags */
    public boolean mouseDrag(Event e, int x, int y) {
        Graphics g = getGraphics( );
        g.drawLine(lastx, lasty, x, y);    // Draw from last position to here
        lastx = x; lasty = y;              // And remember new last position
        return true;
    }
}
```

Example 16-4. Scribble.java (continued)

```java
/** Respond to key presses: Erase drawing when user types 'e' */
public boolean keyDown(Event e, int key) {
    if ((e.id == Event.KEY_PRESS) && (key == 'e')) {
        Graphics g = getGraphics();
        g.setColor(this.getBackground());
        g.fillRect(0, 0, bounds().width, bounds().height);
        return true;
    }
    else return false;
}

/** Respond to Button clicks: erase drawing when user clicks button */
public boolean action(Event e, Object arg) {
    if (e.target == erase_button) {
        Graphics g = getGraphics();
        g.setColor(this.getBackground());
        g.fillRect(0, 0, bounds().width, bounds().height);
        return true;
    }
    else return false;
}
}
```

Exercises

Exercise 16-1. Modify FirstApplet to take advantage of the features of the Graphics class, so that it displays the "Hello World" message in a more visually interesting way.

Exercise 16-2. Modify the Clock applet so that it is configurable via applet parameters, like the Countdown applet is. Your modified applet should read parameters that specify the update frequency for the time display, as well as the font, color, and format of the time display. (See java.text. SimpleDateFormat for a way to format dates and times according to a specified pattern.) Also, add a getParameterInfo() method that describes the applet parameters you define, and modify getAppletInfo() to include a message describing your contribution to the applet.

Exercise 16-3. Modify the Countdown applet so that it responds to mouse clicks: if the mouse is clicked over the timer, it should reset the time to its initial value.

Exercise 16-4. One of the key features of applets is that they are treated as untrusted code and run under a SecurityManager that prevents them from taking malicious actions such as reading sensitive data, deleting files, or using the client machine to send spam out across the network. Take a look again at Example 7-3 in Chapter 7, and write an applet version of that class that attempts to perform restricted actions. Use a TextField or JTextField component to display the applet's output.

17

Sound

On systems that support it, sound can be an important part of many applications. Sound can be used to notify the user that her attention is required, to add the extra dimension of aural feedback to visual GUIs, or for entertainment purposes. Other applications—such as media players, recorders, and editors—are sound-centric and therefore require advanced sound capabilities.

This chapter illustrates Java's sound capabilities, from the simple to the complex:

- Example 17-1 shows how to ring the terminal bell. A simple beep is all that some applications need to attract the user's attention in case of errors or urgent conditions.

- Example 17-2 shows how to play simple audio clips with the java.applet. AudioClip class. This example illustrates a very simple technique that is sufficient to add sounds to many applications, but does not give any control over the playback of the sound.

- Example 17-3 shows how to use the javax.sound.sampled and javax.sound. midi packages to load and play sound clips, how to monitor and change the playback position within the clip, and how to set audio parameters such as volume, balance, and tempo for the clips.

- Example 17-4 shows how to play streaming sounds in both sampled audio and MIDI formats.

- Example 17-5 reads a simple musical score and converts it into a MIDI Sequence, which is then either played on a Sequencer or saved to a file.

- Example 17-6 shows how to make music by directly controlling a MidiChannel of a Synthesizer, bypassing the Sequence and Sequencer used in Example 17-5.

The Java Sound API is a low-level interface to sound, and the default implementation does not support compressed formats such as MP3. In this chapter we'll be working with simple audio files, with types such as *.wav*, *.aiff*, and *.au*. Note that, although Java Sound supports the recording of sounds, there is no recording example in this chapter: setup and configuration problems on different platforms make sound recording a topic that is beyond the scope of this chapter.

Ringing the Bell

In the old days, dumb computer terminals had a bell that would beep when they received the ASCII BEL character (\u0007). Modern computer hardware has retained the ability to create an unpleasant-sounding beep, even if no speakers are plugged in, if audio drivers are misconfigured, or if system volume has been turned down. In a sense, the hardware bell is a sound of last resort, and you can ring it when it is critical that you attract the user's attention.

There are two ways to ring this bell. In modern operating systems, the command-line interface often emulates an old-style terminal, and some of these terminal emulators respond to the BEL character. Thus, on many platforms, a command-line application can make a sound by printing the Unicode character \u0007 to System.out.

Applets and GUI-based applications don't typically do console input and output, and may be launched in such a way that output to System.out is not directed to a terminal emulator. In Java 1.1 and later, these applications can create a beep with the beep( ) method of the java.awt.Toolkit class. (Console-based applications can do this as well, of course, but at the cost of increased startup time to load AWT classes.)

Example 17-1 illustrates both techniques in a console-based application. GUI-based applications should use Component.getToolkit( ) to get a Toolkit object, instead of Toolkit.getDefaultToolkit( ).

Example 17-1. Beep.java

```
package je3.sound;

// Ring the bell!
public class Beep {
    public static void main(String[] args) {
        // In terminal-based applications, this is a non-portable, unreliable
        // way to sound the terminal bell (if there is one) and get the
        // user's attention.  \u0007 is the ASCII BEL or Ctrl-G character.
        System.out.println("BEEP\u0007!");

        // For applications that can use AWT, there is another way
        // to ring the bell.
        String[ ] words = new String[ ] {
            "Shave ", "and ", "a ", "hair", "cut ", "two ", "bits."
        };
        int[ ] pauses = new int[ ] { 300, 150, 150, 250, 450, 250, 1 };

        for(int i = 0; i < pauses.length; i++) {
            // Ring the bell using AWT
            java.awt.Toolkit.getDefaultToolkit( ).beep( );
```

Example 17-1. Beep.java (continued)

```
                System.out.print(words[i]);
                System.out.flush( );
                // Wait a while before beeping again.
                try { Thread.sleep(pauses[i]); } catch(InterruptedException e) { }
            }
            System.out.println( );
        }
}
```

Swing Aural Cues

GUI toolkits, such as Swing, typically play short sounds or cues when specific events occur. The display of an error dialog box will cause an "alert" sound of some sort to let the user know that an error has occurred, for example. And selecting a checkbox might cause a subtle click, to provide a layer of aural feedback and reassure the user that the selection was in fact made. Swing uses a pluggable look-and-feel layer, and any aural cues are the responsibility of the installed look-and-feel. In most cases, no programmatic intervention is required, and the aural cues provided by the look-and-feel can simply be accepted as they are. The API for configuring these aural cues is essentially undocumented. See Example 11-28 for a way to turn aural cues on and off.

Playing Sounds with AudioClip

The sound capabilities of modern computer hardware are usually much more advanced than the dumb terminals of yesterday, and typical users expect their computers to make sounds that are prettier than the coarse console bell. Java programs can do this by loading and playing a file of audio data with the java. applet.AudioClip interface. As the package name implies, the AudioClip interface was originally intended only for applets. Since Java 1.0, applets have been able to call their getAudioClip( ) instance method to read an audio file over the network. In Java 1.2, however, the static java.applet.Applet.newAudioClip( ) method was added to allow any application to read audio data from any URL (including local file: URLs). This method and the AudioClip interface make it very easy to play arbitrary sounds from your programs, as demonstrated by Example 17-2.

Invoke PlaySound with the URL of a sound file as its sole argument. If you are using a local file, be sure to prefix the filename with the file: protocol. The types of sound files supported depend on the Java implementation. Sun's default implementation supports *.wav*, *.aiff*, and *.au* files for sampled sound, *.mid* files for MIDI, and even *.rmf* files for the MIDI-related, proprietary "Rich Music Format" defined by Beatnik.[*]

When you run the PlaySound class of Example 17-2, you may notice that the program never exits. Like AWT applications, programs that use Java's sound capabilities start a background thread and do not automatically exit when the main( )

---

[*] There is no guarantee that the RMF format will continue to be supported.

method returns.* To make PlaySound better behaved, we need to explicitly call System.exit( ) when the AudioClip has finished playing. But this highlights one of the shortcomings of the AudioClip interface: it allows you to play( ), stop( ), or loop( ) a sound, but it provides no way to track the progress of the sound or find out when it has finished playing. To achieve that level of control over the playback of sound, we need to use the JavaSound API, which we'll consider in the next section.

Example 17-2. PlaySound.java

```
package je3.sound;

/**
 * Play a sound file from the network using the java.applet.Applet API.
 */
public class PlaySound {
    public static void main(String[ ] args)
        throws java.net.MalformedURLException
    {
        java.applet.AudioClip clip =
            java.applet.Applet.newAudioClip(new java.net.URL(args[0]));
        clip.play( );
    }
}
```

Finding Music Files

Before you can test PlaySound, you'll need some sound files to play. You probably have lots of sampled audio files sitting around on your computer: they are often bundled with operating systems and applications. Look for files with *.wav*, *.au*, or *.aif* extensions. You may not have MIDI files on your computer, but many MIDI hobbyists make files available for download on the Internet; a quick Internet search will locate many samples you can use.

The JavaSound web page is also worth a visit (*http://java.sun.com/products/java-media/sound/*). This page includes links to an interesting JavaSound demo application that includes source code and its own set of sampled audio and MIDI files. Also of interest here are free downloadable MIDI soundbank files, which may give you richer MIDI sound.

Playing Sounds with javax.sound

To achieve more detailed control over the playback of sounds, including the ability to skip to any specified spot in the sound and control things such as volume and balance, we must use the Java Sound API, which is a much lower-level API than the AudioClip interface. JavaSound consists of the javax.sound. sampled package for sampled audio and the javax.sound.midi package for MIDI-based audio. Example 17-3 demonstrates the basic capabilities of these two packages. It loads a sound file (sampled audio or MIDI) completely into memory and

---

* This is reported to be fixed in Java 1.5.

then displays a GUI that allows you to play it. The GUI makes extensive use of the Swing JSlider component, which allows you both to select the playback position of the sound and to set things such as the volume, balance, and tempo of the sound. The program displays different controls for sampled audio files than it does for MIDI files. Both GUIs are shown in Figure 17-1. You'll notice that the code is substantially different for sampled audio and MIDI files as well.

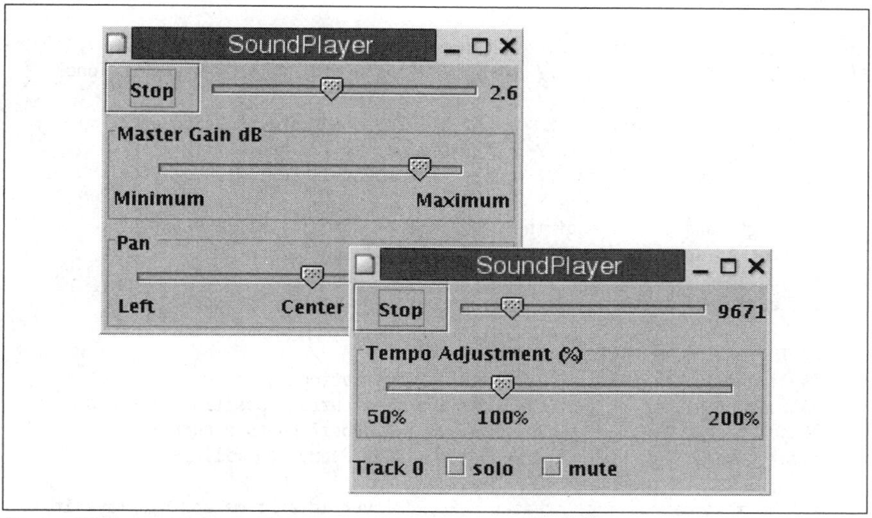

Figure 17-1. SoundPlayer playing sampled audio and MIDI files

A shortcoming of the SoundPlayer class is that it can only play sampled audio files that use PCM encoding. ALAW and ULAW encoded files are not supported, nor are more complex compressed encodings, such as MP3. The JavaSound API attempts to directly mirror the capabilities of sound hardware, and can therefore only play PCM sounds. It does provide a transcoding technique, however, to convert sounds to PCM encoding. We'll see this later in the chapter, in Example 17-4.

Example 17-3. SoundPlayer.java

```
package je3.sound;
import java.io.*;
import java.net.*;
import java.awt.*;
import java.awt.event.*;
import javax.swing.*;
import javax.swing.event.*;
import javax.swing.border.*;
import javax.sound.sampled.*;
import javax.sound.midi.*;

/**
 * This class is a Swing component that can load and play a sound clip,
 * displaying progress and controls.  The main( ) method is a test program.
```

Example 17-3. SoundPlayer.java (continued)

```
 * This component can play sampled audio or MIDI files, but handles them
 * differently. For sampled audio, time is reported in microseconds, tracked in
 * milliseconds and displayed in seconds and tenths of seconds. For midi
 * files time is reported, tracked, and displayed in MIDI "ticks".
 * This program does no transcoding, so it can only play sound files that use
 * the PCM encoding.
 */
public class SoundPlayer extends JComponent {
    boolean midi;            // Are we playing a midi file or a sampled one?
    Sequence sequence;       // The contents of a MIDI file
    Sequencer sequencer;     // We play MIDI Sequences with a Sequencer
    Clip clip;               // Contents of a sampled audio file
    boolean playing = false; // whether the sound is currently playing

    // Length and position of the sound are measured in milliseconds for
    // sampled sounds and MIDI "ticks" for MIDI sounds
    int audioLength;         // Length of the sound.
    int audioPosition = 0;   // Current position within the sound

    // The following fields are for the GUI
    JButton play;            // The Play/Stop button
    JSlider progress;        // Shows and sets current position in sound
    JLabel time;             // Displays audioPosition as a number
    Timer timer;             // Updates slider every 100 milliseconds

    // The main method just creates a SoundPlayer in a Frame and displays it
    public static void main(String[ ] args)
        throws IOException,
               UnsupportedAudioFileException,
               LineUnavailableException,
               MidiUnavailableException,
               InvalidMidiDataException
    {
        SoundPlayer player;

        File file = new File(args[0]);   // This is the file we'll be playing
        // Determine whether it is midi or sampled audio
        boolean ismidi;
        try {
            // We discard the return value of this method; we just need to know
            // whether it returns successfully or throws an exception
            MidiSystem.getMidiFileFormat(file);
            ismidi = true;
        }
        catch(InvalidMidiDataException e) {
            ismidi = false;
        }

        // Create a SoundPlayer object to play the sound.
        player = new SoundPlayer(file, ismidi);

        // Put it in a window and play it
        JFrame f = new JFrame("SoundPlayer");
```

Example 17-3. SoundPlayer.java (continued)

```
        f.setDefaultCloseOperation(JFrame.EXIT_ON_CLOSE);
        f.getContentPane( ).add(player, "Center");
        f.pack( );
        f.setVisible(true);
    }


    // Create a SoundPlayer component for the specified file.
    public SoundPlayer(File f, boolean isMidi)
        throws IOException,
               UnsupportedAudioFileException,
               LineUnavailableException,
               MidiUnavailableException,
               InvalidMidiDataException
    {
        if (isMidi) {        // The file is a MIDI file
            midi = true;
            // First, get a Sequencer to play sequences of MIDI events
            // That is, to send events to a Synthesizer at the right time.
            sequencer = MidiSystem.getSequencer( );  // Used to play sequences
            sequencer.open( );                       // Turn it on.

            // Get a Synthesizer for the Sequencer to send notes to
            Synthesizer synth = MidiSystem.getSynthesizer( );
            synth.open( );  // acquire whatever resources it needs

            // The Sequencer obtained above may be connected to a Synthesizer
            // by default, or it may not.  Therefore, we explicitly connect it.
            Transmitter transmitter = sequencer.getTransmitter( );
            Receiver receiver = synth.getReceiver( );
            transmitter.setReceiver(receiver);

            // Read the sequence from the file and tell the sequencer about it
            sequence = MidiSystem.getSequence(f);
            sequencer.setSequence(sequence);
            audioLength = (int)sequence.getTickLength( ); // Get sequence length
        }
        else {                // The file is sampled audio
            midi = false;
            // Getting a Clip object for a file of sampled audio data is kind
            // of cumbersome.  The following lines do what we need.
            AudioInputStream ain = AudioSystem.getAudioInputStream(f);
            try {
                DataLine.Info info =
                    new DataLine.Info(Clip.class,ain.getFormat( ));
                clip = (Clip) AudioSystem.getLine(info);
                clip.open(ain);
            }
            finally { // We're done with the input stream.
                ain.close( );
            }
            // Get the clip length in microseconds and convert to milliseconds
            audioLength = (int)(clip.getMicrosecondLength( )/1000);
        }
```

Example 17-3. SoundPlayer.java (continued)

```java
        // Now create the basic GUI
        play = new JButton("Play");                     // Play/stop button
        progress = new JSlider(0, audioLength, 0);      // Shows position in sound
        time = new JLabel("0");                         // Shows position as a #

        // When clicked, start or stop playing the sound
        play.addActionListener(new ActionListener( ) {
                public void actionPerformed(ActionEvent e) {
                        if (playing) stop( ); else play( );
                }
        });

        // Whenever the slider value changes, first update the time label.
        // Next, if we're not already at the new position, skip to it.
        progress.addChangeListener(new ChangeListener( ) {
                public void stateChanged(ChangeEvent e) {
                        int value = progress.getValue( );
                        // Update the time label
                        if (midi) time.setText(value + "");
                        else time.setText(value/1000 + "." +
                                        (value%1000)/100);
                        // If we're not already there, skip there.
                        if (value != audioPosition) skip(value);
                }
        });

        // This timer calls the tick( ) method 10 times a second to keep
        // our slider in sync with the music.
        timer = new javax.swing.Timer(100, new ActionListener( ) {
                public void actionPerformed(ActionEvent e) { tick( ); }
        });

        // put those controls in a row
        Box row = Box.createHorizontalBox( );
        row.add(play);
        row.add(progress);
        row.add(time);

        // And add them to this component.
        setLayout(new BoxLayout(this, BoxLayout.Y_AXIS));
        this.add(row);

        // Now add additional controls based on the type of the sound
        if (midi) addMidiControls( );
        else addSampledControls( );
    }

    /** Start playing the sound at the current position */
    public void play( ) {
        if (midi) sequencer.start( );
        else clip.start( );
        timer.start( );
```

Example 17-3. SoundPlayer.java (continued)

```
        play.setText("Stop");
        playing = true;
    }

    /** Stop playing the sound, but retain the current position */
    public void stop() {
        timer.stop();
        if (midi) sequencer.stop();
        else clip.stop();
        play.setText("Play");
        playing = false;
    }

    /** Stop playing the sound and reset the position to 0 */
    public void reset() {
        stop();
        if (midi) sequencer.setTickPosition(0);
        else clip.setMicrosecondPosition(0);
        audioPosition = 0;
        progress.setValue(0);
    }

    /** Skip to the specified position */
    public void skip(int position) { // Called when user drags the slider
        if (position < 0 || position > audioLength) return;
        audioPosition = position;
        if (midi) sequencer.setTickPosition(position);
        else clip.setMicrosecondPosition(position * 1000);
        progress.setValue(position); // in case skip() is called from outside
    }

    /** Return the length of the sound in ms or ticks */
    public int getLength() { return audioLength; }

    // An internal method that updates the progress bar.
    // The Timer object calls it 10 times a second.
    // If the sound has finished, it resets to the beginning
    void tick() {
        if (midi && sequencer.isRunning()) {
            audioPosition = (int)sequencer.getTickPosition();
            progress.setValue(audioPosition);
        }
        else if (!midi && clip.isActive()) {
            audioPosition = (int)(clip.getMicrosecondPosition()/1000);
            progress.setValue(audioPosition);
        }
        else reset();
    }

    // For sampled sounds, add sliders to control volume and balance
    void addSampledControls() {
        try {
```

Example 17-3. SoundPlayer.java (continued)

```java
            FloatControl gainControl =
                (FloatControl)clip.getControl(FloatControl.Type.MASTER_GAIN);
            if (gainControl != null) this.add(createSlider(gainControl));
        }
        catch(IllegalArgumentException e) {
            // If MASTER_GAIN volume control is unsupported, just skip it
        }

        try {
            // FloatControl.Type.BALANCE is probably the correct control to
            // use here, but it doesn't work for me, so I use PAN instead.
            FloatControl panControl =
                (FloatControl)clip.getControl(FloatControl.Type.PAN);
            if (panControl != null) this.add(createSlider(panControl));
        }
        catch(IllegalArgumentException e) { }
    }


    // Return a JSlider component to manipulate the supplied FloatControl
    // for sampled audio.
    JSlider createSlider(final FloatControl c) {
        if (c == null) return null;
        final JSlider s = new JSlider(0, 1000);
        final float min = c.getMinimum();
        final float max = c.getMaximum();
        final float width = max-min;
        float fval = c.getValue();
        s.setValue((int) ((fval-min)/width * 1000));

        java.util.Hashtable labels = new java.util.Hashtable(3);
        labels.put(new Integer(0), new JLabel(c.getMinLabel()));
        labels.put(new Integer(500), new JLabel(c.getMidLabel()));
        labels.put(new Integer(1000), new JLabel(c.getMaxLabel()));
        s.setLabelTable(labels);
        s.setPaintLabels(true);

        s.setBorder(new TitledBorder(c.getType().toString() + " " +
                                     c.getUnits()));

        s.addChangeListener(new ChangeListener() {
                public void stateChanged(ChangeEvent e) {
                    int i = s.getValue();
                    float f = min + (i*width/1000.0f);
                    c.setValue(f);
                }
            });
        return s;
    }

    // For Midi files, create a JSlider to control the tempo,
    // and create JCheckBoxes to mute or solo each MIDI track.
    void addMidiControls() {
```

Example 17-3. SoundPlayer.java (continued)

```java
        // Add a slider to control the tempo
        final JSlider tempo = new JSlider(50, 200);
        tempo.setValue((int)(sequencer.getTempoFactor( )*100));
        tempo.setBorder(new TitledBorder("Tempo Adjustment (%)"));
        java.util.Hashtable labels = new java.util.Hashtable( );
        labels.put(new Integer(50), new JLabel("50%"));
        labels.put(new Integer(100), new JLabel("100%"));
        labels.put(new Integer(200), new JLabel("200%"));
        tempo.setLabelTable(labels);
        tempo.setPaintLabels(true);
        // The event listener actually changes the tempo
        tempo.addChangeListener(new ChangeListener( ) {
                public void stateChanged(ChangeEvent e) {
                    sequencer.setTempoFactor(tempo.getValue( )/100.0f);
                }
            });

        this.add(tempo);

        // Create rows of solo and checkboxes for each track
        Track[ ] tracks = sequence.getTracks( );
        for(int i = 0; i < tracks.length; i++) {
            final int tracknum = i;
            // Two checkboxes per track
            final JCheckBox solo = new JCheckBox("solo");
            final JCheckBox mute = new JCheckBox("mute");
            // The listeners solo or mute the track
            solo.addActionListener(new ActionListener( ) {
                    public void actionPerformed(ActionEvent e) {
                        sequencer.setTrackSolo(tracknum,solo.isSelected( ));
                    }
                });
            mute.addActionListener(new ActionListener( ) {
                    public void actionPerformed(ActionEvent e) {
                        sequencer.setTrackMute(tracknum,mute.isSelected( ));
                    }
                });

            // Build up a row
            Box box = Box.createHorizontalBox( );
            box.add(new JLabel("Track " + tracknum));
            box.add(Box.createHorizontalStrut(10));
            box.add(solo);
            box.add(Box.createHorizontalStrut(10));
            box.add(mute);
            box.add(Box.createHorizontalGlue( ));
            // And add it to this component
            this.add(box);
        }
    }
}
```

Streaming Sounds with javax.sound

Sound files, especially sampled audio files in the uncompressed PCM format, are quite large, and, except for the shortest audio clips, it is not generally a good idea to read the entire file into memory. Instead, these files are typically played in streaming mode so that only the portion of the sound that is currently playing must reside in memory. In exchange for reduced memory consumption, we lose the ability to easily jump to any position within the sound, of course. Example 17-4 is a listing of PlaySoundStream, a program that plays streaming audio data read from the specified URL. It demonstrates streaming techniques for both sampled audio and MIDI data, and also demonstrates a transcoding technique for converting unsupported encodings (such as ALAW and ULAW) into PCM encoding so they can be played. PlaySoundStream is a console-based application with no GUI. Note the use of the wait( ) and notify( ) methods to make streamMidiSequence( ) into a modal method that does not return until the sound has finished playing. Note also that you must use a -m command-line argument in order to play MIDI data.

Example 17-4. PlaySoundStream.java

```java
package je3.sound;
import java.io.*;
import java.net.*;
import javax.sound.sampled.*;
import javax.sound.midi.*;

/**
 * This class plays sounds streaming from a URL: it does not have to preload
 * the entire sound into memory before playing it. It is a command-line
 * application with no gui. It includes code to convert ULAW and ALAW
 * audio formats to PCM so they can be played. Use the -m command-line option
 * before MIDI files.
 */
public class PlaySoundStream {
    // Create a URL from the command-line argument and pass it to the
    // right static method depending on the presence of the -m (MIDI) option.
    public static void main(String[ ] args) throws Exception {
        if (args[0].equals("-m")) streamMidiSequence(new URL(args[1]));
        else streamSampledAudio(new URL(args[0]));

        // Exit explicitly.
        // This is needed because the audio system starts background threads.
        System.exit(0);
    }

    /** Read sampled audio data from the specified URL and play it */
    public static void streamSampledAudio(URL url)
        throws IOException, UnsupportedAudioFileException,
               LineUnavailableException
    {
        AudioInputStream ain = null;   // We read audio data from here
        SourceDataLine line = null;    // And write it here.
```

Example 17-4. PlaySoundStream.java (continued)

```
try {
    // Get an audio input stream from the URL
    ain=AudioSystem.getAudioInputStream(url);

    // Get information about the format of the stream
    AudioFormat format = ain.getFormat();
    DataLine.Info info=new DataLine.Info(SourceDataLine.class,format);

    // If the format is not supported directly (i.e. if it is not PCM
    // encoded), then try to transcode it to PCM.
    if (!AudioSystem.isLineSupported(info)) {
        // This is the PCM format we want to transcode to.
        // The parameters here are audio format details that you
        // shouldn't need to understand for casual use.
        AudioFormat pcm =
            new AudioFormat(format.getSampleRate(), 16,
                            format.getChannels(), true, false);

        // Get a wrapper stream around the input stream that does the
        // transcoding for us.
        ain = AudioSystem.getAudioInputStream(pcm, ain);

        // Update the format and info variables for the transcoded data
        format = ain.getFormat();
        info = new DataLine.Info(SourceDataLine.class, format);
    }

    // Open the line through which we'll play the streaming audio.
    line = (SourceDataLine) AudioSystem.getLine(info);
    line.open(format);

    // Allocate a buffer for reading from the input stream and writing
    // to the line.  Make it large enough to hold 4k audio frames.
    // Note that the SourceDataLine also has its own internal buffer.
    int framesize = format.getFrameSize();
    byte[ ] buffer = new byte[4 * 1024 * framesize]; // the buffer
    int numbytes = 0;                                // how many bytes

    // We haven't started the line yet.
    boolean started = false;

    for(;;) { // We'll exit the loop when we reach the end of stream
        // First, read some bytes from the input stream.
        int bytesread=ain.read(buffer,numbytes,buffer.length-numbytes);
        // If there were no more bytes to read, we're done.
        if (bytesread == -1) break;
        numbytes += bytesread;

        // Now that we've got some audio data to write to the line,
        // start the line, so it will play that data as we write it.
        if (!started) {
            line.start();
```

Example 17-4. PlaySoundStream.java (continued)

```
                started = true;
            }

            // We must write bytes to the line in an integer multiple of
            // the framesize.  So figure out how many bytes we'll write.
            int bytestowrite = (numbytes/framesize)*framesize;

            // Now write the bytes. The line will buffer them and play
            // them. This call will block until all bytes are written.
            line.write(buffer, 0, bytestowrite);

            // If we didn't have an integer multiple of the frame size,
            // then copy the remaining bytes to the start of the buffer.
            int remaining = numbytes - bytestowrite;
            if (remaining > 0)
                System.arraycopy(buffer,bytestowrite,buffer,0,remaining);
            numbytes = remaining;
        }

        // Now block until all buffered sound finishes playing.
        line.drain();
    }
    finally { // Always relinquish the resources we use
        if (line != null) line.close();
        if (ain != null) ain.close();
    }
}

// A MIDI protocol constant that isn't defined by javax.sound.midi
public static final int END_OF_TRACK = 47;

/* MIDI or RMF data from the specified URL and play it */
public static void streamMidiSequence(URL url)
    throws IOException, InvalidMidiDataException, MidiUnavailableException
{
    Sequencer sequencer=null;     // Converts a Sequence to MIDI events
    Synthesizer synthesizer=null; // Plays notes in response to MIDI events

    try {
        // Create, open, and connect a Sequencer and Synthesizer
        // They are closed in the finally block at the end of this method.
        sequencer = MidiSystem.getSequencer();
        sequencer.open();
        synthesizer = MidiSystem.getSynthesizer();
        synthesizer.open();
        sequencer.getTransmitter().setReceiver(synthesizer.getReceiver());

        // Specify the InputStream to stream the sequence from
        sequencer.setSequence(url.openStream());

        // This is an arbitrary object used with wait and notify to
        // prevent the method from returning before the music finishes
        final Object lock = new Object();
```

Example 17-4. PlaySoundStream.java (continued)

```
              // Register a listener to make the method exit when the stream is
              // done. See Object.wait( ) and Object.notify( )
              sequencer.addMetaEventListener(new MetaEventListener( ) {
                      public void meta(MetaMessage e) {
                          if (e.getType( ) == END_OF_TRACK) {
                              synchronized(lock) {
                                  lock.notify( );
                              }
                          }
                      }
              });

              // Start playing the music
              sequencer.start( );

              // Now block until the listener above notifies us that we're done.
              synchronized(lock) {
                  while(sequencer.isRunning( )) {
                      try { lock.wait( ); } catch(InterruptedException e) { }
                  }
              }
          }
          finally {
              // Always relinquish the sequencer, so others can use it.
              if (sequencer != null) sequencer.close( );
              if (synthesizer != null) synthesizer.close( );
          }
      }
}
```

Synthesizing a MIDI Sequence

MIDI audio is quite different from sampled audio. Instead of recording samples of an actual audio waveform, MIDI files record a sequence of keystrokes on a real or virtual synthesizer keyboard. MIDI can't be used to represent voice data, but it is a versatile and compact format for polyphonic electronic music. Many hobbyists transcribe well-known works to MIDI or publish their own compositions as MIDI files. An Internet search will reveal many MIDI samples that you can play with any of the audio player programs we've developed previously in this chapter.

The javax.sound.midi package is useful not only for playback of predefined MIDI files but also for synthesis or playback of MIDI Sequence objects. The program in Example 17-5, PlayerPiano, takes as input a musical score (defined using a simple grammar) and creates a Sequence of MidiEvent objects. It then either plays that Sequence through a Sequencer object or saves the Sequence as a MIDI file for playback with some other sound program.

Invoke PlayerPiano with the score as a single quoted argument. You can use the -o argument to specify a filename to save the MIDI file to. Without this argument, the score will be played instead. Use -i to specify a MIDI instrument number between 0 and 127. Use -t to specify the tempo in beats (quarter notes) per minute. The notes to play are indicated using the letters A through G, with b and # for flat and sharp, respectively, and "." for rests. Notes separated by spaces are played sequentially. Notes that are not separated by spaces are played together, i.e., as a chord. The notation includes modifier characters, which make persistent changes to the way notes are played. Use + and - to increment and decrement the octave. Use > and < to increase and decrease the volume. Use "s" to toggle the damper pedal (to sustain notes) on and off. /1 indicates that the notes following it are whole notes, /2 denotes half notes, and /4, /8, /16, /32, and /64 denote quarter notes, eighth notes, and so on. For example, here the program is invoked to play a scale, followed by a trill and a chord:

```
java je3.sound.PlayerPiano "A B C D E F G +A s/32 D E C D E C /1-->>CEG"
```

One problem with the javax.sound.midi package is that although it represents the fundamental MIDI infrastructure, it does not define symbolic constants for many numbers used in the MIDI protocol. The PlayerPiano program defines some of its own constants as needed.

Example 17-5. PlayerPiano.java

```java
package je3.sound;
import java.io.*;
import javax.sound.midi.*;

public class PlayerPiano {
    // These are some MIDI constants from the spec.  They aren't defined
    // for us in javax.sound.midi.
    public static final int DAMPER_PEDAL = 64;
    public static final int DAMPER_ON = 127;
    public static final int DAMPER_OFF = 0;
    public static final int END_OF_TRACK = 47;

    public static void main(String[] args)
        throws MidiUnavailableException, InvalidMidiDataException, IOException
    {
        int instrument = 0;
        int tempo = 120;
        String filename = null;

        // Parse the options
        // -i <instrument number> default 0, a piano.  Allowed values: 0-127
        // -t <beats per minute>   default tempo is 120 quarter notes per minute
        // -o <filename>           save to a midi file instead of playing
        int a = 0;
        while(a < args.length) {
            if (args[a].equals("-i")) {
                instrument = Integer.parseInt(args[a+1]);
                a+=2;
            }
            else if (args[a].equals("-t")) {
                tempo = Integer.parseInt(args[a+1]);
                a+=2;
            }
            else if (args[a].equals("-o")) {
```

Example 17-5. PlayerPiano.java (continued)

```
            filename = args[a+1];
            a += 2;
        }
        else break;
    }

    char[ ] notes = args[a].toCharArray( );

    // 16 ticks per quarter note.
    Sequence sequence = new Sequence(Sequence.PPQ, 16);

    // Add the specified notes to the track
    addTrack(sequence, instrument, tempo, notes);

    if (filename == null) {  // no filename, so play the notes
        // Set up the Sequencer and Synthesizer objects
        Sequencer sequencer = MidiSystem.getSequencer( );
        sequencer.open( );
        Synthesizer synthesizer = MidiSystem.getSynthesizer( );
        synthesizer.open( );
        sequencer.getTransmitter( ).setReceiver(synthesizer.getReceiver( ));

        // Specify the sequence to play, and the tempo to play it at
        sequencer.setSequence(sequence);
        sequencer.setTempoInBPM(tempo);

        // Let us know when it is done playing
        sequencer.addMetaEventListener(new MetaEventListener( ) {
                public void meta(MetaMessage m) {
                    // A message of this type is automatically sent
                    // when we reach the end of the track
                    if (m.getType( ) == END_OF_TRACK) System.exit(0);
                }
            });
        // And start playing now.
        sequencer.start( );
    }
    else {  // A file name was specified, so save the notes
        int[ ] allowedTypes = MidiSystem.getMidiFileTypes(sequence);
        if (allowedTypes.length == 0) {
            System.err.println("No supported MIDI file types.");
        }
        else {
            MidiSystem.write(sequence, allowedTypes[0],
                            new File(filename));
            System.exit(0);
        }
    }
}

static final int[ ] offsets = {  // add these amounts to the base value
```

Synthesizing a MIDI Sequence | 517

Example 17-5. PlayerPiano.java (continued)

```
    // A   B   C  D  E  F  G
       -4, -2, 0, 1, 3, 5, 7
};

/*
 * This method parses the specified char[ ] of notes into a Track.
 * The musical notation is the following:
 * A-G:   A named note; Add b for flat and # for sharp.
 * +:     Move up one octave. Persists.
 * -:     Move down one octave. Persists.
 * /1:    Notes are whole notes.  Persists 'till changed
 * /2:    Half notes
 * /4:    Quarter notes
 * /n:    N can also be 8, 16, 32, 64.
 * s:     Toggle sustain pedal on or off (initially off)
 *
 * >:     Louder.  Persists
 * <:     Softer.  Persists
 * .:     Rest. Length depends on current length setting
 * Space: Play the previous note or notes; notes not separated by spaces
 *        are played at the same time
 */
public static void addTrack(Sequence s, int instrument, int tempo,
                            char[ ] notes)
    throws InvalidMidiDataException
{
    Track track = s.createTrack( );  // Begin with a new track

    // Set the instrument on channel 0
    ShortMessage sm = new ShortMessage( );
    sm.setMessage(ShortMessage.PROGRAM_CHANGE, 0, instrument, 0);
    track.add(new MidiEvent(sm, 0));

    int n = 0; // current character in notes[ ] array
    int t = 0; // time in ticks for the composition

    // These values persist and apply to all notes 'till changed
    int notelength = 16; // default to quarter notes
    int velocity = 64;   // default to middle volume
    int basekey = 60;    // 60 is middle C. Adjusted up and down by octave
    boolean sustain = false;   // is the sustain pedal depressed?
    int numnotes = 0;    // How many notes in current chord?

    while(n < notes.length) {
        char c = notes[n++];

        if (c == '+') basekey += 12;       // increase octave
        else if (c == '-') basekey -= 12;  // decrease octave
        else if (c == '>') velocity += 16; // increase volume;
        else if (c == '<') velocity -= 16; // decrease volume;
        else if (c == '/') {
```

Example 17-5. PlayerPiano.java (continued)

```
                char d = notes[n++];
                if (d == '2') notelength = 32;  // half note
                else if (d == '4') notelength = 16;  // quarter note
                else if (d == '8') notelength = 8;   // eighth note
                else if (d == '3' && notes[n++] == '2') notelength = 2;
                else if (d == '6' && notes[n++] == '4') notelength = 1;
                else if (d == '1') {
                    if (n < notes.length && notes[n] == '6')
                        notelength = 4;     // 1/16th note
                    else notelength = 64;   // whole note
                }
            }
            else if (c == 's') {
                sustain = !sustain;
                // Change the sustain setting for channel 0
                ShortMessage m = new ShortMessage( );
                m.setMessage(ShortMessage.CONTROL_CHANGE, 0,
                            DAMPER_PEDAL, sustain?DAMPER_ON:DAMPER_OFF);
                track.add(new MidiEvent(m, t));
            }
            else if (c >= 'A' && c <= 'G') {
                int key = basekey + offsets[c - 'A'];
                if (n < notes.length) {
                    if (notes[n] == 'b') { // flat
                        key--;
                        n++;
                    }
                    else if (notes[n] == '#') { // sharp
                        key++;
                        n++;
                    }
                }

                addNote(track, t, notelength, key, velocity);
                numnotes++;
            }
            else if (c == ' ') {
                // Spaces separate groups of notes played at the same time.
                // But we ignore them unless they follow a note or notes.
                if (numnotes > 0) {
                    t += notelength;
                    numnotes = 0;
                }
            }
            else if (c == '.') {
                // Rests are like spaces in that they force any previous
                // note to be output (since they are never part of chords)
                if (numnotes > 0) {
                    t += notelength;
                    numnotes = 0;
                }
```

Example 17-5. PlayerPiano.java (continued)

```
                // Now add additional rest time
                t += notelength;
            }
        }
    }

    // A convenience method to add a note to the track on channel 0
    public static void addNote(Track track, int startTick,
                              int tickLength, int key, int velocity)
            throws InvalidMidiDataException
    {
        ShortMessage on = new ShortMessage( );
        on.setMessage(ShortMessage.NOTE_ON,  0, key, velocity);
        ShortMessage off = new ShortMessage( );
        off.setMessage(ShortMessage.NOTE_OFF, 0, key, velocity);
        track.add(new MidiEvent(on, startTick));
        track.add(new MidiEvent(off, startTick + tickLength));
    }
}
```

Real-Time MIDI Sounds

Example 17-5 played a Sequence of MIDI events through a Sequencer object. It is also possible to synthesize music by directly controlling one or more MidiChannel objects of a Synthesizer object. This technique requires you to turn notes on and off in real time; it is demonstrated in Example 17-6, which turns your computer keyboard into a drum machine. This program uses MIDI channel 10, which is reserved (by the General Midi specification) for percussion. When sending notes to this channel, the different key numbers don't produce a different pitch, but instead make different percussive sounds. The Drums program displays an AWT window that is used to capture java.awt.event.KeyEvent objects. Key down and key up events are translated into noteOn and noteOff calls to the MidiChannel, using the keycode of the key as the number of the percussion instrument to play. The MIDI standard defines percussion instruments for notes 35 through 81, inclusive. You can examine the VK_ constants of KeyEvent to determine which keys produce which codes, or you can just experiment by striking keys at random!

Note that the program also uses the position of the mouse to control the volume of the percussion sounds. Move the mouse to the right side of the window for louder sounds, and move it to the left for softer sounds. If you don't hear anything, be sure that it is correctly positioned in the right side of the displayed window.

You may notice a slight delay between the time you strike a key and the time you hear a sound. This latency is inevitable with software synthesizers. The getLatency( ) method of the Synthesizer object is supposed to return the worst-case latency in microseconds.

Example 17-6. Drums.java

```java
package je3.sound;
import javax.sound.midi.*;
import java.awt.event.*;
import javax.swing.*;

/**
 * This program the MIDI percussion channel with a Swing window.  It monitors
 * keystrokes and mouse motion in the window and uses them to create music.
 * Keycodes between 35 and 81, inclusive, generate different percussive sounds.
 * See the VK_ constants in java.awt.event.KeyEvent, or just experiment.
 * Mouse position controls volume: move the mouse to the right of the window
 * to increase the volume.
 */
public class Drums extends JFrame {
    MidiChannel channel;  // The channel we play on: 10 is for percussion
    int velocity = 64;    // Default volume is 50%

    public static void main(String[] args) throws MidiUnavailableException
    {
        // We don't need a Sequencer in this example, since we send MIDI
        // events directly to the Synthesizer instead.
        Synthesizer synthesizer = MidiSystem.getSynthesizer();
        synthesizer.open();
        JFrame frame = new Drums(synthesizer);

        frame.setDefaultCloseOperation(JFrame.EXIT_ON_CLOSE);
        frame.setSize(50, 128);  // We use window width as volume control
        frame.setVisible(true);
    }

    public Drums(Synthesizer synth) {
        super("Drums");

        // Channel 10 is the GeneralMidi percussion channel.  In Java code, we
        // number channels from 0 and use channel 9 instead.
        channel = synth.getChannels()[9];

        addKeyListener(new KeyAdapter() {
                public void keyPressed(KeyEvent e) {
                    int key = e.getKeyCode();
                    if (key >= 35 && key <= 81) {
                        channel.noteOn(key, velocity);
                    }
                }
                public void keyReleased(KeyEvent e) {
                    int key = e.getKeyCode();
                    if (key >= 35 && key <= 81) channel.noteOff(key);
                }
            });
```

Example 17-6. Drums.java (continued)

```
        addMouseMotionListener(new MouseMotionAdapter( ) {
            public void mouseMoved(MouseEvent e) {
                velocity = e.getX( );
            }
        });
    }
}
```

Exercises

If you want to delve deeper into the Java Sound API, read the JavaSound Programmer's Guide included with the Java SDK documentation bundle. Also visit the *jsresources.org* web site for a useful FAQ and many more example programs. When working with MIDI programs, you may need information from the MIDI specification. Unfortunately, this spec is not available online. It can be ordered in printed form from the official *midi.org* web site, but you can often find the information you need by searching the Web.

These exercises will start you on your way to JavaSound fun:

Exercise 17-1. Convert the Drums program so that it runs as an applet within a web browser.

Exercise 17-2. Modify the PlayerPiano program to play percussion instead of piano notes. Define your own grammar for percussive scores, and have the program play your percussion Sequence repeatedly, creating a rhythm track.

Exercise 17-3. Read up on the details of the PCM audio format, and then implement an AudioInputStream subclass that synthesizes audio data (such as a pure sine wave) in this format. (This is an advanced exercise.)

IV

Enterprise Java APIs

The examples in Part IV illustrate Java APIs that are typically considered server-side or "enterprise" APIs.

This part is titled "Enterprise Java APIs," and the APIs demonstrated here are documented in more detail in *Java Enterprise in a Nutshell*, except for the XML API, which is covered in *Java in a Nutshell*. Despite the name "Enterprise," most of the APIs covered here are part of Java 2 Standard Edition (J2SE). Only the Servlet and JSP APIs are part of Java 2 Enterprise Edition (J2EE).

18

Database Access with SQL

This chapter shows how you can communicate with a database server using the JDBC API of the java.sql package. JDBC is an API that allows a Java program to communicate with a database server using Structured Query Language (SQL) commands. Note that JDBC is a SQL API, not an embedded SQL mechanism for Java.

The java.sql package provides a fairly straightforward mechanism for sending SQL queries to a database and for receiving query results. Thus, assuming that you already have experience working with databases and SQL, this chapter should be relatively easy to understand. On the other hand, if you have not worked with databases before, you'll need to learn basic SQL syntax and some general database programming concepts before you can really take advantage of the examples in this chapter and JDBC in general. I'll try to explain some of the basic concepts as I go along, so that you can get a sense of what is possible with JDBC, but full coverage of database programming is beyond the scope of this chapter. *Java Enterprise in a Nutshell* contains a more thorough introduction to JDBC, a SQL reference, and an API quick-reference for the java.sql package.

In order to run the examples in this chapter, you need access to a database, and you have to obtain and install a JDBC driver for it. If you don't already have a database server to work with, you can use one of the excellent open source databases available today. The examples in this chapter have been tested with MySQL, an open source database available from *http://www.mysql.com*. PostgreSQL, another excellent open source server, is available from *http://www.postgresql.org*. JDBC drivers for these database servers can be downloaded from the same sites. Note that database servers are complex pieces of software. Downloading and installing a database may require significant effort. (Installing the driver, on the other hand, is usually easy: add it to your classpath, or just drop it in the *jre/lib/ext/* directory of your Java installation.)

Once you've decided which database server to use, read the documentation that comes with it. Before running the examples in this chapter, you need to know how to administer the database server. In particular, you need to know how to create a test database (or you need to have your database administrator create one for you). If you are new to databases, figuring out how to do this can actually be more difficult than learning how to program with JDBC.

Accessing a Database

Example 18-1 shows a program that connects to a database and then loops, prompting the user for a SQL statement, sending that statement to the database, and displaying the results. It demonstrates the four most important techniques for JDBC programming: registering a database driver, using the DriverManager class to obtain a Connection object that represents a database connection, sending a SQL statement to the database using the Statement object, and retrieving the results of a query with a ResultSet object. Before we look at the specifics of the ExecuteSQL program, let's examine these basic techniques.

One of the interesting things about the java.sql package is that its most important members—such as Connection, Statement, and ResultSet—are interfaces instead of classes. The whole point of JDBC is to hide the specifics of accessing particular kinds of database systems, and these interfaces make that possible. A JDBC driver is a set of classes that implement the interfaces for a particular database system; different database systems require different drivers. As an application programmer, you don't have to worry about the implementation of these underlying classes. All you have to worry about is writing code that uses the methods defined by the various interfaces.

The DriverManager class is responsible for keeping track of all the JDBC drivers that are available on a system. So the first task of a JDBC program is to register an appropriate driver for the type of database being used. By convention, JDBC driver classes register themselves with the DriverManager when they are first loaded, so, in practice, all you have to do is load the driver class, allowing it to register itself. The Class.forName( ) method provides one easy way of doing this. This method takes a String argument that specifies a class name, so it's simple to pass the driver name to the program on the command line, instead of hardcoding the driver class into your program. Note that this step simply loads a driver and registers it with the DriverManager; it doesn't specify that the program actually use that driver. If a program needs to use multiple databases, it can load multiple driver classes in this step. The driver selection step comes next, when the program actually connects to a database.

After the required driver is loaded (and has registered itself), a JDBC program can connect to the database by calling DriverManager.getConnection( ). You specify the database to connect to with a *jdbc:* URL. This URL has this general syntax:

```
jdbc:subprotocol://host:port/databasename
```

The *subprotocol* of the URL identifies the particular database system that is being used. The DriverManager class uses that part of the URL to select an appropriate JDBC driver from the list of drivers that have been registered. If the DriverManager can't find a JDBC driver for the database, it throws a SQLException.

I used the MySQL database while developing the examples in this chapter, so I had to use a URL like the following to connect to my database:

```
jdbc:mysql://dbserver.mydomain.com:1234/mydb
```

This URL specifies that JDBC should connect to the database named "mydb" stored on a MySQL database server running on the host *dbserver.mydomain.com* and listening for connections on port 1234.

If you are running the database server on the same host your Java program is running on, you can omit the host name portion of the URL. If your database server is listening on its default port (which it usually does), you can omit the port number. For example:

```
jdbc:mysql:///mydb
```

Here's another *jdbc*: URL that works for a local PosgreSQL server:

```
jdbc:postgresql:///mydb
```

DriverManager.getConnection( ) returns an object that implements the Connection interface. This object represents the connection to the database; you use it to interact with the database. The createStatement( ) method of the Connection object creates an object that implements the Statement interface, which is what you use to send SQL queries and updates to the database. The executeQuery( ) and executeUpdate( ) methods of the Statement object send queries and updates, respectively, while the general-purpose execute( ) method sends a statement that can be either a query or an update.

After you send a query to the database, use the getResultSet( ) method of Statement to retrieve an object that implements the ResultSet interface. This object represents the values returned by the SQL query; it is organized into columns and rows like a table. A ResultSet offers its data one row at a time; you use next( ) to move from the current row to the next row. ResultSet provides numerous get*X*( ) methods that allow you to retrieve the data from each column of the current row as a number of different types.

The JDBC API was updated in Java 1.2 to JDBC 2.0. In JDBC 2.0, result sets can be configured to be scrollable, which means that in addition to the next( ) method, you can also use the previous( ) method to move to the previous row, first( ) and last( ) to move to the first and last rows, respectively, and absolute( ) and relative( ) to move to an arbitrary row specified with an absolute or relative row number. If your database server supports scrollable result sets, and if you're using a JDBC 2.0–compliant driver, you can specify scrollable result sets when you create your Statement object. To do this, use the two-argument version of the createStatement( ) method, with code like this:

```
Statement s = connection.createStatement(ResultSet.TYPE_SCROLL_INSENSITIVE,
                           ResultSet.CONCUR_READ_ONLY);
```

There are other possible values for the two arguments to createStatement( ), but a discussion of them is beyond the scope of this chapter. See *Java Enterprise in a Nutshell* for further information.

Now that you understand the basic techniques used in a JDBC program, let's go on to Example 18-1. The ExecuteSQL program uses all the techniques just discussed to connect to a database, execute SQL statements, and display the results. The program parses its command-line arguments to determine the class name of the JDBC driver, the URL of the database, and other parameters necessary to connect to the database. For example, you might invoke the ExecuteSQL program and enter a simple query like this (note that this long Java command line has been broken in two here):

```
% java je3.sql.ExecuteSQL -d com.mysql.jdbc.Driver \
      -u java -p nut jdbc:mysql:///apidb
sql> SELECT * FROM package WHERE name LIKE '%.rmi%'
+----+-------------------------------+
| id |              name             |
+----+-------------------------------+
| 14 | java.rmi                      |
| 15 | java.rmi.dgc                  |
| 16 | java.rmi.registry             |
| 17 | java.rmi.server               |
+----+-------------------------------+
sql> quit
```

Note that this example uses a database table that contains Java package names. If you don't have an existing database with tables to experiment with, you may want to skip ahead to the MakeAPIDB program of Example 18-3 and create some tables to play with.

Notice that ExecuteSQL uses the execute( ) method of its Statement object to execute SQL statements. Since the user can enter any kind of SQL statement, you have to use this general-purpose method. If execute( ) returns true, the SQL statement was a query, so the program retrieves the ResultSet and displays the results of the query. Otherwise, the statement was an update, so the program simply outputs information about how many rows in the database were affected by the update.

The printResultsTable( ) method handles displaying the results of a query. This method gets a ResultSetMetaData object to find out some information about the data returned by the query, so it can format the results appropriately.

There are two other important JDBC programming techniques to note in Example 18-1. The first is the handling of SQLException exceptions that are thrown. The SQLException object supports the standard exception message with getMessage( ), but it may also contain an additional message sent by the database server. You obtain this message by calling the getSQLState( ) method of the exception object.

The second technique is the handling of warnings. The SQLWarning class is a subclass of SQLException, but warnings, unlike exceptions, are not thrown. When a SQL command is executed, any warnings reported by the server are stored in a linked list of SQLWarning objects. You obtain the first SQLWarning object in this list by calling the getWarnings( ) method of the Connection object. If there are any additional SQLWarning objects, you get the next one by calling the getNextWarning( ) method of the current SQLWarning object. In Example 18-1, these warnings are displayed using a finally clause, so that they appear both when an exception is thrown and when execution completes normally.

Example 18-1. ExecuteSQL.java

```java
package je3.sql;
import java.sql.*;
import java.io.*;

/**
 * A general-purpose SQL interpreter program.
 **/
public class ExecuteSQL {
    public static void main(String[] args) {
        Connection conn = null;  // Our JDBC connection to the database server
        try {
            String driver = null, url = null, user = "", password = "";

            // Parse all the command-line arguments
            for(int n = 0; n < args.length; n++) {
                if (args[n].equals("-d")) driver = args[++n];
                else if (args[n].equals("-u")) user = args[++n];
                else if (args[n].equals("-p")) password = args[++n];
                else if (url == null) url = args[n];
                else throw new IllegalArgumentException("Unknown argument.");
            }

            // The only required argument is the database URL.
            if (url == null)
                throw new IllegalArgumentException("No database specified");

            // If the user specified the classname for the DB driver, load
            // that class dynamically.  This gives the driver the opportunity
            // to register itself with the DriverManager.
            if (driver != null) Class.forName(driver);

            // Now open a connection to the specified database, using the
            // user-specified username and password, if any.  The driver
            // manager will try all of the DB drivers it knows about to try to
            // parse the URL and connect to the DB server.
            conn = DriverManager.getConnection(url, user, password);

            // Now create the statement object we'll use to talk to the DB
            Statement s = conn.createStatement();

            // Get a stream to read from the console
            BufferedReader in =
                new BufferedReader(new InputStreamReader(System.in));

            // Loop forever, reading the user's queries and executing them
            while(true) {
                System.out.print("sql> ");     // prompt the user
                System.out.flush();            // make the prompt appear now.
                String sql = in.readLine();    // get a line of input from user

                // Quit when the user types "quit".
                if ((sql == null) || sql.equals("quit")) break;
```

Example 18-1. ExecuteSQL.java (continued)

```java
            // Ignore blank lines
            if (sql.length( ) == 0) continue;

            // Now, execute the user's line of SQL and display results.
            try {
                // We don't know if this is a query or some kind of
                // update, so we use execute( ) instead of executeQuery( )
                // or executeUpdate( ). If the return value is true, it was
                // a query, else an update.
                boolean status = s.execute(sql);

                // Some complex SQL queries can return more than one set
                // of results, so loop until there are no more results
                do {
                    if (status) { // it was a query and returns a ResultSet
                        ResultSet rs = s.getResultSet( );   // Get results
                        printResultsTable(rs, System.out); // Display them
                    }
                    else {
                        // If the SQL command that was executed was some
                        // kind of update rather than a query, then it
                        // doesn't return a ResultSet.  Instead, we just
                        // print the number of rows that were affected.
                        int numUpdates = s.getUpdateCount( );
                        System.out.println("Ok. " + numUpdates +
                                               " rows affected.");
                    }

                    // Now go see if there are even more results, and
                    // continue the results display loop if there are.
                    status = s.getMoreResults( );
                } while(status || s.getUpdateCount( ) != -1);
            }
            // If a SQLException is thrown, display an error message.
            // Note that SQLExceptions can have a general message and a
            // DB-specific message returned by getSQLState( )
            catch (SQLException e) {
                System.err.println("SQLException: " + e.getMessage( )+ ":" +
                                    e.getSQLState( ));
            }
            // Each time through this loop, check to see if there were any
            // warnings.  Note that there can be a whole chain of warnings.
            finally { // print out any warnings that occurred
                SQLWarning w;
                for(w=conn.getWarnings( ); w != null; w=w.getNextWarning( ))
                    System.err.println("WARNING: " + w.getMessage( ) +
                                        ":" + w.getSQLState( ));
            }
        }
    }
    // Handle exceptions that occur during argument parsing, database
    // connection setup, etc.  For SQLExceptions, print the details.
```

Example 18-1. ExecuteSQL.java (continued)

```
        catch (Exception e) {
            System.err.println(e);
            if (e instanceof SQLException)
                System.err.println("SQL State: " +
                                   ((SQLException)e).getSQLState( ));
            System.err.println("Usage: java ExecuteSQL [-d <driver>] " +
                               "[-u <user>] [-p <password>] <database URL>");
        }

        // Be sure to always close the database connection when we exit,
        // whether we exit because the user types 'quit' or because of an
        // exception thrown while setting things up.  Closing this connection
        // also implicitly closes any open statements and result sets
        // associated with it.
        finally {
            try { conn.close( ); } catch (Exception e) { }
        }
    }

    /**
     * This method attempts to output the contents of a ResultSet in a
     * textual table.  It relies on the ResultSetMetaData class, but a fair
     * bit of the code is simple string manipulation.
     **/
    static void printResultsTable(ResultSet rs, OutputStream output)
        throws SQLException
    {
        // Set up the output stream
        PrintWriter out = new PrintWriter(output);

        // Get some "meta data" (column names, etc.) about the results
        ResultSetMetaData metadata = rs.getMetaData( );

        // Variables to hold important data about the table to be displayed
        int numcols = metadata.getColumnCount( ); // how many columns
        String[ ] labels = new String[numcols];   // the column labels
        int[ ] colwidths = new int[numcols];       // the width of each
        int[ ] colpos = new int[numcols];          // start position of each
        int linewidth;                             // total width of table

        // Figure out how wide the columns are, where each one begins,
        // how wide each row of the table will be, etc.
        linewidth = 1; // for the initial '|'.
        for(int i = 0; i < numcols; i++) {                   // for each column
            colpos[i] = linewidth;                           // save its position
            labels[i] = metadata.getColumnLabel(i+1);        // get its label
            // Get the column width.  If the db doesn't report one, guess
            // 30 characters.  Then check the length of the label, and use
            // it if it if it is larger than the column width
            int size = metadata.getColumnDisplaySize(i+1);
            if (size == -1) size = 30;  // Some drivers return -1...
            if (size > 500) size = 30;  // Don't allow unreasonable sizes
```

Example 18-1. ExecuteSQL.java (continued)

```
            int labelsize = labels[i].length( );
            if (labelsize > size) size = labelsize;
            colwidths[i] = size + 1;                 // save the column size
            linewidth += colwidths[i] + 2;           // increment total size
        }

        // Create a horizontal divider line we use in the table.
        // Also create a blank line that is the initial value of each
        // line of the table
        StringBuffer divider = new StringBuffer(linewidth);
        StringBuffer blankline = new StringBuffer(linewidth);
        for(int i = 0; i < linewidth; i++) {
            divider.insert(i, '-');
            blankline.insert(i, " ");
        }
        // Put special marks in the divider line at the column positions
        for(int i=0; i<numcols; i++) divider.setCharAt(colpos[i]-1,'+');
        divider.setCharAt(linewidth-1, '+');

        // Begin the table output with a divider line
        out.println(divider);

        // The next line of the table contains the column labels.
        // Begin with a blank line, and put the column names and column
        // divider characters "|" into it.  overwrite( ) is defined below.
        StringBuffer line = new StringBuffer(blankline.toString( ));
        line.setCharAt(0, '|');
        for(int i = 0; i < numcols; i++) {
            int pos = colpos[i] + 1 + (colwidths[i]-labels[i].length( ))/2;
            overwrite(line, pos, labels[i]);
            overwrite(line, colpos[i] + colwidths[i], " |");
        }

        // Then output the line of column labels and another divider
        out.println(line);
        out.println(divider);

        // Now, output the table data.  Loop through the ResultSet, using
        // the next( ) method to get the rows one at a time. Obtain the
        // value of each column with getObject( ), and output it, much as
        // we did for the column labels above.
        while(rs.next( )) {
            line = new StringBuffer(blankline.toString( ));
            line.setCharAt(0, '|');
            for(int i = 0; i < numcols; i++) {
                Object value = rs.getObject(i+1);
                if (value != null)
                    overwrite(line, colpos[i] + 1, value.toString( ).trim( ));
                overwrite(line, colpos[i] + colwidths[i], " |");
            }
            out.println(line);
        }
```

Example 18-1. ExecuteSQL.java (continued)

```
        // Finally, end the table with one last divider line.
        out.println(divider);
        out.flush( );
    }

    /** This utility method is used when printing the table of results */
    static void overwrite(StringBuffer b, int pos, String s) {
        int slen = s.length( );              // string length
        int blen = b.length( );              // buffer length
        if (pos+slen > blen) slen = blen-pos; // does it fit?
        for(int i = 0; i < slen; i++)        // copy string into buffer
            b.setCharAt(pos+i, s.charAt(i));
    }
}
```

Using Database Metadata

Sometimes, in addition to querying and updating the data in a database, you also want to retrieve information about the database itself and its contents. This information is called *metadata*. The DatabaseMetaData interface allows you to retrieve this kind of information. You can obtain an object that implements this interface by calling the getMetaData( ) method of the Connection object, as shown in Example 18-2.

After GetDBInfo opens a database Connection and obtains a DatabaseMetaData object, it displays some general information about the database server and JDBC driver. Then, if the user just specified a database name on the command line, the program lists all the tables in that database. If the user specified a database name and a table name, however, the program lists the name and data type of each column in that table.

An interesting feature of this GetDBInfo program is how it obtains the parameters needed to connect to the database. The example operates on the premise that at any given site, it is typically used to connect to the same database server, using the same database driver, and may also be used with the same database username and password. So, instead of requiring the user to type all this cumbersome information on the command line each time the program is run, the program reads default values from a file named *DB.props* that is stored in the same directory as the *GetDBInfo.class* file. In order to run Example 18-2, you have to create an appropriate *DB.props* file for your system. On my system, this file contains:

```
# The name of the JDBC driver class
driver=com.mysql.jdbc.Driver
# The URL that specifies the database server.
# It should not include the name of the database to connect to
server=jdbc:mysql:///
# The database account name
user=david
# The password for the specified account, if any.
# Uncomment the line below if you need to specify a password
#password=
```

Lines that begin with # are comments, obviously. The *name=value* format is the standard file format for the java.util.Properties object that is used to read the contents of this file.

After the program reads the default values from the *DB.props* file, it parses its command-line arguments, which can override the driver, server, user, and password properties specified in the file. The name of the database to connect to must be specified on the command line; the database name is simply appended to the server URL. The name of a table in the database can optionally be specified on the command line. For example, you might run the program as follows:

```
% java je3.sql.GetDBInfo api class
DBMS: MySQL 4.0.14-standard
JDBC Driver: MySQL-AB JDBC Driver 3.0.8-stable ($Date: 2004/01/08 16:45:15 $)
Database: jdbc:mysql:///apidb
User: david@localhost
Columns of class:
        id : int
        packageId : int
        name : varchar
```

Example 18-2. GetDBInfo.java

```
package je3.sql;
import java.sql.*;
import java.util.Properties;

/**
 * This class uses the DatabaseMetaData class to obtain information about
 * the database, the JDBC driver, and the tables in the database, or about
 * the columns of a named table.
 **/
public class GetDBInfo {
    public static void main(String[] args) {
        Connection c = null;  // The JDBC connection to the database server
        try {
            // Look for the properties file DB.props in the same directory as
            // this program.  It will contain default values for the various
            // parameters needed to connect to a database
            Properties p = new Properties();
            try { p.load(GetDBInfo.class.getResourceAsStream("DB.props")); }
            catch (Exception e) {}

            // Get default values from the properties file
            String driver = p.getProperty("driver");       // Driver class name
            String server = p.getProperty("server", "");  // JDBC URL for server
            String user = p.getProperty("user", "");       // db user name
            String password = p.getProperty("password", ""); // db password

            // These variables don't have defaults
            String database = null; // The db name (appended to server URL)
            String table = null;    // The optional name of a table in the db
```

Example 18-2. GetDBInfo.java (continued)

```java
// Parse the command-line args to override the default values above
for(int i = 0; i < args.length; i++) {
    if (args[i].equals("-d")) driver = args[++i];      //-d <driver>
    else if (args[i].equals("-s")) server = args[++i];//-s <server>
    else if (args[i].equals("-u")) user = args[++i];  //-u <user>
    else if (args[i].equals("-p")) password = args[++i];
    else if (database == null) database = args[i];    // <dbname>
    else if (table == null) table = args[i];           // <table>
    else throw new IllegalArgumentException("Unknown argument: "
                                            +args[i]);
}

// Make sure that at least a server or a database were specified.
// If not, we have no idea what to connect to, and cannot continue.
if ((server.length() == 0) && (database.length() == 0))
    throw new IllegalArgumentException("No database specified.");

// Load the db driver, if any was specified.
if (driver != null) Class.forName(driver);

// Now attempt to open a connection to the specified database on
// the specified server, using the specified name and password
c = DriverManager.getConnection(server+database, user, password);

// Get the DatabaseMetaData object for the connection.  This is the
// object that will return us all the data we're interested in here
DatabaseMetaData md = c.getMetaData();

// Display information about the server, the driver, etc.
System.out.println("DBMS: " + md.getDatabaseProductName() +
                   " " + md.getDatabaseProductVersion());
System.out.println("JDBC Driver: " + md.getDriverName() +
                   " " + md.getDriverVersion());
System.out.println("Database: " + md.getURL());
System.out.println("User: " + md.getUserName());

// Now, if the user did not specify a table, then display a list of
// all tables defined in the named database.  Note that tables are
// returned in a ResultSet, just like query results are.
if (table == null) {
    System.out.println("Tables:");
    ResultSet r = md.getTables("", "", "%", null);
    while(r.next()) System.out.println("\t" + r.getString(3));
}

// Otherwise, list all columns of the specified table.
// Again, information about the columns is returned in a ResultSet
else {
    System.out.println("Columns of " + table + ": ");
    ResultSet r = md.getColumns("", "", table, "%");
```

Example 18-2. GetDBInfo.java (continued)

```
            while(r.next( ))
                System.out.println("\t" + r.getString(4) + " : " +
                                    r.getString(6));
        }
    }
    // Print an error message if anything goes wrong.
    catch (Exception e) {
        System.err.println(e);
        if (e instanceof SQLException)
            System.err.println(((SQLException)e).getSQLState( ));
        System.err.println("Usage: java GetDBInfo [-d <driver>] " +
                           "[-s <dbserver>]\n" +
                           "\t[-u <username>] [-p <password>] <dbname>");
    }
    // Always remember to close the Connection object when we're done!
    finally {
        try { c.close( ); } catch (Exception e) { }
    }
    }
}
```

Building a Database

Example 18-3 shows a program, MakeAPIDB, that takes a list of class names and uses the Java Reflection API to build a database of those classes, the packages they belong to, and all methods and fields defined by the classes. Example 18-4 shows a program that uses the database created by this example.

MakeAPIDB uses the SQL CREATE TABLE statement to add three tables, named package, class, and member, to the database. The program then inserts data into those tables using INSERT INTO statements. The program uses the same INSERT INTO statements repeatedly, as it iterates though the list of class names. In this type of situation, you can often increase the efficiency of your insertions if you use PreparedStatement objects to execute the statements.

A prepared statement is essentially a blueprint for the statements you need to execute. When you send a SQL statement to the database, the database interprets the SQL and creates a template for executing the statement. If you are sending the same SQL statement repeatedly, only with different input parameters, the database still has to interpret the SQL each time. On database platforms that support prepared statements, you can eliminate this inefficiency by sending a prepared statement to the database before you actually make any calls to the database. The database interprets the prepared statement and creates its template just once. Then, when you execute the prepared statement repeatedly with different input parameters, the database uses the template it has already created. JDBC provides the PreparedStatement class to support prepared statements, but it doesn't guarantee that the underlying database actually takes advantage of them.

You create a PreparedStatement with the prepareStatement( ) method of a Connection object, as shown in Example 18-3. MakeAPIDB passes a SQL statement to prepareStatement( ), substituting ? placeholders for the variable parameters in the statement. Later, before the program executes the prepared statement, it binds values to these parameters using the various setX( ) methods (e.g., setInt( ) and setString( )) of the PreparedStatement object. Each setX( ) method takes two arguments: a parameter index (starting with 1) and a value. Then the program calls the executeUpdate( ) method of the PreparedStatement to execute the statement. (PreparedStatement also provides execute( ) and executeQuery( ) methods, just like Statement.)

MakeAPIDB expects its first argument to be the name of a file that contains a list of classes to be placed into the database. The classes should be listed one to a line; each line must contain a fully qualified class name (i.e., it must specify both package name and class name). Such a file might contain lines like the following:

```
java.applet.Applet
java.applet.AppletContext
java.applet.AppletStub
        ...
java.util.zip.ZipOutputStream
```

The program reads database parameters from a Properties file named *APIDB.props* in the current directory or from an alternate Properties file specified as the second command-line argument. This Properties file is similar to, but not quite the same as, the one used in conjunction with Example 18-2; it should contain properties named driver, database, user, and password. On my system, the *APIDB.props* file looks as follows:

```
# The full classname of the JDBC driver to load: this is a MySQL driver
driver=com.mysql.jdbc.Driver
# The URL of the mysql server (localhost) and database (apidb) to connect to
database=jdbc:mysql:///apidb
# The name of the database user account
user=david
# The password for the database user account.
# Uncomment the line below to specify a password
#password=
```

Note that before you run this program, you must create the database for it on your database server. To do this, you have to follow the instructions provided by your database vendor. You can also use an existing database, as long as it doesn't already contain tables named package, class, or member.

Example 18-3. MakeAPIDB.java

```
package je3.sql;
import java.sql.*;
import java.lang.reflect.*;
import java.io.*;
import java.util.*;

/**
 * This class is a standalone program that reads a list of classes and
 * builds a database of packages, classes, and class fields and methods.
 **/
public class MakeAPIDB {
    public static void main(String args[ ]) {
```

Example 18-3. MakeAPIDB.java (continued)

```
Connection c = null;        // The connection to the database
try {
    // Read the classes to index from a file specified by args[0]
    ArrayList classnames = new ArrayList( );
    BufferedReader in = new BufferedReader(new FileReader(args[0]));
    String name;
    while((name = in.readLine( )) != null) classnames.add(name);

    // Now determine the values needed to set up the database
    // connection. The program attempts to read a property file named
    // "APIDB.props", or one optionally specified by args[1].  This
    // property file (if any) may contain "driver", "database", "user",
    // and "password" properties that specify the necessary values for
    // connecting to the db.  If the properties file does not exist, or
    // does not contain the named properties, defaults will be used.
    Properties p = new Properties( );        // Empty properties
    try {
        p.load(new FileInputStream(args[1])); // Try to load properties
    }
    catch (Exception e1) {
        try { p.load(new FileInputStream("APIDB.props")); }
        catch (Exception e2) { }
    }

    // Read values from Properties file
    String driver = p.getProperty("driver");
    String database = p.getProperty("database");
    String user = p.getProperty("user", "");
    String password = p.getProperty("password", "");

    // The driver and database properties are mandatory
    if (driver == null)
        throw new IllegalArgumentException("No driver specified!");
    if (database == null)
        throw new IllegalArgumentException("No database specified!");

    // Load the driver.  It registers itself with DriverManager.
    Class.forName(driver);

    // And set up a connection to the specified database
    c = DriverManager.getConnection(database, user, password);

    // Create three new tables for our data
    // The package table contains a package id and a package name.
    // The class table contains a class id, a package id, and a name.
    // The member table contains a class id, a member name, and a bit
    // that indicates whether the class member is a field or a method.
    Statement s = c.createStatement( );
    s.executeUpdate("CREATE TABLE package " +
                "(id INT, name VARCHAR(80))");
    s.executeUpdate("CREATE TABLE class " +
                "(id INT, packageId INT, name VARCHAR(48))");
```

Example 18-3. MakeAPIDB.java (continued)

```
            s.executeUpdate("CREATE TABLE member " +
                            "(classId INT, name VARCHAR(48), isField BIT)");

            // Prepare some statements that will be used to insert records into
            // these three tables.
            insertpackage =
                c.prepareStatement("INSERT INTO package VALUES(?,?)");
            insertclass =
                c.prepareStatement("INSERT INTO class VALUES(?,?,?)");
            insertmember =
                c.prepareStatement("INSERT INTO member VALUES(?,?,?)");

            // Now loop through the list of classes and use reflection
            // to store them all in the tables
            int numclasses = classnames.size();
            for(int i = 0; i < numclasses; i++) {
                try {
                    storeClass((String)classnames.get(i));
                }
                catch(ClassNotFoundException e) {
                    System.out.println("WARNING: class not found: " +
                                        classnames.get(i) + "; SKIPPING");
                }
            }
        }
        catch (Exception e) {
            System.err.println(e);
            if (e instanceof SQLException)
                System.err.println("SQLState: " +
                                    ((SQLException)e).getSQLState());
            System.err.println("Usage: java MakeAPIDB " +
                                "<classlistfile> <propfile>");
        }
        // When we're done, close the connection to the database
        finally { try { c.close(); } catch (Exception e) {} }
    }

    /**
     * This hash table records the mapping between package names and package
     * id.  This is the only one we need to store temporarily.  The others are
     * stored in the db and don't have to be looked up by this program
     **/
    static Map package_to_id = new HashMap();

    // Counters for the package and class identifier columns
    static int packageId = 0, classId = 0;

    // Some prepared SQL statements for use in inserting
    // new values into the tables.  Initialized in main() above.
    static PreparedStatement insertpackage, insertclass, insertmember;
```

Example 18-3. MakeAPIDB.java (continued)

```
/**
 * Given a fully-qualified classname, this method stores the package name
 * in the package table (if it is not already there), stores the class name
 * in the class table, and then uses the Java Reflection API to look up all
 * methods and fields of the class, and stores those in the member table.
 **/
public static void storeClass(String name)
    throws SQLException, ClassNotFoundException
{
    String packagename, classname;

    // Dynamically load the class.
    Class c = Class.forName(name);

    // Display output so the user knows that the program is progressing
    System.out.println("Storing data for: " + name);

    // Figure out the packagename and the classname
    int pos = name.lastIndexOf('.');
    if (pos == -1) {
        packagename = "";
        classname = name;
    }
    else {
        packagename = name.substring(0,pos);
        classname = name.substring(pos+1);
    }

    // Figure out what the package id is.  If there is one, then this
    // package has already been stored in the database.  Otherwise, assign
    // an id, and store it and the packagename in the db.
    Integer pid;
    pid = (Integer)package_to_id.get(packagename);  // Check hashtable
    if (pid == null) {
        pid = new Integer(++packageId);             // Assign an id
        package_to_id.put(packagename, pid);        // Remember it
        insertpackage.setInt(1, packageId);         // Set statement args
        insertpackage.setString(2, packagename);
        insertpackage.executeUpdate();              // Insert into package db
    }

    // Now, store the classname in the class table of the database.
    // This record includes the package id, so that the class is linked to
    // the package that contains it.  To store the class, we set arguments
    // to the PreparedStatement, then execute that statement
    insertclass.setInt(1, ++classId);           // Set class identifier
    insertclass.setInt(2, pid.intValue());      // Set package identifier
    insertclass.setString(3, classname);        // Set class name
    insertclass.executeUpdate();                // Insert the class record

    // Now, get a list of all non-private methods of the class, and
    // insert those into the "members" table of the database.  Each
```

Example 18-3. MakeAPIDB.java (continued)

```
            // record includes the class id of the containing class, and also
            // a value that indicates that these are methods, not fields.
            Method[ ] methods = c.getDeclaredMethods( );    // Get a list of methods
            for(int i = 0; i < methods.length; i++) {       // For all non-private
                if (Modifier.isPrivate(methods[i].getModifiers( ))) continue;
                insertmember.setInt(1, classId);            // Set the class id
                insertmember.setString(2, methods[i].getName( )); // Set method name
                insertmember.setBoolean(3, false);          // It is not a field
                insertmember.executeUpdate( );              // Insert into db
            }

            // Do the same thing for the non-private fields of the class
            Field[ ] fields = c.getDeclaredFields( );       // Get a list of fields
            for(int i = 0; i < fields.length; i++) {        // For each non-private
                if (Modifier.isPrivate(fields[i].getModifiers( ))) continue;
                insertmember.setInt(1, classId);            // Set the class id
                insertmember.setString(2, fields[i].getName( )); // Set field name
                insertmember.setBoolean(3, true);           // It is a field
                insertmember.executeUpdate( );              // Insert the record
            }
        }
    }
}
```

Using the API Database

Example 18-4 displays a program, LookupAPI, that uses the database built by the MakeAPIDB program of Example 18-3 and makes interesting SQL queries against it. LookupAPI behaves as follows:

- When invoked with the name of a class member, it lists the full name (including package and class) of each field and/or method that has that name.

- When run with the name of a class, it lists the full name of every class in any package that has that name.

- When called with a portion of a package name, it lists the names of all the packages that contain that string.

- When invoked with the -1 option and a class name, it lists every member of every class that has that name.

- When run with the -1 option and a portion of a package name, it lists all the classes and interfaces in any package that matches that string.

LookupAPI reads the same *APIDB.props* property file MakeAPIDB does. Or, alternatively, it reads a property file specified on the command line following a -p flag. Using the database connection parameters in the property file, the program connects to a database and executes the necessary SQL queries to return the desired information. Note that it calls the setReadOnly( ) method of the Connection object. Doing this provides a hint that the program performs only queries and doesn't modify the database in any way. For some database systems, this may improve efficiency. Other than the setReadOnly( ) method, this example doesn't introduce any new JDBC features. It simply serves as a real-world application of a database and demonstrates some of the powerful database queries that can be expressed using SQL.

Example 18-4. LookupAPI.java

```java
package je3.sql;
import java.sql.*;
import java.io.FileInputStream;
import java.util.Properties;

/**
 * This program uses the database created by MakeAPIDB.  It opens a connection
 * to a database using the same property file used by MakeAPIDB.  Then it
 * queries that database in several interesting ways to obtain useful
 * information about Java APIs.  It can be used to look up the fully-qualified
 * name of a member, class, or package, or it can be used to list the members
 * of a class or package.
 **/
public class LookupAPI {
    public static void main(String[] args) {
        Connection c = null;                    // JDBC connection to the database
        try {
            // Some default values
            String target = null;               // The name to look up
            boolean list = false;               // List members or lookup name?
            String propfile = "APIDB.props";   // The file of db parameters

            // Parse the command-line arguments
            for(int i = 0; i < args.length; i++) {
                if (args[i].equals("-l")) list = true;
                else if (args[i].equals("-p")) propfile = args[++i];
                else if (target != null)
                    throw new IllegalArgumentException("Unexpected argument: "
                                                      + args[i]);
                else target = args[i];
            }
            if (target == null)
                throw new IllegalArgumentException("No target specified");

            // Now determine the values needed to set up the database
            // connection. The program attempts to read a property file
            // named "APIDB.props", or optionally specified with the
            // -p argument.  This property file may contain "driver",
            // "database", "user", and "password" properties that
            // specify the necessary values for connecting to the db.
            // If the properties file does not exist, or does not
            // contain the named properties, defaults will be used.
            Properties p = new Properties();                 // Empty properties
            try { p.load(new FileInputStream(propfile)); } // Try to load props
            catch (Exception e) {}

            // Read values from Properties file
            String driver = p.getProperty("driver");
            String database = p.getProperty("database");
            String user = p.getProperty("user", "");
            String password = p.getProperty("password", "");
```

Example 18-4. LookupAPI.java (continued)

```
                // The driver and database properties are mandatory
                if (driver == null)
                    throw new IllegalArgumentException("No driver specified!");
                if (database == null)
                    throw new IllegalArgumentException("No database specified!");

                // Load the database driver
                Class.forName(driver);

                // And set up a connection to the specified database
                c = DriverManager.getConnection(database, user, password);

                // Tell it we will not do any updates.
                // This hint may improve efficiency.
                c.setReadOnly(true);

                // If the "-l" option was given, then list the members of
                // the named package or class.  Otherwise, lookup all
                // matches for the specified member, class, or package.
                if (list) list(c, target);
                else lookup(c, target);
            }
            // If anything goes wrong, print the exception and a usage message.  If
            // a SQLException is thrown, display the state message it includes.
            catch (Exception e) {
                System.out.println(e);
                if (e instanceof SQLException)
                    System.out.println(((SQLException) e).getSQLState());
                System.out.println("Usage: java LookupAPI [-l] [-p <propfile>] " +
                                   "target");
            }
            // Always close the DB connection when we're done with it.
            finally {
                try { c.close(); } catch (Exception e) {}
            }
        }

        /**
         * This method looks up all matches for the specified target string in the
         * database.  First, it prints the full name of any members by that name.
         * Then it prints the full name of any classes by that name.  Then it
         * prints the name of any packages that contain the specified name
         **/
        public static void lookup(Connection c, String target) throws SQLException
        {
            // Create the Statement object we'll use to query the database
            Statement s = c.createStatement();

            // Go find all class members with the specified name
            s.executeQuery("SELECT DISTINCT " +
                           "package.name, class.name, member.name, member.isField"+
                           " FROM package, class, member" +
                           " WHERE member.name='" + target + "'" +
```

Example 18-4. LookupAPI.java (continued)

```
               "   AND member.classId=class.id " +
               "   AND class.packageId=package.id");

        // Loop through the results, and print them out (if there are any).
        ResultSet r = s.getResultSet( );
        while(r.next( )) {
            String pkg = r.getString(1);        // package name
            String cls = r.getString(2);        // class name
            String member = r.getString(3);     // member name
            boolean isField = r.getBoolean(4);  // is the member a field?
            // Display this match
            System.out.println(pkg + "." + cls + "." + member +
                               (isField?"":"( )"));
        }

        // Now look for a class with the specified name
        s.executeQuery("SELECT package.name, class.name " +
                       "FROM package, class " +
                       "WHERE class.name='" + target + "' " +
                       "   AND class.packageId=package.id");
        // Loop through the results and print them out
        r = s.getResultSet( );
        while(r.next( )) System.out.println(r.getString(1) + "." +
                                            r.getString(2));

        // Finally, look for a package that matches a part of the name.
        // Note the use of the SQL LIKE keyword and % wildcard characters
        s.executeQuery("SELECT name FROM package " +
                       "WHERE name='" + target + "'" +
                       "   OR name LIKE '%." + target + ".%' " +
                       "   OR name LIKE '" + target + ".%' " +
                       "   OR name LIKE '%." + target + "'");
        // Loop through the results and print them out
        r = s.getResultSet( );
        while(r.next( )) System.out.println(r.getString(1));

        // Finally, close the Statement object
        s.close( );
    }

    /**
     * This method looks for classes with the specified name, or packages
     * that contain the specified name.  For each class it finds, it displays
     * all methods and fields of the class.  For each package it finds, it
     * displays all classes in the package.
     **/
    public static void list(Connection conn, String target) throws SQLException
    {
        // Create two Statement objects to query the database with
        Statement s = conn.createStatement( );
        Statement t = conn.createStatement( );
```

Example 18-4. LookupAPI.java (continued)

```java
// Look for a class with the given name
s.executeQuery("SELECT package.name, class.name " +
               "FROM package, class " +
               "WHERE class.name='" + target + "' " +
               "  AND class.packageId=package.id");
// Loop through all matches
ResultSet r = s.getResultSet();
while(r.next()) {
    String p = r.getString(1);  // package name
    String c = r.getString(2);  // class name
    // Print out the matching class name
    System.out.println("class " + p + "." + c + " {");

    // Now query all members of the class
    t.executeQuery("SELECT DISTINCT member.name, member.isField " +
                   "FROM package, class, member " +
                   "WHERE package.name = '" + p + "' " +
                   "  AND class.name = '" + c + "' " +
                   "  AND member.classId=class.id " +
                   "  AND class.packageId=package.id " +
                   "ORDER BY member.isField, member.name");

    // Loop through the ordered list of all members, and print them out
    ResultSet r2 = t.getResultSet();
    while(r2.next()) {
        String m = r2.getString(1);
        int isField = r2.getInt(2);
        System.out.println("   " + m + ((isField == 1)?"":"()"));
    }
    // End the class listing
    System.out.println("}");
}

// Now go look for a package that matches the specified name
s.executeQuery("SELECT name FROM package " +
               "WHERE name='" + target + "'" +
               "  OR name LIKE '%." + target + ".%' " +
               "  OR name LIKE '" + target + ".%' " +
               "  OR name LIKE '%." + target + "'");
// Loop through any matching packages
r = s.getResultSet();
while(r.next()) {
    // Display the name of the package
    String p = r.getString(1);
    System.out.println("Package " + p + ": ");

    // Get a list of all classes and interfaces in the package
    t.executeQuery("SELECT class.name FROM package, class " +
                   "WHERE package.name='" + p + "' " +
                   "  AND class.packageId=package.id " +
                   "ORDER BY class.name");
    // Loop through the list and print them out.
    ResultSet r2 = t.getResultSet();
```

Example 18-4. LookupAPI.java (continued)

```
        while(r2.next( )) System.out.println("  " + r2.getString(1));
    }

    // Finally, close both Statement objects
    s.close( ); t.close( );
    }
}
```

Atomic Transactions

By default, a newly created database Connection object is in auto-commit mode. That means that each update to the database is treated as a separate transaction and is automatically committed to the database. Sometimes, however, you want to group several updates into a single atomic transaction, with the property that either all the updates complete successfully or no updates occur at all. With a database system (and JDBC driver) that supports it, you can take the Connection out of auto-commit mode and explicitly call commit( ) to commit a batch of transactions or call rollback( ) to abort a batch of transactions, undoing the ones that have already been done. Example 21-3 in Chapter 21 uses atomic transactions to ensure database consistency.

Exercises

Exercise 18-1. Before you begin using JDBC, you must first have a database server and a JDBC driver for it, and you must know how to administer the server in order to do such things as create new databases. If you are not already an experienced database programmer, learning to do all this is more difficult than actually programming with JDBC. For this first exercise, therefore, obtain and install a database server if you don't already have one. Obtain and install a JDBC driver for it. Read the documentation for both the server and the driver. Learn the basics of the SQL language, if you don't already know it, and make a note of what SQL subset or SQL extensions are supported by your server and JDBC driver.

Exercise 18-2. Example 18-1 is a general-purpose SQL interpreter program that displays database query results in a rudimentary text-based table format. Modify the program so that it outputs query results using HTML table syntax, resulting in output suitable for display in a web browser. Test your program by issuing queries against some existing database.

Exercise 18-3. Write a program to create a database table of all files and directories stored on your computer (or at least all files and directories beneath a specified directory). Each entry in the database table should include a filename, a size, a modification date, and a boolean value that indicates whether it is a file or a directory. Run this program to generate a database of files. Write a second program that allows a user to make useful queries against this database, such as "list all files larger than 1 megabyte that are older than 1 month," or "list all files with the extension *.java* that were modified today." Optionally, design and create a GUI that allows a user to issue this sort of complicated query without knowing SQL.

19

XML

XML, or Extensible Markup Language, is a meta-language for marking up text documents with structural tags, similar to those found in HTML and SGML documents. XML has become popular because its structural markup allows documents to describe their own format and contents. XML enables "portable data," and it can be quite powerful when combined with the "portable code" enabled by Java.

Because of the popularity of XML, there are a number of tools for parsing and manipulating XML documents. And because XML documents are becoming more and more common, it is worth your time to learn how to use some of those tools to work with XML. The examples in this chapter introduce you to simple XML parsing and manipulation. If you are familiar with the basic structure of an XML file, you should have no problem understanding them. Note that there are many subtleties to working with XML; this chapter doesn't attempt to explain them all. To learn more about XML, try *Java and XML*, by Brett McLaughlin, or *XML Pocket Reference*, by Robert Eckstein, both from O'Reilly.

Parsing with JAXP and SAX

The first thing you want to do with an XML document is parse it. There are two commonly used approaches to XML parsing: they go by the acronyms SAX and DOM. We'll begin with SAX parsing; DOM parsing is covered later in the chapter.

SAX is the Simple API for XML. SAX is not a parser, but rather a Java API that describes how a parser operates. When parsing an XML document using the SAX API, you define a class that implements various "event" handling methods. As the parser encounters the various element types of the XML document, it invokes the corresponding event-handler methods you've defined. Your methods take whatever actions are required to accomplish the desired task. In the SAX model, the parser converts an XML document into a sequence of Java method calls. The parser doesn't build a parse tree of any kind (although your methods can do this, if you want). SAX parsing is typically quite efficient and is therefore often your best choice for most simple XML processing tasks. SAX-style XML parsing is known as "push parsing" because the parser "pushes" events to your event handler methods. This is in contrast to more traditional "pull parsing" in which your code "pulls" tokens from a parser.

The SAX API was created by David Megginson (*http://www.megginson.com/*) and is now maintained at *http://www.saxproject.org*. The Java binding of the SAX API consists of the package org.xml.sax and its subpackages. SAX is a de facto standard but has not been standardized by any official body. There are two versions of the SAX API. Version 2 is substantially different from the original Version 1, and is today the most common. We cover Version 2 in this chapter.

SAX is an API, not an implementation. Various XML parsers implement the SAX API, and in order to use SAX you need an underlying parser implementation. This is where JAXP comes in. JAXP is the Java API for XML Parsing, and was added to J2SE in Java 1.4.* JAXP consists of the javax.xml.parsers package, and also javax.xml.transform, which we'll consider later in this chapter. JAXP provides a thin layer on top of SAX (and on top of DOM, which we'll also see later) and standardizes an API for obtaining and using SAX (and DOM) parser objects. The JAXP package includes default parser implementations but allows other parsers to be easily plugged in and configured using system properties.

Example 19-1 is a listing of *ListServlets.java*, a program that uses JAXP and SAX to parse a web application deployment descriptor and list the names of the servlets configured by that file. We'll see servlets and their deployment descriptors in Chapter 20, but until then you just need to know that servlet-based web applications are configured using an XML file named *web.xml*. This file contains <servlet> tags that define mappings between servlet names and the Java classes that implement them. It also contains <servlet-mapping> tags that map from servlet name to a URL or URL pattern by which the servlet is invoked. The ListServlets program parses a *web.xml* file and stores the name-to-class and name-to-URL mappings, printing out a summary when it reaches the end of the file. To help you understand the what the example does, here is an excerpt from the *web.xml* file developed in Chapter 20:

```
<servlet>
  <servlet-name>Hello</servlet-name>
  <servlet-class>je3.servlet.HelloNet</servlet-class>
</servlet>

<!-- The Counter servlet uses initialization parameters -->
<servlet>
  <servlet-name>Counter</servlet-name>
  <servlet-class>je3.servlet.Counter</servlet-class>
  <init-param>
    <param-name>countfile</param-name>          <!-- where to save state -->
    <param-value>/tmp/counts.ser</param-value> <!-- adjust for your system-->
  </init-param>
```

---

* Prior to Java 1.4, it was available as a standard extension.

```
<init-param>
  <param-name>saveInterval</param-name>       <!-- how often to save -->
  <param-value>30000</param-value>            <!-- every 30 seconds -->
</init-param>
</servlet>

<servlet-mapping>
  <servlet-name>Hello</servlet-name>
  <url-pattern>/Hello</url-pattern>
</servlet-mapping>

<servlet-mapping>
  <servlet-name>Counter</servlet-name>
  <url-pattern>/Counter</url-pattern>
</servlet-mapping>

<!-- Note the wildcard below: any URL ending in .count invokes Counter -->
<servlet-mapping>
  <servlet-name>Counter</servlet-name>
  <url-pattern>*.count</url-pattern>
</servlet-mapping>
```

ListServlets.java includes a main( ) method that uses the JAXP API to obtain a SAX parser instance. It then passes the File to parse, along with an instance of the ListServlets class, to the parser. The parser starts running and invokes the ListServlets instance methods as it encounters XML elements in the file.

ListServlets extends the SAX org.xml.sax.helpers.DefaultHandler class. This superclass provides dummy implementations of all the SAX event-handler methods. The example simply overrides the handlers of interest. The parser calls the startElement( ) method when it reads an XML tag; it calls endElement( ) when it finds a closing tag. characters( ) is invoked when the parser reads a string of plain text with no markup. Finally, the parser calls warning( ), error( ), or fatalError( ) when something goes wrong in the parsing process. The implementations of these methods are written specifically to extract the desired information from a *web.xml* file and are based on a knowledge of the structure of this type of file.

Note that *web.xml* files are somewhat unusual in that they don't rely on attributes for any of the XML tags. That is, servlet names are defined by a <servlet-name> tag nested within a <servlet> tag, instead of simply using a name attribute of the <servlet> tag itself. This fact makes the example program more complex than it would otherwise be. The *web.xml* file does allow id attributes for all its tags. Although servlet engines are not expected to use these attributes, they may be useful to a configuration tool that parses and automatically generates *web.xml* files. In order to demonstrate how to work with attributes in SAX, the startElement( ) method in Example 19-1 looks for an id attribute of the <servlet> tag. The value of that attribute, if it exists, is reported in the program's output.

To run this program, specify the path to a *web.xml* file on the command line. You can use the one included with the servlets examples, which is at *je3/servlet/WEB-INF/web.xml*.

Example 19-1. ListServlets.java

```java
package je3.xml;
import javax.xml.parsers.*;       // JAXP classes for obtaining a SAX Parser
import org.xml.sax.*;             // The main SAX package
import org.xml.sax.helpers.*;     // SAX helper classes
import java.io.*;                 // For reading the input file
import java.util.*;               // Hashtable, lists, and so on

/**
 * Parse a web.xml file using the SAX2 API.
 * This class extends DefaultHandler so that instances can serve as SAX2
 * event handlers, and can be notified by the parser of parsing events.
 * We simply override the methods that receive events we're interested in
 **/
public class ListServlets extends org.xml.sax.helpers.DefaultHandler {
    /** The main method sets things up for parsing */
    public static void main(String[] args)
        throws IOException, SAXException, ParserConfigurationException
    {
        // We use a SAXParserFactory to obtain a SAXParser, which
        // encapsulates a SAXReader.
        SAXParserFactory factory = SAXParserFactory.newInstance();
        factory.setValidating(false);      // We don't want validation
        factory.setNamespaceAware(false); // No namespaces please
        // Create a SAXParser object from the factory
        SAXParser parser = factory.newSAXParser();
        // Now parse the file specified on the command line using
        // an instance of this class to handle the parser callbacks
        parser.parse(new File(args[0]), new ListServlets());
    }

    HashMap nameToClass;     // Map from servlet name to servlet class name
    HashMap nameToID;        // Map from servlet name to id attribute
    HashMap nameToPatterns;  // Map from servlet name to url patterns

    StringBuffer accumulator;                           // Accumulate text
    String servletName, servletClass, servletPattern;  // Remember text
    String servletID;        // Value of id attribute of <servlet> tag

    // Called at the beginning of parsing.  We use it as an init() method
    public void startDocument() {
        accumulator = new StringBuffer();
        nameToClass = new HashMap();
        nameToID = new HashMap();
        nameToPatterns = new HashMap();
    }

    // When the parser encounters plain text (not XML elements), it calls
    // this method, which accumulates them in a string buffer.
    // Note that this method may be called multiple times, even with no
    // intervening elements.
    public void characters(char[] buffer, int start, int length) {
        accumulator.append(buffer, start, length);
    }
```

Example 19-1. ListServlets.java (continued)

```
    // At the beginning of each new element, erase any accumulated text.
    public void startElement(String namespaceURL, String localName,
                             String qname, Attributes attributes) {
        accumulator.setLength(0);
        // If it's a servlet tag, look for id attribute
        if (qname.equals("servlet")) servletID = attributes.getValue("id");
    }


    // Take special action when we reach the end of selected elements.
    // Although we don't use a validating parser, this method does assume
    // that the web.xml file we're parsing is valid.
    public void endElement(String namespaceURL, String localName, String qname)
    {
        // Since we've indicated that we don't want name-space aware
        // parsing, the element name is in qname.  If we were doing
        // namespaces, then qname would include the name, colon and prefix,
        // and localName would be the name without the the prefix or colon.
        if (qname.equals("servlet-name")) {        // Store servlet name
            servletName = accumulator.toString( ).trim( );
        }
        else if (qname.equals("servlet-class")) {  // Store servlet class
            servletClass = accumulator.toString( ).trim( );
        }
        else if (qname.equals("url-pattern")) {    // Store servlet pattern
            servletPattern = accumulator.toString( ).trim( );
        }
        else if (qname.equals("servlet")) {        // Map name to class
            nameToClass.put(servletName, servletClass);
            nameToID.put(servletName, servletID);
        }
        else if (qname.equals("servlet-mapping")) {// Map name to pattern
            List patterns = (List)nameToPatterns.get(servletName);
            if (patterns == null) {
                patterns = new ArrayList( );
                nameToPatterns.put(servletName, patterns);
            }
            patterns.add(servletPattern);
        }
    }


    // Called at the end of parsing.  Used here to print our results.
    public void endDocument( ) {
        // Note the powerful uses of the Collections framework.  In two lines
        // we get the key objects of a Map as a Set, convert them to a List,
        // and sort that List alphabetically.
        List servletNames = new ArrayList(nameToClass.keySet( ));
        Collections.sort(servletNames);
        // Loop through servlet names
        for(Iterator iterator = servletNames.iterator( ); iterator.hasNext( );) {
            String name = (String)iterator.next( );
            // For each name get class and URL patterns and print them.
            String classname = (String)nameToClass.get(name);
            String id = (String)nameToID.get(name);
```

Example 19-1. ListServlets.java (continued)

```java
            List patterns = (List)nameToPatterns.get(name);
            System.out.println("Servlet: " + name);
            System.out.println("Class: " + classname);
            if (id != null) System.out.println("ID: " + id);
            if (patterns != null) {
                System.out.println("Patterns:");
                for(Iterator i = patterns.iterator(); i.hasNext(); ) {
                    System.out.println("\t" + i.next());
                }
            }
            System.out.println();
        }
    }

    // Issue a warning
    public void warning(SAXParseException exception) {
        System.err.println("WARNING: line " + exception.getLineNumber() + ": "+
                           exception.getMessage());
    }

    // Report a parsing error
    public void error(SAXParseException exception) {
        System.err.println("ERROR: line " + exception.getLineNumber() + ": " +
                           exception.getMessage());
    }

    // Report a non-recoverable error and exit
    public void fatalError(SAXParseException exception) throws SAXException {
        System.err.println("FATAL: line " + exception.getLineNumber() + ": " +
                           exception.getMessage());
        throw(exception);
    }
}
```

Parsing and Manipulating with JAXP and DOM

Example 19-1 used the SAX API for parsing XML documents. We now turn to
another commonly used parsing API: the DOM, or Document Object Model. The
DOM API is a standard defined by the World Wide Web Consortium (W3C); its
Java implementation consists of the org.w3c.dom package and its subpackages.
The current version of the DOM standard is Level 2. As of this writing, the DOM
Level 3 API is making its way through the standardization process at the W3C.

The Document Object Model defines the API of a parse tree for XML documents.
The org.xml.dom.Node interface specifies the basic features of a node in this parse
tree. Subinterfaces, such as Document, Element, Entity, and Comment, define the
features of specific types of nodes. A program that uses the DOM parsing model is
quite different from one that uses SAX. With the DOM, you have the parser read
your entire XML document and transform it into a tree of Node objects. Once
parsing is complete, you can traverse the tree to find the information you need.
The DOM parsing model is useful if you need to make multiple passes through

the tree, if you want to modify the structure of the tree, or if you need random access to an XML document, instead of the sequential access provided by the SAX model.

Example 19-2 is a listing of the program *WebAppConfig.java*. Like Example 19-1, WebAppConfig reads a *web.xml* web application deployment descriptor. This example uses a DOM parser to build a parse tree, then performs some operations on the tree to demonstrate how you can work with a tree of DOM nodes.

The WebAppConfig( ) constructor uses the JAXP API to obtain a DOM parser and then uses that parser to build a parse tree that represents the XML file. The root node of this tree is of type Document. This Document object is stored in an instance field of the WebAppConfig object, so it is available for traversal and modification by the other methods of the class. The class also includes a main( ) method that invokes these other methods.

The getServletClass( ) method looks for <servlet-name> tags and returns the text of the associated <servlet-class> tags. (These tags always come in pairs in a *web.xml* file.) This method demonstrates a number of features of the DOM parse tree, notably the getElementsByTagName( ) method. The addServlet( ) method inserts a new <servlet> tag into the parse tree; it demonstrates how to construct new DOM nodes and add them to an existing parse tree. Finally, the output( ) method converts the (possibly modified) tree back into an XML document. It does this using the javax.xml.transform package and subpackages to "transform" the DOM tree into a stream. (Another approach is to visit each node of the tree in order and output its corresponding XML text.)

Example 19-2. WebAppConfig.java

```
package je3.xml;
import java.io.*;            // For reading the input file
import org.w3c.dom.*;        // W3C DOM classes for traversing the document
import org.xml.sax.*;        // SAX classes used for error handling by JAXP
import javax.xml.parsers.*;  // JAXP classes for parsing
import javax.xml.transform.*; // For transforming a DOM tree to an XML file.

/**
 * A WebAppConfig object is a wrapper around a DOM tree for a web.xml
 * file.  The methods of the class use the DOM API to work with the
 * tree in various ways.
 **/
public class WebAppConfig {
    /** The main method creates and demonstrates a WebAppConfig object */
    public static void main(String[ ] args)
        throws IOException, SAXException, ParserConfigurationException,
               TransformerConfigurationException, TransformerException
    {
        // Create a new WebAppConfig object that represents the web.xml
        // file specified by the first command-line argument
        WebAppConfig config = new WebAppConfig(new File(args[0]));
        // Query the tree for the class name associated with the specified
        // servlet name
        System.out.println("Class for servlet " + args[1] + " is " +
                        config.getServletClass(args[1]));
```

Example 19-2. WebAppConfig.java (continued)

```
        // Add a new servlet name-to-class mapping to the DOM tree
        config.addServlet("foo", "bar");
        // And write out an XML version of the DOM tree to standard out
        config.output(new PrintWriter(System.out));
    }

    org.w3c.dom.Document document;  // This field holds the parsed DOM tree

    /**
     * This constructor method is passed an XML file.  It uses the JAXP API to
     * obtain a DOM parser, and to parse the file into a DOM Document object,
     * which is used by the remaining methods of the class.
     **/
    public WebAppConfig(File configfile)
        throws IOException, SAXException, ParserConfigurationException
    {
        // Get a JAXP parser factory object
        javax.xml.parsers.DocumentBuilderFactory dbf =
            DocumentBuilderFactory.newInstance();
        // Tell the factory what kind of parser we want
        dbf.setValidating(false);
        // Use the factory to get a JAXP parser object
        javax.xml.parsers.DocumentBuilder parser = dbf.newDocumentBuilder();

        // Tell the parser how to handle errors.  Note that in the JAXP API,
        // DOM parsers rely on the SAX API for error handling
        parser.setErrorHandler(new org.xml.sax.ErrorHandler() {
                public void warning(SAXParseException e) {
                    System.err.println("WARNING: " + e.getMessage());
                }
                public void error(SAXParseException e) {
                    System.err.println("ERROR: " + e.getMessage());
                }
                public void fatalError(SAXParseException e)
                    throws SAXException {
                    System.err.println("FATAL: " + e.getMessage());
                    throw e;   // re-throw the error
                }
            });

        // Finally, use the JAXP parser to parse the file.  This call returns
        // a Document object.  Now that we have this object, the rest of this
        // class uses the DOM API to work with it; JAXP is no longer required.
        document = parser.parse(configfile);
    }

    /**
     * This method looks for specific Element nodes in the DOM tree in order
     * to figure out the classname associated with the specified servlet name
     **/
    public String getServletClass(String servletName) {
        // Find all <servlet> elements and loop through them.
        NodeList servletnodes = document.getElementsByTagName("servlet");
```

Example 19-2. WebAppConfig.java (continued)

```
        int numservlets = servletnodes.getLength( );
        for(int i = 0; i < numservlets; i++) {
            Element servletTag = (Element)servletnodes.item(i);
            // Get the first <servlet-name> tag within the <servlet> tag
            Element nameTag = (Element)
                servletTag.getElementsByTagName("servlet-name").item(0);
            if (nameTag == null) continue;

            // The <servlet-name> tag should have a single child of type
            // Text.  Get that child, and extract its text.  Use trim( )
            // to strip whitespace from the beginning and end of it.
            String name =((Text)nameTag.getFirstChild( )).getData( ).trim( );

            // If this <servlet-name> tag has the right name
            if (servletName.equals(name)) {
                // Get the matching <servlet-class> tag
                Element classTag = (Element)
                    servletTag.getElementsByTagName("servlet-class").item(0);
                if (classTag != null) {
                    // Extract the tag's text as above, and return it
                    Text classTagContent = (Text)classTag.getFirstChild( );
                    return classTagContent.getNodeValue( ).trim( );
                }
            }
        }
    }

    // If we get here, no matching servlet name was found
    return null;
}

/**
 * This method adds a new name-to-class mapping in in the form of
 * a <servlet> sub-tree to the document.
 **/
public void addServlet(String servletName, String className) {
    // Create the <servlet> tag
    Element newNode = document.createElement("servlet");
    // Create the <servlet-name> and <servlet-class> tags
    Element nameNode = document.createElement("servlet-name");
    Element classNode = document.createElement("servlet-class");
    // Add the name and classname text to those tags
    nameNode.appendChild(document.createTextNode(servletName));
    classNode.appendChild(document.createTextNode(className));
    // And add those tags to the servlet tag
    newNode.appendChild(nameNode);
    newNode.appendChild(classNode);

    // Now that we've created the new sub-tree, figure out where to put
    // it.  This code looks for another servlet tag and inserts the new
    // one right before it. Note that this code will fail if the document
    // does not already contain at least one <servlet> tag.
    NodeList servletnodes = document.getElementsByTagName("servlet");
    Element firstServlet = (Element)servletnodes.item(0);
```

Example 19-2. WebAppConfig.java (continued)

```
        // Insert the new node before the first servlet node
        firstServlet.getParentNode( ).insertBefore(newNode, firstServlet);
    }

    /**
     * Output the DOM tree to the specified stream as an XML document.
     * See the XMLDocumentWriter example for the details.
     **/
    public void output(PrintWriter out)
        throws TransformerConfigurationException, TransformerException
    {
        TransformerFactory factory = TransformerFactory.newInstance( );
        Transformer transformer = factory.newTransformer( );

        transformer.transform(new javax.xml.transform.dom.DOMSource(document),
                        new javax.xml.transform.stream.StreamResult(out));
    }
}
```

Transforming XML with XSLT

We saw the use of the javax.xml.transform package and two of its subpackages in the output( ) method of Example 19-2. There it was used to perform an "identity transform," converting a DOM tree into the corresponding XML file. But transforming the format of an XML document is not the only purpose of these packages. They can also be used to transform XML content according to the rules of an XSL stylesheet. The code required to do this is remarkably simple; it's shown in Example 19-3. This example uses javax.xml.transform.stream to read files containing a source document and a stylesheet, and to write the output document to another file. JAXP can be even more flexible, however: the transform.dom and transform.sax subpackages allow the program to be rewritten to (for example) transform a document represented by a series of SAX parser events into a DOM tree, using a stylesheet read from a file.

Example 19-3. XSLTransform.java

```
package je3.xml;
import java.io.*;
import javax.xml.transform.*;
import javax.xml.transform.stream.*;

/**
 * Transforms an input document to an output document using an XSLT stylesheet.
 * Usage: java XSLTransform input stylesheet output
 **/
public class XSLTransform {
    public static void main(String[ ] args) throws TransformerException {
        // Set up streams for input, stylesheet, and output.
        // These do not have to come from or go to files.  We can also use the
        // javax.xml.transform. {dom,sax} packages use DOM trees and streams of
        // SAX events as sources and sinks for documents and stylesheets.
        StreamSource input = new StreamSource(new File(args[0]));
```

Example 19-3. XSLTransform.java (continued)

```
        StreamSource stylesheet = new StreamSource(new File(args[1]));
        StreamResult output = new StreamResult(new File(args[2]));

        // Get a factory object, create a Transformer from it, and
        // transform the input document to the output document.
        TransformerFactory factory = TransformerFactory.newInstance();
        Transformer transformer = factory.newTransformer(stylesheet);
        transformer.transform(input, output);
    }
}
```

In order to use this example, you'll need an XSL stylesheet. A tutorial on XSL is beyond the scope of this chapter, but Example 19-4 shows one to get you started. This stylesheet is intended for processing the XML log files created by the java.util.logging package. For each <record> tag it encounters in the log file, it extracts the textual contents of the <sequence>, <date>, and <message> subtags, and combines them into a single line of output. This discards some of the log information, but shrinks and simplifies the log file, making it more human-readable.

Example 19-4. simplelog.xsl

```
<?xml version="1.0"?>
<xsl:stylesheet version="1.0" xmlns:xsl="http://www.w3.org/1999/XSL/Transform">
  <xsl:template match="record">
    <xsl:value-of select="sequence"/>
    <xsl:text>: </xsl:text>
    <xsl:value-of select="date"/>
    <xsl:text>: </xsl:text>
    <xsl:value-of select="message"/>
  </xsl:template>
</xsl:stylesheet>
```

An XML Pull Parser

The SAX API for parsing XML is called a "push-parsing" API because the SAX parser "pushes" tokens or events to your code. It is also possible to parse XML using the reverse architecture, in which your code "pulls" tokens from the XML parser as needed. The TAX class of Example 19-6 does just that. TAX is an acronym for Trivial API for XML. It is a pull parser (actually more of a fancy tokenizer) for a subset of XML. Despite its simplicity, it is useful for a variety of XML parsing tasks. The TAX.Parser class relies on the Tokenizer interface (defined in Example 2-8) and on the various implementations of that interface (see Chapters 2, 3, and 6). The TAX class is simply a holder for inner classes and token type constants. In addition to the TAX.Parser class, TAX also holds a Token class, a TokenType class (an enumerated type), and a ParseException class.

Before diving into the details of the TAX parser, it is probably easiest to first study how the parser is typically used. Example 19-5 is a program much like the ListServlets program of Example 19-1: it parses a *web.xml* file and outputs the servlet name-to-class mappings and name-to-URL mappings defined in the file.

Example 19-5. ListServlets2.java

```java
package je3.xml;
import java.io.*;

/**
 * Parse a web.xml file using the TAX pull parser and print out the servlet
 * name-to-class and name-to-url mappings.
 **/
public class ListServlets2 {
    public static void main(String[] args)
        throws IOException, TAX.ParseException
    {
        // Create a TAX.Parser instance to parse the specified file
        TAX.Parser parser = new TAX.Parser(new FileReader(args[0]));
        // By default the parser returns TAG, TEXT and ENDTAG tokens and
        // skips others. Configure it to skip ENDTAG tokens, too.
        parser.ignoreTokens(TAX.ENDTAG);

        // Now loop through all tokens until the end of the file
        for(TAX.Token t = parser.next(); t != null; t = parser.next()) {
            // If it is not a tag, we're not interested
            if (t.type() != TAX.TAG) continue;

            if (t.text().equals("servlet")) {       // We found <servlet>
                parser.expect("servlet-name");   // Require <servlet-name> next
                t = parser.expect(TAX.TEXT);     // Require text token next
                String name = t.text();          // Get text from the token
                parser.expect("servlet-class");  // Require <servlet-class> next
                t = parser.expect(TAX.TEXT);     // Require text token
                // Output name to class mapping
                System.out.println("Servlet " + name +
                                   " implemented by " + t.text());
            }
            else if (t.text().equals("servlet-mapping")) {
                // Now we do the same thing for <servlet-mapping> tags
                parser.expect("servlet-name");
                String name = parser.expect(TAX.TEXT).text();
                parser.expect("url-pattern");
                String mapping = parser.expect(TAX.TEXT).text();
                System.out.println("Servlet " + name +
                                   " mapped to " + mapping);
            }
        }
    }
}
```

Example 19-6. TAX.java

```java
package je3.xml;
import java.util.*;
import java.io.*;
import java.nio.channels.*;
import java.nio.charset.*;
import je3.classes.Tokenizer;
```

Example 19-6. TAX.java (continued)

```java
import je3.classes.CharSequenceTokenizer;
import je3.io.ReaderTokenizer;
import je3.nio.ChannelTokenizer;

/**
 * This class, whose name is an acronym for "Trivial API for XML", is a
 * container for a simple Parser class for parsing XML and its related Token,
 * TokenType and ParseException classes and constants.
 *
 * TAX.Parser is a simple, lightweight pull-parser that is useful for a variety
 * of simple XML parsing tasks. Note, however, that it is more of a tokenizer
 * than a true parser and that the grammar it parses is not actually XML, but a
 * simplified subset of XML. The parser has (at least) these limitations:
 *
 *    It does not enforce well-formedness. For example, it does not require
 *       tags to be properly nested.
 *    It is not a validating parser, and does not read external DTDs
 *    It does not parse the internal subset of the DOCTYPE tag, and cannot
 *       recognize any entities defined there.
 *    It is not namespace-aware
 *    It does not handle entity or character references in attribute values,
 *       not even pre-defined entities such as "
 *    It strips all whitespace from the start and end of document text, which,
 *       while useful for many documents, is not generally correct.
 *    It makes no attempt to do error recovery.  The results of calling next()
 *       after a ParseException is thrown are undefined.
 *    It does not provide enough detail to reconstruct the source document
 *
 * TAX.Parser always replaces entity references with their values, or throws
 * a Tax.ParseException if no replacement value is known.  The parser coalesces
 * adjacent text and entities into a single TEXT token. CDATA sections are
 * also returned as TEXT tokens, but are not coalesced.
 **/
public class TAX {
    // Enumerated type return values for Token.type()
    public static final TokenType TAG = new TokenType("TAG");
    public static final TokenType ENDTAG = new TokenType("ENDTAG");
    public static final TokenType TEXT = new TokenType("TEXT");
    public static final TokenType COMMENT = new TokenType("COMMENT");
    public static final TokenType PI = new TokenType("PI");
    public static final TokenType DOCTYPE = new TokenType("DOCTYPE");
    public static final TokenType XMLDECL = new TokenType("XMLDECL");

    // A type-safe enumeration for token types.  Note the private constructor
    public static class TokenType {
        private static int nextOrdinal = 0;
        private final int ordinal = nextOrdinal++;
        private final String name;
        private TokenType(String name) { this.name = name; }
        public String toString() { return name; }
    }
```

Example 19-6. TAX.java (continued)

```java
// Token objects are the return value of the Parser.next( ) method.
// They provide details about what was parsed and where.
public static class Token {
    TokenType type;      // One of the constants above
    String text;         // Tagname for TAG & XMLDECL,
                         // Complete text minus delimiters for other types
    int line, column;    // Position of start of token
    Map attributes;      // name/value map for TAG and XMLDECL,null otherwise
    boolean empty;       // true for XMLDECL and TAGs ending with "/>".

    // We use this constructor for TAG and XMLDECL tokens
    Token(TokenType t, String s, int l,int c,Map a,boolean e) {
        this(t,s,l,c);
        this.attributes = a;
        this.empty = e;
    }
    // This constructor for other token types
    Token(TokenType type, String text, int line, int column) {
        this.type = type;
        this.text = text;
        this.line = line;
        this.column = column;
    }

    // Property accessor methods
    public TokenType type( ) { return type; }
    public String text( ) { return text; }
    public int line( ) { return line; }
    public int column( ) { return column; }
    public Map attributes( ) { return attributes; }
    public boolean empty( ) { return empty; }
}

// Exceptions of this type are thrown for syntax errors or unknown entities
public static class ParseException extends Exception {
    public ParseException(String msg) { super(msg); }

    static ParseException expected(Token t, String expected) {
        return new ParseException("Expected " + expected + " at line " +
                                  t.line( ) + ", column " + t.column( ));
    }
}

// This is the parser class. It relies internally on a Tokenizer.
// The public constructors allow you to parse XML from a CharSequence,
// a Reader, or a Channel.   By default, it will return tokens of type TAG,
// ENDTAG, and TEXT, and will ignore all others.  You can change this
// behavior by passing token type constants to returnTokens( ) or
// ignoreTokens( ).  By default the parser will replace character entities
// and the pre-defined entities &, <, >, ", and ' with
// their values.  You can define new entity name/replacement pairs by
// calling defineEntity( ).  These configuration methods all return the
```

Example 19-6. TAX.java (continued)

```
    // Parser objects so calls can be chained.  After configuring your Parser,
    // call the next( ) method repeatedly until it returns null.
    public static class Parser {
        Tokenizer tokenizer;   // Used to break up the input
        Map entityMap;          // Map entity name to replacment
        // Should we return tokens of these types?
        boolean[ ] returnTokenType = new boolean[TokenType.nextOrdinal];

        public Parser(CharSequence text) {
            this(new CharSequenceTokenizer(text));
        }
        public Parser(Reader in) {
            this(new ReaderTokenizer(in));
        }
        public Parser(ReadableByteChannel in, Charset encoding) {
            this(new ChannelTokenizer(in, encoding));
        }

        Parser(Tokenizer tokenizer) {
            this.tokenizer = tokenizer;
            tokenizer.tokenizeSpaces(true);  // always tokenize spaces
            tokenizer.trackPosition(true);    // track line and column #
            // We don't always want the tokenizer to tokenize words, but when
            // we do, this is how we want the words formed.
            tokenizer.wordRecognizer(new Tokenizer.WordRecognizer( ) {
                    public boolean isWordStart(char c) {
                        return Character.isLetter(c) || c == '_' || c == ':';
                    }
                    public boolean isWordPart(char c, char first) {
                        if (Character.isLetterOrDigit(c) ||
                            c == '_' || c=='-' || c=='.' || c==':')
                            return true;
                        int type = Character.getType(c);
                        return type == Character.COMBINING_SPACING_MARK ||
                            type == Character.ENCLOSING_MARK ||
                            type == Character.NON_SPACING_MARK ||
                            type == Character.MODIFIER_LETTER;
                    }
            });

            // Set pre-defined entitities
            entityMap = new HashMap( );
            entityMap.put("lt", "<");
            entityMap.put("gt", ">");
            entityMap.put("amp", "&");
            entityMap.put("quot", "\"");
            entityMap.put("apos", "'");

            // Set default values for what token types to return
            returnTokenType[TAG.ordinal] = true;
            returnTokenType[ENDTAG.ordinal] = true;
            returnTokenType[TEXT.ordinal] = true;
        }
```

Example 19-6. TAX.java (continued)

```
    public Parser returnTokens(TokenType t) {
        returnTokenType[t.ordinal] = true;
        return this;
    }

    public Parser ignoreTokens(TokenType t) {
        returnTokenType[t.ordinal] = false;
        return this;
    }

    // Define a mapping from entity name to entity replacement.
    // Note that the entity name should not include the & or ; delimiters.
    public Parser defineEntity(String name, String replacement) {
        entityMap.put(name, replacement);
        return this;
    }

    // This utility method is for reporting parsing errors
    void syntax(String msg) throws ParseException {
        throw new ParseException(msg + " at " +
                                tokenizer.tokenLine() + ":" +
                                tokenizer.tokenColumn());
    }

    // This method returns the next XML token of input or null if there
    // is no more input to parse.
    public Token next() throws ParseException, IOException {
        Token token = null;

        // Otherwise, loop until we find a token we want to return;
        for(;;) {
            // Invariant: we keep the tokenizer on the first unparsed token
            // This means we start our methods by calling tokenType()
            // to examine what we're currently on, not by calling next().
            // But we end by calling next() to consume the stuff we've
            // already seen.
            int t = tokenizer.tokenType();

            // If we're at the tokenizer's start state, then read a token
            if (t == Tokenizer.BOF) t = tokenizer.next();

            // If there is no more input, return null
            if (t == Tokenizer.EOF) return null;

            // Skip any space. This is not technically correct: we don't
            // know if this is ignorable whitespace or not. But in
            // practice, most clients will want to ignore it.
            if (t == Tokenizer.SPACE) {
                tokenizer.next();
                continue;
            }
```

Example 19-6. TAX.java (continued)

XML

```
            // If the token is a open angle bracket, then this is markup
            // otherwise it is text.
            if (t == '<') token = parseMarkup( );
            else token = parseText( );

            // If the token we've parsed is one of the kind to be returned,
            // then return it.  Otherwise, continue looping for a new token
            if (returnTokenType[token.type.ordinal]) return token;
        }
    }

    // Read the next token and return it if it is a TAG with the specified
    // tagname.  Otherwise throw a ParseException
    public Token expect(String tagname) throws ParseException,IOException {
        Token t = next( );
        if (t == null || t.type( ) != TAG || !t.text( ).equals(tagname))
            throw ParseException.expected(t, "<" + tagname + ">");
        return t;
    }

    // Read and return the next token, if it is of the specified type.
    // Otherwise throw a ParseException
    public Token expect(TokenType type) throws ParseException,IOException {
        Token t = next( );
        if (t == null || t.type( ) != type)
            throw ParseException.expected(t, type.toString( ));
        return t;
    }

    // This method called with a current token of '<' to parse various
    // forms of XML markup
    Token parseMarkup( ) throws ParseException, IOException {
        assert tokenizer.tokenType( ) == '<' : tokenizer.tokenType( );
        try {
            // Turn on word tokenizing. It is turned off in finally clause.
            tokenizer.tokenizeWords(true);
            int t = tokenizer.next( );
            if (t == '?') {      // Markup is a PI or XMLDECL
                t = tokenizer.next( );
                if (t != Tokenizer.WORD) syntax("XMLDECL or PI expected");
                if (tokenizer.tokenText( ).equals("xml")) {
                    Token token =
                        new Token(XMLDECL, tokenizer.tokenText( ),
                                  tokenizer.tokenLine( ),
                                  tokenizer.tokenColumn( ) - 2,
                                  parseAttributes( ),
                                  true);

                    if (tokenizer.tokenType( )!='?') syntax("'?' expected");
                    if (tokenizer.next( ) != '>') syntax("'>' expected");
                    return token;
                }
```

Example 19-6. TAX.java (continued)

```
            else {
                Token token = new Token(PI, null,tokenizer.tokenLine(),
                                        tokenizer.tokenColumn( )-2);
                // Read to end of PI
                tokenizer.scan("?>", true, true, false, true);
                token.text = tokenizer.tokenText( );
                return token;
            }
        }

        if (t == '!') {           // Markup is DOCTYPE, CDATA, or Comment
            t = tokenizer.next( );
            if (t == Tokenizer.WORD &&
                tokenizer.tokenText( ).equals("DOCTYPE")) {
                return parseDoctype( );
            }
            else if (t == '[') {
                if (tokenizer.next( ) == Tokenizer.WORD &&
                    tokenizer.tokenText( ).equals("CDATA") &&
                    tokenizer.next( ) == '[') {
                    Token token = new Token(TEXT, null,
                                        tokenizer.tokenLine( ),
                                        tokenizer.tokenColumn( )-8);
                    tokenizer.scan("]]>", true, false, false, true);
                    token.text = tokenizer.tokenText( );
                    return token;
                }
                else syntax("CDATA expected");
            }
            else if (t == '-' && tokenizer.next( ) == '-') {
                // a COMMENT token
                Token token = new Token(COMMENT, null,
                                        tokenizer.tokenLine( ),
                                        tokenizer.tokenColumn( )-4);
                tokenizer.scan("-->", true, false, false, true);
                token.text = tokenizer.tokenText( );
                return token;
            }
            else syntax("DOCTYPE, CDATA, or Comment expected");
        }
        if (t == '/') {     // Markup is an element end tag
            t = tokenizer.next( );
            if (t == Tokenizer.WORD) {
                Token token = new Token(ENDTAG, tokenizer.tokenText( ),
                                        tokenizer.tokenLine( ),
                                        tokenizer.tokenColumn( )-2);

                t = tokenizer.next( );
                if (t == Tokenizer.SPACE) t = tokenizer.next( );
                if (t != '>') syntax("Expected '>'");
                return token;
            }
```

Example 19-6. TAX.java (continued)

XML

```
                    else syntax("ENDTAG expected.");
                }
                if (t == Tokenizer.WORD) { // Markup is an element start tag
                    Token token = new Token(TAG, tokenizer.tokenText( ),
                                        tokenizer.tokenLine( ),
                                        tokenizer.tokenColumn( ) - 1,
                                        parseAttributes( ),
                                        tokenizer.tokenType( ) == '/');

                    if (tokenizer.tokenType( ) == '/') tokenizer.next( );
                    if (tokenizer.tokenType( ) != '>') syntax("'>' expected");
                    return token;
                }

                // If none of the above matched, this is a syntax error
                syntax("Invalid character following '<'");

                // The compiler doesn't realize that syntax( ) never returns,
                // so it requires a return statement here.
                return null;
            }
            finally {
                // restore tokenizer state
                tokenizer.tokenizeWords(false);
                // Get the next token ready
                tokenizer.next( );
            }
        }

    Token parseDoctype( ) throws IOException {
        assert (tokenizer.tokenType( ) == Tokenizer.WORD &&
                tokenizer.tokenText( ).equals("DOCTYPE"));

        int line = tokenizer.tokenLine( );
        int column = tokenizer.tokenColumn( );
        StringBuffer b = new StringBuffer( );

        int t = tokenizer.next( );
        while(t != '>' && t != '[' && t != Tokenizer.EOF) {
            b.append(tokenizer.tokenText( ));
            t = tokenizer.next( );
        }

        if (t == '[') { // If there is an internal subset, scan for its end
            tokenizer.scan("]>", true, true, false, true);
            b.append(tokenizer.tokenText( ));
            b.append(']');
        }

        return new Token(DOCTYPE, b.toString( ), line, column);
    }
```

Example 19-6. TAX.java (continued)

```java
    // Parse a sequence of name=value attributes, where value is always
    // quoted in single or double quotes, and return them as a Map.
    // When this method is called, the tokenizer is looking at the element
    // name, not at the first token to parse.
    // This is used when parsing element start tags and XMLDECLs
    Map parseAttributes() throws ParseException, IOException {
        try {
            // Adjust tokenizer to recognize quotes.
            // Defaults are restored in finally clause below
            tokenizer.quotes("'\"", "'\"");
            int t = tokenizer.next(); // Consume the element name

            // Skip optional space
            if (t == Tokenizer.SPACE) t = tokenizer.next();

            // This is a special case for elements with no attributes
            if (t != Tokenizer.WORD) return Collections.EMPTY_MAP;

            Map m = new HashMap();  // Where we'll store attributes

            while(t == Tokenizer.WORD) {
                String name = tokenizer.tokenText();  // get attribute name
                // The next token must be '='
                if (tokenizer.next() != '=') syntax("'=' expected");
                t = tokenizer.next();
                // The next token must be a quoted string
                if (t != '"' && t != '\'')
                    syntax("quoted attribute value expected");
                // Map attribute name to attribute value.
                // The tokenizer strips the quotes for us.
                // Note that we do not handle entity references here.
                m.put(name, tokenizer.tokenText());
                // Consume the value and skip an optional space after it
                t = tokenizer.next();
                if (t == Tokenizer.SPACE) t=tokenizer.next();
            }
            return m;
        }
        finally { // Always turn off quote tokenizing
            tokenizer.quotes("", "");
        }
    }

    // Coalesce any character data and entity references into a single
    // TEXT token and return it, or throw an exception for undefined
    // entities.  Note that CDATA elements are also returned as TEXT
    // tokens but are not coalesced like this.  When this method is called
    // we know that the tokenizer is looking at a char other than '<'.
    Token parseText() throws ParseException, IOException {
        assert tokenizer.tokenType() != '<' : tokenizer.tokenType();
        // Save line and column info of the start of the text
        int line = tokenizer.tokenLine();
```

Example 19-6. TAX.java (continued)

```
        int column = tokenizer.tokenColumn( );
        StringBuffer b = new StringBuffer( ); // where we accumulate text

        int t;
        while((t = tokenizer.tokenType( )) != '<') {
            if (t == '&') b.append(parseEntityReference( ));
            else {
                // Otherwise we've found some text
                tokenizer.scan("<&",  // scan until we find one of these
                    false, // just match one, not the whole string
                    true,  // extend the token we've already started
                    false, // don't include delimiter char in the token
                    false);// don't skip delimiter; save for next token
                b.append(tokenizer.tokenText( ));
                tokenizer.next( );
            }
        }
        // Strip trailing space and return as a TEXT token
        return new Token(TEXT, b.toString( ).trim( ), line, column);
    }


    // Parse a reference to a general entity or character entity and
    // return its value as a string, or throw an exception for undefined
    // entities. Called when tokenizer is looking at an '&'.
    String parseEntityReference( ) throws ParseException, IOException {
        assert tokenizer.tokenType( ) == '&' : tokenizer.tokenType( );
        String s = null;
        try {
            tokenizer.tokenizeWords(true);
            int t = tokenizer.next( );
            if (t == '#') {  // if it's a character reference
                tokenizer.tokenizeNumbers(true);
                t = tokenizer.next( );
                String text = tokenizer.tokenText( );
                if (t == Tokenizer.NUMBER) {  // a decimal character ref
                    int n = Integer.parseInt(text);  // parse as base-10
                    s = Character.toString((char)n); // convert to string
                }
                else if (t == Tokenizer.WORD && text.charAt(0) != 'x') {
                    // a hexadecimal character reference
                    String hex = text.substring(1);    // skip the 'x'
                    int n = Integer.parseInt(hex, 16); // parse as hex
                    s = Character.toString((char)n);   // convert to string
                }
                else syntax("illegal character following '&#'");
            }
            else { // otherwise a regular entity reference
                if (t != Tokenizer.WORD) syntax("entity expected");
                // look up entity replacement
                s = (String) entityMap.get(tokenizer.tokenText( ));
                if (s == null) syntax("Undefined entity: '&" +
                                    tokenizer.tokenText( ) + ";'");
```

Example 19-6. TAX.java (continued)

```
            }
        }
        catch (NumberFormatException e) {
            // Convert NFE errors to syntax errors
            syntax("malformed character entity");
        }
        finally {  // Restore tokenizer state
            tokenizer.tokenizeWords(false).tokenizeNumbers(false);
        }

        // Require and consume the trailing semicolon
        if (tokenizer.next() != ';') syntax("';' expected");
        tokenizer.next();
        return s;
    }
  }
}
```

Exercises

Exercise 19-1. Two of the examples in this chapter were designed to parse the *web. xml* files (introduced in Chapter 20) that configure web applications. The Tomcat servlet container uses a file named *tomcat-users.xml* to configure its user database. The file shipped by default with Tomcat 5 looks like this:

```
<?xml version='1.0' encoding='utf-8'?>
<tomcat-users>
  <role rolename="tomcat"/>
  <role rolename="role1"/>
  <user username="tomcat" password="tomcat" roles="tomcat"/>
  <user username="both" password="tomcat" roles="tomcat,role1"/>
  <user username="role1" password="tomcat" roles="role1"/>
</tomcat-users>
```

Write a program that uses the SAX API to parse the *tomcat-users.xml* file and output the values of the username and roles attributes of each <user> tag.

Exercise 19-2. Using a DOM parser instead of a SAX parser, write a program that behaves identically to the program you developed in the previous exercise.

Exercise 19-3. Implement the javax.swing.tree.JTreeModel interface on top of a DOM document tree, so that an XML document can be displayed in a Swing JTree component. Write a demonstration program that does this with sample XML files.

Exercise 19-4. The WebAppConfig program of Example 19-2 provides the beginning of a framework for programmatic manipulation of *web.xml* configuration files. Extend this example so that it allows servlets, URL mappings, and initialization parameters to be added to, edited, and removed from the file. Provide a command-line or Swing-based interface to your configuration program.

20

Servlets and JavaServer Pages

A *servlet* is a Java class that implements the `javax.servlet.Servlet` interface or, more commonly, extends the abstract `javax.servlet.http.HttpServlet` class. Servlets, and the Java Servlet API, are an extension architecture for web servers.[*] Instead of serving only static web pages, a servlet-enabled web server can invoke servlet methods to dynamically generate content at runtime. This model offers a number of advantages over traditional CGI scripts. Notably, servlet instances can persist across client requests, so the server is not constantly spawning external processes.

JavaServer Pages (or JSP as it is commonly called) is an architecture built on top of the servlet API. A JSP page contains HTML or XML output intermingled with Java source code, special JSP tags, and tags from imported "tag libraries," including the very useful Java Standard Tag Library, or JSTL. In JSP 2.0, JSP pages may also contain expressions written in a simple "Expression Language" (EL); these expressions are evaluated and are replaced with their values. A JSP-enabled web server compiles JSP pages on the fly, turning JSP source into servlets that produce dynamic output.[†]

This chapter includes examples of both servlets and JSP pages and concludes with an example "web application" that uses Java objects, JSP pages, and a coordinating servlet in a Model-View-Controller (MVC) architecture. The chapter begins, however, by describing the prerequisites for compiling, deploying, running, and serving servlets and JSP pages. For more detailed information about servlets and JSP, see *Java Enterprise in a Nutshell*, *Java Servlet Programming*, by Jason Hunter with William Crawford, and *JavaServer Pages*, by Hans Bergsten, all published by O'Reilly.

---

[*] The `javax.servlet` package can actually be used with any type of server that implements a request/response protocol. Web servers are currently the only common usage of servlets, however, and this chapter discusses servlets in that context only.

[†] It is worth noting that JSP is just one of a general class of Java-based HTML templating tools. WebMacro (*webmacro.org*) and Apache Velocity (*jakarta.apache.org/velocity*) are popular alternatives to JSP.

Servlet Setup

In order to run the examples in this chapter, you need the following:

- A web server to host the examples.
- A *servlet container*, or *servlet engine*, which the web server uses to run the servlets. In order to run the JSP examples, your servlet container must also support JSP pages. Note that most of the JSP examples in this chapter rely on the new features of JSP 2.0. Servlet containers sometimes invert the architecture and include a web server.
- An implementation of the Java Standard Tag Library, so that the JSP examples that use those tag libraries can run correctly.
- The class files for the servlet API, so you can compile servlet classes.
- A *deployment descriptor* that tells your servlet container how to map URLs to servlet classes.

This list looks more daunting than it actually is, as you'll see in the sections that follow.

The Servlet Container

Just as there are many web servers available, there are numerous servlet containers to choose from. I use and recommend Tomcat, an open source product of the Jakarta project. Jakarta is itself a project of the Apache Software Foundation, the organization that produces the open source Apache web server. Tomcat has benefited from substantial contributions by Sun, and the official reference implementations for Sun's Servlet and JSP specifications are built upon the Tomcat codebase. The core of Tomcat is a servlet and JSP container that can be used with the Apache web server, as well as with various commercial web servers. For servlet development, however, Tomcat also includes a powerful pure-Java web server you can run on your local machine.

If you choose to use Tomcat, you can download it from *http://jakarta.apache.org/ tomcat*. At the time of this writing, the current version of Tomcat is 5.x, which implements the Servlet 2.4 and JSP 2.0 specifications. The examples in this chapter were tested with Tomcat 5 and its built-in web server.

Servlets are part of the J2EE platform, and if you have a J2EE 1.4 implementation, then you already have a servlet container (probably Tomcat) suitable for use with the examples in this chapter. This chapter assumes, however, that you have the J2SE platform and are augmenting it with a servlet container, without adopting the entire J2EE platform.

Installing, configuring, and starting a servlet container is beyond the scope of this chapter; you'll need to read the appropriate documentation supplied with your container. If you use Tomcat, however, the process may be as simple as unpacking the download archive and running a startup script from the *bin/* directory. By default, the Tomcat web server listens on port 8080, so once you have started Tomcat, point your web browser at *http://localhost:8080/* or *http://127.0.0.1:8080/*. If everything is working correctly, you should see an introductory page with information about Tomcat. Of course, you should read the instructions that come with your version for full details.

If you already have a working web server and servlet container, go ahead and use it (after you've read the documentation carefully). Note, however, that the examples in this chapter are written to the Servlet 2.4 and JSP 2.0 specifications. If your servlet container does not support these versions of the specifications, some of the examples (particularly the JSP examples) will not work.

Compiling Servlets

In order to compile servlets, you need the class files for the servlet API. If you do not have J2EE installed, you'll need to get these files from your servlet container. With Tomcat 5, they are located in *common/lib/servlet-api.jar*. You need this JAR file to be able to compile the classes in this chapter. Either edit your CLASSPATH environment variable to include the file or, more simply, place a copy of the file in the *jre/lib/ext/* directory of your Java SDK, where the Java VM can find it automatically. Once you have done this, you can compile servlet classes with *javac*, just as you would compile other Java classes.

Using Tag Libraries

Some of the JSP pages in this chapter use the core module of the Java Standard Tag Library (JSTL). They declare that they do this with a line like the following:

```
<%@taglib prefix="c" uri="http://java.sun.com/jsp/jstl/core" %>
```

The URI in this line is the official identifier for the core module of Version 1.1 of the JSTL. To make it work, you'll need the JAR files that implement JSTL 1.1. These JAR files include the implementation classes, as well as the *c.tld* tag library descriptor file that describes the tags in the core module. (It is this *c.tld* file that specifies the URI that officially identifies the library.)

At the time of this writing, the JSTL 1.1 is in the final stages of development. It is not bundled with Tomcat, and there does not yet appear to be a stable home for releases of the library. By the time you read this, the situation ought to be resolved, however. If you have a J2EE 1.4 environment, you should already have a JSTL 1.1 implementation. If an implementation is not included with your servlet container, you should be able to find one at *http://jakarta.apache.org/taglibs* or from *http://java.sun.com/products/jsp/jstl*. At the time of this writing, the JSTL implementation takes the form of two JAR files, named *jstl.jar* and *standard.jar*. You do not need to put these in the *jre/lib/ext* directory, since you never need to compile against them. Instead, you can make them available just to your servlet container. For example, with Tomcat 5, place them in the *common/lib/* directory of the Tomcat installation directory.

Installing and Running Servlets

Once you've obtained and set up a servlet container and the servlet API and taglib JAR files you'll need, you're ready to deploy and run your servlets. Version 2.2 of the Servlet specification standardized servlet deployment, so the process is similar with all servlet containers. Cooperating sets of servlets and the auxiliary files they require are bundled into a "web application" that is deployed into the servlet container. Most web applications include a file named *WEB-INF/web.xml* that provides all the necessary servlet deployment details (simple web applications that consist solely of static HTML pages and JSP pages do not require a *web.xml* file). For ease of distribution and deployment, web applications may be packaged into WAR archives using the JAR archive format. We'll discuss the directory hierarchy for a web application and the contents of the *web.xml* file at the end of this chapter. For now, however, we'll consider just the details you need to run the examples as you read the chapter.

The Java classes in this chapter are in a package named je3.servlet, and the online archive of examples for this book includes those classes and other files from this chapter located in and beneath the directory *je3/servlet/*. The files are organized in a directory hierarchy that is close to the hierarchy required for servlet deployment. To bundle all the examples from the chapter into a single web application, follow these steps:

```
# Compile all classes and put the class files under WEB-INF/classes
# This creates WEB-INF/classes/je3/servlet/*.class
javac -d WEB-INF/classes/ *.java

# Use the jar tool to bundle all necessary files into the je3.war file
# Note that this is a single command line broken across multiple lines.
jar cMf je3.war \
        index.html *.jsp *.jspx \
        ListManager/*.jsp \
        WEB-INF/web.xml \
        WEB-INF/tags/*.tag \
        WEB-INF/classes
```

These *javac* and *jar* commands create a file named *je3.war*, which should contain everything necessary to run all the examples from the chapter. Deploy this file to your servlet container as directed in its documentation. For Tomcat, you simply need to copy the *je3.war* file into the *webapps/* directory in the Tomcat distribution. If Tomcat is running, it should automatically notice and deploy the new web application, and you can force it to do so by stopping and restarting. (You can also deploy web applications in Tomcat using the Tomcat Manager web application included with Tomcat, although running the manager requires some additional Tomcat configuration steps.) If you modify the servlets, you'll need to rebuild the WAR file and redeploy it. Before doing this, you'll need to delete the old WAR file and the unpacked version that Tomcat creates in the *webapps/je3/* directory.

Note that you do not have to create a WAR file to deploy a web application: you can also deploy your working directory. If you want to edit and make changes to the examples in this chapter, it may be easiest to recursively copy the contents of the *je3/servlets/* directory to the Tomcat *webapps/je3* directory and make that your working directory.

With WAR archives, the name of the WAR file is used as a URL prefix for all the servlets and other files in the archive. For example, suppose you deploy the *je3.war* archive in Tomcat's *webapps/* directory. The WAR archive contains a file named *index.html* at the root level, and (assuming that Tomcat is deployed locally) the URL you use to access this file is:

```
http://localhost:8080/je3/index.html
```

Servlet container configuration and web application deployment can be tricky, and this chapter cannot provide a step-by-step tutorial on the process. If the URL just shown does not work for you after building and deploying *je3.war*, you'll want to read your servlet container documentation thoroughly, examine any log files it generates, or consult an experienced servlet guru!

A Hello World Servlet

Example 20-1 is a listing of *HelloNet.java*, which implements a simple "Hello world" servlet, illustrated in Figure 20-1. The HelloNet servlet inherits from javax.servlet.http.HttpServlet and overrides the doGet( ) method to provide output in response to an HTTP GET request. It also overrides the doPost( ) method so it can respond to POST requests in the same way. The doGet( ) method outputs a string of HTML text. By default, this string is "Hello World".

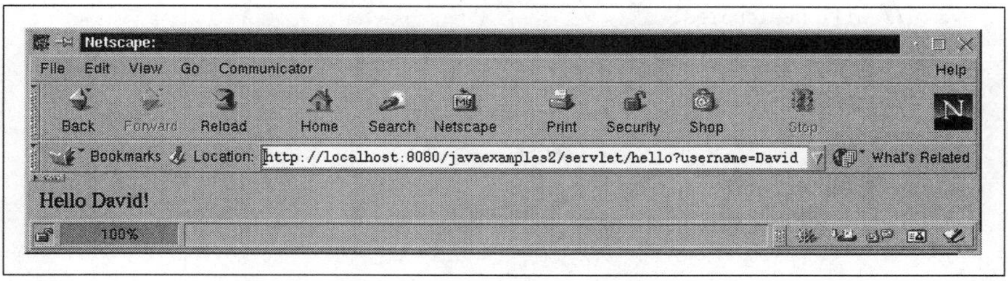

Figure 20-1. The output of the HelloNet servlet

If the HelloNet servlet can determine a username, however, it greets the user by name. The servlet looks for a username in two places, starting in the HTTP request (an HttpServletRequest object), as the value of a parameter named username. If the servlet cannot find a request parameter with this name, it looks for an HttpSession object associated with the request and sees if that object has an attribute named username. Servlet-enabled web servers (i.e., servlet containers) provide a session-tracking layer on top of the stateless HTTP protocol. The HttpSession object allows a servlet to set and query named attributes with a single client session. Later in the chapter, we'll see an example that takes advantage of the session-tracking ability of this HelloNet servlet.

Example 20-1. HelloNet.java

```
package je3.servlet;
import javax.servlet.*;        // Basic servlet classes and interfaces
import javax.servlet.http.*;   // HTTP specific servlet stuff
import java.io.*;              // Servlets do IO and throw IOExceptions

/**
 * This simple servlet greets the user.  It looks in the request and session
 * objects in an attempt to greet the user by name.
 **/
public class HelloNet extends HttpServlet {
    // This method is invoked when the servlet is the subject of an HTTP GET
    public void doGet(HttpServletRequest request, HttpServletResponse response)
        throws IOException
```

Example 20-1. HelloNet.java (continued)

```
{
    // See if the username is specified in the request
    String name = request.getParameter("username");

    // If not, look in the session object.  The web server or servlet
    // container performs session tracking automatically for the servlet,
    // and associates an HttpSession object with each session.
    if (name == null)
        name = (String)request.getSession( ).getAttribute("username");

    // If the username is not found in either place, use a default name.
    if (name == null) name = "World";

    // Specify the type of output we produce.  If this servlet is
    // included from within another servlet or JSP page, this setting
    // will be ignored.
    response.setContentType("text/html");

    // Get a stream that we can write the output to.
    PrintWriter out = response.getWriter( );

    // And, finally, do our output.
    out.println("Hello " + name + "!");
}

// This method is invoked when the servlet is the subject of an HTTP POST.
// It calls the doGet( ) method so that this servlet works correctly
// with either type of request.
public void doPost(HttpServletRequest request,HttpServletResponse response)
    throws IOException
{
    doGet(request, response);
}
}
```

Running the HelloNet Servlet

Before you can run this servlet, you must compile and deploy it as described at the beginning of this chapter. To run a servlet, issue a request for it with a web browser. The URL you use depends on where the web server is running and how you deployed the servlet. If you are running the servlet container on your local machine, if the web server is listening on port 8080, and if you deploy the servlet as part of a web application named je3, using the *web.xml* file shown later in this chapter, you can run the servlet by pointing your browser at:

```
http://localhost:8080/je3/HelloNet
```

This should display a web page that reads "Hello World". For slightly more sophisticated output, provide a request parameter with a URL like the following (which was used to produce the output in Figure 20-1):

```
http://localhost:8080/je3/HelloNet?username=David
```

Another Simple Servlet

You may recall Example 11-18, an error handler utility class that displays Java exceptions to the user in a dialog box and allows them to be reported to a server through a URL. The servlet shown in Example 20-2 is the server-side portion of that example: it handles an HTTP POST request from the ErrorHandler class, deserializes the exception, and returns a response. (The response claims that the exception has been recorded, when in fact it is simply discarded. Saving the exception to a database is left as an exercise; we'll see an example later in the chapter of a servlet that does communicate with a database.)

The code for this example is simple. It demonstrates the use of `ServletRequest.getInputStream( )` to read the body of an HTTP POST request and the use of `HttpServletResponse.sendError( )` to send an HTTP error.

Example 20-2. ErrorHandlerServlet.java

```java
package je3.servlet;
import java.io.*;
import javax.servlet.*;
import javax.servlet.http.*;
import java.sql.*;

/**
 * This servlet is the server-side companion to the
 * ErrorHandler.reportThrowable( ) utility method developed elsewhere in this
 * this book; it responds to the HTTP POST request initiated by that method.
 **/
public class ErrorHandlerServlet extends HttpServlet {
    // This servlet only supports HTTP POST requests
    public void doPost(HttpServletRequest request,
                       HttpServletResponse response) throws IOException
    {
        ObjectInputStream in =
            new ObjectInputStream(request.getInputStream( ));
        try {
            Throwable throwable = (Throwable) in.readObject( );

            // Exercise: save the throwable to a database, along with
            // the current time, and the IP address from which it was reported.

            // Our response will be displayed within an HTML document, but
            // it is not a complete document itself.  Declare it plain text,
            // but it is okay to include HTML tags in it.
            response.setContentType("text/plain");
            PrintWriter out = response.getWriter( );
            out.println("Thanks for reporting your <tt>" +
                        throwable.getClass( ).getName( ) + "</tt>.<br>" +
                        "It has been filed and will be investigated.");
        }
        catch(Exception e) {
            // Something went wrong deserializing the object; most likely
            // someone tried to invoke the servlet manually and didn't provide
            // correct data.  We send an HTTP error because that is the
```

Example 20-2. ErrorHandlerServlet.java (continued)

```
                // easiest thing to do.  Note, however that none of the HTTP error
                // codes really describes this situation adequately.
                response.sendError(HttpServletResponse.SC_GONE,
                                   "Unable to deserialize throwable object");
        }
    }
}
```

Testing the Error Handler

If you use the je3.war file, the ErrorHandlerServlet will be at this URL:

    http://localhost:8080/je3/ErrorHandler

To test it, you can't just enter that URL into a web browser. Doing so would issue an HTTP GET request, which the servlet does not support. Instead, run the ErrorHandler$Test program shown in Example 11-18, and submit a report that way. You should see the servlet's response in the dialog box.

Servlet Initialization and Persistence: A Counter Servlet

Example 20-3 is a listing of *Counter.java*, a servlet that maintains any number of named counters. Each time the value of one of these counters is requested, the servlet increments the counter and outputs its new value. The servlet is suitable for use as a simple hit counter for multiple web pages but can also count any other type of event.

This servlet defines init( ) and destroy( ) methods and saves its state to a file, so it does not lose count when the web server (or servlet container) shuts down. To understand init( ) and destroy( ), you have to understand something about the servlet life cycle. Servlet instances are not usually created anew for each client request. Instead, once a servlet is created, it can serve many requests before it is destroyed. A servlet such as Counter is typically not shut down unless the servlet container itself is shutting down, or the servlet is inactive and the container is trying to free up memory to make room for other servlets.

The init( ) method is invoked when the servlet container first instantiates the servlet, before any requests are serviced. The first thing this method does is look up the value of two *initialization parameters*: the filename of the file that contains the saved state and an integer value that specifies how often to save the state back into that file. Once the init( ) method has read these parameters, it reads the counts (using object serialization) from the specified file and is ready to begin serving requests. The values of the initialization parameters come from the *WEB-INF/web.xml* deployment file. Before running this example, you probably need to edit that file to tell the servlet where to save its state. Look for these lines:

```
<init-param>
    <param-name>countfile</param-name>        <!-- where to save state -->
    <param-value>/tmp/counts.ser</param-value> <!-- adjust for your system-->
</init-param>
```

If the filename */tmp/counts.ser* does not make sense on your system, replace it with a filename that does.

The destroy( ) method is the companion to init( ); it is invoked after the servlet has been taken out of service and there are no more requests being processed by the servlet. The Counter servlet uses this method to save its state, so it can be correctly restored when the servlet container starts the servlet up again. Note, however, that the destroy( ) method is invoked only when the servlet is shut down in a controlled way. In the case of a server crash or power outage, for example, there is no opportunity to save state. Thus, the Counter servlet also periodically saves it state from the doGet( ) method, so it never loses more than a small amount of data.

The doGet( ) method must first determine the name of the counter whose value is to be displayed. Since the Counter servlet is designed for use in a variety of ways, doGet( ) uses three techniques for obtaining the counter name. First, it checks for a parameter sent with the HTTP request. Next, it checks for a request attribute, which is a named value associated with the request by the servlet container or by another servlet that has invoked the Counter servlet. (You'll see an example of this later in the chapter.) Finally, if the servlet cannot find a counter name using either of these techniques, it uses the URL through which it was invoked as the counter name. As you'll see shortly, the servlet container can be configured to invoke the servlet in response to any URL that ends with the suffix *.count*.

Note that the doGet( ) method contains a synchronized block of code. The servlet API allows multiple threads to execute the body of doGet( ) at the same time. Even though many threads representing many different user sessions may be running, they all share a single data structure—the hashtable of named counts. The synchronized block prevents the threads from accessing (and possibly corrupting) the shared data structure at the same time. Finally, note the use of the log( ) method. When asked to start counting with a counter name it has never used before, the servlet uses this method to produce a permanent record of the event in a log file.

Example 20-3. Counter.java

```
package je3.servlet;
import javax.servlet.*;
import javax.servlet.http.*;
import java.io.*;
import java.util.*;

/**
 * This servlet maintains an arbitrary set of counter variables and increments
 * and displays the value of one named counter each time it is invoked.  It
 * saves the state of the counters to a disk file, so the counts are not lost
 * when the server shuts down.  It is suitable for counting page hits, or any
 * other type of event.  It is not typically invoked directly, but is included
 * within other pages, using JSP, SSI, or a RequestDispatcher
 **/
public class Counter extends HttpServlet {
    HashMap counts;      // A hash table: maps counter names to counts
    File countfile;      // The file that counts are saved in
```

Example 20-3. Counter.java (continued)

```java
    long saveInterval;   // How often (in ms) to save our state while running?
    long lastSaveTime;   // When did we last save our state?

    // This method is called when the web server first instantiates this
    // servlet.  It reads initialization parameters (which are configured
    // at deployment time in the web.xml file), and loads the initial state
    // of the counter variables from a file.
    public void init() throws ServletException {
        ServletConfig config = getServletConfig();
        try {
            // Get the save file.
            countfile = new File(config.getInitParameter("countfile"));
            // How often should we save our state while running?
            saveInterval =
                Integer.parseInt(config.getInitParameter("saveInterval"));
            // The state couldn't have changed before now.
            lastSaveTime = System.currentTimeMillis();
            // Now read in the count data
            loadState();
        }
        catch(Exception e) {
            // If something goes wrong, wrap the exception and rethrow it
            throw new ServletException("Can't init Counter servlet: " +
                                       e.getMessage(), e);
        }
    }

    // This method is called when the web server stops the servlet (which
    // happens when the web server is shutting down, or when the servlet is
    // not in active use).  This method saves the counts to a file so they
    // can be restored when the servlet is restarted.
    public void destroy() {
        try { saveState(); }  // Try to save the state
        catch(Exception e) {} // Ignore any problems: we did the best we could
    }

    // These constants define the request parameter and attribute names that
    // the servlet uses to find the name of the counter to increment.
    public static final String PARAMETER_NAME = "counter";
    public static final String ATTRIBUTE_NAME =
        "je3.servlet.Counter.counter";

    /**
     * This method is called when the servlet is invoked.  It looks for a
     * request parameter named "counter", and uses its value as the name of
     * the counter variable to increment.  If it doesn't find the request
     * parameter, then it uses the URL of the request as the name of the
     * counter.  This is useful when the servlet is mapped to a URL suffix.
     * This method also checks how much time has elapsed since it last saved
     * its state, and saves the state again if necessary.  This prevents it
     * from losing too much data if the server crashes or shuts down without
     * calling the destroy() method.
     **/
```

Example 20-3. Counter.java (continued)

```
public void doGet(HttpServletRequest request, HttpServletResponse response)
    throws IOException
{
    // Get the name of the counter as a request parameter
    String counterName = request.getParameter(PARAMETER_NAME);

    // If we didn't find it there, see if it was passed to us as a
    // request attribute, which happens when the output of this servlet
    // is included by another servlet
    if (counterName == null)
        counterName = (String) request.getAttribute(ATTRIBUTE_NAME);

    // If it wasn't a parameter or attribute, use the request URL.
    if (counterName == null) counterName = request.getRequestURI();

    Integer count;  // What is the current count?

    // This block of code is synchronized because multiple requests may
    // be running at the same time in different threads.  Synchronization
    // prevents them from updating the counts hashtable at the same time
    synchronized(counts) {
        // Get the counter value from the hashtable
        count = (Integer)counts.get(counterName);

        // Increment the counter, or if it is new, log and start it at 1
        if (count != null) count = new Integer(count.intValue() + 1);
        else {
            // If this is a counter we haven't used before, send a message
            // to the log file, just so we can track what we're counting
            log("Starting new counter: " + counterName);
            // Start counting at 1!
            count = new Integer(1);
        }

        // Store the incremented (or new) counter value into the hashtable
        counts.put(counterName, count);

        // Check whether saveInterval milliseconds have elapsed since we
        // last saved our state.  If so, save it again.  This prevents
        // us from losing more than saveInterval ms of data, even if the
        // server crashes unexpectedly.
        if (System.currentTimeMillis() - lastSaveTime > saveInterval) {
            saveState();
            lastSaveTime = System.currentTimeMillis();
        }
    } // End of synchronized block

    // Finally, output the counter value.  Since this servlet is usually
    // included within the output of other servlets, we don't bother
    // setting the content type.
    PrintWriter out = response.getWriter();
    out.print(count);
}
```

Example 20-3. Counter.java (continued)

```
    // The doPost method just calls doGet, so that this servlet can be
    // included in pages that are loaded with POST requests
    public void doPost(HttpServletRequest request,HttpServletResponse response)
        throws IOException
    {
        doGet(request, response);
    }

    // Save the state of the counters by serializing the hashtable to
    // the file specified by the initialization parameter.
    void saveState() throws IOException {
        ObjectOutputStream out = new ObjectOutputStream(
                    new BufferedOutputStream(new FileOutputStream(countfile)));
        out.writeObject(counts);  // Save the hashtable to the stream
        out.close();              // Always remember to close your files!
    }

    // Load the initial state of the counters by de-serializing a hashtable
    // from the file specified by the initialization parameter.  If the file
    // doesn't exist yet, then start with an empty hashtable.
    void loadState() throws IOException {
        if (!countfile.exists()) {
            counts = new HashMap();
            return;
        }
        ObjectInputStream in = null;
        try {
            in = new ObjectInputStream(
                    new BufferedInputStream(new FileInputStream(countfile)));
            counts = (HashMap) in.readObject();
        }
        catch(ClassNotFoundException e) {
            throw new IOException("Count file contains bad data: " +
                                        e.getMessage());
        }
        finally {
            try { in.close(); }
            catch (Exception e) {}
        }
    }
}
```

Running the Counter Servlet

Our *web.xml* file assigns the name counter to the Counter servlet. The servlet reads
a request parameter, also named counter, to find the name of the counter variable
to increment and display. Thus, you can test the servlet by pointing your browser
to a URL like the following:

```
http://localhost:8080/je3/counter?counter=numhits
```

The *web.xml* file also specifies that the Counter servlet should be invoked whenever a file ending with the suffix *.count* (and beginning with the web application

---

name) is requested from the web server. (You'll learn how the *web.xml* file specifies this later in this chapter.) In this case, Counter uses the URL itself as the name
of the counter variable. Test this feature by entering a URL like the following:

```
http://localhost:8080/je3/index.html.count
```

By now, you've probably noticed that the Counter servlet doesn't produce very
interesting output: it just displays a number. This servlet is not very useful when
used on its own; it is intended, instead, to have its output included within the
output of other servlets. (We'll explore a couple of ways to do this later in the
chapter.) If your web server supports server-side includes (SSI) and the <servlet>
tag, though, you can use this feature to include the output of the Counter servlet in
web pages. (Tomcat 5 can be configured to support SSI, but does not do so by
default.) To do so, you might create a *test.shtml* file that contains text like the
following:

```
<p>This page has been accessed
  <servlet name='/counter'>
    <param name='counter' value='test.shtml'></param>
  </servlet>
times.
```

Hello JSP

We now transition from servlet examples to JSP examples. One of the shortcomings of any servlet that produces nontrivial output is that they often contain
embedded HTML tags locked up within Java classes where web designers cannot
get to them. JSP is designed to improve this situation: instead of embedding
HTML within Java code, it embeds Java code within HTML pages. (And, as we'll
see, JSP 2.0 and the Java Standard Tag Libraries dramatically reduce the amount
of Java code that must be intermixed with HTML.)

Example 20-4 is a simple JSP page that performs a function similar to the HelloNet
servlet of Example 20-1. If invoked with a parameter named "name", it simply
greets the named user. If there is no parameter, it displays an HTML form to
request the user's name and then greets the user when the form is submitted.

Example 20-4 uses JSP 1.x, and the main thing to note about the example is that it
consists of HTML code intermingled with Java code which is contained within
pseudotags. Remember that JSP pages are compiled into servlet classes. <% and %>
delimit blocks of Java code, which are inserted literally into the body of the
servlet's doGet( ) or doPost( ) method. Note that these "scriptlet" tags can contain
code fragments that are not complete statements. A fragment may end in the
middle of an if block, to be followed by HTML tags (which are inserted literally
into the servlet's output) and then followed by another <%...%> scriptlet that
closes the if block.

The tag <%=...%> is like a scriptlet, but contains a single Java expression (instead
of arbitrary statements) whose value is placed in the servlet's output at that point.
Note also that the example begins with a <%@page...%> directive, which declares
that the JSP page outputs an HTML document. Table 20-1 summarizes the syntax
of JSP 1.x pages.

Table 20-1. JSP 1.x syntax

Tag	Purpose
`<%--...--%>`	A JSP comment. Unlike HTML comments, JSP comments are stripped during the JSP compilation process and never appear in the output page.
`<@page...%>`	The page directive. Every JSP page must have one. Common attributes specify the page language, the content type of the output, the page buffer size, and the list of packages to import.
`<%@include file="URL"%>`	Includes the specified file at compilation time.
`<%@taglib uri="taglibId"prefix="tagPrefix"%>`	Declares a tag library for the page. The `uri` attribute uniquely identifies the library, and the `prefix` attribute specifies the prefix by which it is known on the page.
`<%!...%>`	A declaration tag. These delimiters surround Java code that becomes methods and fields of the resulting servlet class.
`<%=...%>`	An expression tag. Contains a Java expression. The tag is replaced with the expression value at runtime.
`<%...%>`	A *scriptlet*. These delimiters surround Java code that becomes part of the `_jspService( )` method, which is the JSP version of `goGet( )` and `doPost( )`.

Example 20-4. hello.jsp

```
<%@page language='java' contentType='text/html'%>
<% // Begin scriptlet: this is Java code
if (request.getParameter("name") == null) {  // If no name, request one
// Note that the scriptlet ends in the middle of a block.
%>
<%-- Now we switch to HTML tags and java expressions --%>
<form>
<i>Please enter your name: </i><input name="name">
<input type="Submit">
</form>
<%
// Back to Java code
} else {  // Otherwise, if there was a name parameter, greet the user
%>
Hello <%= request.getParameter("name") %>
<% } // end the Java if/else statement %>
```

Displaying a JSP Page

If you use the prepackaged je3.war file for the examples in this chapter, you can try out this example using a URL like this:

```
http://localhost:8080/je3/hello.jsp
```

Servlet containers automatically compile JSP pages as needed (and recompile them when they change, which is very useful during development). You can precompile a JSP page to avoid the compilation overhead on a production web server, but doing that is not covered in this chapter.

Hello JSP2

The JSP 2.0 specification is a major step forward from the 1.x series. It includes support for a simple Java-like expression language (known as "EL"), which replaces awkward <%=...%> tags, and supports the Java Standard Tag Libraries (JSTL), which obviate the need for most <%...%> scriptlets. Example 20-5 is a version of Example 20-4, rewritten using these features. Note that <c:choose> and <c:when> tags serve as an if/else statement and replace the awkwardly intermingled HTML tags and Java scriptlets of Example 20-4. Also, notice that EL expressions are enclosed in ${...}, which is quite a bit friendlier than <%...%>. In this example, the @page directive is joined by an @taglib directive specifying that the page uses the standard "core" tag library and declares its XML namespace to be "c".

Example 20-5. hello2.jsp

```
<%@page contentType='text/html'%>
<%-- The taglib directive specifies that we're using the JSTL 1.1 core taglib.
  -- If you're using 1.0, change to "http://java.sun.com/jstl/core_rt" --%>
<%@taglib prefix="c" uri="http://java.sun.com/jsp/jstl/core" %>
<c:choose>
  <c:when test='${param.name == null}'>
    <form>
    <i>Please enter your name: </i>
    <input name="name"/>
    <input type="Submit"/>
    </form>
  </c:when>
  <c:otherwise>
    Hello ${param.name}!
  </c:otherwise>
</c:choose>
```

Expression Language Syntax

A full tutorial on the Expression Language used in JSP 2 pages is beyond the scope of this chapter; you can find complete details in the JSP 2.0 specification. For now, however, we'll simply note that the language supports expressions and operators much like Java and JavaScript do. The . and [ ] operators can be used to dereference objects. Objects that follow JavaBeans naming conventions behave as if they have properties (rather than accessor methods). Map objects with String keys can also be dereferenced with the . and [ ] operators.

JSP 2.0 defines the predefined objects listed in Table 20-2; these objects can be used in EL expressions.

Table 20-2. JSP 2.0 predefined objects

Object name	Represents
applicationScope	Maps application-scoped attribute names to values. See ServletContext. setAttribute( ) and the JSTL <c:set> tag.
cookie	Maps cookie names to Cookie objects.

Table 20-2. JSP 2.0 predefined objects

Object name	Represents
header	Maps header names to header values as single strings. See `ServletRequest.getHeader( )`.
headerValues	Maps header names to header values as a `String[ ]`. See `ServletRequest.getHeaders( )`.
initParam	Maps initialization parameter names to their `String` values. See `ServletContext.getInitParameter( )`.
pageContext	The `javax.servlet.jsp.PageContext` object for the page.
pageScope	Maps page-scoped attribute names to values. See `PageContext.setAttribute( )` and the JSTL `<c:set>` tag.
requestScope	Maps request-scoped attribute names to values. See `ServletRequest.setAttribute( )` and the JSTL `<c:set>` tag.
sessionScope	Maps session-scoped attribute names to values. See `HttpSession.setAttribute( )` and the JSTL `<c:set>` tag.
param	Maps request parameters to single String values. See `ServletRequest.getParameter( )`.
paramValues	Maps request parameters to `String[ ]` arrays. See `ServletRequest.getParameterValues( )`.

JSP 2.0 also includes support for predefined functions in EL expressions. JSTL 1.1 defines commonly used functions in a module that you can use just a like a tag library. To use these functions, include the following @taglib directive in your page:

```
<%@taglib prefix="fn" uri="http://java.sun.com/jsp/jstl/functions" %>
```

This declaration makes the following functions available to EL expressions. For the most part, these functions behave just like a well-known function of the same name in the core Java API:

```
boolean fn:contains(String, String)
boolean fn:containsIgnoreCase(String, String)
boolean fn:endsWith(String, String)
boolean fn:startsWith(String, String)
int fn:indexOf(String, String)
int fn:length(Object)
String fn:escapeXml(String)
String fn:join(String[ ], String)
String fn:replace(String, String, String)
String fn:substring(String, int, int)
String fn:substringAfter(String, String)
String fn:substringBefore(String, String)
String fn:toLowerCase(String)
String fn:toUpperCase(String)
String fn:trim(String)
String[ ] fn:split(String, String)
```

Displaying JSP Pages that Use Tag Libraries

If you use the je3.war file, the URL to display this example is almost identical to the last one:

```
http://localhost:8080/je3/hello2.jsp
```

Note, however, that in order to make it work, the servlet container must be able to find the tag library implementation classes, as described at the beginning of this chapter. If you are using Tomcat, make sure that you've put the *jstl.jar* and *standard.jar* files (or more current replacements for these files) in the *common/ lib/* directory. Note that the *standard.jar* file contains the necessary tag library descriptor (TLD) files and that the file *META-INF/c.tld* defines the URI used in the @taglib directive in Example 20-5.

Example 20-5 uses Version 1.1 of the JSTL. If you cannot find 1.1 implementation classes, you should be able to make the 1.1 classes work in a 1.0 implementation. To do this, though, you must change your @tablib directive to use the slightly different URL that identifies Version 1.0:

```
<%@taglib prefix="c" uri="http://java.sun.com/jstl/core_rt" %>
```

Finally, note that this example uses only the core module of the JSTL. In addition to the functions module mentioned previously, the JSTL also includes modules of tags for database access ("sql"), XML manipulation ("x"), and internationalized text formatting ("fmt").

Hello XML

The JSP 2.0 example (Example 20-5) looks much cleaner than the original JSP code of Example 20-4. Because of its `<%@page...%>` and `<%@taglib...%>` directives, however, it is not a valid XML document. JSP 2.0 pages can also be written as valid XML documents using a slightly different format illustrated in Example 20-6. `hello3.jspx` (note the file extension) is a rewrite of Example 20-5 using the XML format. It is a valid XML file that, when accessed, outputs a valid XHTML document. It uses the `<jsp:directive.page>` tag instead of the @page directive, and it uses a custom `<tags:xhtml>` tag to output an appropriate XHTML DOCTYPE declaration and `<html>` tag. The definition of this custom `<tags:xhtml>` tag is in the *WEB-INF/tags/* directory of the WAR file, and is not shown here. We'll see more about JSP 2 custom tags later in this chapter.

Example 20-6. hello3.jspx

```
<?xml version="1.0"?>
<tags:xhtml xmlns:tags="urn:jsptagdir:/WEB-INF/tags"
            xmlns:jsp="http://java.sun.com/JSP/Page"
            xmlns:c="http://java.sun.com/jsp/jstl/core"
            xmlns="http://www.w3.org/1999/xhtml">
<jsp:directive.page contentType='text/html'/>
<head><title>Hello</title></head>
  <body>
    <c:choose>
      <c:when test='${param.name == null}'>
        <form action="hello3.jspx">
        <p>Please enter your name:
        <input name="name"/>
        <input type="submit"/>
        </p></form>
      </c:when>
      <c:otherwise>
```

Example 20-6. hello3.jspx (continued)

```
        <p>Hello ${param.name}!</p>
      </c:otherwise>
    </c:choose>
  </body>
</tags:xhtml>
```

The MVC Paradigm for Web Applications

MVC is an acronym for Model-View-Controller, a powerful object-oriented architecture used for graphical user interfaces and also adopted for web applications. The Model is the object or objects upon which that application acts: they are the data. The objects that make up the Model are the core classes of the application. The View is the object or objects that display the model to the user. The Controller is the object that ties everything together, creating view objects for the model and translating the user's interactions with the view into modifications of the model.

In a Java web application, the Controller is a special-purpose servlet and the View, or Views, are JSP pages. The Controller servlet handles all incoming requests, examines them, takes any necessary actions on the Model, and then dispatches the request to an appropriate JSP page, which displays a response to the user. The Model for a web application can be any kind of object, although, by convention, Model objects follow JavaBeans naming conventions with get/set property accessor methods.

The examples that follow constitute a simple web application, named ListManager, for managing a mailing list. As pictured in Figure 20-2, this web application allows users to subscribe to, set delivery preferences for, or unsubscribe from a mailing list. (The example program is not capable of actually sending email to the list subscribers, however.) In the following sections we'll see the Model classes, the Controller servlet, and the JSP views for this web application. Because the Model, Controller, and Views are interdependent, you may need to read through these examples twice in order to understand all the details.

ListManager Model Classes

The ListManager web application uses a User object to model a mailing list subscriber and her mail delivery preferences. The User class does not have a public constructor, however. Instead, User objects are returned from a UserFactory object, which uses a database backend to provide a persistent store for subscriptions and delivery preferences. The four public methods of UserFactory are:

insert( )
    Adds a subscription to the database and returns a User object for it

select( )
    Looks up the User object that corresponds to a specified email address and password

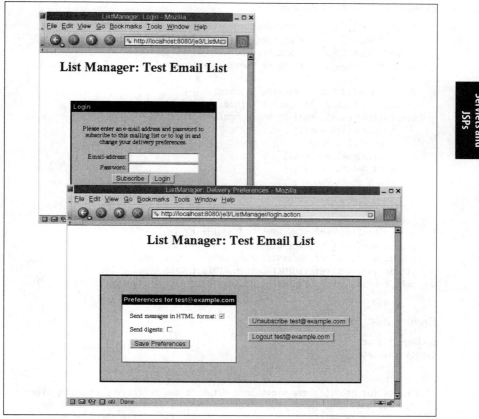

Figure 20-2. The ListManager web application

update( )
>   Updates email delivery preferences in the database to match the current state
>   of the specified User object

delete( )
>   Deletes a subscription from the database, unsubscribing the specified User
>   from the mailing list

Note that these four methods are named after the SQL statements they each use.
The source code for User and UserFactory are listed in Examples 20-7 and 20-8.

Example 20-7. User.java

```
package je3.servlet;

/**
 * This class represents a mailing list subscriber.
 * It has JavaBeans-style property accessor methods.
 */
public class User {
```

Example 20-7. User.java (continued)

```
    String email;       // The user's e-mail address
    boolean html;       // Whether the user wants HTML-formatted messages
    boolean digest;     // Whether the user wants digests
    boolean deleted;    // Set by UserFactory.delete( ); tested by insert( )

    // The constructor is package-private.
    // See UserFactory for public methods to obtain a User object.
    User(String email, boolean html, boolean digest) {
        this.email = email;
        this.html = html;
        this.digest = digest;
        this.deleted = false;
    }

    // The following property accessors follow JavaBeans naming conventions
    public String getEmailAddress( ) { return email; }
    public boolean getPrefersHTML( ) { return html; }
    public boolean getPrefersDigests( ) { return digest; }
    public void setEmailAddress(String email) { this.email = email; }
    public void setPrefersHTML(boolean html) { this.html = html; }
    public void setPrefersDigests(boolean digest) { this.digest = digest; }
}
```

Example 20-8. UserFactory.java

```
package je3.servlet;
import java.sql.*;

/**
 * A class for creating new users in a database and retreiving existing users
 * from the database.  Note that it assumes that a database table with the
 * specified name exists.  You can create such a table with SQL like this:
 *
 *    CREATE TABLE subscribers (
 *        email VARCHAR(64) PRIMARY KEY,
 *        password VARCHAR(20),
 *        html BIT,
 *        digest BIT);
 **/
public class UserFactory {
    Connection db;      // The connection to the database
    String tablename;   // The name of the database table we'll use

    // These prepared statements are created in the constructor, and used
    // in the insert( ), select( ), update( ) and delete( ) methods.
    // PreparedStatements are used for security so that the database cannot
    // be attacked with usernames and passwords that include SQL quotes.
    PreparedStatement insertUser, selectUser, updateUser, deleteUser;

    // Create a new UserFactory object backed by the specified DB table
    public UserFactory(Connection db, String tablename) throws SQLException {
        this.db = db;
        this.tablename = tablename;
```

Example 20-8. UserFactory.java (continued)

```
        // Prepare the SQL statements we'll use later.  Parameters will be
        // subsituted for the question marks in the methods below.
        insertUser = db.prepareStatement("insert into " + tablename +
                                        "(email,password,html,digest) " +
                                        "values(?,?,0,0)");
        selectUser = db.prepareStatement("select * from " + tablename +
                                        " where email=?");
        deleteUser = db.prepareStatement("delete from " + tablename +
                                        " where email=?");
        updateUser = db.prepareStatement("update " + tablename +
                                        " set html=?,digest=? where email=?");
    }

    // Create a new User with the specified e-mail address and password
    public User insert(String email, String password)
        throws UserAlreadyExists, SQLException
    {
        // Check whether the user already exists
        selectUser.setString(1, email);
        ResultSet results = selectUser.executeQuery( );
        if (results.next( )) throw new UserAlreadyExists(email);

        // If not, create a new entry in the database
        insertUser.setString(1, email);
        insertUser.setString(2, password);
        insertUser.executeUpdate( );

        // And return a matching User object to the caller
        return new User(email, false, false);
    }

    // Look up the User object for the specified address and password
    public User select(String email, String password)
        throws NoSuchUser, BadPassword, SQLException
    {
        // Look up the user
        selectUser.setString(1, email);
        ResultSet results = selectUser.executeQuery( );
        // Check that the user exists
        if (!results.next( )) throw new NoSuchUser(email);
        // Check that the password is correct
        String pw = results.getString("password");
        if (!pw.equals(password)) throw new BadPassword(email);
        // Return a User object representing this user and their mail prefs.
        boolean html = results.getInt("html") == 1;
        boolean digest = results.getInt("digest") == 1;
        return new User(email, html, digest);
    }

    // Delete the specified User object from the database
    public void delete(User user) throws SQLException {
        if (user.deleted) return;  // make sure we're not already deleted
```

Example 20-8. UserFactory.java (continued)

```
            // Delete the user from the database
            deleteUser.setString(1, user.getEmailAddress( ));
            deleteUser.executeUpdate( );
            user.deleted = true;  // Don't allow update( ) after delete( )
    }

    // Update the HTML and digest preferences of the specified User
    public void update(User user) throws SQLException {
            if (user.deleted) return;  // Don't allow updates to deleted users
            // Update the database record to reflect new preferences
            updateUser.setInt(1, user.getPrefersHTML( )?1:0);
            updateUser.setInt(2, user.getPrefersDigests( )?1:0);
            updateUser.setString(3, user.getEmailAddress( ));
            updateUser.executeUpdate( );
    }

    // The following are custom exception types that we may throw
    public static class UserAlreadyExists extends Exception {
        public UserAlreadyExists(String msg) { super(msg); }
    }

    public static class NoSuchUser extends Exception {
        public NoSuchUser(String msg) { super(msg); }
    }

    public static class BadPassword extends Exception {
        public BadPassword(String msg) { super(msg); }
    }
}
```

ListManager Controller

The controller class for our `ListManager` application is named `Controller`, and is listed in Example 20-9. When first created, its init( ) method connects to a database and uses that database connection to create the `UserFactory` object that manages mailing list subscriptions. The most important thing to understand about this servlet is that its doGet( ) method handles all requests made to the `ListManager` application. Regardless of what page is displayed in response, the request is first handled through the `Controller` servlet.

The key to making this work is the *WEB-INF/web.xml* configuration file in the *je3. war* web application archive. This file contains the servlet initialization parameters used in the init( ) method to specify how to connect to the database. Most importantly, however, the *web.xml* file includes servlet mappings that specify that the `Controller` servlet should be invoked in response to the filename "ListManager/" (prefixed with the appropriate host, port, and "je3/", of course) and also in response to any filename of the form "ListManager/*.action". The doGet( ) method looks up the name by which the servlet was invoked, and uses that to dispatch to a method that can take the appropriate action. Hyperlinks within the web application all include a ".action" suffix, so they are all directed back to the `Controller` servlet.

The Controller servlet knows how to handle actions named "login", "edit", "unsubscribe", and "logout", and dispatches to methods with the same name. An important point about these method is that they each return a RequestDispatcher object that represents the page—or View—that the servlet should display to represent the new state of the Model. The controller servlet calls the forward( ) method of the RequestDispatcher to forward the request to the new page. (RequestDispatcher also defines a useful include( ) method for including the output of one servlet or JSP page within another.) Note that the comments for the login( ), edit( ), and related methods make a point of specifying exactly which parameters must be included with the request. When we examine the JSP pages that constitute the View objects, we'll see that these pages provide those necessary parameters.

Example 20-9. Controller.java

```
package je3.servlet;
import java.io.*;
import javax.servlet.*;
import javax.servlet.http.*;
import java.sql.*;

/**
 * This is the Controller servlet for the ListManager web application.  It must
 * be configured to be invoked in response to URLs ending with ".action".  When
 * it is invoked this way, it uses the file name it is invoked as
 * ("login.action", "edit.action", etc.) to determine what to do.  Each
 * supported action name has a corresponding method which performs the
 * requested action and returns an appropriate View object in the form of a
 * a RequestDispatcher wrapped around a JSP page. The servlet dispatches to the
 * JSP page which generates an HTML document to display to the user.
 */
public class Controller extends HttpServlet {
    Connection db;                   // Database connection
    UserFactory userFactory;         // Factory for managing User objects

    /**
     * This method is called when the servlet is first created. It reads its
     * initialization parameters and uses them to connect to a database.
     * It uses the database connection to create a UserFactory object.
     */
    public void init( ) throws ServletException {
        // Read initialization parameters from the web.xml deployment file
        ServletConfig config = getServletConfig( );
        String jdbcDriver = config.getInitParameter("jdbcDriver");
        String jdbcURL = config.getInitParameter("jdbcURL");
        String jdbcUser = config.getInitParameter("jdbcUser");
        String jdbcPassword = config.getInitParameter("jdbcPassword");
        String tablename = config.getInitParameter("tablename");

        // Use those parameters to connect to the database
        try {
```

Example 20-9. Controller.java (continued)

```
                // Load the driver class.
                // It registers itself; we don't need to retain the returned Class
                Class.forName(jdbcDriver);

                // Connect to database.  If the database server ever crashes,
                // this Connection object will become invalid, and the servlet
                // will crash too, even if the database server has come back up.
                db = DriverManager.getConnection(jdbcURL, jdbcUser, jdbcPassword);

                // Use the DB connection to instantiate a UserFactory object
                userFactory = new UserFactory(db, tablename);
            }
            catch(Exception e) {
                log("Can't connect to database", e);
                throw new ServletException("Can't connect to database", e);
            }

            // Save an init param where our JSP pages can find it.  They need
            // this so they can display the name of the mailing list.
            ServletContext context = config.getServletContext();
            context.setAttribute("listname",config.getInitParameter("listname"));
    }

    /**
     * If the servlet is destroyed, we need to release the database connection
     */
    public void destroy() {
        try { if (db != null) db.close(); }
        catch(SQLException e) {}
    }

    /* Handle POST requests as if they were GET requests */
    public void doPost(HttpServletRequest req,HttpServletResponse resp)
        throws IOException, ServletException
    {
        doGet(req, resp);
    }

    public void doGet(HttpServletRequest req, HttpServletResponse resp)
        throws IOException, ServletException
    {
        // Look up the information we need to dispatch this request
        // We need to know what name we were invoked under and whether there
        // is already a User object in the session.
        String name = req.getServletPath();
        User user = (User) req.getSession(true).getAttribute("user");

        // This will hold the page we dispatch to for the response
        RequestDispatcher nextPage;

        // If no user is defined yet, go to the login page.
        // Otherwise, dispatch to one of the methods below based on the name
```

Example 20-9. Controller.java (continued)

```
        // by which we were invoked (see web.xml for the mapping).  The page
        // to display is the return value of the method we dispatch to.
        try {
            if (name.endsWith("/login.action"))
                nextPage = login(req, resp);
            else if (user == null)
                nextPage = req.getRequestDispatcher("login.jsp");
            else if (name.endsWith("/edit.action"))
                nextPage = edit(req, resp);
            else if (name.endsWith("/unsubscribe.action"))
                nextPage = unsubscribe(req, resp);
            else if (name.endsWith("/logout.action"))
                nextPage=logout(req, resp);
            else {
                // If we don't recoginze the name we're invoked under,
                // send a HTTP 404 error.
                resp.sendError(HttpServletResponse.SC_NOT_FOUND, "Not Found");
                return;
            }
        }
        catch(SQLException e) {
            // If anything goes wrong while processing the action, then
            // output an error page.  This demonstrates how a servlet can
            // produce its own output instead of forwarding to a JSP page.
            // We could also use resp.sendError( ) here to send an error code.
            resp.sendError(HttpServletResponse.SC_INTERNAL_SERVER_ERROR);
            resp.setContentType("text/html");
            PrintWriter out = resp.getWriter( );
            out.print("<h1>Error</h1>");
            out.print("An unexpected error has occurred.<pre>");
            out.print(e);
            out.print("</pre>Please contact the webmaster.");
            return;
        }
        // Now send the nextPage as the response to the client.
        // See the RequestDispatcher class.
        nextPage.forward(req, resp);
    }

    // This method handles "/login.action", which is either a request to
    // subscribe a new user, or a request to log in an existing subscriber.
    // A form that links to "/login.action" must define a parameter named
    // "email" and a parameter named "password".  If this is a subscription
    // request for a new user, the parameter "subscribe" must also be defined.
    RequestDispatcher login(HttpServletRequest req, HttpServletResponse resp)
        throws ServletException, IOException, SQLException
    {
        // This action can dispatch to one of two pages
        RequestDispatcher loginPage = req.getRequestDispatcher("login.jsp");
        RequestDispatcher editPage = req.getRequestDispatcher("edit.jsp");

        // Get parameters from the request
        String email = req.getParameter("email");
```

Example 20-9. Controller.java (continued)

```java
        String password = req.getParameter("password");

        // Make sure e-mail address is not the empty string!
        if (email.length( ) == 0) {
            req.setAttribute("loginMessage",
                                "You must specify an e-mail address");
            return loginPage;
        }

        // Now try to subscribe or login.  If all goes well, we'll end up
        // with a User object
        User user = null;
        try {
            // This action is either for subscribing a new user or for
            // logging in an existing user.  It depends on which submit button
            // was pressed.
            if (req.getParameter("subscribe") != null) {
                // A new subscription
                user = userFactory.insert(email, password);
            }
            else {
                // A login
                user = userFactory.select(email, password);
            }
        }
        // If anything goes wrong, we send the user back to the login page
        // with an error message.
        catch(UserFactory.NoSuchUser e) {
            req.setAttribute("loginMessage", "Unknown e-mail address.");
            return loginPage;
        }
        catch(UserFactory.BadPassword e) {
            req.setAttribute("loginMessage", "Incorrect Password");
            return loginPage;
        }
        catch(UserFactory.UserAlreadyExists e) {
            req.setAttribute("loginMessage", email + " is already subscribed");
            return loginPage;
        }

        // If we got here, the user is subscribed or logged in. Store the User
        // object in the current session and move on to the edit page.
        HttpSession session = req.getSession(true);
        session.setAttribute("user", user);
        return editPage;
    }

    // This method handles the URL "/edit.action".
    // A form that links to this URL must define parameters "html" and
    // "digest" if the user wants HTML messages or digests.
    RequestDispatcher edit(HttpServletRequest req, HttpServletResponse resp)
        throws ServletException, IOException, SQLException
```

Example 20-9. Controller.java (continued)

```
    {
        // Update the user's email delivery preferences based on request params
        User user = (User) req.getSession( ).getAttribute("user");
        user.setPrefersHTML(req.getParameter("html") != null);
        user.setPrefersDigests(req.getParameter("digest") != null);
        // Ask the factory to save the new preferences to the database
        userFactory.update(user);
        // And re-display the edit page
        return req.getRequestDispatcher("edit.jsp");
    }

    // This method handles the URL "/unsubscribe.action"
    // No parameters are necessary for this action.
    RequestDispatcher unsubscribe(HttpServletRequest req,
                                  HttpServletResponse resp)
        throws ServletException, IOException, SQLException
    {
        // Get the User object from the session
        User user = (User) req.getSession( ).getAttribute("user");
        // Note the e-mail address before destroying it.
        String email = user.getEmailAddress( );
        // Delete the user from the database
        userFactory.delete(user);
        // Terminate the session
        req.getSession( ).invalidate( ); // log out
        // Now display the login page again with an unsubscribed message
        req.setAttribute("loginMessage",
                    email + " unsubscribed and logged out.");
        return req.getRequestDispatcher("login.jsp");
    }

    // This method handles the URL "/logout.action".
    // No parameters are necessary for this action.
    RequestDispatcher logout(HttpServletRequest req, HttpServletResponse resp)
        throws ServletException, IOException, SQLException
    {
        // Destroy the session object, and return to the login page with
        // a "logged out" message for confirmation.
        User user = (User) req.getSession( ).getAttribute("user");
        req.setAttribute("loginMessage", user.getEmailAddress( )+" logged out");
        req.getSession( ).invalidate( ); // delete session
        return req.getRequestDispatcher("login.jsp");
    }
}
```

ListManager Views

The View classes used by the ListManager application are JSP pages. Although the Controller class can handle four actions (login, edit, unsubscribe, and logout) the web application requires only two views, *login.jsp* and *edit.jsp*, which are shown in Examples 20-10 and 20-11.

login.jsp displays a login form, obviously. As part of the form, it displays an optional message, specified by the `Controller` servlet with the `HttpServletRequest.setAttribute()` method. This message explains errors ("Incorrect Password") or provides confirmation ("logged out"). The login form has input fields for an email address and password, and has buttons to log in and edit an existing subscription or to subscribe a new address to the list. Whichever button the user clicks, the email address and password are sent to the "login.action" URL, which is handled by the `login()` method of the `Controller` servlet.

The `edit.jsp` page includes a form that allows the user to edit his mail preferences; this form POSTs to the "edit.action" URL, which is handled by the `edit()` method of the `Controller`. It also includes buttons that POST to the "logout.action" and "unsubscribe.action" URLs, which are handled by the `logout()` and `unsubscribe()` methods of the `Controller`.

Note that both *login.jsp* and *edit.jsp* clearly document their inputs and outputs. This helps integrate these View objects with the action methods of the `Controller` servlet. This technique is particularly helpful for large web applications in which a Java programmer is developing the `Controller` and a web designer is developing the JSP pages that constitute the View objects.

Example 20-10. login.jsp

```
<%-- --------------------------------------------------------------------
   - login.jsp: Displays a login form for the ListManager web application.
   -
   - Inputs: The page expects the name of the mailing list in
   - ${applicationScope.listname} (the "listname" attribute of ServletContext).
   - It also looks for an optional error or status message in
   - ${requestScope.loginMessage} (the "loginMessage" attribute of the
   - ServletRequest)
   -
   - Outputs: When submitted, the form POSTs to "login.action", and defines
   - parameters named "email" and "password". If the user submits with the
   - Subscribe button, it defines a "subscribe" parameter. Otherwise, if the
   - user submits with the Login button, it defines a "login" parameter.
   -------------------------------------------------------------------- --%>
<%@taglib prefix="tags" tagdir="/WEB-INF/tags" %><%-- custom tag directory --%>
<html>
<head><title>ListManager: Login</title></head>
<body>
<div align="center">
<%-- Get list title from ServletContext attribute --%>
<h1>List Manager: ${applicationScope.listname}</h1>

<%-- Use the custom "box" tag to highlight the login form --%>
<tags:box title="Login" bgcolor="#ccf" border="3" margin="70" padding="20">
<%-- Get login message from request attribute and highlight with a tag. --%>
<tags:attention>${requestScope.loginMessage}</tags:attention>
<%-- The rest of the file is standard HTML --%>
<p>
Please enter an e-mail address and password to subscribe to this
mailing list or to log in and change your delivery preferences.
```

Example 20-10. login.jsp (continued)

```
<form action='login.action' method="post">
  <table>
    <tr>          <%-- First row: email address --%>
      <td align='right'>Email-address:</td>
      <td><input name='email'></td>
    </tr><tr>     <%-- Second row: password --%>
      <td align='right'>Password:</td>
      <td><input type='password' name='password'></td>
    </tr><tr>     <%-- Third row: buttons --%>
      <td align='center' colspan=2>
        <input type=submit name="subscribe" value='Subscribe'>
        <input type=submit name="login" value='Login'>
      </td>
    </tr>
  </table>
</form>
<%-- Demonstrate <jsp:include> to include servlet output in a page --%>
This page has been accessed
<jsp:include page="/Counter">
<jsp:param name="counter" value="login.jsp"/>
</jsp:include> times.
</tags:box>
</div>
</body>
</html>
```

Example 20-11. edit.jsp

```
<%-- ------------------------------------------------------------------------
   - edit.jsp: Edit subscription preferences, unsubcribe, or log out
   -
   - Inputs: this page expects a user to be logged in and ${sessionScope.user}
   - (the "user" attribute of HttpSession) to be the User object for that user.
   - It expects ${applicationScope.listname} to contain the name of the mailing
   - list.
   -
   - Outputs: This page displays 3 forms which POST to "edit.action",
   - "logout.action" and "unsubscribe.action" respectively.  The edit form
   - includes HTML checkboxes, and defines a parameter "html" if the user
   - indicates that she prefers HTML-formatted e-mail.  It defines the
   - parameter "digest" if the user prefers to receive message digests.
   - The logout and unsubscribe forms define no parameters.
   ------------------------------------------------------------------------ --%>
<%@ taglib prefix="tags" tagdir="/WEB-INF/tags" %><%--custom tags directory--%>
<html>
<head><title>ListManager: Delivery Preferences</title><head>
<body><div align="center">
  <h1>List Manager: ${applicationScope.listname}</h1>
  <tags:box bgcolor="#ccf" border="3" margin="75" padding="20">
    <!-- This table puts the edit form on the left and stacks the -->
    <!-- unsubscribe and logout buttons on the right. -->
    <table><tr><td>
```

Example 20-11. edit.jsp (continued)

```
<!-- Custom tag creates a titled box for the edit form -->
<tags:box
      bgcolor="#fff" border="1" margin="25" padding="20"
      title="Preferences for ${sessionScope.user.emailAddress}">
  <!-- The edit form -->
  <form action="edit.action" method="post">
    Send messages in HTML format:
    <%-- Note the use of a ${} EL expression inside these tags to --%>
    <%-- set the default state of the checkboxes --%>
    <input type="checkbox" name="html"
           ${sessionScope.user.prefersHTML?"checked":""}>
    <p>
    Send digests:
    <input type="checkbox" name="digest"
    ${sessionScope.user.prefersDigests?"checked":""}>
    <p>
    <input type="submit" value="Save Preferences">
  </form>
</tags:box>
</td><td>
  <!-- The unsubscribe form -->
  <form action="unsubscribe.action" method="post">
    <input type="submit"
    value="Unsubscribe ${sessionScope.user.emailAddress}">
  </form>
  <p>
  <!-- The logout form -->
  <form action="logout.action" method="post">
    <input type="submit" value="Logout ${sessionScope.user.emailAddress}">
  </form>
</td></tr></table>
</tags:box>
</div></body></html>
```

Custom Tags in JSP 2.0

The JSP pages in Examples 20-10 and 20-11 use the custom tags <tags:attention> and <tags:box>. In both cases, the JSP files include an @taglib directive that maps the tags: prefix to a directory in the *WEB-INF/* directory of the web application. Within that directory are files named *attention.tag* and *box.tag*, which provide expansions for the two tags. Note that the tag names are defined by the filenames of the .tag files.

The <attention> tag is a trivial one; its very short body is the subject of Example 20-12. It consists simply of a <span> tag and some CSS style attributes that are wrapped around the contents to which the user's attention should be drawn. In the tag body, the <jsp:doBody/> tag is a placeholder for the contents of the <attention> tag.

Example 20-12. attention.tag

```
<span style="color:#f00; font-weight: bold;">
<jsp:doBody/>
</span>
```

The *box.tag* file of Example 20-13 is somewhat more complex because it can accept attributes. The @attribute directives at the top of the file declare these attributes. The bulk of the file consists of HTML <div> tags and CSS styles for the box with optional color, border, margins, and title. Expressions in ${ } place the attribute values into the CSS style attributes as needed. Note that the expressions use the ?: ternary operator to provide default values when the attribute is undefined. Again, the <jsp:doBody/> tag is used as a placeholder for the contents of the box.

Note that the custom tags shown here are a JSP 2.0 feature. Prior to JSP 2.0, custom tags had to be defined as Java classes and configured with a TLD (tag library descriptor) file. While this can be useful for tags with advanced features, many useful custom tags are simple templates like these, and JSP 2.0 makes them much easier to define.

Example 20-13. box.tag

```
<%@ attribute name="bgcolor" %>
<%@ attribute name="border" %>
<%@ attribute name="padding" %>
<%@ attribute name="margin" %>
<%@ attribute name="title" %>
<div style="
    background-color: ${bgcolor!=null?bgcolor:"transparent"};
    border: solid black ${border!=null?border:"0"}px;
    margin: ${margin!=null?margin:"5"}px;

">
<div style="
    background-color: #000;
    color: ${bgcolor!=null?bgcolor:"transparent"};
    margin: 0;
    padding: ${title!=null?4:0}px;
    font-family: sans-serif;
    font-weight: bold;
    text-align: left;
">
${title}
</div>
<div style="padding: ${padding!=null?padding:"5"}px;">
<jsp:doBody/>
</div>
</div>
```

Packaging a Web Application

Now that we've considered each of the pieces that constitute our ListManager web application, we'll look at how those pieces are put together into a web application WAR file. For completeness, we'll include all the servlets and JSP pages from this chapter, not just the ones that implement the mailing list manager. In order to do this, we must:

1. Write a *web.xml* file that configures all the servlets
2. Arrange that configuration file—along with the servlet implementation classes, JSP pages, and related files—in their correct places in a directory hierarchy
3. Zip them all up (with the *jar* tool) to create a WAR file

Recall from the start of this chapter that we used these commands to compile the servlet classes and create the WAR file:

```
javac -d WEB-INF/classes/ *.java
jar cMf je3.war \
        index.html *.jsp *.jspx ListManager/*.jsp \
        WEB-INF/web.xml WEB-INF/tags/*.tag WEB-INF/classes
```

We'll consider the directory hierarchy of the web application first, and then look at the *web.xml* file.

Web Application Directory Structure

Our *je3* web application is structured as follows:

/
> This is the root directory for the application. The servlet container will map a file *x* in this directory to a URL like this:
>
> > `http://localhost:8080/je3/x`

/index.html
> The default file served for the URL "je3/". This is just a plain HTML file that contains links to the various examples contained in the web application.

/.jsp*
> The hello.jsp, hello2.jsp and hello3.jspx examples go here.

/ListManager/
> A directory for the ListManager application, which serves to keep it separate from this chapter's other servlet and JSP examples.

/ListManager/login.jsp
> The ListManager login page.

/ListManager/edit.jsp
> The ListManager edit preferences page.

/WEB-INF/
> Most web applications have a *WEB-INF/* subdirectory for configuration information, servlet class files, and other auxiliary files. The servlet container does not expose these files to the client (although a servlet may do so if it chooses),

---

so it is reasonably safe to store sensitive configuration information (such as passwords) beneath this directory.

/WEB-INF/web.xml

The all-important configuration file that maps servlet names to Java class names and URLs to servlet names. It also defines servlet initialization parameters and maps tag library URIs to the actual location of the TLD file.

/WEB-INF/classes/je3/servlet/.class*

Java class files for the `Controller` servlet, its `User` and `UserFactory` model classes, and also the `HelloNet`, `ErrorHandlerServlet`, and `Counter` servlets.

/WEB-INF/tags/.tag*

.tag files defining the custom JSP 2.0 tags used in the web application.

The web.xml Configuration File

The *WEB-INF/web.xml* file is the main configuration file for a web application. In a well-designed web application, this is the only file that may need customization when deploying the application to a new server or in a new network environment. The *web.xml* file for the servlet and JSP examples in this chapter, including the ListManager web application, is shown in Example 20-14.

The bulk of the *web.xml* file consists of <servlet> tags, which map servlet implementation classes to servlet names and define initialization parameters for servlets that need them. Note that it is perfectly legal to define multiple names for the same servlet implementation class. Creating multiple named instances of the same servlet implementation in this way allows you to specify different initialization parameters for each instance. You might set up multiple copies of the ListManager Controller servlet to manage multiple mailing lists, for example.

The other important tags in the configuration file are the <servlet-mapping> tags, which map servlet names to the URLs by which they may be invoked. Note that there can be more than one <servlet-mapping> tag for each servlet and that a <servlet-mapping> can include wildcard characters. <servlet> and <servlet-mapping> are the most important tags for a *web.xml* file, but they are by no means the only ones. The example illustrates a few others; see the Servlet specification for full details on the syntax of this file.

Example 20-14. web.xml

```
<?xml version="1.0" encoding="ISO-8859-1"?>
<web-app xmlns="http://java.sun.com/xml/ns/j2ee"
    xmlns:xsi="http://www.w3.org/2001/XMLSchema-instance"
    xsi:schemaLocation="http://java.sun.com/xml/ns/j2ee web-app_2_4.xsd"
    version="2.4">

<!-- This is descriptive information about the webapp as a whole -->
<display-name>Java Examples in a Nutshell</display-name>
<description>
    Servlet and JSP examples from Java Examples in a Nutshell, 3rd
    edition, including a simple web application to allow users to
    subscribe and unsubscribe from a mailing list, and to set their mail
    delivery preferences.
</description>
```

Example 20-14. web.xml (continued)

```
<!-- Next come servlet tags that map class files to servlet names and -->
<!-- also define servlet initialization parameters -->
<servlet>
  <servlet-name>Hello</servlet-name>
  <servlet-class>je3.servlet.HelloNet</servlet-class>
</servlet>

<servlet>
  <servlet-name>ErrorHandler</servlet-name>
  <servlet-class>je3.servlet.ErrorHandlerServlet</servlet-class>
</servlet>

<!-- The Counter servlet uses initialization parameters -->
<servlet>
  <servlet-name>Counter</servlet-name>
  <servlet-class>je3.servlet.Counter</servlet-class>
  <init-param>
    <param-name>countfile</param-name>           <!-- where to save state -->
    <param-value>/tmp/counts.ser</param-value> <!-- adjust for your system-->
  </init-param>
  <init-param>
    <param-name>saveInterval</param-name>        <!-- how often to save -->
    <param-value>30000</param-value>             <!-- every 30 seconds -->
  </init-param>
</servlet>

<!-- The Controller servlet for the ListManager application needs -->
<!-- initialization parameters to specify the database to be used. -->
<!-- You'll need to set these before you can use the application. -->
<servlet>
  <servlet-name>Controller</servlet-name>
  <servlet-class>je3.servlet.Controller</servlet-class>
  <init-param> <!-- the JDBC driver class to use -->
    <param-name>jdbcDriver</param-name>
    <param-value>com.mysql.jdbc.Driver</param-value>
  </init-param>
  <init-param> <!-- The database to connect to -->
    <param-name>jdbcURL</param-name>
    <param-value>jdbc:mysql:///test</param-value>
  </init-param>
  <init-param> <!-- The username to connect as -->
    <param-name>jdbcUser</param-name>
    <param-value></param-value>
  </init-param>
  <init-param> <!-- The password to use -->
    <param-name>jdbcPassword</param-name>
    <param-value></param-value>
  </init-param>
  <init-param> <!-- the database table to use -->
    <param-name>tablename</param-name>
    <param-value>testlist</param-value>
  </init-param>
```

Example 20-14. web.xml (continued)

```
      <init-param> <!-- the name of the mailing list -->
        <param-name>listname</param-name>
        <param-value>Test Email List</param-value>
      </init-param>
    </servlet>

    <!-- Next we map URLs and URL patterns to servlet names -->
    <servlet-mapping>
      <servlet-name>Hello</servlet-name>
      <url-pattern>/Hello</url-pattern>
    </servlet-mapping>
    <servlet-mapping>
      <servlet-name>ErrorHandler</servlet-name>
      <url-pattern>/ErrorHandler</url-pattern>
    </servlet-mapping>
    <servlet-mapping>
      <servlet-name>Counter</servlet-name>
      <url-pattern>/Counter</url-pattern>
    </servlet-mapping>
    <!-- Note the wildcard below: any URL ending in .count invokes Counter -->
    <servlet-mapping>
      <servlet-name>Counter</servlet-name>
      <url-pattern>*.count</url-pattern>
    </servlet-mapping>

    <!-- These are the different URLs that invoke the ListManager Controller -->
    <!-- Note that we could also use wildcards here. -->
    <servlet-mapping>
      <servlet-name>Controller</servlet-name>
      <url-pattern>/ListManager/</url-pattern>
    </servlet-mapping>
    <servlet-mapping>
      <servlet-name>Controller</servlet-name>
      <url-pattern>/ListManager/login.action</url-pattern>
    </servlet-mapping>
    <servlet-mapping>
      <servlet-name>Controller</servlet-name>
      <url-pattern>/ListManager/logout.action</url-pattern>
    </servlet-mapping>
    <servlet-mapping>
      <servlet-name>Controller</servlet-name>
      <url-pattern>/ListManager/edit.action</url-pattern>
    </servlet-mapping>
    <servlet-mapping>
      <servlet-name>Controller</servlet-name>
      <url-pattern>/ListManager/unsubscribe.action</url-pattern>
    </servlet-mapping>

    <!-- ListManager sessions timeout after 15 minutes of inactivity -->
    <session-config>
      <session-timeout>15</session-timeout>
    </session-config>
</web-app>
```

Exercises

Exercise 20-1. Modify the HelloNet servlet so that it behaves like the *hello.jsp* page. That is, if it is invoked without a name parameter specified, it should prompt the user to enter her name and then displays a greeting. Although you are writing a single servlet, it should be able to display two distinct pages of output: a greeting page and a login page. The login page displays an HTML form, and the servlet should be able to handle submissions from this form.

Exercise 20-2. Modify the HelloNet servlet again, as in the last exercise. This time, however, do not hardcode the HTML for the greeting and login pages in the servlet itself. Instead, implement the contents of these pages in JSP files, and use the servlet as the controller that processes the input and decides when each page should be displayed. Your servlet class should use a RequestDispatcher to forward the request to the appropriate JSP page for display. It can use the session object or request attributes to pass data from the servlet to the JSP pages.

Exercise 20-3. Modify the Counter servlet to use a database, rather than a local file, as its persistence mechanism. Write a CounterAdmin servlet that is an administrative interface for the Counter servlet; it should display (but not update) each of the counts stored in the database. The CounterAdmin servlet should be password-protected and should display a JSP-based login page that requires the user to log in before the current counts are displayed. Use a servlet initialization parameter from the *web.xml* file to specify the password for the servlet.

Exercise 20-4. This chapter combines the ListManager web application with various stand-alone examples and then packages them all into a single WAR file. Repackage the ListManager web application by itself, and deploy two independent instances of it on a web server to manage subscriptions to two different mailing lists.

Exercise 20-5. The Controller servlet examines the name under which it was invoked and uses that name to dispatch to an action method defined within the servlet. Modify this class so that each action is defined as a separate object. Define an interface named ServletAction with an action( ) method that accepts servlet request parameter and response arguments and returns a RequestDispatcher, just as the current methods of the Controller servlet do. Then change those methods into implementations of this new interface. Modify the servlet so it maintains a Map of URL action names to ServletAction objects. Initialize the map in the servlet's init( ) method.

Exercise 20-6. Extend the ListManager web application by adding a password-protected administrative interface that displays all subscribers and their preferences. The administrative password should be stored as an initialization parameter, of course.

21

Remote Method Invocation

This chapter presents examples of the remote method invocation (RMI) capabilities of the java.rmi and java.rmi.server packages. Remote method invocation is a powerful technology for developing networked applications without having to worry about the low-level networking details. RMI transcends the client/server model of computing with a more general remote object model. In this model, the server defines objects that clients can use remotely. Clients invoke methods of a remote object exactly as if it were a local object running in the same virtual machine as the client. RMI hides the underlying mechanism for transporting method arguments and return values across the network. An argument or return value can be a primitive value or any Serializable object.

To develop an RMI-based application, you need to follow these steps:

1. Create an interface that extends the java.rmi.Remote interface. This interface defines the exported methods that the remote object implements (i.e., the methods the server implements and clients can invoke remotely). Each method in this interface must be declared to throw a java.rmi. RemoteException, which is the superclass of many more specific RMI exception classes. Every remote method must declare that it can throw a RemoteException, because there are quite a few things that can go wrong during the remote method invocation process over a network. (Actually, in Java 1.2 and later, this requirement is loosened: remote methods may instead throw one of the superclasses of RemoteException: IOException or Exception.)

2. Define a subclass of java.rmi.server.UnicastRemoteObject (or sometimes a related class) that implements your Remote interface. This class represents the remote object (or server object). Other than declaring its remote methods to throw RemoteException objects, the remote object doesn't need to do anything special to allow its methods to be invoked remotely. The UnicastRemoteObject and the rest of the RMI infrastructure handle this automatically.

3. Write a program (a server) that creates an instance of your remote object. Export the object, making it available for use by clients, by registering the object by name with a registry service. This is usually done with the java. rmi.Naming class and the *rmiregistry* program. A server program may also act as its own registry server by using the LocateRegistry class and Registry interface of the java.rmi.registry package.

4. After you compile the server program with *javac*, use *rmic* to generate a stub and a skeleton for the remote object. With RMI, the client and server don't communicate directly. On the client side, the client's reference to a remote object is implemented as an instance of a stub class. When the client invokes a remote method, it is a method of this stub object that is actually called. The stub does the necessary networking to pass that invocation to a skeleton class on the server. This skeleton translates the networked request into a method invocation on the server object, and passes the return value back to the stub, which passes it back to the client. This can be a complicated system, but fortunately, application programmers never have to think about stubs and skeletons; they are generated automatically by the *rmic* tool. Invoke *rmic* with the name of the remote object class (not the interface) on the command line. It creates and compiles two new classes with the suffixes _Stub and _Skel.

5. If the server uses the default registry service provided by the Naming class, you must run the registry server, if it is not already running. You can run the registry server by invoking the *rmiregistry* program.

6. Now you can write a client program to use the remote object exported by the server. The client must first obtain a reference to the remote object by using the Naming class to look up the object by name; the name is typically an *rmi*: URL. The remote reference that is returned is an instance of the Remote interface for the object (or more specifically, a stub object for the remote object). Once the client has this remote object, it can invoke methods on it exactly as it would invoke the methods of a local object. The only thing that it must be aware of is that all remote methods can throw RemoteException objects, and that in the presence of network errors, this can happen at unexpected times.

7. Finally, start up the server program, and run the client!

The following sections of this chapter provide two complete RMI examples that follow the steps outlined here. The first example is a relatively simple remote banking program, while the second example is a complex and lengthy multiuser domain (MUD) system (a kind of extensible chat-room universe). These examples are followed by a short discussion of advanced RMI features that are not demonstrated in this chapter.

Remote Banking

Example 21-1 shows a class, Bank, that contains inner classes and interfaces for a remote bank client/server example. In this example, the RemoteBank interface defines remote methods to open and close accounts, deposit and withdraw money, check the account balance, and obtain the transaction history for an account. The Bank class contains all of the classes and interfaces required for the example, except for the server class, which is the class that actually implements the RemoteBank interface. This server class is shown in Example 21-2.

Example 21-1 defines the following inner classes and interfaces:

RemoteBank

The Remote interface implemented by the bank server and used by the bank client.

FunnyMoney

A trivial class that represents money in this banking example. It is nothing more than a wrapper around an int, but it serves to demonstrate that Serializable objects can be passed as arguments to remote methods and returned by remote methods.

BankingException

A simple exception subclass that represents banking-related exceptions, such as "Insufficient funds." It demonstrates that remote method implementations on a server can throw exceptions that are transported across the network and thrown in the client program.

Client

This class is a standalone program that serves as a simple client to the bank server. It uses Naming.lookup( ) to look up the desired RemoteBank object in the system registry and then invokes various methods of that RemoteBank object, depending on its command-line arguments. It is really as simple as that; the use of RMI is almost transparent.

A session using the Bank.Client class might look as follows (note that the command-line argument "david" is the account name and "javanut" is the password that protects the account):

```
% java je3.rmi.Bank\$Client open david javanut
Account opened.
% java je3.rmi.Bank\$Client deposit david javanut 1000
Deposited 1000 wooden nickels.
% java je3.rmi.Bank\$Client withdraw david javanut 100
Withdrew 100 wooden nickels.
% java je3.rmi.Bank\$Client balance david javanut
You have 900 wooden nickels in the bank.
% java je3.rmi.Bank\$Client history david javanut
Account opened at Wed Jul 12 15:30:12 PDT 2000
Deposited 1000 on Wed Jul 12 15:30:31 PDT 2000
Withdrew 100 on Wed Jul 12 15:30:39 PDT 2000
% java je3.rmi.Bank\$Client close david javanut
900 wooden nickels returned to you.
Thanks for banking with us.
```

In this example session, the bank client is running on the same host as the server. This need not be the case; the Client class looks for a system property named bank to determine which bank server to connect to. So you could invoke the client program like this (one long command line that has been broken into two lines):

```
% java -Dbank=rmi://bank.trustme.com/TrustyBank \
je3.rmi.Bank\$Client open david javanut
```

Example 21-1. Bank.java

```java
package je3.rmi;
import java.rmi.*;
import java.util.List;

/**
 * This class is a placeholder that simply contains other classes and
 * interfaces for remote banking.
 **/
public class Bank {
    /**
     * This is the interface that defines the exported methods of the
     * bank server.
     **/
    public interface RemoteBank extends Remote {
        /** Open a new account, with the specified name and password */
        public void openAccount(String name, String password)
            throws RemoteException, BankingException;

        /** Close the named account */
        public FunnyMoney closeAccount(String name, String password)
            throws RemoteException, BankingException;

        /** Deposit money into the named account */
        public void deposit(String name, String password, FunnyMoney money)
            throws RemoteException, BankingException;

        /** Withdraw the specified amount of money from the named account */
        public FunnyMoney withdraw(String name, String password, int amount)
            throws RemoteException, BankingException;

        /** Return the amount of money in the named account */
        public int getBalance(String name, String password)
            throws RemoteException, BankingException;

        /**
         * Return a List of Strings that list the transaction history
         * of the named account
         **/
        public List getTransactionHistory(String name, String password)
            throws RemoteException, BankingException;
    }

    /**
     * This simple class represents a monetary amount.  This implementation
     * is really nothing more than a wrapper around an integer.  It is useful
     * to demonstrate that RMI can accept arbitrary non-String objects as
     * arguments and return them as values, as long as they are Serializable.
     * A more complete implementation of this FunnyMoney class might bear
     * a serial number, a digital signature, and other security features to
     * ensure that it is unique and non-forgeable.
     **/
    public static class FunnyMoney implements java.io.Serializable {
```

Example 21-1. Bank.java (continued)

```java
    public int amount;
    public FunnyMoney(int amount) { this.amount = amount; }
}

/**
 * This is a type of exception used to represent exceptional conditions
 * related to banking, such as "Insufficient Funds" and  "Invalid Password"
 **/
public static class BankingException extends Exception {
    public BankingException(String msg) { super(msg); }
}

/**
 * This class is a simple stand-alone client program that interacts
 * with a RemoteBank server.  It invokes different RemoteBank methods
 * depending on its command-line arguments, and demonstrates just how
 * simple it is to interact with a server using RMI.
 **/
public static class Client {
    public static void main(String[] args) {
        try {
            // Figure out what RemoteBank to connect to by reading a system
            // property (specified on the command line with a -D option to
            // java) or, if it is not defined, use a default URL.  Note
            // that by default this client tries to connect to a server on
            // the local machine
            String url = System.getProperty("bank", "rmi:///FirstRemote");

            // Now look up that RemoteBank server using the Naming object,
            // which contacts the rmiregistry server.  Given the url, this
            // call returns a RemoteBank object whose methods may be
            // invoked remotely
            RemoteBank bank = (RemoteBank) Naming.lookup(url);

            // Convert the user's command to lower case
            String cmd = args[0].toLowerCase();

            // Now, go test the command against a bunch of possible options
            if (cmd.equals("open")) {              // Open an account
                bank.openAccount(args[1], args[2]);
                System.out.println("Account opened.");
            }
            else if (cmd.equals("close")) {        // Close an account
                FunnyMoney money = bank.closeAccount(args[1], args[2]);
                // Note: our currency is denominated in wooden nickels
                System.out.println(money.amount +
                                   " wooden nickels returned to you.");
                System.out.println("Thanks for banking with us.");
            }
            else if (cmd.equals("deposit")) {   // Deposit money
                FunnyMoney money=new FunnyMoney(Integer.parseInt(args[3]));
                bank.deposit(args[1], args[2], money);
```

Example 21-1. Bank.java (continued)

```
                System.out.println("Deposited " + money.amount +
                                    " wooden nickels.");
            }
            else if (cmd.equals("withdraw")) {  // Withdraw money
                FunnyMoney money = bank.withdraw(args[1], args[2],
                                            Integer.parseInt(args[3]));
                System.out.println("Withdrew " + money.amount +
                                    " wooden nickels.");
            }
            else if (cmd.equals("balance")) {   // Check account balance
                int amt = bank.getBalance(args[1], args[2]);
                System.out.println("You have " + amt +
                                    " wooden nickels in the bank.");
            }
            else if (cmd.equals("history")) {   // Get transaction history
                List transactions =
                    bank.getTransactionHistory(args[1], args[2]);
                for(int i = 0; i < transactions.size(); i++)
                    System.out.println(transactions.get(i));
            }
            else System.out.println("Unknown command");
        }
        // Catch and display RMI exceptions
        catch (RemoteException e) { System.err.println(e); }
        // Catch and display Banking related exceptions
        catch (BankingException e) { System.err.println(e.getMessage()); }
        // Other exceptions are probably user syntax errors, so show usage.
        catch (Exception e) {
            System.err.println(e);
            System.err.println("Usage: java [-Dbank=<url>] Bank$Client " +
                                "<cmd> <name> <password> [<amount>]");
            System.err.println("where cmd is: open, close, deposit, " +
                                "withdraw, balance, history");
        }
    }
  }
 }
}
```

A Bank Server

Example 21-1 defined a RemoteBank interface and a bank client program. Example 21-2 is a RemoteBankServer class that implements the RemoteBank interface and acts as a server for the Bank.Client program. This class includes a main() method so it can be run as a standalone program. This method creates a RemoteBankServer object and registers it with Naming.rebind(), so that clients can look it up. It reads the system property bankname to determine what name to use to register the bank, but uses the name FirstRemote by default. (This is the same name that the Bank.Client uses by default as well.)

RemoteBankServer implements the RemoteBank interface, so it provides implementations for all remote methods defined by that interface. It also defines some utility methods that are not remote methods, but that are used by the remote methods. Note that RemoteBankServer includes an inner Account class that stores all the information about a single bank account. It maintains a hashtable that maps from account names to Account objects. The various remote methods look up the named account, verify the password, and operate on the account in some way. Any RMI remote object must be able to handle multiple, concurrent method invocations because multiple clients can be using the object at the same time. RemoteBankServer uses synchronized methods and synchronized statements to prevent two clients from opening, closing, or modifying the same account at the same time.

Before you can run this RemoteBankServer program, you must compile it, generate stub and skeleton classes, and start the *rmiregistry* service (if it is not already running). You might do all this with commands like the following (on a Unix system). Note the -d argument to *rmic*: it tells the RMI compiler where to put the stub and skeleton classes. Assuming the *RemoteBankServer.class* file is in the current directory, the usage shown here puts the generated classes in the same directory.

```
% javac RemoteBankServer.java
% rmic -d ../../../../ je3.rmi.RemoteBankServer
% rmiregistry &
% java je3.rmi.RemoteBankServer
FirstRemote is open and ready for customers.
```

Note that Example 21-2 contains a fatal flaw: if the bank server crashes, all bank account data is lost, which is likely to result in angry customers! Example 21-3 is another implementation of the RemoteBank interface; this implementation uses a database to store account data in a more persistent way.

Example 21-2. RemoteBankServer.java

```java
package je3.rmi;
import java.rmi.*;
import java.rmi.server.*;
import java.util.*;
import je3.rmi.Bank.*;

/**
 * This class implements the remote methods defined by the RemoteBank
 * interface.  It has a serious shortcoming, though: all account data is
 * lost when the server goes down.
 **/
public class RemoteBankServer extends UnicastRemoteObject implements RemoteBank
{
    /**
     * This nested class stores data for a single account with the bank
     **/
    class Account {
        String password;                      // account password
        int balance;                          // account balance
        List transactions = new ArrayList();  // account transaction history
        Account(String password) {
```

Example 21-2. RemoteBankServer.java (continued)

```java
            this.password = password;
            transactions.add("Account opened at " + new Date());
        }
    }

    /**
     * This hashtable stores all open accounts and maps from account name
     * to Account object.  Methods that use this object will be synchronized
     * to prevent concurrent access by more than one thread.
     **/
    Map accounts = new HashMap();

    /**
     * This constructor doesn't do anything, but because the superclass
     * constructor throws an exception, the exception must be declared here
     **/
    public RemoteBankServer() throws RemoteException { super(); }

    /**
     * Open a bank account with the specified name and password
     * This method is synchronized to make it thread safe, since it
     * manipulates the accounts hashtable.
     **/
    public synchronized void openAccount(String name, String password)
        throws RemoteException, BankingException
    {
        // Check if there is already an account under that name
        if (accounts.get(name) != null)
            throw new BankingException("Account already exists.");
        // Otherwise, it doesn't exist, so create it.
        Account acct = new Account(password);
        // And register it
        accounts.put(name, acct);
    }

    /**
     * This internal method is not a remote method.  Given a name and password
     * it checks to see if an account with that name and password exists.  If
     * so, it returns the Account object.  Otherwise, it throws an exception.
     * This method is synchronized because it uses the accounts hashtable.
     **/
    synchronized Account verify(String name, String password)
        throws BankingException
    {
        Account acct = (Account)accounts.get(name);
        if (acct == null) throw new BankingException("No such account");
        if (!password.equals(acct.password))
            throw new BankingException("Invalid password");
        return acct;
    }
```

Example 21-2. RemoteBankServer.java (continued)

```java
/**
 * Close the named account.  This method is synchronized to make it
 * thread safe, since it manipulates the accounts hashtable.
 **/
public synchronized FunnyMoney closeAccount(String name, String password)
    throws RemoteException, BankingException
{
    Account acct;
    acct = verify(name, password);
    accounts.remove(name);
    // Before changing the balance or transactions of any account, we first
    // have to obtain a lock on that account to be thread safe.
    synchronized (acct) {
        int balance = acct.balance;
        acct.balance = 0;
        return new FunnyMoney(balance);
    }
}

/** Deposit the specified FunnyMoney to the named account */
public void deposit(String name, String password, FunnyMoney money)
    throws RemoteException, BankingException
{
    Account acct = verify(name, password);
    synchronized(acct) {
        acct.balance += money.amount;
        acct.transactions.add("Deposited " + money.amount +
                              " on " + new Date( ));
    }
}

/** Withdraw the specified amount from the named account */
public FunnyMoney withdraw(String name, String password, int amount)
    throws RemoteException, BankingException
{
    Account acct = verify(name, password);
    synchronized(acct) {
        if (acct.balance < amount)
            throw new BankingException("Insufficient Funds");
        acct.balance -= amount;
        acct.transactions.add("Withdrew " + amount + " on "+new Date( ));
        return new FunnyMoney(amount);
    }
}

/** Return the current balance in the named account */
public int getBalance(String name, String password)
    throws RemoteException, BankingException
{
    Account acct = verify(name, password);
    synchronized(acct) { return acct.balance; }
}
```

Example 21-2. RemoteBankServer.java (continued)

```
/**
 * Return a Vector of strings containing the transaction history
 * for the named account
 **/
public List getTransactionHistory(String name, String password)
    throws RemoteException, BankingException
{
    Account acct = verify(name, password);
    synchronized(acct) { return acct.transactions; }
}

/**
 * The main program that runs this RemoteBankServer.
 * Create a RemoteBankServer object and give it a name in the registry.
 * Read a system property to determine the name, but use "FirstRemote"
 * as the default name.  This is all that is necessary to set up the
 * service.  RMI takes care of the rest.
 **/
public static void main(String[] args) {
    try {
        // Create a bank server object
        RemoteBankServer bank = new RemoteBankServer();
        // Figure out what to name it
        String name = System.getProperty("bankname", "FirstRemote");
        // Name it that
        Naming.rebind(name, bank);
        // Tell the world we're up and running
        System.out.println(name + " is open and ready for customers.");
    }
    catch (Exception e) {
        System.err.println(e);
        System.err.println("Usage: java [-Dbankname=<name>] " +
                            "je3.rmi.RemoteBankServer");
        System.exit(1); // Force exit because there may be RMI threads
    }
}
}
```

A Persistent Bank Server

The RemoteBankServer class of Example 21-2 does not have a persistent store for customer account data. We solve that problem here with the PersistentBankServer class of Example 21-3. In addition to reiterating RMI programming techniques, this class also demonstrates the use of SQL atomic transactions to ensure database consistency.

After the PersistentBankServer creates its Connection object, it calls setAutoCommit() with the argument false to turn off autocommit mode. Then, for example, the openAccount() method groups three transactions into a single, atomic transaction: adding the account to the database, creating a table for the account history, and adding an initial entry into the history. If all three transactions are successful (i.e.,

---

they don't throw any exceptions), openAccount( ) calls commit( ) to commit the transactions to the database. However, if any one of the transactions throws an exception, the catch clause takes care of calling rollback( ) to roll back any transactions that succeeded. All remote methods in PersistentBankServer use this technique to keep the account database consistent.

In addition to demonstrating the techniques of atomic transaction processing, the PersistentBankServer class provides further examples of using SQL queries to interact with a database. In order to run this example, you need to create a properties file named *BankDB.props* with database connection information, like those used in Chapter 18. Before you run the server for the first time, you also need to create an accounts table in the database. You can do this using the ExecuteSQL program of Example 18-1 or by using any other database administration tool to execute this SQL statement:

```
CREATE TABLE accounts (name VARCHAR(20), password VARCHAR(20), balance INT);
```

Since this is an RMI server as well as a database client, you must run the *rmic* compiler to generate stub and skeleton classes and start the *rmiregistry* service, just as you did for RemoteBankServer.

Example 21-3. PersistentBankServer.java

```java
package je3.rmi;
import java.rmi.*;
import java.rmi.server.*;
import java.rmi.registry.*;
import java.sql.*;
import java.io.*;
import java.util.*;
import java.util.Date; // import explicitly to disambiguate from java.sql.Date
import je3.rmi.Bank.*;  // Import inner classes of Bank

/**
 * This class is another implementation of the RemoteBank interface.
 * It uses a database connection as its back end, so that client data isn't
 * lost if the server goes down.  Note that it takes the database connection
 * out of "auto commit" mode and explicitly calls commit( ) and rollback( ) to
 * ensure that updates happen atomically.
 **/
public class PersistentBankServer extends UnicastRemoteObject
    implements RemoteBank
{
    Connection db;   // The connection to the database that stores account info

    /** The constructor.  Just save the database connection object away */
    public PersistentBankServer(Connection db) throws RemoteException {
        this.db = db;
    }

    /** Open an account */
    public synchronized void openAccount(String name, String password)
        throws RemoteException, BankingException
```

Example 21-3. PersistentBankServer.java (continued)

```
{
    // First, check if there is already an account with that name
    Statement s = null;
    try {
        s = db.createStatement();
        s.executeQuery("SELECT * FROM accounts WHERE name='" + name + "'");
        ResultSet r = s.getResultSet();
        if (r.next()) throw new BankingException("Account name in use.");

        // If it doesn't exist, go ahead and create it Also, create a
        // table for the transaction history of this account and insert an
        // initial transaction into it.
        s = db.createStatement();
        s.executeUpdate("INSERT INTO accounts VALUES ('" + name + "', '" +
                        password + "', 0)");
        s.executeUpdate("CREATE TABLE " + name +
                        "_history (msg VARCHAR(80))");
        s.executeUpdate("INSERT INTO " + name + "_history " +
                        "VALUES ('Account opened at " + new Date() + "')");

        // And if we've been successful so far, commit these updates,
        // ending the atomic transaction.  All the methods below also use
        // this atomic transaction commit/rollback scheme
        db.commit();
    }
    catch(SQLException e) {
        // If an exception was thrown, "rollback" the prior updates,
        // removing them from the database.  This also ends the atomic
        // transaction.
        try { db.rollback(); } catch (Exception e2) { }
        // Pass the SQLException on in the body of a BankingException
        throw new BankingException("SQLException: " + e.getMessage() +
                                    ": " + e.getSQLState());
    }
    // No matter what happens, don't forget to close the DB Statement
    finally { try { s.close(); } catch (Exception e) { } }
}

/**
 * This convenience method checks whether the name and password match
 * an existing account.  If so, it returns the balance in that account.
 * If not, it throws an exception.  Note that this method does not call
 * commit() or rollback(), so its query is part of a larger transaction.
 **/
public int verify(String name, String password)
    throws BankingException, SQLException
{
    Statement s = null;
    try {
        s = db.createStatement();
        s.executeQuery("SELECT balance FROM accounts " +
                        "WHERE name='" + name + "' " +
                        " AND password = '" + password + "'");
```

Example 21-3. PersistentBankServer.java (continued)

```
        ResultSet r = s.getResultSet( );
        if (!r.next( ))
            throw new BankingException("Bad account name or password");
        return r.getInt(1);
    }
    finally { try { s.close( ); } catch (Exception e) { } }
}

/** Close a named account */
public synchronized FunnyMoney closeAccount(String name, String password)
    throws RemoteException, BankingException
{
    int balance = 0;
    Statement s = null;
    try {
        balance = verify(name, password);
        s = db.createStatement( );
        // Delete the account from the accounts table
        s.executeUpdate("DELETE FROM accounts " +
                    "WHERE name = '" + name + "' " +
                    "  AND password = '" + password + "'");
        // And drop the transaction history table for this account
        s.executeUpdate("DROP TABLE " + name + "_history");
        db.commit( );
    }
    catch (SQLException e) {
        try { db.rollback( ); } catch (Exception e2) { }
        throw new BankingException("SQLException: " + e.getMessage( ) +
                            ": " + e.getSQLState( ));
    }
    finally { try { s.close( ); } catch (Exception e) { } }

    // Finally, return whatever balance remained in the account
    return new FunnyMoney(balance);
}

/** Deposit the specified money into the named account */
public synchronized void deposit(String name, String password,
                            FunnyMoney money)
    throws RemoteException, BankingException
{
    int balance = 0;
    Statement s = null;
    try {
        balance = verify(name, password);
        s = db.createStatement( );
        // Update the balance
        s.executeUpdate("UPDATE accounts " +
                    "SET balance = " + balance + money.amount + " " +
                    "WHERE name='" + name + "' " +
                    "  AND password = '" + password + "'");
```

Example 21-3. PersistentBankServer.java (continued)

```
        // Add a row to the transaction history
        s.executeUpdate("INSERT INTO " + name + "_history " +
                        "VALUES ('Deposited " + money.amount +
                        " at " + new Date() + "')");
        db.commit();
    }
    catch (SQLException e) {
        try { db.rollback(); } catch (Exception e2) { }
        throw new BankingException("SQLException: " + e.getMessage() +
                                   ": " + e.getSQLState());
    }
    finally { try { s.close(); } catch (Exception e) { } }
}

/** Withdraw the specified amount from the named account */
public synchronized FunnyMoney withdraw(String name, String password,
                                        int amount)
    throws RemoteException, BankingException
{
    int balance = 0;
    Statement s = null;
    try {
        balance = verify(name, password);
        if (balance < amount)
            throw new BankingException("Insufficient Funds");
        s = db.createStatement();
        // Update the account balance
        s.executeUpdate("UPDATE accounts " +
                        "SET balance = " + (balance - amount) + " " +
                        "WHERE name='" + name + "' " +
                        "  AND password = '" + password + "'");
        // Add a row to the transaction history
        s.executeUpdate("INSERT INTO " + name + "_history " +
                        "VALUES ('Withdrew " + amount +
                        " at " + new Date() + "')");
        db.commit();
    }
    catch (SQLException e) {
        try { db.rollback(); } catch (Exception e2) { }
        throw new BankingException("SQLException: " + e.getMessage() +
                                   ": " + e.getSQLState());
    }
    finally { try { s.close(); } catch (Exception e) { } }

    return new FunnyMoney(amount);
}

/** Return the balance of the specified account */
public synchronized int getBalance(String name, String password)
    throws RemoteException, BankingException
{
    int balance;
```

Example 21-3. PersistentBankServer.java (continued)

```
        try {
            // Get the balance
            balance = verify(name, password);
            // Commit the transaction
            db.commit();
        }
        catch (SQLException e) {
            try { db.rollback(); } catch (Exception e2) { }
            throw new BankingException("SQLException: " + e.getMessage() +
                                       ": " + e.getSQLState());
        }
        // Return the balance
        return balance;
    }

    /** Get the transaction history of the named account */
    public synchronized List getTransactionHistory(String name,
                                                   String password)
        throws RemoteException, BankingException
    {
        Statement s = null;
        List list = new ArrayList();
        try {
            // Call verify to check the password, even though we don't
            // care what the current balance is.
            verify(name, password);
            s = db.createStatement();
            // Request everything out of the history table
            s.executeQuery("SELECT * from " + name + "_history");
            // Get the results of the query and put them in a Vector
            ResultSet r = s.getResultSet();
            while(r.next()) list.add(r.getString(1));
            // Commit the transaction
            db.commit();
        }
        catch (SQLException e) {
            try { db.rollback(); } catch (Exception e2) { }
            throw new BankingException("SQLException: " + e.getMessage() +
                                       ": " + e.getSQLState());
        }
        finally { try { s.close(); } catch (Exception e) { } }
        // Return the Vector of transaction history.
        return list;
    }

    /**
     * This main() method is the standalone program that figures out what
     * database to connect to with what driver, connects to the database,
     * creates a PersistentBankServer object, and registers it with the registry,
     * making it available for client use
     **/
    public static void main(String[] args) {
```

Example 21-3. PersistentBankServer.java (continued)

```
    try {
        // Create a new Properties object.  Attempt to initialize it from
        // the BankDB.props file or the file optionally specified on the
        // command line, ignoring errors.
        Properties p = new Properties();
        try { p.load(new FileInputStream(args[0])); }
        catch (Exception e) {
            try { p.load(new FileInputStream("BankDB.props")); }
            catch (Exception e2) { }
        }

        // The BankDB.props file (or file specified on the command line)
        // must contain properties "driver" and "database", and may
        // optionally contain properties "user" and "password".
        String driver = p.getProperty("driver");
        String database = p.getProperty("database");
        String user = p.getProperty("user", "");
        String password = p.getProperty("password", "");

        // Load the database driver class
        Class.forName(driver);

        // Connect to the database that stores our accounts
        Connection db = DriverManager.getConnection(database,
                                              user, password);

        // Configure the database to allow multiple queries and updates
        // to be grouped into atomic transactions
        db.setAutoCommit(false);
        db.setTransactionIsolation(Connection.TRANSACTION_READ_COMMITTED);

        // Create a server object that uses our database connection
        PersistentBankServer bank = new PersistentBankServer(db);

        // Read a system property to figure out how to name this server.
        // Use "SecondRemote" as the default.
        String name = System.getProperty("bankname", "SecondRemote");

        // Register the server with the name
        Naming.rebind(name, bank);

        // And tell everyone that we're up and running.
        System.out.println(name + " is open and ready for customers.");
    }
    catch (Exception e) {
        System.err.println(e);
        if (e instanceof SQLException)
            System.err.println("SQL State: " +
                               ((SQLException)e).getSQLState());
        System.err.println("Usage: java [-Dbankname=<name>] " +
                  "je3.rmi.PersistentBankServer " +
                          "[<dbpropsfile>]");
```

Example 21-3. PersistentBankServer.java (continued)

```
            System.exit(1);
        }
    }
}
```

A Multiuser Domain

A multiuser domain, or MUD, is a program (a server) that allows multiple people (clients) to interact with each other and with a shared virtual environment. The environment is typically a series of rooms or places linked to each other by various exits. Each room or place has a textual description that serves as the backdrop and sets the tone for the interactions between users. Many early MUDs were set in dungeons, with place descriptions reflecting the dark, underground nature of that imaginary environment. In fact, the MUD acronym originally stood for "multiuser dungeon." Some MUDs serve primarily as chat rooms for their clients, while others have more of the flavor of old-style adventure games, where the focus is on exploring the environment and problem solving. Others are exercises in creativity and group dynamics, allowing users to add new places and items to the MUD.

Examples 21-4 through 21-8 show classes and interfaces that define a simple user-extensible MUD system. A program like this MUD example clearly demonstrates how the RMI programming paradigm transcends the client/server model. As we'll see, MudServer and MudPlace are server objects that create the MUD environment within which users interact. But at the same time, each user within the MUD is represented by a MudPerson remote object that acts as a server when interacting with other users. Rather than having a single server and a set of clients, then, this system is really a distributed network of remote objects, all communicating with each other. Which objects are servers and which are clients really depends on your point of view.

In order to understand the MUD system, an overview of its architecture is useful. The MudServer class is a simple remote object (and standalone server program) that defines the entrance to a MUD and keeps track of the names of all the places within a MUD. Despite its name, the MudServer object doesn't provide the services most users think of as "the MUD." That is the job of the MudPlace class.

Each MudPlace object represents a single place within the MUD. Each place has a name and a description, and lists the items in the place, the people (users) currently in the place, the exits from the place, and the other places to which those exits lead. An exit may lead to an adjoining MudPlace on the same server, or it may lead to a MudPlace object in a different MUD on a different server altogether. Thus, the MUD environment that a user interacts with is really a network of MudPlace objects. It is the descriptions of places and items, and the complexity of the linkages between places, that give the MUD the richness that makes it interesting to a user.

The users, or people, in a MUD are represented by MudPerson objects. MudPerson is a remote object that defines two methods. One method returns a description of the person (i.e., what other people see when they look at this person), and the other method delivers a message to the person (or to the user that the MudPerson represents). These methods allow users to look at each other and to talk to each other. When two users run into each other in a given `MudPlace` and begin to talk to each other, the `MudPlace` and the server on which the MUD is running are no longer relevant; the two `MudPerson` objects can communicate directly with each other through the power of RMI.

The examples that follow are long and somewhat complex, but are worth studying carefully. Given the complexity of the MUD system being developed, however, the classes and interfaces are actually surprisingly simple. As you'll see, remote method invocation techniques are very powerful in systems like this one.

Remote MUD Interfaces

Example 21-4 is a `Mud` class that serves as a placeholder for inner classes and interfaces (and one constant) used by the rest of the MUD system. Most importantly, `Mud` defines three `Remote` interfaces: `RemoteMudServer`, `RemoteMudPerson`, and `RemoteMudPlace`. These define the remote methods that are implemented by the `MudServer`, `MudPerson`, and `MudPlace` objects, respectively.

Example 21-4. Mud.java

```
package je3.rmi;
import java.rmi.*;
import java.util.Vector;
import java.io.IOException;

/**
 * This class defines three nested Remote interfaces for use by our MUD game.
 * It also defines a bunch of exception subclasses, and a constant string
 * prefix used to create unique names when registering MUD servers
 **/
public class Mud {
    /**
     * This interface defines the exported methods of the MUD server object
     **/
    public interface RemoteMudServer extends Remote {
        /** Return the name of this MUD */
        public String getMudName() throws RemoteException;

        /** Return the main entrance place for this MUD */
        public RemoteMudPlace getEntrance() throws RemoteException;

        /** Look up and return some other named place in this MUD */
        public RemoteMudPlace getNamedPlace(String name)
            throws RemoteException, NoSuchPlace;

        /**
         * Dump the state of the server to a file so that it can be restored
         * later. All places, and their exits and things, are dumped, but the
         * "people" in them are not.
         **/
        public void dump(String password, String filename)
            throws RemoteException, BadPassword, IOException;
    }
```

Example 21-4. Mud.java (continued)

```
/**
 * This interface defines the methods exported by a "person" object that
 * is in the MUD.
 **/
public interface RemoteMudPerson extends Remote {
    /** Return a full description of the person */
    public String getDescription( ) throws RemoteException;

    /** Deliver a message to the person */
    public void tell(String message) throws RemoteException;
}


/**
 * This is the most important remote interface for the MUD.  It defines the
 * methods exported by the "places" or "rooms" within a MUD.  Each place
 * has a name and a description, and also maintains a list of "people" in
 * the place, things in the place, and exits from the place.  There are
 * methods to get a list of names for these people, things, and exits.
 * There are methods to get the RemoteMudPerson object for a named person,
 * to get a description of a named thing, and to go through a named exit.
 * There are methods for interacting with other people in the MUD.  There
 * are methods for building the MUD by creating and destroying things,
 * adding new places (and new exits to those places), for linking a place
 * through a new exit to some other place (possibly on another MUD server),
 * and for closing down an existing exit.
 **/
public interface RemoteMudPlace extends Remote {
    /** Look up the name of this place */
    public String getPlaceName( ) throws RemoteException;

    /** Get a description of this place */
    public String getDescription( ) throws RemoteException;

    /** Find out the names of all people here */
    public Vector getNames( ) throws RemoteException;

    /** Get the names of all things here */
    public Vector getThings( ) throws RemoteException;

    /** Get the names of all ways out of here */
    public Vector getExits( ) throws RemoteException;

    /** Get the RemoteMudPerson object for the named person. */
    public RemoteMudPerson getPerson(String name)
        throws RemoteException, NoSuchPerson;

    /** Get more details about a named thing */
    public String examineThing(String name)
        throws RemoteException,NoSuchThing;

    /** Use the named exit */
    public RemoteMudPlace go(RemoteMudPerson who, String direction)
        throws RemoteException,NotThere,AlreadyThere,NoSuchExit,LinkFailed;
```

RMI

Example 21-4. Mud.java (continued)

```java
/** Send a message of the form "David: hi everyone" */
public void speak(RemoteMudPerson speaker, String msg)
    throws RemoteException, NotThere;

/** Send a message of the form "David laughs loudly" */
public void act(RemoteMudPerson speaker, String msg)
    throws RemoteException, NotThere;

/** Add a new thing in this place */
public void createThing(RemoteMudPerson who, String name,
                        String description)
    throws RemoteException, NotThere, AlreadyThere;

/** Remove a thing from this place */
public void destroyThing(RemoteMudPerson who, String thing)
    throws RemoteException, NotThere, NoSuchThing;

/**
 * Create a new place, bi-directionally linked to this one by an exit
 **/
public void createPlace(RemoteMudPerson creator,
                        String exit, String entrance,
                        String name, String description)
    throws RemoteException,NotThere,
           ExitAlreadyExists,PlaceAlreadyExists;

/**
 * Link this place (unidirectionally) to some existing place.  The
 * destination place may even be on another server.
 **/
public void linkTo(RemoteMudPerson who, String exit,
                   String hostname, String mudname, String placename)
    throws RemoteException, NotThere, ExitAlreadyExists, NoSuchPlace;

/** Remove an existing exit */
public void close(RemoteMudPerson who, String exit)
    throws RemoteException, NotThere, NoSuchExit;

/**
 * Remove this person from this place, leaving them nowhere.
 * Send the specified message to everyone left in the place.
 **/
public void exit(RemoteMudPerson who, String message)
    throws RemoteException, NotThere;

/**
 * Put a person in a place, assigning their name, and sending the
 * specified message to everyone else in the place.  The client should
 * not make this method available to the user.  They should use go()
 * instead.
 **/
public void enter(RemoteMudPerson who, String name, String message)
    throws RemoteException, AlreadyThere;
```

Example 21-4. Mud.java (continued)

```
    /**
     * Return the server object of the MUD that "contains" this place
     * This method should not be directly visible to the player
     **/
    public RemoteMudServer getServer( ) throws RemoteException;
}

/**
 * This is a generic exception class that serves as the superclass
 * for a bunch of more specific exception types
 **/
public static class MudException extends Exception { }

/**
 * These specific exception classes are thrown in various contexts.
 * The exception class name contains all the information about the
 * exception; no detail messages are provided by these classes.
 **/
public static class NotThere extends MudException { }
public static class AlreadyThere extends MudException { }
public static class NoSuchThing extends MudException { }
public static class NoSuchPerson extends MudException { }
public static class NoSuchExit extends MudException { }
public static class NoSuchPlace extends MudException { }
public static class ExitAlreadyExists extends MudException { }
public static class PlaceAlreadyExists extends MudException { }
public static class LinkFailed extends MudException { }
public static class BadPassword extends MudException { }

/**
 * This constant is used as a prefix to the MUD name when the server
 * registers the mud with the RMI Registry, and when the client looks
 * up the MUD in the registry.  Using this prefix helps prevent the
 * possibility of name collisions.
 **/
static final String mudPrefix = "je3.rmi.Mud.";
}
```

The MUD Server

Example 21-5 shows the `MudServer` class. This class is a standalone program that starts a MUD running; it also provides the implementation of the `RemoteMudServer` interface. As noted before, a `MudServer` object merely serves as the entrance to a MUD: it is not the MUD itself. Therefore, this is a fairly simple class. One of its most interesting features is the use of the serialization classes of java.io and the compression classes of java.util.zip to save the state the MUD, so that it can be restored later.

Example 21-5. MudServer.java

```
package je3.rmi;
import java.rmi.*;
```

Example 21-5. MudServer.java (continued)

```java
import java.rmi.server.*;
import java.rmi.registry.*;
import java.io.*;
import java.util.Hashtable;
import java.util.zip.*;
import je3.rmi.Mud.*;

/**
 * This class implements the RemoteMudServer interface.  It also defines a
 * main() method so you can run it as a standalone program that will
 * set up and initialize a MUD server.  Note that a MudServer maintains an
 * entrance point to a MUD, but it is not the MUD itself.  Most of the
 * interesting MUD functionality is defined by the RemoteMudPlace interface
 * and implemented by the RemotePlace class.  In addition to being a remote
 * object, this class is also Serializable, so that the state of the MUD
 * can be saved to a file and later restored.  Note that the main() method
 * defines two ways of starting a MUD: one is to start it from scratch with
 * a single initial place, and another is to restore an existing MUD from a
 * file.
 **/
public class MudServer extends UnicastRemoteObject
    implements RemoteMudServer, Serializable
{
    MudPlace entrance;   // The standard entrance to this MUD
    String password;     // The password required to dump() the state of the MUD
    String mudname;      // The name that this MUD is registered under
    Hashtable places;    // A mapping of place names to places in this MUD

    /**
     * Start a MUD from scratch, with the given name and password.  Create
     * an initial MudPlace object as the entrance, giving it the specified
     * name and description.
     **/
    public MudServer(String mudname, String password,
                     String placename, String description)
        throws RemoteException
    {
        this.mudname = mudname;
        this.password = password;
        this.places = new Hashtable();
        // Create the entrance place
        try { this.entrance = new MudPlace(this, placename, description); }
        catch (PlaceAlreadyExists e) {} // Should never happen
    }

    /** For serialization only.  Never call this constructor. */
    public MudServer() throws RemoteException {}

    /** This remote method returns the name of the MUD */
    public String getMudName() throws RemoteException { return mudname; }
```

Example 21-5. MudServer.java (continued)

```java
    /** This remote method returns the entrance place of the MUD */
    public RemoteMudPlace getEntrance() throws RemoteException {
        return entrance;
    }

    /**
     * This remote method returns a RemoteMudPlace object for the named place.
     * In this sense, a MudServer acts like an RMI Registry object,
     * returning remote objects looked up by name.  It is simpler to do it this
     * way than to use an actual Registry object.  If the named place does not
     * exist, it throws a NoSuchPlace exception
     **/
    public RemoteMudPlace getNamedPlace(String name)
            throws RemoteException, NoSuchPlace
    {
        RemoteMudPlace p = (RemoteMudPlace) places.get(name);
        if (p == null) throw new NoSuchPlace();
        return p;
    }

    /**
     * Define a new placename to place mapping in our hashtable.
     * This is not a remote method.  The MudPlace() constructor calls it
     * to register the new place it is creating.
     **/
    public void setPlaceName(RemoteMudPlace place, String name)
        throws PlaceAlreadyExists
    {
        if (places.containsKey(name)) throw new PlaceAlreadyExists();
        places.put(name, place);
    }

    /**
     * This remote method serializes and compresses the state of the MUD
     * to a named file, if the specified password matches the one specified
     * when the MUD was initially created.  Note that the state of a MUD
     * consists of all places in the MUD, with all things and exits in those
     * places.  The people in the MUD are not part of the state that is saved.
     **/
    public void dump(String password, String f)
        throws RemoteException, BadPassword, IOException
    {
        if ((this.password != null)&& !this.password.equals(password))
            throw new BadPassword();
        ObjectOutputStream out = new ObjectOutputStream(
                            new GZIPOutputStream(new FileOutputStream(f)));
        out.writeObject(this);
        out.close();
    }
```

Example 21-5. MudServer.java (continued)

```
/**
 * This main( ) method defines the standalone program that starts up a MUD
 * server.  If invoked with a single argument, it treats that argument as
 * the name of a file containing the serialized and compressed state of an
 * existing MUD, and recreates it.  Otherwise, it expects four command-line
 * arguments: the name of the MUD, the password, the name of the entrance
 * place for the MUD, and a description of that entrance place.
 * Besides creating the MudServer object, this program sets an appropriate
 * security manager, and uses the default rmiregistry to register the
 * the MudServer under its given name.
 **/
public static void main(String[ ] args) {
    try {
        MudServer server;
        if (args.length == 1) {
            // Read the MUD state in from a file
            FileInputStream f = new FileInputStream(args[0]);
            ObjectInputStream in =
                new ObjectInputStream(new GZIPInputStream(f));
            server = (MudServer) in.readObject( );
        }
        // Otherwise, create an initial MUD from scratch
        else server = new MudServer(args[0], args[1], args[2], args[3]);

        Naming.rebind(Mud.mudPrefix + server.mudname, server);
    }
    // Display an error message if anything goes wrong.
    catch (Exception e) {
        System.out.println(e);
        System.out.println("Usage: java MudServer <savefile>\n" +
                        "   or: java MudServer <mudname> <password> " +
                        "<placename> <description>");
        System.exit(1);
    }
}

/** This constant is a version number for serialization */
static final long serialVersionUID = 7453281245880199453L;
}
```

The MudPlace Class

Example 21-6 is the MudPlace class that implements the RemoteMudPlace interface
and acts as a server for a single place or room within the MUD. It is this class that
holds the description of a place and maintains the lists of the people and items in
a place and the exits from a place. This is a long class, but many of the remote
methods it defines have simple or even trivial implementations. The go( ),
createPlace( ), and linkTo( ) methods are among the more complex and interesting methods; they manage the network of connections between MudPlace
objects.

Note that the `MudPlace` class is `Serializable`, so that a `MudPlace` (and all places it is connected to) can be serialized along with the `MudServer` that refers to them. However, the names and people fields are declared transient, so they are not serialized along with the place.

Example 21-6. MudPlace.java

```java
package je3.rmi;
import java.rmi.*;
import java.rmi.server.*;
import java.rmi.registry.*;
import java.io.*;
import java.util.*;
import je3.rmi.Mud.*;


/**
 * This class implements the RemoteMudPlace interface and exports a
 * bunch of remote methods that are at the heart of the MUD.  The
 * MudClient interacts primarily with these methods.  See the comment
 * for RemoteMudPlace for an overview.
 * The MudPlace class is Serializable so that places can be saved to disk
 * along with the MudServer that contains them.  Note, however that the
 * names and people fields are marked transient, so they are not serialized
 * along with the place (because it wouldn't make sense to try to save
 * RemoteMudPerson objects, even if they could be serialized).
 **/
public class MudPlace extends UnicastRemoteObject
    implements RemoteMudPlace, Serializable
{
    String placename, description;         // information about the place
    Vector exits = new Vector();           // names of exits from this place
    Vector destinations = new Vector();    // where the exits go to
    Vector things = new Vector();          // names of things in this place
    Vector descriptions = new Vector();    // descriptions of those things
    transient Vector names = new Vector(); // names of people in this place
    transient Vector people = new Vector(); // the RemoteMudPerson objects
    MudServer server;                      // the server for this place

    /** A no-arg constructor for de-serialization only.  Do not call it */
    public MudPlace() throws RemoteException { super(); }

    /**
     * This constructor creates a place, and calls a server method
     * to register the object so that it will be accessible by name
     **/
    public MudPlace(MudServer server, String placename, String description)
        throws RemoteException, PlaceAlreadyExists
    {
        this.server = server;
        this.placename = placename;
        this.description = description;
        server.setPlaceName(this, placename);  // Register the place
    }
```

Example 21-6. MudPlace.java (continued)

```java
/** This remote method returns the name of this place */
public String getPlaceName() throws RemoteException { return placename; }

/** This remote method returns the description of this place */
public String getDescription() throws RemoteException {
    return description;
}

/** This remote method returns a Vector of names of people in this place */
public Vector getNames() throws RemoteException { return names; }

/** This remote method returns a Vector of names of things in this place */
public Vector getThings() throws RemoteException { return things; }

/** This remote method returns a Vector of names of exits from this place*/
public Vector getExits() throws RemoteException { return exits; }

/**
 * This remote method returns a RemoteMudPerson object corresponding to
 * the specified name, or throws an exception if no such person is here
 **/
public RemoteMudPerson getPerson(String name)
    throws RemoteException, NoSuchPerson
{
    synchronized(names) {
        // What about when there are 2 of the same name?
        int i = names.indexOf(name);
        if (i == -1) throw new NoSuchPerson();
        return (RemoteMudPerson) people.elementAt(i);
    }
}

/**
 * This remote method returns a description of the named thing, or
 * throws an exception if no such thing is in this place.
 **/
public String examineThing(String name) throws RemoteException, NoSuchThing
{
    synchronized(things) {
        int i = things.indexOf(name);
        if (i == -1) throw new NoSuchThing();
        return (String) descriptions.elementAt(i);
    }
}

/**
 * This remote method moves the specified RemoteMudPerson from this place
 * in the named direction (i.e. through the named exit) to whatever place
 * is there.  It throws exceptions if the specified person isn't in this
 * place to begin with, or if they are already in the place through the
 * exit or if the exit doesn't exist, or if the exit links to another MUD
 * server and the server is not functioning.
 **/
```

Example 21-6. MudPlace.java (continued)

```java
public RemoteMudPlace go(RemoteMudPerson who, String direction)
    throws RemoteException, NotThere, AlreadyThere, NoSuchExit, LinkFailed
{
    // Make sure the direction is valid, and get destination if it is
    Object destination;
    synchronized(exits) {
        int i = exits.indexOf(direction);
        if (i == -1) throw new NoSuchExit();
        destination = destinations.elementAt(i);
    }

    // If destination is a string, it is a place on another server, so
    // connect to that server.  Otherwise, it is a place already on this
    // server.  Throw an exception if we can't connect to the server.
    RemoteMudPlace newplace;
    if (destination instanceof String) {
        try {
            String t = (String) destination;
            int pos = t.indexOf('@');
            String url = t.substring(0, pos);
            String placename = t.substring(pos+1);
            RemoteMudServer s = (RemoteMudServer) Naming.lookup(url);
            newplace = s.getNamedPlace(placename);
        }
        catch (Exception e) { throw new LinkFailed(); }
    }
    // If the destination is not a string, then it is a Place
    else newplace = (RemoteMudPlace) destination;

    // Make sure the person is here and get their name.
    // Throw an exception if they are not here
    String name = verifyPresence(who);

    // Move the person out of here, and tell everyone who remains about it.
    this.exit(who, name + " has gone " + direction);

    // Put the person into the new place.
    // Send a message to everyone already in that new place
    String fromwhere;
    if (newplace instanceof MudPlace) // going to a local place
        fromwhere = placename;
    else
        fromwhere = server.getMudName() + "." + placename;
    newplace.enter(who, name, name + " has arrived from: " + fromwhere);

    // Return the new RemoteMudPlace object to the client so they
    // know where they are now at.
    return newplace;
}

/**
 * This remote method sends a message to everyone in the room.  Used to
```

Example 21-6. MudPlace.java (continued)

```java
 * say things to everyone.  Requires that the speaker be in this place.
 **/
public void speak(RemoteMudPerson speaker, String msg)
    throws RemoteException, NotThere
{
    String name = verifyPresence(speaker);
    tellEveryone(name + ":" + msg);
}

/**
 * This remote method sends a message to everyone in the room.  Used to
 * do things that people can see. Requires that the actor be in this place.
 **/
public void act(RemoteMudPerson actor, String msg)
    throws RemoteException, NotThere
{
    String name = verifyPresence(actor);
    tellEveryone(name + " " + msg);
}

/**
 * This remote method creates a new thing in this room.
 * It requires that the creator be in this room.
 **/
public void createThing(RemoteMudPerson creator,
                        String name, String description)
    throws RemoteException, NotThere, AlreadyThere
{
    // Make sure the creator is here
    String creatorname = verifyPresence(creator);
    synchronized(things) {
        // Make sure there isn't already something with this name.
        if (things.indexOf(name) != -1) throw new AlreadyThere();
        // Add the thing name and descriptions to the appropriate lists
        things.addElement(name);
        descriptions.addElement(description);
    }
    // Tell everyone about the new thing and its creator
    tellEveryone(creatorname + " has created a " + name);
}

/**
 * Remove a thing from this room.  Throws exceptions if the person
 * who removes it isn't themself in the room, or if there is no
 * such thing here.
 **/
public void destroyThing(RemoteMudPerson destroyer, String thing)
    throws RemoteException, NotThere, NoSuchThing
{
    // Verify that the destroyer is here
    String name = verifyPresence(destroyer);
    synchronized(things) {
```

Example 21-6. MudPlace.java (continued)

```
        // Verify that there is a thing by that name in this room
        int i = things.indexOf(thing);
        if (i == -1) throw new NoSuchThing();
        // And remove its name and description from the lists
        things.removeElementAt(i);
        descriptions.removeElementAt(i);
    }
    // Let everyone know of the demise of this thing.
    tellEveryone(name + " had destroyed the " + thing);
}

/**
 * Create a new place in this MUD, with the specified name and description.
 * The new place is accessible from this place through
 * the specified exit, and this place is accessible from the new place
 * through the specified entrance.  The creator must be in this place
 * in order to create a exit from this place.
 **/
public void createPlace(RemoteMudPerson creator,
                        String exit, String entrance, String name,
                        String description)
    throws RemoteException,NotThere,ExitAlreadyExists,PlaceAlreadyExists
{
    // Verify that the creator is actually here in this place
    String creatorname = verifyPresence(creator);
    synchronized(exits) {  // Only one client may change exits at a time
        // Check that the exit doesn't already exist.
        if (exits.indexOf(exit) != -1) throw new ExitAlreadyExists();
        // Create the new place, registering its name with the server
        MudPlace destination = new MudPlace(server, name, description);
        // Link from there back to here
        destination.exits.addElement(entrance);
        destination.destinations.addElement(this);
        // And link from here to there
        exits.addElement(exit);
        destinations.addElement(destination);
    }
    // Let everyone know about the new exit, and the new place beyond
    tellEveryone(creatorname + " has created a new place: " + exit);
}

/**
 * Create a new exit from this mud, linked to a named place in a named
 * MUD on a named host (this can also be used to link to a named place in
 * the current MUD, of course).  Because of the possibilities of deadlock,
 * this method only links from here to there; it does not create a return
 * exit from there to here.  That must be done with a separate call.
 **/
public void linkTo(RemoteMudPerson linker, String exit,
                   String hostname, String mudname, String placename)
    throws RemoteException, NotThere, ExitAlreadyExists, NoSuchPlace
{
```

Example 21-6. MudPlace.java (continued)

```java
        // Verify that the linker is actually here
        String name = verifyPresence(linker);

        // Check that the link target actually exists.  Throw NoSuchPlace if
        // not.  Note that NoSuchPlace may also mean "NoSuchMud" or
        // "MudNotResponding".
        String url = "rmi://" + hostname + '/' + Mud.mudPrefix + mudname;
        try {
            RemoteMudServer s = (RemoteMudServer) Naming.lookup(url);
            RemoteMudPlace destination = s.getNamedPlace(placename);
        }
        catch (Exception e) { throw new NoSuchPlace(); }

        synchronized(exits) {
            // Check that the exit doesn't already exist.
            if (exits.indexOf(exit) != -1) throw new ExitAlreadyExists();
            // Add the exit, to the list of exit names
            exits.addElement(exit);
            // And add the destination to the list of destinations.  Note that
            // the destination is stored as a string rather than as a
            // RemoteMudPlace.  This is because if the remote server goes down
            // then comes back up again, a RemoteMudPlace is not valid, but the
            // string still is.
            destinations.addElement(url + '@' + placename);
        }
        // Let everyone know about the new exit and where it leads
        tellEveryone(name + " has linked " + exit + " to " +
                     "'" + placename + "' in MUD '" + mudname +
                     "' on host " + hostname);
    }

    /**
     * Close an exit that leads out of this place.
     * It does not close the return exit from there back to here.
     * Note that this method does not destroy the place that the exit leads to.
     * In the current implementation, there is no way to destroy a place.
     **/
    public void close(RemoteMudPerson who, String exit)
        throws RemoteException, NotThere, NoSuchExit
    {
        // check that the person closing the exit is actually here
        String name = verifyPresence(who);
        synchronized(exits) {
            // Check that the exit exists
            int i = exits.indexOf(exit);
            if (i == -1) throw new NoSuchExit();
            // Remove it and its destination from the lists
            exits.removeElementAt(i);
            destinations.removeElementAt(i);
        }
        // Let everyone know that the exit doesn't exist anymore
        tellEveryone(name + " has closed exit " + exit);
    }
```

Example 21-6. MudPlace.java (continued)

```java
    /**
     * Remove a person from this place.  If there is a message, send it to
     * everyone who is left in this place.  If the specified person is not here,
     * this method does nothing and does not throw an exception.  This method
     * is called by go( ), and the client should call it when the user quits.
     * The client should not allow the user to invoke it directly, however.
     **/
    public void exit(RemoteMudPerson who, String message)
        throws RemoteException
    {
        String name;
        synchronized(names) {
            int i = people.indexOf(who);
            if (i == -1) return;
            names.removeElementAt(i);
            people.removeElementAt(i);
        }
        if (message != null) tellEveryone(message);
    }

    /**
     * This method puts a person into this place, assigning them the
     * specified name, and displaying a message to anyone else who is in
     * that place.  This method is called by go( ), and the client should
     * call it to initially place a person into the MUD.  Once the person
     * is in the MUD, however, the client should restrict them to using go( )
     * and should not allow them to call this method directly.
     * If there have been networking problems, a client might call this method
     * to restore a person to this place, in case they've been bumped out.
     * (A person will be bumped out of a place if the server tries to send
     * a message to them and gets a RemoteException.)
     **/
    public void enter(RemoteMudPerson who, String name, String message)
        throws RemoteException, AlreadyThere
    {
        // Send the message to everyone who is already here.
        if (message != null) tellEveryone(message);

        // Add the person to this place.
        synchronized (names) {
            if (people.indexOf(who) != -1) throw new AlreadyThere( );
            names.addElement(name);
            people.addElement(who);
        }
    }

    /**
     * This final remote method returns the server object for the MUD in which
     * this place exists.  The client should not allow the user to invoke this
     * method.
     **/
    public RemoteMudServer getServer( ) throws RemoteException {
```

Example 21-6. MudPlace.java (continued)

```java
        return server;
    }

    /**
     * Create and start a thread that sends out a message to everyone in this
     * place.  If it gets a RemoteException talking to a person, it silently
     * removes that person from this place.  This is not a remote method, but
     * is used internally by a number of remote methods.
     **/
    protected void tellEveryone(final String message) {
        // If there is no one here, don't bother sending the message!
        if (people.size() == 0) return;
        // Make a copy of the people here now.  The message is sent
        // asynchronously and the list of people in the room may change before
        // the message is sent to everyone.
        final Vector recipients = (Vector) people.clone();
        // Create and start a thread to send the message, using an anonymous
        // class.  We do this because sending the message to everyone in this
        // place might take some time, (particularly on a slow or flaky
        // network) and we don't want to wait.
        new Thread() {
                public void run() {
                    // Loop through the recipients
                    for(int i = 0; i < recipients.size(); i++) {
                        RemoteMudPerson person =
                            (RemoteMudPerson)recipients.elementAt(i);
                        // Try to send the message to each one.
                        try { person.tell(message); }
                        // If it fails, assume that that person's client or
                        // network has failed, and silently remove them from
                        // this place.
                        catch (RemoteException e) {
                            try { MudPlace.this.exit(person, null); }
                            catch (Exception ex) { }
                        }
                    }
                }
        }.start();
    }

    /**
     * This convenience method checks whether the specified person is here.
     * If so, it returns their name.  If not it throws a NotThere exception
     **/
    protected String verifyPresence(RemoteMudPerson who) throws NotThere {
        int i = people.indexOf(who);
        if (i == -1) throw new NotThere();
        else return (String) names.elementAt(i);
    }

    /**
     * This method is used for custom de-serialization.  Since the vectors of
     * people and of their names are transient, they are not serialized with
```

Example 21-6. MudPlace.java (continued)

```
 * the rest of this place.  Therefore, when the place is de-serialized,
 * those vectors have to be recreated (empty).
 **/
private void readObject(ObjectInputStream in)
    throws IOException, ClassNotFoundException {
    in.defaultReadObject( );  // Read most of the object as normal
    names = new Vector( );    // Then recreate the names vector
    people = new Vector( );   // and recreate the people vector
}

/** This constant is a version number for serialization */
static final long serialVersionUID = 5090967989223703026L;
}
```

The MudPerson Class

Example 21-7 shows the MudPerson class. This is the simplest of the remote objects in the MUD system. It implements the two remote methods defined by the RemoteMudPerson interface and also defines a few nonremote methods used by the MudClient class of Example 21-8. The remote methods are quite simple: one simply returns a description string to the caller, and the other writes a message to a stream where the user can see it.

Example 21-7. MudPerson.java

```
package je3.rmi;
import java.rmi.*;
import java.rmi.server.*;
import java.io.*;
import je3.rmi.Mud.*;

/**
 * This is the simplest of the remote objects that we implement for the MUD.
 * It maintains only a little bit of state, and has only two exported
 * methods
 **/
public class MudPerson extends UnicastRemoteObject implements RemoteMudPerson {
    String name;              // The name of the person
    String description;       // The person's description
    PrintWriter tellStream;   // Where to send messages we receive

    public MudPerson(String n, String d, PrintWriter out)
        throws RemoteException
    {
        name = n;
        description = d;
        tellStream = out;
    }

    /** Return the person's name.  Not a remote method */
    public String getName( ) { return name; }
```

Example 21-7. MudPerson.java (continued)

```
/** Set the person's name.  Not a remote method */
public void setName(String n) { name = n; }

/** Set the person's description.  Not a remote method */
public void setDescription(String d) { description = d; }

/** Set the stream that messages to us should be written to. Not remote. */
public void setTellStream(PrintWriter out) { tellStream = out; }

/** A remote method that returns this person's description */
public String getDescription() throws RemoteException {
    return description;
}

/**
 * A remote method that delivers a message to the person.
 * I.e. it delivers a message to the user controlling the "person"
 **/
public void tell(String message) throws RemoteException {
    tellStream.println(message);
    tellStream.flush();
}
}
```

A MUD Client

Example 21-8 is a client program for the MUD system developed in the previous examples. It uses the `Naming.lookup()` method to look up the `RemoteMudServer` object that represents a named MUD on a specified host. The program then calls the `getEntrance()` or `getNamedPlace()` method of this `RemoteMudServer` object to obtain an initial `MudPlace` object into which to insert the user. Next, the program asks the user for a name and description of the `MudPerson` that will represent him in the MUD, creates a `MudPerson` object with that name and description, and then places it in the initial `RemoteMudPlace`. Finally, the program enters a loop that prompts the user to enter a command and then processes the command. Most of the commands that this client supports simply invoke one of the remote methods of the `RemoteMudPlace` that represents the user's current location in the MUD. The end of the command loop consists of a number of catch clauses that handle the large number of things that can go wrong.

In order to use the `MudClient` class, you must first have a `MudServer` up and running. You should be able to accomplish that with commands like the following:

```
% cd je3/rmi
% javac Mud*.java
% rmic -d ../../../../ je3.rmi.MudServer
% rmic -d ../../../../ je3.rmi.MudPlace
% rmic -d ../../../../ je3.rmi.MudPerson
% rmiregistry &
% java je3.rmi.MudServer MyMud muddy Lobby \
    'A large marble lobby with ficus trees'
```

Having started the server with these commands, you can then run the client with a command like this:

```
% java je3.rmi.MudClient localhost MyMud
```

Example 21-8. MudClient.java

```java
package je3.rmi;
import java.rmi.*;
import java.rmi.server.*;
import java.rmi.registry.*;
import java.io.*;
import java.util.*;
import je3.rmi.Mud.*;

/**
 * This class is a client program for the MUD.  The main( ) method sets up
 * a connection to a RemoteMudServer, gets the initial RemoteMudPlace object,
 * and creates a MudPerson object to represent the user in the MUD.  Then it
 * calls runMud( ) to put the person in the place, begins processing
 * user commands.  The getLine( ) and getMultiLine( ) methods are convenience
 * methods used throughout to get input from the user.
 **/
public class MudClient {
    /**
     * The main program.  It expects two or three arguments:
     *   0) the name of the host on which the mud server is running
     *   1) the name of the MUD on that host
     *   2) the name of a place within that MUD to start at (optional).
     *
     * It uses the Naming.lookup( ) method to obtain a RemoteMudServer object
     * for the named MUD on the specified host.  Then it uses the getEntrance( )
     * or getNamedPlace( ) method of RemoteMudServer to obtain the starting
     * RemoteMudPlace object.  It prompts the user for their name and
     * description, and creates a MudPerson object.  Finally, it passes
     * the person and the place to runMud( ) to begin interaction with the MUD.
     **/
    public static void main(String[ ] args) {
        try {
            String hostname = args[0]; // Each MUD is uniquely identified by a
            String mudname = args[1];  //    host and a MUD name.
            String placename = null;   // Each place in a MUD has a unique name
            if (args.length > 2) placename = args[2];

            // Look up the RemoteMudServer object for the named MUD using
            // the default registry on the specified host.  Note the use of
            // the Mud.mudPrefix constant to help prevent naming conflicts
            // in the registry.
            RemoteMudServer server =
                (RemoteMudServer)Naming.lookup("rmi://" + hostname + "/" +
                                               Mud.mudPrefix + mudname);

            // If the user did not specify a place in the mud, use
            // getEntrance( ) to get the initial place.  Otherwise, call
            // getNamedPlace( ) to find the initial place.
```

Example 21-8. MudClient.java (continued)

```
                RemoteMudPlace location = null;
                if (placename == null) location = server.getEntrance( );
                else location = (RemoteMudPlace) server.getNamedPlace(placename);

                // Greet the user and ask for their name and description.
                // This relies on getLine( ) and getMultiLine( ) defined below.
                System.out.println("Welcome to " + mudname);
                String name = getLine("Enter your name: ");
                String description = getMultiLine("Please describe what " +
                                        "people see when they look at you:");

                // Define an output stream that the MudPerson object will use to
                // display messages sent to it to the user.  We'll use the console.
                PrintWriter myout = new PrintWriter(System.out);

                // Create a MudPerson object to represent the user in the MUD.
                // Use the specified name and description, and the output stream.
                MudPerson me = new MudPerson(name, description, myout);

                // Lower this thread's priority one notch so that broadcast
                // messages can appear even when we're blocking for I/O.  This is
                // necessary on the Linux platform, but may not be necessary on all
                // platforms.
                int pri = Thread.currentThread( ).getPriority( );
                Thread.currentThread( ).setPriority(pri-1);

                // Finally, put the MudPerson into the RemoteMudPlace, and start
                // prompting the user for commands.
                runMud(location, me);
        }
        // If anything goes wrong, print a message and exit.
        catch (Exception e) {
                System.out.println(e);
                System.out.println("Usage: java MudClient <host> <mud> [<place>]");
                System.exit(1);
        }
    }

    /**
     * This method is the main loop of the MudClient.  It places the person
     * into the place (using the enter( ) method of RemoteMudPlace).  Then it
     * calls the look( ) method to describe the place to the user, and enters a
     * command loop to prompt the user for a command and process the command
     **/
    public static void runMud(RemoteMudPlace entrance, MudPerson me)
        throws RemoteException
    {
        RemoteMudPlace location = entrance;  // The current place
        String myname = me.getName( );       // The person's name
        String placename = null;             // The name of the current place
        String mudname = null;               // The name of the mud of that place
```

Example 21-8. MudClient.java (continued)

```
    try {
        // Enter the MUD
        location.enter(me, myname, myname + " has entered the MUD.");
        // Figure out where we are (for the prompt)
        mudname = location.getServer().getMudName();
        placename = location.getPlaceName();
        // Describe the place to the user
        look(location);
    }
    catch (Exception e) {
        System.out.println(e);
        System.exit(1);
    }

    // Now that we've entered the MUD, begin a command loop to process
    // the user's commands.  Note that there is a huge block of catch
    // statements at the bottom of the loop to handle all the things that
    // could go wrong each time through the loop.
    for(;;) {  // Loop until the user types "quit"
        try {     // Catch any exceptions that occur in the loop
            // Pause just a bit before printing the prompt, to give output
            // generated indirectly by the last command a chance to appear.
            try { Thread.sleep(200); } catch (InterruptedException e) { }

            // Display a prompt, and get the user's input
            String line = getLine(mudname + '.' + placename + "> ");

            // Break the input into a command and an argument that consists
            // of the rest of the line.  Convert the command to lowercase.
            String cmd, arg;
            int i = line.indexOf(' ');
            if (i == -1) { cmd = line; arg = null; }
            else {
                cmd = line.substring(0, i).toLowerCase();
                arg = line.substring(i+1);
            }
            if (arg == null) arg = "";

            // Now go process the command.  What follows is a huge repeated
            // if/else statement covering each of the commands supported by
            // this client.  Many of these commands simply invoke one of
            // the remote methods of the current RemoteMudPlace object.
            // Some have to do a bit of additional processing.

            // LOOK: Describe the place and its things, people, and exits
            if (cmd.equals("look")) look(location);
            // EXAMINE: Describe a named thing
            else if (cmd.equals("examine"))
                System.out.println(location.examineThing(arg));
            // DESCRIBE: Describe a named person
            else if (cmd.equals("describe")) {
```

Example 21-8. MudClient.java (continued)

```
                    try {
                        RemoteMudPerson p = location.getPerson(arg);
                        System.out.println(p.getDescription());
                    }
                    catch(RemoteException e) {
                        System.out.println(arg + " is having technical " +
                                            "difficulties. No description " +
                                            "is available.");
                    }
                }
                // GO: Go in a named direction
                else if (cmd.equals("go")) {
                    location = location.go(me, arg);
                    mudname = location.getServer().getMudName();
                    placename = location.getPlaceName();
                    look(location);
                }
                // SAY: Say something to everyone
                else if (cmd.equals("say")) location.speak(me, arg);
                // DO: Do something that will be described to everyone
                else if (cmd.equals("do")) location.act(me, arg);
                // TALK: Say something to one named person
                else if (cmd.equals("talk")) {
                    try {
                        RemoteMudPerson p = location.getPerson(arg);
                        String msg = getLine("What do you want to say?: ");
                        p.tell(myname + " says \"" + msg + "\"");
                    }
                    catch (RemoteException e) {
                        System.out.println(arg + " is having technical " +
                                            "difficulties. Can't talk to them.");
                    }
                }
                // CHANGE: Change my own description
                else if (cmd.equals("change"))
                    me.setDescription(
                            getMultiLine("Describe yourself for others: "));
                // CREATE: Create a new thing in this place
                else if (cmd.equals("create")) {
                    if (arg.length() == 0)
                        throw new IllegalArgumentException("name expected");
                    String desc = getMultiLine("Please describe the " +
                                            arg + ": ");
                    location.createThing(me, arg, desc);
                }
                // DESTROY: Destroy a named thing
                else if (cmd.equals("destroy")) location.destroyThing(me, arg);
                // OPEN: Create a new place and connect this place to it
                // through the exit specified in the argument.
                else if (cmd.equals("open")) {
                    if (arg.length() == 0)
                        throw new IllegalArgumentException("direction expected");
                    String name = getLine("What is the name of place there?: ");
```

Example 21-8. MudClient.java (continued)

```
                String back = getLine("What is the direction from " +
                                "there back to here?: ");
                String desc = getMultiLine("Please describe " +
                                name + ":");
                location.createPlace(me, arg, back, name, desc);
            }
            // CLOSE: Close a named exit.  Note: only closes an exit
            // uni-directionally, and does not destroy a place.
            else if (cmd.equals("close")) {
                if (arg.length( ) == 0)
                    throw new IllegalArgumentException("direction expected");
                location.close(me, arg);
            }
            // LINK: Create a new exit that connects to an existing place
            // that may be in another MUD running on another host
            else if (cmd.equals("link")) {
                if (arg.length( ) == 0)
                    throw new IllegalArgumentException("direction expected");
                String host = getLine("What host are you linking to?: ");
                String mud =
                    getLine("What is the name of the MUD on that host?: ");
                String place =
                    getLine("What is the place name in that MUD?: ");
                location.linkTo(me, arg, host, mud, place);
                System.out.println("Don't forget to make a link from " +
                                "there back to here!");
            }
            // DUMP: Save the state of this MUD into the named file,
            // if the password is correct
            else if (cmd.equals("dump")) {
                if (arg.length( ) == 0)
                    throw new IllegalArgumentException("filename expected");
                String password = getLine("Password: ");
                location.getServer( ).dump(password, arg);
            }
            // QUIT: Quit the game
            else if (cmd.equals("quit")) {
                try { location.exit(me, myname + " has quit."); }
                catch (Exception e) { }
                System.out.println("Bye.");
                System.out.flush( );
                System.exit(0);
            }
            // HELP: Print out a big help message
            else if (cmd.equals("help")) System.out.println(help);
            // Otherwise, this is an unrecognized command.
            else System.out.println("Unknown command.  Try 'help'.");
        }
        // Handle the many possible types of MudException
        catch (MudException e) {
            if (e instanceof NoSuchThing)
                System.out.println("There isn't any such thing here.");
```

Example 21-8. MudClient.java (continued)

```
                    else if (e instanceof NoSuchPerson)
                        System.out.println("There isn't anyone by that name here.");
                    else if (e instanceof NoSuchExit)
                      System.out.println("There isn't an exit in that direction.");
                    else if (e instanceof NoSuchPlace)
                        System.out.println("There isn't any such place.");
                    else if (e instanceof ExitAlreadyExists)
                        System.out.println("There is already an exit " +
                                           "in that direction.");
                    else if (e instanceof PlaceAlreadyExists)
                        System.out.println("There is already a place " +
                                           "with that name.");
                    else if (e instanceof LinkFailed)
                        System.out.println("That exit is not functioning.");
                    else if (e instanceof BadPassword)
                        System.out.println("Invalid password.");
                    else if (e instanceof NotThere)      // Shouldn't happen
                        System.out.println("You can't do that when " +
                                           "you're not there.");
                    else if (e instanceof AlreadyThere)  // Shouldn't happen
                        System.out.println("You can't go there; " +
                                           "you're already there.");
                }
                // Handle RMI exceptions
                catch (RemoteException e) {
                    System.out.println("The MUD is having technical difficulties.");
                    System.out.println("Perhaps the server has crashed:");
                    System.out.println(e);
                }
                // Handle everything else that could go wrong.
                catch (Exception e) {
                    System.out.println("Syntax or other error:");
                    System.out.println(e);
                    System.out.println("Try using the 'help' command.");
                }
            }
        }
    }

    /**
     * This convenience method is used in several places in the
     * runMud( ) method above.  It displays the name and description of
     * the current place (including the name of the mud the place is in),
     * and also displays the list of things, people, and exits in
     * the current place.
     **/
    public static void look(RemoteMudPlace p)
        throws RemoteException, MudException
    {
        String mudname = p.getServer( ).getMudName( ); // Mud name
        String placename = p.getPlaceName( );          // Place name
        String description = p.getDescription( );       // Place description
        Vector things = p.getThings( );                 // List of things here
```

Example 21-8. MudClient.java (continued)

```
        Vector names = p.getNames( );              // List of people here
        Vector exits = p.getExits( );              // List of exits from here

        // Print it all out
        System.out.println("You are in: " + placename +
                           " of the Mud: " + mudname);
        System.out.println(description);
        System.out.print("Things here: ");
        for(int i = 0; i < things.size( ); i++) {   // Display list of things
            if (i > 0) System.out.print(", ");
            System.out.print(things.elementAt(i));
        }
        System.out.print("\nPeople here: ");
        for(int i = 0; i < names.size( ); i++) {    // Display list of people
            if (i > 0) System.out.print(", ");
            System.out.print(names.elementAt(i));
        }
        System.out.print("\nExits are: ");
        for(int i = 0; i < exits.size( ); i++) {    // Display list of exits
            if (i > 0) System.out.print(", ");
            System.out.print(exits.elementAt(i));
        }
        System.out.println( );                     // Blank line
        System.out.flush( );                       // Make it appear now!
    }

    /** This static input stream reads lines from the console */
    static BufferedReader in =
        new BufferedReader(new InputStreamReader(System.in));

    /**
     * A convenience method for prompting the user and getting a line of
     * input.  It guarantees that the line is not empty and strips off
     * whitespace at the beginning and end of the line.
     **/
    public static String getLine(String prompt) {
        String line = null;
        do {                          // Loop until a non-empty line is entered
            try {
                System.out.print(prompt);           // Display prompt
                System.out.flush( );                // Display it right away
                line = in.readLine( );              // Get a line of input
                if (line != null) line = line.trim( ); // Strip off whitespace
            } catch (Exception e) { }               // Ignore any errors
        } while((line == null) || (line.length( ) == 0));
        return line;
    }

    /**
     * A convenience method for getting multi-line input from the user.
     * It prompts for the input, displays instructions, and guarantees that
     * the input is not empty.  It also allows the user to enter the name of
```

Example 21-8. MudClient.java (continued)

```
 * a file from which text will be read.
 **/
public static String getMultiLine(String prompt) {
    String text = "";
    for(;;) {  // We'll break out of this loop when we get non-empty input
        try {
            BufferedReader br = in;        // The stream to read from
            System.out.println(prompt);    // Display the prompt
            // Display some instructions
            System.out.println("You can enter multiple lines.  " +
                               "End with a '.' on a line by itself.\n" +
                               "Or enter a '<<' followed by a filename");
            // Make the prompt and instructions appear now.
            System.out.flush();
            // Read lines
            String line;
            while((line = br.readLine()) != null) {    // Until EOF
                if (line.equals(".")) break;  // Or until a dot by itself
                // Or, if a file is specified, start reading from it
                // instead of from the console.
                if (line.trim().startsWith("<<")) {
                    String filename = line.trim().substring(2).trim();
                    br = new BufferedReader(new FileReader(filename));
                    continue;  // Don't count the << as part of the input
                }
                // Add the line to the collected input
                else text += line + "\n";
            }
            // If we got at least one line, return it.  Otherwise, chastise
            // the user and go back to the prompt and the instructions.
            if (text.length() > 0) return text;
            else System.out.println("Please enter at least one line.");
        }
        // If there were errors, for example an IO error reading a file,
        // display the error and loop again, displaying prompt and
        // instructions
        catch(Exception e) { System.out.println(e); }
    }
}

/** This is the usage string that explains the available commands */
static final String help =
    "Commands are:\n" +
    "look: Look around\n" +
    "examine <thing>: examine the named thing in more detail\n" +
    "describe <person>: describe the named person\n" +
    "go <direction>: go in the named direction (i.e. a named exit)\n" +
    "say <message>: say something to everyone\n" +
    "do <message>: tell everyone that you are doing something\n" +
    "talk <person>: talk to one person.  Will prompt for message\n" +
    "change: change how you are described.  Will prompt for input\n" +
    "create <thing>: create a new thing.  Prompts for description \n" +
```

Example 21-8. MudClient.java (continued)

```
        "destroy <thing>: destroy a thing.\n" +
        "open <direction>: create an adjoining place. Prompts for input\n"+
        "close <direction>: close an exit from this place.\n" +
        "link <direction>: create an exit to an existing place,\n" +
        "       perhaps on another server.  Will prompt for input.\n" +
        "dump <filename>: save server state.  Prompts for password\n" +
        "quit: leave the Mud\n" +
        "help: display this message";
}
```

Advanced RMI

There are several advanced features of RMI that are beyond the scope of this book but are important to know about. I'm only going to describe these features briefly here; you should consult *Java Enterprise in a Nutshell* for details.

Remote Class Loading

Ideally, a client of a remote object should need only direct access to the remote interface; it should not need to know anything about the implementation of that interface. In the examples we've seen in this chapter, however, the client requires access to the implementation stub class as well. (And in practice, you've probably run the client and the server on the same machine with the same class path, so they shared all classes.)

Having to distribute implementation stubs with RMI client programs can be a burden, especially when the server implementation changes. Fortunately, RMI provides a mechanism that allows a client to remotely load the stub classes it needs from a network server. Unfortunately, making this work takes a fair bit of effort. First, you must have a web server running and make the stub classes available for download from that server. Second, you must install a security manager in all your clients to protect against malicious code in the downloaded stub classes (and remember that an RMI server that uses other remote objects is itself an RMI client). Third, since you've installed a security manager, you must explicitly specify a security policy that allows your RMI clients to make the network connections they need to communicate with remote objects. See *Java Enterprise in a Nutshell* for all the details.

Activation

In the RMI examples of this chapter, the process that implements a remote object must be running all the time, waiting for connections from clients. As of Java 1.2, the RMI activation service enables you to define remote objects that don't run all the time, but that are instantiated and activated only when needed. Activation also enables persistent remote references that can remain valid even across server crashes.

In order to implement an activateable remote object, you extend the java.rmi.activation.Activatable class, rather than the UnicastRemoteObject class that we've used in this chapter. When you subclass Activatable, you must define an initialization constructor that specifies a location from which the class can be loaded. You must also define an activation constructor (with different arguments) that the activation service uses to activate your object when it is requested by a client.

Once you have implemented your activateable remote object, you can instantiate an initial instance of it and register it with the activation service, or you can create an ActivationDesc object that tells the activation service how to instantiate it when it is needed. In either case, the activation service itself must be running. You run this service with the *rmid* command that ships with the Java SDK in Java 1.2 and later. Conveniently, *rmid* can also perform the function of the *rmiregistry*.

All the details described here are server-side details: the client can't tell the difference between an activateable remote object and a regular remote object. This section has outlined only the process of creating activateable objects; see *Java Enterprise in a Nutshell* for more information.

CORBA Interoperability with RMI/IIOP

One of the weaknesses of traditional RMI remote objects is that they work only when Java is used for both the client and the server. (This is also a strength, in that it keeps the remote method infrastructure simple and easy to use.) A new technology called RMI/IIOP allows you to use RMI remote objects with the IIOP network protocol. IIOP is the Internet Inter-ORB Protocol: the protocol used by the CORBA distributed object standard. RMI/IIOP is implemented in the javax.rmi package, and is a standard part of Java 1.3 and later.

RMI remote objects can't automatically use the IIOP protocol: you must implement them specially by subclassing the javax.rmi.PortableRemoteObject class and following a number of other steps. Although there is extra work involved, using RMI/IIOP can be of great value if you are working in a heterogeneous environment and want to connect Java remote objects with legacy remote objects implemented using the CORBA standard. See *Java Enterprise in a Nutshell* for an overview, and see *http://java.sun.com/products/rmi-iiop/* and the RMI/IIOP documentation in the Java SDK for complete details.

Exercises

Exercise 21-1. Modify the remote banking example in this chapter so that bank customers are allowed to borrow money from the bank against some maximum line of credit, and so they can also apply money from their account to pay off their debt. Add borrow( ) and repay( ) methods to the RemoteBank interface, implement these methods with RemoteBankServer or PersistentBankServer, and modify the client so that it can call these methods when the user requests them.

Exercise 21-2. The *rmiregistry* program provides a simple name service for RMI programs; it allows servers to register names for the remote objects they serve, and it allows clients to look up those remote objects by name. Because it is a global registry, shared by any number of remote services, there is a possibility of name collisions. For this reason, if a service needs to define names for a number of remote objects, it should usually provide its own custom registry. That way, a client can use the global registry to look up the service's custom naming registry, and then it can use this custom registry to look up particular named objects for that service.

Use RMI to write a server that provides such a custom naming service. It should export remote methods that correspond to the bind( ), rebind( ), unbind( ), and lookup( ) methods of the Naming class. You will probably want to use a java.util.Map object to associate names with remote objects.

Exercise 21-3. The MUD example of this chapter uses remote objects to represent the rooms or places in the MUD and the people interacting in the MUD. Things that appear in the MUD, however, are not remote objects; they are simply part of the state of each room in the MUD.

Modify the example so that things are true remote objects. Define a MudThing interface that extends Remote. It should have a getDescription( ) method that returns the description of a thing. Modify the MudPlace interface and RemoteMudPlace class to have methods that allow MudThing objects to be added to and removed from a place.

Define a trivial implementation of MudThing that simply returns a static string from its getDescription( ) method. Then, define another implementation of MudThing, named Clock. This class should have more dynamic behavior: whenever its getDescription( ) method is called, it should return a string that displays the current time. Modify the MUD server so that it places a Clock object in the entrance to the MUD.

Exercise 21-4. Modify the MUD example again so that MudPerson objects can pick up MudThing objects they find in a MudPlace, carry them around, drop them in other places, and give them to other people. Implement at least three new methods: pickup( ), drop( ), and give( ). Modify the MUD client so that it supports pickup, drop, and give commands.

22

Example Index

This is an index of the examples presented in this book. If you want to find an example that uses a particular class, package, or method, or an example that performs a particular task, look it up here. The numbers shown in this index are example numbers, not page numbers. You can also use this index if you know the name of the example you want but do not know where it appears in the book.

Symbols

% operator, 1-2

A

abstract classes, 2-9
abstract methods, 2-9
AbstractTokenizer.java, 2-9
accessor methods, 2-5
Action, 11-15, 11-21, 11-25
ActionListener, 9-2, 11-12, 15-3, 16-3
ActionMap, 14-2
ActionParser.java, 11-25
actions
    defined with reflection, 11-16
AdjustmentListener, 8-1
AffineTransform, 12-7, 12-10, 12-18
AffineTransformOp, 12-13
Alignment.java, 15-2
AlignmentEditor.java, 15-7
alpha transparency, 12-14
AlphaComposite, 12-12

animation

    bouncing circle, 12-4
    clock, 16-2
    in a message line, 11-21
    with Timer, 12-19
AnswerEvent.java, 15-4
AnswerListener.java, 15-5
AntiAlias.java, 12-11
antialiasing, 12-11
Applet, 16-1, 16-2, 16-3, 16-3
    getAppletInfo( ), 16-2, 16-3
    getAudioClip( ), 16-3
    getDocumentBase( ), 16-3
    getImage( ), 16-3
    getParameter( ), 16-3
    getParameterInfo( ), 16-3
    init( ), 16-2, 16-3, 16-3
    newAudioClip( ), 17-2
    paint( ), 16-1
    showStatus( ), 16-3
    start( ), 16-2, 16-3
    stop( ), 16-2, 16-3

F

FactComputer.java, 1-11
Factorial.java, 1-7
Factorial2.java, 1-8
Factorial3.java, 1-9
Factorial4.java, 1-10
FactQuoter.java, 1-12
Fibonacci series, 1-3
Fibonacci.java, 1-3
Field, 9-1, 18-3
fields
    protected, 2-9
File, 3-1, 3-2
    delete( ), 3-1
    deleteOnExit( ), 6-1
file locking, 6-1
FileChannel, 6-1, 6-2, 6-3, 6-7, 6-9
    locking, 6-1
    map( ), 6-3, 6-7
    transferTo( ), 6-2
    tryLock( ), 6-1
FileCopy.java, 3-2
FileCopy2.java, 6-2
FileCopy3.java, 6-4
FileFilter, 11-21
FileInputStream, 3-2, 6-2
FileLister.java, 3-4
FileLock, 6-1
FileOutputStream, 3-2, 6-2
FileReader, 3-3, 3-7
files
    compressing, 3-5
    copying, 3-2, 6-4
    deletion, 3-1
    displaying text, 3-3
    memory mapping, 6-3
    random access, 3-8
    reading from, 3-2
    reading text, 3-3
    copying, 6-2
    locking, 6-1
    memory mapping, 6-7

FileTransferHandler.java, 14-3
FileViewer.java, 3-3
FileWriter, 3-7
filling shapes, 12-10
FilterReader, 3-6
FirstApplet.java, 16-1
FizzBuzz.java, 1-2
FizzBuzz2.java, 1-6
FloatControl, 17-3
FlowLayout, 11-2
FlowLayoutPane.java, 11-2
FocusListener, 14-2
Font, 8-1, 11-28, 12-1, 12-2, 16-3
    decode( ), 16-3
    deriveFont( ), 12-10
FontChooser.java, 11-17
FontList.java, 12-2
FontMetrics, 12-1, 13-4, 15-1
fonts
    font families, 11-17
    in Java 1.1, 12-2
    logical fonts, 12-2
    selecting with dialog, 11-17
    unicode character set, 8-1
FontUIResource, 11-28
for loop, 1-2

G

GatheringByteChannel, 6-13
GeneralPath, 12-7, 12-8, 12-17
GenericClient.java, 5-5
GenericPaint.java, 12-18
GetDBInfo.java, 18-2
GetURL.java, 5-1
GetURLInfo.java, 5-2
glue, 11-5
GlyphVector, 12-10, 12-17
GradientPaint, 12-10, 12-14
Graphics, 12-1
    dispose( ), 13-1
    drawLine( ), 11-10, 11-11
    drawString( ), 8-1
    setColor( ), 11-11

I

I/O

see input/output

I/O streams, 3-2

i18n

see internationalization

Icon, 11-15, 11-16

IllegalArgumentException, 1-9

Image, 12-1, 12-13, 16-3

ImageIcon, 12-13, 16-3

ImageIO, 12-14

ImageOps.java, 12-13

immutable class, 2-5

IndexOutOfBoundsException, 4-2

InetAddress, 5-11

InetSocketAddress, 6-9, 6-10, 6-11

inheritance, 2-4

inner classes, 2-8

input/output

archiving directories, 3-5

basic decode loop, 6-5

bulk transfers with FileChannel, 6-2

byte buffers, 6-1

compressing files, 3-5

converting bytes to chars, 6-5, 6-6

copying bytes between channels, 6-4

copying files, 3-2, 6-2, 6-4

custom streams, 3-6, 13-4

file deletion, 3-1

listing directories, 3-4

locking files, 6-1

memory mapped files, 6-3

multi-line console input, 21-8

parsing XML, 19-6

random access files, 3-8, 6-1

reading from console, 1-12, 5-7, 21-8

reading text files, 3-3

temporary files, 6-1

converting chars to bytes, 6-10

memory mapped files, 6-7

multiplexed, 6-11, 6-13

nonblocking, 6-11, 6-13, 6-14

reading binary data, 5-6

writing binary data, 5-6

InputMap, 14-2

InputStream, 3-2

InputStreamReader, 8-2

InputStreamWriter, 8-2

Insets, 15-9

instanceof operator, 2-7

Integer, 1-11

parseInt( ), 1-11

interfaces, 2-8

implementing via proxy, 9-3

internationalization

character encodings, 8-2

currency, 8-3

date formats, 8-3

localized formatting, 8-3

localized messages, 8-5

localizing GUI resources, 11-22

menus, 8-4

message formats, 8-5

number formats, 8-3

resource bundles, 8-4

unicode, 8-1

IntList.java, 2-7

introspection, 15-10

Introspector, 11-19, 15-10

InvocationHandler, 9-3

invoking methods, 9-2

ItemChooser.java, 11-14

ItemListener, 11-14

J

JApplet, 16-3

java.applet

Applet, 16-1, 16-2, 16-3, 16-3

Applet.getAppletInfo( ), 16-2, 16-3

Applet.getAudioClip( ), 16-3

Applet.getDocumentBase( ), 16-3

Applet.getImage( ), 16-3

Applet.getParameter( ), 16-3

Applet.getParameterInfo( ), 16-3

Applet.init( ), 16-2, 16-3, 16-3

Applet.newAudioClip( ), 17-2

Applet.paint( ), 16-1

Applet.showStatus( ), 16-3

Index

We'd like to hear your suggestions for improving our indexes. Send email to *index@oreilly.com*.

B

About the Author

David Flanagan is a computer programmer who spends most of his time writing about Java. His other books with O'Reilly & Associates include the bestselling *Java in a Nutshell*, *Java Foundation Classes in a Nutshell*, *Java Enterprise in a Nutshell*, *JavaScript: The Definitive Guide*, and *JavaScript Pocket Reference*. David has a degree in computer science and engineering from the Massachusetts Institute of Technology. He lives in the U.S. Pacific Northwest between the cities of Seattle, Washington and Vancouver, British Columbia.

Colophon

Our look is the result of reader comments, our own experimentation, and feedback from distribution channels. Distinctive covers complement our distinctive approach to technical topics, breathing personality and life into potentially dry subjects.

The animal on the cover of *Java Examples in a Nutshell*, Third Edition, is an alligator. There are only two species of alligator: the American alligator (*Alligator mississippiensis*), found in the southeastern coastal plain of the United States, and the smaller Chinese alligator (*Alligator sinensis*), found in the lower valley of the Yangtze River. Both alligators are related to the more widely distributed crocodile.

The alligator is a much-studied animal, so a great deal is known about its life cycle. Female alligators lay 30 to 80 eggs at a time. The mother allows the sun to incubate the eggs, but stays nearby. After about 60 days the eggs hatch, and the young call out for their mother. The mother then carries or leads them to the water, where they live with her for a year.

Alligators eat a varied diet of insects, fish, shellfish, frogs, water birds, and small mammals. Alligator attacks on humans are rare. Although normally slow-moving animals, alligators can charge quickly for short distances when they or their young are in danger.

Alligators have been hunted extensively for their skin. The American alligator was placed on the endangered species list in 1969, then declared to be out of danger in 1987. The Chinese alligator remains on the endangered list.

Genevieve d'Entremont was the production editor and copyeditor for *Java Examples in a Nutshell*, Third Edition. Emily Quill, Reg Aubry, and Claire Cloutier provided quality control. Jamie Peppard and Matt Hutchinson provided production assistance. Julie Hawks updated the index.

Edie Freedman designed the cover of this book. The cover image is a 19th-century engraving from *Old Fashioned Animal Cuts*. Emma Colby produced the cover layout with QuarkXPress 4.1 using Adobe's ITC Garamond font.

Melanie Wang designed the interior layout, based on a series design by David Futato. This book was converted by Joe Wizda to FrameMaker 5.5.6 with a format conversion tool created by Erik Ray, Jason McIntosh, Neil Walls, and Mike Sierra that uses Perl and XML technologies. The text font is Linotype Birka; the heading font is Adobe Myriad Condensed; and the code font is LucasFont's TheSans Mono Condensed. The illustrations that appear in the book were produced by Robert Romano using Adobe Photoshop 6. This colophon was written by Clairemarie Fisher O'Leary.

Related Titles Available from O'Reilly

Java

Ant: The Definitive Guide

Enterprise JavaBeans, *3rd Edition*

Head First Java

Head First EJB

J2EE Design Patterns

J2ME in a Nutshell

Java and SOAP

Java & XML Data Binding

Java & XML

Java Cookbook

Java Data Objects

Java Database Best Practices

Java Enterprise Best Practices

Java Enterprise in a Nutshell, *2nd Edition*

Java Extreme Programming Cookbook

Java in a Nutshell, *4th Edition*

Java Management Extensions

Java Message Service

Java Network Programming, *2nd Edition*

Java NIO

Java Performance Tuning, *2nd Edition*

Java RMI

Java Security, *2nd Edition*

Java ServerPages, *2nd Edition*

Java Servlet Programming, *2nd Edition*

Java Swing, *2nd Edition*

Java Web Services in a Nutshell

JXTA in a Nutshell

Learning Java, *2nd Edition*

Mac OS X for Java Geeks

NetBeans: The Definitive Guide

Programming Jakarta Struts

Tomcat: The Definitive Guide

O'REILLY®

Our books are available at most retail and online bookstores.
To order direct: 1-800-998-9938 • *order@oreilly.com* • *www.oreilly.com*
Online editions of most O'Reilly titles are available by subscription at *safari.oreilly.com*

Keep in touch with O'Reilly

1. Download examples from our books

To find example files for a book, go to:
www.oreilly.com/catalog
select the book, and follow the "Examples" link.

2. Register your O'Reilly books

Register your book at *register.oreilly.com*

Why register your books? Once you've registered your O'Reilly books you can:

- Win O'Reilly books, T-shirts or discount coupons in our monthly drawing.
- Get special offers available only to registered O'Reilly customers.
- Get catalogs announcing new books (US and UK only).
- Get email notification of new editions of the O'Reilly books you own.

3. Join our email lists

Sign up to get topic-specific email announcements of new books and conferences, special offers, and O'Reilly Network technology newsletters at:

elists.oreilly.com

It's easy to customize your free elists subscription so you'll get exactly the O'Reilly news you want.

4. Get the latest news, tips, and tools

http://www.oreilly.com

- "Top 100 Sites on the Web"—PC Magazine
- CIO Magazine's Web Business 50 Awards

Our web site contains a library of comprehensive product information (including book excerpts and tables of contents), downloadable software, background articles, interviews with technology leaders, links to relevant sites, book cover art, and more.

5. Work for O'Reilly

Check out our web site for current employment opportunities:

jobs.oreilly.com

6. Contact us

O'Reilly & Associates, Inc.
1005 Gravenstein Hwy North
Sebastopol, CA 95472 USA

TEL: 707-827-7000 or 800-998-9938
(6am to 5pm PST)

FAX: 707-829-0104

order@oreilly.com
For answers to problems regarding your order or our products.
To place a book order online, visit:
www.oreilly.com/order_new

catalog@oreilly.com
To request a copy of our latest catalog.

booktech@oreilly.com
For book content technical questions or corrections.

corporate@oreilly.com
For educational, library, government, and corporate sales.

proposals@oreilly.com
To submit new book proposals to our editors and product managers.

international@oreilly.com
For information about our international distributors or translation queries. For a list of our distributors outside of North America check out:
international.oreilly.com/distributors.html

adoption@oreilly.com
For information about academic use of O'Reilly books, visit:
academic.oreilly.com

O'REILLY®

Our books are available at most retail and online bookstores.
To order direct: 1-800-998-9938 • *order@oreilly.com* • *www.oreilly.com*
Online editions of most O'Reilly titles are available by subscription at *safari.oreilly.com*